Macworld® Mac® Upgrade and Repair Bible

Macworld® Mac® Upgrade and Repair Bible

Todd Stauffer

IDG Books Worldwide, Inc.

An International Data Group Company

Foster City, CA ◆ Chicago, IL ◆ Indianapolis, IN ◆ New York, NY

Macworld® Mac® Upgrade and Repair Bible

Published by
IDG Books Worldwide, Inc.
An International Data Group Company
919 E. Hillsdale Blvd., Suite 400
Foster City, CA 94404
www.idgbooks.com (IDG Books Worldwide Web site)

Library of Congress Catalog Card Number: 98-72476

ISBN: 0-7645-3217-0

Printed in the United States of America

10 9 8 7 6 5 4 3 2 1

1B/QT/QZ/ZY/FC

Distributed in the United States by IDG Books Worldwide, Inc.

Distributed by Macmillan Canada for Canada; by Transworld Publishers Limited in the United Kingdom; by IDG Norge Books for Norway; by IDG Sweden Books for Sweden; by Woodslane Pty. Ltd. for Australia; by Woodslane (NZ) Ltd. for New Zealand; by Addison Wesley Longman Singapore Pte Ltd. for Singapore, Malaysia, Thailand, Indonesia, and Korea; by Norma Comunicaciones S.A. for Colombia; by Intersoft for South Africa; by International Thomson Publishing for Germany, Austria, and Switzerland; by Toppan Company Ltd. for Japan; by Distribuidora Cuspide for Argentina; by Livraria Cultura for Brazil; by Ediciencia S.A. for Ecuador; by Ediciones ZETA S.C.R. Ltda. for Peru; by WS Computer Publishing Corporation, Inc., for the Philippines; by Unalis Corporation for Taiwan; by Contemporanea de Ediciones for Venezuela; by Computer Book & Magazine Store for Puerto Rico; by Express Computer Distributors for the Caribbean and West Indies. Authorized Sales Agent: Anthony Rudkin Associates for the Middle East and North Africa.

For general information on IDG Books Worldwide's books in the U.S., please call our Consumer Customer Service department at 800-762-2974. For reseller information, including discounts and premium sales, please call our Reseller Customer Service department at 800-434-3422.

For information on where to purchase IDG Books Worldwide's books outside the U.S., please contact our International Sales department at 650-655-3200 or fax 650-655-3297.

For information on foreign language translations, please contact our Foreign & Subsidiary Rights department at 650-655-3021 or fax 650-655-3281.

For sales inquiries and special prices for bulk quantities, please contact our Sales department at 650-655-3200 or write to the address above.

For information on using IDG Books Worldwide's books in the classroom or for ordering examination copies, please contact our Educational Sales department at 800-434-2086 or fax 317-596-5499.

For press review copies, ███ontact our Public Relations department at ██

For authorization to phot███lease contact Copyright Clearance Cent██0-4470.

IDG BOOKS WORLDWIDE is a trademark under exclusive license to IDG Books Worldwide, Inc., from International Data Group, Inc.

ABOUT IDG BOOKS WORLDWIDE

Welcome to the world of IDG Books Worldwide.

IDG Books Worldwide, Inc., is a subsidiary of International Data Group, the world's largest publisher of computer-related information and the leading global provider of information services on information technology. IDG was founded more than 25 years ago and now employs more than 8,500 people worldwide. IDG publishes more than 275 computer publications in over 75 countries (see listing below). More than 90 million people read one or more IDG publications each month.

Launched in 1990, IDG Books Worldwide is today the #1 publisher of best-selling computer books in the United States. We are proud to have received eight awards from the Computer Press Association in recognition of editorial excellence and three from *Computer Currents'* First Annual Readers' Choice Awards. Our best-selling ...For Dummies® series has more than 50 million copies in print with translations in 38 languages. IDG Books Worldwide, through a joint venture with IDG's Hi-Tech Beijing, became the first U.S. publisher to publish a computer book in the People's Republic of China. In record time, IDG Books Worldwide has become the first choice for millions of readers around the world who want to learn how to better manage their businesses.

Our mission is simple: Every one of our books is designed to bring extra value and skill-building instructions to the reader. Our books are written by experts who understand and care about our readers. The knowledge base of our editorial staff comes from years of experience in publishing, education, and journalism — experience we use to produce books for the '90s. In short, we care about books, so we attract the best people. We devote special attention to details such as audience, interior design, use of icons, and illustrations. And because we use an efficient process of authoring, editing, and desktop publishing our books electronically, we can spend more time ensuring superior content and spend less time on the technicalities of making books.

You can count on our commitment to deliver high-quality books at competitive prices on topics you want to read about. At IDG Books Worldwide, we continue in the IDG tradition of delivering quality for more than 25 years. You'll find no better book on a subject than one from IDG Books Worldwide.

IDG BOOKS WORLDWIDE

John Kilcullen
CEO
IDG Books Worldwide, Inc.

Steven Berkowitz
President and Publisher
IDG Books Worldwide, Inc.

Eighth Annual Computer Press Awards ≥1992

Ninth Annual Computer Press Awards ≥1993

Tenth Annual Computer Press Awards ≥1994

Eleventh Annual Computer Press Awards ≥1995

IDG Books Worldwide, Inc., is a subsidiary of International Data Group, the world's largest publisher of computer-related information and the leading global provider of information services on information technology. International Data Group publishes over 275 computer publications in over 75 countries. More than 90 million people read one or more International Data Group publications each month. International Data Group's publications include: **ARGENTINA:** Buyer's Guide, Computerworld Argentina, PC World Argentina; **AUSTRALIA:** Australian Macworld, Australian PC World, Australian Reseller News, Computerworld, IT Casebook, Network World, Publish, Webmaster; **AUSTRIA:** Computerwelt Osterreich, Networks Austria, PC Tip Austria; **BANGLADESH:** PC World Bangladesh; **BELARUS:** PC World Belarus; **BELGIUM:** Data News; **BRAZIL:** Annuário de Informática, Computerworld, Connections, Macworld, PC Player, PC World, Publish, Reseller News, Supergamepower; **BULGARIA:** Computerworld Bulgaria, Network World Bulgaria, PC & MacWorld Bulgaria; **CANADA:** CIO Canada, Client/Server World, ComputerWorld Canada, InfoWorld Canada, NetworkWorld Canada, WebWorld; **CHILE:** Computerworld Chile, PC World Chile; **COLOMBIA:** Computerworld Colombia, PC World Colombia; **COSTA RICA:** PC World Centro America; **THE CZECH AND SLOVAK REPUBLICS:** Computerworld Czechoslovakia, Macworld Czech Republic, PC World Czechoslovakia; **DENMARK:** Communications World Danmark, Computerworld Danmark, Macworld Danmark, PC World Danmark, Techworld Denmark; **DOMINICAN REPUBLIC:** PC World Republica Dominicana; **ECUADOR:** PC World Ecuador; **EGYPT:** Computerworld Middle East, PC World Middle East; **EL SALVADOR:** PC World Centro America; **FINLAND:** MikroPC, Tietoverkko, Tietoviikko; **FRANCE:** Distributique, Hebdo, Info PC, Le Monde Informatique, Macworld, Reseaux & Telecoms, WebMaster France; **GERMANY:** Computer Partner, Computerwoche, Computerwoche Extra, Computerwoche FOCUS, Global Online, Macwelt, PC Welt; **GREECE:** Amiga Computing, GamePro Greece, Multimedia World; **GUATEMALA:** PC World Centro America; **HONDURAS:** PC World Centro America; **HONG KONG:** Computerworld Hong Kong, PC World Hong Kong, Publish in Asia; **HUNGARY:** ABCD CD-ROM, Computerworld Szamitastechnika, Internetto online Magazine, PC World Hungary, PC-X Magazin Hungary; **ICELAND:** Tolvuheimur PC World Island; **INDIA:** Information Communications World, Information Systems Computerworld, PC World India, Publish in Asia; **INDONESIA:** InfoKomputer PC World, Komputek Computerworld, Publish in Asia; **IRELAND:** ComputerScope, PC Live!; **ISRAEL:** Macworld Israel, People & Computers/Computerworld; **ITALY:** Computerworld Italia, Macworld Italia, Networking Italia, PC World Italia; **JAPAN:** DTP World, Macworld Japan, Nikkei Personal Computing, OS/2 World Japan, SunWorld Japan, Windows NT World, Windows World Japan; **KENYA:** PC World East African; **KOREA:** Hi-Tech Information, Macworld Korea, PC World Korea; **MACEDONIA:** PC World Macedonia; **MALAYSIA:** Computerworld Malaysia, PC World Malaysia, Publish in Asia; **MALTA:** PC World Malta; **MEXICO:** Computerworld Mexico, PC World Mexico; **MYANMAR:** PC World Myanmar; **NETHERLANDS:** Computer! Totaal, LAN Internetworking Magazine, LAN World Buyers Guide, Macworld Netherlands, Net, WebWereld; **NEW ZEALAND:** Absolute Beginners Guide and Plain & Simple Series, Computer Buyer, Computer Industry Directory, Computerworld New Zealand, MTB, Network World, PC World New Zealand; **NICARAGUA:** PC World Centro America; **NORWAY:** Computerworld Norge, CW Rapport, Datamagasinet, Financial Rapport, Kursguide Norge, Macworld Norge, Multimediaworld Norge, PC World Ekspress Norge, PC World Nettverk, PC World Norge, PC World ProduktGuide Norge; **PAKISTAN:** Computerworld Pakistan; **PANAMA:** PC World Panama; **PEOPLE'S REPUBLIC OF CHINA:** China Computer Users, China Computerworld, China InfoWorld, China Telecom World Weekly, Computer & Communication, Electronic Design China, Electronics Today, Electronics Weekly, Game Software, PC World China, Popular Computer Week, Software Weekly, Software World, Telecom World; **PERU:** Computerworld Peru, PC World Profesional Peru, PC World SoHo Peru; **PHILIPPINES:** Click!, Computerworld Philippines, PC World Philippines, Publish in Asia; **POLAND:** Computerworld Poland, Computerworld Special Report Poland, Cyber, Macworld Poland, Networld Poland, PC World Komputer; **PORTUGAL:** Cerebro/PC World, Computerworld/Correio Informático, Dealer World Portugal, Mac*In/PC*In Portugal, Multimedia World; **PUERTO RICO:** PC World Puerto Rico; **ROMANIA:** Computerworld Romania, PC World Romania, Telecom Romania; **RUSSIA:** Computerworld Russia, Mir PK, Publish, Seti; **SINGAPORE:** Computerworld Singapore, PC World Singapore, Publish in Asia; **SLOVENIA:** Monitor; **SOUTH AFRICA:** Computing SA, Network World SA, Software World SA; **SPAIN:** Communicaciones World España, Computerworld España, Dealer World España, Macworld España, PC World España; **SRI LANKA:** Infolink PC World; **SWEDEN:** CAP&Design, Computer Sweden, Corporate Computing Sweden, Internetworld Sweden, it.branschen, Macworld Sweden, MaxiData Sweden, MikroDatorn, Natverk & Kommunikation, PC World Sweden, PCaktiv, Windows World Sweden; **SWITZERLAND:** Computerworld Schweiz, Macworld Schweiz, PCtip; **TAIWAN:** Computerworld Taiwan, Macworld Taiwan, NEW ViSiON/Publish, PC World Taiwan, Windows World Taiwan; **THAILAND:** Publish in Asia, Thai Computerworld; **TURKEY:** Computerworld Turkiye, Macworld Turkiye, Network World Turkiye, PC World Turkiye; **UKRAINE:** Computerworld Kiev, Multimedia World Ukraine, PC World Ukraine; **UNITED KINGDOM:** Acorn User UK, Amiga Action UK, Amiga Computing UK, Apple Talk UK, Computing, Macworld, Parents and Computers UK, PC Advisor, PC Home, PSX Pro, The WEB; **UNITED STATES:** Cable in the Classroom, CIO Magazine, Computerworld, DOS World, Federal Computer Week, GamePro Magazine, InfoWorld, I-Way, Macworld, Network World, PC Games, PC World, Publish, Video Event, THE WEB Magazine, and WebMaster; online webzines: JavaWorld, NetscapeWorld, and SunWorld Online; **URUGUAY:** InfoWorld Uruguay; **VENEZUELA:** Computerworld Venezuela, PC World Venezuela; and **VIETNAM:** PC World Vietnam.
5/7/98

Credits

Acquisitions Editor
Michael Roney

Development Editor
Katharine Dvorak

Technical Editor
Dennis Cohen

Copy Editor
Ami Knox

Project Coordinator
Susan Parini

Book Designer
Murder By Design

Graphics and Production Specialist
Sue Defloria
Stephanie Hollier

Graphics Technicians
Linda J. Marousek
Hector Mendosa

Quality Control Specialists
Constance Petros
Mark Schumann

Illustrator
Jesse Coleman

Proofreader
Annie Sheldon

Indexer
C² Editoral Services

About the Author

Todd Stauffer is the author or coauthor for over a dozen computer books including *Small Business Office 97 For Dummies* (IDG Books Worldwide). He's the cohost of the nationally televised "Disk Doctors" call-in computing show on JEC Knowledge TV. Todd is also a contributor to *The Mac Report*, *NetProfessional*, and *Inside Line* and the Mac columnist for *Peak Computing Magazine* and the Webintosh online news service. Before moving to Colorado, Todd was editor-in-chief of *Texas Computing* magazine, a freelance magazine writer, an advertising copy writer, and a technical editor.

To Donna. Thanks for making the writing process livable, life fun to live, and for being not only a well-rounded renaissance woman, but also the coolest Mac chick in the world.

Foreword

There's an old joke, based on fact, that goes like this: According to NASA scientists, given its ratio of body mass to wingspan, the ordinary bumblebee is technically incapable of flight. But the bumblebee doesn't know that, so it goes ahead and flies anyway.

And so it is with the Mac. Thanks to strident reporting in the mainstream press, Apple is supposed to be dead, Microsoft triumphant, and the Macintosh extinct. But we 20 million Mac fans don't know that, so we go right on happily using our Macs.

Part of our happiness with Macs is due to their not becoming obsolete nearly as quickly as Windows computers. The average Windows user must buy a new machine every two years; the average Mac fan keeps a Mac model running for five.

This book points out a prime reason why: The Mac's simplicity extends beyond its software design to its hardware. With a bit of good information and surprisingly little money, the Mac on your desk today can be accelerated, expanded, fixed, and given lease after new lease on life. In this age of cheap memory, G3 processor upgrades, and plummeting prices on every conceivable piece of add-on gear, keeping your Mac forever young is a more attractive option than ever.

Macworld Mac Upgrade and Repair Bible is clearly a labor of love, months in the making; it is rich with model-by-model advice, vast amounts of troubleshooting expertise, and enough background to help you make informed choices. I predict you'll be surprised, as I was, at the breadth of the coverage; my only suggestion to the editors was that they consider a more accurate title, along the lines of *Mac Upgrade, Repair, Troubleshooting, ISDN, Multimedia, Networking, SCSI, USB, Windows-Compatibility, and Hardware Bible*.

They told me the cover would have to be 17 inches wide.

Anyway, here's hoping that you and your Macs remain partners for years to come. Thanks to this book, that future is a distinct possibility.

—David Pogue

Preface

It feels so good to be right.

Although I'm a die-hard believer in Macintosh superiority, there was one particular day when I finally knew — in spite of the widespread counterintelligence I read daily in business and technology publications — that I'd made the correct decision when I bought a Macintosh. It was the day that a Mac-oriented peripheral manufacturer announced a PowerPC G3 upgrade card for my Power Macintosh 6100 computer.

I bought that Power Macintosh 6100 soon after it was released in 1994, becoming an early adopter of PowerPC technology. I was on the cutting edge, I thought, and I computed happily for nearly three-and-a-half years using that Mac — quite a long time for a business computer, especially when you consider I make my living writing about computers. But after that many years, my Mac was ready for retirement.

Then came the announcement of a G3 upgrade. Six months later, after testing one of those upgrade cards in the 6100, I can report that it will add years to the life of that machine. Although I now work daily on a newer Mac, that 6100 is still in my office, used by interns and contractors for design, Adobe Photoshop work, and Web programming. And it's more powerful and useful than Macs many years younger.

Upgrading a Mac is more than satisfying — it's fun. The actual upgrade is rarely difficult, it almost always works, and it's not even terribly expensive most of the time. By performing various upgrades, you can end up with a machine that is not only faster; it might also be more capable and more exciting.

You can do so many interesting things with a Macintosh to make it faster, more productive, or more powerful. Upgrading and troubleshooting a Mac isn't just about keeping up with the Joneses via speed boosts. It's about raising your awareness level of other things you can accomplish with your Mac, and then going out and making those new things happen. Want a bigger monitor? More RAM? A network between your Macs or faster Internet access? You can have any of these things, and in many cases these upgrades don't require any special tools.

Not all Macs are a joy to work with, but many models are wonders of industrial design. The Color Classic, the PowerBook, and the iMac include some amazingly well-implemented design features (although not without some trade-offs) that make them a joy to upgrade, if you can get your hands on the correct parts. Other

Macs — workhorses such as the Mac IIvi, the Quadra 650, the Power Macintosh 7500, and the Power Macintosh G3 Minitower — are metal and plastic testimonials to high-end power computing. You can do a lot inside these machines to extend their power and usefulness, and you can accomplish quite a bit with them.

The ultimate goal of *Macworld Mac Upgrade and Repair Bible* is to give you a more enjoyable computing experience. With a little understanding of the basics and a few golden rules to live by, you'll be able to upgrade and troubleshoot any Mac out there, adding years to its life and discovering many exciting new things you can do.

Above all else, this book will help you to continue to enjoy that Mac.

Who Should Use This Book?

Have you ever wanted to do something with your Mac, but weren't sure if it was possible? Things like recording CDs, adding RAM, using a cable modem, getting better 3D video performance for games, printing photographs, or implementing a sophisticated backup plan? Or maybe you need to troubleshoot a particular Mac (or number of different Macs) that keeps crashing, bombing, freezing, or having trouble starting up.

If so, this is the book for you.

But who, specifically, is *qualified* to read this book? Obviously, Mac folks or people who need to work with Macs. You should probably know the basics of using your Mac — how the hard-drive icon works, how to enter data, and how to move around on the screen. If you have that basic level of Mac knowledge, you may be surprised at your ability to grasp computer troubleshooting. It certainly isn't as complicated as carpentry, modern dance, or auto repair (at least, not often). In most cases, computer troubleshooting is much more straightforward and, in some cases, much less likely to cause minor injuries.

Here are some of the people who should consider this book:

♦ *Creative types.* If you're a writer, artist, editor, producer, publisher, or other creative type who uses a Mac often, you'll find this book handy for upgrading and troubleshooting day-to-day and catastrophic problems alike.

♦ *Professionals.* If you're a real estate, finance, marketing, public relations, or senior-level professional business person, you may find it very convenient to use a Mac on a day-to-day basis, but less than convenient to have it fail for some reason. Flip through this book quickly to find the answers you need to get back to work sooner.

◆ *Small business owners/workers.* In small-business settings, you can't always afford a network administrator or consultant. This book may serve as a palatable substitute. Get up and running with new capabilities or fix serious problems quickly, even when your business may be on the line. Plus, there's coverage of topics such as sharing printers, obtaining high-speed Internet access, and managing your backup strategy.

◆ *Hobbyists/home users.* If you're a Mac aficionado, you'll enjoy learning some new things about your Mac, including its inner workings and opportunities to increase performance. If you use a Mac at home, you may find that learning more about it helps you upgrade it for less money, makes it more useful when used in the off hours, or gives you a leg up at work or in school.

◆ *Technology professionals.* If you're in charge of managing Macs, getting them connected to networks, or working with them in a cross-platform (Mac and Intel-compatible PC) environment, this book should be a big help. It discusses not only upgrading and repair, but also network configuration and troubleshooting, along with DOS/Windows compatibility issues.

Ultimately, *Macworld Mac Upgrade and Repair Bible* is designed for any Mac owner, user, or administrator who wants to learn more about how Macs work and how they can be upgraded or fixed. This is a no-nonsense, comprehensive guide to just about everything you can do to augment a Mac OS computer, along with tips and instructions for actually getting the job done. It's also a resource for you if you have an immediate or chronic problem with your Mac that needs to be isolated and fixed.

Here are a few of the upgrading issues this book will help you resolve:

◆ Should you upgrade your Mac, and is it something you'll feel comfortable doing?

◆ What different upgrade paths does your particular Mac offer?

◆ What are the bottlenecks in your particular Mac, and what's the smartest way to upgrade to get the best bang for the buck?

◆ What capabilities can you add to your Mac? Will they alleviate your current limitations?

◆ Why do things go wrong with Macs?

◆ How can you pinpoint and isolate problems?

◆ What's the best way to troubleshoot problems with your Mac?

◆ How can you get an "unhappy" Mac to start up so you can recover data or continue working?

◆ What's the best approach to preventative maintenance?

A large part of this book is focused on the actual technologies you can use to upgrade your Mac, as well as hints, advice, and step-by-step instructions for performing an upgrade. I believe this book will give you a strong feel for all sorts of upgrades, allowing you to apply some wit and wisdom to the instructions that come with the upgrades that you buy for your Mac. It'll also help you decide which upgrades are best for you and where you should focus your upgrading energy.

Another huge part of this book focuses on troubleshooting problems — both hardware and software — to help you figure out what's happening when something goes wrong. Not only do I cover known issues that crop up in the cases of particular peripherals, Mac models, and software combinations, but I also give you the tools you need to explore Mac troubleshooting on your own.

Here's the bottom line. You can use this book in two ways: First, you can refer to individual chapters to find the answers to specific questions or problems that involve upgrading and/or troubleshooting. Second, you can read all or part of the book to understand quite a bit about how Macs work and how they can be upgraded or repaired. This general knowledge can be useful if you'll be working with Macs (or any computer) as a hobbyist or a professional.

What's in This Book?

This book is organized into four parts. The book can certainly be read from cover to cover, but you'll find that the parts differ somewhat in their approach, making some of them more narrative than others. The first two parts are primarily about upgrading, whereas the second two parts cover troubleshooting:

◆ *Part I: Getting Ready to Upgrade.* Many beginning-to-intermediate users may find this part interesting to read from start to finish. It begins with the very basics — reasons for upgrading and the subsystems of a Macintosh that can be upgraded. It then provides a primer on how a Macintosh works, including the various add-ons and upgrades you can use to augment your Mac. The next step is to get serious about *bottlenecks,* or the slowdowns that your particular Mac is experiencing. With those identified, you can plan your upgrades, deciding what to do immediately, what can wait, and what needs to be sent out to a service center. Finally, you take a look inside most Macintosh models, including how to get the case open and where to find certain parts of the computer.

◆ *Part II: Performing the Upgrade.* Organized more as a reference tool, this part includes individual chapters that each discuss different types of upgrades: what's possible, what's necessary, and how to perform them. Each chapter discusses a particular upgrade goal or subsystem of the Macintosh (for example, printing, sound, networking, storage), along with the related technologies and different possible upgrades. These chapters tell you what technologies are available, how they work, and even give a little help when it comes to deciding which upgrade technology is best for you. You'll also learn about related software topics, such as implementing a backup system, getting on the Internet, and creating a local area network.

◆ *Part III: Troubleshoot and Repair.* This part begins with a discussion of the most general level of troubleshooting: deciding whether the problem is most likely in the hardware or in the software. If yours is a software-only problem, you'll probably find the solution in Part IV. In the remainder of Part III, hardware and software/hardware integration issues are discussed. This entails anything from hard drive and scanner problems to downed networks and troubled PowerBooks. These chapters also feature information and advice on major troubleshooting issues, such as what to do when the Sad Mac icon appears or when you have trouble with the logic board, power supply, and system memory.

◆ *Part IV: Tweak and Recover the Mac OS.* If your problem is in the Mac's operating system software, the solution will likely be found in these pages. Part IV introduces you to the basic techniques and specific problems associated with the Mac OS, including how to troubleshoot crashing programs, freezes in the Finder, and specific error messages. You'll also take a look at preventative measures you can take to avoid system software problems, including intelligent approaches to managing your System Folder and other parts of the Mac OS installation. Finally, if that installation needs a complete refresher, you'll find strategies for backing up your Mac and starting all over again with a clean installation of (or an upgrade to) your Mac OS software.

You'll find there's a logical progression to the parts and the chapters. In almost every case, the primary knowledge you need to understand a concept or topic is found either in an earlier chapter or earlier in a particular chapter that covers something highly technical. Although you certainly don't need to read from cover to cover, if you find you're reading something that confuses you, flip back a few pages to see if it's explained in better detail.

Navigating This Book

This book is designed to make it easy for you to get as little or as much information as you want on a particular topic. Each part offers a short explanation at the beginning; each chapter features introductory points that explain the chapter's overall themes and a complete summary at the end. Use these to help you determine whether or not a particular chapter has the information you're seeking.

Within each chapter you'll encounter different icons in the margin of the text. These alert you to the adjacent paragraphs, which offer extra information, tips, and warnings, depending on the icon:

These paragraphs are generally filled with related information that's of particular importance for some or all Mac owners. These can include cautionary notes, sideline information, or something that might help you pinpoint a particular problem or issue.

This tidbit offers a shortcut, interesting fact, or other information that will help you get the most out of the component, peripheral, or procedure being discussed.

This icon alerts you to a resource on the World Wide Web that offers additional information. Fire up your Web browser and check out the suggested site if it interests you. (If you find a site that seems to have changed or disappeared, let me know through my Web site or e-mail address, both of which are listed towards the end of the Preface.)

If you see this icon, the software being discussed can be installed from the CD-ROM that accompanies this book. It also should be catalogued on the Mac-Upgrade.com Web site, just in case your Mac can't work with CDs.

In some cases, I'll discuss an item or concept that's more fully explained in another section or chapter. If you see this icon, you can turn to the recommended section or chapter to learn more about the topic being discussed.

Interesting tangents and tips appear in sidebars

You'll also find other important and interesting information in sidebars throughout the book, although this information usually isn't necessary to complete the task at hand or to finish troubleshooting the problem; it's more often another way to do or think about the current topic.

On the CD-ROM

In the back of this book you'll find a CD-ROM that includes many of the shareware and freeware programs recommended throughout these pages. I hope you'll find the CD-ROM contains some welcome additions to your library of utilities for keeping a Mac happy, as well as a few surprises for getting your Mac to fork over information and otherwise cooperate.

The authors and publishing companies represented on the included CD-ROM have all generously allowed me to present their software to you in this convenient format; in that spirit, I recommend you pay the shareware author for any shareware program on the CD-ROM that you find useful. This will likely entitle you to the latest version, more features, and, perhaps, individualized support for using the software product.

The CD-ROM features an HTML interface that nearly any Mac user should have no trouble using; in fact, the CD-ROM includes Netscape Navigator to enable you to view the contents of the CD-ROM if you don't already have an HTML (Web) browser. Insert the CD-ROM, and double-click the Read Me file for more information, instructions, and last minute changes. Appendix C also discusses the CD-ROM in detail.

Experts and Evangelistas

In 1996, Guy Kawasaki, Apple Fellow and Chief Evangelist, started an e-mail mailing list called the Evangelist. Every day, people write to a special e-mail address at Apple, where messages are gathered together, judged for their interest and appeal to a larger Macintosh community, and then dispersed through the Internet to tens of thousands of mailing-list recipients. These folks, called Evangelistas, read the message, and then respond as appropriate.

Often Evangelistas respond to individual requests for help from Mac users — problems they're having convincing their officemates to buy Macs for their department, issues they're having with a technical glitch, or requests for information on a product that can perform a particular task. The typical Evangelist question will often get tens or hundreds of responses from friendly Mac aficionados and experts.

In the course of writing this book, I tapped this enormous resource by sending my own requests to the list for tips and anecdotes about Macintosh upgrading. The best and most pertinent of those are included in sidebars throughout this book, along with the names of the senders and some information about them. I did this for two reasons: first, to let you in on some great tips that were new to me when I read them and deserve to be heard; second, to let you know that such a valuable resource exists for you, too, and that I certainly recommend reading the Evangelist if you have an interest in working with and maintaining Macs.

For more information on the Evangelist, see `www.evangelist.macaddict.com` on the Web.

Getting More Information

With the advent of the World Wide Web, information dissemination and publishing have changed somewhat dramatically. When I first started writing computer books, it wasn't common for authors to include an e-mail address in their prefaces. These days, something above and beyond that is usually necessary to properly satisfy the rights and needs of readers. In the case of a topic like upgrading and troubleshooting Macs, I believe this book needs to continue to breathe and expand beyond the snapshot of history that's enclosed within its shiny covers. On the World Wide Web, I'm able to do that.

The Mac-Upgrade.com Web site is designed to fill two needs: First, it will be a forum for discussion of this book and related topics, allowing me to chat directly with you about upgrading and repairing Macs. Second, it will allow readers to discuss problems among themselves or directly with the manufacturers and experts. You'll find coverage of newer Mac models, tips, explanations of new upgrades, news of new technologies, and more.

The site will also serve as the official errata and bug-report page for this book. I recommend that you periodically stop by the pages specific to this book to see if anything about the printed copy has changed or has been updated.

The Mac-Upgrade.com site URL is `www.mac-upgrade.com`. For book-specific updates only, enter `www.mac-upgrade.com/bible/` in your Web browser. This book also features a number of different resources for instant answers to your upgrading and repairing questions. See Appendix B for the best places to find help on the Web.

You can also write me directly with questions or comments, although I'd certainly recommend you check the Web site first. I love getting mail, and I'm happy to answer any question — but I'm only one person, and it can take me a few days to respond. If you happen to be asking a frequently asked question, it's probably already answered on the Web site, so you'll be better served by checking there first and getting the answer immediately.

If the Web site has not answered your question, however, send me a message at questions@mac-upgrade.com. In the subject line of your message, let me know how urgent the question is and tell me something about its content, as in: "3 days: Error on Page 59?" In the body of your message, tell me everything you can about your Mac (if relevant) and describe the problem in as much detail as possible.

If for some reason you can't reach me through the preceding address, I will always maintain the e-mail address tstauffer@aol.com on America Online (at least, as long as AOL continues to exist). Please send your message with a similarly complete subject line and description.

Feedback

This is a first edition of *Macworld Mac Upgrade and Repair Bible*, and as such, your feedback is most welcome and very necessary at this stage in the book's development. I certainly hope to have the opportunity to update this book frequently and comprehensively, but I can't do that without learning your opinions on the subject matter, organization, and coverage. Please feel free to send any and all criticism my way. You can even toss in a complement every now and then. I'll read every e-mail and try to incorporate as many suggestions as possible.

If you can, send the message to feedback@mac-upgrade.com and put the words "Bible Feedback" in the subject line. Or, check out the Feedback page on the IDG Books Worldwide Web site at www.idgbooks.com, or send postal mail care of *Macworld Mac Upgrade and Repair Bible*, IDG Books Worldwide, 919 E. Hillsdale Blvd. Suite 400, Foster City, CA 94404.

Acknowledgments

This was an amazing opportunity to take a stab at writing a good book on a topic I really enjoy, which isn't something I always get to say about my computer book projects. For this book I had a good schedule, quality conspirators, and access to the world's greatest computing network — the Mac community. Many people put a lot of time into this project to end up with the book that we did, and I'm very proud of the results.

First, I'd like to thank Michael Roney and Katharine Dvorak at IDG Books Worldwide for helping me all the way through the book-writing and editing process, including some important decisions and some great editorial calls as we decided how this book would be structured. Their advice and encouragement were invaluable, and their organization is one of the most professional I've dealt with in this business. With supporting help from Ami Knox and Steve Klett, it's no surprise that IDG's books are as well regarded as they are.

For technical expertise I relied on a number of different individuals, not the least of whom was technical editor Dennis Cohen, whose criticism of every single page of the manuscript was inestimable. I'd also like to thank Rich Voelker and Rob Blair of Voelker Research in Colorado Springs, Colorado. Both of them spent hours with me hashing out the best answers to some sticky Mac problems. On top of that, Rich went beyond the call of duty in giving me free reign in his Mac repair shop to take pictures, explore different Mac models, and pick his brain. It was a valuable experience that certainly proved beneficial to the book. Ryan Bruels, another of Rich's employees, was also helpful with preliminary troubleshooting research.

I'd like to thank a number of people, most of them industry experts and/or Mac Evangelistas, who offered tips, advice, and anecdotes for inclusion in the book. Those people include: Kevin Patfield, Mark Boszko, Rich Barron, Tony Hines, Dave Johnson, Mike Kent, Scott Barber, Jim Cox, Lisa Devlin, Philip Accas, Ronald D. Leppke, Doug Holmes, Doug Dickeson, Etienne Michaud, Rick Emery, David Lublin, Bill Smith, Bob Boyle, J. Brian Rowe, Allan M. Schwartz, Mark Marinello, Hunt Sidway, Andy Hendrickson, John Brassfield, Bob Patterson, Eric Wesselman, Peter Trzcinski, Gerald Wilson, Guido Korber, Don Miller, Nancy L. Spoolman, Yuval Kossovsky, Garry Halliday, Glenn Schunemann, Reed Jackson, George Pluimakers, Jon Steltenpohl, Wayne H. Deese, Martin Step, and Skillman Hunter.

It's also important to note that very few of these tips would have reached my desk if it weren't for the Evangelist, an Apple-sponsored electronic mailing list created by Guy Kawasaki and run by John Halbig. They've both done a valuable service by offering a virtual meeting place for that elusive and amazing group of folks known as the Mac Community. Ever wondered why the Mac is the best computer platform out there? It's the people involved.

Speaking of Apple people, I'd like to thank Keri Walker, Kim Strop, Jeremy Buschine, and the rest of the Apple public relations staff for responding to my frantic requests for Apple products, including a number of the Macs and peripherals pictured and discussed in this text. Other companies that helped with the production of this book include Polaroid, which provided an excellent 35mm slide scanner used in the book's production, as well as Techworks, Iomega, CH Products, SyQuest, Yamaha, Caere, RAMP Networks, Asante, Sonnet Technology, Kensington, Wacom, and CalComp, among others. Most of the photos in this book were shot with either a Canon PowerShot or an Apple QuickTake 200 digital camera.

The CD-ROM's organization, design, and HTML were conceived and implemented by Kevin Wiley, who was also responsible for securing permission to use the shareware and freeware titles found on the book's CD-ROM, as well as helping me set up, install, and test the products that are discussed throughout this book. He also served as Web master for my Web sites and network administrator for our offices, and proved invaluable in many other ways, including research and opinions for the book's content. This book would not have been as complete or as useful without his involvement.

I'd also like to thank David Rogelberg and Brian Gill from the Studio B agency for helping me secure this opportunity to write a book that I really wanted to write. Not to mention the coup the two of them pulled off by putting me together with a publisher that really wanted to give me the chance to do it well and enjoy the experience.

Finally, I'd like to thank Donna Ladd for everything else, including being a wonderful partner and friend throughout this entire process. Aside from reading and editing every page of this book, Donna was there constantly to support, critique . . . and help me forget about this effort and get out to see a movie every once in a while. Not only would this book be the worse for her not having been a part of my life, but I'd probably still be stuck somewhere around Chapter 12, mired in my own self-pity.

Contents at a Glance

Contents

Part II: Performing the Upgrade   141

Getting Ready to Upgrade

This part begins with the very basics — reasons for upgrading and the subsystems of a Macintosh that can be upgraded. It then provides a primer on how a Macintosh works, including the various add-ons and upgrades you can use to augment your Mac. The next step is to get serious about *bottlenecks,* or the slowdowns that your particular Mac is experiencing. With those identified, you can plan your upgrades, deciding what to do immediately, what can wait, and what needs to be sent out to a service center. Finally, in this part you take a look inside most Macintosh models, including how to get the case open and where to find certain parts of the computer.

Is It Time to Upgrade?

Should you upgrade? That's not the easiest question in the world to answer. If you're like me — scared to death of missing out on cutting edge technology — then it's a question you'll ask yourself all the time. If you're like some other Mac owners I know, the question almost never comes up — your Mac works and that's that.

But it is something you should ask yourself every once in a while. And, in general, it's an easy question to answer. However, here's a more clever way to ask it. Instead of "Should I upgrade?" ask yourself this: "Is my current Mac driving me crazy?"

Even if your Mac is driving you just a little crazy, you've probably identified a potential for an upgrade. If there's anything you want to do but can't — or if everything is just too slow for you to bother — then you're a candidate for an upgrade. Whether you're interested in speed, new capabilities, or better response times from hardware and software you already have, you can probably add these things to your existing Mac at a reasonable cost. All it takes is a little know-how and a logical approach. First and foremost, you need to follow the scientific method one learns in grade school: Identify the problem.

Does Your Computer Meet Your Needs?

You probably spent an absurd amount of money on your Macintosh when it first came out, and back then it probably met every one of your needs. Thousands of dollars were dropped in a store, or sent in the mail, and a shiny new system ended up in the trunk of your car, on your doorstep, or otherwise on your desk. For quite some time, everything hummed along nicely (see Figure 1-1).

Figure 1-1: I bought this Power Macintosh 6100/60AV in 1994. At the time, it was a serious screamer. These days, it might be sitting in a closet if it weren't for a couple of key upgrades that make it still very useful and usable.

As time went by, though, updates to the system software appeared, new versions of programs came out, and cool, new applications (such as those for Web browsing, 3D rendering, and high-end graphics) started popping up. Then one day, you realized you were drinking a lot of coffee or nervously swiveling in your chair every time you launched a program, saved a file, or started to print.

When this happens to many computer users, they just grin and bear it, assuming that upgrades or a new system would be an expense best left for next year, or somewhere down the road. Waiting to upgrade is not necessarily a good idea, however.

The Investment Principle

I encourage you to think seriously about your computer as an important investment. I know you spent quite a bit of money up front, but you may have used up those investment dollars already, especially if it's been a few years.

What's your time worth to you now? If you're doing something basic such as entering your finances and storing a household inventory, maybe you don't desperately need to spend much money on upgrading. But if you sit in front of your computer for hours and hours per day—as I do—you need to think carefully about the worth of your time and how much of it your computer is chewing up.

Tip

Here's a suggestion: Check your calendar for an upcoming day during which you will be required to use your computer for a lengthy stretch of time. While you work that day, keep a pen and paper handy. Make note of every time it takes your computer a few extra seconds to "think" about something: printing, copying, loading a program, signing on to the network. Assign a dollar amount to your hourly wage, and then multiply the dollar amount by the amount of time you were waiting on your Mac.

The trick then is to quantify your computing experience. Say your computer wastes $20 of your time per day. If $20 represents time wasted on an average business day, the computer is wasting about $5,000 of your time per year.

$20 x 250 working days per year = $5,000

That may seem like an extreme example, and it tends to assume you're not wasting much time on your own. In addition, you need to understand that not all upgrades are going to *completely* do away with wasted time. Even the fastest Macs force you to wait a few seconds for this and that. Nevertheless, it's still a useful number for gauging how beneficial it might be to upgrade for better productivity.

Next, take into account all the other issues you might have with your current computer setup, such as:

✦ *Anything that just drives you crazy.* Is there something in your setup (printer, modem, keyboard) that you want to replace now?

✦ *Anything that could be harming you.* Is your monitor fuzzy? Is your mouse cramping your wrist? These sorts of upgrades should be considered whenever using your computer isn't comfortable or pleasing to you. Remember, you probably work on your Mac for hours at a time. It should be a physically comfortable experience.

✦ *Any upgrade that could significantly increase productivity.* I used to have an inkjet printer that I swore by—I claimed that anyone who owned a laser printer was just asking for trouble and wasting money. But I'm also well-known for pushing deadlines. Every few weeks, during a book project, I'd need to print 75 to 100 pages of text and images to send to a publisher. I would usually start that process at about four o'clock in the afternoon to make the 7 p.m. FedEx drop-off time. I often missed it.

These days, with a laser printer, I can print 50 pages in about ten minutes. The printer cost a bit up front, but I feel much more productive on deadline days. And—surprise!—each page printed using the laser printer's toner is cheaper than a page printed using an inkjet's ink.

✦ *Anything you think might be really cool.* Might as well toss this one in. Would you like to upgrade for video conferencing? How about adding a digital camera or a scanner to help post images on the Web or place them in your newsletters? Whatever you want, include it in your list—especially if you think you deserve it.

By now you must have at least $7,000 worth of justification for a new system. (If you've got a corporate-based Mac, jump out of your cubicle, storm into the boss' office, and demand a new computer right now.) Even if you can't come up with that much money immediately, you now know it's probably worthwhile to perform some choice upgrades right away. The question is, which upgrades should you perform?

The 75/25 Rule

I made this rule up, and over the years more than a few of my computer-book–writing colleagues have disagreed with me. But I still think it stands, and I offer it here for your perusal. It's the 75/25 Rule.

Note

Why do a lot of computer book writers disagree with this rule? I can only assume it's because they constantly get cool computer toys to play with — for free — from the public relations departments of various computer companies. They then go on to proclaim that every computer user should spend thousands of dollars each year to upgrade to the latest and greatest. Fortunately, that isn't usually necessary — especially in the Mac world. Less expensive upgrades can often make your computing experience enjoyable again.

Basically, the rule goes like this: If you're on a limited budget for computing, you should make sure your equipment works very well for at least 75 percent of the things you do. The other 25 percent is where you can scrimp, if necessary.

Let me elaborate, using my own setup as an example. I'm a writer, and as such, I need a good monitor. My Main Mac has a very, very nice Sony 17" monitor, shown in Figure 1-2, which is incredibly crisp, displays millions of colors, and doesn't strain my eyes.

I'm also a *freelance* writer, so I spend a lot of time using the Internet for e-mail and accessing the World Wide Web for research. For this reason I have a very fast modem connection for my computer and would consider a higher-speed option if it were currently offered up here in the Rocky Mountains.

I also like to work with graphics and building Web sites, so I have a nice scanner. And, as should nearly everyone who works with important data and stores large files, I have a removable media drive (an Iomega Zip drive, currently) to help me back up all these important documents. I've also spent a little extra money for a comfortable, well-designed keyboard that promotes decent hand posture and doesn't annoy me with funny clicking sounds or oddly placed keys.

Figure 1-2: I deal with some graphics, but I'm not a professional artist, so this 17" monitor is the perfect size for my work.

What don't I have? I'm not a serious gamer, so I don't have a 3D-enhancing video card, an ultra-fast processor, or a major joystick or flight controller. (Actually, I did have all three of these while writing this book, because a couple different companies sent me their evaluation units. I may soon become a serious gamer.) I'm also not a high-end artist, so I don't need an expensive video card capable of extremely high resolution and acceleration. Likewise, I don't create many digital movies, so I don't need a full-blown audio/visual setup.

For me, the things I do that take up 75 percent of my time—looking at a monitor, writing, communicating, working with graphics, backing up data, printing—are all handled by equipment that's more than adequate. In fact, I enjoy using a fast Internet connection, a good monitor, and an expensive keyboard.

The things I only do 25 percent of the time—playing games, creating images, and working with video—aren't handled by the best and fastest add-ons. My computer is capable of doing these things, but it's not a barn burner.

Why different people need different computers

You can see from the description of my 75/25 distribution that different sorts of tasks require different types of computers. My computer tends to focus on input and output, because I mainly use it to write and print things. In fact, the demands I typically place on a Mac don't come near to requiring the high power that you can get in today's microprocessors.

On the other hand, a graphic artist, especially one using Photoshop for imaging or 3D programs for creating animations or illustrations, definitely needs a computer with a powerful processor. A high-end artist also needs a good monitor and scanner, but might only use a printer for proofing work, so a less-expensive color inkjet would suffice. Whereas an artist might need only the most minimal of modems, he or she will require access to high-end Jaz or SyQuest removable cartridges for storing huge data files.

In general, you can separate computers into a few different categories. Although your ideal Mac may borrow from two or more of these categories, this should give you a starting point for deciding what sort of focus your Mac should have:

✦ *Input/Output oriented.* Good for designers, writers, administrators, and professionals. This sort of Mac is capable of dealing with graphics, but is not designed specifically for that function. It has a midrange monitor, a good printer, a good keyboard, a decent scanner, and a mouse or trackball. It also has a modem and/or a basic network connection (if it's located in an office setting).

✦ *Graphics oriented.* This Mac is designed for artists, multimedia specialists, and architects. It features a huge monitor (or two or more monitors), a powerful graphics subsystem on an expansion card, a lot of RAM memory, and probably a special input tablet for freehand drawings. This computer also uses a high-speed processor and a reasonably high-capacity hard drive. The inkjet or dye-sublimation printer may only be for color proofing, and a minimum modem or network connection is necessary for e-mail or light browsing. In most cases, files are transferred using removable cartridges that can handle huge documents.

✦ *Multimedia oriented.* The audio/video (AV) professional or hobbyist, depending on the specialty, might need a special video-in card to help receive and compress live video signals for editing on the Mac. Multimedia-oriented computers need high-end processors, lots of RAM, and, quite often, expensive expansion cards for video editing. The monitor may not be particularly special, and the printer may not even be necessary, except for the occasional script or memo. There's probably not much reason for such a computer to be on a network (unless you have an office full of these AV monsters), but it will need a high-capacity removable drive. The modem is optional, as is a scanner and cool input device, although a graphics tablet and pen is nice for selecting and playing back video segments on screen.

✦ *Communications oriented.* This Mac is good for the home office or small business, salespeople, telecommuters, managers, and executives. It's perfectly good for reports, memos, and spreadsheets, but isn't designed for ten hours of use per day. Instead, it has a smaller monitor, decent keyboard, and typical mouse. The printer is a low-end laser or a fast inkjet, a scanner is either page-fed (for faxing through the computer) or nonexistent, and the processor is midrange. The modem or other Internet connection is fast, though, and this computer might even be equipped with telephony devices to keep an electronic log of long-distance calls, track appointments, and identify incoming calls using Caller ID information.

✦ *Home/Games oriented.* The home machine is midrange, enabling it to perform a variety of tasks — it can be used for business communications, desktop publishing, and connecting to the Internet. But its focus is on affordability and, in many cases, multimedia for games and educational titles. The printer, modem, and keyboard are all adequate, but a gamer's Mac will feature a quality joystick, a midsized monitor, and a special video card. Even a 3D-oriented gaming card can be plugged into this machine. It also features a fast processor, a fast CD-ROM drive, and good speakers. That's not just for gaming; you can also play audio CDs over this high-quality system while entering checkbook information or creating a database for your volunteer organization.

Where do you fit in? Perhaps with none of them — or several of them all at once. But you can see where your system is most likely hybridized, and what you'd typically want to concentrate on for a given task. If you're dealing with a tight budget, pick 75 percent of those tasks you most need to accomplish and build a Mac that tackles them elegantly and completely.

Should you upgrade or buy something new?

This is a tough question to answer, because it depends on a number of different factors, including what you already own, what you do with it, and how interested you are in spending money on the computer. The Macintosh is well known for its ability to stay useful for many, many years, even without significant upgrades. Macs built ten years ago can still be upgraded to all but the very latest Mac operating systems. That sure isn't the case with many other computers, including Intel-compatible PCs. But eventually you may need to take a look at your system and determine whether or not you should try to upgrade it now or just buy a new one.

Note

This section assumes you know a bit about the different processors and other technologies your Mac is based on. If numbers like PowerPC 601 and 68040 are foreign to you, read about them in Chapter 2, "Figure Out Your Mac."

Here are some starting points:

✦ *How old is your computer?* You're either satisfied with an older Mac or you're not. If you're not, you can do only a certain number of things with it before buying a new Macintosh. In the Mac world, the term *old* can apply to two different types of setups. The first is a computer based on a 68030 (or earlier) processor. That includes most of the Mac Classics, Mac II series, and LCII

series, and the even older Mac SE/30, SE, and Mac Plus series (see Figure 1-3).
Although these computers can be upgraded a bit, few of them can be
upgraded to PowerPC technology. The fastest speeds they can generally reach
were state-of-the-art around 1993. (Computers based on 68040 machines can
often be upgraded to PowerPC or better.) Certain original equipment,
PowerPC-based Power Macintosh setups make up the second type of "old"
Macintosh. If you've got a first generation Power Macintosh or PowerPC-
based Performa, your options may be a bit limited.

Figure 1-3: The Macintosh Plus can't be upgraded to the latest
PowerPC technology, but it can still be made into a reasonably
useful computer.

✦ *How upgradeable is your computer?* It may sound like a silly question, but
it's not. For instance, the Quadra 650 is an older-technology 68040-based
computer that was very popular with professionals, art firms, and corporate
graphics departments. It's also very upgradeable, with three NuBus slots and
the ability to accept 136MB of system RAM. Apple even built a special
PowerPC Upgrade card for that Quadra. Compare that system to the Quadra
660AV, which was an amazing system for its time. With built-in audio/visual
capabilities and a special digital signal processing chip, it was the standard
for media professionals in 1994 — a late-generation 68040 Mac with Power-

PC-like abilities. Unfortunately, it wasn't quite as upgradeable, with a fixed amount of video RAM, room for only 68MB of system RAM, and only one path to PowerPC: Pull the entire logic board and install a new one.

Although I intend to cover the upgradeability of most models in depth throughout this book, one way to get a quick snapshot of your system's configuration is to head to Apple's Web site. Buried there you'll find a gem called the AppleFacts Online Archive at `http://product.info.apple.com/productinfo/datasheets/indexhtml` on the Web. You can look up your current system's specifications and some of the upgrades Apple has made available over the years, and check for a match. (If you have a clone machine, you should check Appendix B and the included CD-ROM for links to sites that can help you determine the upgradeability of your particular model.)

✦ *How much will it cost to upgrade?* The basic problem with upgrading nearly any computer is newer computers tend to be pretty cheap to begin with — sometimes cheaper than the cost of getting your older Mac back in fighting shape. You can always spend a little less, but make sure the money you're spending is contributing to either satisfaction of the 75/25 rule or staving off insanity until you get a large enough windfall to buy a new Mac. Otherwise, you might as well squirrel that money away at 4 percent interest and save up for a new computer.

✦ *How happy will you be with an upgraded system?* It's not just the shiny chrome and the new tires — there's a good chance you really will be more productive with a new machine. If you look at all your options and realize you're just not getting the bang for your upgrading buck — or if you think all your current equipment is too dingy and you want some of that new stuff — you should probably start shopping the computer stores or some of the Mac-oriented Web-based stores.

With all that in mind, it's important to decide what exactly you need to upgrade, about how much it'll cost, and whether or not it'll be worth it. If you decide it is a good idea to upgrade, just keep Ol' Faithful computing. If you decide to buy a new system, continue reading to arm yourself with some valuable tips on what components are important in your Mac and what to look for while you're shopping.

Don't forget, there's a thriving aftermarket for used Macs sold among individuals. Check your local classifieds, the America Online Mac classified message boards (if you're an AOL member), or type `news:comp.sys.mac.wanted` in your Usenet message group reader program or your Web browser. If you need to know how much a system is really worth, check out the American Computer Exchange's regular listings at `www.amcoex.com` on the Web.

The What and Why of Upgrades

Before you can decide what upgrades are right for you — and how much they cost — you need to know a little about the different upgrades that are even possible with most Mac models. In this section, you'll look closely at the different reasons to upgrade your computer, and then you'll see many of the specific upgrade tasks that can be performed, including:

✦ Software upgrades

✦ Upgrading for increased speed

✦ Enhancing your productivity with upgrades

✦ Doing more things with your Mac

Great places to shop for Mac stuff on the Web

Other good stops may pop up along the way, but I find myself regularly visiting all the following Web sites in my constant pursuit of the perfect peripheral. At these sites you're bound to find plenty of great supplies, accessories, and, if necessary, new Power Macs and PowerBooks:

✦ The Apple Store (http://store.apple.com) — Some call it the "Great Configurator" because it's so much fun to shop the site for great systems and components, and then head back to the other Web stores, where they are cheaper.

✦ Club Mac (www.club-mac.com) — A fairly consistent player in the Mac-Web market so far, Club Mac really does feel like a club, of sorts, especially when you sign up for their weekly e-mail sales sheet. Plus, they often have great prices, discounts, and closeouts.

✦ Cyberian Outpost (www.cyberian.com) — A complete resource for software, books, accessories, Macs, and peripherals. Another good place to shop, Cyberian Outpost is known for its "Coming Soon" lists, long rosters of not-yet-released products that have been announced by their manufacturers.

✦ Other World Computing (www.macsales.com) — This site has been improving its look and feel for quite a while now, but you often can't beat Other World for great prices on Macs, PowerBooks, and other equipment. It's a no-frills kind of Web site, but that's part of what makes it fun.

Keep in mind that your particular model may not be able to handle every type of upgrade outlined in this section, although nearly every Macintosh model offers some level of upgrading ability that can improve performance and capabilities.

Cross-Reference

Obviously, most of what you'll see in this section is just the tip of the iceberg; if any of these upgrades confuse you or if you'd like to learn more about them, check out the chapters in Part II of this book. In those chapters, you'll find details for nearly every imaginable upgrade (and how most Mac systems can benefit).

Is your problem a hardware or a software issue?

Although most folks automatically assume upgrading requires buying new hardware for their computers, that's not always the case. In some instances, it's perfectly possible that a quick software fix will speed up your computer or otherwise give it a little more life. But how do you know if your problems can be addressed with a software fix? Here are some guidelines:

✦ *You haven't upgraded the Macintosh operating system in quite some time.* The Mac OS (or System, as it used to be called) is responsible for all the computing and interaction between the various components of your Mac. As newer versions have come out, Apple's engineers have occasionally made improvements that increased the performance of older Mac hardware. Assuming you have enough RAM to support the system update — and your system hasn't aged beyond the support of the latest Mac OS (only a few have) — you might seriously consider updating the operating system before doing anything else. (This is discussed in more depth in Chapter 31.)

✦ *You haven't checked for system-specific updaters.* Apple has to make little tweaks to the Mac OS for every single Macintosh computer model it creates. Sometimes, Apple improves those tweaks or releases new ones as bugs are found or new capabilities are created. In these cases, it's often up to you to find the updates and apply them yourself. The best way to start is to head over to www.apple.com/support where Apple has posted updated files on the Web. (This is also discussed in Chapter 31.)

Tip

Here's one that people miss a lot. If you have a GeoPort-style modem (or any modem that you bought directly from Apple), Apple tends to post the upgrades for the modem software on the Support Web site just listed. Apple also includes them on upgrades to the Mac OS. Believe it or not, you may be able to use a software upgrade to increase your modem speed for free. (See Chapter 16 for a lot more on modems and GeoPort adapters.)

✦ *You haven't checked for new device drivers in a while.* For many of the peripherals your Mac uses — such as the printer, scanner, and modem — special software drivers are loaded as extensions and/or Control Panels that help your Mac communicate with those devices. Over time, the manufacturers of those devices will often release new versions of the drivers that can improve reliability and speed, or even add (or activate) new features. Check the Web sites or call the customer-support lines of the manufacturers of your peripherals to check for possible updates.

✦ *You haven't updated your applications in a while.* Again, many applications go through completely free update versions intended to improve performance, fix problems, and add new features. These aren't always heavily publicized, so you should stop by the Web sites put up by the publishers of your favorite (and/or most often used) software programs.

✦ *You have a Power Macintosh and some older programs you use a lot.* When Apple switched to the PowerPC processor in Power Macs, it built in the ability to use the same programs that older Macs — such as Mac IIs and LCs and Quadras — had been using. However, these programs don't run very fast on PowerPC computers, because they aren't optimized for the new CPU. Instead, the Power Mac emulates an old-style 68040 Mac, which slows everything down (at least, relative to running PowerPC-based applications — the latest Power Macs still run 68040 applications faster than the original 68040 machines). To avoid this, you need to upgrade older software applications that weren't optimized for PowerPC when you got them. Upgrading some of them will be free — just consult the publisher's Web site. Others may charge for the privilege, but it's a great way to get better performance from a PowerPC.

✦ *You do a lot of copying from one hard drive to another.* Using some third-party utilities, it's possible to make your file copies run smoother and more efficiently. For instance, SpeedDoubler, a utility package from Connectix, increases copying speeds by more effectively using free RAM. Of course, Mac OS 8 and above also feature improved copying speeds, so it may just take upgrading to the latest version of the OS to see an improvement.

✦ *Your only real problem is you don't have enough RAM to run more programs at once.* Most Macs using System 7.0 and above (and certain, late versions of System 6.0.*x*) have the built-in ability to run more than one program at once, a capability called *multitasking*. The problem is each program needs its own fixed amount of RAM memory in which to run. Often hardware presents the solution — you need to install more RAM. And RAM can be pretty cheap these days. In some cases, though, it might be more useful to use Connectix's RAMDoubler, a program that causes your Mac to believe it has more RAM than it really does. This enables you to run more small programs at one time than you otherwise might be able to. It's not recommended for slower Macs, but if all you want to do is work with one or two more programs on a faster Mac, it might solve the problem. (See Chapter 6 for more on RAM upgrades and RAMDoubler.)

How do I know what version I have?

If you're following some of these suggestions for upgrading software, you may have noticed that many of the ideas require you to compare the *version* of a piece of software you currently have to any new versions that might be available. But how do you find out which version you have?

There are three basic ways to figure out what version you have of a program or driver software. The first way makes use of the Get Info command in the Mac's Finder. Find the program, extension, or Control Panel for which you need to know the version number. Next, use the File ➪ Get Info command. In the Get Info dialog box that results, you should see the version number of that particular program (see Figure 1-4).

The second way to determine the version number of most applications is to start the program itself. Next, from the Apple menu—in the top-left corner of the screen—select the About command. (The command's name actually changes for each program, so the command for Microsoft Word would be About Microsoft Word.) In the resulting alert box, you'll see the version number of the program (see Figure 1-5). You can usually click the OK button or just click the alert itself to return to the program.

The third option? Look at the floppy disk or CD-ROM that the program came on. You'll often find the version number printed on it. This method is low-tech, granted, but it often works like a charm.

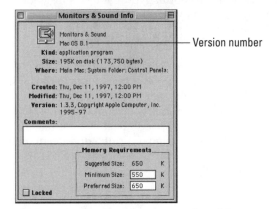

Figure 1-4: The Get Info command enables you to determine the version number of a particular Mac program or extension.

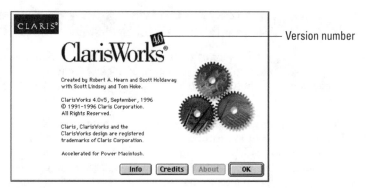

Figure 1-5: Another option for finding version numbers is to view the program's About box.

Knowing all these things can help you in the first part of your upgrade quest — deciding whether your problem is hardware or software. The best place to begin (usually because it's the cheapest) is scouting the Web and other resources (such as America Online, local Mac user groups, your local library or university, or even a Mac guru you may know) for updates to your system software, drivers, and any applications you use frequently. You may also find programs such as SpeedDoubler and RAMDoubler help you get through a rough patch in your upgrading plans, at least for the time being. But if all this comes to nothing, or if you're sure your software is already up-to-date, your problem may be on another front — hardware.

Speed up your Mac

One of the main reasons to upgrade the hardware in your Macintosh is to simply speed it up. That can mean a lot of things — you'll need to know a little about the specific slowdown before you can identify what about your computer needs to be upgraded. In general, though, a computer needs a speed boost when it takes a long time to load programs, spends quite a while preparing to print a document, drives you crazy while you wait for a new Web page to come up — anything like this. Usually, these sorts of problems can be fixed.

I'll begin by discussing some of the components of an aging Mac that tend to slow down the system, and what you can do to upgrade or otherwise improve those speeds. Chapter 2 discusses the actual workings of these items, but for now I just want you to be aware of the different options you have for increasing the speed and performance of your Mac.

✦ **Memory.** Believe it or not, the RAM memory in your computer can be the most important upgrade you make to increase the speed of your computer. Not only is it an easy upgrade, but it's also relatively inexpensive. I've seen posters that said, "You can never be too thin or have too much RAM." It's true (at least, the part about RAM). Adding a few megabytes of RAM can really free up your computer to do more things while speeding everything up a little bit. Chapter 6 discusses your RAM needs in depth.

✦ **Processor.** One of the main reasons your computer might slow down is the processor, or Central Processing Unit (CPU). It's here that everything is calculated — from what should be drawn on the screen to how to calculate a formula in a spreadsheet, how to change the spacing of text in a desktop publishing document to how to change the direction of an enemy plane in a flight simulation game. If these calculations seem slow, it might be time to upgrade the processor. In many Macs, the processor can be easily upgraded. Nearly all modern Power Macs include some sort of upgrading solution, as do many older Macs. Not all Macs are easily upgraded; you'll need to find out about your specific setup. Most of them are detailed in Chapter 6.

✦ **Logic board.** The logic board, or main circuit board, is the control center of your Mac, and may be worth upgrading in certain situations (especially when you move from Quadra-level Mac to Power Mac). In this sort of upgrade, you generally also get a faster processor; in fact, almost everything speeds up a little bit. This is a good upgrade because it essentially gives you a new computer, but at the same time enables you to keep the hard drive, video cards, and anything else you may have invested in significantly. The down side: Logic boards can be really tough to install. Additionally, upgrading the logic board can be expensive. (See Chapter 5 for details on the logic board.)

✦ **Hard drive.** An older hard drive can slow down a lot of things — loading programs, saving data, even playing QuickTime movies and multimedia games — because the computer wastes time trying to retrieve the data before it can compute and show you the results. Fast, new hard drives are especially important to graphics and multimedia professionals, because they're the folks who tend to save the largest files. However, even home users and gamers can benefit from faster hard drives.

✦ **Modem.** In a home office or small business, you probably use a modem to connect to the outside world and the Internet. Modems are all about speed — some fairly speedy modems are available, and you need them for a high-quality Internet experience. Even America Online users can benefit from a faster modem.

✦ **Networking.** If you already have your Macs networked, you can get a big speed boost by changing the type of hardware you use for your network. A lot of Macs still use LocalTalk — the basic telephone-wire-and-printer-port networking that Macs have always had. Move up to Ethernet, though, and you'll see an extreme difference. In special situations, you might even consider Fast Ethernet, which can really move files quickly.

✦ **Video.** If you work with complicated drawings and paint images on the computer screen, you may be well served with a new video card. Many new cards are designed with tons of memory to display millions of colors, along with special 2D and 3D acceleration capabilities, which enables them to draw images on the screen more quickly. You can also get specialty cards designed to help you render 3D images and add effects to video more quickly.

✦ **Printing.** Move up from an inkjet (or a dot matrix) printer to a laser printer, and you'll see a speed boost. Or, if you already have a laser printer, you can get a faster laser printer (especially if you've added computers to your workgroup) or connect your networked laser printer via Ethernet instead of LocalTalk networking hardware.

Improve your productivity

Obviously, you'll probably be increasing your productivity if you speed up your Mac. But that's not the only way to increase productivity. You can also add interesting and sometimes unique products to your machine that will help you do things with your computer that you haven't done before, perhaps making you more efficient or productive. For example:

✦ **Telephony and Internet.** Using certain modem and telephone upgrades, you can integrate your computer with your telephone, enabling you to track calls, take messages, get CallerID information, and automatically add callers to a database of contacts. Access to the Internet or online services can often save a trip to the library when it's time to research current events or check the address of a contact.

✦ **Scanning.** Adding a scanner to your computer can increase productivity in a number of ways: You can scan documents for electronic storage (making them easier to retrieve than paper-based files), you can scan text and use optical character recognition to translate the scan into a word processing document, or you can scan documents for faxing directly from your computer (thereby saving the cost of a fax machine and avoid the time wasted by standing over the machine to feed pages).

✦ **Printers and Accessories.** The faster the printer, the more productive you might be. But what about color? Having a color printer, a printer capable of legal-sized pages, or even a printer with an envelope-feeder could increase your ability to be productive with your computer.

✦ **Input Devices.** A new keyboard, more comfortable mouse, or pen-based input device can help anyone be more productive with their Macs.

✦ **Backup/Storage Devices.** The worst way to lower your productivity levels is to lose documents and have to recreate them because you didn't save them on a backup device. To stay productive with your Mac, you must implement a strong backup plan. That usually involves upgrading your system to include a removable media drive such as a tape drive or a Zip drive. You can also toss in some backup software to help you keep on top of your backup needs.

✦ **Networking.** If you've got a couple of Macs in your office, being able to share files and print to a high-speed printer without swapping floppy disks or Zip disks can be a major boon to productivity, because it keeps you planted in your seat while you work. (Of course, you should still get up and stretch occasionally.)

Do more things with your Mac

This last category of things to do with your Mac may or may not enable you to be productive. Some Mac users report they've gotten into completely new businesses because they started playing with their Mac one day. (I know Web designers and Mac programmers who started out that way.) And, you might also want to add some hardware to your Mac that's designed for nothing more than having fun with it.

Here are some upgrades that add capability to your Mac:

✦ **Multimedia.** This can be for work or for play. Card upgrades enable you to save digital video to your hard drive so you can edit the video and send it back out to a VCR as an edited presentation. Or, you can add 3D cards for rendering images, special accelerators for gaming, and surround-sound speaker systems. Of course, plenty of joysticks and weapon control systems are available for adding realism to the gaming experience.

✦ **DOS and Windows emulation.** A number of hardware solutions enable you to install an actual Intel (or clone company) processor inside your Mac. With a quick keystroke combination, you can switch between Windows (or DOS) and the Mac OS — in fact, both can be running simultaneously. This can be productive, too — especially if your company has some Windows-only programs you need to run. Or, it can be strictly for gaming. PowerMacs can even run software-only solutions (such as VirtualPC or SoftWindows) that give them similar capabilities at lower cost. And, yes, most of these solutions can run Windows 95, as shown in Figure 1-6.

✦ **PowerBooks.** Upgrades for the PowerBook run the gamut, from docks that make it simple to plug your PowerBook into a full-size monitor and keyboard to PC Card expansion cards that make short work of adding modems and Ethernet to your notebook. In addition, some PowerBooks can be upgraded with new processors (the PowerBook 500 can even be upgraded to a PowerPC processor!), and most of them can accept new RAM, external CD-ROM drives, and removable media.

✦ **CD-ROM and DVD-ROM.** Speaking of CD-ROM and DVD-ROM drives, if you don't have one, you've got to change that situation. Most new programs come on CD-ROM, and having a CD-ROM drive (any CD-ROM drive) makes upgrading your software, your Mac OS, or your utilities much easier than using floppy disks to do the same thing. Plus, tons of cool programs, clip art galleries, sound clips, shareware libraries, and even more serious stuff (law libraries and magazine archives, for example) are available on CD-ROM. The best titles are also being released on DVD-ROM media, which allow for even more data to be stored, including video and audio for full-length movies and realistic multimedia software.

So, that's what upgrading means, and that's what's possible with a little cash and some know-how. I hope you've decided you're ready to tackle an upgrade that's been haunting you for a while—or maybe you've come across some new ideas that will add to your Mac experience. If either is the case, you're ready to move on to Chapter 2, which discusses how your Mac works and what everything in your Mac does.

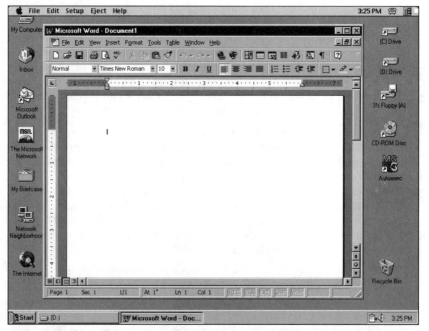

Figure 1-6: That's right . . . if you absolutely have to, you can run Windows 95 applications on many Mac models.

Summary

✦ When do you upgrade your Mac? When it's driving you crazy. Even if you're on a budget, your Mac should perform at least 75 percent of its tasks quickly, flawlessly, and in a pleasing way. It can struggle a bit with the other 25 percent, but if it has more trouble than that, it's time to upgrade.

✦ You probably need a Mac setup that is different from what many other people might need. Whoever you are, you're special, and your Mac should reflect that. Get to know all your upgrade options so you can make an informed choice.

✦ Upgrading and repair doesn't just refer to the nuts and bolts of your Mac — it can mean upgrading your software and your Mac's operating system, too. In fact, a lot of improvements can be accomplished for very little money by installing free upgrades and patches on your Mac's hard drive.

✦ There are many different reasons to upgrade your Mac, including gaining computing speed, increasing your productivity, and doing more things with your computer.

✦　　✦　　✦

Figure Out Your Mac

Before you can upgrade and/or repair your Mac, it is helpful to know a little about how your Mac works. If you're already up-to-speed on your Mac's innards, feel free to skim this chapter and move right on to Chapter 3. If you're more of an intermediate user, and you haven't quite learned everything there is to know about a Mac's hardware, you can delve a bit deeper into those topics here; this will make the terminology a bit easier to stomach when you get around to upgrading and troubleshooting your Mac in upcoming chapters.

How Your Mac Computes

You may have been clicking and typing away for years on your Mac without ever really wondering what process is underneath that makes everything happen. You press a key, for instance, and most of the time a character shows up on the screen. You choose Save from a program's menu, and an open file is stashed away for use some other day. Fire up America Online or your Web browsing program, and somehow your modem (or network connection) manages to talk to a distant computer and exchange information.

So how does all this work?

Your Mac can be seen as three different subsystems working together to make everything happen that needs to happen. Each of these subsystems communicate data back and forth at amazing speed, making the operating of your computer appear seamless. These subsystems are as follows:

♦ **Processing.** The processing subsystem is the brains of the system, ultimately responsible for all the computations your Mac makes to display things on the screen. These computations might include recalculating an average in a spreadsheet, deciding how to rotate a

3D object in a game program, or determining the correct spacing for a particular font face and kerning setting in a desktop publishing program.

✦ **Input/Output.** This subsystem is responsible for communicating with human beings and the outside world. It includes devices such as a keyboard, mouse, digital drawing tablet, modem, monitor, network interface, or printer. Any of these devices is designed either to get information into the computer (like a keyboard) or to send information from the computer (like a printer).

✦ **Storage.** All Macs also have a subsystem that is responsible for storing relevant data so that it might be used again. Storage devices include floppy drives, hard disk drives, CD-ROM drives, Zip drives, SyQuest drives, and anything else that can store data in a permanent way. The storage subsystem then keeps track of the Mac OS, your applications, and any data files or documents that you specifically save while you're working.

Take, for instance, the process of starting up ClarisWorks (or AppleWorks, if you have a newer version), opening a saved document, and working with that document. Doing so involves all three subsystems, which work together to create the experience, as follows:

1. You begin by using the mouse (input/output) to double-click the ClarisWorks icon in the Finder.

2. The Finder, on receiving this command, decides how it will load ClarisWorks (processing). ClarisWorks is found on the hard drive (storage) and started.

3. You then choose the Open command (input/output), and ClarisWorks responds by bringing up a dialog box (processing). The file you choose is loaded from the hard drive (storage). You then edit it using the keyboard (input/output and processing).

4. Finally, you choose the Print command (input/output), ClarisWorks creates a printer image (processing) and sends the image to the printer, which prints the document (input/output).

This description could go on forever, but you get the point. Essentially, these three subsystems work together to enable you to get data into and out of the computer so you can get work done, as shown in Figure 2-1.

Mac's Subsystems Working Together

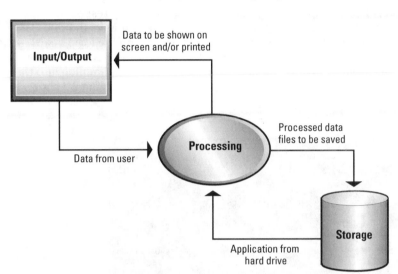

Figure 2-1: I/O peripherals, the processor subsystem, and storage devices all work together to help your Mac compute.

Within each subsystem are various components important to the function of that particular subsystem. In fact, many, many different components can exist in your Mac, more than I'll have space to discuss in this chapter. Throughout the rest of the book, however, I cover nearly all the components you are able to install in your Mac.

Ultimately, upgrading your Mac requires digging into each subsystem and replacing various components. What you'll find, though, is it's important to look at each subsystem as a whole, making sure you're upgrading in the most efficient way. To do that, you'll need to understand the internal workings of each subsystem.

Processor and Memory

The first subsystem I'll discuss is the processing system, which comprises the central processing unit (CPU), Random Access Memory (RAM), and other types of memory, such as cache RAM, you may have installed in your system. These three components work in concert to perform all of the data manipulation your Mac undertakes.

The CPU

At the heart of any computer is the CPU, which is ultimately responsible for processing all of the data the computer deals with. In your Mac, the CPU is a relatively small, square computer chip that sits directly on the logic board—the main circuit board in your Mac's computer. (Actually, some Mac's CPUs are installed on *daughtercards*, which are smaller circuit boards that plug into the main logic board. This is discussed in more depth in Chapter 6.) Figure 2-2 shows a logic board and CPU.

Figure 2-2: A Macintosh logic board (a Performa 6200 series board)

The CPU is the brain of your Mac, enabling it to perform mathematical operations, reorder data, or step through logical processes that, when taken together, add up to something useful in a computer application.

Note

Plenty of Mac owners refer to their Mac's entire case and power supply (the box with switches and disk drive openings built in) as their Mac's "CPU." This isn't exactly accurate, as the CPU is actually just a little chip that's attached to the Mac's logic board. You can still call it that, but it's probably more accurate to say, "I'm going to install a new hard drive in my Mac's case," than it is to say, "I'm going to install a new hard drive in my Mac's CPU."

If you actually planned to install something in the CPU, you'd need much, much smaller tools.

CPU speed

One of the foremost concerns most owners have with their CPU is gauging the speed at which it runs. Two different factors contribute to the speed of a CPU. One of those factors is the megahertz speed of the CPU's clock.

The speed at which a particular CPU computes is governed by a quartz clock crystal that is installed on the logic board. This crystal oscillates at a given frequency, in megahertz, acting as a timing mechanism for the CPU. As long as two processors are basically the same internally, you can compare their speeds by comparing their megahertz (MHz) levels, for example, a 68030 running at 25MHz is slightly slower than a 68030 running at 33MHz.

But you can't just compare two completely different CPUs by their megahertz speeds. For instance, a Macintosh running a 68030 processor at 33MHz would not be faster than a 68040 running at 25MHz, because the 68040 is a more advanced processor, capable of many more instructions than a 68030 at the same (or even at a slightly lower) megahertz level.

Note

The Motorola 680x0 family ranges from the 68000 processor (the original Mac and Mac Plus) to the 68040 processor (Quadras and Centris models), with stops at 68020 (Mac II) and 68030 (SE/30, Mac IIx, and others) along the way. Each series got progressively faster, even at the same megahertz level.

CPU architecture

The Macintosh OS has actually run on two different series of CPUs. While the Mac OS itself is *backward compatible* (meaning the current Mac OS can run most of the programs that have ever been written for older Mac OS versions), the two different series of processors are not compatible.

✦ **The Motorola 680x0 series.** From the first Macintosh model (the Mac 128K) through the powerful and popular Quadra and PowerBook 500 series, the Motorola 680x0 processors reigned supreme. These processors were based on Complex Instruction Set Computing (CISC) architecture, a popular way to build microprocessors in the 1970s and 1980s. By comparison, the Intel x86 family of processors (including the Pentium processors, to a degree) also use CISC architecture.

Tip

It's not a hard-and-fast rule, but Motorola processors are generally referred to (when speaking) by their last three numbers, each digit read individually, as in "Oh-Four-Oh" when discussing a 68040. (You'll also hear it said "Oh-Forty.") If you wanted to include the megahertz level of the processor, you could say, "I have a 25 megahertz oh-four-oh in my Quadra," and come off sounding like a pro.

✦ **The IBM/Motorola PowerPC series.** Starting in early 1994, Apple introduced a new line of CPUs to their customers — the PowerPC processors built by Motorola and IBM. Based on the more advanced Reduced Instruction Set Computing (RISC) architecture, these chips were able to run faster than the older Motorola series. Additionally, Apple has been able to increase the abilities of new PowerPC chips in an exponential fashion, going from 60MHz processors to 300MHz processors (and beyond) in about four years' time.

Like the 680x0 series, the PowerPC has also been through a few different iterations. Each new numbered series has made improvements on the former, in most cases including a boost in speed. Table 2-1 shows how the currently available PowerPC processors stack up.

Table 2-1
PowerPC Processors Used in Mac OS Computers

PowerPC Processor	Megahertz Range	Improvements
601	60–120MHz	Original PowerPC chip
603/603e	75–300MHz	Consumes less power, slightly faster than 601
604/604e	120–350MHz	Faster than 601, 603; 604e is low-power
740/750	233–300 (and above)MHz	Low-power, faster than 601, 603, 604

Note that the PowerPC 740 and PowerPC 750 processors are generally referred to by Apple as the *G3* processors, presumably meaning *third generation*.

Apple's transition to PowerPC

In the late 1980s and early 1990s, Apple recognized a growing need in the future of Macintosh computers. The Motorola 680x0 architecture, on which Apple had relied for years, wasn't getting much faster. It was taking a long time for newer, exciting processors to come out — so long that Apple was concerned they'd lose customers to the Intel standard. So they reconfigured Macs to use a completely new and exciting chip designed jointly by Motorola and IBM, with a little help from Apple.

But the new PowerPC architecture created some interesting challenges for Apple. Because the PowerPC was completely different from the old Motorola chips, regular Mac software — even the Mac OS — wouldn't run on PowerPC chips. For programs to run on the PowerPC architecture, which is a completely different type of processor from the older Motorola 680x0 chips, Apple had to rewrite the Mac OS so it would do two things.

First, the new PowerPC-enabled Mac OS had to run applications that were specially rewritten to take advantage of the fast PowerPC processor architecture. These are called *native* applications, because they're written specifically for the PowerPC processor that's native to a Power Macintosh. (If you were a Mac owner around 1994, you might have heard a lot about "Made for PowerMac" and "PowerPC Native" software.)

Second, Apple enabled older applications to run on the new PowerPC machines in an emulation mode. In essence, the Apple team rewrote the Mac OS so that it could, if necessary, pretend the PowerPC processor was actually one of the older Motorola chips. That is, older programs could be fooled into running correctly.

The only caveat: Emulating the old chip is slow. Even on newer Power Macs, it's always recommended that you upgrade any 680x0-style programs to a PowerPC-native version. The speed improvement is very noticeable.

Main memory

The CPU isn't the only component in the processing subsystem. An important part of this process involves the RAM installed in your Mac. RAM is one of the places in which the processor keeps documents and application data that is currently being processed. The CPU can't process everything simultaneously, so important stuff is put into a holding pattern until the processor is ready.

In this way, computer memory is a lot like human memory—at least, short-term human memory. Things you remember for a long time, like a bygone birthday or your high school graduation, are events that would be more appropriate for a computer's storage subsystem; things need to be written to a storage device, like a hard drive, if a computer is expected to "remember" it for a long time.

But RAM, on the other hand, is the short-term memory of a computer. For instance, everything you see at any given time on your computer screen is actually in RAM—as is a good portion of the document you're working on in a word processing program or the image you're editing in Photoshop. RAM is a repository of space that's used by the processor to keep track of *current* data the processor needs for the task at hand.

That's why adding RAM can significantly boost the performance of your computer. The reason? RAM is much faster than any storage option—even a high-speed hard drive. The more RAM (short-term memory) your Mac has, the less it has to access the hard drive (long-term memory) to fetch an important piece of data. Every time your computer stops to check something on the hard drive, it slows things down a bit. The more RAM you have, the less this speed bump shows up.

The RAM module

So what is RAM? Physically, RAM is usually a collection of chips, called *DRAMs* (for Dynamic Random Access Memory), placed on a module that can then be easily installed in a RAM socket on the logic board of your Mac. The module, depending on its design, is either a Single Inline Memory Module (SIMM) or a Dual Inline Memory Module (DIMM) (see Figure 2-3). SIMMs have been the standard with nearly all Mac models since the Macintosh Plus (the first Mac with upgradeable memory) was first introduced. DIMMs are relative newcomers, common only on high-end PowerPC 604 and PowerPC 750 (and above) Macs.

Figure 2-3: On top, a SIMM; below, a DIMM

RAM modules are designed to be easily added to a Mac's logic board, allowing the amount of RAM to be flexible to your needs — although there are limits for most Mac models. PowerBooks are the exception; they generally don't use standard SIMM or DIMM designs, but each particular PowerBook model requires particular upgrade modules.

Nearly every Mac model has slightly different RAM requirements. You'll want to check your manual carefully and read Chapter 6 in this book before buying RAM for your system; depending on the model, your Mac may not be able to accept additional RAM. If you can add RAM, though, it tends to be one of the easiest upgrades to accomplish (see Figure 2-4), and the additional RAM can have a significant impact on the performance of your computer.

Figure 2-4: A RAM SIMM being installed in a free SIMM socket. This is usually all it takes to add RAM to your Mac.

Measuring RAM

RAM is measured in megabytes (MB), each of which represent roughly millions of bytes. A byte is the amount of computer memory necessary to store one text character, like the letter g. Millions of bytes, then, represent millions of characters.

Note

Kilobytes (K), or thousands of bytes, is also an important measurement in computing, but not so much when discussing system RAM. (It's been over a decade since a viable computer had less than one megabyte of system RAM.) Other types of RAM (discussed a bit later in this chapter) are measured in kilobytes, however.

In general, SIMMs are available in increments of 1MB. Common SIMM sizes include 1-, 2-, 4-, 8-, 16-, 32-, 64-, and 128MB modules.

Other memory

Aside from short-term computational needs, your computer uses RAM for a couple of other purposes. In fact, your Mac usually has more than one set of RAM modules, with modules designed for different purposes aside from the main system memory. One of those purposes, video RAM, is discussed later in the "Input and Output" section of this chapter. Another use for RAM, called *cache memory*, is an important part of most modern Mac processing subsystems.

I mentioned before that having a sufficient amount of RAM can speed up your system. Any time the computer can't find data in RAM, it has to seek it out on the hard drive, which slows everything down. Adding RAM makes your Mac less likely to consult the hard drive, making operations proceed more smoothly.

Cache memory takes that theory one step further. Just as a squirrel might have a cache of nuts close by for easy consumption in the winter, many modern Macintosh processors take advantage of a bit of cache RAM that holds frequently needed data, making it available at a moment's notice. This cache RAM is usually a higher speed than common system RAM, and it uses sophisticated mathematical formulas to attempt to determine what data will be necessary for the processor's next functions. When the processor is forced to consult standard RAM for data, the process is somewhat slower than when it consults cache RAM. So, every *hit,* or successful cache RAM prediction, speeds the computer a bit more.

Cache RAM is also much more expensive than typical system RAM — usually three to five times more expensive. That's why it's used more sparingly. Where you might have 64MB of RAM for your main system, you might only have 1MB of cache RAM.

Types of cache

To add to the overall complication, there are actually a few different types, or *levels*, of cache memory:

✦ **Level 1.** Level 1 cache is a small bit of memory — usually 8 or 16 kilobytes — that sits on the processor chip itself. This memory is used by the processor to hold the very next instructions and/or data that will be needed so the flow of data isn't impeded by slower forms of RAM.

✦ **Level 2.** Level 2 cache is a larger amount of very high-speed RAM — between 256 kilobytes and 2 megabytes — that acts as a buffer between the processor's on-board cache and the system's main RAM. Level 2 is usually a module of faster, more expensive RAM. In many newer Macs, it can be added or upgraded to increase performance. Level 2 cache RAM is often added using a specially designed module that plugs into the Mac's logic board.

✦ **Level 3.** Level 3 cache only shows up in the rare system, although it's becoming a bit more common. Level 3 cache is really identical to level 2 cache — a high-speed RAM module on the logic board. The difference is level 3 cache refers to this type of RAM only when another level 2 cache module is also present. This happens most often with PowerPC 750 and similar processors that feature level 2 cache on the processor daughtercard. If both types of cache are present, the cache on the logic board is level 3. (Level 3 cache is rarely useful and most often disabled when a new level 2 source is installed in an upgradeable Mac.)

What is backside cache?

With the popularity of the PowerPC 750 has come a new type of cache memory that has entered the Mac maven's lexicon — backside cache. So, what's the difference?

You already know that traditional level 2 cache RAM is a very fast memory module designed to hold data that the computer believes the processor will be using over and over again — thus cutting down on relatively slow requests to the system RAM for new data. Backside cache works the same way (and, in fact, is also level 2 cache), but it's even faster.

Whereas regular level 2 cache lives on the motherboard, backside cache lives on a special daughtercard, right next to the processor. In fact, both the processor and the cache are on their own separate memory bus, enabling them to transfer data at very high speeds — usually between 50 percent and 100 percent of the processor's clock speed. (So, a 300MHz processor might have a backside cache that runs between 150 and 300MHz.) This makes accessing a backside cache much quicker than accessing a traditional level 2 cache, which is limited to the speed of the system bus (40–83MHz or so).

Storing Data on Your Mac

One of your Mac upgrade priorities is likely its storage capabilities — that is, the ability to save information, applications, and data that you use in your daily computing. Although your system's hard drive is the most obvious form of storage in your Mac, you might need to upgrade or augment others as well. In many cases you'll know when you need a new storage solution: Either you're unable to store as many applications and data files as you need to store, or you're having a lot of trouble storing and transporting files between locations, service bureaus, or among friends and colleagues. In that case, you'll want to know your options and upgrade your Mac to handle your current storage requirements.

Types of storage

Although your Mac likely came with a floppy disk drive and a hard drive (and perhaps a CD-ROM drive), you certainly have other options to consider. Before you can decide exactly how to add storage to your machine, though, you need to know what's available. Consider the major types of storage:

✦ **Hard drive.** The hard disk drive, sometimes called a fixed disk or hard disk, is the main storage unit for many Mac users. The hard drive is generally capable of storing many different data and application files — both large and small — and files on a hard drive can easily be erased and overwritten. It's certainly possible (and fairly easy) to add an external hard drive to your Mac, which you could conceivably take with you and attach to another Mac, if necessary. However, hard drives are generally considered less portable than other types of storage.

✦ **Floppy drive.** Also called floppy disk drives, every desktop Mac model and most PowerBooks feature a floppy drive capable of storing data on removable floppy disks, as shown in Figure 2-5. (Actually, the disks don't seem floppy at all, because they feature a hard plastic shell, but the disk on the inside of the casing is floppy.) Floppy disks are for storing a few smaller files or (in some cases) applications. Whereas floppy disks can only store a fraction of the files that a hard drive can handle, the floppy is much more portable and easily exchanged with colleagues or friends.

Note

At the time of writing Apple was just beginning to introduce Mac models that don't come with floppy drives, specifically the consumer-oriented iMac. In the past, only PowerBook Duos, the PowerBook 100, and the PowerBook 2400 have been released without built-in floppy drives, requiring an external drive to access a floppy disk.

Figure 2-5: A floppy disk being inserted into a Mac floppy drive

✦ **Compact Disc drives.** Although the most common CD-based drives for Macs are Compact Disc–Read Only Memory (CD-ROM) drives, they're not the only type. CD-based drives are able to store hundreds of megabytes of data that can be retrieved at speeds fast enough to run multimedia applications — such as showing digital video on screen. CD-ROM drives can only read that data, however. Instead, a special drive like a CD-Recordable (CD-R) drive or a CD-Rewritable (CD-RW) drive is necessary for storing data on a CD. CDs are capable of around 700MB of storage and are easily transported and shared.

✦ **DVD drives.** Alternatively called *digital video disc* and *digital versatile disc*, DVD is a standard for CD-like discs that can store many, many times the information of a standard CD. Like CD-ROM drives, most consumer DVD-ROM drives are read-only; however, recordable drives do exist for media professionals and others. DVDs can hold many large files and are easily transported and shared. (Note that DVD drives require Mac OS 8.1 or greater.)

✦ **Removable media drives.** Although in a class similar to CD and DVD technologies, removable drives run a wider gamut of formats, capacities, and capabilities. In general, removable media drives include an easily removed cartridge or media container that, like a floppy disk or a CD, can be transported and shared. Popular versions of removable media drives include the Iomega Zip drive (shown later in Figure 2-7) and the SyQuest SyJet drive. SyQuest is also the pioneer of older SyQuest removable technologies that are popular with many Mac users, prepress houses, and print shops.

✦ **Tape drives.** Although not as popular in the Mac world as in the Intel-compatible PC industry, tape drives are still a viable alternative for users wanting inexpensive back-up capabilities. Whereas tape is transportable and can store quite a bit of information, it is also more difficult to deal with than regular removable media, often using proprietary file formats. In addition, tape drives are much slower than other removable media drives.

✦ **DAT and 8mm tape.** These tape drives (*DAT* stands for *digital audio tape*) are a little different, offering large capacities and higher-speed retrieval. Although mostly found in larger offices, these high-end tape mechanisms offer a convenient and reasonably affordable way to back up large amounts of data on a regular basis.

Reasons to add storage

There are a couple of reasons to upgrade your Mac's storage capabilities, and certain recommendations I can make based on those needs. See which category fits you most completely:

✦ *Add storage space for permanent files and applications.* Sometimes you simply run out of space on your hard drive. Upgrades to older applications tend to require more space, and you're constantly creating and storing data files as you compute. In cases where a lot of storage is more important than transportability, your best solution is usually to upgrade by adding a larger hard drive. (You can also replace your existing drive, but desktop Macs are very easily upgraded by simply adding a new drive.) You might also consider a removable media drive, like the Iomega Jaz, which is capable of storing 1GB (1,024MB) of data or more on a removable cartridge.

✦ *Transport files to others.* Many creative Mac owners have a need to carry with them large graphics and animation files that are to be processed by others who specialize in preparing the files for print or media production. Business people and professionals might have similar needs, or they might simply want to transport their work home without lugging the computer along with it. In these cases, a removable media drive usually serves them well, with capacities ranging from the 100- or 200MB Zip drives to 2.5GB media and beyond. In some cases, it can also be worthwhile to create writable or rewritable CDs for distributing to a large organization or among friends and coworkers.

✦ *Back up important files.* One of the most important reasons to upgrade your storage capabilities is to add a complete back-up solution to your Mac system. Backing up files is one of the most important tasks in a professional or creative setting, yet not enough small and large businesses (or home offices) have a complete, workable back-up plan. Either inexpensive tape drives, DAT drives, or removable media drives can be useful in creating your back-up system.

Hard drives

Hard disk drives are small, self-contained metal boxes responsible for the main storage duties of almost every desktop and laptop Macintosh computer made. The drives themselves contain disks, or platters, that are covered in a special coating. A magnetized head — something like a magnetic version of a phonograph's needle — passes over the platter, reading and writing tiny bits of data, and then sending those bits to the main system RAM, where it can then be processed by the CPU.

Drive capacity

Very early hard drives — those that came as add-ons to the first few Mac models — held about 10- to 20MB. Since then, Macs have featured a variety of popular sizes, from 40MB and 80MB to 230MB, 500MB, and even 810MB. These days, hard drives tend to be measured in the gigabytes of data they can store; a typical new Macintosh computer can come with hard drives that can store anywhere from two to nine gigabytes of data, or more. Add-on drives you buy for expansion purposes tend to offer a similar range of capacities. Hard drive technology is continually improving, suggesting that capacities will continue spiraling up for a number of years. Figure 2-6 shows an internal hard drive.

Drive technology

For years nearly every Mac that had a hard drive was relying on Small Computer System Interface (SCSI) technology. SCSI hard drives tend to be a bit quicker than the alternatives, whereas the SCSI bus in Macs offers a number of interesting expansion options. (Not only can you add hard drives, for instance, but also scanners, CD-ROM drives, removable media drives, and other more specialized devices, too.)

Figure 2-6: A typical internal hard drive—this one came directly from a Power Macintosh 6100.

Some modern, midrange Macs offered by Apple and a few of the clone vendors feature Integrated Drive Electronics (IDE) hard drives and internal interfaces. IDE, a popular interface for Intel-compatible PCs, is a more inexpensive technology that offers good performance. Most of these Macs, however, can accept external SCSI devices for expansion purposes.

Drive speed

A number of different statistics, taken together, give you an idea of a drive's overall speed. These numbers are only reasonably interesting; nearly any modern hard drive designed for SCSI- or IDE-based Macs is going to prove fast and capable enough, as long as you buy a drive with a large enough capacity for your tastes. There are reasons to worry over these numbers, though. The faster the drive, the more capably it will run more storage-intensive applications, such as those for recording digital audio and video. If you expect to make professional-caliber QuickTime movies, for instance, you'll want a fast drive.

Here are the specific statistics to watch for:

✦ **Seek time.** This is the average amount of time it takes a drive to find a particular piece of data. What's measured here is the elapsed time, in milliseconds, that it takes the read/write head to find data on the spinning platter inside the drive. Seek times between 8 and 17 milliseconds are optimal.

✦ **RPMs.** The revolutions per minute (RPMs) statistic is an important measurement of overall speed. This number represents the speed at which the drive's spindle (on which the platters are mounted) spins. Speeds of 4,800 and 5,400 RPMs are typical; speeds of 9,600 RPMs or greater are generally considered AV-rated.

Floppy drives

Every Mac, with the exception of a few mini-PowerBook models and the iMac, has a floppy drive built right in. Depending on the age of your Mac, its floppy drive may have certain capacities and features that differentiate it from other models' drives, but for the most part the drives accept 3.5" floppy disks to which they can read and write data. Some of the differences over the years are listed here:

✦ **Capacity.** Original Macs featured floppy drives capable of storing 400 kilobytes of data on a single disk. Later Macs (Mac 512e, Plus, and early Mac II series) featured double-density 800K drives capable of reading and writing both to 400K and 800K disks. Finally, the Mac IIx and up are capable of reading and writing to high-density 1.44MB floppy disks as well as 800K and 400K disks. (Some modern floppy drives can only read, not write to, 400K disks.)

✦ **Injection.** All Apple Macintosh floppy drives have an auto-eject feature, which automatically ejects the disk from the floppy drive once the disk is no longer needed by the Mac OS. Early Macs (up to and including some Centris and Quadra models) offered *auto-inject* as well, meaning a disk would be grabbed by the floppy drive and pulled in through its opening when placed there. Later Quadra and all Power Macintosh models use less expensive drives that require you to push the disk completely into the drive.

✦ **SuperDrive.** The 1.4MB high-density drives in most Mac models are called *SuperDrives* because, with the correct software (called PC Exchange, part of the Mac OS since System 7.5), these drives are capable of reading, writing, and formatting MS-DOS, ProDOS (Apple II), and similar formats. That makes it possible for you to stick a DOS-formatted disk into your Mac, read data from it, write data to it, and return it to a friend who uses an Intel-compatible computer.

Compact disc and DVD

These removable disc drives — especially the CD-ROM drive — have become pretty much standard issue for most modern Macs, and were optional in most new Quadra, Centris, LCIII, and Power Mac models. As a result, CD-ROMs are becoming a standard format for commercial software and Mac OS system software installations; rarely do programs and updates arrive on floppy disk nowadays. For the most part, these installations are much less time-consuming and troublesome for the user, enabling you to insert the CD-ROM into the drive, begin the installation program, and move on to another task while allowing the installation to complete.

This convenience also makes CD-ROM drives a fairly important upgrade. If your system doesn't already feature a CD-ROM drive, adding one is certainly recommended, especially if you plan to use your Mac for multimedia or gaming applications, or if you need to install new applications on a fairly regular basis. Both external and internal CD-ROM drives can be added to many systems. Most Macintosh-oriented CD-ROM drives use SCSI technology for connecting to the Mac.

DVD drives are backward-compatible with CD-ROM drives, meaning you can insert a disc using either CD-ROM or DVD technology and have no trouble reading it with your Macintosh. If you expect to run games, watch commercial movies, or use multimedia educational (or reference) titles, a DVD drive would be a good upgrade.

CD technologies

Aside from reading data from compact discs, CD-based drives have other capabilities, each slightly different:

✦ **Compact Disc–Read Only Memory (CD-ROM).** These very common drives are for reading CD-ROM material only. Most modern Macs come equipped with these drives, enabling program CD-ROMs to be used for installations and reference CD-ROMs to be used for data access.

✦ **Compact Disc–Recordable (CD-R).** These drives are capable of writing data to special CD-R media. The drives can only write data once, however, and special software is required. The media is reasonably inexpensive, enabling you to distribute or archive information in CD format to share with friends or colleagues.

✦ **Compact Disc–Rewriteable (CD-RW).** Often, drives are both CD-R and CD-RW capable, depending on the media. CD-RW media tends to be quite a bit more expensive, but in exchange you get the added ability to overwrite data you've previously saved to the CD. This makes using the drive for backing up or temporary archiving a more viable solution.

✦ **Digital Versatile Disc–Read Only Memory (DVD-ROM).** As the DVD standard emerges, the most affordable DVD drives are actually DVD-ROM drives, capable of reading both CD-ROM and DVD-ROM media, but incapable of writing data to either.

✦ **Digital Vesatile Disc–Random Access Memory (DVD-RAM).** This is another emerging standard using DVD media. In this case, the media can be written to by your Mac.

CD speeds

For comparison purposes, CD-ROM drives offer two important statistics —
throughput levels and seek times:

✦ **Throughput.** CD-ROM drives measure throughput in kilobytes per second
(KBps), but in practical terms this number is usually expressed as a multiple
of audio CD speeds; for instance, a 4x, or *4 speed,* drive is four times the data
throughput rate of an audio CD player. Audio CD players transmit data at 150
KBps, so a 4x drive is capable of transmitting 600 KBps. In more recent years,
the speed at which CD-ROMs are capable of transferring data has skyrocketed
to 24x and beyond. The popularity of DVD, in addition, has driven the prices
of CD-ROM drives down to the point that even the fastest made are very
inexpensive.

✦ **Seek time.** Not often reported by the manufacturer's marketing department,
seek time is still a reasonable gauge of a CD-ROM drive's speed. Times of 150
milliseconds or less are adequate.

Removable media

Many different standards and types of removable media exist, including the popular
Syquest, Bernoulli, and Zip systems. In general, the point with any removable media
is to enable you to store a good chunk of data (tens or hundreds of megabytes) on
one removable element. You can then transport that data, share it with others, or
store it in a safe place for backup purposes.

The following are some of the more common types of removables and their
typical uses:

✦ **SyQuest.** SyQuest, Inc.'s SyQuest cartridge drives were a popular standard for
Mac creative professionals in the late 1980s and early 1990s. The removable
SyQuest cartridges work a little like hard disk drives, with a drive head and a
platter. Popular capacities include 44MB, 88MB, and 200MB, along with
smaller 135MB, 230MB, and 270MB SyQuest cartridges. Although these
cartridge drives have been supplanted somewhat by new offerings from
SyQuest (like the 1.5GB SyJet drive) and competitor Iomega, they are still very
popular with creative agencies and prepress services.

✦ **Bernoulli.** This competing standard by Iomega was similar to SyQuest drives
in form and function. Sizes ranged from 35MB to 150MB.

✦ **Magneto Optical.** A popular buzzword in the early 1990s, this drive
technology was heralded as a laser-based replacement for many drive
technologies because of its ability to reach higher into impressive storage
capacities. Other drive technologies, however, have largely stolen its
thunder, although it's made something of a comeback in recent times.

✦ **Zip and Jaz.** Taking the industry by storm, Iomega introduced and fiercely marketed the Zip drive as an inexpensive 100MB storage solution to supplant the floppy drive. Since then, millions of Zip drives have sold, including many that are now preconfigured in Apple and clone Mac OS machines. The Jaz drive, Zip's bigger brother, is a 1–2GB drive capable of hard drive speeds. Figure 2-7 shows a Zip drive.

Figure 2-7: The Zip drive, popular for both its convenience and its blueness (on external versions), is preinstalled in many Power Mac models. (Photo courtesy Iomega Corp., www.iomega.com)

✦ **SyJet and EZ Flyer.** Not to be outdone, SyQuest has retaliated with a similar line-up of high-speed removables. The EZ Flyer works at hard drive speeds (faster than a Zip drive) and stores 230MB of data, whereas the SyJet stores 1.5–3GB of data at a higher speed still. Unfortunately, SyQuest hasn't been able to grab the mindshare that Iomega has, making it less likely that a print shop or service bureau can accept one of these cartridges. They remain, however, great for personal transporting and backup.

Input and Output

Your Mac computes, and your Mac stores data. So far, so good. But to think this is all your Mac does is to overlook the most important part of most computing tasks — interaction with human beings. That's where input and output come into play.

Input means getting data into the computer — and this can be done through any number of different devices: keyboards, mice, trackballs, graphics tablets. Macs have traditionally been graphically oriented, so input devices have followed suit by attempting to duplicate other interfaces — like pencil and paper — found in the artist's real world (see Figure 2-8). Even scanners and cameras can be used to get digital data into your Mac.

Figure 2-8: Graphics tablets are a great substitute for a mouse — especially for freehand artists and other tactile types.

Output means the different ways your computer turns data into something more tangible by human senses: In most cases, that's sound or visual display. To generate output, you need special output devices — such as monitors, printers, and a sound interface — that can take computer data and turn it into something a little more interesting and meaningful to people.

Hooking up I/O devices

Input/output devices (or I/O devices, for short) are generally external devices that hang off your computer's case (some of these things can be built in, too). In general, these devices are connected to your Mac in one of five ways:

✦ **Serial Ports.** Your Mac has at least one and probably two serial ports, located on the back of the computer. On most models, one of the ports is labeled with a picture of a phone, whereas the other one features a small printer icon.

✦ **SCSI.** All Macs also feature an external SCSI port, enabling you to hook up multiple SCSI devices by daisy chaining them together. SCSI devices can include hard drives, CD-ROM drives, scanners, cameras, and other devices.

✦ **ADB Ports.** ADB, or Apple Desktop Bus, is a special port used for keyboards, mice, and graphics tablets, and serves as a power source for some other peripherals (some modems, for example). ADB can also accept multiple devices daisy chained together.

✦ **Peripheral-specific ports.** Most Macs also feature a monitor port, a port for speakers, a line-in (microphone or audio device) port and, in some cases, a telephone jack or an Ethernet networking port. All these are designed to accept particular types of peripherals to expand the Mac's capabilities.

✦ **Expansion cards.** Modern Macs also feature the capability to accept internal cards, enabling you to add circuit boards, called *expansion cards,* that add input/output capabilities to your Mac. Three major types of expansion cards exist: processor direct slot (PDS) cards, NuBus slot cards, and Peripheral Component Interconnect (PCI) cards. Which type of card you get depends on the type of expansion slots your Mac has to offer (see Chapter 4 for more details).

Note

The very latest Macs—so new that they haven't shipped at the time of writing—promise to offer two new ways to connect devices to your Mac: Firewire and USB ports. Firewire is the next generation of SCSI, and it promises fewer headaches and higher speeds for applications like digital video production. Universal Serial Bus (USB) is a new, cross-platform take on the old idea of serial ports, offering higher speeds and more compatibility. Both are expected, at some point, to replace their aging counterparts in future Mac models.

Types of I/O devices

It's odd to think of the Macintosh in any shape or form as a relative of the huge mainframe computers of the 1960s, 1970s and 1980s. (A few are still around, believe it or not.) But both types of machine are computers. And both need to use input and output devices to interact with humans. Whereas the creators of supercomputing dynamos probably never worried about allowing you to scan family pictures to add them to a Web page, they did have to enable basic input and output devices to connect to the computer, just as your Mac does.

Although several devices might come to mind immediately — keyboards, mice, monitors — you'll probably find a number of different I/O devices you've never heard much about. Adding different ways to communicate with your Mac (or simply going with a higher quality of I/O devices) can go a long way to making you more productive and/or more pleased with time spent computing. Let's look at four basic categories:

✦ *Getting data into the computer.* Using keyboards, touchpads, trackballs, mice, joysticks, and graphics tablets, you can get all sorts of data into your computer.

✦ *Getting images and sound into the computer.* Using digital cameras, MIDI devices, AV capabilities, and scanners, you can add images to your documents, file them away in databases, or use sound in your presentations. Power Macs and a few other models can even accept voice commands using special software and an Apple PlainTalk microphone.

✦ *Receiving visual results from the computer.* Monitors and printers are popular upgrades for serious Mac users. The more you sit in front of your computer or you look at the printed pages it spits out, the higher you'll probably want the quality of these devices to be.

✦ *Receiving audible results from the computer.* Using the Mac's built-in sound (on most models), you can hook up a stereo receiver or powered speakers to hear sounds that are generated digitally. You can also hook up MIDI devices on which your Mac can actually play songs. Or, your Mac can speak selections of text using Apple's Text-to-Speech technology.

Keyboards

The keyboard is generally considered requisite by nearly everyone but Apple, who made a play at selling Macs without them in the early 1990s. (This unbundling was actually done to lower the suggested price and allow users to buy a keyboard they preferred on their own, but it's still a bit odd.) Most of us probably use a keyboard for the majority of our input needs, although a few other options exist.

Keyboards are connected to Macs using the ADB port located on the back of the Macintosh's case. Most ADB devices can be daisy chained, enabling you to do things such as hooking a keyboard to your Mac, and then hooking a mouse to your keyboard. The ADB is a Mac exclusive; it's not compatible with the majority of keyboards in the Intel-compatible PC world, which rely on two other connecting standards (PC serial ports and the IBM PS/2 connector). Although you can adapt PC keyboards to work with Macs, it's often a more expensive solution than even the most pricey Mac keyboard. With newer Macs, USB ports enable you to share input devices between Macs and PCs.

Although earlier keyboards offered fewer keys, these days the 105-key extended keyboard is standard for most Mac configurations. Such a keyboard includes a numeric keypad, inverted-T cursor keys, and a row of function keys from F1 to F15. In addition, Mac keyboards are set apart from other keyboards by including three special keys — Control, Option, and Command (⌘) — on either side of the space bar. (Figure 2-9 shows a standard 105-key layout.)

Figure 2-9: A typical 105-key extended keyboard, designed for a Macintosh.

Obviously, keyboards other than the standard U.S. English QWERTY keyboard exist, supporting non-English characters, high-performance layouts (like Dvorak-style keyboards), and even some devices that can be operated with one hand or by individuals with limited mobility. Many of these keyboards are available in ADB versions compatible with Macs, although some may follow a PC standard, which would then have to be adapted to ADB. (Doing so is discussed in Chapter 10.)

Mice and pointing devices

The standard Mac mouse is a single-button, ADB device that can be either connected directly to a Macintosh's ADB port or daisy chained by connecting it to an available input on a Mac-compatible keyboard. Earlier mice (for systems like the Mac Plus and before) were serial devices that connected directly to a 9-pin port on the back of the machine.

A ball in the base of a Mac's mouse tracks across the tabletop or mousepad as you drag the mouse. Those movements are translated into digital signals, which the Mac interprets and responds to by moving the on-screen mouse pointer in relation to the movement you make with the mouse. Because the mouse tracks relative movement, you can pick the mouse up and put it back down in another location without affecting the position of the mouse pointer. (This is not true of all pointing devices.)

Nearly all Mac systems include a mouse as part of the package; it's difficult to get by without one. Alternatives to the mouse, however, abound. For a variety of reasons, a new mouse or another ADB (or USB) pointing device is certainly an upgrade to consider:

✦ **Two-button programmable mice.** Mice with two or more buttons are becoming more popular among Mac owners who have upgraded to Mac OS 8.0 and beyond. The latest versions of the Mac OS support contextual menus that pop up whenever the user holds down the Control key while clicking. This Ctrl-click can be programmed into some mice, enabling a second button to be used to bring up the contextual menu.

✦ **Ergonomic mice.** Some users and manufacturers have found that paying close attention to how a mouse fits in your hand can go a long way to avoid strain and wrist injuries. Special mice have resulted that offer different sizes and contours.

✦ **Trackballs and trackpads.** Both of these types of devices enable you to use a few fingers to move the mouse pointer around on the screen instead of dragging a mouse around on your desktop. Although these devices still promote repetitive movements, some users feel less strain than with mice. Others simply feel more comfortable or accurate using these input choices.

✦ **Joysticks.** Usually used for games, many Mac joysticks can also double as mouse-like pointing devices, enabling you to use the joystick to manipulate the mouse pointer on screen.

✦ **Drawing tablets.** Probably the most fun of these optional pointing devices is the drawing tablet, which enables you to use pen-to-paper motion to move the mouse pointer around on the screen. Useful for intensely graphical projects, these tablets also come in inexpensive consumer versions that can just as easily be used by professionals or home users.

✦ **Touch screens.** Special monitors or add-ons to existing monitors can be used to upgrade your Mac to include touch-screen capabilities, allowing the mouse pointer (and/or mouse clicks) to be manipulated by pointing at or touching the screen.

Scanners

All the data your Mac works with is *digital* data, meaning it's been translated into 1s and 0s for interpretation by a computer. When it comes to a digital picture, your Mac has no real understanding of the overall image; instead, it knows the digits that represent that image as a grid of pixels composed of light, brightness, and color levels. This is especially easy to believe with a program like Adobe Photoshop or Macromedia FreeHand, which enables you to edit those pixels as you work.

But what about a printed 35 mm photograph? Or a charcoal sketch? For a Mac to work with medium like this, it has to turn it from something solid into something digitally rendered. To make this conversion happen, Macs require the services of an input device called a *scanner*.

Like photocopiers, scanners use special light-sensitive receptors to pass over a printed image, collecting information about the lights and darks, the color values of red, blue, and green in the image, and the dimensions of the grid of pixels it's trying to create. Although scanners can vary greatly in quality, the price of most models has been coming down rapidly, allowing nearly everyone to get their hands on a scanner that will fill their needs. Types of scanners include the following:

- ✦ **Handheld scanners.** These scanners are increasingly rare. At one point a very popular alternative to flatbed scanners, handhelds included the scanning internals in a unit about five inches wide that could be dragged slowly down a document to scan it into the computer.

- ✦ **Flatbed scanners.** These scanners have seen amazing price drops over the past few years, causing the market for handheld scanners to disappear. Flatbed scanners enable you to lay a document or open book face down on glass, like a photocopier, and then scan the image into your Mac. Flatbed scanners tend to offer the best quality and color reproduction.

- ✦ **Page scanners.** A relatively new class of scanners, page scanners are designed to be small, unobtrusive scanners that are fed a page at a time. Most of the scanning mechanisms are less sophisticated than a flatbed's, resulting in lower overall image quality. Page scanners are inexpensive, though, and offer a good solution for professionals and home users who want to scan documents for nongraphic tasks such as copying, faxing, and digital archiving. Figure 2-10 shows a page scanner.

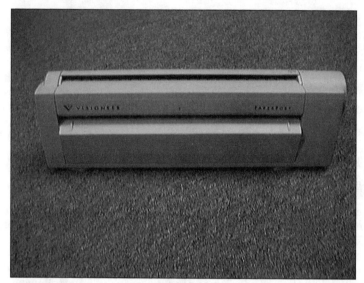

Figure 2-10: The PaperPort page scanner is a convenient way to make lower-quality scans for faxing by modem or making printed copies.

Most flatbed scanners connect to Macs using the external SCSI interface, because they have a lot of information to transfer. Many page scanners, on the other hand, use a serial (modem/printer) port for transferring the image back to the Mac; this is done for the sake of convenience, enabling you to use the scanner with more than one Mac. Some page scanners, however, do feature SCSI connections for increased speed. And there are other specialty scanners, too, designed to scan 35mm slides, transparencies or other special media.

Digital cameras

Growing steadily more popular each year is a new class of digital camera geared to small business and consumer users. First spearheaded by Apple with the original QuickTake camera (codeveloped with Kodak), consumer digital cameras have become a popular hardware niche featuring companies such as Kodak, Olympus, Nikon, Casio, and Canon.

Digital cameras don't require film. Instead, they use camera-like lenses and settings to capture digital information, which is then stored in static RAM or on cards or expansion modules of some kind (the type of memory used by the camera can vary widely). The picture can then be transferred to a computer, viewed on a television screen (with many models), or, occasionally, saved to a disk or printed to a color inkjet printer.

Most of the time, you'll want to transfer the images to your Mac for editing in Photoshop or a similar program. They can then be used for desktop publishing, Web publishing, digital archiving, or other tasks.

Most digital cameras communicate with Macs using a serial port. Some models can also use a Video In connection (on AV-equipped Macs) to transfer still images and/or live motion video to your Mac.

Tethered cameras

Also called *digital video cameras* or *videoconferencing cameras,* these popular add-ons for Macs tend to have small camera lens that can be focused on a computer user while he or she is viewing the Mac's monitor, as shown in Figure 2-11.

Figure 2-11: The QuickCam is a popular, low-cost tethered camera for Web-based video conferencing. (Figure courtesy Connectix Corporation, www.connectix.com)

Such cameras are useful for sending live video images over phone lines or the Internet or for digitizing video to be sent via removable media. Many of these cameras are also capable, like digital cameras, of taking still images. The difference: Tethered cameras have to stay connected to your Mac at all times for them to work. They're usually connected via a serial port or a Video In connector on AV-equipped Macs.

AV upgrades

Many Mac models in the past few years have come with onboard audio/visual features, usually in the form of inputs for video using RCA-style (or S-video and stereo miniplug) adapters and cables. These inputs enable you to hook up a TV, VCR, camcorder, or other compatible video source for getting video streams into your Mac. Whereas nearly all Macs have sound input, AV Macs feature stereo sound inputs that can be used in conjunction with the video inputs to digitize the audio along with video images.

The most basic AV cards do little on their own, instead relying on Apple's QuickTime multimedia software working together with an application program designed to digitize the video that comes in from your video source. Your Mac then digitizes the video by applying a special video compressor/decompressor (CODEC) to compress the amount of storage space required by the movie. The video is then stored as digital information on a large disk drive.

Some higher-end upgrades, however, feature circuitry designed to speed the Mac's ability to turn the video signal into digital information by supporting various codecs with acceleration hardware. This hardware acceleration enables the movie to be digitized more quickly, at the same time creating smaller files on the hard drive. This means the movie can be larger on the screen than a movie digitized by a Mac equipped with basic AV capabilities.

AV upgrades come in the form of expansion cards (using either the older NuBus interface or the newer PCI standard, depending on what your Mac supports) that you install inside your Mac. A few Mac models have the basic capability built in, but also allow you to add expansion cards that speed the digitizing process.

Mac video upgrades

To display a video image on a computer monitor, most Mac models come with some sort of video capability included: Either the video circuitry is built into the logic board or it comes on an installed expansion card. What I'm talking about here is different from the capability to display images on a TV screen, which requires different circuitry. (That's called *video out* and it's usually included on AV Mac or AV upgrade cards.)

Just because this monitor-driving ability is included doesn't mean it can't be upgraded. In fact, there are a number of reasons to consider upgrading your Mac's computer video capability:

✦ **More colors.** Depending on the size of your screen (and the resolution of the display, as described next), your Mac's onboard video may be limited to a certain amount of colors — often the limitation is either 256 colors or "thousands" of colors. For true professional results, you may want to be able to view millions of different colors on the screen at once. In cases like that, you need to upgrade your video capabilities, usually by adding a special memory module to your video circuitry.

✦ **Higher resolution.** The larger your Mac's monitor, the more desktop space you can display at one time. An original compact Mac has a 9-inch (diagonal) monitor, making it nearly impossible to view (and read) an entire page of text at once. Large monitors used for desktop publishing can be more like 20 inches diagonally. That allows you to easily view an entire page because the monitor shows you more of the Mac's desktop. To get all this desktop space on a 20-inch monitor, you may need to upgrade your video's memory or add an expansion card. Otherwise, you may be stuck at a lower resolution, meaning the image is larger, but you can see less of it at one time.

✦ **Use two monitors.** If you've never seen this in action, you're missing something. Nearly any Macintosh can actually use two or more monitors at once, employing all of the space as workspace on the screen. (For instance, you could put your e-mail program on the screen to your right, but design Web pages on the screen to the left.) To do this, all you need is more than one computer video output. Some Macs already have more than one (especially the AV Mac and many PowerBook models), but others require an expansion card update.

✦ **Better response times.** Finally, you can upgrade (or add) a video card in your Mac to take advantage of accelerator technologies built into new cards. Some accelerate 2D manipulations (such as in drawing programs), whereas others accelerate 3D applications (such as computer-aided design [CAD] modeling or gaming). Whichever you opt for requires an additional expansion card, although some accelerators work together with your existing video card.

Video circuitry is built into many Macs, but that circuitry may be able to accept expansion memory modules. Video circuitry can also be added using a NuBus or PCI expansion card, depending on the card technology supported by your Mac.

Monitors

You can use a computer without a monitor. Trust me. But there isn't much point, unless it's a computer sitting somewhere in a closet acting as a file server or Web server. Otherwise, for most people, most of the time, Macs need monitors.

Monitors are another very popular upgrade, because a lot of computer users tend to find over time that the monitor they bought originally isn't as crisp, large, or capable as they'd like it to be. Before people become serious about their Macs, they tend to think a nice monitor is a luxury they don't need. After users become more serious, they're more likely to decide that a good monitor is worth having. (After all, you spend hours and hours looking at it!)

Over the years, monitors have been made in many shapes, sizes, and forms. Although some of that variation no longer exists, you still need to consider a number of factors when you buy a new or used monitor for your Mac, as follows.

✦ *Multiscan or fixed?* Depending on the age of your Mac, its video circuitry probably supports both multiscan monitors or fixed-resolution monitors. The difference is multiscan monitors can synchronize to different resolutions, making it possible for the monitor to change the size of the Mac desktop pictured on screen. This can be used to make more working space available or to make the images on the screen bigger for easier reading. Older Macs may require a special adapter to work with certain multiscan monitors.

✦ *Color or grayscale?* Although very few monitors these days aren't color, some very interesting used monitors display only shades of gray instead of colors. It may not sound like it, but they're not impossible to work with, especially for certain applications (reading e-mail, typing letters, or watching over a network of other Macs, for example).

✦ *What size?* Monitors come in various display sizes, measured diagonally. In recent years, monitor vendors have been required to detail the specific dimensions of the viewable area of their monitor (for example, 13.7 inches), but monitors are still known by more general, accepted sizes (for example, 15 inches). Traditionally, Mac monitors have fallen into one of these sizes: 12, 14, 16, 19, or 21 inches. More recently, Macs have been designed or adapted to work with the popular and widely available VGA and SuperVGA monitors used by Intel-compatible PCs. So now sizes such as 15, 17, and 20 inches are common, too.

✦ *What dot pitch?* The distance between the red, green, and blue dots on a color monitor can affect the overall appearance and quality of that monitor. Most modern monitors have a dot pitch of .28 millimeters or lower, which is perfectly adequate. Larger monitors (16 inches and above) can get by with a .31 millimeter dot pitch. Monitors above this dot pitch level can be harder to look at for an extended period of time.

✦ *CRT or Trinitron?* Sony's Trinitron technology uses stripes instead of pixels on the screen (along with some other technological differences) that creates an image pleasing to many computer users' eyes. Although high-quality CRTs are certainly available, you might want to compare them to a flat Trinitron display before making your final decision.

Monitors are always connected to Macs via computer video ports (assuming the monitor isn't built into the Mac itself). These ports are either built into the logic board or are part of an expansion card. Only one monitor per port is allowed, but additional monitors can be hooked up to other available ports connected to different video circuitry.

Printers

Once you get something interesting on the screen, you may find reason to print it out and take it with you. Printers have been at the heart of Macintosh computing since the very beginning, when the Mac and Adobe PageMaker ushered in the desktop publishing revolution. Apple introduced the original LaserWriter around that time, making professional output from a computer a reality.

Since then, printing technology has gone in all sorts of directions. Printers exist for many different needs and desires. You should consider a few different technologies in printing:

✦ **Dot-matrix printers.** The original Apple ImageWriter was a dot-matrix printer, meaning it used pins to create small dots on a ribbon that was pressed against paper, somewhat in the same method employed by modern typewriters. These printers are fairly cheap to keep running, but very, very uncommon. They tend to be slow, loud, and the quality of their output is low. They are useful for multipart (carbon copy) forms, however, because the pins actually strike the page.

✦ **Inkjet printers.** Available in both black-and-white and color varieties, inkjets represent a low initial investment (rarely more than a few hundred dollars) that can result in great image and text quality. Inkjets are also the only affordable way to print color documents. Inkjets can be reasonably speedy, but they don't compete with laser printers. They're also somewhat more expensive to equip with such consumables as paper and ink.

✦ **Laser printers.** These also come in a variety of shapes and sizes, ranging from hundreds to many thousands of dollars. Although color lasers aren't yet common, Apple does make a few for more professional endeavors. On the lower end, lasers are a fast, inexpensive way to print black-and-white pages quickly. Consumables (like laser toner) can be expensive one-time purchases, but they last much longer than inkjet inks.

Macs can actually use two different types of printers (directly), and those printers can be connected to the Mac in two different ways. *QuickDraw* printers use the Mac's own screen and page description technology to print a page, meaning the printers can be cheaper and easier to service. It also means the printer can only be connected to a Mac and can't be easily shared with a network of Intel-compatible PCs. Additionally, it uses TrueType font technology, which is a decent font technology, but not always the best choice for graphics professionals.

Postscript printers, on the other hand, use the standard Adobe Postscript page description language to print the page. This usually means more professional quality. It also means that other computers, such as those based on Windows and UNIX, can print to the printer, too.

Some Mac printers (especially QuickDraw printers) can be connected directly to the printer port on the back of the Mac. Others can be networked using LocalTalk or Ethernet cabling. Ethernet is especially useful for powerful network printers that need to be shared with groups of Macs and/or Mac and Intel-compatible users.

Speakers

Most Macs can accept speakers connected to the Sound Out port on the back panel of the Mac. The speakers can't be garden variety, though. They need to be somewhat special.

The connector on the back of a Macintosh is actually a line-out connector, meaning it needs to be sent to an amplifier before it can be played over speakers. Powered computer speakers can be used in this case; the speakers have to plug into a wall power outlet or run on batteries. Your other option: Hook your Mac up to your home stereo system's amplifier.

Computer speakers should also be properly shielded so that the magnets inside the speakers don't affect any of the surrounding computer equipment. Magnets can distort monitor images and erase data from floppy disks and removable media.

MIDI sound

The Musical Instrument Digital Interface (MIDI) specification enables you to hook electronic instruments, such as keyboard synthesizers, up to your Mac using a special converter box. The box itself is usually connected to a serial (modem/printer) port, and then the device is hooked into the converter box.

This allows you to play notes on the instrument that are then recognized by specialized MIDI software. The music isn't just recorded by your Mac, however. MIDI software can actually differentiate the notes and, for instance, display them as annotation on a music staff. You can have your computer write, transpose, harmonize, and do many different things with music, ultimately enabling you to compose directly on the screen. The resulting music can then be played through your Mac's speakers or sent back out to the instrument and played automatically.

Communication Between Computers

One other form of input/output hasn't really been mentioned so far — input and output to-and-from other computers. Although your Mac will probably spend a lot of time interacting with you, you may also want it to interact with other computers (especially when it's younger). Not only will it grow up to be well adjusted, but it will enable you to access the Internet, work with files from other platforms (such as DOS and Windows), and even run programs written for other computers.

Communicating with other computers

At some point you'll want to move your Mac from its isolated little island out into the world of network communications. Or maybe it's already networked, and you want it to go faster. In either case, you can upgrade to get your Mac talking directly to other Macs, Intel-compatible PCs, or all sorts of computers out on the Internet.

Modems

A modem (*mod*ulator/*dem*odulator) is the most basic form of networking, enabling you to call other computers over regular phone lines and share data. Modems work by turning digital information into an analog (or audible) signal that can be transmitted over phone lines. When the data gets to another modem, it's translated back into a digital signal that can be interpreted by its computer.

Modems come in different speeds, measured by the number of kilobits they can transmit per second (Kbps). Although modems were once made to communicate at rates as low as 150 bps, the current range for acceptable performance is 14.4 Kbps to 56 Kbps. Technological limitations may keep modems at 56 Kbps for the foreseeable future, although these sorts of hurdles are usually overcome eventually.

Modems connect to the modem port on the back of your Mac and then directly to a phone line.

Digital modems

Although there's really no such thing as a digital modem (a modem by definition means a digital-to-analog conversion), it's popular to call some long-distance networking devices "modems" because they're for use in homes or small businesses over existing lines of communication — phone lines, satellites, or cable TV lines. These technologies include the following:

✦ **ISDN.** Integrated Services Digital Network is a refit of the current telephone service designed to offer more services than a typical phone line as well as high-speed computer communications. Typical ISDN modems can transfer data at about 128 Kbps.

✦ **xDSL.** An emerging technology that allows for very fast digital transmissions over existing telephone lines. Speeds vary but run in the hundreds of Kbps.

✦ **Cable.** Offered by your cable TV provider, these modem-like connections offer high-speed Internet access over the existing cable line. Speed varies depending on the number of subscribers in a given area, but averages at least a few hundred Kbps.

✦ **Satellite.** A satellite dish (usually the smaller 18-inch version) is used to receive Internet-related transmissions. Usually high-speed in one direction (toward your Mac) but requires a traditional slower modem connection to send data back to the Internet.

For the most part, these digital modems are still emerging, and standards and/or capabilities may change dramatically. Currently, those that are available use either an expansion card slot, an Ethernet connection, or the modem port to connect to your Mac.

Local Area Networks

When you connect a number of Macs (or Macs and Intel-compatible PCs) in an office, you're creating a local area network, or LAN. You can do this to share files, send e-mail, collaborate on documents, or share other resources, such as printers or Internet access. To create a LAN, though, you'll need to string some cable between all your machines.

Small, slower networks can use LocalTalk cabling, which directly connects Macs using special LocalTalk (or PhoneNet) adapters and cabling that stretches between them. Usually Macs are connected together in a daisy chain (or *bus* topology) so that one Mac accepts a connection from another Mac before it extends a connection to the next Mac in line. The Macs at either end have terminators that force the data to bounce back down the cabling, if necessary. LocalTalk can be a bit slow, sending data at about 230 Kbps.

Larger networks can use Ethernet cabling for a much higher speed connection (ideally, 10 Mbps, or megabits per second). In this case, it may be necessary to install a network hub, which is used to help data find its way to the appropriate Mac. Fast Ethernet cabling and connectors bump that speed up to 100 Mbps, but require Fast Ethernet equipment for all connected Macs.

Special software is also necessary. An all-Mac network can use AppleTalk for sharing files and printers, whereas add-on software may be necessary to incorporate Intel-compatible PCs into your LAN.

LocalTalk runs directly off the printer ports of nearly every Mac made, but Ethernet can sometimes require an expansion card. Ethernet capabilities are built into many business Macs (Centris, Quadra, most Power Macintoshes), although you may still need to buy a special adapter.

Working with DOS and Windows

The other part of being a well-rounded communicator is learning to read, write, and think in other languages. The Mac equivalent of a foreign tongue includes files and disks formatted for use in the MS-DOS and Microsoft Windows world. Fortunately, most modern Macs are fully equipped to handle just about anything a Windows user can throw at them. Some Macs go even further, offering enhancements that can enable you to actually run Windows and DOS software on your Mac.

Files and floppies

At its most basic, nearly every Mac (beyond the Mac Plus and original Mac II) features a special floppy drive, called the Superdrive, that is capable of reading floppy disks in formats other than that specific to Macintosh. Using PC Exchange, a Macintosh control panel that ships with System 7.5 and above, your Mac can actually accept and read a PC-formatted floppy disk with no real intervention on your part. Just pop the floppy in the drive. The PC-formatted disk appears on your desktop, as shown in Figure 2-12.

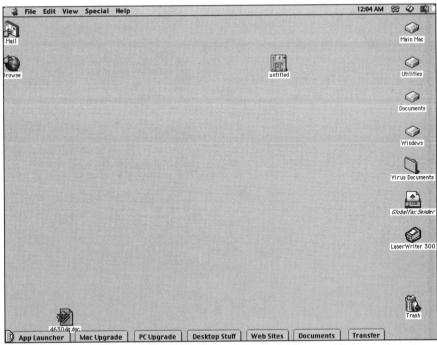

Figure 2-12: The PC floppy appears on the desktop with a special icon.

How do you get PC files into your Mac applications? For your Mac to read the PC-based files, it needs a compatible program. For instance, Microsoft Word 98 for Macintosh can easily read just about any sort of Microsoft Word for Windows file (Word 97, Word 95, Word 6.0) that you'll come across. Plus, updates for new versions of Word for Windows can usually be downloaded from Microsoft's site in a timely fashion. Similarly, a program like ClarisWorks has built into it the ability to read and write data files in PC-oriented formats like Microsoft's RTF and WordPerfect for DOS.

Check www.microsoft.com/macoffice for updates and other information on Word and other Microsoft Office applications.

If you have Mac OS 7.6 or above, you may also have received MacLinkPlus, a bundled set of translators that can be used with most Mac applications to load files created by different Mac or PC applications. In this case, you have an entire arsenal of file translators at your disposal, enabling you to load a ton of different file formats into the Macintosh application of your choice. Figure 2-13 shows my ClarisWorks File Open dialog box, enhanced by MacLinkPlus.

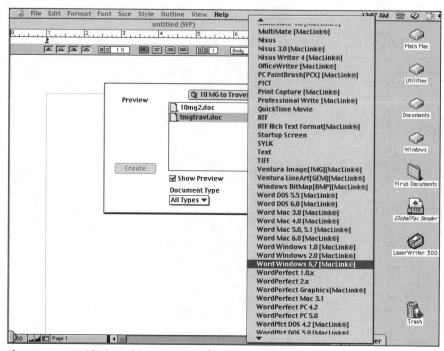

Figure 2-13: With the addition of MacLinkPlus, your Mac applications can load and work with many, many PC file formats.

Note

In most cases, you'll want to use a program that's actually similar in function to the application that originally created the data file you're trying to import. If someone sent you a PC-based Lotus 1,2,3 (spreadsheet) document, you should probably try to open it using Microsoft Excel or ClarisWorks' spreadsheet tools.

Windows/PC emulation software

As advanced PowerPC processors have tons of power to burn, some enterprising software companies have come up with a way to allow Windows and DOS programs to actually run on top of the Mac OS. Double-click a file, and you've suddenly got Windows 95 (or the operating system of your choice) chugging along in a window. Not only are these emulators used for playing games (which is certainly a popular reason to own one of these programs), but these Windows solutions are great for professional Mac owners who need access to an occasional Windows application or an in-house DOS program. They're also a good idea for telecommuters who want to dial into their Windows network using a home-based Macintosh.

SoftWindows 95, from Insignia Corporation, is a popular example of this software, enabling users to run nearly any Windows 95 application on top of their Mac OS desktops. It can require a bit of RAM to operate (at least 20MB of free RAM is recommended for good performance), but it's a good way to run Windows if you have a pressing need. (Figure 2-14 shows SoftWindows in action.)

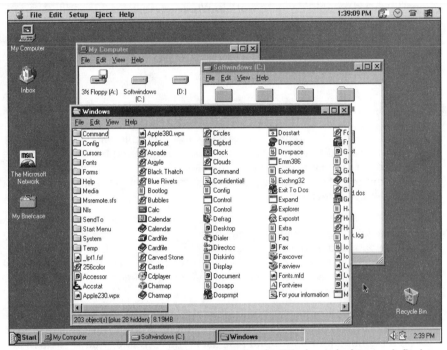

Figure 2-14: SoftWindows enables you to resize the Windows desktop so it fits in a window along with your other Mac applications.

Although SoftWindows emulates Windows itself, other programs have also been written to emulate an actual Intel-compatible PC on your Mac. It doesn't look much different—the PC environment still runs in a window on your Mac's desktop—but the result is an emulator that's more flexible in its ability to run DOS, Windows, OS/2, Linux, OpenStep, and almost any other operating system designed to work on a typical PC. Insignia makes one of these applications, called RealPC. Connectix, of RAMDoubler and SpeedDoubler fame, offers a popular alternative to RealPC called Virtual PC.

DOS-compatible cards

The final option for DOS compatibility is a specially designed expansion card called a *DOS-compatible card*. Made by companies like Apple, Reply, and Orange Micro, these cards are NuBus or PCI expansion cards that feature an actual Intel-compatible processor on the card. Using a keystroke sequence (usually ⌘-Return), the control of your monitor, keyboard, and mouse is transferred to the DOS-compatible card, enabling you to work in Windows, DOS, or (sometimes) another PC-based operating system. You can even add a second monitor to observe the DOS card's progress while you work on the Mac, and then use the keystroke sequence to return to the DOS side.

Summary

✦ Three major subsystems — processing, input/output, and storage — work together to make your Mac compute. Data is gathered by the input devices, placed in memory, processed by the central processing unit (CPU), and sent back out to the user via output devices. It can then be saved for a later date using storage devices.

✦ The "brains" of your Mac include the CPU, main system memory (RAM), and any cache memory your Mac may have. This is the "short-term" memory, where data and instructions are stored until your Mac has the opportunity to compute based on that data. RAM is probably the most necessary and useful upgrade a Mac owner can make, although upgrading the CPU can certainly speed up your computing experience.

✦ All Macs include some sort of storage device — a floppy drive, hard drive, CD-ROM drive, or all three — but the included storage options sometimes aren't enough for the intrepid Mac user. The technology now exists to store 100MB or even 2GB of data on a single, removable cartridge that's easy to carry with you or store for safe-keeping. Plus, they're usually reasonably inexpensive.

✦ There are plenty of different devices to help you get data into and out of your Mac, including keyboards, mice, scanners, monitors, and printers. More exciting options include drawing tablets, digital cameras, and audio/visual technology that can even be used to digitize and edit movies or recorded audio.

✦ What else do you need to do? A Mac can be hooked up to other computers using modems and networking cables, and it can access the Internet. Or, you can read PC-formatted floppies if you need to share files with friends and colleagues. In fact, many Power Macs (and a few earlier models) can even run Windows and DOS programs in a window, right along side your Mac applications. All you need is the right upgrade.

✦   ✦   ✦

Find Your Bottlenecks

As any computer ages, it begins to exhibit signs of slowing down. Some of these signs can be attributed to maintenance issues: It's important to upgrade your operating system, delete unused files, and run disk-utility programs to maintain order inside your Mac. Over time, however, it's inevitable that computers will begin to slow down without more extreme measures, usually involving a hardware upgrade.

When it's time to upgrade, the key to doing it successfully is finding where exactly the traffic jams are occurring in your system. What subsystems are slowing down? Processing? Storage? Are a number of different factors coming together to slow down your Mac's operation?

You've got to know where the slowdowns — the bottlenecks — are occurring before you can make an informed decision to upgrade.

Why Is My Mac Slowing Down?

Once you understand the various components in your Mac and the possible upgrades you can perform (as discussed in Chapter 2), you might still be left puzzling over the common question, "Why is my Mac getting slower?" After all, when you bought your Mac, chances are you were perfectly happy with its speed. At that time it ran the Mac OS and all your applications, the windows snapped around the screen, and it didn't even take terribly long to print. But since that time (especially if it's been quite a while), things seem to be taking longer.

There are two main reasons a computer begins to slow down over time:

✦ *The Mac's storage subsystem is poorly maintained or overloaded.* Having a well-maintained hard drive, with at least 5 to 15 percent free space, is important to the operation of any computer. As a hard disk becomes filled, it has a tendency to become fragmented, forcing the disk's read/write heads to race around more and more to find the necessary data. All this hard drive accessing (called *thrashing* by nerdy types) can severely affect the Mac's performance. Figure 3-1 shows an example of fragmentation.

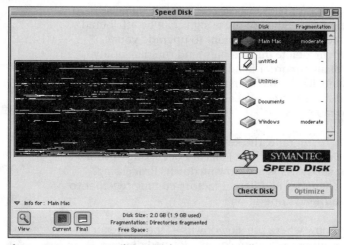

Figure 3-1: Norton Utilities' Disk Doctor can tell you the level of fragmentation on your drive.

What does fragmentation mean?

When your Mac writes data — either application files or documents — to its hard disk, it does its best to write the data sequentially. When you first buy (or reformat) a hard drive, this sequential writing is relatively easy to do. The drive simply finds some free space and begins writing; more than likely, enough space occurs in one area so that the data file can be put down in its entirety.

But once a hard disk has seen quite a bit of use, those free spaces become more scarce. As a result, the Mac is forced to write data wherever it can manage to find some empty space — even if it can't write the whole file sequentially. Instead, it will keep track of the various places, all over the hard drive, where it was able to squeeze in some data. These haphazardly written data files are then considered *fragmented*, because small fragments are littered all over the drive.

This can happen even when the hard drive isn't full, especially after months of use. As you add and delete files, the linear, sequential areas on the drive get filled and wiped and filled again, to the point that even a drive that's only half full is forcing files to be saved all over the place. To further illustrate, imagine working with a stenographer's pad and pencil. If you fill the pad and then use the pencil's eraser to do away with every third paragraph, the pad is only two-thirds full. But filling it again would require writing only in the available space, resulting in a lot of page turning, which would slow your note-taking.

To speed up a fragmented drive, it should be defragmented using Norton Utilities or a similar program. These programs rearrange the data files sequentially so that they're no longer as fragmented. As an added bonus, the free space is organized sequentially, too, so that new data files are also written in the most efficient manner. If your drive is heavily fragmented, you might get a nice little speed boost from running such a utility program.

✦ *You've added new programs, system software enhancements, or new tasks that require more advanced technology.* This is the real reason most Macs seem to slow down. Whereas new Mac OS versions can sometimes actually speed things up a bit (especially for Power Macintoshes), often Apple adds new features and technologies that can slow down older computers. Other applications can do the same thing by adding new features that become more and more power hungry. Microsoft Word 5.1, for instance, ran on most Mac II series computers with plenty of gusto. Mac Word 6.0, however, required even faster Quadra and Centris machines. Mac Word 98, taking things even further, doesn't run particularly speedily on anything below a second-generation (PowerPC 603- or 604-based) Power Mac.

Even if you've been diligent in your fight against hard-disk fragmentation, the fault for your Mac's slowdown can be laid squarely on your shoulders. If you didn't want all those new-fangled software programs, you wouldn't be in the performance crunch you are now! A Mac Plus running Mac System 6.0.1, PageMaker 1.0, and MacPaint would still be a perfectly serviceable machine. Not a very exciting one, but it wouldn't be incredibly slow. Of course, if you've already used the later versions, you're probably hooked on the features. To speed up all that new software, you'll need to find your hardware bottlenecks.

Understanding bottlenecks

A bottleneck is a point of congestion that retards or halts free movement, such as a traffic jam. In fact, the use of the term "bottleneck" in computing may be directly related to the high frequency of automobile traffic jams in the computing mecca of California. (California's famous traffic jams actually seem to attract millions of people to the state, apparently so they can be seen talking on a cellular telephone.)

In much the same way that too many distracted cell-phone users can cause a bottleneck on California's highways, a relatively minor part of your Mac's subsystems can easily create an impasse that *retards* or *halts* the free movement of data between your Mac's processor, storage devices, and input/output devices. This is especially true if, by using newer programs, Mac OS versions, or more unwieldy data files, you're causing the pathways inside your Mac to deal with more data than they have in the past.

Note

Of course, another way to illustrate the problem with bottlenecks is to remind you that the term is meant to conjure the image of the neck of a bottle. The neck is usu-ally thinner than the rest of the bottle, retarding the flow of liquid out of the bottle (especially if you turn the bottle completely upside-down). When you do away with the bottleneck in your computing subsystems, you can likely speed the flow of data in your Mac.

That's a computing bottleneck. Determining which bottlenecks are likely occurring in your Mac is part of the process you need to go through to get the most bang for your upgrading buck.

For example, a very common bottleneck for many Mac owners is not having enough RAM; without enough RAM, even a normally speedy Power Macintosh can slow way down. RAM is necessary for running more than one program, dealing with large documents (like digital images), and even setting a disk cache or RAM disk that can speed the flow of data through your Mac (see Figure 3-2).

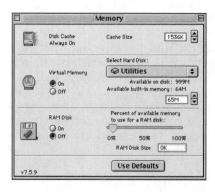

Figure 3-2: Using the Memory control panel, you can change a number of RAM-related settings. The more RAM you have, the more effectively these settings can speed up your Mac.

Knowing this about RAM, you might be inclined to run out and buy RAM right now. (Always a good idea, by the way, unless your Mac is already at its maximum or you don't have an available RAM upgrade slot.) But if you hadn't considered this bottleneck, you might have incorrectly assumed your processor needs upgrading—it may not, depending on the sorts of tasks you perform. A new motherboard or CPU upgrade is considerably more expensive than 16 or 32 more megabytes of RAM. And you'd find, even if you bought and installed the processor upgrade, you might still need extra RAM to get it working at full speed.

Finding the bottleneck

Finding the bottleneck usually amounts to determining what has changed in your system and what subsystem has been affected by the change. In Chapter 1, I mention the 75/25 rule. If your system is now too slow for comfort, something about your needs has changed. Perhaps you're creating many more flyers, but you haven't updated your printer. Or maybe you're working with much more advanced graphics, but you don't have a specialized video accelerator. In any case, you need to get back to the point where at least 75 percent of your computing tasks are handled with grace and speed by your Mac.

Most likely, you've upgrading a piece of software or two (or you've upgraded the Mac OS), and that software now requires more advanced Mac hardware to run at an acceptable speed. Table 3-1 shows some examples of popular Mac software and how, from one version to the next, software can require you to upgrade your Mac's hardware to keep up. The question is, what exactly is slowing the software down? That's what you'll need to determine before upgrading.

Table 3-1
Up the Ante: Software Requirements from Version to Version

Software Title	Version	Requirements	Version	Requirements
ClarisWorks	4.0	68020, 4MB RAM	5.0	68020, 8MB RAM, 55MB HD
MS Office	4.2.1	68030, 8MB RAM, 62MB HD	98	PowerPC, 16MB RAM, 120MB HD
Quicken	7.0	68030, 6MB RAM, 12MB HD	98	68030, 16MB RAM, 45MB HD
HyperCard	2.3.5	68000, 2MB RAM	2.4	68020, 16MB RAM

For starters, take a look at some common bottlenecks:

✦ **RAM.** It's a fact of computing: New programs simply require more RAM. Mac OS 8 and later, for instance, require that at least 16MB of RAM be present in your Mac, just for starters — and that certainly doesn't guarantee optimum performance. RAM is the most common bottleneck in most Mac systems, and it's among the easiest upgrades.

✦ **Cache.** Cache RAM, if your Mac is capable of accepting it, can speed up your computing considerably. In many cases, a Mac's processor isn't being fully tasked, even if your system is slowing down. The problem may be that the processor is waiting for data to arrive. When that's the case, cache RAM can certainly help.

✦ **Processor.** If your processor is aging, it may begin to choke on all the new instructions, features, and lines of programming code in newer applications. The more 3D, image manipulation and number crunching your applications do, the more your CPU can become a bottleneck.

✦ **Network.** If you're using LocalTalk for your network, you're not communicating at a tenth of the speed you could be using Ethernet. You should also have an efficient network setup—with file and print servers, if necessary—to speed things along, especially in a larger workgroup.

✦ **Modem.** If you use a dial-up connection for access to networks or the Internet, a slow modem can mean the difference between frustration and productivity. Even the latest Power Macs can be brought to their knees by slow modem connections.

✦ **Video card.** Accelerated video cards can jazz up the performance of Macs for artists, designers, multimedia professionals, and, of course, gamers. By off-loading some of the processing requirements relative to graphics, accelerated video cards enable the system's CPU to devote time to other tasks.

✦ **Hard drive.** If you're running out of space on your hard drive, you may be affecting your Mac's ability to use Virtual Memory (megabytes of storage space on your hard drive reserved for use by the Mac OS), which could affect performance when you're working with many different applications open at once. Older hard drives can also be relatively slow, making audio/visual and QuickTime-related tasks crawl along.

✦ **Printer.** If your Mac hums along just fine, but you're waiting interminable amounts of time for your final work to appear in print, you may need to upgrade your printer (by installing more printer RAM, for instance). You might also need to buy a completely new printer with a faster page-per-minute rating.

✦ **Port choice.** Serial ports (printer/modem ports) are much slower than some other upgrade options you may have, such as an internal card or a SCSI connection. Some devices, such as certain page scanners (those little scanners that can sit in front of your monitor and be fed a page at a time, like a fax machine) connect via slow serial cable connections. The faster ones use a SCSI cable to connect.

Obviously, other bottlenecks may exist—for instance, you may find a specialized digital video card helps you record and edit video at a faster pace. These bottlenecks may be important to you or not, depending on the specific work you're doing. (Eventually, I discuss them all in this book.) But the main bottlenecks just discussed are those that most Mac users will encounter when it's time to upgrade.

Speed versus quality

The other important question to ask when it comes to upgrading your Mac is whether the problems you're having are more related to speed or quality. Although most bottlenecks are about speed, you can also have quality bottlenecks if the quality of your computing experience or the output your computer generates is affecting your productivity or livelihood. Some quality issues are related to your actual time sitting in front of the computer: Maybe you're squinting at a low-quality monitor or you're trying to hear your computer through inadequate speakers. In these cases, productivity might be affected because you and the computer don't get along. Other quality issues have to do with the usefulness and professionalism of the output generated by your computer.

Upgrading to improve the quality of your work—buying an exceptional printer, for instance—might enable you to get better clients, do a better job of teaching, or manage your team more effectively. A quality-related upgrade might also keep you from running out to your local print shop or calling a consultant every time you need a particular task accomplished. Whatever the reason, you should not only consider the speed bottlenecks that physically affect your Macintosh system or network, but also take into account the quality bottlenecks that might be slowing your day-to-day productivity.

Improve Your Mac's Speed

If you've identified speed as your major interest in upgrading, your next step is to determine the exact bottlenecks slowing your system down. To do this, you need to spend time observing your Mac as you work—deciding specifically when it performs well and when it doesn't. It may surprise you where the bottlenecks really lie.

Diagnosis: Slow computer

To decide where the slowdowns in your Mac are occurring, you need to take careful note of the symptoms it's exhibiting. Understanding these symptoms can help you find the right upgrade path to address your Mac's particular bottlenecks. Here are some of the slowdown symptoms you may encounter:

✦ *My Mac is slow when I have a lot of programs running at once.* Although a processor or logic board can help this situation, the most important upgrade is RAM. Memory is necessary for you to run more than one program at once—the more RAM you have, the more programs you can run (see Figure 3-3).

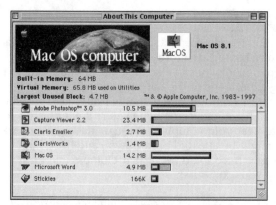

Figure 3-3: The About This Computer dialog box (found in the Apple menu when the Finder is active) shows you how much RAM you have available and how much is being used by the programs you have running.

✦ *My Mac is slow when I'm dealing with a 2D graphic document.* These sorts of files — found in Photoshop or a similar program — can be serious memory hogs. If you don't have much RAM, the graphics program is forced to write a lot of data to the hard drive, slowing everything down. Get more RAM first and a processor second. You might also consider a floating-point unit (FPU) upgrade if you have a 68030 or older machine.

✦ *My Mac is slow when I work with 3D graphics, multimedia programs, and games.* This can take RAM and a speedy processor, but you might also look into a video card upgrade. Newer video cards offer better 3D performance for graphics and games. Cards specifically designed for multimedia professionals can speed up 3D rendering and video editing, too.

✦ *My Mac is slow when I load and save documents.* Your RAM could be low, your processor could be aging, but the real problem may be that your hard drive is too slow — especially if you're dealing with very large files. A new SCSI hard drive using Fast/Wide technology or higher-speed RPMs might help you save those large documents more quickly. (You may also need a SCSI expansion card to take full advantage of a high-speed drive.) A cache RAM upgrade may also help you here, especially with newer Macs.

✦ *My Mac is slow when I try to work with almost any document.* If typing is slow when working with a relatively short word processing document, or it takes a while for the cursor to move to the next cell in your spreadsheet program, you're using software that is taxing your Mac's ability to process information. (Also, not enough RAM may be available.) When most or all your applications are unbearably slow, that's a good indicator a processor or logic board upgrade is necessary.

✦ *My Mac is slow when using a Web browser or AOL.* This can be a RAM and processor issue, but it's most likely a slow connection to the Internet or online service. For home users, that means a faster modem (or a different modem technology, like cable or xDSL) is needed. For corporate users, it may mean you should look into an Ethernet connection to the Internet. (Realize that this isn't always the case. Sometimes your Internet connection will be slow because of bottlenecks on the Internet itself. If you experience chronic slowness instead of occasional slowdowns, you're a better candidate for an upgrade.)

✦ *My Mac is slow when I copy files over the network.* If you're still using LocalTalk connections, you may have outgrown them. Consider using Ethernet cards and cabling. Also, troubleshoot your network to make sure you're using the latest AppleTalk and Internet access software.

✦ *My Mac is slow when it prints.* If you're using an inkjet or personal laser printer, you might need more RAM or a processor upgrade for your Mac. If you're using a PostScript laser printer, you might get away with a RAM upgrade or processor upgrade for the printer itself. You should also consider a faster connection for network-style printers — Ethernet is much quicker for printing than LocalTalk.

✦ *My Power Mac is slow.* Although aging Power Macs can use a speed boost from more RAM or a new processor, you can also breathe new life into any Power Mac by upgrading its cache RAM. Power Macs make very efficient use of cache RAM to speed operations considerably. Power Macs also tend to speed up slightly with each new Mac OS release and perform much more quickly with *native applications*, that is, Mac OS programs that are accelerated for the PowerPC processor.

Speed options

Once you've determined the bottleneck(s), you decide what action to take to eliminate them. Take into account a couple of different things while you decide what bottlenecks need to be attacked and in what order:

✦ *Should I get a new logic board?* If you identify a number of different bottlenecks that are all choking your system — the speed of your expansion cards, your processor, your RAM, and your cache, for instance — you may need to consider a complete upgrade of the logic board. Moving to a faster logic board can bring along speed benefits of all sorts, including the chance to address many of these bottlenecks at once. Of course, updating some Mac logic boards can be both expensive and difficult. Make sure you're comfortable performing such an upgrade and that a logic board upgrade is available for your Mac model. If one isn't, you may need to consider a new Mac.

✦ *What are my priority bottlenecks?* If you need to be productive immediately, you may find that adding RAM, plugging in a cache RAM module, or adding a SCSI peripheral will result in an immediate speed boost that can help you get through a crunch; you can then spend time upgrading more complex components later.

✦ *Can it be fixed with a simple upgrade card?* Say you want faster 2D or 3D gaming capability. Video speed problems can usually be fixed quickly with an upgrade card. PowerPC upgrade cards exist for some Quadra, Mac II, and Performa models, too. You'll need to make sure your Mac can handle another upgrade card (do you have a free slot?) and that you get the right type of card — PDS, NuBus, or PCI. (See Chapter 4 for information on expansion cards.)

✦ *Am I willing to perform the upgrade?* If your Mac is still under warranty (and the upgrade would void that warranty), you may need to factor in the cost of consulting a qualified Apple technician. Or, if you're simply not sure you want to perform the upgrade yourself, remember that getting help can add to the overall cost of upgrading.

✦ *Should I just get a new Mac?* If you suddenly realize you'll be spending quite a bit of money for the upgrade, don't forget to consider the possibility of buying a new or used Mac. New Macs tend to have a nice amount of RAM, a fast processor, and a new logic board, which, when they're all put together, can add up to much better speeds than you get when you upgrade an older system.

Improve Your Mac's Quality

The flip-side of upgrading involves improving the quality of work you're able to do with your Mac. You won't necessarily speed up with these sorts of upgrades, but you may find that you're more productive. In most cases, these upgrades are also easier to perform, because they tend to involve either expansion cards or external peripherals. Quality — especially of the output you generate from working — is an important part of any business or home Mac. The better your final product, the happier you'll be with your Mac's abilities.

Diagnosis: Poor quality

What follows are some common complaints about a Mac's ability to generate quality output or otherwise make the computing experience enjoyable. If any of these apply, you can begin to see what you'll need to do to improve life with your Mac, and decide which upgrades, if any, are worthwhile.

✦ *My monitor is difficult to look at.* Some older monitors can be too small, too fuzzy, or too dim to enjoy working with for long periods of time. The solution, in most cases, is to buy a new monitor. You can also do a few other things to revive a monitor, detailed in Chapter 25. But if you have the budget, you should certainly consider getting a new monitor if you find that yours bothers your eyes or affects your ability to concentrate.

✦ *My Mac doesn't display enough colors.* You might find when you're dealing with computer images, whether on Web pages or in a program like Photoshop, your Mac isn't capable of displaying as many colors as you might like. Although the fix could be as simple as changing a control panel or similar setting (see Chapter 25), it's true that some Macs simply don't have enough video RAM (VRAM) to display more than hundreds or thousands of colors. You might be able to upgrade that VRAM, however, or add another video card.

✦ *I'd like more desktop space in which to work.* You could get a larger monitor, or you can hook up additional monitors to your Mac. If you add a video card and a second monitor, it's possible to extend the virtual desktop of your Mac so that you're using both screens at the same time (see Figure 3-4).

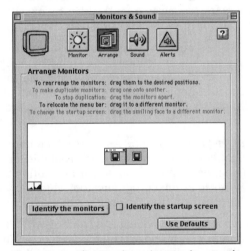

Figure 3-4: The Monitors (or Monitors and Sound on some Macs) control panel can be used to choose which monitor is positioned where and how the virtual desktop will be arranged.

✦ *My print quality is low.* If you have a dot matrix printer, an old inkjet, or even an aging laser printer, you may not be completely happy with the quality. In most cases, the best plan is to upgrade to a new printer, although you should also test your printer thoroughly to ensure you're getting the most out of your ink or toner cartridges. (Printer troubleshooting is covered in Chapter 26.)

✦ *I want my inkjet to print in color.* A few Apple and Hewlett Packard inkjets (especially if they're a few years old) shipped as black-and-white printers, but could be upgraded to color using a special add-on kit. If you fit in this group, you can upgrade very quickly to color. Others will probably need to buy a new printer, though.

✦ *I need Postscript quality output, but my printer isn't capable of it.* The confusing world of Mac fonts rears its head every once in a while, resulting in jagged print, confusing problems, and poor print quality. But you can try a few other things before you rush out to buy a new printer, including software add-ons and font fixes.

✦ *I need to print more images on a page, but my laser printer can't do it.* If you don't have enough printer RAM or your printer's settings are a tad screwy, you might not be using the RAM most effectively. A laser printer needs enough RAM to create a digital image of the entire page before it can be printed. If the printer runs out of RAM before it's ready to print, you get an error message, and an incomplete page comes out of the printer.

✦ *I hate my keyboard.* You can easily buy and install a new keyboard for your Mac. You can even install it many feet away from the Mac, along with a monitor and other peripherals for presentations or kiosks, if necessary.

✦ *I want a new mouse.* Mac OS 8 and above includes *contextual menus,* which pop up when you Ctrl-Click a window or document on your Mac. With an ADB mouse that has two or more buttons, you can often program a button to do the Ctrl-Click for you, making it a simple matter to pop up contextual menus all over the place. Figure 3-5 shows the Kensington Turbo Mouse program in action.

✦ *I hate driving, flying, shooting with the keyboard.* All sorts of gaming controls, such as steering wheels, flight yokes, and joysticks, are available for the Mac. Some of them work in conjunction with your mouse (or in addition to it), enabling you to use the devices in normal programs, too, which may be helpful for people with wrist pain, arm trouble, or other physical challenges.

✦ *I need to work with Intel-compatible PCs.* Reading and working with PC floppies takes nothing more than System 7.5 (or above) and the correct settings in software. To run PC (DOS, Windows, OS/2) programs, you'll need a software emulator or a hardware upgrade card that includes a Pentium processor (or Pentium-like processor from Cyrix Corp.) and connectors that let you hook up PC peripherals. You can also network your Mac to a PC local area network, network a PC into a Mac workgroup, or print from a Mac to a PC printer — all with the correct hardware add-ons, of course.

✦ *My Mac doesn't sound very good.* Most Macs have stereo outputs that can be used with stereo receivers or powered speakers to enrich the multimedia experience. If you need it, you can also add expansion cards that enable you to use your Mac as a digital mixing board, accepting multiple inputs and mixing them together as they're digitally recorded. Or, hook up a MIDI device and have your Mac read music and play instruments automatically.

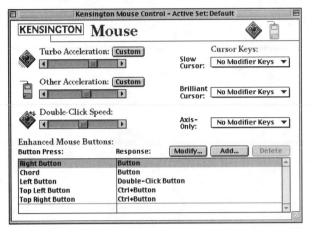

Figure 3-5: Using a programmable mouse, you can add functions to mouse buttons to make them more convenient than keystroke combinations or selecting menu items.

None of these are bottlenecks in your Mac system itself; instead, they're bottlenecks that keep you from getting quality work done. Any of these upgrades that you consider important should be addressed just as you might address speed issues. In fact, you might want to upgrade or repair a couple of these problems *before* you focus on speed. If your business is about writing, designing, or printing, for instance, you may want to get a better monitor, printer, or scanner right now — even before you boost the processor in your Mac.

Summary

✦ A big part of upgrading is determining the bottlenecks in your system. Like automobile traffic, bottlenecks are jams in your system that don't allow data to flow quickly and efficiently. Sometimes freeing up a relatively insignificant bottleneck results in great performance for your entire Mac.

✦ Your Mac may seem to be slowing down for one of two reasons: First, you haven't properly maintained your hard drive. Or, it can slow down if you install newer programs that require more RAM and processing power than the older programs that you're replacing.

✦ Determining the exact nature of your bottleneck means diagnosing the problem based on the symptoms. What slowdowns or quality problems is your Mac exhibiting?

✦   ✦   ✦

File Your Upgrade Flight Plan

Many Mac owners make the mistake of upgrading without a proper plan of attack. That's not to say I'm much of a list writer or flowchart guy myself — but I do try to ruminate a bit over additions to my Mac. After all, you want to get the best performance and quality you possibly can for the least amount of money, and you need to do it in a way that makes sense for the way you compute. That's why it's important to know what upgrades are possible, understand how your Mac works, and learn the secrets of rooting out your Mac's bottlenecks.

If you've read the chapters before this one, you probably have that much knowledge under your belt. Now you're ready to make the upgrading (and repair) decisions that will affect your system. You'll then need to prepare for the upgrade itself, including a look at the tools you'll want to have handy and some of the software diagnostics that might help you in your quest.

Determining Your Needs and Wants

As discussed in Chapter 3, bottlenecks can be any single part of your Mac that slows down the entire system because, like a traffic jam, that component doesn't let enough data get through. After you've identified the potential bottlenecks in your system, it's important to figure out exactly which need to be addressed immediately and which should be dealt with later, especially if budget is an issue. In this case, you need to decide what you absolutely have to upgrade right away (to maintain acceptable productivity levels) and what you want to upgrade as soon as possible (to maintain acceptable fun-to-work-with levels).

Unless you'll have to grab money out of your family's weekly food budget to upgrade your Mac, I recommend that you consider any productivity-enhancing tool a "need-to-have-it" upgrade. That includes things like drawing tablets, faster printers, and big monitors (if these things could possibly help). I also want you to consider upgrades that are more comfortable, ergonomically pleasing, or just a tad bit of fun to work with. You may not have the budget for all these things immediately, but these "wants" should really be high enough on the list that you consider them soon.

Now make your list. Fire up ClarisWorks, SimpleText, or just grab a pen and make a note of the upgrades you think fall in the "Need" column and those that go in the "Want" column. Don't forget to prioritize based not just on preference, but also on which bottlenecks are most extreme in your system. If you desperately need RAM, put it at the top of the needs list. If you really think a new CPU would help immeasurably, put it high on the needs list, too. If you can't think of anything cooler than a fighter pilot's joystick, consider putting that one high on the wants list. Maybe you can get around to it if your needs don't overwhelm your budget first.

What will it cost?

With your list in hand, you're ready to figure out how the upgrade can be accomplished and how much, roughly, it will cost. Table 4-1 focuses on the major upgrades for overcoming speed and quality bottlenecks.

Table 4-1
Upgrade Possibilities, Results, and Costs

Upgraded Component	Subsystem Affected	How Upgraded	Cost
Memory	Processing	RAM module	$2–$10 per MB
CPU	Processing	Expansion card	$500–$2,000
		Daughterboard	$500–$2,000
		Clock enhancement	$75–$250
		Chip upgrade	$250–$1,000
Cache RAM	Processing	RAM module	$75–$250 per MB
Logic board	Processing	Replace board	$500–$2,000+
Hard drive	Storage	Internal/External drive	$50–$150 per GB

Upgraded Component	Subsystem Affected	How Upgraded	Cost
Removable drive	Storage	Internal/External drive	$100–$1,500
Modem	Input/Output	Internal/External device	$50–$400
Network adapter	Input/Output	Expansion card	$100–$400
Network transceiver	Input/Output	External cabling	$25–$150
Hub	Input/Output	Connect networked Macs	$50–$500
ISDN adapter	Input/Output	Internal/External device	$250–$750
Video card	Input/Output	Expansion card	$250–$2,000+
Video accelerator	Input/Output	Expansion card	$150–$500
Printer	Input/Output	External device	$200–$5,000
Monitor	Input/Output	External device	$300–$2,500
Scanner	Input/Output	External device (serial); External device (SCSI)	$100–$500; $250–$2,000
Speakers	Input/Output	External device (sound-out)	$25–$500
Microphone	Input/Output	External device (sound-in)	$5–$250
MIDI	Input/Output	External switch box	$50–$150

Take each item and add it to your list, prioritizing based not only on need, but also on cost. If you find that your list is getting out of hand costwise, you have a different decision to consider first — whether you should spend a great deal of money up front for an overhaul or a new system.

Obviously, there's quite a bit of play in many of these prices. One way to get the latest prices is to pick up a copy of a recent Mac-oriented magazine (such as *Macworld*) and check the pages of ads that generally appear toward the back of the magazine. Once you know how much these upgrades are going to set you back, you can make a better decision as to what needs to be upgraded immediately and what can wait for a while.

List for my Power Macintosh 6100 system

As I write this, I'm personally interested in upgrading a Power Macintosh 6100 system for use as a workstation here in my office for people I bring in as Web designers and for other jobs. It needs to be capable of handling graphics, but it doesn't have to be decked out for a high-end artist. It's already an AV model, meaning it includes a video card that can accept video input from a VCR or camcorder. I don't use it that much, but, along with built-in video, this 6100 can already drive two monitors—one can even be a 20" monitor with millions of colors.

What it's lacking though, is hard drive space and speed. So, for my list, I'm looking at a few different options (text in parentheses represents an alternative choice):

To Be Upgraded	What Upgrade?	Cost
Processor	To G3	$700
(Processor	To 604e	$400)
(Cache RAM	To 512k	$75)
(Processor clock	To 83MHz	$75)
Hard drive	Add 2GB	$250

Adding a 604e processor and cache RAM would amount to nearly $500, so I'm probably better off going with the high-end G3 upgrade. (The cache RAM is rendered fairly useless once a G3 upgrade is installed.) I could also choose to boost the clock speed on the 6100 from 60MHz to 83MHz, which might result in a 30 percent gain in processing power. Along with the cache RAM, the clock upgrade would offer a slightly perceivable speed gain. It wouldn't last as long as a G3 upgrade, though, which offers a 500 to 800 percent speed gain and might make the system very usable for two or three more years.

More hard drive space is immediately necessary. Because of the nature of the Power Mac 6100's case, I'm limited to either replacing the existing hard drive or installing an external SCSI model. I'll opt for the external drive, even though it's a bit more expensive than an internal drive, because it will bring the total drive space to about 2.5GB for this Mac.

For me, this is a business Mac that still has about one-and-a-half years of (tax-related) depreciation left before its been completely written-off. So, I'm going to invest for a long-haul solution that can make the Mac worth using for at least two years or so. Otherwise, I might opt for a cheaper solution that would keep the machine in service only six months or a year, especially if I see reason to buy a new system down the road.

Don't forget to check the Web-based stores mentioned in Chapter 1 if you're trying to find pricing for upgrades to your Mac.

How can you upgrade?

Before you can move forward with your upgrading, your plan needs to include a look at your current system and your options for upgrading. Every Mac system is slightly different, with different types and numbers of upgrade slots, different RAM requirements and capabilities, and, occasionally, even different ports on the back of the machine.

You may decide that you're more adept at external upgrades than internal ones, or that you only have a certain amount of available slots and ports, and you'd like to save one of the internal slots for a more important upgrade. Or, maybe your Mac has a special slot for a particular upgrade — knowing that beforehand can help you decide what sort of add-on you need and how much it'll cost you.

Upgrading questions

To plan your upgrade, you'll need to know a few things about your particular Mac. Specifically, you need to ask yourself the following:

✦ *What slots do I have available?* Whether you're upgrading by adding a RAM module, an expansion card, or even a CPU daughtercard, you'll need to know how many slots your Mac came with and how many you have available for a particular upgrade. Consult the chapter in Part II that relates to the upgrade you're trying to perform to learn more about the slots available in most Mac models.

✦ *What ports do I have available?* Again, different Macs have varying numbers of ports and types of connections available. If your SCSI port is already taken by a number of external peripherals, are you able to add another SCSI device to that chain of devices? Does your Mac include a stereo sound-in port, or would you need to add a sound card for audio recording? Depending on your needs, you'll need to explore the back side of your Mac to see what ports you have to work with.

✦ *Is anything full or overloaded?* If you have a non-network printer and an external modem, your serial ports (modem and printer ports) are probably completely full. If you want to add a page scanner, you'll need to either consider a SCSI version or some sort of contraption to help you switch between one or the other of your peripherals (see Figure 4-1). If you have a few internal SCSI devices, you may be filling up that chain; you'll need to determine what SCSI addresses, if any, are left. You also need to avoid overloading any one port or expansion card with devices — you may be slowing your SCSI chain down if it includes several small hard drives (you'd be better off with one large one), or you might have to switch your ports so often that it becomes tiresome and counterproductive.

Figure 4-1: A simple data switch (this is a Mac serial version made by Belkin Components) can be used to switch a serial port between two devices, such as a printer and a page scanner.

Specific upgrade paths

Almost every Mac model has its own unique upgrading abilities, although some later Mac models share similar characteristics. Over the years Apple's approach has been reactionary — designing machines that complied with customers' wishes as they were made known. The original Mac 128k was hardly upgradeable at all — an interesting gambit that was later overturned with the six-slot Mac II. Since that time, nearly every Mac and Mac OS clone model makes it easy for you to get into the case for a little user upgrading, although the options for upgrading can vary widely.

Table 4-2 shows you many of the more popular Macintosh and Mac OS clone models and their basic component upgrade paths.

If your model isn't listed, it may be too new for inclusion. Check http://www.mac-upgrade.com for updates.

Table 4-2
Upgrade Slots and Ports for Major Mac OS Models

Mac OS Model	Modem Port?	Printer Port?	ADB Port?	Other Ports?	Slots?
Mac 128k	Yes[1]	Yes[1]	No	N/A	None
Mac 512k	Yes[1]	Yes[1]	No	N/A	None
Classic	Yes	Yes	Yes	N/A	None
Classic II	Yes	Yes	Yes	N/A	None
Color Classic	Yes	Yes	Yes, 2	N/A	1 LC PDS
Plus	Yes	Yes	No	N/A	None
SE	Yes	Yes	Yes, 2	N/A	1 SE PDS
SE/30	Yes	Yes	Yes, 2	N/A	1 SE/30 PDS
Mac II, IIx	Yes	Yes	Yes, 2	N/A	6 NuBus
IIci, IIcx	Yes	Yes	Yes, 2	N/A	3 NuBus
IIfx	Yes	Yes	Yes, 2	N/A	6 NuBus, 1 PDS
IIsi	Yes	Yes	Yes	N/A	1 NuBus or PDS
IIvi, IIvx, Performa 600 /600CD; Centris 650, Quadra 650	Yes	Yes	Yes, 2	N/A	3 NuBus, 1 PDS
Performa 400, 405, 410, 430, 450; Performa 475, 476; LC, LC 475, LC 520	Yes	Yes	Yes	N/A	LC PDS
Performa 550, 560; LC 550	Yes	Yes	Yes, 2	N/A	LC PDS
Performa 575, 577, 578; LC 575	Yes	Yes	Yes	N/A	LC PDS, comm
Performa 580; LC 580	Yes	Yes	Yes	N/A	LC PDS, comm, video
LC II	Yes	Yes	Yes	N/A	LC PDS

(continued)

Table 4-2 (continued)

Mac OS Model	Modem Port?	Printer Port?	ADB Port?	Other Ports?	Slots?
Performa 450, 460; LC III	Yes	Yes	Yes	N/A	LC III PDS, Quadra 605
Mac TV	Yes	Yes	Yes, 2	N/A	None
Performa 630, 630CD, 631CD, 635CD, 636CD, 637CD, 638CD; LC 630	Yes	Yes	Yes	N/A	LC PDS, comm, video
Performa 630/640DOS	Yes	Yes	Yes	PC game[4]	comm, video
Quadra 610/610DOS	Yes	Yes	Yes, 2	PC game[4]	LC PDS
Quadra 630	Yes	Yes	Yes	N/A	LC III PDS, comm, video, TV
Centris, Quadra 600AV	GeoPort	Yes	Yes	Video in/out	NuBus or PDS[3]
Quadra 700	Yes	Yes	Yes, 2	N/A	2 NuBus, 1 PDS
Quadra 800	Yes	Yes	Yes	N/A	3 NuBus, 1 PDS
Quadra 840AV	GeoPort	Yes	Yes	Video in/out	3 NuBus
Quadra 900/950	Yes	Yes	Yes	N/A	5 NuBus, 1 PDS
PM 6100, 6100AV, Performa	GeoPort	GeoPort	Yes	Video in/out[4]	1 6100DOS; NuBus or PDS[23]
M 7100, 7100AV	GeoPort	GeoPort	Yes	Video in/out[4]	PDS, 3 NuBus[2]
PM 8100, 8100AV	GeoPort	GeoPort	Yes	Video in/out[4]	3 NuBus[5]
Performa 6200, 6218	Yes	Yes	Yes	N/A	LC III PDS, comm, video
Performa 6205, 6214CD, 6290; PM6200	Yes	Yes	Yes	N/A	LC III PDS, comm, video, TV

Mac OS Model	Modem Port?	Printer Port?	ADB Port?	Other Ports?	Slots?
Performa 6216, 6220, 6230	Yes	GeoPort[6]	Yes	N/A	Comm, video, tuner
Performa 6300, 6320	Yes	GeoPort[6]	Yes	N/A	LC III PDS, comm, video, TV
Performa 6360	Yes	Yes	Yes	N/A	PCI, comm, video, TV
Performa 6400, PM 6400	GeoPort	GeoPort	Yes	N/A	2 PCI, comm, video, TV
Performa 5215CD, 5260	Yes	GeoPort[6]	Yes	N/A	LC III PDS, comm, video
LC 5200/5300	Yes	Yes	Yes	N/A	LC III PDS, comm, video, TV
LC 5500, PM 5500	GeoPort	GeoPort	Yes	N/A	PCI (7"), PCI-based comm, video, TV
PM 4400, 4400PC	GeoPort	GeoPort[6]	Yes	PC game[4]	2PCI[2]
PM 6500	GeoPort	GeoPort[6]	Yes	N/A	2 PCI, PCI comm, video, TV
PM 7200	GeoPort	GeoPort	Yes	N/A	2 PCI
PM 7200/ 120, 7200PC	GeoPort	GeoPort	Yes	PC game[4]	3 PCI[2]
PM 7500, 7600	GeoPort	GeoPort	Yes	Video in/out	3 PCI, DAV codec
PM 7300, 7300PC	GeoPort	GeoPort	Yes	PC game	
PM 8500, 8600	GeoPort	GeoPort	Yes	Video in/out	3 PCI, DAV codec
PM 9500, 9600	GeoPort	GeoPort	Yes	N/A	6 PCI
iMac	N/A	N/A	N/A	USB, 2	N/A

(continued)

Table 4-2 (continued)

Mac OS Model	Modem Port?	Printer Port?	ADB Port?	Other Ports?	Slots?
20th Mac	GeoPort	GeoPort	Yes	Video in/out	PCI (7"), PCI-based comm, video, TV
PM G3	GeoPort	GeoPort	Yes	video(8) in/out	3 PCI
Mac	N/A	N/A	N/A	USB, 2	N/A

Power Computing Systems

Power 100/120	GeoPort	GeoPort	Yes	N/A	3 NuBus, 1 PDS
PowerBase 180, 200, 240	GeoPort	GeoPort	Yes	PS/2 mouse/key	3 PCI
PowerWave 120, 132, 150	GeoPort	GeoPort	Yes	N/A	3 PCI[2]
PowerCurve 120; 3 PCI PowerCenter 150/166/180	GeoPort	GeoPort	Yes	N/A	120/132;
PowerCenter Pro 180, 210, 240	GeoPort	GeoPort	Yes	N/A	3 PCI[2]
PowerTower Pro; 180, 200, 225, 250	GeoPort	GeoPort	Yes	N/A	6 PCI[2]

Motorola Systems

StarMax 3000 MT	GeoPort	GeoPort	Yes	N/A	5 PCI[2]
StarMax 3000 DT	GeoPort	GeoPort	Yes	N/A	3 PCI
StarMax 4000	GeoPort	GeoPort	Yes	N/A	5 PCI[2]
StarMax 5000	GeoPort	GeoPort	Yes	N/A	5 PCI PCI[27]

UMAX Systems

c500 series	GeoPort	GeoPort	Yes	N/A	2 PCI
c600 series	GeoPort	GeoPort	Yes	N/A	3 PCI
c600x/240	GeoPort	GeoPort	Yes	N/A	3 PCI[2]

Mac OS Model	Modem Port?	Printer Port?	ADB Port?	Other Ports?	Slots?
c600x/280	GeoPort	GeoPort	Yes	N/A	3 PCI[7]
j700 series	GeoPort	GeoPort	Yes,2	N/A	4 PCI[2]
s900 series	GeoPort	GeoPort	Yes,2	N/A	6 PCI[2]
S900/250, S900i/ 250, S900DP/250	GeoPort	GeoPort	Yes,2	N/A	6 PCI[7]

1 Early Macs had a 9-pin serial port configuration that differs from the rounded Din-8 connectors of modern Macs.

2 A DOS-compatible, AV, Video or SCSI card fills one available expansion slot.

3 Requires NuBus adapter for PDS slot.

4 Only on AV or DOS-compatible model.

5 Features high-speed NuBus burst mode.

6 Used by Communications Slot modem.

7 Two expansion slots are already filled.

Although most PCI cards are 7-inch cards, it's important to know the size of the card and the available slots in your Mac before upgrading. In some cases, a 12-inch slot is required, and your Mac may or may not have a 12-inch slot available. Other caveats include Macs that are built with cases too low to hold NuBus or PCI cards that themselves are built to a nonstandard height—check your Mac's documentation to ensure correct sizing. And, you may notice that some of the "pizza box" style of Macs (that is, those that have very low profile cases—Quadra 610 and Power Macintosh 6100, for example) often require an adapter for their one PDS slot so that it can accept a NuBus card. (The adapter actually enables you to install the card sideways so that it will fit in the low-slung case.)

Most Power Macintosh–equivalent computers feature GeoPort-compatible serial ports, allowing for faster throughput and some unique features when compared to older Macs. GeoPort Macs can use the Apple GeoPort adapter, for instance, and connect to online services and the Internet without using a dedicated modem; instead, the modem is emulated by the Mac's PowerPC processor. (In the cases of non-PowerPC AV Macs, modem capabilities are emulated on a separate multimedia processor.) This also enables you to hook the Mac up to a phone line and use it as a speaker phone, a digital answering machine, and more—all without a modem. Figure 4-2 shows a GeoPort adapter.

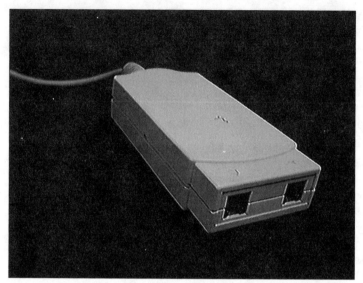

Figure 4-2: The GeoPort adapter, often called a *pod*, can be used to connect your AV or Power Mac to a phone line, forgoing the need for a modem.

Nearly all Macs also feature Apple Desktop Bus (ADB) ports, which enable you to install additional peripherals, usually for input and output. The ADB port is used for the keyboard and mouse, but other devices—drawing tablets, trackballs, telephony devices, and even some modems—use the ADB port to connect to the Mac and draw enough electricity to operate.

If your Mac is a DOS-compatible version, it most likely includes additional ports for Windows or DOS to work with, including a PC game port (which can accept two PC joysticks for game play) and a special VGA port for hooking up PC video. Most DOS cards enable you to use either two monitors (one for DOS, one for Mac) or a single monitor, employing a special patch cable to connect both the Mac's internal video and the PC's video connector to a single monitor.

The iMac, introduced in the summer of 1998, has none of the traditional Mac ports, opting instead for two Universal Serial Bus (USB) ports that will support the keyboard, mouse, and all upgrading options. The iMac has a proprietary internal slot.

Expansion cards: PDS, NuBus, and PCI

When the original Mac 128k was designed, a conscious decision was made (many say it was made specifically by Steve Jobs) to avoid including an expansion slot, even though such slots were available and popular on the existing Apple II series of computers. The thinking seemed to be that Macs were supposed to be the easiest computers in the world to use, so they should not have confusing technical capabilities like internal expansion.

Yet despite the potential for confusion, enough early Mac users and potential Mac users requested slot upgrades to warrant a complete change in tactics by Apple. The Mac SE featured a special PDS slot. The Mac II was an even more radical change from the original Mac philosophy, rolling off the assembly line with a total of six NuBus slots.

Since that time, nearly every Mac made (aside from PowerBooks, Mac Classic models, and the Mac TV) has had some number of internal slots, although the number certainly varies widely. If you've already looked up your Mac earlier in Table 4-2, you're aware of the slots you have available for internal upgrading. The question becomes this: Why are there so many different kinds of slots?

Processor Direct Slots

PDS slots were first introduced in the Mac SE, enabling that model of Mac to be upgraded for better video capabilities or faster processing. As would eventually be the case with most PDS slots in Macs, the SE's slots were designed specifically to accept a card created for the SE. In fact, because a PDS slot is directly tied to the processor in a Mac, it must be designed specifically to work with your Mac model (or a series of similar models). Unlike PDS cards, NuBus and PCI cards both use an intermediary on the logic board for communicating with the processor; this is why NuBus and PCI cards are interchangable between Mac models.

Table 4-3 shows the different types of PDS cards that must be used with particular Mac models.

Table 4-3
Mac Models and PDS Types

Mac Model/Series	PDS Type	Looks Like	Notes
Mac SE	SE PDS	96-pin connector	
Mac LC	LC PDS	120-pin connector	Many PDS slots are LC-compatible, including Performa and PowerMac models
Mac SE/30	SE/30 PDS	120-pin connector	Compatible with some IIfx, IIsi cards
Mac IIfx	IIfx PDS	120-pin connector	Compatible with some SE/30, IIsi cards
Mac IIsi	IIsi PDS	120-pin connector	Compatible with some SE/30, IIfx cards
LC II, LC III	030 PDS	96-pin connector	Also LCIII PDS; compatible with LC PDS
Quadra, Centris	040 PDS	140-pin connector	On all 040 models except Powerbooks and AV Macs (The Centris/Quadra 610/660AV can share some PDS cards.)
Power Macintosh 6100, 7100, 8100	601 PDS	91-pin connector	Also on Performa 61xx series

NuBus cards

A NuBus card is a 32-bit-wide expansion technology that sits on an expansion bus — that is, it doesn't have a direct line to the processor, like a PDS slot does. That also means you can have more than one NuBus slot. Theoretically, the limit is 16 NuBus slots, although no Mac model has ever come close. The most you'll see in a shipping model is 6 slots (Mac II, Mac IIfx), and that many NuBus slots is pretty rare. More often, Macs are configured with 3 NuBus slots or so, as shown in Figure 4-3.

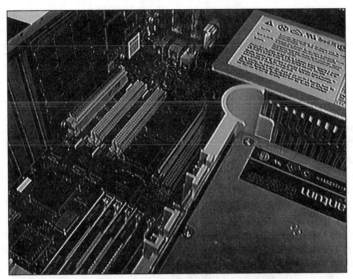

Figure 4-3: The NuBus slots in a Mac II series computer

NuBus cards are self-configuring: You simply install them in their slots and start up your Mac to begin using them. The Mac OS Slot Manager software assigns each NuBus card a slot number as the Mac goes through its startup process. Data is then transferred between the CPU and the NuBus cards by way of bus interface units, or chips on the logic board that are responsible for managing the data flow.

NuBus is a Texas Instruments standard that was used pretty much exclusively by Apple in Macintosh computers, enabling it to be optimized for use with Macs in later iterations. Both the NuBus '90 and the PowerPC NuBus standards enabled the cards to work more quickly as new, faster Macs were released.

Although still immensely popular for upgrading aging Macs, NuBus isn't quite the star of the Mac OS industry that it once was. Instead, the PCI standard has taken over for both Macs and Intel-compatible PCs.

PCI cards

If your Mac is a Power Macintosh or a Performa — or Mac OS clone — based on the second-generation PowerPC processors (the 603 and 604 family of processors), your Mac also comes with a PCI expansion bus. This bus, originally developed by Intel Corporation as a replacement for the ISA bus, fits in very nicely in Macs, as well as in Intel-compatible PCs. (Note that not all Performa models include an available PCI card slot, even though they use the PCI bus.)

This means two things: First, the PCI standard allows for faster connections and throughput than NuBus cards, making it better for video, multimedia, and network communications cards that can take advantage of the extra speed. Second, adhering to the PCI standard means that in many cases all an Intel-compatible PCI card vendor has to do is write Mac OS driver software for their card, and it can then be used in a Macintosh. That results in more choices for Mac users.

Having trouble finding a Mac-compatible PCI card? Apple's Tech Info Library (http://til.info.apple.com) recommends that you look for a blue "Designed for Macintosh computers with PCI" sticker on the box of the expansion card. Apple also advises that certain cards, originally designed for Intel-compatible PCs, can be easily repurposed for Macs, so long as they don't have to be active as your Mac starts up (for instance, a video card needs to be active, but a communications card doesn't). Check the manufacturer's Web site for Mac driver software you can download.

PCI cards come in two basic sizes — 7 inches and 12 inches — and which to use depends on how much circuitry is required to get the board up and running. Some Mac systems aren't equipped to handle the full 12-inch cards. You should find out about your system before you buy a PCI upgrade card. (Figure 4-4 shows both card sizes.)

Figure 4-4: Make sure the PCI card you buy will fit your Mac.

Special slots for special Macs

PCI, NuBus, and PDS are the standard types of upgrade cards in the Mac industry—but they're not the only ones. In the past, Apple has also offered computers special upgrade slots designed specifically for one function or another, instead of being upgrade generalists like PCI- and NuBus-standard slots.

For the most part, these special slots have been in the Performa line of Macs. These home-oriented systems were given special slots that could be used with Apple brand and some third-party upgrades for high-end capabilities like networking, adding a TV tuner, and capturing digital video. Instead of the more expensive professional versions of these cards, Apple's upgrades were cheaper (usually less than $200 new) and easy to add to the consumer-oriented Performa systems.

These days, upgrades for the Performa Communications (comm) slot, the video in/out slot, and the TV tuner slot are harder to come by, but not impossible. If you own a compatible Performa or Power Mac series computer that includes comm slots, and want to upgrade using these slots, your best bet is to shop the Mac catalog stores and Mac-oriented classified ads.

Can You Do It Yourself?

For quite some time I've hosted a radio call-in show dedicated to answering people's questions about both Intel-compatible PC and Macintosh upgrading. And just as often as I get a caller who seems to be incredibly excited about upgrading his or her system, I come across another who isn't thrilled at the prospect of opening the computer's case and messing around with the innards.

In fact, I've talked to folks who would rather just sell a computer and start over before they tackle something like upgrading. "Should I get more RAM or just buy a new computer?" sure isn't a dumb question, but it does suggest a certain trepidation.

Three types of upgrades

Just in case you need some reassurance, here it is: You can easily perform most upgrades on your own. Most of them barely even involve a screwdriver (you can thank Apple's engineers for that), and the upgrades that do require some assembly are still designed for regular folks to accomplish. In fact, I look on upgrading as having three basic levels. Anyone can accomplish any of these, but if upgrading makes you uncomfortable, you can decide to leave the more complex operations to the professionals. Here are the three types of upgrades:

✦ **External upgrades.** Rarely requiring any special tools, an external upgrade usually involves plugging a peripheral into an available port on the back of your Mac.

✦ **Slot upgrades.** These require you to open your Mac's case, but they're usually very straightforward: If you have a free slot, you just plug the expansion card into it. This goes for RAM, too, which is easily inserted into a SIMM or DIMM socket without requiring a degree in any of the hard sciences.

✦ **Logic board-level upgrades.** These can get a bit more serious, but they're by no means frightening. Replacing a CPU chip, daughtercard, ROM chip, PRAM battery, and similar upgrades do require that you ground yourself electrically and dig into the innards of your Mac. But it's certainly not impossible to do. In fact, some folks find it fun to get into their Mac, add a small chip or two, and fire the computer back up at twice its old speed!

Tip

External upgrades are a cakewalk. Anyone should feel comfortable doing them. The only real rule of thumb to remember is this: Turn off your Mac before plugging or unplugging peripherals into ports on the back of your Mac. There's enough power discharge possible to damage the ports. I've seen it happen.

The other two require tools, and you will need to get inside your Mac. It can be fun though, even if you're not the Indiana Jones of silicon. Go ahead and explore a bit, as long as you take the precautions discussed in the following sections.

Tools you'll need

You do have to admit that, in many ways, computers are weird. What other major electronic devices are we actually *encouraged* to take apart and mess with ourselves? Any individual caught taking a screwdriver to the back of a television set is immediately branded an engineer or a daredevil, if not worse. The idea of popping a few more chips into your VCR is equally ludicrous. But with computers — even Macs — it's de rigueur. Never mind that what you paid for your Mac would probably keep you in TVs and VCRs for decades.

If you're planning to upgrade, you'll need to get inside that case. And while you're there, you'll be making a few changes, so you'll need tools for that. For the most part, you don't need to buy specialized Mac or PC upgrading tools from the computer store. Instead, a few typical household tools will suffice, along with a specialty item or two:

✦ Flathead screwdriver

✦ Phillips-head screwdriver

✦ Small flashlight

✦ Paper clip

✦ Antistatic containers/bags

✦ Grounding strap

Flathead screws aren't terribly typical on your standard Mac, but flathead screwdrivers can be useful nonetheless. Many Mac cases are designed to be pried open with no tools other than your fingers. Unfortunately, it seems that in some cases Apple didn't actually mean *human* fingers, as their cases can stick together sometimes, even if they were designed with the best intentions. In those cases a flathead screwdriver can be used to gently create space between a Mac's chassis and its outer shell of plastic. (With the original Mac classic form-factor Macs, a putty knife or case spreader is a better option.)

The Phillips screwdriver is used more conventionally — to remove screws. Whether or not your Mac has a quick-release case, it'll still probably need to have some screws removed, because they're used for everything from mounting hard drives to keeping expansion cards inline.

The flashlight can be a penlight or something slightly bigger, just to help you look around inside a full Mac. Get enough expansion cards and internal drives in your Mac and you'll find that a little light is necessary to see components on the logic board.

The jack-of-all-trades in your arsenal is a common, but sturdy, paper clip. Paper clips are handy for at least two situations — reaching hard to switch DIP switches (on/off switches usually used to change SCSI ID numbers on storage devices) and ejecting problem disks from floppy drives and removable drives.

You may also want a can of compressed air handy for blowing dust out of the case and away from your internal components. Remember that compressed air can be very cold and cause condensation, so don't spray it directly on or closely to circuit boards and other exposed electronics. Instead, keep it a few feet away and just blow the dust out. An amazing amount of dust in a system can cause overheating and/or sporadic behavior from the Mac.

Note If you have a classic-style (all-in-one) Mac or a PowerBook, you'll also need a Torx screwdriver if you plan to open the case. The process is described in Chapter 5 for Mac Classics and Chapter 20 for PowerBooks.

The screwdrivers make sense, but what about that other stuff? Most likely, any hardware upgrade you receive will come with an antistatic bag or packaging of some sort. If you're taking a component out of your Mac, try to place it immediately in such an antistatic bag or container. (If one didn't come with the components you've bought, you can probably buy or borrow an antistatic bag from a local computer store.) Static electricity discharge — even from your fingers — can be very damaging to computer components, potentially rendering them useless.

That's also why you'll want a grounding strap for serious upgrading. A grounding strap is fixed to your wrist or ankle, effectively grounding you against static discharge. That enables you to work with computer components without fear that you'll discharge electricity into any of the components.

The great "plug-it-in" debate

A grounding strap should be your first line of defense in upgrading, but it's not necessarily the most popular way to guard against static electricity — at least among a certain school of upgraders. Another way to avoid discharge damage is to keep the computer electrically ground. That means leaving it plugged into the wall socket while you work on its innards.

While a computer is plugged in, touching any metal part of the power supply of chassis will discharge static, enabling you to work in relative peace — except that there's now electrical current running the computer and trickling through other components.

I know from personal experience that you can create quite a light show if you have your Mac plugged in and you drop a screwdriver on the logic board. It's not a pretty light show though, because it could give you a jolt, and it's almost always expensive when a computer component fries.

I think the best advice I've heard on the subject is this: Keep your Mac plugged in if you're more worried about your components getting shocked than you are about your body getting shocked. If you feel very strongly that your person should not be exposed to any electric shock, work with a grounding strap instead.

Tips for the upgrade

Finally, let's take a look at some advice, both compiled from experts and from my personal experience, that I can offer you before you undertake your upgrade. In almost every case, your upgrade should come off without a hitch — after all, these are Macs. But just to ensure success, take a look at these hints:

✦ *Take your time*. Give yourself quality, quiet time to complete the upgrade. Studies show that nearly every task takes two-and-a-half times longer than you thought it would to complete. When it comes to computer upgrading, we can comfortably round up the time it will take to complete an upgrade to at least three times longer than expected. If something goes wrong, it's best that it goes wrong during a slow evening, weekend, or some other time you've set aside for improvements. Don't start upgrading right before a big deadline.

✦ *Back up your important data.* I know it seems silly to backup your data if you're installing a new 3D video card, but it's not. If you fry the computer and render it useless, you'll be wishing you had a removable media backup (like a Jaz cartridge or a rewritable CD) that includes all your important spreadsheets, songs, and journal entries. Otherwise, your Mac might be going to the repair shop for a few days along with your important files.

✦ *Make space for upgrading.* I like to have an entire table top, completely clear of obstructions and junk, to finish an important upgrade. Give yourself six feet by three feet or so, and don't clutter the table with stuff you don't need. Include just your tools, hardware, instructions, and enough space for this book.

✦ *Keep an empty bowl or coffee cup handy.* Well, you've got to have someplace to drop loose screws. A coffee cup or two for the screws you take out of your system will save you the trouble of finding them again in the carpet — or the, uh, pain of finding them again for those of you decide to store them in a pocket or in your mouth. (You can use paper cups, but that's not very eco-conscious of you.)

✦ *Think things through.* Here's something I've actually done before: "I'll just get the instructions off the Internet while I'm upgrading." The problem: I can't get on the Internet if my computer is lying in two on the table in front of me. A little planning can go a long way in cases like these. Print out relevant information, and don't take your computer apart if you're expecting an important e-mail or fax.

✦ *Make one change at a time.* If you plan to install both new RAM and a new video card, for instance, install each separately, and then piece things together and test them out. Change one thing at a time, and then test between each upgrade. This helps keep variables to a minimum if you need to troubleshoot your Mac after completing each upgrade.

✦ *Don't leave the case off.* It's usually OK to leave your Mac's case cover off while you're testing a new upgrade, but don't compute long-term with the case cover off. Mac cases are designed so that air flows a specific way, and the case requires its outer shell to make that happen. If the air doesn't flow, your components may overheat, regardless of the temperature in the room.

Finally, read the chapters in this book carefully and check out the sidebars containing advice from the professionals. Someone somewhere has probably been through a particular upgrade before and passed that information on, so you don't have to make the same mistakes.

Summary

✦ Before you upgrade, you should have a plan. Determine your needs and wants, and then come up with a plan for attacking your Mac's bottlenecks while staying within your budget.

✦ Every Mac is a little different. Check yours for ports, slots, and other ways of upgrading, and know what options you have available before you start shopping for the upgrade.

✦ Know your cards. Does your Mac have a PDS slot or NuBus slot, or does it need PCI cards for upgrading?

✦ Get the right tools. You'll need a few common household items and one or two things from the computer store before you begin your upgrading adventure.

✦ Lastly, take a few tips along for the ride. Before you start peeling that case apart in the next chapter, take a moment to reflect on all the things others such as myself have done wrong in their upgrading career. Most importantly, take it slow and have fun.

✦   ✦   ✦

Inside Your Mac

Ready to take your Mac apart? In this chapter, you'll focus almost completely on your Mac's case — what's on the outside of it, how you get it off, and what's inside when you get there. You'll determine the model of Macintosh that you have so you can know exactly what upgrade paths you have at your disposal. Once you know the model, you're ready to take the case off and peer inside.

With the case open, you'll see what the internals of your Mac look like, including the power supply, upgrade slots, memory sockets, and CPU. Most importantly, opening the case gives you an idea of what options you have left. What's already been upgraded, what slots are open still, and is there room for internal peripherals like hard drives or CD-ROM drives? You'll know by the end of this chapter.

Determine Your Mac Model

The key to your Mac's identity is the type of model and model number found on the name badge that your Mac proudly displays right up front for all to see (at least it's up front on most models). This model name and number will determine what upgrades you can use, what system software you can load, and what programs you can buy off the shelves at computer stores.

The Mac model will also be useful for telling you what processor you have, what upgrade options you have, and other tidbits, such as how much RAM you can use and what sort of memory modules you need to buy for upgrading. The model name and number will also help you determine what ports you have available and, in some cases, what the limitations are on speed and storage upgrades.

Note   Knowing your Mac's model number will prove vital to using this book. Nearly every upgrading chapter in Part II includes a comprehensive chart that tells you the vital statistics involving your Mac or the Macs you support. You'll want to know your model pretty intimately so you can find it easier on those charts.

I'll discuss the naming conventions used by both Apple and the major clone vendors. They always follow some sort of logic, but it may not be the logic you were hoping for.

What's in an Apple's name?

You can make two generalizations about the way Apple comes up with model names. First, the word portions of the names almost always indicate the market to which Apple plans to sell the machine — which means the model names are not necessarily indicative of the power that particular Macintosh offers. Second, the numbers should go *up* when a Mac offers more speed and features, and they often do. But numbers usually only go up relative to a product that Apple believes the new product is replacing. Bottom line: Apple's product numbers can end up being more confusing than this paragraph.

I'll try to elaborate. Apple has had about eight different product brand names over the years, for example, Mac II, Mac LC, Performa, and so on. For the most part (at least, since about 1989) these names have been designed to suggest which market Apple is trying to sell the machine to. In many cases, the actual computer will be identical (like the Quadra 630, Performa 630, and LC 630), with the only difference being the peripherals that come with the machine and the bundled software.

Take a look at the different Mac brands and how they fit into Apple's marketing plans and their history. It's an interesting story.

Macintosh

The original Macs weren't really aimed at a particular market, because, for a while at least, only one or two Mac models were being sold at a time. These Macs rarely had numbers, opting instead to denote the amount of RAM the Mac had (such as the Mac 512k) before moving on to exciting name add-ons, such as Mac Plus, Mac SE, and Mac SE/30. (Mac SE/30 isn't a product number. The number is meant to suggest that the SE/30 model uses a Motorola 68030 processor, unlike the 68000 in its predecessors.)

I'm including the Mac Classic models in this category, although you could certainly debate that the Macintosh Classic series was a slightly different brand. After all, the Classic line would go on to include the Mac Classic II, the Mac Color Classic, and others. They all fit the all-in-one form factor though, so it's safe enough to call them all just Macintosh when it comes to branding.

Let me also toss four other odd-ball machines in here that Apple has made over the years — the Mac TV, the Mac Portable, the 20th Anniversary Macintosh, and the iMac. Although each of them couldn't be any more different from the other, they've all had a unique place in Apple's marketing and history of trying to reinvigorate the amazing design success enjoyed by the original Macintosh. Apple's latest attempt, the iMac (see Figure 5-1), fits this category because I like it here; whether or not the iMac becomes a strong model name that features add-on words or numbers as Apple releases improved models remains to be seen.

Figure 5-1: The iMac is Apple's PowerPC G3-based foray into the world of inexpensive but stylish home computers.

Macintosh II

Apple may have originally envisioned continuing the Mac series with a Mac II and a Mac III, but ultimately this Mac series with the roman numeral came to be a brand unto itself. The Mac II series represented an expandable Mac with a separate monitor, making it distinct from the regular all-in-one Mac line of computers. The Mac II also followed a unique lettering scheme for calling out different models.

Instead of the Mac II Plus, Apple opted to append lowercase letters to the *II* for successors to the original Mac II, as in Mac IIci, Mac IIsi, and Mac IIfx. Unfortunately, the lettering scheme seemed to have absolutely no basis in logic: The IIci is more powerful than the IIcx, for instance, and the IIx is one of the earlier Mac II series computers, whereas the IIsi came along later. See what I mean? Clearly the established order of the English alphabet had little influence on Apple's naming scheme.

The funny thing is, there really is some reasoning behind it, according to technical editor Dennis Cohen. (I didn't know any of this stuff myself.) Here's the deal: The IIcx was the IIx in a *compact* form, hence the addition of the *c*. The IIci was a *compact* II with *internal* video, so it gets both a *c* and an *i*. The IIfx was the *faster* IIx; the IIsi was a *smaller* Mac II with *internal* video. Now you know.

Note

Although it was never official, rumor had it that a Mac advertising campaign centering on music sensation Lawrence Welk's late 1980s comeback was part of the original naming scheme. "And a Mac, and a Mac II..." were tough for the seasoned band director to spit out on a steady beat, so the idea was canned after a few rehearsals. (Okay, I made that up.)

Macintosh LC

LC originally stood for low cost, I believe, but historically LC is the Mac brand that's marketed directly to education customers. Although Apple doesn't use the LC brand much anymore, at the time regular retail consumers couldn't really get their hands on LC equipment unless it was through a "parent buy" program or some similar promotion out of Apple's education sales group.

The early LC models included roman numerals (LC II, LC III) but eventually turned to product numbers that usually related to similar Quadra, Performa, or Power Macintosh computers. The Quadra 630 and LC 630 are similar machines, for instance, as are the LC 575 and the Performa 575. LC systems can include a monitor, and many of the 500 and 5000 series LCs have built-in monitors (usually larger 14- and 15-inch models). But that's not a hard-and-fast rule—LC models just as often don't include monitors. LCs often come with Ethernet, differentiating them slightly from the consumer models (which usually include modems). Today, Apple tends to offer different models of the Power Macintosh line for education customers only (for instance, the Power Macintosh 5500 line), but even that seems to be a dying trend, as Apple continues to offer more build-to-order systems to all its customers.

Centris/Quadra

Although two separate brand names, the Centris line was fairly short-lived and, occasionally, the same exact machine as the like-numbered Quadra. These were all 68040-based Macs that were the progeny of the Mac II line and the predecessors to the original Power Macintosh line. Aimed at business and creative professionals, the Quadras and Centrises (Centrisi?) usually came without monitors or keyboards and with very little software. They were powerhouses for their time and relied on a fairly straightforward numbering scheme that told you both the form factor (tower, desktop, big desktop) and relative speed.

As far as numbers went, some made perfect sense: The Quadra 605, 610, 630 and 650 all stepped up in speed and features (although the 630 was a later addition than the others). Other numbered schemes were a bit more odd—the Quadra 700 is less powerful than the 650, but comes in a tower case (it was also introduced earlier than the 650). The 660AV offered a less powerful processor than the 650, used a 610's case, but offered advanced multimedia abilities and upgraded serial ports. Go figure.

The Quadra 650 and 800: Upgrade heaven

A lot of Quadra 650s and Quadra 800s were sold in the early 1990s. These were very popular machines made in the heyday of Mac market share and sales volumes, and they offered plenty of room for expansion, upgrades, and add-ons. Funny thing is, they're still good machines to own for a lot of these reasons.

Both the 650 and 800 can take on over 100MB of RAM, they both can accept PowerPC upgrade cards, and both have logic boards that can be swapped out for Power Macintosh 7100 and 8100, respectively: that means not only first generation PowerPC performance, but 604e or G3 performance with upgrade cards from Sonnet and Newer Technologies.

There are other tweaks, too, including plenty of NuBus slots for adding graphics cards and other speed enhancements. In many cases, you can do this upgrading for less than the cost of a new system — especially if you're already heavily invested in NuBus cards and peripherals for your 650 or 800. If you've got one of these Macs, hold on to it. Or, if you're shopping the used market, you might consider grabbing one of these Macs for a rock-bottom price, and then upgrading it. (Early Power Macs, like the 6100 and 7100, are great upgradeable secondhand buys, too.)

Performa

Performa is the long-running consumer brand that Apple has traditionally offered in home electronics and department stores such as Sears and Best Buy. The Performa brand lasted about as long as Apple's presence in these stores, ending its reign as the consumer brand in early 1997 (in early 1998, Apple announced an exclusive retail relationship with CompUSA, pulling its products from many consumer-electronics stores). The name *Performa* is all about branding in Apple's eyes; Performas often come with monitors, always come with keyboards and mice, usually feature modems, and always include a broad range of home computing and educational software titles. The Performa 5400, for instance, offered a little bit of all these things (see Figure 5-2).

The Performa line has often overlapped with the business and education brands from Apple, including similar product numbers in many cases. For instance, the Performa 6116 and the Power Macintosh 6100 are nearly identical computers. The Performa has been around so long that it's impossible to call it more or less powerful than other Mac brands — some Performas are the same power level as LCs, Mac IIs, Quadras, and even Power Macintoshes. The Performa 6400, last in the Performa line, was based on a second-generation PowerPC 603e processor, no speed slouch for its time. The Performa 400, by contrast, was the same basic computer — processor, monitor, features — as the Mac Classic II.

Figure 5-2: Not only does the Performa 5400 feature a built-in monitor and a home software package, but it honored another Performa tradition of sharing its design with other Mac models. It's a relabeled version of the Power Macintosh 5400, which is available only to education customers (in the U.S.).

In almost all cases, a Performa will not feature built-in Ethernet for networking, as do most business-oriented Macs. Instead, Performas almost always include a bundled internal or external modem that can be used to access online services and the Internet over phone lines.

You might notice something else unique about the Performa line — tons and tons of model numbers. The expansion chart back in Chapter 4 showed entries like "Performa 575, 576, 577, 578" — many more model numbers than you'd generally find for other Mac models. (There was only an LC 575 and LC 580, by contrast.) This is because Performa numbers changed slightly based on the software bundle and (sometimes) the hardware included. A particular model, say the Performa 631CD, might include a faster modem, slightly different software, and a larger hard drive compared to the similar 630CD. This might be because it was a follow-on product or because it was sold in a different venue; at one time, Apple had different models for computer stores versus electronics stores versus department stores.

Since that time, Apple's focus on consolidating its brands has resulted in a two-step process for consumer brands. First, the Performa brand was rolled into the Power Macintosh line — specifically, the Performa 6400 became the Power Macintosh 6400 (briefly) followed by the Power Macintosh 6500 series. The 6500 series was sold as Home, Small Business, and Creative Studio models, depending on included expansion cards and the software included.

Once Apple moved to a build-to-order system, a single brand name became applicable for pretty much the entire line of Macs offered — the Power Macintosh G3 series. (The follow-on to this will likely be the Power Macintosh G4 series.) With the build-to-order system in place, a customer can configure a Power Macintosh in many different ways, according to their individual needs. This makes it convenient for all sorts of customers, as well as for Apple, because the company no longer has to create different brands and bundles to try to please all comers.

The only caveat in this plan so far is the iMac, a consumer-and-education-oriented Mac (in some ways, a successor to the Performa) that comes in a single, standard configuration. Whether the iMac becomes its own series of models (like Mac II and Mac LC eventually did) remains to be seen. Apple is likely, though, to continue sticking to only a few product names, at least for a while, as their business model has become more oriented toward simplicity in recent years.

Power Macintosh

The Power Macintosh line began in early 1994 with the release of the first Mac models based on the PowerPC processor and architecture. Originally positioned as business machines only (and fairly expensive ones at that), Power Macintosh computers used Quadra-style cases, were sold without keyboards and didn't include hefty software bundles. Eventually, however, the Power Macintosh line would encompass most of the computers sold through business and consumer retail outlets, including online stores and the Web-based Apple Store. First generation Macs were the 6100, 7100, and 8100 models, all based on preexisting Quadra cases and form factors. These Macs used NuBus expansion cards, enabling Mac owners to make the transition more comfortably to the new PowerPC architecture.

The Power Macintosh has gone through at least one significant transition since the jump to the PowerPC processor — the second-generation Macs (unofficially called "G2") featured PowerPC 603 and 604 processors along with being the first Macs to use the Intel-compatible standard PCI expansion bus. This generation of Macs includes the Power Macintosh 6500, which represented the inclusion of Performa-style machines in the Power Macintosh lineup. Other second-generation Power Macs include the 4400, 7300, 7600, 8600, and 9600 models.

Second generation Power Macs have another thing going for them — unprecedented upgrade capabilities. With the exception of the 4400 and 6500 models, all these Macs can accept daughtercard processor upgrades, allowing the addition of a faster PowerPC 604 or a PowerPC 750 (G3) processor to the computer by simply swapping an internal circuit board. This has resulted in quite an aftermarket of processor upgrades.

The Power Macintosh G3 line is the third generation of Power Macintosh computers, featuring the PowerPC 750 processor (alternatively called the Power PC G3 processor) — a high-speed processor capable of reaching well beyond 300MHz. The PowerPC 750 processor is also specially optimized for the Mac OS, enabling it to perform remarkably well for a low-power, low-cost processor. The G3 and G4 processors beyond it hold serious promise for a new era of 500MHz to 1GHz (gigahertz) computing.

PowerBook

The PowerBook line of Macs represent Apple's second foray into the world of a portable Macintosh (the third, actually, if you include the original all-in-one Macs that could be carried around in a huge bag). The Macintosh Portable was a rather large Mac with a handle — somewhat in the spirit of an IBM Selectric typewriter — that never really took off with consumers. (More successful was the Outbound 2030, an early attempt at a portable Mac OS clone machine. The Outbound was very much like a laptop with a 33MHz 68030 processor, 14MB of RAM, and a decent 9-inch screen. Outbound bought old Mac Plus machines to retrieve the ROMs in order to run the Mac OS legally on a clone. Outbound went out of business sometime after Apple introduced its very popular first round of PowerBook computers.)

The PowerBook was a completely different story. Beginning with the simultaneous release of the PowerBook 100, 140, and 170, the PowerBook was an almost overnight sensation, with a reputation as a technology tool that was also a status symbol in urban centers around the world. Later PowerBooks added to that mystique when the 500 series became one of the most lauded portable computer designs in the industry. (See Figure 5-3).

Figure 5-3: The PowerBook 500 series offered a sleek case, upgrade options, and stereo sound, making it a popular Mac OS portable.

Apple made the transition to PowerPC with the PowerBook 5300 series, which was notable for more bad characteristics than good, included some issues that are still covered by Repair Extension Programs implemented by Apple. Later, the PowerBook 1400 and 3400 series pulled Apple's reputation for great PowerBooks back out of the mud, followed by the raging success of the G3 and faster models.

The PowerBook had offered another branding element aside from the numbering scheme — the Duo moniker had been used for a smaller line of compact PowerBooks. PowerBook Duos offered no built-in floppy drive, for instance, but tended to be a few pounds lighter than regular PowerBooks. The Duo series also had the ability to hook up to a special Duo Dock, enabling the portable computer to be used with a full-size monitor, keyboard, and additional peripherals.

The Duo line has been discontinued, although the PowerBook 2400 extends many of its metaphors, as does the compact Apple eMate and its progeny. (Although the Newton OS is no longer being developed as of this writing, a "consumer portable" device is expected from Apple to fill the need for an ultra-compact Mac portable.) Apple will most likely continue to make compact PowerBook and notebook computer solutions into the foreseeable future, probably under the PowerBook brand name.

What about the clones?

A thriving Mac OS clone market existed for only a few years in the mid-1990s. These compatibles had their own names and numbering schemes to help buyers understand their branding. Although each company had a unique (and occasionally annoying) methodology for naming their machines, most of them were easy to grasp if only because they didn't offer as many models as Apple.

In this book, I focus almost exclusively on the three largest Mac OS vendors — Power Computing, Motorola, and UMAX. Other Mac OS vendors tended to base their systems on the offerings of the later two companies anyway, because Motorola and UMAX both have had the right to sublicense the Mac OS.

The most complete reference I've seen regarding Mac OS models is a site called EveryMac (www.everymac.com), where host Brock Kyle maintains detailed technical, configuration, and pricing information on every Mac model in the world.

Power Computing

Power Computing Corporation (PCC) was the original Mac clone manufacturer and, over time, the most successful. In late 1997, when Apple decided to curtail the sale of Mac clones, it did so by buying the assets of Power Computing for over $100 million. Apple is now responsible for maintaining Power Computing tech notes and Web-based support, and any warranties are handled by a third party.

Web

Power Computing information is maintained as a part of the Apple Tech Info Library, available at `http://til.info.apple.com`.

In its time as a Mac OS clone vendor, Power Computing came up with seven different model names: Power, PowerWave, PowerBase, PowerCurve, PowerCenter, PowerCenter Pro, and PowerTower Pro. Table 5-1 shows the differences.

Table 5-1 Power Computing Corporation Models		
Model Name	**Model Numbers**	**Description**
Power	100, 120	First PCC machines, based on PowerPC 601
PowerWave	120, 132, 150	PCC's first PCI-based Mac, based on PowerPC 604
PowerCurve	120	PCC's second PCI-based Mac, based on PowerPC 601
PowerBase	180, 200, 240	PCC's consumer-oriented PCI Mac, based on PowerPC 603e
PowerCenter	120, 132, 150, 166, 180	PCC's third PCI series, based on PowerPC 604
PowerCenter Pro	180, 210, 240	Update of PowerCenter for speed, based on PowerPC 604e
PowerTower Pro	180, 200, 225, 250	PCC's high-end graphics workstation, based on PowerPC 604e

No other vendor's machines are based directly on the Power Computing models. They tend to be fairly well behaved and were popular until Power Computing went out of business (after Apple had paid for its core assets). The models can have occasional odd problems due mostly to performance tweaks Power Computing engineered on logic boards sold to them by Apple. Apple will probably be tracking Power Computing–related issues for some time to come.

Every Power Computing machine sold is daughtercard-upgradeable, meaning you can add higher-speed processors to existing Power Computing machines. These cards are available from a number of upgrade vendors, although slight differences between Apple, Power Computing, and other Mac OS models make it necessary that you read carefully before buying an upgrade daughtercard for a PCC machine. Very little trouble has been reported for PCC compatibles that have been upgraded to high-end 604e and G3 processors.

Motorola

Motorola clones are generally based on the Tanzania motherboard, sharing traits with the Power Macintosh 4400 computer. Motorola's marketing strategy focused on selling Macs into the corporate sector, both for creative and regular business tasks. Motorola machines are generally not daughtercard-upgradeable, and the models that Motorola mass produced were rarely performance leaders. Motorola did have a CHRP-compatible Mac OS machine that was introduced shortly before Apple refused to upgrade Motorola's clone license to include Mac OS 8.0. The Motorola CHRP system would have used G3 technology well before Apple's own offerings, making it one of the faster desktop computers available in late 1997.

Motorola's shipping models featured straightforward names; they were all called StarMax, and numbers were used to suggest the power levels associated with the machines. In the case of the 3000 and 4000 series machines, both series were available in desktop and minitower cases — the numbers don't suggest physical form, just processor type and market placement. Table 5-2 shows the Motorola models.

What's CHRP?

The *Common Hardware Reference Platform*, or CHRP, was a specification hacked out by Motorola, IBM, Apple, and other companies to enable Mac OS computers to incorporate traditionally Intel-compatible hardware, including PS/2-style ports and PC-style serial and parallel ports. The big news was the clone vendors would have been able to run the Mac OS on PowerPC-based hardware that didn't require special Mac OS ROM chips for operation, meaning they wouldn't have had to rely on Apple for hardware parts in their clone machines.

Unfortunately (at least, for consumers), Apple has shied away from the CHRP platform and shut down most Mac OS cloners. Apple's high-end operating system, currently known by its code name, Rhapsody, promises to run on a variety of hardware platforms, including both PowerPC and Intel-compatible machines. At the same time, Apple has begun incorporating more Intel-compatible ports and specifications (such as PCI slots and USB ports), giving Macs access to a much greater variety of computer peripherals and add-ons.

Table 5-2
Motorola StarMax Product Numbers and Features

Product Number	Megahertz Levels	Features
StarMax 3000 series	180, 200, 240	Desktop or minitower, based on PowerPC 603e
StarMax 4000 series	160, 200	Desktop or minitower, based on PowerPC 604e
StarMax 5000 series	300	Minitower, based on PowerPC 603e

Motorola appended the letter *S* to the end of a product name (for example, StarMax 3000/180/S) to suggest it came bundled with the SOHO package, which included software and hardware appropriate for a home office. The letter *E* was used in the same way to suggest an Enterprise package bundle.

UMAX

Emerging from the Mac licensing wars of 1997 relatively unscathed, UMAX was the last Mac OS clone maker, having decided to slowly work it's way out of the Mac OS clone business throughout 1998. You may still be able to find new UMAX systems to purchase, especially as direct-mail catalog vendors deplete their inventories.

UMAX systems seem to be aimed directly at Apple's main markets — consumers, creative professionals, and small enterprise settings. UMAX Mac OS desktop systems are actually sold under the familiar SuperMac brand, which was originally a different company name and brand of Apple Macintosh–compatible peripherals (along with some software, like the first color paint program for Macintosh). The models are differentiated using single alphabetic letters, followed by numbers that don't quite seem to represent anything. Table 5-3 shows the UMAX models.

Table 5-3
SuperMac Mac OS Compatible Models and Features

Product	Megahertz Levels	Features
C500 series	140, 160, 200, 240	Desktop case, based on PowerPC 603e, CPU upgradeable
C600 series	180, 200, 240, 280	minitower case, based on PowerPC 603e, CPU upgradeable
J700 series	150, 180, 233	desktop case, based on PowerPC 604e, CPU upgradeable
S900 series	150, 180, 200, 233, 250, 250DP	Tower case, based on PowerPC 604e, CPU upgradeable

UMAX uses a number of different letter codes to represent various things in the model name (for example, C500i/200). An *i* usually means Internet (that is, the model includes a modem), an *e* is for enterprise (the model includes Ethernet), *vPC* means the model includes Virtual PC software, and *DP* means dual processing (the model includes two PowerPC processors that can be used simultaneously by some programs and operating systems, such as the BeOS, if they support that particular model).

The BeOS is an alternative operating system designed to run on many PowerPC-based Macintosh models. Check out www.be.com on the Web for more information.

Is your Mac PowerPC-based?

This is probably the first thing you'll want to know about your Mac once you've learned the model name and number. In some ways, it's vital to know whether your Mac uses a PowerPC processor, because that fact can determine quite a bit about how to troubleshoot and speed up your Mac.

How can you tell? With Apple products it's easy — every Mac that was originally sold with a PowerPC processor (not including special aftermarket upgrades) has a four-digit model number, except those that include information about the chip right in the name (like the Power Macintosh G3 — a dead giveaway). Performa, LC, PowerBook, and any other models that feature four digits (in other words, the PowerBook 5300, the Performa 6400) are PowerPC-based.

Also, all major Mac OS clones are PowerPC-based, because Mac OS licensing didn't begin until after Apple had transitioned completely to PowerPC processors. The last new Macintosh computer made to support the 68040 processor was the PowerBook 190, introduced in 1995. It is now a discontinued product, as are all non-PowerPC Macs.

What type of expansion bus does your Mac use?

Part of getting to know the model and specifications of your Mac includes determining what sort of expansion bus — NuBus, PDS or PCI — the Mac uses. This is of vital importance if you plan to upgrade using internal expansion cards. In nearly all cases, a Mac designed for a certain expansion technology is incapable of using cards designed for another expansion technology. (There are add-on adapters for some special cases.)

If your Mac is a second-generation Apple Power Macintosh or newer, a second-generation Power Computing machine or newer, or nearly any other Mac OS clone, it is probably based on the PCI bus. Older Apple Macs and the first Power Computing models usually accept NuBus cards, but not always. PDS is the norm for many Performa, LC, and a few Power Macintosh models.

Chapter 4 has a more in-depth explanation of the different bus technologies.

Is your Mac AV capable?

Another capability that varies from Mac to Mac is AV capability. Usually, this means the Mac's ability to receive video input (from a VCR, camcorder, or similar device) and digitize it into a QuickTime movie that can be saved to the Mac's hard drive. This enables the user to edit the movie, add effects and titling, and then output the movie to another video source for taping or compress the video file and transfer it to other computers for use as a movie or presentation.

To determine if your Mac is AV capable, consult Table 4.2 in Chapter 4, looking for Video In capabilities listed in the Other Ports column. Also, note that many 68040 and PowerPC-based Performa and LC models include a special video slot that enables them to be easily upgraded to AV functions.

Oddly enough, even though these Macs are called AV Macs (suggesting that they have special audio and visual capabilities), the only real differentiator is usually enhanced video capabilities. Because most Macs have advanced audio built in, this isn't really a feature special to AV Macs.

If your Mac isn't an AV-enhanced model, it can probably still be upgraded to AV capability. Check Chapter 13 for more on the subject.

Your Mac's hard disk technology

Yet another important fact to know is the hard disk technology used by your particular Mac model. Once you know the name and model number of your Mac, use it to determine the type of hard disk technology options you have for upgrading your Mac. (See Table 7-1 in Chapter 7.) There are basically two types to concern yourself with: IDE and SCSI.

SCSI is the faster and more capable of the two, whereas IDE is a bit less expensive and the Intel-compatible standard, making IDE drives more readily available. Most Macs offer SCSI technology for upgrading, although many newer Macs come with internal IDE drives. Even these Macs, as a rule, offer external SCSI upgrading for adding external hard drives and other SCSI peripherals.

Opening Your Mac's Case

Macintosh computer cases have been many and varied over the years. As Apple's philosophy regarding user upgrades of Mac systems has changed (the company now thinks it's an okay, if not a great, idea for consumers to upgrade their Macs), so has the ease-of-entry for cases. With some exceptions, corporate and professionally aimed Macs have been pretty easy to open and upgrade — especially the bread-and-butter Mac II, Quadra, and Power Macintosh series computers. Original Macs can be very tough, LCs vary somewhat, and Performas can range from simple to downright scary, depending on the configuration.

Mac OS clone machines tend to vary less, although they also don't usually use very creative cases. Borrowing from the lower-cost case designs in the Intel-compatible world, clone vendors such as Power Computing, Motorola, and UMAX have generally opted for simple case designs, in either desktop or tower configurations, that are taken apart by removing a few screws and lifting the case off the computer's chassis. With these cases, your best bet is to consult the manual that came with your Mac OS clone computer to learn exactly how you open it. Once opened, it'll look a lot like some Apple Macintosh models.

Opening any computer's case

Before looking at the specifics, it's important to first discuss some universal rules for opening any computer's case. In general, these rules are designed to keep both the computer systems and the humans involved out of harm's way.

Whenever you prepare to open your Mac's case, follow these guidelines:

✦ Create a good workspace with room on a flat tabletop. Mac cases and equipment can be sharp-edged, so protect the table from damage. Don't use conductive materials like fabric, plastic, or metal under the systems — nonconductive rubber mats or wood surfaces are best.

✦ Keep food and drink away from open Mac systems, and try to avoid the possibility of spills on or in your Mac.

✦ Electrically ground yourself when upgrading any computer components. A wrist or ankle grounding strap is the best alternative.

✦ Avoid static electricity at all costs — it can kill computer components. Try not to upgrade in a carpeted room. When upgrading, touch a shielded computer power supply (or other metal surface) to discharge static often, and don't wear clothing that promotes static electricity.

✦ When handling computer components, avoid touching the metal contacts or other parts of a circuit board. Handle boards and drives by their edges and corners as much as possible.

✦ Use the right tools. Make sure you do your best not to strip the screws used to hold your Mac together. Use hand tools to tighten and loosen screws on your Mac's case. Don't use power tools, so as to avoid stripping and overtightening. You should also avoid magnetized tools for working inside a computer.

✦ Handle circuit boards with care. Avoid dragging objects across the surface of the logic board or other circuit boards.

✦ Hang onto screws, wires, and connectors. Keep containers on hand for holding small parts so they don't get lost.

✦ Label everything. If you remove or unplug any components, be ready with labels and/or masking tape and a pen to label wires or connectors. Also, when possible, label the direction in which a connector should be reattached.

Open your Apple Macintosh case

Apple cases have gone through many, many iterations, and all the various nuances can't quite be covered here. I will try to hit the most popular models, including some of the original Macs that were never specifically designed for upgrading.

If you have your original manuals, they may be of some help. You'll find that some Mac models make it difficult for you to get to the RAM sockets or cache RAM slots for upgrading, even once you have the case off. (The Power Macintosh 8100 is a wonderful example of a very tough upgrade, requiring you to pull all the cables connecting the logic board to the rest of the Mac to do something simple, like upgrading RAM.)

Note   Instructions for upgrading an iMac model Macintosh were not available at the time of writing, although early indications are that these Macs can be upgraded using methods similar to those for upgrading other Mac all-in-one designs, due to a slide-out logic board on the back of the machine. Check your iMac's documentation for details.

Can I use my Mac while the case is off?

You can definitely start up and test your Mac with the case off, as long as you take care to avoid touching any internal components while power is streaming through the system. Shut down your Mac and take proper precautions before touching or installing anything internally.

That said, you definitely should not run your Mac with the case off all the time. Apple or the clone manufacturer designed that case with the flow of air over components in mind. That's why the power supply has a fan and the Mac case has a little opening with grilles. Leaving the case off disrupts the flow of air and—regardless of the room's temperature—can actually cause the Mac to overheat.

Your Mac is designed to run with the case on, so put it back on and leave it properly installed once your upgrading session is finished.

Mac Classic form factor

These are the original all-in-one Macs, including the Mac SE, Mac SE/30, Mac Classic, Mac Classic II, and the Performa 400. These models require a T-15 Torx screwdriver to open them. It's recommended that you wear a grounding strap when working with these Macs.

Caution

The CRT connections inside a pre–Mac SE model (Mac Plus, Mac 512k, Mac 128k) can be very dangerous. I don't recommend upgrading these machines on your own — instead, have a qualified technician look at them for you. In the case of a Mac SE or newer, you should wait 30 seconds after powering down the Mac before attempting the open the case, which gives the Mac enough time to discharge electricity that's built up in the CRT. Even this is sometimes not enough, though. Professionals dissipate this charge with a grounding tool, as shown in Figure 5-4. Without this, the Mac could potentially hold a charge for months that could hurt or (possibly) kill you. Again, I don't recommend upgrading these machines yourself. If you do, either properly discharge the CRT or avoid touching it at all costs.

Figure 5-4: You should always wait at least 30 seconds after powering down a Mac before attempting to open the case. Professionals dissipate the charge with a grounding tool.

Here's how to open a Classic form-factor Mac:

1. Place the Mac screen-down on your workbench.

2. Loosen the Torx screws on the back of the Mac (you'll find two of them up under the Mac's handle).

3. Remove the plastic reset switch (on the right side) of the Mac. It lifts straight out of the air vents (you may need to pry it up a bit).

4. Using a case spreader (there's a special Mac "cracker" tool you may be able to get from Mac shops) or a flat wall scraper/putty knife, gently pry the front plastic away from the back of the case, as shown in Figure 5-5.

Figure 5-5: Carefully pull the front plastic from the rest of the case to avoid scratches and cracks.

5. Remove the foil base from the Mac (depending on the model).

You now have the logic board exposed. To install more RAM or otherwise upgrade, follow instructions in later chapters specific to your desired upgrade.

Color Classic, Color Classic II

The Color Classic offers more expandability than the original Classic series, enabling you to easily pop open the back and pull out the logic board for adding RAM or an expansion card.

To open the Color Classic, follow these steps:

1. Unplug any wires attached to ports on the back panel.

2. Remove the two retaining screws on either side of the back panel.

3. Push down and pull on the tabs (see Figure 5-6).

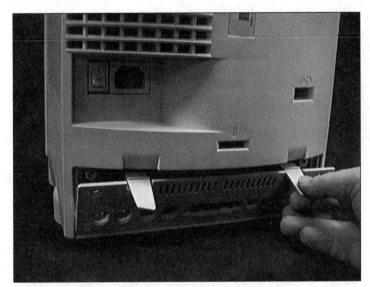

Figure 5-6: The Color Classic's rear panel swings off for easy access to the logic board.

4. The rear panel should pop open, giving you access to a small handle for the logic board. Pull that handle straight outward to upgrade components (like RAM) located on the logic board.

Mac II, IIx, IIfx

The larger form factor Mac II series boasts 6 NuBus slots for expansion, so the case needs to be fairly easy to get into—and it is.

To open one of these Mac II series machines, follow these steps:

1. Remove the retaining screw, which holds the top of the case and the rear panel together.

2. Press in on the tabs located on their side of the rear panel, near the top of the case.

3. While pressing, lift up on the top of the case, as shown in Figure 5-7. It should lift completely off.

Figure 5-7: The top of the Mac II chassis lifts completely off, affording plenty of room for expansion.

Mac IIcx, IIci, Quadra 700

The slightly more compact IIcx, IIci, and Quadra 700 are also fairly easy to get into for upgrading purposes. Although these cases are designed to include a retaining screw, the case will stay together without it, so you may find yours no longer has one.

Here's how to get it open:

1. Remove the retaining screw (if there is one). It's located in the center of the rear panel, near the top of the case.

2. Pull up simultaneously on the two tabs on either side of the retaining screw (see Figure 5-8).

3. Lift the top of the case up and off of the rest of the chassis.

Mac IIsi

A machine all to its own, the Mac IIsi is also a bit tougher to get into than some of its II series siblings. The thought is the same, but the case itself takes a bit more brawn.

To open the Mac IIsi, follow these steps:

1. Remove the retaining screw (if there is one). The screw is near the top of the rear panel, just to the left of the air-vent grille.

2. Snap up each of the tabs holding the top of the case to the rear panel. To do this most effectively, place your thumb on the small plastic ledge near the tab, and then use your forefinger to lift the tab with a slight twisting motion (see Figure 5-9).

Figure 5-8: This more compact Mac II (and early Quadra) is also designed for easy upgrading.

Figure 5-9: Releasing one of the tabs on the Mac IIsi (You can use both hands to release both tabs at the same time.)

LC, LC II, LC III, Quadra 605, Performa 400 series

These low-slung, pizza-box-style Macs still manage to offer a few reasons to get inside of them. Doing so is similar to the Mac II series, but you'll need to put a little elbow grease into it:

1. Remove the retaining screw in the top center of the rear panel of the case.

2. Snap the tabs on the case top up from the rear panel. Note that this is easiest to do if you place your arm on top of the case and pull back to release the tabs (as shown in Figure 5-10).

Figure 5-10: Getting into an LC's case is a little like popping the top on a can of soda.

Mac IIvx, IIvi, Centris 650, Quadra 650, Performa 600, Power Macintosh 7100, Workgroup Server(WGS) 70, WGS 7150

One of the more popular cases with Apple's manufacturing folks (and one of the more enduring case designs), this form factor is also somewhat unpopular with upgrading experts. I've been told by Mac upgrading experts that this case is the worst of them all.

Actually, the case itself is quite easy to open. The problem is the case doesn't often give you much access to the logic board in these Macs, which is often obscured by the hard drive and CD-ROM drive, if one is installed. That means you have to remove them to get to the logic board. For more on the exciting upgrading tasks that await the owner of one of these machines, consult your user's guide.

To open the case, follow these steps:

1. Remove the large retaining screw located in the top center of the Mac's back panel.

2. Slide the case slightly forward, as shown in Figure 5-11.

Figure 5-11: Unlike earlier Macs, this case needs to be slid forward a bit before it's lifted off the chassis.

3. Now, lift the case directly up and off the Mac's chassis.

Centris 610/660AV, Quadra 610/660AV, Power Macintosh 6100, Performa 6110 series, WGS 60

The other Mac pizza boxes (Mac folks in general can't seem to decide which series more rightly deserves the name, although this second series corresponds more to the shape of the large, deep-dish pizza favored by tech types) offer fairly easy access. And, once you get the case off, the upgrade slots and sockets could be more convenient in these machines.

To open these Macs, follow these steps:

1. Release the tabs that hold the case's top to the back panel of the Mac. You may find it easier to release these tabs by placing your arm on the lid while you pull up on the tabs (see Figure 5-12).

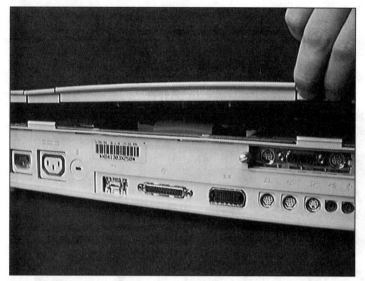

Figure 5-12: These tabs can take a little muscle to release the first few times.

2. Lift the case's top slightly, and then slide the case forward a bit to move it away from the undercarriage of the case and allow it to clear the front panel of the Mac's chassis.

3. Grab the top of the case from both the back and the front and lift it completely off the Mac's chassis.

Quadra/Centris 630, Performa 630, 6200, 6300 series

This was also a popular form factor, especially for Performa series Macs that could be upgraded with a TV tuner card. The case itself is designed for easy upgrading (Performa-style), enabling you to pull the logic board out of the machine without removing the entire case.

To pull the logic board for upgrading:

1. Locate the two tabs on the back panel of the Mac and push them down until they release from the case.

2. Pull the tabs until the small panel covering the Mac's ports comes apart from the rest of the back panel (see Figure 5-13).

3. Remove the retaining screws that hold the logic board in place. (There are generally two, located at the top left and right corners of the metallic surface.)

4. Grab the small metal handle (you may have to press down on it a bit to unlock it from its casing) and pull straight out of the machine. The logic board should slide out easily, as shown in Figure 5-14.

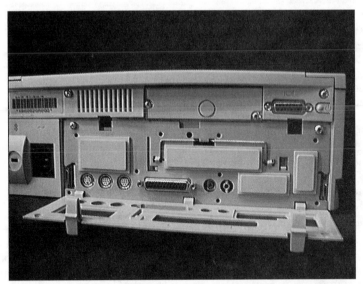

Figure 5-13: This small panel swings away, enabling you to get at the logic board.

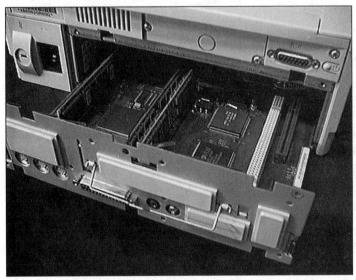

Figure 5-14: Slide-out logic boards on this and similar Mac designs makes it really simple to add RAM and other board-level components.

Of course, this process only really helps you get to the logic board of your Mac. What if you want to get at the internal hard drive or other components? First, be warned—this isn't nearly as easy, and you need to be careful to avoid bending or breaking the plastic housing on your Mac.

Note   If you do break the housing on your Mac, run down to your local Mac repair shop and ask them if you can buy another housing. You don't want to run your Mac for long without it because it can affect airflow, resulting in an overheated Mac and/or components.

Here's what you do:

1. Locate the two tabs under the front panel of the Mac. They should look something like those shown in Figure 5-15.

2. Using a screwdriver, gently lift one of the tabs up into the front panel while pulling the panel away from the Mac's chassis slightly. (This is a delicate operation, but once it works the front panel should move toward you a half-inch or so.)

Figure 5-15: Use the screwdriver to press up on the tab slightly so it can release from the Mac's chassis.

3. Do the same with the other tab. Once both are released, the front panel should come easily away from the Mac's chassis, exposing the internal drives.

Who needs access to a Performa's internal drive, anyway?

I was close to a deadline on an important project a while back when the power supply on our Performa 6215 went down for the count. Unable to get it up and running without a service call, I was helpless to recover the data on that Performa's hard drive. Unless . . .

I rolled into a major computer chain store, got lucky with a floor model, and walked out only a few pounds lighter in the wallet, but with a brand new (at the time) Performa 6400 minitower. Because both machines use internal IDE drives, we swapped the drives in the two Performas and booted the 6400 using the 6215's drive. The work was done on time, the Performa 6215 was fixed, and both machines are now used daily — although their hard drive transplant has never been reversed.

By the way, I speak from experience about breaking this front panel. I broke the panel on the Performa 6215 while performing this drive swap. Fortunately, the machine had to be serviced anyway and the local shop gave me a new front panel for a nominal fee.

Quadra 800, Quadra 840AV, WGS 80, Power Macintosh 8100, WGS 8150

The first real tower case (with apologies to the Quadra 700) from Apple is somewhat less upgrade-friendly than you might imagine, with thumbscrews replacing the quick-release tabs that other Mac models tend to sport. Still, it's certainly not that tough:

1. Unscrew the four thumbscrews on the back panel of the Mac.

2. Slide the case forward a few inches to pull it away from the screws in back and from the drive opening in front.

3. Tilt the back of the case's lid up a bit, and then lift the case's lid completely off the Mac's chassis, as shown in Figure 5-16.

Quadra 900/950, WGS 90, Power Macintosh 9500, WGS 9150

On these huge server-oriented Macs, the entire side panel will come off for your upgrading pleasure. Most feel these are pretty nice enclosures to work in — not as easy as the newer minitowers, but not as small either. These six-slot machines can take a lot of upgrading for server duties, digital video, and other important tasks.

Figure 5-16: Thumbscrews aren't common to most Mac models, but they don't make it too tough to get into the Apple's first real minitower enclosure.

To open one of them, follow these steps:

1. Remove the retaining screw, if you can find one (the slot for it is to the left of the large cooling grille on the back panel, but there's rarely an actual screw there).

2. Push in the small tabs at the top and bottom of the side panel where it meets the back panel.

3. Slide the side panel away from the back panel (as shown in Figure 5-17), and then remove it completely.

Performa 6400, Power Macintosh 6500

These Macs, in the Performa tradition, feature pull-out logic boards that make it fairly simple to add RAM and upgrade cards. But what about hard drives and the like? To work with those, you'll need to remove the front facing.

To pull the logic board, follow these steps:

1. Remove the retaining screws found next to the two tabs on the back panel of the Mac.

2. Grasp the tabs and pull directly back away from the Mac (see Figure 5-18).

Figure 5-17: Although the case was left upright for this image, feel free to put your Mac on its side for easier upgrading.

Figure 5-18: The logic board on these Macs is simple to access.

To remove the front panel on these Macs, follow these steps:

1. Grab the front panel from below and feel for the two buttons up underneath the panel.

2. Push those buttons in as far as possible while simultaneously pulling the panel away from the bottom of the case (see Figure 5-19).

3. Once it's free of the buttons on the bottom, remove the panel completely.

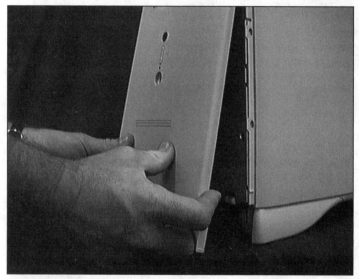

Figure 5-19: Don't be shocked if this makes a little noise — it's tough to do the first few times.

Note

You'll find that it's easy to upgrade the logic board on many of the relatively simple-to-upgrade Performa and all-in-one models, but a real bear to upgrade internal drives and such. If you're intimidated by the process, feel free to simply pass on opening the case and install external SCSI hard drives instead. If you do mess up the plastic on your Mac, though, don't worry about it too much. A local Mac service center should be able to sell you the front panel for popular models at a reasonable price.

LC and Performa 520, 550, 575, 580, MacTV

In the spirit of the original Mac, these 68040-based (MacTV has a 68030) all-in-one units were popular choices for schools and homes that wanted machines that were easy to work with and somewhat less cumbersome than typical units. They also turned out to be machines that are a bit less upgradeable than others, although access to the logic board is generally simple.

To access the logic board in an all-in-one Mac, follow these steps:

1. Remove the retaining screws that hold the back plate to the back panel of the Mac. (Remove any cables that are plugged into the ports on the back of the Mac, too.)

2. Press down on the tabs at the top of the back plate and pull, as shown in Figure 5-20.

Figure 5-20: The all-in-one Macs offer quick access to the logic board.

3. Grab the exposed metal handle and pull straight back to reveal the logic board.

Performa and Power Macintosh 5200/5300 series

These PowerPC versions of the all-in-one Macintosh are a little larger, a bit more capable, and usually feature larger screens than their predecessors. They're only about as expandable, however, offering similar logic-board access.

Here's how to get at the logic board:

1. Remove the two retaining screws on the back plate that hold it to the Mac's back panel.

2. Reach under the back plate, locate the tabs, and press down to release them.

3. Lift the plate up and off the back panel, as shown in Figure 5-21.

4. Grab the exposed metal handle and pull straight back to reveal the logic board.

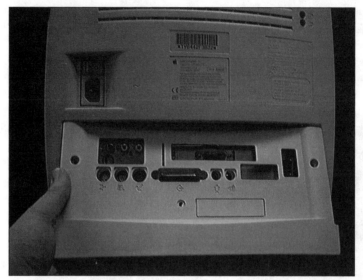

Figure 5-21: Unlike most all-in-one models, the back plate for this series is latched at the bottom.

Power Macintosh 7200, 7300, 7500, 7600, G3 Desktop, WGS 7250/7350

Another popular case design, these Macs aren't the most pleasant to get into, but they're very much easier to work inside of than are the similar cases they replace — the long-lived IIvx to Power Mac 7100 desktop case. This one releases without screws, but watch out for the metal retaining braces that like to jump off the drives in the front of the case.

To open this case, follow these steps:

1. Reach up under the front panel and locate the tabs.

2. Push the tabs up while simultaneously sliding the case toward you, as shown in Figure 5-22.

3. Slide the case completely off the machine (if desired) to gain access to the internal drives and logic board.

It's interesting to note that you can actually flip this case completely open by swinging the drive cage up and away from the logic board (see Figure 5-23). The instructions that follow show how to open it up.

Figure 5-22: Pull slowly on the case to get it to slide smoothly away from the front-mounted internal drives.

Figure 5-23: One of Apple's more interesting cases, the 7300 (and similar) series enables easy access to the logic board.

1. Unplug the Mac—it can't be swung open if it's plugged in.

2. Releasing the foot that helps the drive cage to stand. The foot looks like a small, square box that might be designed for holding screws or thumbtacks or something. Swing it around so that it's settled outside of the case. Once you swing up the drive cage, the foot will rest on the table surface, enabling you to leave the logic board exposed without being forced to hold the drive cage up.

3. Find the releases on the other side of the drive cage. These are green, plastic tabs that, when pushed down, release the drive cage from its lockdowns in the sides of the case.

4. Grab the cage's handle and swing it away from the logic board.

Power Macintosh 8600, 9600, and G3 Minitower

This minitower case is as innovative as the Power Macintosh 7300 series case; it also allows you to swing components out of the way to get at the logic board. If there's any competition at all for the top spot, this minitower case wins out by a hair for its simplicity.

Here's how to open this case:

1. Place the case on its side. The side housing the large green button should be on top. Unplug the Mac.

2. Press the green button down into the case while pulling that side of the Mac away from the rest of the case.

3. Pull the side completely off the case by carefully opening it completely until it comes free.

4. To expose the logic board, release the two tabs that anchor the drive cage to the rest of the case.

5. Swing the drive cage up and away from the logic board. (Figure 5-24 shows how to swing these drive cages out of their cases.)

The Innards Revealed

Once you have your Mac opened up and exposed to the world, you'll probably want to take a look around and familiarize yourself with things. Not everything in here is replaceable or repairable, but a lot of it is. And if your primary motivation is upgrading, you'll definitely want to explore some parts of the Mac.

Figure 5-24: One of Apple's most innovative cases, the 8600 is easy to get apart.

For some, the innards of a computer may seem like a strange world, but it's really rather tame. You have components that need to be connected to the Mac (so it can manage them), you have expansion cards that need to be connected to the logic board, and you have wiring that does the connecting. Taken separately, they all make a lot of sense.

Components

To begin, let's look at the different components you may encounter when upgrading a Mac. The Power Mac 6100 isn't representative of all Macs, but it's a great place to get started, because it's very open and easy to view. Take a look at Figure 5-25, which shows the Power Mac 6100 with its case off.

For the most part, these are the components you'll be working with when upgrading: the hard drive, floppy drive, CD-ROM drive, RAM sockets, cache RAM sockets, the PRAM battery, and upgrade slots. You'll also want to know where the power supply, SCSI controller, and CPU are, because you may have reason to use them in conjunction with other upgrades to accomplish your goals.

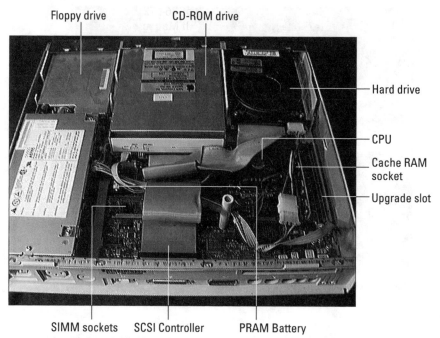

Figure 5-25: Some of the elements you'll typically find when you open a Mac's case.

Here's a quick rundown on identifying each:

✦ **Power supply.** The power supply is always a metallic box set into the case of the Mac you're working with. It should have power connectors for a three-prong power cable coming out the back of the Mac, with smaller power connectors (usually four colored wires and a connector) coming into the case for connecting to internal components.

✦ **Hard drive.** An enclosed metal box with no openings, connected to the Mac by a power connector and a SCSI (or IDE) ribbon cable.

✦ **CD-ROM drive.** Similar to the hard drive, but has an opening on the front (exposed through the front of the Mac's case) for the CD tray or caddy.

✦ **Floppy drive.** Similar to a hard drive and a CD-ROM drive, but with an opening for a 3.5-inch floppy disk in the front.

✦ **SCSI controller.** Usually on either the motherboard or an expansion card, the SCSI controller offers a 50-pin connector for attaching a ribbon cable that then is used to connect SCSI internal drives.

Note

Some Macintosh systems (including many Performa models, the Power Macintosh 4400, 6500, and many Power Macintosh G3 systems) offer IDE hard drives instead of SCSI. Most of these Macs still offer external SCSI connections, and those that include free internal expansion bays often offer an internal SCSI connection as well.

✦ **Memory sockets.** Memory sockets accept 36-, 72-, or 128-pin modules, depending on your Mac model. Almost all Mac models offer at least two of these sockets, generally located right next to one another.

✦ **Cache RAM.** Level 2 cache RAM is usually added to a Mac using either a special memory module or an expansion card (especially on older models). This generally adds 256K to 2MB of high-speed RAM that can be used as a repository for frequently needed information, enabling the processor to avoid waiting to retrieve this data from the hard drive.

✦ **Upgrade slot.** Most Macs have at least one upgrade slot, whereas others offer more than one. These allow cards in standard sizes, usually between 6 and 12 inches long, to be installed in the Mac, adding functionality. The cards must be of the same type as the available slot — PDS cards fit in PDS slots, NuBus cards fit in NuBus slots, and PCI cards fit in PCI slots. (Some Macs offer other specialized slots.) Upgrade slots are generally found directly on the motherboard and usually offer access to the back side of the Mac (see Figure 5-26).

Figure 5-26: Upgrade slots in a Performa 6200 series Mac include a special communications slot and room for a Performa-specific video input card.

✦ **CPU.** The CPU is a fairly sizable chip on the motherboard or an attached daughtercard. In newer Mac models, it's usually obscured by a heat sink, a special device that dissipates heat quickly while the computer is running. The CPU should be labeled clearly as either a 680x0-level processor or as a particular PowerPC processor.

✦ **PRAM battery.** This small lithium-ion battery sometimes looks like a battery for a wristwatch or camera, and other times looks like a slightly warped C battery. This battery offers a continuous trickle of power to your Mac's Parameter RAM (PRAM), where boot-up settings such as the system date, AppleTalk preferences, and screen resolution are all stored. If this battery fails, you'll experience interesting symptoms, most of which are outlined in Chapter 22.

Wiring and cables

In most Macs, you'll find three different types of wire. The power wires run between the Mac's power supply and any internal components that require power. The second type of wires are ribbon cables, which are used to connect components — like hard, floppy and CD-ROM drives — to the logic board or an input/output expansion card. The third internal wire is a thin, low gauge wire used to connect the logic board to indicator lights and switches that are wired into the case. These wires can also be used for things like connecting the Mac's sound capabilities to a CD-ROM drive. Figure 5-27 shows these different wires and cables.

Externally, you'll probably find yourself dealing with a few different styles of cables. These cables are usually used to connect external components to your Mac — components like removable storage drives, modems and network connections. Figure 5-28 is a quick identification guide to some of the cabling you'll come across.

✦ **SCSI cable.** Used to connect external storage devices (and some others, like scanners) to your Mac. Usually has a 25-pin connection to the Mac and 25 or 50-pin connection to peripherals.

✦ **Modem/serial cable.** Standard Mac cables have small, round DIN-8 connectors for connecting to the Mac and to peripherals.

✦ **Ethernet.** Ethernet cabling actually comes in two different types: 10Base2 (coax) cable, which resembles the cabling used for cable TV hookups, and 10BaseT (twisted-pair) cable, which looks a little like telephone wire. 10BaseT cabling uses a different connector than telephone wire, and the cable itself is slightly thicker.

✦ **Audio.** Most Mac audio patch cables (between speakers and the Mac or the Mac and a receiver) use ⅛-inch stereo RCA connectors. Macs require specially built line-level microphones, some of which are sold under the Apple brand.

✦ **ADB.** ADB cables are used to connect a variety of input/output devices — keyboards, trackballs, mice — to the Mac. The ADB is also a source of power for some other devices, like modems and telephony managers.

✦ **Mac video.** This cable ends in a 15-pin connector, which can be used to hook an Apple monitor to a Macintosh computer. Many non-Apple monitors require a VGA adapter, which allows the monitor to sync with the Apple built-in video. Some video cards include both Mac video and VGA ports on the card.

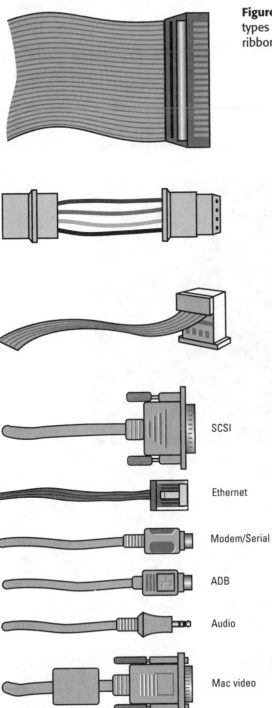

Figure 5-27: The three different types of internal wiring: (from the top) ribbon cable, power cable, device wiring

SCSI

Figure 5-28: Cables used to connect components to the back of your Mac for external upgrades

Ethernet

Modem/Serial

ADB

Audio

Mac video

Expansion cards

Chapter 4 discusses the different technologies that a Mac might use for its expansion card capabilities. Once you get your Mac open, you may want to see for yourself what expansion cards look like and how you go about installing them.

What expansion cards look like

In Figure 5-25 you can see the PDS slot for the Power Macintosh 6100. Figure 5-29 shows the PCI slots available in a Power Macintosh 7300.

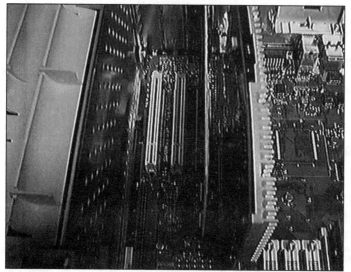

Figure 5-29: PCI slots are actual slots instead of socket-style connectors, which are used in NuBus.

Some basic differences include:

✦ **NuBus.** Connectors are usually gray in appearance and are actually sockets that accept pins from the card. The card's connector housing fits over the connector on the logic board. The number of NuBus slots varies between one and six, depending on the Mac model.

✦ **PDS.** Connectors are usually black in appearance and are actual slots, accepting a flat circuit-board connector that slips into the slot from the card. All Macs with PDS slots have only one PDS slot.

✦ **PCI.** Similar to PDS slots in appearance, but usually white in color. Most PCI-based Macs have either three or six slots, although some Mac models have one specialized PCI slot that can only accept certain types of upgrade cards (such as the PCI communications slot on Performa 6200/6300 models).

Installing expansion cards

Installing an expansion card is usually a straightforward process, and it tends to work the same for any sort of board. Give yourself a little time for adding an expansion board — at least 10 or 15 minutes to get the case off and the card installed for testing. Also, keep track of your screws — there's a chance you'll be dealing with at least a few when you install a new card.

Here's how it all works:

1. Shut down your Mac and electrically ground yourself.

2. Open the Mac's case and locate an empty expansion slot. (Visually inspect it to ensure it's the right type of slot for your card.)

3. Remove the screw and metal dust plate that covers the hole in back of the case for the slot you'll be using.

4. Position the card so that the card's interface is directly over the slot. If it's a NuBus card, make sure the card's housing fits over the NuBus slot on the logic board. If it's a PDS or a PCI card, make sure the card's connector fits snugly in the slot.

5. Press down lightly and uniformly on the top corners of the expansion card until it's firmly installed in the slot.

 Be sure that the card is fully installed in the slot. If one end is higher than the other, parts of the connector may not be making proper contact, and the card will fail to work.

6. Try restarting your Mac while the case is still off and see if the card is recognized. If all goes well, the card should be installed and working with no trouble. (You can use the Apple System Profiler to check.) Shut down the computer and reinstall the case.

 An Internet link to download the Apple System Profiler is available on the included CD-ROM and is usually installed with Mac OS 7.6 or higher — check your Apple menu or the Apple Extras folder on your main hard drive.

Serial ports

Your Mac likely has two serial ports — a printer port and a modem port. In some ways, these ports are the same. They can both accept any sort of serial device and they can both (on AV Macintosh and Power Macintosh models) accept GeoPort devices. There is one difference — the printer port is also designed to be a LocalTalk connection for printer and network connections. The modem port isn't.

Generally, connecting devices to these ports is simple; you power down your Mac, align the serial connector so that the arrow (or other logo) is pointing toward the top of the port, and then insert the connector. If it doesn't go in easily, you probably have it slightly misaligned. (If you have a non-Apple Macintosh, you may also find that the manufacturer had an interesting definition for the word *top* when it comes to finding the top of the port. Try rotating the connector 90 degrees or more.)

From there, whatever is connected to the port is managed by its software drivers, usually in the form of a control panel. You may be asked to tell the control panel which port the device is connected to — printer or modem. In almost every case, expanding via a serial port is simple. (See the chapter on the particular device in question for more help.)

There's only one problem that you'll often encounter with working serial ports that come right out of the box with your Mac — there's only two of them, the modem port and the printer port. (And that's on desktop models — many PowerBooks have *one*.) Sometimes, you'll need more than two of them.

A lot of peripherals can require the use of a serial port, including modems, printers, some scanners, some small printers, digital cameras, PDA docking devices (for a PalmPilot or Newton, for instance), or, of course, a LocalTalk network. If you have more than two of these peripherals — or any others than I didn't mention — you'll need some way to switch between them.

Here's what to do when you need a free serial port:

✦ *Shuffle.* One way to get around this problem is to change the way you're hooking things up. For instance, if you have a laser printer that *could* be connected via Ethernet, you could disconnect it from the printer port, connect it via an Ethernet connection, and then use the printer port for something else.

✦ *Get a switch box.* Manual switch boxes for serial ports are reasonably inexpensive and generally available in good computer stores (remember to get the Mac's Din-8 serial port variety). These boxes feature a manual A-B switch that enables you to pick between two different serial peripherals at any one time. There are a few caveats — some printers (many Hewlett-Packard models come to mind) don't like to be on a switch box, and you may have poor connections to some other peripherals, such as digital cameras and PDA docking devices. Overall they work pretty well though, as long as you remember to load *only* the correct driver (don't tell two control panels that they can both have the serial port at the same time) and, of course, you need to remember to switch to the device you want to use.

✦ *Try powered switching.* If the switch box doesn't work for you, try a powered switching device instead. These boxes sense which device you're trying to use (using their own control panels), and then route the data to that device. The PortDoubler series from Momentum, Inc. (www.momentuminc.net/) and the Port Xpander offerings from MacAlly (www.macally.com/) both boast these capabilities as well as being compatible with more devices than typical switch boxes.

✦ *Add more ports.* Ready for the big guns? You can actually add more serial ports using an expansion card, such as the PCI offerings from Keyspan (www.keyspan.com/), which also plans to sell a USB card that will be available to Macs that don't yet have USB ports.

Summary

✦ Before you can upgrade or troubleshoot your Mac, it's a good idea to know what model you have. This knowledge will go a long way to help you out not only in your Mac repair shop or parts store, but also with this book. Most chapters feature a chart that helps you run through the system specifications for upgrading your particular Mac model.

✦ Almost every Mac has a slightly different procedure for opening the case, and certain rules apply both to specific Mac models and to opening any computer.

✦ You need to have certain tools on hand before upgrading. You should also carefully consider your surroundings and make sure you're ready to put forth the time, energy, and organization required to upgrade successfully.

✦ Finally, you should know some universals about upgrading Macs, including the wires you're going to find inside the system, what cabling to use on the outside, and how to identify the different types of upgrade cards. Now, at long last, you're ready to upgrade.

✦   ✦   ✦

Performing the Upgrade

P A R T

✦   ✦   ✦   ✦

In This Part

Chapter 6
Processor and Memory

Chapter 7
Hard Drives

Chapter 8
CD-ROMs, Recordable
CDs, and DVD

Chapter 9
Removable Drives and
Backup

Chapter 10
Input Devices

Chapter 11
Scanners and Digital
Cameras

Chapter 12
Monitors and Monitor
Cards

Chapter 13
Digital Video

Chapter 14
Sound, Speech,
and MIDI

Chapter 15
Printers and Print
Sharing

Chapter 16
Modems and Internet
Access

Chapter 17
Networking

Chapter 18
Multimedia and Gaming

Chapter 19
Dealing with DOS and
Windows PCs

Chapter 20
PowerBooks

✦   ✦   ✦   ✦

Part II includes individual chapters that each discuss different types of upgrades — what's possible, what's necessary, and how to perform them. Each chapter discusses a particular upgrading goal or subsystem of the Macintosh — printing, sound, networking, storage — along with the related technologies and different possible upgrades. These chapters tell you what a technology is, how it works, and even give a little help when it comes to deciding which upgrade technology is best for you. You'll also learn about related software topics — things such as implementing a backup system, getting on the Internet, and creating a local area network.

Processor and Memory

If you're upgrading to change the speed of your Mac, this chapter is certainly one of the places to start. The Mac's logic board and processor are responsible for most of the technology that your Mac uses to "think," or process data. The logic board includes the *system bus* (the path for data to travel around the logic board) and the *expansion bus*, which determines what sort of expansion cards you'll be able to use: PDS, NuBus, or PCI. The logic board also houses the processor or processor daughtercard, and is responsible for making sure the processor and the rest of the Mac communicate well with one other.

The speed of the processing subsystem in a Macintosh is based on the coming together of a number of different variables, including the system bus speed, the processor, the amount of RAM in the system and the amount of cache RAM that's installed. With these four factors covered, you can considerably speed up the performance of a given Mac.

Of course, that also depends on an important condition — exactly how upgradeable your particular Mac model is. Some models are capable of amazing leaps in technology, whereas others are rather limited in what they can do. In most cases, Macs can accept more RAM, even if they require the replacement of existing RAM modules to do it. However, the various Mac models differ in their capacity to accept new processors and cache RAM.

This chapter discusses all the processing subsystem upgrades you can perform on a Macintosh. Read on to find out what all your particular Mac model is capable of doing and how you can go about boosting your Mac's processing speed.

The Processor and Logic Board

The processor and logic board in a particular Macintosh model were designed very specifically to go together. The logic board is the heart of the Mac, responsible for dealing with everything else that makes up the computer, including the storage subsystem, video, expansion cards, RAM, cache RAM—even the battery for Parameter RAM (PRAM) settings.

Note   *Parameter RAM* is a small section of memory reserved for permanent settings on the Macintosh, most of which are governed by your control panels. These settings have to be maintained when the Mac is shut down, so a small battery is used to constantly power the RAM that the settings inhabit.

All these components need to work together with the processor to make the computer's processing tasks run smoothly. This, too, is managed by the logic board.

In fact, the logic board and processor are so intertwined that the two must have a speed-based relationship for them to work together. The processor's speed is measured in megahertz, as first mentioned in Chapter 2. For the processor and the logic board to work together, the speed of the logic board's system bus (which gets data to and from the processor) needs to be in line with the speed of the processor: Either the speeds must be identical or the processor speed needs to be an exact multiple of the speed of the logic board. This is one way computer companies decide what the exact speeds of their processors are going to be.

The speed game

Consider that a processor can be the same speed as the logic board's system bus. In pre–Power Macintosh computers, this was almost always the case. A 25MHz 68030, like the Mac IIci, has a 25MHz system bus.

In later systems, though, it became popular for processors to be *clock-multiplied,* meaning they actual run internally at a clock speed that is an exact multiple of the system bus speed. The first time this really became common was with the 68040 chips in the Quadra and LC series, in which the processors were clock-doubled. In many cases, that meant they featured a 66MHz processor running on a 33MHz system bus. In fact, even the Quadra 800 and 650 models, which were advertised as 33MHz systems, were actually clock-doubled so that the internal processor ran at 66MHz.

Note   It's interesting to note that Apple was originally shy about advertising the internal speed of its processors, even though its competition in the Intel-compatible PC world was already making a science of it with the 486DX2-66–style naming conventions. (DX2 suggested a clock-doubled processor.)

With the advent of the Power Macintosh models, Apple started focusing less on marketing the bus speed of Macs and more on pushing the processor speeds, especially as it became common for the processor speeds to reach multiples beyond double-speed. The 66MHz PowerPC 601 in the Power Macintosh 6100 was still a clock-doubled processor (the system bus ran at 33MHz), but the next generation of Power Macs started going beyond double — such as the Power Macintosh 7200/120, which featured a 40MHz bus, meaning the processor was clock-tripled. The 300MHz PowerPC 750 processor, available in some Power Macintosh G3 configurations, is actually cheating just slightly; it's based on a 66MHz bus and 4.5 as a multiplier. Do the math and you get to about 297MHz.

Actually, the 66MHz bus is about 66.6MHz, resulting in a 4.5 multiplier that brings the Power Macintosh G3 to 299.7MHz. And if you're not willing to give them that one, multiply it by a 66.66MHz bus. Now it's 299.97. Fair enough?

The point is two-fold. First, it's important to realize that processor speed and system bus speed are this closely related — especially when you get into upgrading those Mac models that have upgradeable processors. In many cases, the cards enable you to choose speeds for the processor and system bus that will affect both performance and stability. When you're picking numbers for the system bus, you may pick something slightly higher than the original rating, which could result in crashes. Scale that back a bit and you may actually hit a range that will enable you to use a multiplier that gives you a higher processor speed, even at a lower bus speed.

For instance, a 66MHz bus setting might work at 231MHz, but a 60MHz bus setting might allow you to boost the processor to 240MHz. It may not speed things up much, but people do this sort of thing anyway for the bragging rights.

Upgradeable processors

This and the previous discussion assume you're in a position to choose processor and system bus speeds because you have a Macintosh capable of accepting the upgrade. This is certainly not true in many cases, although a surprising number of Mac models truly are upgradeable. Exactly *how* upgradeable is another issue.

Some general things can be said about processor upgrading. First of all, it's rare that you can jump more than one major revision in the technology. For instance, a lot of Mac II series machines can be upgraded using a PDS card that increases the processor to the 68040 level, making it capable of running at 50- or 66MHz, depending on the bus speed of the original Mac II series machine. But a Mac II series machine — except in isolated incidents — can't be upgraded to a PowerPC-based Mac.

Many 68040 machines can be upgraded to Power Macs. Likewise, PowerPC 601-based machines can be upgraded to PowerPC 604e machines (which is actually a direct generational leap, because the PowerPC 603e is not the logical successor of the 601), and PowerPC 604e machines can be upgraded to G3-level PowerPC 750 processors. One of the few exceptions to this rule is the first generation (6100, 7100, 8100) Power Macintosh models, which can be upgraded to G3 processing power using special PDS cards from Sonnet Technologies and Newer Technologies.

Where else can you get upgrades? See Table 6-1 for a little help. (Note that the Level of Products category represents the products currently shipping as of this writing. The companies listed may have shipped products designed for earlier Macs in the past, but have since stopped selling them new.)

Table 6-1 Processor Upgrade Manufacturers		
Company	Level of Products	URL
Apple Computer	PPC	www.apple.com/products/
Sonnet Technologies	030, 040, PPC, G3	www.sonnettech.com/
Newer Technologies	PPC, G3	www.newertech.com/
MacTell	PPC, G3	www.mactell.com/
PowerLogix	PPC, G3	www.powerlogix.com/
XLR8	PPC, G3	www.xlr8.com/
Micromac	030, 040, PPC	www.micromac.com/

Note

Aside from selling a wide variety of upgrading products, Micromac also offers an excellent specifications search service on their Web site. Just choose your Mac model from a menu, and the site will give you all the specifications for the model, including RAM types and possible upgrades.

Types of upgrades

Before looking at the specific upgrades available for the various Macintosh models, take a look at the different types of upgrades you'll encounter when you set out to augment your system. There are really only four major types of upgrades out there, although they vary a bit within each type. You'll likely only have one choice, although a number of mid-life Macs — those built in the early 1990s — offer a few choices.

Here are the types of upgrades:

✦ **Expansion card.** It's rare-to-never that you'll see an expansion card upgrade that's based on NuBus or PCI, but the processor direct slot (PDS) that was popular on earlier Mac models has proved to be a big hit with upgrade manufacturers. From the Color Classic to the Power Macintosh 8100, PDS slots can almost always be filled with an upgrade that takes your model to the next level. The only exception to this rule are some PowerPC-based Performa models that offer PDS slots but never really used them for much of anything. Unfortunately, those models don't seem very upgradeable. Figure 6-1 shows a processor upgrade expansion card.

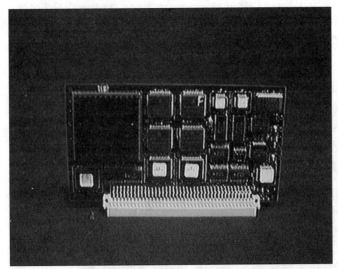

Figure 6-1: The Sonnet Presto 040 is a PDS expansion card for many of the Mac II series computers.

✦ **Logic board.** In this case, the entire logic board needs to be replaced for the Mac to be upgraded. A logic board upgrade is a tough but not impossible task; Apple generally recommends that the logic board upgrade be completed by an authorized service center. Depending on your Mac model (and how much interest you have in keeping the Mac under warranty and/or functional), you can probably manage the logic board upgrade yourself. Unfortunately, you're unlikely to find logic board upgrades at the retail level, requiring you to shop the used market and the used/refurbished computer mail-order houses.

✦ **Processor.** A Mac's processor is usually either *soldered* on the motherboard— meaning it's affixed by heating metal that then cools to form a seal—or it's socketed, meaning it's installed in such a way that it could, if necessary, be removed from its socket. This second sort of processor is interesting, because it means — if a manufacturer expends enough ingenuity to solve the problem — you can often add a different processor to make the Mac operate at higher speeds. This is exactly the approach taken to upgrading many Mac II series machines to 68040 and some Performa-series machines to PowerPC. It's also the approach used to upgrade G3-level machines to higher speeds.

✦ **Daughtercard.** This last type of upgrade is the most common with later systems. In most Apple and many clone models based on the PowerPC 604e processor, the CPU is actually mounted on an expansion card complete with settings, heat sinks, and (sometimes) cache RAM. To upgrade the processor, all you have to do is pull the existing daughtercard and plug in the new one. With some daughtercards, it's even possible to set the speed of the system bus (within certain parameters dictated by the logic board). Figure 6-2 shows a CPU daughtercard.

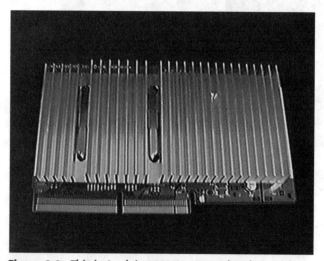

Figure 6-2: This is Apple's 200MHz 604e daughtercard. Notice the heat sink that covers the processor and other components.

It's almost laughably simple to upgrade most Macs when they provide an upgrade path. Personally, I think most Mac processor upgrades are a joy to perform because you just open the Mac, install the upgrade, and start computing at incredible new speeds.

Still, there are a few caveats, which I'll cover after you take a look at the options available for your particular system.

Individual upgradeability

Time for one of those big tables. Table 6-2 shows you the upgradeability of major Macintosh models including some of the clones. When a particular Mac is upgradeable, all the ways in which it can be upgraded are listed in the Upgradeable? column. 030 stands for 68030, 040 stands for 68040. Note that if a computer is already a 68030 and the table indicates it's upgradeable to a 68030, this is usually because the upgrade doubles the speed of the processor (or better), usually via a PDS card.

Table 6-2
Macintosh Processor Upgrades

Mac OS Model	Processor	Speed	Upgradeable?	Upgrade Technology
Mac 128k	68000	8MHz	No	N/A
Mac 512k	68000	8MHz	No	N/A
Classic	68000	8MHz	No	N/A
Classic II	68030	16MHz	No	N/A
Color Classic	68030	16MHz	030, 040	PDS
Color Classic II	68030	33MHz	040	PDS
Plus	68000	8MHz	No	N/A
SE	68000	8MHz	030	PDS
SE/30	68030	16MHz	030	PDS
Mac II	68020	16MHz	030	CPU
Mac IIx	68030	16MHz	030	CPU
IIcx	68030	16MHz	040	PDS
IIci	68030	25MHz	040	PDS
IIsi	68030	20MHz	040	PDS
IIvi	68030	20MHz	040, PPC 601	PDS, logic board
IIvx	68030	32MHz	040, PPC 601	PDS, logic board
IIfx	68030	40MHz	N/A	N/A
LC	68020	16MHz	030, 040	CPU, PDS

(continued)

Table 6-2 *(continued)*

Mac OS Model	Processor	Speed	Upgradeable?	Upgrade Technology
LC II	68030	16MHz	030, 040	CPU, PDS
LC III/III	68030	25/33MHz	040	Logic board (LC475)
LC 520	68030	25MHz	040, PPC 601	Logic board, CPU[1]
LC 550, Performa 550, 560	68030	33MHz	040, PPC 601	Logic board, CPU[1]
Performa 200	68030	16MHz	No	N/A
Performa 250, 400, 405, 410, 430	68030	16MHz	040	Logic board (LC 475)
Performa 450	68030	25MHz	040	Logic board (LC 475)
Performa 600, 600CD	68030	32MHz	040, PPC 601	PDS, logic board (7100)
Performa 460, 466, 467	68030	33MHz	N/A	Logic board (LC 475)
Performa 475, 476	68LC040	50MHz	PPC 601	CPU
Performa 520	68030	25MHz	N/A	N/A
Performa 575, 577, 578 LC 575	68LC040	66MHz	PPC 601	CPU
Performa 580, 588, LC 580	68LC040	66MHz	PPC 601	CPU
Mac TV	68030	33MHz	No	N/A
Performa 600/ 600CD	68030	33MHz	040, PPC 601	PDS, logic board
Performa 630, 0 630CD, 631CD, 3 635CD, 636CD, 637CD, 638CD, LC 630, Quadra 6	68LC040	66MHz	PPC 601	CPU
Quadra 605	68LC040	50MHz	PPC 601	CPU
Centris 610	68LC040	40MHz	040, PPC 601	CPU, PDS/logic board[2]
Quadra 610/ 610DOS	68040	50MHz	040, PPC 601	CPU, PDS/logic board[2]

Mac OS Model	Processor	Speed	Upgradeable?	Upgrade Technology
Centris 650, Quadra 650	68040	66MHz	040, PPC 601	CPU, PDS/logic board[2]
Centris, Quadra 660AV	68040	50MHz	040, PPC 601	CPU, logic board
Quadra 700	68040	50MHz	040, PPC 601	CPU, PDS
Quadra 800	68040	66MHz	PPC 601, 604	PDS, logic board (8500)
Quadra 840AV	68040	80MHz	PPC 601, 604	Logic board (8500)
Quadra 900	68040	50MHz	040, PPC 601	CPU, PDS
Quadra 950	68040	66MHz	PPC 601	PDS
PM 6100, 6100AV, 6100/DOS, Performa 6110, 6112, 6115, 6116, 6117, 6118	PPC 601	60/66MHz	PPC 604, G3	PDS
PM 7100, 7100AV	PPC 601	66/80MHz	PPC 604, G3	PDS
PM 8100, 8100AV, 8110, 8115	PPC 601	80/100/ 110MHz	PPC 604, G3	Logic board (8500), PDS
Performa 5200, 5210, 5215, 5220, Power Mac 5200/75	PPC 603	75MHz	No	N/A
Performa 5260, 5270, 5300, Power Mac 5260/100, 5300/100	PPC 603e	100MHz	No	N/A
Performa 5260/120, 5280, 5320, 5400, 5410, 5420, PM 5260/120, 5400/120	PPC 603e	120MHz	No	N/A
Performa 5400/160, 5430	PPC 603e	160MHz	No	N/A
Performa 5400/ 180, 5440, PM 5400/180	PPC 603e	180MHz	No	N/A
PM 5400/200	PPC 603e	200MHz	No	N/A
PM 5500/225	PPC 603e	225MHz	No	N/A
PM 5500/250	PPC 603e	250MHz	No	N/A

(continued)

Table 6-2 *(continued)*				
Mac OS Model	**Processor**	**Speed**	**Upgradeable?**	**Upgrade Technology**
Performa 6200, 6205, 6210, 6214, 6216, 6218, 6220, 6230	PPC 603	75MHz	No	N/A
Performa 6260, 6290, 6300, 6310	PPC 603e	100MHz	No	N/A
Performa 6320	PPC 603e	120MHz	No	N/A
Performa 6360	PPC 603e	160MHz	No	N/A
Performa 6400/180, 6410	PPC 603e	180MHz	No	N/A
Performa 6400/200, 6420	PPC 603e	200MHz	No	N/A
PM 4400/160	PPC 603e	160MHz	No	N/A
4400/200, 4400PC	PPC 603e	200MHz	No	N/A
PM 6500	PPC 603e	200–300MHz	No	N/A
PM 7200, 7215	PPC 601	75–120MHz	PPC 604e	Logic board (7600)
PM 7220/200	PPC 603e	200MHz	PPC 604e	Logic board (7600)
PM 7300	PPC 604e	166–200MHz	PPC 604e, G3	Daughtercard
PM 7500/100	PPC 601	100MHz	PPC 604e, G3	Daughtercard
PM 7600	PPC 604e	120–200MHz	PPC 604e, G3	Daughtercard
PM 8500, 8600	PPC 604/604e	120–300MHz	PPC 604e, G3[3]	Daughtercard
PM 9500, 9600	PPC 604e	120–350MHz	PPC 604e, G3[3]	Daughtercard
PM 9500/9600MP	2 PPC 604e	180–200MHz	2 PPC 604e	Daughtercard
PM G3 series	G3 (PPC 750)	233–300MHz	G3	CPU

Power Computing Systems

Power 100/120	PPC 601	100–120MHz	PPC 604e	PDS
PowerBase 180, 200, 240	PPC 603e	180–240MHz	PPC 604e, G3	Daughtercard
PowerWave 120, 132, 150	PPC 604	120–150MHz	PPC 604e, G3	Daughtercard
PowerCurve 120, PowerCenter 120, 132 150/166/180	PPC 604	120–180MHz	PPC 604e, G3	Daughtercard

Mac OS Model	Processor	Speed	Upgradeable?	Upgrade Technology
PowerCenter Pro 180, 210, 240	PPC 604e	180–250MHz	PPC 603e, G3	Daughtercard
PowerTower Pro 180, 200, 225, 250	PPC 604e	180–250MHz	PPC 604e, G3	Daughtercard
UMAX Systems				
c500 series	PPC 603e	140–240MHz	PPC 604e, G3	CPU
c600 series	PPC 603e	180–280MHz	PPC 604e, G3	CPU
j700 series	PPC 604e	150–233MHz	PPC 604e, G3	Daughtercard
s900 series	PPC 604e	150–250MHz	PPC 604E, G3	Daughtercard

1 Must be upgraded with a logic board upgrade to an LC 575 or Performa 570 series before the processor upgrade can be installed.

2 These Macs can be upgraded to PowerPC using either a PDS card or a logic board upgrade to a Power Macintosh 6100.

3 The Mach 5 series of 604e processors (which boosted speeds to 300- and 350MHz in the shipping versions of some 8600 and 9600 model Power Macs) can't be upgraded with 604e processors, because more powerful 604e processors were never made (they can still be upgraded to G3 and beyond).

As you can see from the table, upgrades are slightly more popular and viable in Macs than you may have realized. A lot of models have some sort of upgrade path to keep them up to speed for many years. It's especially interesting to note that the Mac market has gone through some fairly definitive transition points that trace the contemporary theory (and market demands) that governed upgradeability. Some major issues in the history of the Mac market can suggest why certain models are added to in one way whereas others are upgraded in another.

First, many 68030 machines (especially those intended for business use) can be upgraded to 68040-level processors, making them capable, in many cases, of running Mac OS 8.0. (Mac OS 8.0 was the first Mac OS to exclude 68030 machines.) This upgradeability is almost always offered by third-party vendors and really became popular only after vendors realized that the PDS slot was a good way to boost performance to 68040 levels or better. The 68040 was a slight departure from the earlier 68000 series processors, with a different cache scheme and slightly more advanced internals. This made it attractive for an upgrade, especially after a lot of software programs were upgraded to 040 compatibility. These upgrades remain popular because the Mac OS has stopped supporting processors older than 68040s in Mac OS 8.0. Some cards can upgrade to 68040 but don't support later Mac OS versions, so shop for that capability if it interests you.

Unofficial upgrades: Logic boards and clock chipping

Table 6-2 pretty much focuses on "official" upgrades, by which I mean upgrades offered by Apple or another reasonably well-received vendor that seem to have gone through an engineering and testing phase on the released product.

If you find you're stuck with a machine that's not officially upgradeable, there might be other ways to go about speeding things up—but you'll need to be a bit handy with electronics.

One way to upgrade a nonupgradeable Mac is to simply swap motherboards with a similar model that uses the same case, cabling, and other miscellany. This isn't always the easiest thing to do; there are minor differences in many Mac models that seem similar. But you'll find that, in some cases, you might be lucky with this approach. For instance, you might be able to upgrade an aging 68LC040-based Performa all-in-one model (like the Performa 630) with a similar pull-out logic board from a Performa 6200 series. At least, I've heard of that working. I've also heard of it not working. Many Performa and education-oriented Power Macintosh machines have similar logic board designs, making it possible to upgrade through many leaps in technology. I've seen a Performa 575 running a 200MHz 603e processor; an upgrade like changing a Performa 6200 into a 300MHz 603e (from a Power Macintosh 6500) should be a no-brainer.

Check around in Usenet newsgroups and on the Web to see what type of motherboard swaps have brought people luck, but realize that you're taking matters into your own hands—like your warranty and the likelihood that certified technicians will tell you to fly a kite if something goes wrong. So where do you find the boards? For starters, try Shreve Systems (www.shrevesystems.com/), NEXCOMP (www.nexcomp.com/), MilagroMac (www.milagromac.com/upgrades.html) or We Love Macs (www.lovemacs.com/). Usenet and used Mac Web sites are also good bets.

If you're really a hobbyist type, you might enjoy clock chipping your Macintosh's processor. *Clock chipping* is a process that increases the clock speed at which your Mac's processor runs, based on the assumption the processor was originally set at a lower clock rate than the Mac's logic board can handle to avoid quality-control problems. This is usually a safe bet, but it doesn't necessarily make clock chipping a great idea.

If you're the sort of person who will perform a clock-chipping upgrade anyway (the basic process replaces the existing quartz oscillating clock on your logic board with a faster—or a variable—clock), this won't deter you. I'm not actually against the process. In my view, the problem is two-fold: Clock chipping too often introduces errors, including heat problems, that affect stability. Plus, it usually just isn't that overwhelming of a speed gain. Instead of clock chipping, I recommend saving your pennies for more RAM or cache—or even a new Mac.

Second, the transition from 68040 to PowerPC was a big deal in the Mac world in 1993 and 1994, with many models of that time reflecting Apple's desire to give everyone upgrade options. Most of those cards and logic board upgrades are no longer available for retail sale; you'll need to comb the upgrade mail-order houses and the used markets to see if you can find what you're looking for.

Third, most Macs based on the 604e processor are easily upgradeable to faster 604e and/or G3-level processors, with the exception of the Motorola clones and others based on Motorola sublicenses. Those particular models don't really have much of an upgrade path at all for the time being, other than extra system and cache RAM.

Performing the upgrade

If you've gotten your hands on the information and parts you need to move ahead with your upgrading task, you're pretty much ready to roll. In all cases, you'll probably need to review the instructions in Chapter 5 for getting your particular Mac model open and exposed for the upgrading. You'll likely be working through an enjoyable experience that's free of Mac internal headaches, but you'd best have a set of tools on hand anyway to contend with Phillips-head screws, the occasional flathead screw, and, in rare instances, a T15 Torx screw or two.

Here are a few other things you'll want to consider before performing the upgrade:

+ *Back up your data.* Even if you don't want to, you should back up the system you're about to upgrade. There's a chance you'll either destroy the Mac, and then run screaming out the room with your arm on fire (in which case neither I, Apple, nor IDG Books can claim any culpability), or you might install a processor upgrade that goes nuts and starts overwriting everything on the drive. Although these things aren't terribly likely, I imagine some folks have managed to live through worse and were very pleased that they'd decided to back up their hard drives.

+ *Electrically ground yourself.* Even if you take a cavalier approach to static electricity around your RAM, hard drive, and small pets, remember that a grounding strap costs about $10, whereas a new high-speed processor is usually worth hundreds or thousands of dollars. It's the most expensive component in most Macs, so you should handle your processor with static-free care.

+ *Handle with care.* Use the antistatic bags, software packaging, and anything else that comes with your processor upgrade to store it until you're ready to install it. Then, if you're replacing a card or daughtercard that you've removed from your Mac, store that component in the same antistatic bag and software packaging to keep it safe. (You may need it again or decide to sell it.)

✦ *Know your system.* When you're upgrading the logic board or processor, it's incredibly important to know what's really going on inside your Mac. Get a good feel for what components you're supposed to be removing or replacing, and make sure you're doing everything according to procedure.

✦ *Label everything.* If you're in doubt when you're inside your Mac, label something with a piece of masking tape or an office-supply sticky label. (Don't use Post-It-style stickies, because they'll fall off of hot surfaces and wiring.)

✦ *Consider a clean install.* If you perform a clean install of the Mac OS soon after installing your upgrade (and making sure it's fairly problem free), you may have better luck with it over the long haul. Any assumptions the Mac OS made about your computer (certain portions of the OS can only be installed on Macs with particular power capabilities) might be changed when you reinstall with your upgrade in place.

The most important advice I can give you is to know your limits. If you're not comfortable performing this upgrade, admit that to yourself and move on. Most of these processor upgrades aren't complicated, but they do involve very expensive, somewhat delicate components. If you consign the task to an official Apple authorized dealer, they're responsible if something gets messed up. They'll also perform the upgrade by the book, test it, and perhaps even guarantee the workmanship for a period of time.

Expansion card upgrades

This sort of processor upgrade is, bar none, the simplest to complete. All you really need to do is locate the available PDS slot in your Macintosh and plug in the upgrade. You'll then install a little software that will activate the card, accelerating the Mac the next time you restart.

The only real issue with PDS upgrades is you'll need the PDS slot to be available for you to perform the upgrade. If the slot is taken up by something else — such as a video or multimedia card — you'll have to remove it before you can install the processor upgrade. This can be an important issue if the card is critical to your work or if you don't have any available NuBus slots for similar cards.

Some Macs will also require an adapter (the Mac IIsi comes to mind, as well as some other Macs in slimline cases), so make sure you get the adapter when you purchase the accelerator.

The following walks through a Mac IIci upgraded with the Presto 040 card from Sonnet Technologies. In this case the new processor is a clock-doubled 68040 processor that runs internally at 80MHz but communicate with the rest of the system at 40MHz. That's quite a boost over the standard Mac IIci, which runs with a 25MHz 68030 processor. Read the warnings in the "Performing the upgrade" section, and then follow these steps:

1. Shut down the Mac, ground yourself, and pull the power cord. Remove the Mac's cover.

2. Locate the PDS slot, which should be labeled. (Make sure you've chosen the PDS slot and not a NuBus slot.) If there's a card already in the slot, remove it. (Make sure it isn't connected to any wires through the back of the case, and then grab the card at each top corner and pull straight up.)

3. Make sure you've discharged static electricity, and then open the static-free bag that contains the upgrade card. Remove the card.

4. Line the card up carefully over the PDS socket. Note the notches in PDS connector on the card and how they match up correctly in only one direction relative to the PDS slot.

5. Press the card into the socket (see Figure 6-3). It should go in fairly easily. If you find yourself forcing it too hard, you may have the card facing the wrong direction. Look at the connector on the card and on the logic board to orient the card correctly, and then install the card again.

Figure 6-3: Press the card gently into the socket with even pressure on each side of the top of the card.

6. Close up the case (or you can test your Mac for a short time with the case open), and then plug the Mac in and start it up.

7. You probably won't experience a speed boost until you install the software that came with the accelerator. Install that software, and restart the Mac.

Now you can sit back and watch the Mac to see if things seem accelerated. The startup process may not seem very speedy—it involves the hard drive, ROM, and a number of different things that you haven't sped up with the accelerator. Instead, watch for telltale signs in applications that, in the past, ran a bit slow.

If you're having trouble just getting started, read the instructions and any troubleshooting issues in the accelerator's documentation closely. Remember that you've changed the processor after you've installed the Mac OS, so it may be a bit confused about things—specifically, issues like 32-bit addresses (in the Memory control panel) and the 040 cache setting (in its own control panel). Other model-specific settings may get confused, too.

If you really feel as though you're not seeing much acceleration, you should troubleshoot the card by isolating the card's extension and restarting. Next, test a particularly tough processing challenge (something like recalculating a spreadsheet, creating a complicated chart, or performing a Photoshop special effect). Then, test with the extension enabled and see if the card does things faster. If not, check to make sure the extension is loading as the Mac starts up. Shut down the Mac and open it up to make sure the card is seated correctly.

If everything looks good and it still seems things aren't working, you might need to troubleshoot for a conflict or software problem (see Chapters 30 through 33) or call the manufacturer to see if they have new software drivers and/or troubleshooting tips for the particular Mac model and accelerator you're using.

Note   Don't forget that RAM is a big part of speeding up your Mac, as discussed in Chapter 2. If you're squeezed for RAM, you may not see the speed boost you're expecting from your accelerator card.

Logic board upgrades

Although a walkthough of a complete logic board upgrade is beyond the scope of this book (the main problem is that every different Mac case requires a different procedure), I hit some high points here on this subject. Most importantly, don't approach a logic board upgrade lightly. In one sense it's a great idea if you know that the logic board will fit correctly in the case; if you install the new, factory-built logic board, there really can't be a conflict that crops up, because you're not using a third-party accelerator or something similar.

Installation is critical, however. It's not impossible to do, by any stretch of the imagination, but you'll need to take some precautions. Most of all, consider whether or not you want to spend the time it'll take for the upgrade. Also, rather than putting a used motherboard in your Mac, why not just buy and use the complete, newer Mac from which it came?

Note

Of course, if you have a slide-out logic board (like many all-in-one and Performa models), you probably don't have too much to worry about in this arena. Just be carefully grounded and prepared with antistatic materials when you pull the logic board out according to the instructions in Chapter 5. (Don't forget to transfer RAM and cache RAM to the new logic board.) Slide the new logic board back into the Mac. If all goes well, you'll have a new, faster computer.

If you've gotten past those issues, here are some other things to consider:

✦ *Read the warnings in the "Performing the upgrade" section.*

✦ *Check the ratings.* Make sure the case and power supply are really rated to handle the new logic board. Just because the cases look the same doesn't always mean the innards are. Specifically, check the rating on the power supply to make sure your old case's supply can handle the new logic board.

✦ *Be organized.* A real pro at this sets aside a few hours for the changeover, reads up on the particular models in question, and even keeps a written log of what he or she does throughout the surgery.

✦ *Root around to find out if anything in your current Mac is incompatible or known to cause trouble with the logic board you'll be installing.* For instance, is the new logic board known to have a conflict with the hard drive model in your Mac? (This could be a tough one to answer, but you might find help in Usenet discussion groups or on Mac acceleration-oriented Web sites.)

✦ *Ground yourself electrically and be very careful with components inside your computer.* In particular, keep metal from coming in contact with the logic board or scraping across it, particularly if it's still plugged in. You'll have to unplug the Mac to remove the logic board, so a grounding strap is absolutely necessary.

✦ *Keep track of everything!* If you go into this upgrade without a plan, you will either (a) lose a screw or (b) have a screw left over. Don't count on yourself to remember where everything went or keep track of parts left on the table or in the carpet. Instead, label everything (cables, wiring, ribbon cables) and keep glasses or cups around to hold screws and parts. Also, make a note of the *direction* that something is connected or plugged into something else, especially if it can clearly go more than one way. Labels that tell you which side is "left" or "up" are perfect, as long as you decide before hand what exactly "left" and "up" are going to mean in this context.

✦ *Know what you're doing.* Before removing a cable or touching a setting, reason out what, exactly, the function of that particular gizmo is. If you know what something is supposed to do, you'll be less likely to forget where it goes when you're reinstalling it later.

Assuming you've grounded yourself, opened the case, and you're ready to do the swap, here's a very general description of the process:

1. Remove any expansion cards and store them safely in a static-free area.

2. You'll need to focus on removing any connections to the logic board. This includes labeling the ribbon cables for your drives and removing them, labeling and removing the power connection to the logic board from the power supply (note carefully how they're connected), and labeling and removing any small wires that connect LED lights and the speaker to the logic board. You should also label and remove any port connections — serial, SCSI, and so on — to the logic board (at least, those that aren't already part of the logic board).

3. You'll need to remove obstructions from the logic board. If necessary, remove the hard drive and floppy drive. (They may swing out, they may be anchored to the logic board, they may not be in the way at all.) Keep track of screws and learn how the drive assembly or drive cage is pulled apart and put back together. You may also need to remove the power supply. Be aware that everything in a Mac isn't always held together by screws; often there are levers and notches that you need to push or pull to get things to pop apart.

4. Make note of how the logic board is connected to the case. (A diagram on your notepad can be a good idea.) It probably uses a combination of plastic standoffs, screws, washers and other mounting braces or parts. Once you've got it figured out, carefully disassemble it, and then remove the logic board.

You've got everything out. Now, just reverse the preceding process to reinstall everything along with the new logic board. Once you're done and it seems everything has been a big success, you might want to do any other transferring you need to do between logic boards — RAM, cache, accelerators, and so on — and then test the Mac with the box open so you can get back in if something isn't right. You'll likely have a cable or two backward — check all the lights, sounds, and other indicators on your Mac. If they're not working or are working in an odd way, you may have messed up a connection. Shut down, and head back into the machine to fix things.

CPU upgrades

Again, these are very specific to the model of Macintosh that's being upgraded, as well as being reasonably rare compared to the other types of upgrades. Although I recommend you strongly consider having a professional install your logic board (and preferably a professional who is then financially responsible for any errors), I *really* recommend it for CPU upgrades. Actually, it's not amazingly difficult to install a processor upgrade — just amazingly delicate. A CPU chip connects to the logic board by way of some very spindly little pin connectors that can easily bend or break. And when you bend or break one, you're well on your way to having ruined the processor, which can be worth quite a bit of money.

On newer Macs, the CPU chip is installed in a Zero Insertion Force (ZIF) socket, which is a bit easier to work with. These sockets are designed so that a small lever, located on the side of the socket, can be easily lifted. Once it's lifted, the pressure that holds each pin in place in the socket is released, and the CPU can be pulled out with just one finger on each side of it. Reinserting the CPU is just as easy: You properly align the chip, and then give it a tiny tap. As a result, the chip will slide into the socket, enabling you to lower the lever and tighten the chip back into place.

Interestingly, touching these ZIF sockets, when installed new on a Power Macintosh G3, for instance, will void the Apple warranty. Apple puts a seal over the ZIF socket that must be broken to access the processor. Even though ZIF is a better way to go, Apple still believes it's complicated enough that you should take the machine to an authorized service center to upgrade the processor chip.

But in most cases, you won't have to worry about that, because your chip upgrade will probably not involve a ZIF socket or any of that stuff. Yours will be much, much tougher.

Seriously, with older Macs, you'll need a chip puller and some patience (work the chip slowly out of the socket, moving to one side, lifting a slight amount, and then moving to the next side and lifting a slight amount). You'll also need good instructions; if you're performing a chip upgrade using a third-party kit, make sure the kit is designed specifically for your Mac model and the instructions are complete. Go slowly, ground yourself, and don't bend a pin.

 Note   If you do bend a pin—but you don't break it—stop right there and take the whole mess immediately to a service center. They should be able to salvage the CPU.

Daughtercard upgrades

These, thank the maker, are easy enough to accomplish. A daughtercard is really a simple extension of the PDS idea—instead of being an open slot on the logic board for various upgrades, it's a single slot designed to take a board that contains the Mac's CPU. This makes Macs incredibly easy to upgrade and has become something of a fixture in new systems, at least for the time being.

Every daughtercard-upgradeable Mac is a Power PC 604e or above, so you'll only be using this method on the more recent machines. When you're shopping for a daughtercard upgrade, you need to be careful that the particular upgrade you're looking at supports your Mac model, as the bus speeds and processor speeds need to sync up in an exact multiple. (A 50MHz bus will work with a 200MHz processor, but not with a 233MHz processor.) Some daughtercards have auto-synching bus and processor speeds that enable you to just drop one card in a number of different Mac models, where it will sync itself to the best speed possible.

There's another type of processor upgrade you'll encounter—the variable speed daughtercard upgrade. With these, you have a dial or other sort of setting that enables you to try to push the envelope a bit; you can set the bus speed and processor speed to see if you can sweat the last little bit of performance out of your machine. Personally, I'd walk away from one of these cards if it was more expensive, unless you want the flexibility to put the card in different systems. If you like the idea of all the settings, though, grab one of these cards and get ready to install it.

Installing a daughtercard is a pretty straightforward process. With the exception of the Power Computing Power Center Pro (I can't speak for other models in the Power Computing, but that particular machine, which I own, is a bear), every daughtercard-upgradeable Mac has had a very clear, wide-open way to get at the card. This example shows a Sonnet Crescendo G3 upgrade card being installed in a Power Macintosh 7300.

As far as precautions, there are only a few:

✦ Read the warnings in the "Performing the upgrade" section.

✦ Be aware of static electricity discharge and wear a grounding strap. Be aware of your surroundings as well (get rid of any liquid, kids, and free-flowing molten lava), because the cards you're holding in your hands are likely worth hundreds or thousands of dollars.

✦ Speaking of hands, don't reach into a Mac that's been running awhile and grab the daughtercard—the accordion-like metal all over the card is a heat sink, designed to dissipate heat from the processor. Wait for it to cool for a few minutes or more before touching it, and then be careful at first.

Here's how to install the typical daughtercard upgrade:

1. Shut down the Mac, ground yourself, and pull the power cord. Remove the Mac's cover and open the case so you can see the daughtercard.

2. The current processor will already be in the daughtercard slot. Check it to make sure it's not hot. Make sure you've discharged electricity, grab it by each top edge, and remove it from the slot. Put it down in a safe and static-free area on your desktop or work table.

3. Open the static-free bag that contains the upgrade card. Unwrap the card.

4. Line the card up carefully over the daughtercard slot. The card will only fit in one direction because one section of the card's interface is slightly larger than the other part.

5. Press the card into the socket (see Figure 6-4). It should go in fairly easily. If you find yourself forcing it too hard, you may have the card facing the wrong direction or misaligned.

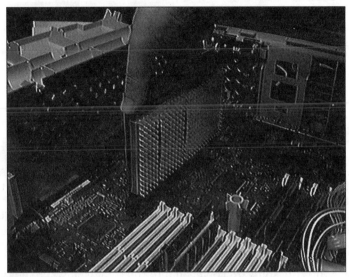

Figure 6-4: Press the daughtercard into the socket with even pressure on each side of the top of the card.

If your daughtercard doesn't have special settings, all that's left is to button up the Macintosh and start it up. In some cases, you might experience the speed gain immediately. In others, you'll need to load the included software so that the accelerator's extensions are installed, and then restart the Mac to enjoy your newfound wonder machine.

If your daughtercard does feature settings for the bus speed and processor speed, you might want to experiment with the case open for a while. Following the instructions that came with the card, pick and choose to find the best settings for your particular Mac. While you search for the best settings, look for a balance between over-revving your Mac and getting the best speeds that keep the system stable. If you suspect there's extra crashing as a result of the daughtercard, try backing it down a notch or so in bus and processor speed, and then make sure you're using the most recent version of the card's extensions and utilities.

Remember that the card is the only processor you've got in the machine, which is different from some upgrades, where both the old and new processors can be in the Mac at the same time. If you experience trouble getting the Mac to start up, check the card. If it isn't plugged in correctly, your Mac doesn't have a processor, making it less than useful.

Other difficulties may be attributable to problems with the extension software (especially if you've recently upgraded the Mac OS) or to the card not being completely compatible with your Mac. If you have such trouble, contact the manufacturer to see if they recommend another unit or a slightly slower one that might prove more compatible.

Upgrading Memory

Maybe I should have made this section appear first in this chapter. After all, in almost all cases, memory is the most important upgrade. Too often the RAM requirements are spiraling past our aging machines, leaving them slower than they really need to be, if only because they don't have enough RAM to really shine. Once you've used all the physical RAM in your Mac, you're left with solutions like Virtual Memory and Connectix RAMDoubler — solutions that take processor time to implement and access the hard drive constantly, which slows down everything.

So, if your Mac runs the software you need it to run (that is, if you're not upgrading so you can still take advantage of the latest Mac OS version or to move up to some level of PowerPC performance), and your Mac just seems a little sluggish, you should look into getting more RAM for your system.

Of course, there are other things you can do with memory that can increase your Mac's speed, including managing well the memory you do have in your system and adding cache RAM. (For more on the basics of RAM, see Chapter 2.)

System RAM

In fact, RAM can be useful for more than just running programs. You can hand RAM over to your Mac's disk cache, which tends to speed up accesses to the hard drive. You can also use RAM to create a RAM disk, which acts as a regular floppy or hard disk, but is accessed at the speed of RAM. This is a great way to speed up a Web browser, for instance, enabling it to place all its browser data files on the RAM disk so that they can be easily accessed when you visit a particular Web page more than once.

The amount of RAM your Mac needs keeps going up and up. At the time of writing, Apple doesn't seem willing to sell a Mac OS system with less than 32MB of RAM and that's a reasonable, if not stellar, minimum. Recently, a glut of RAM (and minor improvements in RAM technology) has kept prices so low for months and months that programmers and computer manufacturers are getting used to RAM being cheap. This means they're willing to be a bit frivolous with it when they're creating their programs or adding features to operating system versions.

So, if you use your Mac on a daily basis in a professional capacity, you probably want between 48- and 64MB of RAM to work with office applications like Microsoft Office and FileMaker Pro. If you use your Mac for professional graphics and layout work, relying on Photoshop, PageMaker, QuarkXPress or similar programs, you might want 64MB as a lower limit, with 128MB of RAM not being an unreasonable amount.

For high-end tasks such as full-time Photoshop work, running a server computer, rendering animation, and application development, you're more likely to want 256MB of RAM. Apple has made Macs capable of accepting 1GB of RAM, which is quite a lot, but probably won't seem so in just a few more months or years (especially with more and more convergence between video production, audio production, and computing). QuickTime on its own will likely drive people to install much more RAM, as desktop video and audio production slowly become as popular as desktop publishing.

Check your RAM settings

If you're not sure how much RAM you currently have in your Mac, it's easy enough to find out. In the Finder, choose About This Computer (or About This Macintosh) from the Apple menu. In the resulting dialog box, you can see all the applications that are currently running and how much space each of them takes up (see Figure 6-5).

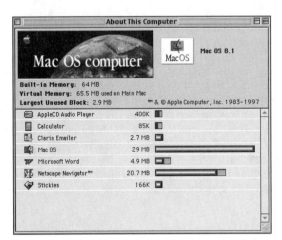

Figure 6-5: The amount of RAM you currently have and how much each application takes up

Notice that this dialog box tells you a number of things, including the amount of built-in RAM (based on the physical, actual RAM chips) that's installed in your Mac and the amount of Virtual Memory available, if you have Virtual Memory turned on in the Memory control panel. Virtual memory enables you to use hard drive space as a way to increase the amount of system RAM available to your Mac; this way it can quickly swap programs that aren't being used or bits of data to the hard drive, and then make room for something that is being used. Although convenient, because it allows you to run more demanding programs than you might other wise be able to, Virtual Memory, no matter how sophisticated, will always slow your Mac down.

You can set Virtual Memory on or off via the Memory control panel, as well as decide how much of the hard drive you'd like set aside for virtual memory. Usually, setting it right at 1MB over the amount of physical RAM you have in your Mac is a good balance between speed and usefulness. You can set it higher if your Mac is struggling to run a particular program or two, and you're willing to take a performance hit.

The Memory control panel will also enable you to create a RAM disk and manage the amount of RAM you dedicate to a cache. This cache reads ahead on the hard drive and tries to store data — in high speed RAM — that it thinks your programs may need next. If it's right, that's a *hit* to the cache, which gives you a little speed burst. If it's right often enough every second, you'll begin to see a decent speed increase as you work on the Mac. The rule of thumb is to add about 96K of cache for every megabyte of physical RAM you have in your system. If you're running low on RAM for your programs, though, you can get a little more back by turning down your cache settings.

A RAM disk is great if you've got some extra RAM to play with. Create a RAM disk and you can store data files in a portion of RAM that's been set aside to act as though it's a floppy disk or a small hard drive (see Figure 6-6). The difference is, it's really RAM, which is must faster than any sort of physical storage. Of course, the downside is that a RAM disk is just as volatile as RAM itself; although a RAM disk's data will survive a soft restart (Special ➪ Restart), it won't survive the Mac being shut down. In that case, you'll lose what's on the RAM disk. The best plan? Place data that isn't mission-critical, such as files from a game program or Web browser cache files, on the RAM disk to provide speedy access.

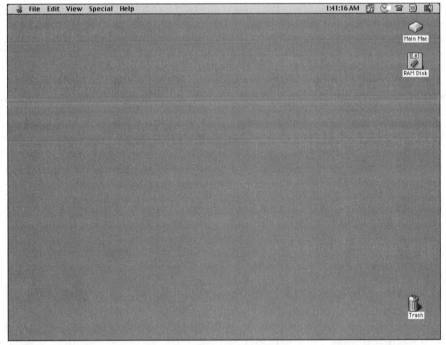

Figure 6-6: I always have a RAM disk on my desktop to store noncritical files where I can get at them quickly.

Working with RAM

Your Mac's programs have to actively deal with RAM too. In fact, they have to request RAM whenever they're launched so that they have space in memory to store their data and programming code. Without enough RAM, the program won't run well or at all; with too much RAM, the program is hoarding system memory from the rest of your programs.

You can check a program's RAM allocation by selecting the program's actual icon (not an alias) in the Finder and choosing File ➪ Get Info. You'll then see the memory requirements for the program in the lower-right corner of the Get Info box.

You can change those settings to something higher if you are getting "Out of Memory" error messages when working with the program or if it runs more slowly than you believe it should. You can also set the requested value to a higher number so that the application tries to get a lot of memory, but will take less if you're already running many other programs.

Interestingly, all of this allocating and reallocating of RAM can lead to a fairly common problem that people have with their Macs — fragmented memory. In the last section of this book, you'll read about software problems that can be caused by a hard drive becoming *fragmented:* Too many files have been written and rewritten to portions of that drive so that there are small, left-over fragments everywhere. That same sort of thing can happen in RAM.

If you've opened and closed a lot of applications (usually over days or weeks) since the last time you shut down or restarted your Mac, little bits of that memory may not have been deallocated every time a program was shut down. After a little time, this fragmentation can cause trouble when you launch other applications. Eventually, you'll get "Out of Memory" error messages or other more problematic crashes. If you experience something similar, and you've been using your Mac nonstop for quite some time, consider restarting in order to defragment memory. (When you shut down or restart, most of your Mac's system memory gets wiped clean, and you can start over again.)

Adding RAM

If you've decided you're ready to dig in and change the amount of RAM in your Mac, you'll need to figure out how much RAM your Mac can handle. That's what Table 6-3 is for, and the information it contains will also tell you what sort of RAM to buy and how many RAM modules you need to add at once.

Note

If you're serious about adding RAM, I recommend you download the Apple Memory Guide document from Apple's Support Web site (`www.apple.com/suppport/`). It not only has memory requirements for different Macs, but it even includes diagrams that show you how and where to add RAM to your particular Mac system.

The RAM Table

Each Mac model ships with a certain amount of RAM and generally offers at least one slot for upgrading (often some of the Mac's base RAM is soldered onto the logic board). Each model also has a certain type of RAM technology that it needs to use, and the RAM has to be a certain speed, in nanoseconds. Finally, in some cases you can't just install one RAM module. Instead, you're forced to install two or more to fill a memory *bank* or series of modules that are accessed as one.

Table 6-3
Macintosh RAM Upgrades

Model	Base RAM	Max RAM	Slots	Type	Speed	Groups of...
Mac 128k	128K	128K	0	N/A	N/A	N/A
Mac 512k	512K	512K	0	N/A	N/A	N/A
Classic	1MB	4MB	2	30-pin SIMM	120 ns	2
Classic II	2MB	10MB	2	30-pin SIMM	100 ns	2
Color Classic	4MB	10MB	2	30-pin SIMM	100 ns	2
Color Classic II	4MB	36MB	1	72-pin SIMM	80 ns	1
Plus	1MB	4MB	4	30-pin SIMM	150 ns	2
SE	1MB	4MB	4	30-pin SIMM	150 ns	2
SE/30	1MB	32MB	8	30-pin SIMM	120 ns	4
Mac II	1MB	20MB	8	30-pin SIMM	120 ns	4
Mac IIx	1MB	32MB	8	30-pin SIMM	120 ns	4
IIcx	1MB	128MB	8	30-pin SIMM		
IIci	1MB	128MB	8	30-pin SIMM	80 ns	4
IIsi	1MB	17MB	4	30-pin SIMM	100 ns	4
IIvi, IIvx	4MB	68MB	4	30-pin SIMM	80 ns	4
IIfx	4MB	128MB	8	64-pin[1] SIMM	80 ns	4
Mac TV	4MB	8MB	1	72-pin SIMM	80 ns	1
LC, Performa 200	2MB	10MB	2	30-pin SIMM	100 ns	2

(continued)

Table 6-3 (continued)

Model	Base RAM	Max RAM	Slots	Type	Speed	Groups of...
LC II, Performa 250, 400, 405, 410, 430	4MB	10MB	2	30-pin SIMM	100 ns	2
LC III/III+, 475, 520, 550, 575; Performa 275, 450, 460, 466, 467, 475, 476, 520, 550, 560, 575, 577, 578	4MB	36MB	1	72-pin SIMM	80 ns	1
Performa 600	4MB	68MB	4	30-pin SIMM	80 ns	1
Performa 580, 588, LC 580	8MB	52MB	2	72-pin SIMM	80 ns	1
Performa 630, 630CD, 635CD, 636CD, 637CD, 638CDLC630, Quadra 630	4MB	36MB	1	72-pin SIMM	80 ns	1
Performa 630DOS, 631CD, 640DOS	8MB	52MB	2	72-pin SIMM	80 ns	1
Quadra 605	4MB	36MB	1	72-pin SIMM	80 ns	1
Centris 610, Quadra 610, 610DOS	4MB	68MB	2	72-pin SIMM	80 ns	1
Centris 650, Quadra 650	4MB[2]	132MB[2]	4	72-pin SIMM	80 ns	1
Centris, Quadra 660AV	4MB	68MB	2	72-pin SIMM	70 ns	1
Quadra 700	4MB	20MB	4	30-pin SIMM	80 ns	4
Quadra 800	8MB	136MB	4	72-pin SIMM	60 ns	1
Quadra 840AV	4MB	128MB	4	72-pin SIMM	60 ns	1

Model	Base RAM	Max RAM	Slots	Type	Speed	Groups of...
Quadra 900, 950	4MB	256MB	16	30-pin SIMM	80 ns	4
PM 6100, 6100AV, 6100/ DOS; Performa 6110, 6112, 6115, 6116, 6117, 6118	8MB	72MB	2	72-pin SIMM	80 ns	2
PM 7100, 7100AV	8MB	136MB	4	72-pin SIMM	80 ns	2
PM 8100, 8100AV, 8110, 8115	8MB	264MB	8	72-pin SIMM	80 ns	2
PM 8100/110	16MB	264MB	8	72-pin SIMM	80 ns	2
Performa 5200, 5210, 5215, 5220, 5260, 5270 PM 5200/75	8MB	64MB	2	72-pin SIMM	80 ns	1
Performa 5260, 5270, 5300, 5320, Power Mac 5260/100, 5260/ 1205300/100	16MB	64MB	2	72-pin SIMM	80 ns	1
Performa 5400, 5400/160, 5400/180, 5410, 5420, 5430, 5440, PM 5400/ 120, 5400/180	16MB	136MB	2	168-pin DIMM	70 ns	1
PM 5400/200	24MB	136MB	2	168-pin DIMM	70 ns	1
PM 5500/ 225, 5500/250	32MB	128MB	2	168-pin DIMM	60 ns	1
Performa 6200, 6205, 6214, 6216, 6260, 6290	8MB	64MB	2	72-pin SIMM	80 ns	1

(continued)

Table 6-3 (continued)

Model	Base RAM	Max RAM	Slots	Type	Speed	Groups of...
Performa 6210, 6218, 6220, 6230, 6300, 6310, 6320	16MB	64MB	2	72-pin SIMM	80 ns	1
Performa 6360	16MB	136MB	2	168-pin SIMM	70 ns	1
Performa 6400/ 180, 6400/ 200, 6410	16MB	136MB	2	168-pin SIMM	70 ns	1
Performa 6420	24MB	136MB	2	168-pin SIMM	70 ns	1
PM 4400/160	16MB	96MB	3	168-pin DIMM	60 ns	1
PM 4400/200	16MB	160MB	3	168-pin DIMM	60 ns	1
PM 4400PC	32MB	160MB	3	168-pin DIMM	60 ns	1
PM 6500 series	32MB[3]	128MB	2	168-pin DIMM	60 ns	1
PM 6500/300	64MB	128MB	2	168-pin DIMM	60 ns	1
PM 7200 series	8MB	256MB	4	168-pin DIMM	60 ns	1
PM 7215/90	16MB	256MB	4	168-pin DIMM	70 ns	1
PM 7220/200	16MB	160MB	3	168-pin DIMM	60 ns	1
PM 7220/200PC	32MB	160MB	3	168-pin DIMM	60 ns	1
PM 7300/ 166, 7300/180	16MB	512MB	8	168-pin DIMM	70 ns	1
PM 7300/ 180PC, 7300/ 200	32MB	512MB	8	168-pin DIMM	70 ns	1
PM 7500, 7600	8MB	512MB	8	168-pin DIMM	70 ns	1
PM 7600/200	32MB	512MB	8	168-pin DIMM	70 ns	1

Model	Base RAM	Max RAM	Slots	Type	Speed	Groups of...
PM 8200/100	8MB	256MB	4	168-pin DIMM	70 ns	1
PM 8200/120	16MB	256MB	4	168-pin DIMM	70 ns	1
PM 8500	16MB	512MB	8	168-pin DIMM	70 ns	1
PM 8515	32MB	512MB	8	168-pin DIMM	70 ns	1
PM 8600	32MB	512MB	8	168-pin DIMM	70 ns	1
PM 9500/120, 9500/132, 9500/200	16MB	768MB	12	168-pin DIMM	70 ns	1
PM 9500/ 150 9515/132	8MB	768MB	12	168-pin DIMM	70 ns	1
PM 9500/ 180MP	32MB	768MB	12	168-pin DIMM	70 ns	1
PM 9600/200, 9600/200MP, 9600/233	32MB	768MB	12	168-pin DIMM	70 ns	1
PM 9600/300, 9600/350	64MB	768MB	12	168-pin DIMM	70 ns	1
PM G3 Desktop	32MB	192MB	3	168-pin DIMM	10 ns[4]	1
PM G3 MT	32MB	384MB	3	168-pin DIMM	10 ns[4]	1
20th Anniversary	32MB	128MB	2	168-pin DIMM	60 ns	1

1 The IIfx requires a unique 64-pin SIMM.

2 The Quadra 650 later came with 8MB of base RAM, which raised its limit to 136MB.

3 The Power Macintosh 6500 Small Business Edition bundle came with 48MB of RAM.

4 G3 series computers use high-speed SO-DIMMs.

Before you run out and buy more RAM for your Mac, it's always a good idea to pop open your Mac's case and take a look at how your RAM is distributed, it's possible, for instance, to have 4MB of RAM that's filling your four RAM slots, because you have four 1MB SIMMs. Or, you could have one 128MB DIMM in your Mac and still have one or two RAM slots open for even more upgrading.

Note   You should also read your Mac's manual to check and see if *interleaving* will increase the performance of your Mac. In some models that are capable of being upgraded one RAM module at a time, you can get a better performance gain if you install *two* at a time, because each module then becomes a separate part of the main memory allowing the Mac to take advantage of interleaving. When that happens, the processor can alternate between the modules when it retrieves data, thus speeding up the process of gathering data from RAM. The speed boost usually hovers around 10 to 15 percent.

Adding the RAM

Adding RAM is certainly one of the easier upgrades, at least in most cases. You won't void your warranty or upset Apple or your clone's manufacturer if you add RAM—unless you have a very special circumstance or a new system yet-to-be-introduced when this was written. (Check your manual just to be safe.) In general, anyone can add RAM to a Mac.

The things you need to be careful of are the same things you worry about with other upgrades—electrically grounding yourself; keeping your RAM modules away from static, liquid, or other trauma; and not forcing or breaking anything inside the Mac. Otherwise, RAM is very straightforward. The only problem you'll have may be getting your Mac's case open and the RAM module slots exposed so you can reach them (Apple and the clone vendors haven't done a great job on every Mac in this respect).

You also shouldn't touch the contacts on a RAM module—handle it by the top corners instead.

From there, adding RAM is straightforward in most systems, although one or two of them can be slightly more challenging. Consult your manual and/or the Apple Memory Guide document available from their Support Web site for more details on your particular machine. SIMMs and DIMMs can be a little different, so take note. (Also, don't forget my admonishment regarding earlier compact Macs—Plus, SE, SE/30—back in Chapter 5. Upgrading the RAM in these models ranges from tough and annoying to simply dangerous. Strongly consider taking these Macs to a qualified service center.)

If it were a perfect world, every single RAM SIMM upgrade would go like this:

1. Shut down the Mac, ground yourself electrically, and unplug the Mac.

2. Open the Mac's case. Find an empty RAM module slot.

3. Make sure you've got the module turned the right direction. To fit into the memory slot, the modules should go in at a 45-degree angle to the logic board (see Figure 6-7).

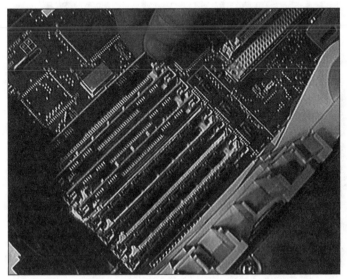

Figure 6-7: Inserting a SIMM in a memory slot

4. With the module pushed into the memory slot at a 45-degree angle, tilt the module up until it locks into the slot at 90 degrees. In some cases, little metal or plastic hooks will grab the module and hold it in place.

5. Insert any other modules if your Mac requires more than one at a time.

That's all you need to do. You can close your Mac and start it up to test if the RAM module is working correctly and recognized by the Mac. Check the About This Computer window or the Apple System Profiler to see the added RAM.

For a RAM DIMM installation, things are sometimes slightly different.

If it were a perfect world, every single RAM DIMM upgrade would go like this:

1. Shut down the Mac, ground yourself electrically, and unplug the Mac.

2. Open the Mac's case. Find an empty RAM DIMM slot.

3. You'll install the DIMM directly into the DIMM slot (not at an angle), so you need to visually line up the notches on the bottom of the DIMM with the ridges in the DIMM slot to make sure it'll fit.

4. Push the DIMM down into the slot. If all goes well, the release lever on the side of the DIMM should lock into place (see Figure 6-8).

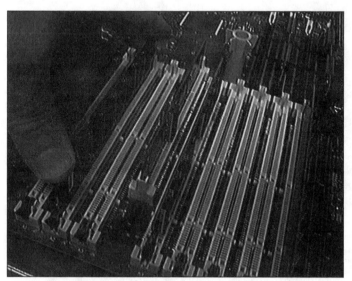

Figure 6-8: Inserting a DIMM into a memory slot

To release the DIMM, simply push down on the locking lever on the side of the DIMM slot. This should pop the DIMM right out.

Note   Does the RAM module just not seem to fit? It happens. These slots and modules are supposed to be pretty standard, but that's not always the case. Try to buy RAM from a Mac-knowledgeable dealer who can tell you which modules are best for your particular model. But if you get a module that doesn't fit, don't try to force it. Return it for an exchange, probably on a slightly different make or brand of module.

Cache RAM

Cache RAM, as discussed in Chapter 2, is incredibly high-speed memory that's designed to hold important information between regular RAM and the processor, such that the processor is almost always accessing this high-speed memory instead of regular RAM. That keeps the processor running at peak performance, instead of forcing it to slow down while it waits for data to arrive from the main memory.

Many Mac systems can accept cache RAM upgrades that are placed in a special cache RAM slot on the logic board. Check your manual to see if your Mac has a socket for cache RAM. If it does, you can upgrade it the same as you would a regular RAM module. Just shop for a cache RAM module for your particular Mac model instead of a regular RAM module. (Cache RAM is usually much more expensive than regular RAM. A megabyte of RAM can cost $3–$5, whereas 512 kilobytes of cache RAM can cost $25–$75, depending on the Mac model.)

Other Macs, especially older models, can accept a cache PDS card, which usually helps to speed the machine up by 10 to 20 percent or so. If you're pretty sure you aren't interested in investing in a processor upgrade that fits in the PDS slot of your Mac II series machine (or if you have a model that can't be upgraded by a PDS processor card), you might want to pop in a cache RAM PDS card to get a decent speed increase over regular performance.

Note

You can't really do much about the cache in a G3 system, as most G3 processors use a backside cache that's built onto the computer's daughtercard. But in earlier Power Macs, a decent-sized level 2 cache is a *must*, even with Performa models and some others in which Apple didn't originally install a cache module. If you have a Performa 6000 series Mac or a Power Macintosh of any type with no cache or only 128- or 256K of cache, you should seriously consider upgrading to 512K or 1MB of cache. Your PowerPC will thank you.

Summary

✦ If you want speed when you're using your applications and the Mac's Finder, then upgrading your processor is certainly one way to do that. Actually, adding RAM is usually the first step, but many Mac models can be upgraded to handle a processor that's a generation ahead of the processor originally shipped with the machine. Not only can that speed things up, but such an upgrade might even enable you to use a Mac OS version that has been upgraded so that it no longer supports your original machine. (This was true of 68030-based Macs and Mac OS 8.0 and above, which no longer support those earlier Macs, but do support some of those Macs when they're upgraded to 68040 processors.)

✦ There are four different types of processor upgrade: expansion card upgrades, processor upgrades, daughtercard upgrades, and logic board upgrades. Expansion cards and daughtercards are the easiest, whereas processor upgrades are the most delicate and logic board upgrades are the toughest. That last trade-off is worth something, though, because a logic board upgrade is the only upgrade that can give you *all* the features of a new Mac, like support for more RAM, built-in AV features (if they exist), and other extras.

✦ Upgrading with an expansion card or daughtercard is easy, but you should really think twice before performing a processor or logic board upgrade on your own. If you're not mechanically inclined — or if you're simply not inclined to risk ruining a card worth thousands of dollars — consult an Apple

Authorized Service center and see if they can upgrade it for you quickly and safely.

✦ RAM is even more important than processor upgrades, if only because the fastest processor out there needs the breathing room that enough RAM affords it. RAM and processor upgrades go hand-in-hand. Plus, RAM is one of the easiest internal upgrades there is. Cache RAM isn't much tougher, and it can easily boost your Mac's performance in an appreciable way.

✦   ✦   ✦

Hard Drives

At one time, hard drives were incredibly expensive components and it was difficult for the average user to afford upgrading one. Instead, energy would be focused on external removable drives, floppies, and tape backup. A few years ago, Mac users pined for software solutions that would compress data and applications while working with them, saving precious hard drive space.

I'm not trying to be cavalier about this, but you should forget all that stuff. Hard drives are really cheap these days. Although removable drives are definitely still a good idea, you should feel much more free about upgrading your Mac's hard drive capacity when you reach your current limits. The drives are much cheaper these days, and there's really no way to get faster storage options for your Mac.

This can be really important if the Mac is going to be used for graphics manipulation, desktop publishing, or multimedia work. Fast, huge drives are necessary for those of us who play with audio on a daily basis — not to mention people creating video presentations, professional advertising layouts and building kiosk presentations or burning CD-ROMs. All these applications can require tons of hard drive space.

In addition, you'll need some speed. Hard drive upgrades can easily be tailored to the individual user, allowing you to focus on simply adding more space, adding space for use in professional multimedia, adding space for use in a workgroup server situation or adding space for the ultimate in speed and security. Each technology gets progressively more complicated, but I'll try to wade through them all, and you can go as deep as you want to go. Whether you're just upgrading a home system or looking to add a video-editing studio to your mix of Mac tasks, there's a hard drive upgrade to help you.

Hard Drive Types and Upgrades

It's perfectly amazing how much hard drive space one person can use these days. My current machine has 6GB of hard drive space, and the LAN in my office features about 20GB of space on which I can drop files for backup, archiving, and transferring between the different Macs. This book alone has over 75MB of space dedicated to it to handle all the digital images and screenshots. And that doesn't even include the CD-ROM's contents, which are being developed on yet another Mac.

Whereas the purpose of most of the storage upgrades in my office has been to add space (I've added internal and external drives to these Macs, most of the time just to get a little more room for regular documents and applications), I've also had to prioritize the types of hard drives, the speed of their interfaces, and the amount of space dedicated to such activities as digital imaging and audio production. For some jobs, hard drives need to be *faster*, not just bigger. In other cases, the drives need to be easier to work with and more convenient.

Although it may not seem so, there are actually a number of different types of hard drive upgrades, and just as many reasons to perform a hard drive upgrade in the first place. It's important to know not just the technologies involved in hard drive upgrades, but the actual reasons for upgrading. You'll also need a little information on how to upgrade your particular machine; refer to Table 7-1, which appears later in this section.

Reasons to upgrade

Aside from the obvious ("I need more space!"), you probably have some specific reasons in mind for upgrading. Let's take a look at those reasons, and then consider the types of hard drive technologies best suited for solving your problem.

✦ *I need more space for my home/home-office/small-business computer.* In this case, you probably just need to store more documents, newer programs, or more e-mail. Depending on your computer system, you have two or three choices. First, you can upgrade the drive that's currently your main, internal hard drive. Second, you can add an additional hard drive internally, if your computer has that capacity. Third, you can add an external hard drive using the SCSI connector on the back of your Mac. In any of these cases, you'll need a basic IDE or SCSI hard drive, depending on the technology used in your Mac.

✦ *I need more space for professional images, desktop layout, or multimedia.* This midrange need means you require a faster drive than the average, but you don't exactly have a contract with Disney yet (that is, you're not doing any heavy-duty video or audio editing). In this case, you want to focus on the available SCSI technology in your computer. If it has an internal hard drive option, chances are it offers you fairly speedy SCSI connections inside the machine. Determine exactly what type of SCSI that is, and then get a hard drive to match.

✦ *I need space for editing digital video, digital audio, and crazy stuff like that.* This time maybe you do have a contract with Disney (or Pixar). Your Mac's built-in SCSI technologies may not suffice. Instead, you're likely going to call in the heavy guns — an upgrade card that features Fast, Wide, or Ultra SCSI technologies. You'll then need to get a drive to match it. Of course, you should make sure your Mac doesn't already feature some advanced SCSI before you jump out there and spend money on an upgrade card.

✦ *I'm really serious about high-end digital work.* Look into an AV drive — not just a high-speed drive, but a drive that actually only allows data to be written sequentially. These drives act a little like tape recording mechanisms: They lay every piece of data down right after the last bit. That way, the drive doesn't skip around to find more space. They're also a bit tougher to work with and can't be used for anything other than audio and video production. (These AV drives are less common these days, what with the faster speeds available in general-purpose SCSI drives and RAID setups.)

✦ *You won't believe my high-speed, huge-capacity needs.* If you're in this boat, whether it's for digital work or high-end serving needs, you might need to consider a Redundant Array of Inexpensive Disks (RAID) that can either speed up your access, maintain the security of your data or a little of both. RAIDs use special software to mirror data on a number of different high-speed disks at once, enabling the disks to share the load necessary to speed up saves. They're also good for mirroring data on different drives, so that a single drive failure can't pull down your digital editing bay or your file server. This is complex stuff, no doubt.

Hard drive technologies

After determining why you want to upgrade, the next step is figuring out how to upgrade. You'll need a quick primer, though, so you know exactly what to look for when you're shopping for your hard drive upgrade. (You may also need a new hard drive interface card, especially if you're looking to move up to some professional-level artistry.) Not only do different Macs rely on different drive technologies, but they can even rely on different levels within those technologies, such as the increasingly powerful levels of the SCSI standard.

IDE technology

IDE stands for *Integrated Drive Electronics*, and it represents a speedy but less expensive drive technology that Apple has only recently begun using. Seeing some action in PowerPC-based Performa machines, IDE gained popularity by being included in the Performa 6400, Power Macintosh 6500, and the early G3-level Power Macintosh computers.

IDE is actually the most popular Intel-compatible drive technology, which makes the drives a bit less expensive while allowing them to be comparable in speed to standard SCSI drives. (SCSI, discussed in the next section, is the prevailing standard in the Mac industry). A lot of Mac veterans scoff at IDE, but the derision is only partly warranted. Having SCSI in a Mac is a definite advantage, because it's a bit easier to add SCSI devices than it is to add IDE devices, and you can add more SCSI devices to a single Mac. SCSI also tends to be a bit quicker and is more extensible — high-end SCSI technologies can offer very high transfer speeds.

Apple has mitigated most of these disadvantages, however. The IDE drives that ship with Apple's Macs can be a bit slower, but they're usually tolerable. IDE expansion in Macs is usually severely limited — most Macs that ship with IDE drives don't offer any additional drive bays. And nearly every Mac that's ever shipped with an IDE drive still offers a SCSI interface, so you can upgrade using SCSI drives. So it's not as scary as some folks think.

If you do need to buy an IDE drive as a replacement drive for your system (check Table 7-1 later in this chapter to see if your Mac features IDE technology), you'll want to know a couple of tidbits about Apple's implementation of IDE. In many cases you'll probably shop for an IDE drive from a retailer or mail-order house that sells IDE drives for Intel-compatible PCs. If this is the case, you'll need to watch out for some of the ways Macs integrate IDE technology that differ slightly from the Intel-compatible world:

✦ Apple's internal IDE hard drives use the standard 40-pin ribbon connector found in Intel-compatible computers.

✦ You can use IDE drives made by other companies as long as they support the *identify* command, work at least at *PIO mode 2* performance level, and have *write caching* turned on. The most important distinction, though, is the drive must support Logical Block Addressing (LBA). This allows IDE drives to get past an inherent 520MB limit. Be sure to ask the retailer or the manufacturer of the drive if these settings are all available in the particular drive you're considering — for the most part, they're very common default settings.

✦ Some early Mac systems that include IDE drives (Apple specifically mentions the PowerBook 150, Macintosh 630 series, and Power Macintosh 5200/75 LC) employ an internal IDE controller that may limit those machines to using the first 2GB of their IDE drive (assuming you install one rated higher than 2GB). Newer Macs shouldn't suffer from this limit as long as the drive is otherwise compatible. For instance, the Macintosh G3 series originally shipped with 4- and 6MB IDE options.

✦ In the Power Macintosh G3 and below, Apple doesn't specifically support any of the high-speed IDE interface standards like Ultra-DMA. These technologies increase the speed of IDE drives in Intel-compatibles, but Apple hasn't written any drivers to support these drives.

✦ Although some Macs do have enough internal expansion to support a second IDE drive, carefully read the specifications and manual for your specific machines. In some cases — the Power Macintosh 4400 and the G3 machines, for example — the IDE bus is full, because the model has an IDE hard drive and an IDE CD-ROM drive. (The Mac's IDE interface can generally only handle two devices.) On these systems, Apple usually includes an internal SCSI adapter that enables you to add SCSI devices internally in any open drive bays.

Obviously, you could have some luck walking into an Intel-compatible-oriented store and buying a bigger IDE drive for your Macintosh. The drives used in IDE-capable Macs aren't significantly different from those used in Intel-compatibles. My one caveat: Choose a store with a good return policy. In most cases, those drives aren't tested in Macs, so any number of small issues could keep them from performing optimally.

Note

You may have heard of the unfortunately named *master/slave* configuration settings that Intel-compatible users focus on when adding or upgrading IDE devices. No such system exists in Macintosh machines that include IDE technology. Although master/slave configurations allow two different IDE devices to coexist on the same bus (one is set to be master and the other to slave, usually via a jumper or dip switch on the drives themselves), Mac systems avoid this potential headache by only allowing one IDE device per IDE bus. That's why Intel-compatibles can often support four IDE devices (in machines rated for Extended IDE capabilities) whereas Macs only support two. That means you work with fewer inexpensive IDE devices, but it also means you get to avoid setting near-microscopic jumper sleeves on the drives' control pins, a task most Mac loyalists like to leave in the Intel-compatible sphere where it belongs. (Note: This is all true at the time of writing. However, I've heard rumors that the newer Power Macintosh G3 models may have this capability. If your G3 has an internal IDE Zip drive or one was offered when you bought the G3, you may have the ability to support two IDE drives per bus. This may also be true in the future Power Macintoch models.)

Should you upgrade your internal IDE drive?

It sure can be tempting. Those IDE drives on sale in the computer stores are usually fifty to a hundred bucks cheaper than their SCSI counterparts. However, the Mac just doesn't quite support IDE like Intel-compatible PCs do. Plus, you're going to have to swap the IDE drive that's already in your machine and toss it or sell it in the classifieds: Most Macs only support one internal IDE hard drive, and any external hard drives have to be SCSI. What to do?

If you're going to be adding a significant amount of space — say you're going from 1GB of storage to 6GB — then certainly consider choosing a new IDE drive and swapping it for your existing internal IDE drive. Just be aware of all the issues surrounding such a move, like the fact that early IDE-based Macs can only address 2GB on an IDE drive. (Swapping an internal drive is covered later in this chapter.)

(continued)

(continued)

If the move isn't as significant, I'd encourage you to look into an external SCSI drive for your Mac. All Macs (barring the first few models in the mid-1980s and the iMac) support external SCSI drives, and there are two advantages to this approach. First, you keep the same startup drive that you've always had (and that Apple installed in your system), minimizing your exposure to incompatibility problems. Second, an external drive is handy and portable, giving you the option of grabbing the drive and connecting it to another Mac if your computer ever fails or if you decide to upgrade to a new machine. The downside? The external SCSI bus on most Macs operates at 5MBps, which is slower than the internal SCSI bus in many modern Macs. Fortunately, the speed difference is not terribly noticeable when compared to Apple's IDE drive performance.

SCSI technology

The old standard in the Mac world is Small Computer System Interface (SCSI) technology, which varies quite a bit from IDE in both its performance characteristics and flexibility. It also varies somewhat from IDE in terms of price, and SCSI support continues to be one reason Apple's Macintosh systems are generally priced at a premium over Intel-compatible machines that don't include SCSI capabilities. Far be it for me to editorialize, but I certainly feel the presence of SCSI is worth the extra cost.

Where IDE is limited to two internal drives (in Apple's current implementation), SCSI allows up to 7 devices to coexist on a single bus (chain of devices wired together). In Macs with two SCSI buses, that means (theoretically) 14 devices could coexist on the same Mac — a feat that IDE technology is unlikely to accomplish during this millennium, if at all. Most Macs are limited to about 6 devices, however, and SCSI headaches can be some of the worst troubleshooting for the typical Mac users or administrator, so be warned.

Note

According to Apple, the grand-poobah of SCSI was the Workgroup Server 95 (and presumably the WGS 9150), capable of dealing with a full 20 SCSI devices attached to it. Other Macs that can handle 14 include the Power Macintosh 8100/8150/9150. Newer Macs like the 7300, 7500, 7600, 8600, and 9600 can handle a theoretical 14 as well, but space limitations keep the practical limit closer to 8 or so. Earlier Macs with internal drive bays (like the Quadra and Centris series) actually used two SCSI buses, but treated them like one, meaning you still couldn't have duplicate SCSI IDs. As always, check your manual.

SCSI terms and basics

A number of terms are bandied about when discussing SCSI, so let's get the basics out of the way right now. Let me start, though, by saying that adding and troubleshooting SCSI devices (covered extensively in Chapter 23) is certainly not as difficult as some computing tasks can be. In fact, it makes perfect sense. You do need something of a grasp on the terms and concepts, though, to make sure you pull through a SCSI operation unscathed.

A SCSI *bus* is simply a data path for information to flow between the computer and peripherals. For every SCSI bus, there's a SCSI controller that's responsible for being a traffic cop for data on that bus. (Newer Macs feature dual-channel asynchronous SCSI, enabling a single controller to run two buses, but that's only mildly interesting.)

Okay, now here's a challenge for you. Pick up a book about Macs — any book about Macs — and try to figure out what I'm about to tell you. If you didn't have me, you'd tear your hair out. (Actually, *Macworld Mac Secrets, 5th Edition* by David Pogue and Joseph Schorr [IDG Books Worldwide, 1998] does a pretty good job, and not just because it's another Mac title that would look good on your bookshelf right next to this one.)

Each SCSI bus can have up to eight different SCSI IDs that are assigned to devices on the bus. Those IDs are numbered 0 through 7. On any given bus, however, only seven of the eight IDs are available, because the host Macintosh has to have one of the IDs (usually number 7) on each bus. The Mac has to be a device on the bus, after all, if it's going to talk to other devices.

So, you have seven SCSI IDs available for devices. Remember, though, that preexisting devices also rate a SCSI ID number, so your internal hard drive takes up another ID number (often number 0). An internal CD-ROM drive takes another number (usually number 3). Now, if your Mac has only one SCSI bus, you're down to five devices that you can install either internally or externally. If you have an internal Zip drive, say "see ya" to another SCSI ID.

But if your Mac has two SCSI buses, one is probably an *internal* bus and the other is an *external* bus. In this case, you need to be careful that you know not only what the SCSI ID number is for a given device, but also what bus that particular device is on. For instance, my Power Computing PowerCenter Pro not only has a regular SCSI bus for connecting internal and external peripherals, it also has an Adaptec UltraSCSI card, which offers high-speed 20MBps connections internally. This creates a second bus, meaning another set of SCSI ID numbers 0 through 7. You can see what that looks like in Figure 7-1.

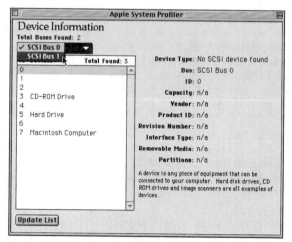

Figure 7-1: The Apple System Profiler shows two different SCSI buses, each with its own set of SCSI ID numbers.

SCSI ID numbers

When you install a new SCSI device, it has to have a new SCSI ID number. Amazing problems (data integrity problems, crashes, freezes) can result when you assign the same SCSI ID number to two different devices. That's to be avoided at all costs. Otherwise, not too many rules govern SCSI ID numbers.

Most external devices offer a small switch that enables you to change the SCSI ID number (see Figure 7-2). External devices may also have dip switch settings or a similar switch for choosing ID numbers.

Internal devices, on the other hand, usually rely on jumper settings. You place a plastic sheath over two or more tiny metal posts on the drive to choose settings. Jumpers are a barrel of laughs to play with, but important to know about if you plan to add a second drive to your Mac. Most SCSI drives come from the factory set to SCSI ID 0. However, that's no good if you're adding a second drive, because the original drive that shipped with your Mac is set to SCSI ID 0. You'll have to change the new drive's number.

In case you're wondering, there isn't much method to choosing SCSI IDs. Technically, the higher the SCSI ID, the higher the priority — but that doesn't really matter often, because the Macintosh itself is the only device that really has priority over the others. That said, if you have trouble with a SCSI drive showing up, mounting, or working as a startup disk, you might try setting it to a higher SCSI ID — or any different SCSI ID at all — and see if that changes things. (I'll cover SCSI troubleshooting extensively in Chapter 23. And I mean pages and pages worth!)

Figure 7-2: SCSI IDs are usually simple to set on external devices.

Types of SCSI

The second major concern when you want to add a SCSI device is the exact nature of the SCSI connections you have available in your Mac. These come down to the different types of SCSI technology that have been developed over the years to improve — you guessed it — the speed of the SCSI connection. I'll start, though, by complaining about how confusing this can all be.

In the SCSI world, there have been three standards: SCSI (or SCSI-1), SCSI-2 and SCSI-3. These names and numbers are, for the most part, completely irrelevant to our lives. The standards are only given names, according to rumor, so that in-the-know computer scientists can laugh at the rest of us.

More important are the SCSI transfer protocols, which coincide somewhat with the SCSI standards. It may help to know that SCSI-1 was ratified in 1985, SCSI-2 in 1990 and SCSI-3 is still a developing standard (at this writing) but seems intended only to extend the SCSI-2 standard, not replace it. The standards, then, are only interesting as dates in time. What you'll hear more often are references to the transfer protocols, as outlined here:

✦ **SCSI.** Although people use the word SCSI to mean just about any sort of SCSI device (regardless of its standards or speeds), it's probably most useful to think of SCSI as "basic SCSI," or the protocol that was part of the SCSI-1 standard. In this standard, data is transferred along 8-bit wide data paths at about 5MB per second. In this case, the SCSI bus speed is 5MHz.

✦ **Fast SCSI or Fast SCSI-2.** Part of the SCSI-2 specification, Fast SCSI is a transfer protocol that doubles the speed of basic SCSI to 10MHz, still using an 8-bit path. That results in a maximum throughput of 10MB per second.

✦ **Wide SCSI or Wide SCSI-2.** Wide SCSI interfaces use a 16-bit bus at 5MHz to transfer data. This also results in a maximum throughput of 10MB per second, but it also means that Wide SCSI buses can support up to 16 devices per bus (instead of the regular 8 devices). Wide SCSI is usually internal only, and requires a special 68-pin cable to communicate with Wide SCSI devices. (Many Wide SCSI cards also feature a 50-pin or 25-pin external connector for adding slower external SCSI devices to the bus.)

✦ **Fast/Wide SCSI or Fast/Wide SCSI-2.** Put these two SCSI-2 technologies together and you get a 16-bit bus running at 10MHz. That results in maximum transfers of 20MBps, along with support for 16 devices.

✦ **Ultra SCSI or Ultra SCSI-3.** Part of the emerging SCSI-3 standard, Ultra SCSI uses an 8-bit bus at 20MHz for a maximum transfer rate of 20MBps.

✦ **Ultra/Wide SCSI or Ultra/Wide SCSI-3.** As you might guess, this is a 20MHz, 16-bit SCSI bus capable of data transfers up to 40MBps and support for 16 devices. This also requires a 68-pin cable for the highest-speed connections.

Technically, SCSI interfaces and drives should be backward compatible. That is, a fast drive can plug into a slow interface and run at the slower speed, and, by the same token, a slow drive could also be plugged into a fast SCSI interface and continue to work. In practice, this seems to be generally true, although the early SCSI-1 devices were reportedly quite a mess (you're probably better off shying away from drives and SCSI interfaces built before the late 1980s). Of course, those drives tend to be small in capacity and cumbersome in the amount of space they take up.

What is of interest here is buying the right drive for your Mac's SCSI interface — or, if you're not happy with its built-in capabilities, maybe you want to add an upgrade card for better SCSI performance and for the ability to support faster drives. If you're not sure what SCSI technology your Mac offers, take a look at Table 7-1 later in this chapter.

SCSI cables and connections

You may already have gathered that SCSI, while high speed and only getting faster, can also be a bit temperamental. Along with Postscript font handling, many an avid Mac fan thinks of the SCSI chain as the *dark side* of a Mac's personality. It's here where even the slightest inequities can result in poor or absolutely zero performance.

FireWire: *Mega, Super, Ultra* SCSI

Even as huge drives based on the Ultra/Wide SCSI standard spew megabytes-per-second of recorded audio and video in production studios everywhere, it's still not enough. According to a recent interview I read featuring George Lucas of *Star Wars* fame, he expects that the last movie in the second trilogy of Star Wars films will be shot completely digitally—no actual film will be used. Unfortunately, says Lucas, the technology hasn't been invented quite yet to make that happen. It will be, though.

FireWire, which is less glamorously known as Serial SCSI, is the next step in SCSI technology that may help Mr. Lucas's quest. As the SCSI bus speeds up beyond 20MHz, complexities make it more practical to use serial technology (where data bits are sent one at a time) instead of parallel technology (where data bits are sent 8 or 16 at a time, hence 8-bit and 16-bit buses of traditional SCSI). Although it seems like a step backward, it isn't because the speed of a serial bus could reach beyond 1,000MHz and into the gigahertz (GHz) range. Meanwhile, parallel technology is having trouble getting past 20MHz.

FireWire is also less complex, requiring a simple 6-pin connector to operate, and it's much smarter about termination issues, which tend to be the bane of current SCSI connections. Already FireWire is emerging not just as a hard drive technology, but as a popular way to connect digital cameras to computers for transferring images. Eventually, perhaps, we'll reach throughput speeds of 50MBps, 100MBps, or something greater for these connections to finally quench the cinematographic desires of Mr. Lucas.

The biggest factors for SCSI involve the cabling used and the need for termination. Both of these can contribute to interference on the line that can ultimately bog down performance.

First, SCSI cables need to be high quality, offering the proper shielding and components. Apple points out in their Tech Info Library (located at `http://til.info.apple.com`) that poor quality cables are often responsible for seemingly mysterious SCSI problems.

Cable length is also an issue. Even though you can daisy chain SCSI devices, the overall length of a SCSI chain should never exceed 20 feet, and a chain longer than 10 feet can be problematic. For this reason, cable lengths of 12 to 24 inches are recommended between devices, with 6 feet being the absolute maximum for most devices (some devices simply won't work with cables over 24 inches long). If you need a SCSI device (for example, a scanner) to be placed farther away from your Mac than that, you should consider placing another Mac closer to it or opting for a network-based scanner that's connected by technology such as Ethernet.

Also, take note whenever you buy cabling for your SCSI devices: The external connector on your Mac uses a 25-pin connection, but many SCSI devices use the standard (called *Centronics*) 50-pin connector. In some cases, you may need to buy an adapter cable so you can hook a device to your external SCSI connector. After that, most devices can be daisy chained using 50-pin to 50-pin cables. But don't take my word for it—Iomega Zip and Jaz drives, for instance, opt for 25-pin cables. Check your devices closely to ensure you get the right cable and/or adapter.

SCSI termination

After you've connected your drives, you'll need termination. Because SCSI is capable of daisy chaining devices, the SCSI bus actually works a bit like a network, with address numbers (the SCSI IDs) allowing devices to communicate with the Macintosh itself. But the SCSI bus also needs to know its limits. When data gets to one of the ends of a SCSI chain, it "bounces" back, causing interference. Special resistors, called *terminators*, prevent this problem. The last device in a SCSI chain needs to be terminated; instead of having a cable that connects it to another device, a special terminator is plugged into (or activated) within the device so that data doesn't try to go further downline (see Figure 7-3).

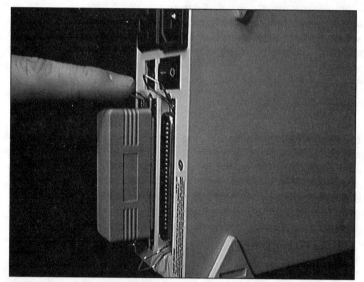

Figure 7-3: A SCSI terminator keeps stray data bits from causing interference on the line.

SCSI termination can also be important at different points in the connection. For most chains, the bus should be terminated at both ends. The exception is a chain that's less than 18 inches or so in length. (And it should probably still be terminated, just to be safe.)

For most of Mac users, that means terminating the last device in the external chain of SCSI devices. For many Macs, the internal drive acts as the first termination point, and the last external device is the second. If your SCSI chain reaches beyond 10 feet, adding a third terminator at about the 10-foot point can be useful if (and only if) you're having SCSI-related errors. If you're installing a second internal drive, there's a good chance you'll need to play with the termination settings, because your current internal drive is terminated. If you can add the internal drive in the middle of the internal SCSI chain, so much the better.

You should know a few exceptions to these rules. The Mac Plus has no internal termination (as it has no internal drive) so the *first* external SCSI device in the chain should be terminated, as should the last (but only terminate the drive once if it's your only SCSI device). The Mac IIfx requires a bizarre 200-ohm terminator that is different from every other Mac's and almost every other device (it's also used for connecting hard drives to Apple LaserWriter IIf/IIg and LaserWriter Pro 630 printers). This special terminator is black (when Apple makes it) to differentiate it from regular external terminators, which are traditionally gray.

Aside from knowing the color, you'll need to figure out what these terminators look like and how they work. SCSI terminators come in three basic flavors:

- ✦ **Built-in terminators.** These terminators are resistors built into or connected directly to the SCSI device. Generally used for internal devices, they can either be removed or switched off when another device is added to the SCSI chain. Read your documentation carefully though, as these terminators can be damaging if incorrectly reinstalled.

- ✦ **External terminator plugs.** These terminators plug into the cabling connectors on your external SCSI devices, or between the SCSI cable and a particular device's SCSI connector.

- ✦ **Logic board terminators.** These often look like memory modules. They plug into the SCSI port on the Macintosh when no internal hard drive is present. Otherwise, the hard drive's internal terminator is sufficient.

Good termination of the SCSI bus can be the difference between a no-problem upgrade and error after error. In that spirit, let me iterate and reiterate a few cautionary notes:

- ✦ Don't terminate devices twice. This can be an easy mistake to make on a device that features both built-in termination and a second SCSI connector. If you terminate at the connector while internal termination is active, you could have big problems. You could damage devices or lose data.

- ✦ Be aware that some devices offer an automatic or internal termination that can sometimes be controlled by software. Read your hard drive's manual carefully to make sure it doesn't offer some unique termination system.

✦ Check the manual on your Mac before installing a SCSI device that sends termination power (TERMPWR) to the SCSI bus. Some modern Macs don't like that at all.

✦ Look into drives and devices that offer *active termination*. This means the device will decide on its own whether or not termination is necessary under the circumstance. Often these devices (if they're designed to be installed externally) also feature an LED or readout that tells you what its termination decision was. If you're not happy with its decision, you can discipline it as necessary.

Mac books dedicate untold pages to SCSI problems and troubleshooting — and this one is no exception. Check Chapter 23 for starters, and then flip through the rest of the troubleshooting chapters in Part III for advice on troubleshooting all sorts of SCSI devices.

Add a Hard Drive

If you're ready to add some serious storage space to your Mac, a hard drive is a good bet. These days a hard drive is a cheap, effective and fast way to add gigabytes and gigabytes of storage. Although removable media and recordable CDs are okay for backup and trading data, nothing beats a high-speed hard drive for day-to-day data retrieval.

Which brings you to your first issue: How fast of a hard drive can your Mac handle? Specifically, you're interested in knowing the drive technology you'll want to use for your new drive (IDE or SCSI) and, if it's a SCSI connection, what transfer technology it uses (Fast SCSI, Wide SCSI, Ultra SCSI, and so on). Armed with this knowledge, you'll have a better idea of which drive to buy.

And you'll want to decide whether to upgrade internally or externally. If you've been reading this chapter from the beginning, you may already be aware of these advantages and disadvantages:

✦ **External.** External drives communicate more slowly with your Mac than do internal drives most of the time (very early Macs had similar speeds both internally and externally). External drives are easy to install, portable, and usually have cool external cases (see Figure 7-4).

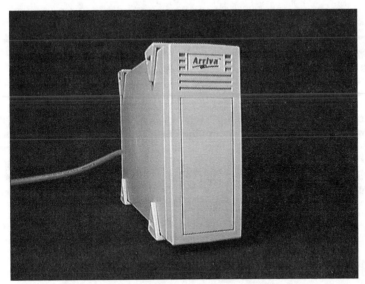

Figure 7-4: An external hard drive will have its own casing, power cable, and obvious SCSI connectors and SCSI ID controls.

✦ **Internal.** Internal drives can be faster, can use advanced SCSI technologies, and don't add another box to your computer setup. You'll need an extra drive bay in your Mac, though, and internal drives can be much tougher to add, usually requiring a screwdriver, good lighting and, in some cases, plenty of patience. In addition, internal drives are naked compared to external drives, showing up without plastic cases and LED indicators.

Evangelista tip: External hard drives

What if you feel like adding an internal drive, but you want an enclosure for your old internal drive so that it can live a second life as an external drive? Well, you can call one of those hard drive specialists in the marketplace ads in the back of *Macworld*, but there's another way. Here's a hint from Kevin Patfield, one of the corp of elite Evangelistas out there on the Internet who give solid advice to Mac users:

"This one's pretty obvious, yet I still see people asking about it. The question usually goes something like this: 'Where's the best place to buy an enclosure for a hard disk? I've just installed a new quintillion gigabyte internal in my Mac and I'd like to use my old quadrillion gigabyte drive as an external.' The answer is to first buy an *external* drive and swap it with the original internal drive. This is almost always cheaper than buying an internal drive and an enclosure. It has an additional advantage in that you can easily back up everything onto your new drive before you even reach for a screwdriver."

(continued)

(continued)

One caveat is that not all internal drives will fit in external enclosures. When you buy the external drive enclosure, ask the vendor or manufacturer if it's designed to accept a standard 3.5" hard drive from your Mac. If the vendor knows Macs and Mac upgrading, you should be able to get a straight answer to this question.

Also, realize that the drive in your Mac is often an Apple-specific drive that uses Apple's hard disk driver software. Replacing it with another drive isn't impossible, but it does add another layer of complexity, requiring you to update the driver software without help from Apple's Mac OS installation CDs, for instance. You may also have trouble getting Apple's included utilities (such as Disk First Aid) to troubleshoot the drive, so you'll need to have the drive's own utilities handy at all times. (Make sure you have a backup diskette or bootable CD-ROM that includes those utilities.)

What hard drive should you buy?

The short answer: You'll probably want to buy a Fast SCSI drive for upgrading most Macs in most situations. If you're looking at a need for serious high-speed data transfers, you might want an Ultra/Wide SCSI card and an Ultra/Wide SCSI drive to go with it. If you're replacing an internal drive, you'll need a new drive that uses the same technology (IDE or SCSI) as the old drive. If you want an external drive, it's probably going to be a plain SCSI model, unless you buy a special upgrade card that enables you to hook up an external Wide SCSI drive.

The longer answer: When you go on your quest for a hard drive, you'll need to be armed with a little information. First, does your Mac accept IDE hard drives, SCSI hard drives, or both? If you'll be upgrading externally, you need a SCSI drive, and most likely you can get away with a slower drive — most Macs' SCSI ports still transfer data at SCSI-1 speeds. New Macs are an exception, especially those that feature SCSI on an expansion card instead of built into the motherboard. Check your manual; your SCSI card may transfer data externally at Fast SCSI or even Ultra/Wide SCSI speeds, so you'll want to buy a hard drive to match. Remember, any sort of Wide SCSI requires a 64-pin connector.

The fact that you need this information can only mean one thing — it's chart time. Table 7-1 has the details about the various Mac models and the info you need to upgrade your hard drive, including whether or not there's room for an internal hard drive and what technology the Mac's main drive uses. Because all Macs (aside from the first two) offer a 5MBps SCSI port externally, that information isn't included in the chart.

Note The iMac, Apple's recently announced all-in-one consumer Macintosh, doesn't support any sort of external SCSI. Other consumer Mac models may follow suit in the future.

Table 7-1 Hard Drive Upgrade Paths for Major Mac OS Models			
Model	**Main Drive**	**Available Bays?**	**Internal SCSI Speed**
Mac 128, 512, Plus	None	No	N/AN/A
Mac Classic series (includes, SE, Plus, and so on)	SCSI	No	5MBps
Mac II series, Quadra 700	SCSI	No	5MBps
LC series.C/Q605, Performa 400 series	SCSI	No	5MBps
Mac IIvi, IIvx, Q/C650, 0 Performa 600, WGS70; PM 7100, WGS 715	SCSI	5.25"[1]	5MBps
C/Q610, 660AV, PM6100, Performa 6100 series	SCSI	5.25"[1]	5MBps
Q630, Performa 630, LC 630, 6200, 6300 series	IDE	No	N/A
Q800, 840AV, PM 8100, WGS 8150	SCSI	5.25"[1], 3.5"	5MBps
Q900/950, WGS 90, PM 9500; WGS 9150	SCSI	5.25"[1], two 3.5"	10MBps
Performa 6400, PM 6500	IDE[2]	5.25"	5MBps
LC/Performa 500 series; MacTV	SCSI[3]	No	5MBps
Performa/PM 5200/5300	IDE	No	N/A
PM 7200, 7300, 7500, 7600, WGS 7250/7350, 8500	SCSI	3.5"[4]	10MBps
G3 Desktop, G3 Desktop Server	IDE[2]	3.5"[4]	5MBps
PM 8600, 9600	SCSI	Three 5.25"[4]	10MBps
G3 Minitower; G3 Minitower Server	IDE[2]	Three 5.25"[4]	5MBps

(continued)

Table 7-1 *(continued)*

Model	Main Drive	Available Bays?	Internal SCSI Speed
Power Computing			
Low-profile systems	SCSI	3.5″[14](5)	See below
Desktop systems	SCSI	5.25″, 3.5″[14](5)	See below
Minitower systems	SCSI	two 5.25″, 3.5″ [14](5)	See below
PowerCurve, PowerBase; PowerCenter	SCSI	See cases above	5MBps
Power, PowerWave, PowerTower	SCSI	See cases above	10MBps
PowerCenter Pro	SCSI	See cases above	20MBps
Motorola			
Desktop systems	SCSI	Varies	Varies
Minitower systems	SCSI	Varies	Varies
UMAX			
c500 series	IDE	None	N/A
c600 series	IDE[2]	Two 5.25″, two 3.5″	5MBps
j700 series	SCSI	5.25″, 3.5″	10MBps
s900 series	SCSI	5.25″, three 3.5″	10MBps

1 One 5.25″ bay filled by factory CD-ROM on certain models.

2 Internal expansion bays are prewired for SCSI devices.

3 IDE on 580 series models.

4 One available bay is filled by a factory Zip drive on certain models.

5 Power Computing machines allow two half-height drives to fit in each full-height bay, so only half of the listed bay may be available, depending on configuration. (Nearly all Power Computing machines can accept an additional 3.5″ SCSI hard drive, assuming a power connector is available.)

If you plan to add a drive to your Mac (instead of simply replacing the old drive) you'll probably need to buy a SCSI drive, even if your Mac uses IDE technology. In every case I've encountered, a Mac using IDE features an internal SCSI connection for additional drives if that model supports additional internal drives. (Check your Mac's manual.) And, as always, external drives are SCSI every time.

So, in just about every Mac out there, you'll probably be upgrading with a SCSI drive, and, unless your Mac has a special Ultra/Wide SCSI card or a similar upgrade, you'll most likely be fine if you buy a Fast SCSI hard drive. (They're as cheap as any other drive.) Focus on the 50-pin connector, even for an internal drive. That'll most likely work in nearly any Mac you could get your hands on.

If you own a G3 Macintosh or a UMAX S900 (among a few others), you might have a 68-pin Ultra/Wide card — it's a popular build-your-own upgrade for these machines. Check your documentation. If you do have one of these cards, you'll likely want to buy a higher-end Wide SCSI drive for better performance.

Note

Read the documentation that came with your Ultra/Wide SCSI card carefully. Some of these cards offer 68-pin ports externally as well, yet they sometimes can't handle an actual external device because of wiring limitations. The original G3 Ultra/Wide upgrade card is an example of one of these cards that limits you to internal Wide SCSI upgrades.

Finally, owners of clone machines that use PC-style cases should be warned of one other caveat: Just because you have a free drive bay doesn't necessarily mean you'll have a SCSI connector and/or a power cable that can be used for that drive bay. However, you can buy a power connector splitter from your local computer store that will increase the number of peripherals you can connect. (Plus, you should be able to get SCSI ribbon cables that offer more connectors, as long as you limit your SCSI IDs to the number available to your Mac.) You'll want to check the rating on your power supply before adding too many power splitters, though, to make sure you're not adding more of a power drain than your Mac can handle.

Do you need a new SCSI card?

In most cases, you don't need any new expansion cards for your Mac. If it has an available internal drive bay, you should also have an available internal SCSI connector. Even if you don't have an available drive bay, you can always hook up an external SCSI drive, if you have any SCSI ID numbers left on your SCSI bus. With most Mac models, you should have an available SCSI ID if you don't have seven SCSI devices, including internal drives, already hooked up.

Tip

If you do have a full SCSI bus, or if you're interested in a high-speed SCSI connection, you should look into a SCSI expansion card.

You can find SCSI cards for most Macs, including versions for NuBus and PCI expansion slots. (PDS cards are more rare, but you'll find them through specialty shops and Macintosh classified/used sources.) Look for a card that offers the level of SCSI performance that you're interested in — Fast, Fast/Wide, Ultra, and so on.

Once you've got the card, you shouldn't have much trouble installing it. The process is the same as for almost any upgrade card:

1. Shut down your Mac and electrically ground yourself.

2. Open the Mac's case and locate an empty expansion slot. (Visually inspect it to ensure it's the right type of slot for your card.)

3. Remove the screw and metal dust plate that covers the hole in back of the case for the slot you'll be using.

4. Position the card so that its interface is directly over the slot. If it's a NuBus card, make sure the card's housing fits over the NuBus slot on the logic board. If it's a PDS or a PCI card, make sure the card's connector fits snugly in the slot.

5. Press down lightly and uniformly on the top corners of the expansion card until it's firmly installed in the slot.

Note

Be sure the card is fully installed in the slot. If one end is higher than the other, parts of the connector may not be making proper contact, and the card will fail to work.

6. Attach the SCSI cable. The red line on the SCSI cable should line up with the left side of the SCSI connector on the card itself (see Figure 7-5).

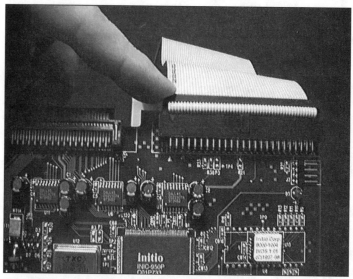

Figure 7-5: You'll need to hook the SCSI cable up to the SCSI card correctly so you can install additional SCSI devices.

7. Try restarting your Mac while the case is still off and see if the card is recognized. You may need to install a software driver or extension that enables you to control the card.

Use the Apple System Profiler to check for the presence of the card — you should find that installing a SCSI upgrade card created a new SCSI bus (probably SCSI bus 1 or 2). Notice also the bus is completely empty, except for the Macintosh, which is automatically assigned SCSI ID 7. The Apple System Profiler is installed with Mac OS 8.0 and above, or you can use the link on the CD-ROM to download it from Apple's Internet servers.

Upgrading and installing a hard drive

Whether or not you've installed a new SCSI card, you may be itching to create more storage space by adding an internal hard drive to your Mac's case. It's easy enough to do, as long as you have everything you need to get started. First, you'll need to make sure your Mac is ready for the upgrade, and that includes considering some important SCSI issues. If you're just planning to replace your older drive, you'll want to take out your old drive.

Before you install the drive

You should know about a few important issues before you remove or install a hard drive. The first two focus on SCSI, but note that the second two are applicable to IDE and SCSI. Here are some preliminaries:

✦ Using a program like the Apple System Profiler or any SCSI probing software that comes with your new SCSI drive, check to see what SCSI ID numbers are available in your Macintosh. If you'll be replacing the internal drive, its number is likely SCSI ID 0. Otherwise, you'll want to pick an available number for this additional drive. (Actually, you should probably make note of two or three SCSI ID numbers that are available, just in case you run into big problems that make it difficult to get back into the System Profiler program.)

✦ Shut down your Mac, ground yourself, open the case and take a look inside. Make sure the Mac has a free drive bay for your installation. Also make sure a SCSI connection (usually in the middle of the SCSI ribbon cable) and a free power connector are available.

✦ Also make a visual confirmation that the bay you have is the correct size for your drive. A standard 3.5" drive can fit in any available bay (unless it's a PowerBook's drive bay), but a 5.25" drive needs a 5.25" bay. (If you have a 3.5" drive destined for a 5.25" bay, you'll need to get an adapter or mounting kit for the drive.)

✦ Take a look at how your Mac is designed for installation of the drive. Notice, for instance, the sort of mechanism that's used to slide the drive in and out of its bay. You'll need this sort of kit (it may be included with your drive or available from a Macintosh dealer) to complete the upgrade. Some drives simply screw into a drive cage inside the machine. Others require more elaborate plastic or metal guides or rails (see Figure 7-6). If you have trouble finding an appropriate mounting kit, try Proline Distribution (www.proline.com) or an online Mac-oriented store.

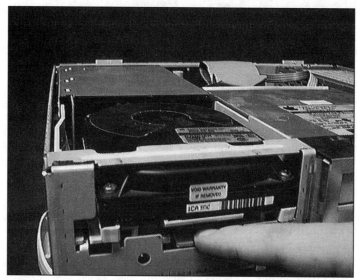

Figure 7-6: Many Macs take a high-end approach to hard drive mounting hardware. One type is released by pressing down on a plastic tab, and then sliding the drive forward.

Caution   If you're replacing your older, main startup drive with a new one, don't forget that the new drive is going to need a Mac OS System Folder on it so that it can load the Mac OS for you once you have it installed. Of course, you can also use a Mac OS or utilities CD-ROM to boot your system, but be sure you have the hard drive utilities you need handy (on floppy disk or bootable CD-ROM) so you can use them to format and partition the drive.

Remove the old drive

Removing an older hard drive so you can install a newer one is a fairly simple process. If you don't plan to use the old drive anymore, you can even use the same hardware to install your new drive. Here's the procedure:

1. Shut down your Mac, unplug it, ground yourself, and remove the case.

2. Find the original hard drive and take a look at the type of guide attached to the drive bay.

3. Remove the SCSI (or IDE) cable and the power connector from the back of the drive (see Figure 7-7). Always grab the connector and pull—don't yank on the cables or wires.

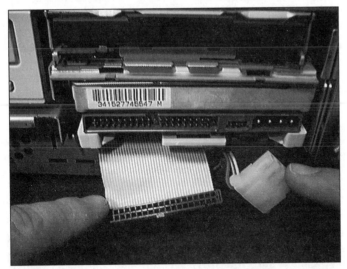

Figure 7-7: Remove the connectors gently from the drive. Note their orientation for installation of the new drive.

4. If necessary, unscrew any retaining screws holding the drive to its drive bay (quick-release plastic drive rails won't have any screws to worry about.)

5. Release the drive from its drive bay and slide it out of the bay. Depending on your Mac model, you may find that sliding the drive out of the front of its bay is easier, even if the cables are hooked up at the back of the bay (see Figure 7-8).

Figure 7-8: Once the drive is unfettered, slide it straight out of its bay.

There's really nothing else to do. If you are replacing an old drive with a new one, remove the guide rails from the drive and attach them to the new drive. (You may have trouble getting them to fit, in which case you should contact the vendor or manufacturer to see if they have a kit for your particular Mac model.)

SCSI installation

Installing a SCSI drive is basically the reverse of removing one, except you'll need to worry a bit about the drive's SCSI ID and its termination. Here are the rules:

✦ If you removed your original SCSI drive, you'll need to make sure your new drive is terminated (it may be auto-terminating or it may require an additional step — check your drive's manual). You probably *won't* have to change the SCSI ID on the drive, because most internal SCSI drives come set to SCSI ID 0. (You should still double-check, though.)

✦ If you didn't remove your old drive, make sure you're installing your drive in the *middle* of the SCSI ribbon cable. If you are, termination shouldn't be necessary, so make sure your drive *isn't* terminated (check the drive's manual for termination details). You will need to set a unique SCSI ID, probably using jumpers (see Figure 7-9).

Figure 7-9: You'll probably have to check the drive's manual carefully for the jumper settings that enable you to change SCSI ID numbers.

✦ Install the correct rails. You'll need to attach your new drive to a drive bay, either by screwing it into place (this is more likely on non-Apple machines) or getting some guide rails that help you slide the drive into place. If the latter's the case, get the proper installation kit for your Mac, and then screw it onto the drive.

Connecting the drive

Finally, you're ready to install the SCSI or IDE drive. This will most likely be anti-climactic, because it's not tough once you've got everything set correctly:

1. Make sure your Mac is shut down, unplugged, and you're electrically grounded. Remove the Mac's case.

2. Slide the new drive into an available drive bay. *Note:* There's usually an upside and downside for the drive. It's unlikely to cause a problem from being installed upside down, though it'll probably be tough to install it upside down if your Mac uses guide rails. But take a glance at your manual and make sure you have the drive facing the correct direction, just to be sure you're installing it correctly. Also, the drive should be installed with its SCSI or IDE interface and power ports facing the interface and power cables. On some Macs the cables are actually near the front of the drive bay—and therefore near the front of the case—instead of at the back of the drive bay.

3. Connect the SCSI or IDE cable to the drive. Make sure you orient the cable correctly, with the red stripe on the SCSI or IDE cable lining up with the leftmost Pin 1 on the connector.

4. Connect the power wires to the drive. They can only be installed in one direction, so if you have trouble plugging the connector into the drive, try flipping it over.

5. Make sure the drive is firmly seated in its bay and reinstall any protective metal plates that cover the drive bay.

You can test the drive with the Mac's case still off, but shut your Mac down again and replace the case once you're sure everything is working.

Working with the new drive

If you're lucky, you were able to get a hard drive that came preformatted for Macintosh computers. Once it boots up and *mounts,* or appears on your Mac's desktop, you can simply double-click its icon and start using it (there may even be some software utilities already on the drive). Check your manual to determine whether your drive was preformatted for Macintosh.

If the drive isn't Mac-formatted, you may be asked by your Mac if you want to erase the disk. This formats it for the first time—you can click OK if you're absolutely sure the dialog box is referring to the new drive. The Format menu item should give you a clue by showing you the capacity of the drive. Click Cancel if you'd prefer to run some other formatting or hard drive utility software.

Getting info off the older drive

If you're upgrading your system by replacing your older drive, you may be concerned about transferring data between the two drives. After all, on many Macs there's only room for one internal drive. What are your options?

The best plan is to back up the data from the original drive to an Iomega Jaz cartridge, a recordable CD, or something similar. Copy all the data you need to one of these GB-sized solutions, and then copy it all back to the new drive once everything is installed. If you don't have such a removable drive and you can't borrow or rent one, you have another interesting solution.

If your Mac has a built-in CD-ROM drive, use this sneaky little tactic to solve this problem. Just unhook your CD-ROM drive and uninstall it, and then reinstall your older hard drive in the CD-ROM drive's place. You don't really need to install the guide rails and get it all to fit perfectly—just make sure the drive won't fall, get liquid spilled on it, or get knocked around, and then hook up the SCSI or IDE cable and power connector. Fire up your Mac and copy data between the two drives. Immediately afterward, disconnect the drive and reconnect the CD-ROM drive. (Note that this sort of configuration is never a long-term solution.)

If you're using SCSI drives, one additional word of caution—don't forget to choose an available SCSI ID for the older drive, as it's not the main disk (ID 0) anymore. If you're temporarily replacing the internal CD-ROM, ID 3 should be available.

Most likely your new drive came with drive utilities to help you get up and on your way, such as Apple's Drive Setup (for Apple-branded hard drives), Silverlining, or the FWB Toolkit for third-party drives. Such a program will enable you to set all sorts of parameters, including the number of partitions (virtual hard drives) you're going to create, their capacities and whether or not they'll support other computer formats (like Apple II ProDOS or Intel-compatible DOS formats).

If you don't have much experience formatting and partitioning hard drives, you might want to flip to Chapter 23 and read about your options.

Adding a RAID

If you have serious multimedia or server storage needs, a single hard drive—even a large, fast, wide, and rather handsome SCSI drive—may not be enough. Instead, you may be ripe for a Redundant Array of Inexpensive Drives or a RAID.

There are two basic reasons to have a RAID: speed and data integrity. Using two or more drives, RAID software is capable of writing data in parallel over two different SCSI buses, which is reason number one to have a second SCSI card or a dual-channel Mac such as a Quadra 900/950 or a Power Mac 8600 or 9600. Writing data this way—it's called *data striping*—allows you to store data at twice the rate of a single SCSI drive. For speed, RAIDs are generally used by graphics, publishing, scientific, and film professionals.

You can also set up a RAID to offer *data mirroring*, which simply means the software writes every file to each individual drive at the same time. If one drive goes down or breaks, the other is there as a backup. Data mirroring is an obvious favorite for servers, especially Web commerce servers or workgroup servers that have a mission-critical responsibility to keep a company or organization running.

Either way, the RAID appears on your desktop as a single drive, even though you'll need two drives or more to create it. You'll also need to buy Ultra/Wide or Fast/Wide drives; for the most part, it's pointless to set up a RAID with slow drives. After all, you want to get speeds *faster* than are currently available from the fastest SCSI-3 drives by using two or more in tandem.

Setting up RAID

RAID software offers different *levels* that correspond to the type of RAID you'll be creating. RAID level 0 is data striping. RAID level 1 is data mirroring, and RAID levels 2 through 5 are combinations of the two, either to speed up data mirroring or add more physical drives to increase the speed or data integrity.

If you don't already have RAID software (Apple includes AppleRAID or SoftRAID on WorkGroup Server systems and in other server software bundles they sell), you'll need to get some. An example of RAID software is Conley's SoftRAID, driver software that enables you to take two or more high-speed drives and use them for data striping or mirroring. You may also need a second SCSI card (or a RAID-specific SCSI card) for your system, such as Initio's Miles card (www.initio.com), which includes SoftRAID (see Figure 7-10).

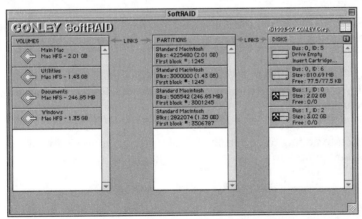

Figure 7-10: SoftRAID software makes it easy to install and monitor a RAID for high-speed and data-sensitive operations.

Using SoftRAID, you can set up flexible RAID situations, using drives on separate SCSI buses or on the same bus. The process is straightforward: You install new drivers for each physical hard drive, and then you (usually) initialize the drive. With that accomplished, you create partitions on the drives that you can use for mirroring or striping other paritions. Finally, you tell SoftRAID which partition is for what purpose, and then let it do its work.

Note

As much as it seems like it, RAIDs really aren't a good substitute for a backup system. For one, a RAID writes the same data to both drives (when mirroring), including data you might not want written to both drives — for example, a virus. Also, a catastrophic system error, configuration problem, or a partially saved document appears on both drives. And one drive in a RAID will rarely enable you to reload an earlier version of something you've deleted. You'll need a solid backup strategy for your system as well as a RAID for total data security.

Summary

✦ You've got two different types of hard drive technology in the Mac-compatible world: IDE and SCSI. Although Macs have historically used SCSI, IDE is becoming popular as a low-cost alternative. Because IDE is the Intel-compatible standard, it's easier to find and usually cheaper than comparable SCSI drives. SCSI technology is much more flexible, so all Macs still incorporate some SCSI connections, even if their main drives are IDE-based.

✦ SCSI can be both amazing and annoying at the same time. There's a lot to know about the technology to connect a drive successfully, including how the SCSI ID numbering system works, how SCSI devices are connected, and how to properly terminate a chain of SCSI devices. You may also want to know the different types of SCSI technology so you can get the best one (or fastest one) that suits your needs.

✦ Before you can buy the drive, though, you'll need to know what your Mac can handle. This chapter's chart shows you the type of technology your Mac's main drive uses, what other drive technologies are available to you, and whether you'll be able to add an internal drive.

✦ Finally, it's on to adding the drive. Electrically ground yourself, follow the guidelines, and jump into your system and add that storage space!

✦   ✦   ✦

CD-ROMs, Recordable CDs, and DVD

Just as the audio compact disc (CD) replaced the LP record in most home stereos (assuming the current vinyl comeback remains the domain of audiophiles), the CD-ROM (short for compact disc — read only memory) has slowly taken over the duties once reserved for floppy disks. CD-ROMs are the standard for delivering new applications to computer users, as well as the basis for nearly all games, multimedia titles, art libraries, sound collections, and utilities.

Computer-related CD technology has been upgraded and updated constantly to make it faster, more reliable and more widely applicable. A big part of increasing the usability of the standard has been to add recording capabilities to drives that use CD media. This enables individuals and workgroups to create archives of data on long-lasting CD media, as well as creating their own low-cost CDs for distribution.

You may even find you have reason to create your own audio CDs or data CD-ROMs, whether you're recording as a music professional, cutting the first CD for your garage band, or creating a CD-ROM of reference data for your volunteer organization. The technology exists for doing this affordably, and it's not at all difficult to integrate such technologies into your Macintosh setup.

The latest CD-like technology, DVD (digital versatile disc is the definition for this acronym, although the industry has yet to agree on a standard definition), is growing in leaps and bounds, promising to offer unprecedented storage space on a disc the same size as a CD. This is not only opening up CD-like technology to more storage options, but it's making it possible to deliver better-than-ever multimedia — even full-length movies — for playback on DVD set-top players and DVD computer peripherals.

This chapter covers the basics of CD technology including CD-ROM, recordable CDs, and CDs that can be written to over and over again. You'll also see how to install an internal or external CD-ROM drive, how to add CD recording technology to your Mac, and how to use CD recording software. Finally, you'll take a look at CD-ROM toolkit and acceleration software you can add to your Mac.

CD Technologies

The basic idea behind an audio CD (take digital music data and press it onto a disc that is then read by a laser) has been manipulated, cajoled, and extended by computer peripheral manufacturers into the computing CD standards of today. Today's CD-ROM and related technologies offer higher access speeds, quick transmission of data, and a nonlinear data retrieval option that is more convenient than many comparable technologies. Additionally, recent times have shown that the overall price of CD-related technology — especially for individual recording of CDs — has come down incredibly over the past months and years.

CDs and DVDs of all sorts have made a strong showing in computing and other consumer electronics tasks. If you don't already have a CD-ROM drive for your Mac, you almost certainly should add one if you plan to buy any software, games, or multimedia titles in the future. If you have aspirations to become your own multimedia producer, or if you want a nice, reliable way to backup your hard drive or network (especially for long-term archiving) you should look into recordable CD technologies.

Finally, if you're into the latest games, digital movies, and multimedia titles, you might want to upgrade your Mac with a DVD-ROM drive.

How CD technology works

All CD technology employs the same basic premise: using an optical sensor and a laser, a read-only head (in most of the implementations) passes over the disc as it spins, reading the disc. It looks for microscopic *pits* — tiny indentations — in the media, which translate as slightly less light reflected back to the optical sensor. These variances in light represent digital data — ones and zeros that, ultimately, are turned into something meaningful for the Mac to feed to its processor and display on screen. A typical CD-ROM uses this technology to store up to 650MB of digital information in the form of audio, video, or computer applications and data.

CD-ROM media is designed to be written once, using special tools, and read many times using a CD-ROM drive. To create a CD-ROM, the pits and *lands* — the parts of a CD that remain flat — are pressed into the media by a special CD-ROM press. The press creates identical copies of a master CD after the master has been *burned* — a process in which a laser that's considerably stronger than the laser used in consumer CD-ROM drives creates the microscopic pits that represent data. Each pressed

CD-ROM now has a data imprint that's identical to the master CD's, impressed upon a polycarbonate substrate at the heart of the disc itself.

After a CD-ROM is pressed, a thin aluminum coating is added on the top (that's the shiny part that often receives a painted label), and a clear plastic coating is added on the bottom. It's interesting to note that a typical CD or CD-ROM is actually read by a laser that sweeps along the bottom of the disc, which explains why scratches and painted labels on the top don't interfere with the reading of data. Scratches can be compensated for and dealt with on the lower layer, as well (turn over one of your CDs and see if it doesn't have a scratch or two), but drives are more sensitive to damage on the underside of a CD.

When you place a CD in a CD-ROM drive, the drive spins up to its rated speed in revolutions per minute (RPMs). Depending on where the data is on the CD, however, that RPM level can change to maintain a steady stream of data. This is called *constant linear velocity* and it grows out of a very basic need that audio CDs exhibit — a uniform transfer rate. Because the concentric circles of data on a CD are much smaller toward the middle of the media than at the outside (see Figure 8-1), it's important to speed up the RPMs of the disc the closer the head gets to the center of the disc to maintain a constant flow of data.

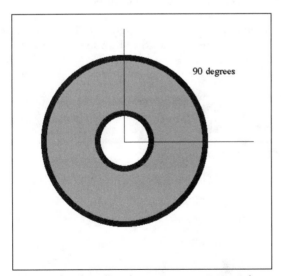

Figure 8-1: The disc shape means a CD needs to slow down to read the same amount of data on the outside tracks as it does on the inside tracks.

Audio CDs do this to maintain a constant flow because they're playing music. Traditionally, CD-ROMs were based on this mechanism to offer constant data rates as well, even at much faster speeds. The very latest drives, however, have switched over to the *constant angular velocity* approach used by floppy drives and hard drives: The media spins at the same speed all the time, meaning data is transferred faster from the edges of the CD and slower from the inner parts of the disc. This is seen as an acceptable trade-off because the high RPM rates of today's drives make it tough to change the speed at a moment's notice. The constant RPMs also result in an overall speed gain, allowing drive manufacturers to claim higher transfer speeds.

CD-ROM speeds

Drives are marketed and sold according to their data transfer rate. (Some CD technology manufacturers also mention *seek time*, or the amount of time it takes the CD to jump to a new set of data, which I'll discuss in a moment.) Data transfer rate's magic number is actually a *multiplier:* It's a number that suggests how much faster than an audio CD player the CD-ROM drive is. Originally, CD-ROM drives transferred data at the same rate as audio CD players — a constant 150 kilobytes per second (KBps). This speed was too slow for many applications, such as transferring video clips, so manufacturers found a way to push the drives to 2x speeds, or two times an audio CD player. That's about 300 KBps.

These days, CD-ROM drives can reach up to 24 KBps or higher (although speeds over 12x generally reflect best-case data rates). Table 8-1 shows you the data rates associated with particular speed multipliers.

Table 8-1
Theoretical Transfer Rates at a Given Multiplier

Speed Multiplier (versus Audio CD)	Transfer Rate
1	150 KBps
2	300 KBps
4	600 KBps
6	900 KBps
8	1.2 MBps
12	1.8 MBps
16	2.4 MBps
24	3.6 MBps

Again, I emphasize that these data rates are best case scenarios. Ignoring things such as the load on your Mac's processor, the SCSI bus to which the drive is connected, the amount of L2 and disk cache used in conjunction with the CD-ROM drive, and other factors that involve the computer, remember also that the drives themselves have limitations. Drives rated 12x and above tend to use constant angular velocity, so their maximum data rate is only applicable to the outer edge of the CD. (Data on the inside of the CD may transfer at only slightly over 50 percent of that rate.)

Another problem with this metric: Many CD-ROMs on the market today have been optimized for 4x or slower drives. That means data is placed on the disc in such a way that the slower drive can get to it quickly, giving faster drives no inherent advantage except faster RPMs. That isn't to say a fast drive isn't a good thing; it does mean that incremental upgrades, as in upgrading from an 8x to a 12x drive, are almost always a waste of money.

The bottom line is this: The multiplier is only good for telling you some relative things about the speed of a drive. It probably isn't important to upgrade your CD-ROM drive unless you have a 2x or slower drive. If you have the opportunity to buy a faster drive at a reasonable cost, do so, realizing that the specific switch from 12x to 16x can actually result in a slight slowdown due to the change to constant angular velocity. Great drives can be had in the 8x to 12x range, and then again at 24x.

Note

You may even suffer some interesting slowdowns with 24x drives. If you ever have the opportunity to load a CD-ROM in a 2x drive and a 24x drive at the exact same time, try it, assuming both machines use the same version of the Mac OS. The 24x drive takes longer to mount on the desktop. Why? Because it has to spin up all the way to those 24x RPM heights, a process that takes a little extra time. In very informal tests I've conducted on my systems, a 2x drive in a Power Mac 6100 brings a CD-ROM to the desktop about one second faster than a 24x drive in a Power Mac 8600/300. The 12x drive in a 7300/200 fared better, beating the 8600 by about two seconds.

Aside from comparing the multiplier ratings in a general way, the other important measurement to look at is the seek time, or how long it takes the drive (on average) to find a particular data frame. This is especially critical if you use CD-ROMs for nonlinear tasks, such as accessing a database, looking up info in reference materials, or playing adventure games. Lawyers who use legal references on disc, teachers who use electronic encyclopedias, and anyone who works with software such as Microsoft Bookshelf (with its quotations, almanac, thesaurus, Zip code lookup) will benefit from drives with faster (lower in milliseconds) seek times. Linear tasks such as installing applications, watching digital videos, and playing audio samples are much less affected by seek time.

CD-Recordable

So far the discussion has centered on CD-ROM technology, which doesn't allow the CD to be overwritten with new data; this is due to the CD burning process being reasonably cost-prohibitive, and read-only drives being cheaper to install in new computers geared for consumers. Recordable CD technologies have become less expensive in recent years, however, enough so that hobbyists and freelancers can afford to add them to their Mac workstations. Others recordable CD solutions are designed for studio and production use, but are still more affordable — and easier to use — than they were just months ago.

There are two basic methods for recording to CDs — CD-R (CD-*Recordable*) and CD-RW (CD-*Rewritable*). The differences in functionality and price between the two are fairly significant.

CD-R is a *WORM* (write-once read-many) technology. It allows you to write data to a special CD-R disc once, and then read the data back as often as necessary. Most CD-R software supports *multisession* writes, which simply means you don't have to fill the contents of the disc at once; you can go back and write again and again to the disc until you fill it up. What you can't do is overwrite data you've already written to the disc. Once it's on the disc, it stays there.

CD-R media, in fact, are slightly different from CD-ROM media. Both have the polycarbonate substrate, the reflective aluminum backing (or gold backing on very high-quality CD-R discs), and the plastic protective layer. Between the substrate and the aluminum, however, CD-R media have another layer made of organic dye. The dye is "burned" by a special laser to create slightly different light reflections that represent the changes from ones to zeros in binary data. In this way, CD-R media is different from CD-ROMs, as no actual pits and lands are created. They remain compatible with most CD-ROM drives, however, because the changes in dye composition reflect light much the same way as physical pits and lands do, so that the media appears identical to a pressed CD-ROM as far as a typical CD-ROM drive is concerned.

CD-R creation is a lot like burning master CDs for CD-ROM production, except the media is slightly different and the process a little more forgiving. The files and documents are arranged in a special program (such as Adaptec's Toast) that then writes the data sequentially to the CD-R media. Essentially, the software enables you to create a "master disk" on your hard drive that is then burned onto the CD-R media.

Note that this is different from the mass-production pressing method used to create consumer CD-ROMs. CD-R drives aren't designed for high-speed duplication as CD presses are. It also means you can't interrupt the process once a burn begins to take place — the data must be written in a smooth, sequential fashion. Many drives manage to do this by including large RAM buffers or advanced caching techniques or creating "image files" that place all the data needed in one contiguous section of the hard drive.

CD-R drives were once very expensive compared to CD-ROM technology, but these days they're typically only about twice as expensive as CD-ROM drives, with CD-R media being reasonably affordable as well. This makes them an interesting solution for someone who has room for the drive (see Figure 8-2) and the inclination to create CDs for archiving or for distribution.

Figure 8-2: This CD-R drive, from Yamaha (www.yamaha.com) doubles as a 6x CD-ROM drive and attaches to the external SCSI chain. (Photo courtesy Yamaha Corp.)

CD-Rewritable

Of course, the problem with CD-R is you can only write to it once. You can't reuse the disc once it's been recorded to (except to add another recording session to it if there's still room). CD-RW, on the other hand, is designed to be erasable.

CD-RW does this by replacing the recordable layer of CD-R (created by burning in a special dye, as previously mentioned) with a new type of rewritable layer than can be changed back to its original state. This CD-RW rewritable layer uses a chemical compound that crystallizes when heated to a particular temperature, but returns to a noncrystal state when made even hotter, and then cooled.

The major problem with this approach is it's much more expensive to work with than CD-R and the media isn't quite as backward compatible, because this approach doesn't mirror the pits and lands of CD-ROM technology quite as faithfully as does CD-R technology. Still, it's great for sharing CD-RW discs with other CD-RW–capable drives or as a backup mechanism to be used with a particular drive.

DVD

Digital Versatile Disc (abbreviated DVD, and also known as Digital Video Disc) is, at its most basic, a bigger, meaner version of CD-ROM technology. Capable of holding a minimum of 4.7GB of data and a current maximum of about 17GB — depending on the technology used to create the DVD-ROM — DVD is being aimed at a number of different applications, just as CD technology was. Where CDs quickly became a digital audio standard, DVD is projected to become the digital video standard, edging out both VHS tape in home entertainment systems and CD-ROM technology on personal computers.

DVD drives are backward compatible with CD-ROM drives, enabling them to play audio CDs, CD-ROMs, and CD-R media (some early DVD drives can't play CD-R). DVD relies on the MPEG-2 standard for video compression, so it can't play back full-screen video on a computer that lacks MPEG-2 decompression hardware. (Stand-alone DVD players for home entertainment centers include this technology.) It can, however, be used without MPEG-2 hardware for transferring data stored in databases or storing large-scale adventure games and clip art collections, just as CD-ROM technology can. Most DVD-ROM drives do ship with MPEG-2 cards, however, with some notable exceptions. For instance, Apple's first DVD-ROM drives were installed in Power Macintosh G3 machines without MPEG-2 decompression hardware.

Note   The DVD standard also calls for support for the AC-3 Dolby Surround Sound standard for audio, which the decoding hardware should also be capable of outputting to a stereo receiver. Most DVD decompression cards offer S-video, composite, and audio connectors. Even with this hardware, DVD tends to require a powerful Macintosh (PowerPC 604 in most cases), built on a PCI expansion bus.

DVD drives transfer data at about 1.2 MBps, or approximately the rate of speed of a 9x CD-ROM drive. This is data throughput good enough for MPEG-2 compressed video streams that are then decompressed quickly using dedicated hardware. At 4.7GB, that's about 2 hours of MPEG-2 compressed video — at 17GB, about 24 hours of MPEG-1 video (which offers quality similar to VHS) can be stored.

Although the DVD medium is about the same size and appearance as a CD, technological advances have increased its capacity considerably. The basic manufacturing process is similar; in fact, CD-ROM manufacturers can retool fairly easily to support DVD production. However, the basic technology has advanced considerably since the CD specification was finalized.

For one thing, DVD media can be both dual-layer and dual-sided. Using a semitransparent layer that sits over a lower layer of data, a single side of a DVD can store about 9GB as opposed to the single-sided, single-layer capacity of 4.7GB. Double that again (nearly) if the media is double-sided and double-layered.

The capacity of a single layer, however, has been improved by making more data fit in the same amount of space as a CD-ROM. The minimum pit length of a CD is 0.83 micro meters; on a DVD it's 0.4 micrometers. The tracks of pits and lands don't have to be as far apart, either, with only 0.74 micrometers required for DVD vs. 1.6 micrometers for CD technology.

And there are DVD recording solutions on the horizon, as well. DVD-R drives allow write-once capabilities to DVD disks as large as 3.9GB, whereas rewritable DVD-RAM will allow either 2.6GB or 5.2GB of storage per disc, depending on whether or not the disc is double-sided. DVD-RAM works much like the CD-RW standard to enable you to write to DVD media. As of this writing the standard is still in flux, with a competing standard, DVD+RW, promising 3.0GB capacity per side.

Note   As of this writing, DVD technology is still slow to arrive in the Macintosh. Early out of the gate are three companies: Apple, with DVD drives for Power Macs and PowerBooks; e4 (www.e4.com), with the Cool-DVD kit; and Pioneer (www.pioneer.com), with DVD-ROM and DVD-R units.

Add CD-ROM Technology to Your Mac

If you don't already have a CD-ROM drive for your Mac, I wholeheartedly recommend you look into adding one (or even a DVD-ROM drive, if one is available for a reasonable price) as quickly as you can. You'll need one — at least, if you ever plan to update the system software on your Mac, play multimedia titles, or browse a CD-based encyclopedia. Will you be installing Microsoft Office, for instance? In that case, I recommend a CD-ROM drive. (I'm not sure if Office 98 even comes on floppies, but if it does, it probably takes at least 50 of them.) Same goes for installing the Mac OS.

In fact, one of the best reasons for installing a CD-ROM drive might be to take advantage of all those CD-ROMs that are being bundled with Macintosh, programming, and Web development magazines these days. If you have a slower Internet connection, these CDs can be doubly handy, giving you access to the latest OS updates, utilities, and code samples without forcing an all-night download on you.

If I haven't yet tempted you, don't forget you can use a CD-R drive to put together your own CDs of music, talk, or whatever else you'd like to create or produce. If you're one of the growing numbers who has only got a CD player in your car, maybe you'd like to transfer some tapes to CD-R for those long driving trips. (Of course, observe all copyright laws in doing so.)

Evangelista tip: Boot from a CD-ROM

If you're installing a third-party or external CD-ROM drive, you'll still want it to act like a built-in Apple CD-ROM when it comes to rebooting off the CD media. There are plenty of reasons for this: You can boot off a Mac OS CD-ROM to run Disk Tools or reinstall parts of the system, or you can boot from the TechTool or Norton Utilities CD-ROM so you can run some tests on your boot drive.

With an internal CD-ROM mechanism, all you have to do is hold down the C key as the machine starts up and it'll boot from the internal CD-ROM drive. But if you've got either a third-party drive or an external drive, Evangelista Mark Boszko, owner of DragonF/X, has a tip for you:

(continued)

(continued)

"Most of the time, if you want to upgrade your system software or run a disk utility on the Mac's internal hard drive, you'll want to boot from the CD-ROM drive. I've found that some third-party external CD-ROM drives won't boot from the CD-ROM when you hold down the C key.

"I've found, though, that holding down the ⌘-Opt-Shift-Del keys will usually do the trick, unless you have another external drive with a System file on it—then you'll have to press ⌘-Opt-Shift-Del *and* C."

Choosing a drive

Let me quickly give you an overview of the factors involved in choosing a CD-ROM or DVD solution. You need to know a number of different things about your setup before you can move on to buying and installing the drive:

✦ **Available space.** Do you need an external SCSI model of CD-ROM or DVD-ROM drive, or do you have an available drive bay? And, what technology do you need for your drive? If it's DVD, there's a good chance it'll require an EIDE interface, so you'll need to have a free EIDE connector in your Power Macintosh 4400 or G3 or above system. Otherwise, external SCSI drives are a bit more expensive, but much easier to add.

Note

If you plan to replace the CD-ROM drive in a very new Power Macintosh system, you'll likely be freeing up an EIDE connector. (Check your documentation.)

✦ **Functionality.** If you want to be able to record CDs, you'll need to choose a CD-R or CD-RW drive. Don't forget to shop around for the best media prices and take that into consideration. In some cases, CD-R can be a lot less expensive and more compatible with older CD-ROM drives. You can also get CD-ROM changers that can hold more than one CD-ROM and switch them on demand.

✦ **Speed.** As discussed in the previous section, you should balance speed with price in a CD-ROM drive and make sure you're not upgrading for an insignificant speed boost. Drives in the 8x to 12x range are perfectly acceptable for use with most any games or multimedia titles. Don't forget to check the seek time (usually measured in milliseconds) and compare it to others if you plan to use the drive for reference and database lookups.

Finally, you'll find when shopping for drives that the brand name on the drive doesn't always match the brand name of the actual components used to create the drive; you might be more interested in the component manufacturer. These drives are made by companies such as Sony, Panasonic, Phillips, NEC, and Mitsumi, but they're branded and distributed (often) by companies such as APS Technologies, Club-Mac, and Mactell.

If you want to know the specifications for a particular drive, ask for the brand name and model number of the drive mechanism, and then check out the manufacturer's Web site for details.

Installing a CD-ROM drive

Installing a CD-ROM drive doesn't differ much from installing a hard drive, whether it's internal or external. If there's any major difference, it's that you'll probably need special driver software for the CD-ROM drive (which is often, but not always, true for new hard drives), and there's a slightly higher chance that you'll want to install a CD-ROM or DVD drive that uses an EIDE interface instead of a SCSI connection.

External drives

If you're installing an external CD-ROM drive, it's going to be a SCSI model. You add it just as you would a SCSI hard drive:

1. Identify an available SCSI ID number using the Apple System Profiler or a similar tool.

2. Shut down the Macintosh and ground yourself electrically.

3. Determine where in the SCSI chain you'd like to put the drive, and then plug the SCSI cables into the connectors on the back of the drive. If you have the correct cabling, you can add it to the middle of your chain to avoid moving terminators around. If this is your only SCSI device, connect the SCSI cable to the SCSI port on the back of the Mac, and then connect it to the drive (see Figure 8-3).

DVD: Special installation

These instructions, by the way, should work for any of the drives mentioned in this chapter—CD-R, CD-RW, DVD-ROM. The only additional issue regards internal DVD drives which (often) need to be connected to a special expansion card responsible for MPEG-2 and AC-3 digital audio decompression.

The card installs in a free PCI slot and is connected to the DVD drive via an included cable (consult the drive's documentation). Video-out and audio-out ports on the back of the card can then be used to connect the drive to a television, stereo receiver, or home entertainment system, if desired.

Figure 8-3: External drives need little more than a SCSI connection.Shown here is a Toshiba XM-6201B 32x CD-ROM drive (www.toshiba.com).

4. Terminate the drive connector if necessary. Some drivers are self-terminating, and others offer a switch on the back of the drive to enable termination. Still others require a special plug for terminating the device.

5. With the SCSI chain properly connected and terminated, restart your Macintosh.

6. Install the software drivers that came with the drive. They should help you identify that the Mac recognizes the drive and is making it available for use on the SCSI chain.

7. Restart your Mac.

After restarting, your Mac should load the extensions necessary to use the CD-ROM drive. Test it by inserting a CD-ROM to see if the disc's icon appears on the desktop. If it does, you've successfully installed the drive.

Internal drives

Installing an internal drive can be quite a bit more difficult than working with an external drive. Depending on the type of case your Mac has and the drive bay itself, you may have trouble getting the drive to fit correctly.

Some of Apple's Macs were made to accept only a CD-ROM drive built by Apple, end of story. An example of these included all-in-one Power Macintosh machines and the Performa 630, 640, 6200, 6300 series of Macs. Take a close look at your Apple Macintosh and notice that the button for the drive is actually built into the front plastic of the Mac — it's not on the face of the drive itself. Most third-party drives are all-in-one units with a button on the face. To replace an Apple CD-ROM drive, you'll need an Apple CD-ROM drive (see Figure 8-4). The exception is a Mac that has a bezel, or front plastic facing, you can remove to reveal an available drive key for the CD-ROM drive (see Figure 8-5).

Figure 8-4: On the top: front view of a typical Panasonic drive mechanism. On the bottom: CD-ROM drive built into an Apple Performa 6200 series.

If that works out for you, you'll probably be able to upgrade (or add) an internal CD-ROM drive. Just make sure a bezel kit or a complete mounting kit is available for your particular Mac model. In the Mac world, one of the main purveyors of these bezels and mounting kits is Proline Distribution (www.proline.com). You'll find their kits sold wherever internal Macintosh drives are sold, including popular Web sites.

Figure 8-5: Pulling the bezel off the CD-ROM bay for a Power Macintosh 6100

Because most Macs come with a CD-ROM or DVD drive, there isn't as much of an aftermarket for these drives and their mounting kits as there are for, say, Zip and Jaz drives. You'll need to shop carefully for the mounting kit, making sure you do your best to match the manufacturer of the drive you're adding with the bezel/mounting kit that you're buying. You'll also have to buy a bezel/mounting kit designed for your particular Macintosh model. Otherwise, the drive itself shouldn't be too hard to find; most of the major CD-ROM manufacturers make SCSI internal CD-ROM drives. (Certain Mac modeis have an internal EIDE connection available.)

Note   If you buy a drive that isn't part of a kit designed specifically for a Macintosh, you may need to buy software that can add a Mac driver for your CD-ROM drive. FWB CD Toolkit (discussed later in this chapter) handles most major manufacturer's drives.

With the kit and drive in hand, you're ready to fit the two together. Here's how to install an internal drive:

1. Choose a SCSI ID number that won't conflict with any of the other devices in your Mac. (Make sure you choose one on the correct bus, too, if your Mac has both an internal and an external bus.)

2. Shut down your Mac, ground yourself electrically, and unplug the machine.

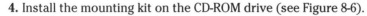

3. Remove the case and locate the open drive bay for the CD-ROM. (If necessary, remove the existing CD-ROM.) Remove the front bezel that covers the bay you'll be using.

4. Install the mounting kit on the CD-ROM drive (see Figure 8-6).

Note

You won't necessarily have to install a mounting kit on some Mac clone machines that use Intel-compatible PC-type enclosures. In that case, you'll likely just slide the drive into its bay (make sure the front of the drive is flush with the front of the case) and then screw the drive into its drive cage. In most cases, holes in the drive cage will line up with screw holes in the drive.

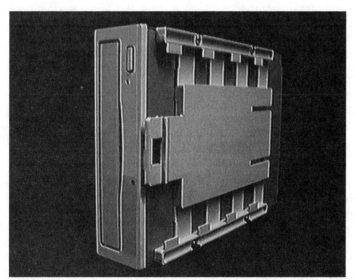

Figure 8-6: The CD-ROM mounting kit will enable the drive to slide into your particular Mac's drive bay.

5. Select the correct SCSI ID for the drive. You'll likely do this by setting a jumper or switching a series of dip switches. (The drive's manual should tell you how.)

6. Slide the drive into its bay. Lock it into place (with most mounting kits the drive slides into the bay, locking into a plastic tab or lever).

7. Plug the SCSI cable into the SCSI connector and the power cable into the power connector, both of which are on the back of the drive.

8. Reassemble the case and install the new front bezel. Test it carefully to make sure it lines up correctly with the new drive; otherwise, you may need to try remounting or realigning the drive.

9. Reinstall the case. (You can skip this step for testing purposes.)

10. Plug the Mac in and start it up.

11. Run any software that was included with the CD-ROM drive. If no Macintosh drivers were included, run FWB CD Toolkit to install drivers.

12. Restart the Macintosh.

If all goes well, your drive should be recognized by its drivers and available once the Mac has completely booted up. Check it using the Apple System Profiler or by installing a CD in the drive to see if it mounts to the desktop correctly.

CD-Related Software

There are plenty of CD-ROM and DVD titles out there for you enjoy, whether you're a teacher, a researcher, a professional, or a gamer — or, perhaps you're a little of all those. However, another class of software may merit your attention when you're ready to upgrade your CD-ROM, CD-R, or DVD equipment — CD utilities.

Some utilities are necessary just to get third-party CD-ROM and DVD drives up and running. Other utilities help it run a little faster and might be worth some consideration if you think your drive is too slow. Still other utilities work with CD-R and CD-RW drives to properly record, or burn, data into the CD for safekeeping.

CD Utilities

This category is dominated by FWB, Inc., makers of the Hard Drive Toolkit and its sibling, the CD-ROM Toolkit. If you buy a third-party hard drive or CD-ROM drive that includes Mac software, FWB is probably the source of that software.

If you didn't get the software with your CD-ROM, you might consider looking into it. The CD-ROM Toolkit makes it possible for you to install third-party drives from various vendors to serve as emergency boot drives or for system maintenance. Table 8-2 shows the manufacturers supported by the CD-ROM Toolkit.

Table 8-2
CD-ROM Manufacturers Supported by the FWB CD-ROM Toolkit

Vendor	Drive Type
Apple	CD-ROM
Chinon	CD-ROM
Hitachi	CD-ROM
NEC	CD-ROM
Panasonic	CD-ROM
Philips	CD-ROM
Pioneer	CD-ROM
Pinnacle Micro	CD-R
Plextor	CD-ROM
Ricoh	CD-R
Sanyo	CD-ROM
Sony	CD-ROM, CD-R
Teac	CD-ROM
Toshiba	CD-ROM
Yamaha	CD-R

The Toolkit also features a number of speed enhancements, including flexible cache settings that enable you to decide how much RAM to use for look-ahead, directory storage and other caching techniques. The more RAM (and/or hard drive space) you dedicate to the CD-ROM cache, the faster it will seem to run: Data is moved from the CD to RAM in the background, and then accessed directly from the much-faster RAM when more data is needed.

The CD-ROM Toolkit gives you access to other options as well, such as the different types of disc formats it should attempt to mount, whether or not to have the CD-ROM tray eject whenever the Mac is shut down, and whether you want to be warned when a badly mastered CD-ROM has been inserted in the drive.

Casa Blanca Works (www.proline.com/cbwindex.html) offers a rival program, CDWorks, that also acts as a driver for most SCSI CD-ROM drives, and includes the capability to boot from the drive and to alter cache settings to speed up CD-ROM access. CDWorks also touts a feature that enables you to disable Apple's built-in cache, resulting in a speed-up, according to the company's literature.

A third utility, CD Mounter Plus, comes from Software Architects (www.softarch.com). This one features a special audio CD remote for easy playback of audio CDs, as well as offering all the typical support for CD-ROM drive brands and SCSI mounting.

Creating CD-R

Adaptec, Inc., leads the market for CD burning with a number of different software offers, the most obvious of which is Adaptec Toast. Toast helps you do all the things necessary to put together a good CD-R — organize the data, get it ready to be sent to the CD-R disc, and manage the data flow so that it writes correctly, smoothly, and sequentially. That's how you create CDs for distribution or sharing among typical CD-ROM drives.

Toast isn't the only way to create CD-Rs. New technology from Adaptec and others, called *packet writing*, focuses on individual packets of data that can be stored, instead of a continuous data stream. This allows you to treat a CD-R more like a typical hard drive: You just drag and drop new files onto the CD-R. The end result is burning a CD-R becomes a lot more like saving files to a typical removable media device.

Drives have to be certified to run with DirectCD, Adaptec's software for this sort of drag-and-drop CD-R creation. At issue is the fact that DirectCD and similar incremental CD-R approaches use the Universal Disc Format (UDF) to make their magic possible. (In the Mac OS, this magic translates to the ability to simply drag and drop files onto CD-R media in the Finder — a vast improvement for novice and occasional use.) UDF essentially circumvents the need for multiple sessions every time you write to the CD-R, allowing you to leave the session "open" until you're ready to remove the CD-R disc from the drive or use it on another computer.

The CD-R drive you use must support UDF and the ability to open and close an ISO 9660 (PC file format) session without shutting down the drive. Because many CD-ROM drives aren't capable of reading the UDF format, the CD-R must be translated into ISO 9660 if it is to be distributed to other users. DirectCD includes the ability to read and write directly to UDF format drives, and the Mac OS now supports UDF natively with Mac OS 8.1 and above.

If you've got all the requisites for DirectCD, you simply install it and configure its control panel (see Figure 8-7). You'll then be able to drag files you want to store on a CD-R directly onto that disc in the Finder.

Figure 8-7: DirectCD makes CD-R recording almost fun.

Summary

✦ If you don't already have a CD-ROM drive, there's a good chance you'll need one. Most new programs today are distributed on CD-ROM, as are most games, reference, and multimedia software titles. A very old Mac may be able to survive without CD technology, but a newer Mac shouldn't. In fact, owners of the latest Power Macs might even want to look into DVD, the latest in digital disc technologies.

✦ If you've already got a CD-ROM drive, think before you upgrade; there's usually not an amazing increase in the speeds of the drives. At least, the increase usually isn't dramatic enough to warrant a hefty upgrade price. If you don't have a CD-ROM drive at all, though, very fast drives are very affordable and generally easy to add. All you really need to decide is whether you'll install the drive internally or externally. If you want to install an internal drive, you'll need to find out if your Mac will support SCSI or IDE for the connection.

✦ With the drive in place, you might want to look into some CD-related software upgrades that can speed up your access and help you manage your drives.

✦ You may also want to create your own CDs for others to play back or even record to. If that's the case, you'll need to get special software that enables you to record CDs in conjunction with special drives (CD-R and CD-RW drives) designed for the task.

✦   ✦   ✦

Removable Drives and Backup

Although removable media devices have always been a good idea for professionals and Mac artists dealing in large files, it's only been in the last few years that removable drives have become a viable way to significantly extend home or office system storage capacity. At one time, the floppy disk was a great way to transport files and backup important documents, because the files tended to be small enough to fit on a floppy. These days, though, other alternatives are necessary. In response to these demands, removable media devices have become easier to use, work as fast as typical hard drives, and offer reasonable enough costs and capacities that they're worthwhile to cart around or use for backing up and archiving.

The Iomega Zip drive isn't completely responsible for this revival, but it's fair to say that it's done its part. In fact, with the overwhelming popularity of the Zip drive, it's likely to become a defacto standard replacement for floppies. (Already I'm surprised when a colleague doesn't have a Zip drive available, especially if we plan to swap Web site data or graphics.) It does have some heated competition, including the LS120 standard, a revamp of the original floppy drive that handles both high-capacity 120MB floppy disks and the standard 1.44MB floppies that everyone is used to.

The bottom line is this: If you don't have a removable drive for your Mac, you should get one (unless you're struggling along without something even more important like a joystick or cool speakers). I'd recommend a Zip drive even for old Macs like the Mac Plus or Mac SE. In fact, I'd recommend them, in some cases, instead of a hard drive for those models (see the Note that follows).

But whatever your Mac, some sort of removable drive is a good idea, whether it's for moving files around, backing files up, or both. The Zip drive may be tough to resist (especially because it's built into many Macs), and it's certainly a good choice. But consider some of the other drives as well — some of the latest store 1.5- or 2.0GB of data per disk or cartridge, which can be a great way to back up a lot of important data all at once.

Note   Why recommend a Zip drive as a hard drive for a classic Mac (Mac Plus, the early Mac SE)? As those Macs don't all have internal drive options, your only hard drive options are external. Most modern SCSI drives, however, are too fast for the older Macs; although you can use the drives, you have to purposefully slow the rate at which data is transferred by those drives. At the same time, older (used) drives are usually in 40- or 80MB capacities for those machines. Zip drives are a tad slower than modern drives — a deficit that works well with older Macs. Plus, Zips offer a lot of flexibility for those older Macs, making it easy to get an additional 100MB of storage every time you buy a new cartridge.

Removable Drives Explained

The Mac's ability to easily add SCSI devices, along with the popularity of storage-intensive images and desktop publishing files, made removable drives an early, popular upgrade for Mac professionals. Back when Intel-compatible PCs were still focused on number-crunching and word processing using a character-based operating system, the Mac was encouraging users to add photographic-quality images to their layouts and presentations. This required removable media technologies though, because getting the file to the local print shop or prepress house was necessary for preparing it for public consumption. Professional Mac users needed an easy way to do this.

This state of affairs encouraged companies like Iomega and SyQuest to come up with a new sort of storage device — the removable cartridge device or removable hard drive. Using fairly large cartridges and special external SCSI drives, Mac users could write data to cartridges that could hold 20MB, 44MB, and in some cases 88MB of data at once. You could then take the cartridge with you to your final destination. (Figure 9-1 shows a newer SyQuest model that can work with these cartridges.)

Figure 9-1: SyQuest cartridges made it easy to transport data from one place to another.

These days, people have largely moved on from the original SyQuest and Iomega drives (especially the Bernoulli models). They're slower, smaller-capacity technologies than many of the more exciting new approaches. You'll still find the drives and cartridges for sale, of course, as they're around for posterity and many shops still make use of the drives for backing up and transporting documents.

As the technology has progressed, the three factors that typify computing have worked their magic on removable media: It's become faster, smaller, and able to hold greater capacities. Now, the inexpensive Iomega Zip drive and the SyQuest EZFlyer drives can hold between 100MB and 230MB (depending on the model and manufacturer) on cartridges that are barely larger than floppy disks (see Figure 9-2).

Speed, size, and capacity have all reached a point where removable media drives make sense for just about anybody, because a Zip or SyQuest disk can easily be used for transporting files, backing up files, or simply extending the capacity of your computer.

Figure 9-2: Zip disks are thicker than floppies, but not much larger.

If you like computer games, for instance, but don't have room for them on your main hard drive, you can just grab the Jaz disk that holds all your games and pop it into your Jaz drive; it won't run much slower, and you'll have your main hard drive available for other data. Plus, if you've got kids, getting the games away from them (or using the games as a reward for completed homework) is as easy as taking control of the Jaz cartridge. You might similarly create a Jaz disk that has all your Web development tools and documents on it, so you can pop it in and continue working on a Web project. Or a Zip with all your personal documents on it might be a convenient way to move from workstation to workstation on campus or while traveling.

The other factor that's made removable media popular is its ease of use. Tape drives — though still available and popular as a backup medium — are notorious for being difficult to use, requiring special software and some downtime while the backup takes place. And tapes often don't work like regular disks, so you can't just use the Finder to save to them. Jaz, Zip and SyQuest technologies just pop up on your desktop as icons, allowing you to open them, copy files to and from them and launch programs from them. This similarity to hard drives is part of what's driving their success, especially with consumers and small businesses.

But they're not the only technologies worth looking into. Magneto-optical drives can hold a great amount of information on CD-like media that lasts a long time in storage, isn't terribly volatile, and can be used for fairly fast retrieval. Digital audio tape (DAT) and tape cartridge backup devices also have their niche as cheap media. If you need to back up an entire network for safekeeping, you'd need quite a few Jaz cartridges to get it done. With tape, it's a different story. So, although you're likely to want one of the popular, hip removable drives that's on the market currently, you'll still want to shop around for the one that's best for you.

Removable cartridge drives

It's hard to know what exactly to call the Zip and SyJet class of drives. The name is already taken by actual removable hard drives that the industry has experimented with in the past, along with the PCMCIA (or PC Card) standard of hard drives that can be plugged into PowerBooks, eMates and other portable computers. At the same time, *high-density floppy drives*, although another popular way to refer to these drives, is extending the use of the word *floppy* to the point of being ridiculous. There's nothing floppy about any of these hard plastic cartridges. (A typical 3.5-inch floppy disk actually contains a floppy disc inside its shell, but these newer cartridges offer completely different mechanisms.)

So I suppose I'll just call them removable cartridge drives. Whatever you call them, they're important to computing. Iomega has sold millions of Zip drives, and I've seen reports that they continue to crank out over a million per month. With Zip well on its way to becoming a de facto standard, the others are vying for more specialized niches, but they're important, too.

So how do they work? For the most part, these drives are actually combinations of different technologies — a little magneto-optical here, a little hard-drive-like mechanism there. (In fact, the original SyQuest cartridges actually were removable hard drives of a sort, with little platters and spindles just like what hard drives have.)

First, take a look at a chart that shows you the specifications and speeds of each (see Table 9-1). In the following sections, I introduce you to the most popular of these drives.

Table 9-1
Popular Removable Cartridge Drives and Performance

Drive	Capacity	Interface	Max. Speed	Internal Available?
Iomega Zip	100MB	SCSI-1	1.4 MBps	Yes
Iomega ZipPlus	100MB	SCSI-1	1.4 MBps	No
SyQuest EZFlyer	230MB	Fast SCSI	2.4 MBps	No
Iomega Jaz 1GB	1GB	Fast SCSI	6.6 MBps	Yes
Iomega Jaz 2GB	2GB	Ultra SCSI	6.7 MBps	Yes
SyQuest SyJet	1.5GB	Fast SCSI	6.9 MBps	Yes
SyQuest Quest	4.8GB	Ultra/Wide SCSI	10.6 MBps	Yes
Castlewood Orb	2.16GB	Ultra SCSI	12.2 MBps	Yes

Note that the maximum speed number in the table is the maximum sustained transfer rate that's claimed by the company in their technical specifications — most of the time, the average rate will be much lower. Also, although performance is important, it's not the only factor in choosing a removable cartridge drive. All these drives offer hard-drive-like performance, although the high-end models are certainly better suited for multimedia and similar needs.

Note

In-depth statistics weren't available at the time of writing regarding the SuperDisk, a USB-based LS120 floppy drive announced shortly after the iMac was announced. The SuperDisk should work with both 120MB LS120 disks as well as standard 1.44MB disks in both Intel-compatible PC and Mac formats. The first of these drives has been announced as a joint effort between Panasonic and Imation (www.imation.com).

Iomega Zip

Currently available in a 100MB capacity, the Zip drive may never increase that number (at least, it will probably always be compatible with the 100MB cartridges). After all, these are the most popular removable media drives ever — with apologies to floppy disk drives and CD-ROM drives — and part of this success relies on turning Zip cartridges into commodities. That is, you ought to be able to exchange a Zip disk with anyone and have them be able to immediately read the disk.

Note

Apple itself addressed the issue of swapping Zip disks with the release of Mac OS 8.1, which included a new version of the PC Exchange system extension. Not only does the Mac OS support Windows 95 long file names, but it also has the ability to read Windows and DOS-formatted Zip cartridges (and other removable media).

The Iomega drive comes in both internal and external versions. The internal SCSI version usually requires a mounting kit that's specific to your Mac's model. If you opt for the external model, it'll connect directly to your external SCSI bus. You'll have to set the Zip's SCSI ID externally — you get a choice of ID number 5 or number 6 on most models. You can also use the Zip as a pass-through connector to other SCSI devices on the SCSI bus. The drive has only 25-pin SCSI connectors, however, so you may need an adapter for some SCSI cables.

The second generation of Zip drives — the ZipPlus drive — switches back and forth between SCSI and Intel-compatible parallel connections, enabling you to use the drive with either platform. It also offers an on-off switch for users who'd like to power down between uses.

The Zip disks (or Zip cartridges) have a 100MB capacity when unformatted, which is lowered to about 95MB after the formatting process. You can buy the cartridges preformatted for the Macintosh, but if you can't find such cartridges, you can use DOS-formatted cartridges and reformat them for the Macintosh. (Or, with Mac OS 8.1 or greater, you can simply save files to the DOS-formatted cartridge.) You use the included Zip Tools software to reformat the disk, and this takes about ten minutes on a Mac for a full reformat (including a test of the cartridge) or a minute or so for a quick format. (See Figure 9-3.)

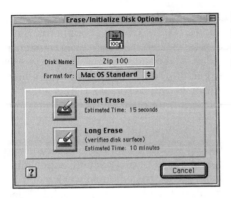

Figure 9-3: The Zip drive comes with its own software, including tools for formatting, backing up and other tasks.

Chapter 23 discusses formatting Zip disks and other removable disks.

If you've ever flipped a Zip cartridge over and looked at the back, right-hand corner, you may have noticed a little clear plastic section. What's it for? All it does is tell the Zip drive it's dealing with an actual Zip disk that's been inserted. Without this identifier, the drive won't clamp down, thereby preventing it from engaging its read/write head on some other sort of media that could damage the drive.

Iomega Jaz

The Jaz drive currently offers capacities of 1GB and 2GB of data storage per cartridge—quite an amount for media professionals or for backing up your Macs. (The Jaz was originally released with support 500MB cartridges, which are rare these days but still useful.) The Jaz offers high-speed access to your data, on par with a typical hard drive. This makes it a reasonable alternative to buying another hard drive for secondary storage—especially if you like the idea of being able to swap out one cartridge for another and start over again with another one or two gigabytes of free space.

Not just Iomega anymore

The Zip drive is so popular that Iomega has seen fit to allow a number of companies to build Zip-compatible drives and use their own brand names on them. Epson America (www.epson.com) is the most visible clone maker, offering actual Zip-compatible drives for internal and external use. Other companies focus on the media; Zip disks are made by both Sony (www.sony.com) and FujiFilm (www.fujifilm.com). All these devices and media should be compatible with one another, so even if you have an Iomega drive you can feel secure buying media made by another company and vice versa.

The Jaz 2GB version is the first to offer an Ultra SCSI connector, allowing you to hook the external drive up to your Mac using a 50-pin to 50-pin connector. (For best results you'll need an expansion card SCSI interface with an external connector that supports Ultra SCSI speeds. Most built-in Mac SCSI connectors are limited to 5MB per second.) Sustained transfer rates can reach up to 8.7 MBps, with quick bursts getting all the way up to the Ultra SCSI limit of 20 MBps. The Jaz 1GB is slightly slower, offering a Fast SCSI interface with a burst rate of 10 MBps and a maximum sustained rate of 6.6 MBps.

Jaz drives provide an extremely flexible backup solution. Just the opportunity to back up one or two gigabytes of data at one time is incredibly useful, especially in workgroup situations. You'll also find that it's easy to back up a workgroup server on Jaz disks because they're fast, reliable, and can store quite a bit of data. (If necessary, you can always compress the data using a backup utility or a compression tool like StuffIt Deluxe from Aladdin Systems — www.aladdinsys.com.) In many ways, the convenience of Jaz and its ilk beats the other options, including magneto-optical and tape-backup technologies. Jaz drives work just like hard drives and offer a higher transfer rate, making them easier to work with than some of the other backup solutions. Of course, the cartridges can also be a bit more expensive.

SyQuest EZFlyer

Seen as a competitor to the Iomega Zip drive, the EZFlyer is a removable cartridge drive capable of higher transfer speeds and capacities than the Zip drive, with a 230MB cartridge capacity that's backward compatible with older EZ135 135MB cartridges. Unfortunately, the EZFlyer isn't compatible with the Zip's media, and hasn't caught on the way the Zip drive has.

The EZFlyer is very fast for its price range and is currently capable of over double the capacity of a Zip drive. Many users find it's a great choice for simple backup and data storage solutions or for restoring stored applications and data to lab-based computers.

So, although you won't be sharing your data with as many people, the EZFlyer is still a great solution for a number of tasks, including quick and easy backup onto media that's cheaper than the one-to-two gigabyte removable drives such as the Iomega Jaz and SyQuest SyJet. For day-to-day backup of a single Mac, you can't beat the EZFlyer. It's also a nice solution for aging Macs that never have had much storage in the first place, enabling you to store applications, games, or data files on the EZFlyer cartridge and then run them directly.

SyQuest SyJet

SyQuest's competitor to Iomega's Jaz drive offers many of the same characteristics and advantages, while competing on price and performance. Offering good speed, 1.5GB of storage space and features like a special A/V mode (for high sustained rates of throughput), the SyJet offers a similar level of convenience and efficiency for backup and data-sharing tasks. The 1.5GB media makes it another ideal choice for workgroups, graphics professionals, and multimedia artists. (See Figure 9-4).

Figure 9-4: The SyQuest SyJet drive and cartridge. Both are a little bigger than the Zip, but they store a lot more data (www.syquest.com).

SyQuest Quest

The Quest is currently one of the higher-capacity removable media drives in existence, offering the ability to save up to 4.7GB of data on a single cartridge. This fast removable drive is aimed at media professionals and larger servers and workgroups that need the capability to back up large amounts of data quickly. All-digital recording studios, video editing workstations, and Macs in multimedia studios can benefit from the Ultra/Wide SCSI connection offered by the Quest, with sustained rates around 10 MBps and burst rates that can reach 40 MBps.

Although SyQuest builds the Quest, its real market is as an Original Equipment Manufacturer (OEM) device, meaning other companies are focusing on packaging and selling the drive in their own enclosures or adding them to systems internally. The Ultra/Wide interface demands an internal connection and special high-end SCSI capabilities (see Chapter 7 for more on SCSI type). If you're interested in something like this, shop the Mac stores and catalogs to see what companies are making the Quest available.

Castlewood Orb

The Orb, although not an offering from one of the big hitters, Iomega or SyQuest, promises to be a special removable drive. Described as a magneto-resistive drive, the Orb is a high-speed, high-capacity drive focused squarely on users who want such a drive at a low cost. The Orb competes right up there with the Quest and similar high-capacity, high-speed drives.

Learn more about the Orb at www.castlewoodsystems.com.

Magneto-optical drives

Magneto-optical (M-O) drives certainly aren't as popular as the low-cost, high-performance removable cartridge drives that have swept the industry. But, rather quietly, M-O technology has come back into vogue for certain applications, offering very high capacities and an incredibly long storage life, which makes it popular for long-term archiving.

At one point, these drives languished in capacities of only a few hundred megabytes, and historically they're known for being very slow. Yet M-O has come into its own recently. Now, transfer rates approach those of hard drives and high-end removable cartridge drives, with many M-O drives in the 1-4 MBps range. Capacities are ranging upward too, with popular M-O drives offering capacities of 230MB, 640MB, 2.6GB, and 4.6GB. Popular drive vendors include Pinnacle Micro (www.pinnaclemicro.com) and APS Technologies (www.apstech.com).

Magneto-optical, like nearly any other drive technology designed for Macintosh, offers SCSI and Fast SCSI implementations. You'll usually find the drives in external casing but can occasionally come across an internal version. Although they certainly are rivaled by the increased appearance of CD Rewritable solutions, M-O will probably be around for quite some time, thanks to increased capacities and speed improvements.

Tape drives

Consider, if you will, the two reasons to buy a tape drive for your backup solution — and the two reasons to avoid tape backup at all costs. These days, tape drives are being designed to hold amazing amounts of data in a single cartridge. In certain implementations, tapes can hold 30-, 40-, or 70GB of data. Tape cartridges are traditionally very cheap, too, offering data backup at pennies per megabytes.

Now the cons. Tape is slow, slow, slow. And, along with being slow, it's a *near-line* solution, meaning it doesn't actually appear as a drive on your computer. That is, it dosen't pop up on your Mac's desktop like a Zip, Jaz, or M-O cartridge will. Instead, you have to use special software to save your data to tape.

Tape can't reasonably be used to transfer data between computers, because, by necessity, it has to write all its data sequentially. This means, as with a cassette tape of music, you have to fast forward through the tape to find a particular file or document. If you wanted to quickly share, say, five different documents with a colleague, you'd have to wait quite a while as the tape skipped around to various sections to find the documents and retrieve them.

But that's really not what tape backup is about. Instead, it's an inexpensive media for last-ditch, offsite backup storage — the type of backup that's done automatically, late at night, and then filed away in a fireproof box the next day so that the network can be recovered some time in the future if something dramatically bad happened.

So, how do you add tape? Here are the three major tape formats you might concern yourself with:

✦ **QIC.** The popular standard for inexpensive backups is QIC technology. Pronounced "quick," QIC is an impressive-sounding acronym until you realize it stands for "quarter-inch cartridge," after which maybe you're not so impressed. But QIC's various standards (ranging from QIC-40 to QIC-3220) enable you to use tapes that store up to 10GB. Some innovative drive makers have sped these drives up, too, resulting in throughput of 20 or 30 megabytes per second. Not bad.

✦ **DAT.** Digital audio tape is popular for backups as well as for high-end audio recording. Transfer rates aren't barn burners, usually hovering around 0.5 MBps. The tape capacities range from a few gigabytes to 12GB or more, with data compression as a popular option. Lastly, although good and relatively speedy, DAT drives are expensive and have stayed that way for a number of years.

✦ **DLT.** Digital linear tape is changing the tape game a bit, offering huge capacities and high (2.5 MBps) speeds. Capacities for these sorts of drives range from 20GB to 70GB with the media costing around a dollar per gigabyte or less. This is truly one of the best ways to back up entire workgroups and servers with a hands-off system of automated software and safe physical storage. But it's also the ultimate in expensive backup systems, often doubling the price of already costly DAT drives.

Adding a Removable Media Drive to Your Mac

Attaching most external removable media drives to your Mac is a cakewalk, especially if you have experience adding a scanner or external hard drive. The only exceptions occur when the drive you're using isn't particularly designed to work with a Macintosh or offers less-than-stellar software drivers. Most of the popular removable cartridge drives rarely suffer from such deficiencies, and, in fact, many of them can be used as startup drives or even be used to read DOS-formatted media directly.

You may also decide that you'd prefer to install an internal removable device. Aside from not taking up space on your desktop, an internal upgrade has the added advantage of being able to access the faster internal SCSI buses on newer Macs. This will go a long way toward making your removable drive feel as though it offers speeds that rival a hard drive.

Adding an external removable media drive

External removable media drives attach to the SCSI port on the back of your Mac. (In the case of an iMac or similar USB-equipped Mac, you may find an external drive designed to hook up to a USB port. Chapter 10 explains USB in more detail.) Depending on the Mac model, you may need an adapter — in general, the removable drive will include a cable or adapter that connects to the standard 25-pin SCSI port on the back of most Macs. (50-pin Fast SCSI and 64-pin Wide SCSI ports may also be supported by the removable drive and are desirable for best performance.)

To install an external drive:

1. Unpack the drive and check for all the necessary parts. Pay close attention to any cards or inserts that the manufacturer installs in the drive for shipping (check your manual carefully). You'll need to remove any of these retaining devices before you turn on your drive.

2. Using the Apple System Profiler or a similar SCSI probe tool, check to ensure you have a free SCSI ID available for the drive (see Figure 9-5). (Remember to select the correct bus if you have both an internal and external SCSI bus in your Mac.)

Note

To access the SCSI device information in the Apple System Profiler, choose Select ➪ Device Information from the program's menu bar.

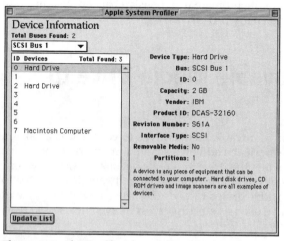

Figure 9-5: The Profiler shows that SCSI ID 5 is available on my Mac's SCSI bus.

3. Change the SCSI ID on the back of your drive to the ID number you've identified as available in your Mac (see Figure 9-6).

Figure 9-6: Most external removable media devices have a SCSI indicator with an up and a down button for changing SCSI IDs.

4. Turn off your computer. Apple and other Mac peripheral companies recommend that you never have your computer on when installing or uninstalling SCSI devices.

5. Decide where you'll be installing the drive in your SCSI chain. (If this is your only external SCSI device, skip to step 6.) If you have another external device, for instance, decide whether you'll be installing this drive using the existing device's SCSI port or if you'll be plugging your new drive directly into your Mac. Remember that you should only have one terminator at the end of your SCSI chain, so don't allow more than one of your external devices to be terminated.

6. Plug the SCSI cable into the SCSI IN port on the back of your removable media drive (see Figure 9-7). If it doesn't have a port specifically labeled SCSI IN, you can likely use either port.

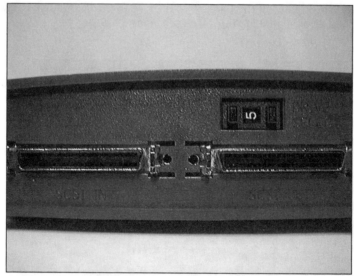

Figure 9-7: Check your SCSI connections for some indication that one is the In port and one is the Out port. (Shown is a SyQuest SyJet.)

7. Plug the other end of the SCSI cable into your Mac, or plug it into the next SCSI device in your SCSI chain if you have other devices.

8. If this removable drive is the last device in your SCSI chain, you'll need to terminate it. Either add a terminator to its SCSI OUT port, flip the termination switch, or, if the drive offers auto-sensing termination, do nothing at all. (Don't forget to remove or deactivate any terminators you've installed or activated on devices installed earlier in the chain.)

9. Plug the drive into an electrical socket (preferably a surge protector).

10. Turn on the drive and wait for it to spin up. (It should flash its lights, make a little noise for a moment or two, and then calm down.) If your drive has no power switch, skip to 11.

11. Start up your Mac.

12. With the Mac activated and the drive on, install any software that came with the drive. You may need to restart your Mac.

To test the installation, you can probably insert the appropriate cartridge for your new drive and see if it mounts the cartridge on your Mac's desktop in the Finder. If it does, all went well. (You may have to format the media cartridge before it will work properly.) If you don't see the drive, check the Apple System Profiler to make sure it's been mounted using the SCSI ID number you expected. If it has, and the drive still doesn't work, consult your manual for any specifics this drive requires.

If your drive doesn't appear to be mounted, you can troubleshoot it as you would any SCSI device:

✦ Visually inspect the SCSI ID setting to ensure it's set for the expected number. If it isn't (or if it's set for an ID number that is already taken in your Mac), shut down immediately, change the ID number on the drive to an ID that's available in your Mac, and restart.

✦ Check the cable connection to your device and check all the cable connections in your SCSI chain.

✦ Make sure only the last device in an external SCSI chain is terminated.

If the drive still won't work, consult your drive's manual and check some of the other SCSI troubleshooting tips in Chapter 23.

Adding an internal removable media drive

You'll notice that this process is very similar to installing an internal hard drive. Usually the only difference is a removable media drive generally needs a full 5.25-inch drive bay in your Mac OS computer. You'll also need a special mounting kit for most Mac models to make the slightly smaller facing of the internal drive fit flush with the front of your computer.

Here's a few things to know before you get started:

✦ As with an internal hard drive, consider where exactly you're putting the drive on the internal SCSI chain. Make sure you have an available SCSI connection on the ribbon cable, as well as an available power connection inside your Mac.

✦ If you will be installing it in the middle of the SCSI cable that's inside your Mac, the drive should not be terminated. If it's on the end of the SCSI cable, you'll need to terminate the drive, while making sure that no other drives inside the Mac remain terminated.

✦ You'll also want to make sure the SCSI ID is set correctly on the internal drive. Check the Apple System Profiler for an available ID, and then consult the drive's manual for instructions on setting the SCSI ID. (It's likely set to SCSI ID 4 or 5, which should be fine if only the Mac's original SCSI devices are installed — unless the Mac already has a factory-installed removable drive.)

✦ Make sure you have the appropriate mounting kit for your Mac model.

Macs that can accept internal removable drives include the Performa 6400, Power Macintosh 6500, 7200, 7300, 7500, 7600, 8600, 9600, G3 Desktop, G3 Minitower and G3 Server series, and subsequent full-size Mac desktop and minitower computers. Nearly all Mac OS clone models can accept an internal drive, if there's still a free expansion bay in the case and the appropriate power and SCSI connectors are available inside — just be sure to order the correct mounting kit for your particular Mac or Mac clone model when you buy the drive. Some expandable Quadra-level machines might have room for a removable drive if they don't already have an internal CD-ROM drive, as the minitower machines (Quadra 840AV, 950, and so on) should support an internal removeable drive, assuming you can find a mounting kit and front bezel to fit that model.

To install an internal drive:

1. Make sure your Mac is shut down and unplugged, and you're electrically grounded. Remove the Mac's case.

2. Install the mounting hardware on the drive so it can slide into its drive bay.

3. Slide the drive into its bay.

4. Connect the SCSI cable to the drive. Make sure you orient the cable correctly, with the red strip on the SCSI cable lining up with Pin1, the leftmost pin on the connector.

5. Connect the power wires to the drive. They can only install in one direction, so if you have trouble plugging the connector into the drive, try flipping it over.

6. Make sure the drive is firmly seated in its bay, and then install the mounting kit's faceplate so that it's flush with the front of the case (see Figure 9-8).

7. Start up your Mac and install any software that came with the drive. Restart the computer if necessary.

Now insert a cartridge to test the drive. If things don't seem to be working, check your manual, the troubleshooting tips at the end of the section "Adding an external removable media drive," or most of Chapter 23.

As when installing any internal device, you can test the drive with the Mac's case still off, but shut your Mac down again and replace the case once you're sure everything is working.

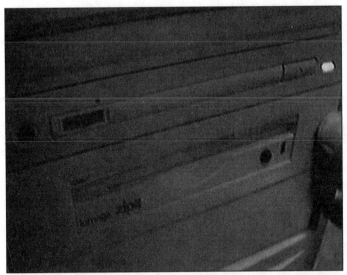

Figure 9-8: The front plate fits around the front of the removable drive to provide an opening for inserting cartridges (shown is an internal Zip drive).

Implement Your Backup Plan

Here's a true story: While working in the science department at my alma mater after graduation, a major outage occurred on the administration's server computer (an Intel-compatible PC) during a fairly stormy weekend. Perhaps due to a lightning hit or some similar electric shock issue, the main hard drive in the server went completely dead. The data on it, barring an incredibly expensive excavation, was irretrievable.

Of course, we had a backup. The system administrator had diligently run a tape backup program weekly on the server over the past year since its installation, and the process was going strong. A cartridge of all our data existed. This was not just a tragedy, but an opportunity; our system administrator, the consummate professional, had done the right thing and was likely going to impress the dean and high-ranking academics. Foresight had won over chance.

Actually, chance had another card up its sleeve. As it turns out, the tape cartridge that the system administrator had used for the most recent backup (about four days old) was bad. He couldn't get any data from it. To make matters worse, he had done something that isn't exactly recommended—he'd used that same cartridge for all his backups in the department for the last nine months. That's nine *whole* months.

Hard drives can (and eventually *will*) go bad. It's an engineering fact — they're mechanical devices with a limited lifespan. But tape and other backup devices can *also* go bad. In our science department, anything that wasn't saved on individual hard drives was forcibly reverted to files and folders that had been backed up nine months prior to that time. Entire projects, budgets, file entries and papers were lost. There was a backup plan in place, but it wasn't a terribly good one. Instead, it only provided a false sense of security.

Note   DriverSavers (`www.drivesavers.com`) is a company that's renowned for its ability to revive destroyed drives. If you're ever in a situation where you have to get data off a drive that's been waterlogged, burned, dropped, run over, or exposed to any other fury of nature, contact Drivesavers and see what they can do. A bullet-proof backup plan is a lot cheaper, though.

What to back up

You don't *have* to back up everything on your hard drive. After all, in most cases (especially those where you've legally bought and licensed your software) you won't need to back up applications, because you have the originally floppy disks or CD-ROMs. You also may not need to back up the System Folder, because you have your Mac OS CD handy and you could, in a pinch, reinstall the operating system.

So what do you need to back up? Of course, you should *consider* backing up absolutely everything on your hard drive(s) or network. (See sidebar that follows for some interesting ideas.) But if you just can't spare the space, here's what you should make a point of backing up:

✦ **Documents.** Anything you create using your hands and your brain should be backed up. Likewise, back up anything anyone else has created that's saved on your hard drive. You don't want to have to recreate the documents if you lose your main hard drive.

✦ **Upgrades and updates.** You'll likely download upgrades and updates to your existing software programs at times when you find something new on the manufacturer's Web site. Make a point of quickly dragging those files to a handy Zip or SyJet cartridge while you're busy installing them. This includes new extensions, control panels, and fonts you install in the System Folder.

✦ **Bookmarks.** If you use your Web browser extensively, make a point of backing up the Bookmarks file that's in that browser's folder in the Preferences folder, which is located in the System Folder.

✦ **E-mail.** If you're like me, you like to keep your old e-mail. It allows you to root around for an old phone number, keep a paper trail of communications, and dig up that Web address someone sent you once. I keep hundreds of megabytes of e-mail saved, and I back it up (and archive it) regularly so I don't miss a beat.

✦ **Preferences.** It won't kill you to lose these, but you might want to back up the preference files for your favorite applications — especially if you've got them set just right. Preferences are in the Preferences folder in the System Folder.

✦ **Saved Games.** Do you want to start over on level one? I thought not.

How to back up

Two different backup terms get bandied about often and deserve definitions. Not everyone uses these terms as strictly defined as I'm suggesting here, but it's how I'll try to use the terms in this book:

✦ **Backing up.** By this I mean copying files currently on your Mac or your network to another type of media on a regular basis, according to a predefined system that rotates the backup media over a fixed period of time. Backups are created using either a *mirroring* system (where an exact copy of your folders and documents is copied to the backup media) or an *incremental* system (where only folders and documents that have changed since the last backup session are copied to the backup media).

✦ **Archiving.** In this case, I'm talking about copying files from your hard drive or network to another media, with the intention of deleting the files from your hard drive and storing the archival media in a safe place. This is useful for holding onto older files that you no longer need on a day-to-day basis, but may need down the road.

Obviously, both have their place. But the single most common error in backing up data is what I described happened in my alma mater's science department — archiving when one means to back up. A lot of programs that call themselves backup programs will perform something very convenient for you — incremental backups. They'll only update files that have changed since the last time you archived. This is a great feature but, by itself, is neither archiving nor a complete backup system.

Evangelista tip: Self-extracting System Folder

It's true that the most important files to back up on your Mac are data files, as you can't recreate them without hours of work once they're gone. And, if you're into economy backups, you can usually skip things like applications and the System Folder. They can be reinstalled from disks and installation CD-ROMs.

But backing up those files, too, really isn't such a bad idea, especially if there's a decent chance that your Mac could get messed up — whether it's on public display, used in a lab setting, or if you tend to install a bunch of beta software. System administrator Rich Barron (from both the CSU Fullerton — Art Department and Santa Ana College in Southern California) has a great tip — use the self-extracting archive option in the programs StuffIt Lite or StuffIt Deluxe to create an archive that can open itself on most any Mac in your organization, resulting in a ready-made System Folder:

"I do a normal install on the Mac. I run it through its paces in all the programs and work out all the glitches I catch. Next I take the System Folder and make a duplicate that I compress and turn into a self-extracting archive (.sea) so it is not dependent on its 'mother' program to help it uncompress. I also make a very stripped-down version (few extensions, no fonts, few control panels, and so on) of the same System Folder. The remaining software is also compressed program by program in the same .sea format."

You might also find that the program ShrinkWrap, from Aladdin Systems (www.aladdin-sys.com), is a useful way to create System folder backups; instead of self-extracting archives, you can create disk images that you can double-click and mount on the desktop, causing them to act exactly like large floppy disks that you can then install or copy files from.

Use the Zip disk as a Startup disk (⌘-Option-Shift-Del keys can be used together to skip the internal hard drive and boot off an external system disk), and then copy the compressed System Folder to the newly formatted (or otherwise repaired) hard drive. Double-click to decompress the System Folder, and then restart. You should have a new system, ready to let you get some work done. (The second half of this tip, including information for restoring systems for Mac workgroups, can be found in Chapter 33.)

If you just continue to mirror the changes you make on your hard drive onto a single backup cartridge, you can't use that cartridge to retrieve a document that became corrupted or was inadvertently deleted a few weeks ago, as you could if you created an archival tape or cartridge, and then stored it away. At the same time, incrementally copying updated files to the same cartridge isn't a proper backup system, either, because a flaw in the cartridge itself negates any advantage to performing the backup.

In a serious backup situation, you need a *generational* approach to copying your data from your hard drive(s) or network to the backup media. Depending on your level of paranoia you can introduce as many generations as you want into the equation. The bottom line is you always need to have more than one backup to choose from at a given moment.

Note   Aladdin Systems seems to offer a lot of software entries in this category, but I've got another one to discuss. Although it's not technically a backup utility, you may find FlashBack (www.aladdinsys.com) to be convenient for archiving different *versions* of the same document, allowing you to move backward through your document's different saves to find a version you like more. Other utilities, like Michael Kamprath's Super Save (www.kamprath.net/claireware) will actually save each *keystroke* you make in text documents, enabling you to pour back through them to recreate documents if necessary. (It helps to be a great typist, naturally.)

A generational system

Here's how a three-generation backup system would work. You start with three different cartridges. One Monday, mirror your hard drive or network to the first cartridge. On Wednesday, mirror your hard drive to the second cartridge. On Friday, mirror the drive to the third cartridge. Now, a good idea would be to drop the Monday cartridge out of the rotation and store it away (offsite, in a fireproof casing, in a safe deposit box, and so on). You might do this once a week or once a month, depending on how many cartridges you feel safe using.

Next, with a new cartridge, mirror your drives on Monday. When Wednesday rolls around, do your mirroring on the Wednesday cartridge; on Friday, mirror over the Friday cartridge. And so on. (Note that these Wednesday and Friday backups could be incremental, too, but for the sake of this example they're all fresh, complete mirroring backups.)

Notice what you're doing here. Every other business day, you have a fresh new backup. If the network fails on Thursday, you can back up using the Wednesday cartridge — if the Wednesday cartridge is no good, you can try the Monday cartridge. Plus, you've got an extra little bonus — those archival cartridges that slipped out of the rotation. If suddenly you find a corrupt or virus-infected file, then you have the option of fishing through your archives for a copy that wasn't corrupted, even if the corruption happened weeks ago.

Note

Obviously, if you're not backing up incredibly important business files or an entire network, you might be able to get away with backing up once or twice a week. But seriously consider being vigilant about backing up, even if it's only a home system. Your Quicken data or salary spreadsheet can change a lot in few weeks, and I guarantee you'll appreciate having that data backed up if you ever run into trouble. At the very least, home users should set a weekly or semi-weekly alarm to remind them to backup to a removable cartridge drive. Just remember to use a fresh cartridge every few weeks and use the old one as an archive.

A software approach

If you're a system administrator or in a similar position of responsibility, your first order of business should be to think seriously about your backup issues. You will probably also want to grab some software to help you out. Retrospect, from Dantz Corp (www.dantz.com), is among the most popular for Mac users and networks (see Figure 9-9). For other levels of users, Dantz offers Disk Fit Pro and Disk Fit Direct, for backing up the individual Macs of professional and personal users, respectively. Disk Fit Direct tends to be bundled with removable media drives — check the product material if this interests you.

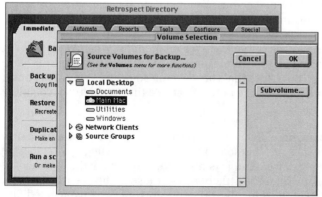

Figure 9-9: Retrospect offers industrial-style backup capability for networks and server computers.

If you feel you'd like to work up to professional-level software, or if you'd like to give something a bit cheaper a try, you might look into a shareware solution. Be aware that the shareware author may not offer any guarantees about the usefulness or accuracy of the software. (Then again, most big companies don't either.) You can try some of the downloadable options or grab one or two off the CD. One I've found useful is called Drag 'n' Back.

Drag'n'Back and Drag'n'Back Lite (with fewer features) are located on the CD-ROM included with this book.

Drag'n'Back offers two options that you'll find on the pro-level software, too — the ability to update incrementally and the ability to update using an archival system (see Figure 9-10).

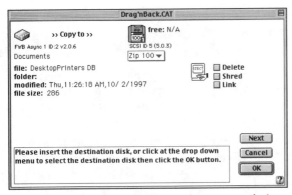

Figure 9-10: Drag'n'Back offers a shareware solution to professional backup issues.

Incremental updates

In fact, most backup programs offer the ability to update incrementally. Remember, incremental updates add only the files that have changed since the last time the data was mirrored to the cartridge in question. It's okay to use this feature as long as you continue to swap cartridges in a generational pattern. Consider the following scenario (which assumes you've already been backing up for at least a week):

1. You do a full backup to a new cartridge on Monday the 6th (of a particular month).

2. You change an important file on Tuesday.

3. On Wednesday the 8th, you do an incremental backup to the Wednesday cartridge. This cartridge was last updated on Wednesday the 1st, so the changed file (on Tuesday the 7th) is noted and backed up.

4. On Friday the 10th, you do an incremental backup to the Friday cartridge. The change has occurred since last Friday (the 3rd), so it is noted and backed up here as well.

Now, if you have pulled the cartridge used on Monday and replaced it with a new one for the next Monday, you'll have an old copy of the file (the one that was recorded on the 6th), and two new copies of the program (on the 8th and the 10th). Both bases are covered — if a user needs the older copy of the file, you have it. If they lose the newer version, you've got that, too. If you're the system administrator for a large network, eventually you'll be a hero.

Caution

Don't get too cocky, though. Remember one last warning. Test your media regularly, especially if you're using it over and over again. Even those Wednesday and Friday cartridges (or whatever days you ultimately settle on) should be checked every few weeks to see if they can really be used to restore data. If you do run into trouble and need to restore data, you'll be glad you've tested your updates recently.

Evangelista and Expert tips: Thou shalt back up

As you might imagine, Evangelistas and experts alike have plenty of horror stories resulting in lapses in their backup routines. Here's a quick look at some of the best of those, including some times for quick and better backups—plus the requisite scare tactics to get you to promise yourself that you'll implement a backup plan:

"Obviously, you'll want to back up your data regularly, but why back up corrupted files? Just before doing a backup, run your diagnostic tools, such as Tech Tool Pro or Norton Utilities for a bootable disk. Repair all broken files, and then do your backup. That way, you'll know that you have a clean backup."—Win Stiles

"'I Lost My Entire Thesis...and it was due two hours ago!' Losing an important document is a common complaint among McGill students and faculty. As Murphy's Law would have it, the likelihood of losing a paper is directly proportional to the importance it bears to the author and inversely proportional to the number of backup copies the user has made.

"Here are several points to keep in mind: Hard disk drives are typically warranted for a maximum of five years. It's not a matter of if they fail, but when they fail.

"Each time your computer hangs, freezes, or crashes, there's a good chance that at least one file on your computer is slightly corrupted, and an even better chance that it's one of the files that you were just working on.

"Accidents happen, like saving another document with the same filename or inadvertently putting your file in the trash. Why tempt fate? You only have so much time to waste on recovering your thesis when it was due two hours ago. Why not do your best to prevent the situation from ever happening? It's not difficult and it only takes minutes to do. The Golden Rule: Always have a backup of your work. Consider the effort of backing up versus the effort of retyping or rewriting your entire thesis when it was due two hours ago."—James A. Connolly, McGill University Computing Centre

(continued)

(continued)

"Backing up doesn't need to be complicated. With at least two physical hard drives, you can back up just the data partition to the other drive. That way if one drive dies, you've still got the data on the other. It won't help if your house burns down, but the backup tape on your shelf wouldn't help then, either." — Marc Zeedar

Want some more expert advice on backing up? Craig Issacs from Dantz Corporation (the same folks that make Retrospect and Disk Fit) has a few choice tips for people putting together their backup plans. He tells me his one hope is that you will be encouraged to create a backup of your data before attempting any upgrade or fix. Here are his top tips:

Automate your backups. Get a backup device that holds about twice as much as your hard disk so you can schedule backups for times when you're not there.

Back up every hard disk. Every hard disk contains critical data so don't just back up servers. And make sure you include portable computers.

Back up more than just documents. Don't limit backups to just certain files — you'll inevitably need one that wasn't backed up. Good backup software only backs up files that are new or modified.

Make several copies. Make at least three different sets of your data. Even an old copy is better than no copy at all.

Keep a backup set offsite. You never know when a fire, flood, theft, or earthquake makes your offsite copy your only copy.

Verify your backup. You need confidence in your backups. Make sure your backup software has full read-back verification. And try restoring a few files yourself, just in case.

Implement a network backup strategy. If you're on a network, network backup software lets you share a storage device and ensures every Macintosh is backed up.

Don't procrastinate. Far too many new Dantz customers are people who recently lost data. Develop your backup plan now!

Summary

✦ Removable media drives have become very popular among all sorts of Mac owners in the past few years, in part because of breakthroughs in their speed, capacity, and usability. These days, little cartridges store hundreds of megabytes or even gigabytes of data, but they work pretty much like a regular hard drive.

✦ Removable cartridge drives come in many shapes and sizes, including the incredibly popular Iomega Zip drive and the equally famous Jaz and SyQuest SyJet drives. Other drives offer even more capacity and faster access. Although removable cartridge drives are easily the most popular, they aren't the only type of drives on the market. Magneto-optical and tape-backup technologies are equally as viable for certain tasks.

✦ Once you pin down the sort of removable media drive you'd like to use, you'll want to install it. Both internal and external drives exist, so pick your versions and install away. Be warned, though, that installing these drives never fails to involve the magical world of SCSI.

✦ With the drive in place and working properly, you're ready to start backing up your Mac or your workgroup. To do that requires some forethought and a smart plan, as well as an awareness of the terminology. Of course, new software won't hurt, either.

✦   ✦   ✦

Input Devices

So far we humans haven't perfected the "Computer! I'd like tea. Earl Grey — hot!" sort of speech-recognition that the Star Trek characters are able to use when dealing with a computer. We're getting close, though, and it sure won't take 400 years to get to that point, either. Of course, it isn't completely clear that voice command is necessarily the perfect interface (in all cases) for dealing with computers, because we already have plenty of talking going on in the office and down in the academic computer lab. Until we do come up with something better, then, we're forced to focus on the input tools we have — different types of mice, keyboards, trackpads, and touch-sensitive devices.

Every Mac comes with a mouse, and, aside from a bizarre period of cost-conscious years in the early 1990s, all Macs come with keyboards. These are the basic means that we use for communicating directly with the Mac OS. But there are other ways.

If you've never explored the different options available to you for input, you may be missing out on something special. I personally enjoy using a trackball for my daily mousing needs, and the one I have offers extra programmable buttons I can use for a variety of tasks. In Mac OS 8 and above, the operating system will actually respond to two different sorts of mouse clicks (a regular click and a Ctrl+click) that can be programmed into some mice to make the process more convenient. My mouse has still another button which, when pressed, pops up a quick-and-easy application switching menu that lets me change the current application without heading to the Application menu (see Figure 10-1).

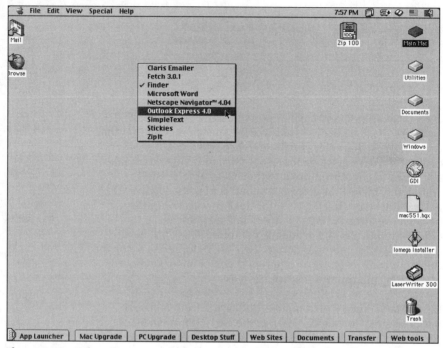

Figure 10-1: Using a programmable Kensington Turbo Mouse, I'm able to bring up a custom menu that enables me to switch between programs.

First, let's discuss how the Mac's input/output technology, the Apple Desktop Bus, works. I'll then move on to choosing and installing input devices.

The Apple Desktop Bus

The Apple Desktop Bus (usually redundantly referred to as the *ADB bus*) is another one of those fabulously simple and useful innovations on the Mac side of the computing arena that hasn't taken off with Intel-compatible PCs. ADB has many similarities to SCSI, as it is a peripheral bus architecture that enables you to daisy chain devices together, allowing them to all communicate with the Mac as necessary. ADB has something else in common with SCSI: it's an asynchronous bus, meaning data can be sent back and forth between devices and the Mac at any time —the device simply requests the Mac's attention, and then proceeds to send the data once it has received the go-ahead.

ADB is dissimilar to SCSI in one notable way: It's very, very slow. According to Apple's specifications, the ADB bus transmits at 154 bytes per second. (Compare that to a 5MB per second maximum on the slowest SCSI bus.) ADB offers very little bandwidth to data, communicating serially—that is, one data bit at a time. This isn't usually a problem, because ADB is used to hook up fairly simple devices, such as keyboards and mice, that don't need to communicate a ton of complex data. It does mean, though, that there's a practical limit to the number of devices you can hook up to the ADB port, although that's mitigated somewhat by the fact that it's difficult to use more than two input devices at once. (Just try it.)

ADB connections

ADB is certainly capable, though. Most recent Macs have a single ADB port, although Mac II and Centris/Quadra models, among others, often offered two ADB ports. Both are on the same bus, however, and most ADB devices offer more than one ADB connection, so you can daisy chain the devices to one another (see Figure 10-2).

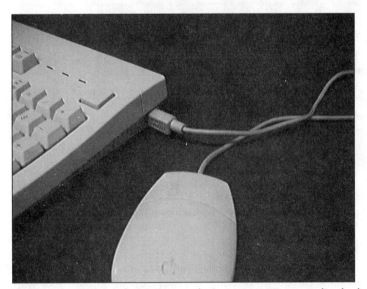

Figure 10-2: A daisy chain of input devices: An ADB mouse hooked up to the Mac, ultimately, via its attachment to an ADB keyboard

The ADB cable uses a 4-pin DIN connector on both sides for connecting devices to the Mac or to each other. No specific termination is necessary to make the devices work correctly, although you may run into a practical termination—ADB devices that don't thoughtfully provide a second ADB port. In these cases, you may have to rearrange your devices so that the single-port device is at the end of your chain.

You may also notice the tendency in the Mac world for some manufacturers to use the ADB port as a source of power for their other, reasonably unrelated, devices. Modems are a prime candidate: some models not only plug into the modem port to communicate with the Mac, they also plug into the ADB port to draw a bit of power. Usually a device that does this will also have a pass-through connector (see Figure 10-3). In these cases, you can connect your keyboard or mouse wiring directly to the back of the pass-through connector to provide power.

Don't think, however, that you can connect as many devices as you want with these pass-through connectors. You'll find there's a practical limit of about three or four devices — even though the theoretical limit is about 14 devices — on an ADB bus before things start to get sluggish.

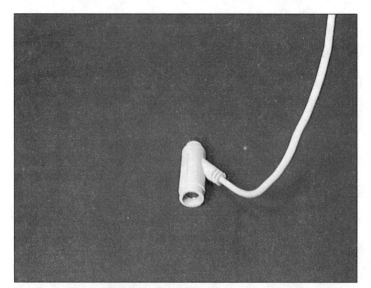

Figure 10-3: Some devices offer special ADB pass-through ports for connecting other devices.

Note

Apple warns that signal degradation could set in if you attach more than three ADB devices to your Mac, although I've personally worked with at least four with no problems. If you do notice sluggishness or the occasionally lost character when typing, you might try working with fewer ADB devices connected to see if that solves your trouble.

One other note about ADB connections — ADB connections are not *hot-swappable*, meaning you need to turn the computer off before plugging and unplugging devices. Although many Mac users report having no trouble connecting and disconnecting devices while the Mac is still powered up, I can only tell you what Apple tells us: This is not recommended.

ADB numbers

Although it's not terribly important in most cases, ADB, like SCSI, addresses its devices with special numbers. These numbers enable the Mac to identify the device that needs attention and listen for its input. As a user, it's not something you generally have to worry about. If prompted though, it can be useful to know that the Mac keyboard is generally device number 2, whereas a mouse is usually device number 3. (The occasionally third-party input device driver software has been known to ask for this information.)

A couple of other numbers are important. The limit to the length of all your cables should be about 5 meters, says Apple's technical specs, which means you'll need to buy special add-on devices if you plan to use a keyboard and/or mouse any farther away from your Mac than that. ADB devices (when added together) can't draw more than 500 milliamperes (mA) total for all devices. For comparison, Apple says the Apple Standard Keyboard draws a maximum of 100 mA, and the Apple Extended Keyboard draws a maximum of 85 mA. You can check the technical specifications of your other ADB devices, and then add their consumption numbers together.

Input Devices

So what can you hook up using those ADB ports? Quite a lot, actually. Aside from the typical input devices — mice, trackballs, keyboards — you'll find some interesting devices to consider purchasing. Input devices can range from graphics pads, which enable you to input data using a pen, to touch screens, and even special devices for the physically challenged.

Where do you find these devices? Obviously the local computer store only carries a few different keyboards and mice, usually those that appeal to the widest audience of people. For more specialized devices, you'll often have to look around a little bit. Try the Mac-based catalog vendors and their associated online services. Also, specifically for Mac peripherals, check out some of these companies:

✦ **MacAlley** (www.macally.com) makes a number of Mac ADB peripherals, including keyboards, mice, touchpads, joysticks, and gamepads. It's also a good place to find storage devices, cables, and adapters for Macs.

✦ **APS Technologies** (www.apstech.com) builds some peripherals, but they're also a catalog company and clearing house for special items such as advanced mousing controllers, cables, and the like.

✦ **Adesso, Inc.** (www.adessoinc.com) specializes in ergonomic keyboards and mice for Macs and PCs.

✦ **Microspeed** (www.microspeed.com) offers trackpads, mice, and Mac keyboards.

✦ **Qtronix** (www.qtronix.com) makes mice, trackballs, and unique keyboard solutions with built-in mousing devices.

✦ **Kensington** (www.kensington.com), best known for trackballs, also offers other accessories and mousing solutions.

Keyboard

The original Mac classic form factor usually went hand-in-hand with a smallish 58-key keyboard that looked a whole lot like a disembodied typewriter. Later, Apple made the transition to larger keyboards, including some middling designs, and eventually adopted the typical form factor of today, the 104-key extended keyboard. Nearly any Mac keyboard you buy these days includes a Power key in the upper right-hand corner, function keys across the top of the keyboard, and a numeric keypad on the right-hand side. That still gives manufacturers some room to play with, so keyboards tend to come in all shapes and sizes.

Evangelista tip: Keyboards and ADB, susceptible to static

Does the carpet in your office develop a pretty strong static electricity charge? If you live in a dry climate and/or you notice you get little shocks when you touch the door knobs, filing cabinets, or computer components in your workspace, you might need to take extra precautions to make sure you're not damaging computer equipment with static electricity.

Evangelista Tony Hines had this to say about his workplace and their creative solution:

"About two years ago, our ad agency moved into a freshly carpeted office space; we promptly discovered that said carpet had a knack for developing strong jolts. After knocking out two keyboards and one mouse, we knew we had to do something to get rid of the static.

"We invested in two large humidifiers, but didn't notice much of a difference. Then, the guy who maintains our phone systems passed along a tidbit that proved to be the ideal solution: fabric softener. No, we don't put fabric softener on our Macs. We simply bought a large, cheap bottle of fabric softener at the local grocery store, and then mixed it half-and-half with water in a spray bottle. About once a week, we spray the carpets in our offices, and it works great. Plus, the office carpets smell 'spring fresh'!"

Keyboard layouts

One thing you may already know about your Mac is its ability to support keyboard layouts other than the standard QWERTY format to which English-speaking typists have grown accustomed. If you use a keyboard with an international layout, you can change many of the layouts using just the Keyboard control panel, as shown in Figure 10-4, along with the menu bar–based layout switcher. (If your version of the Mac OS is a localized one, you'll probably see other options.)

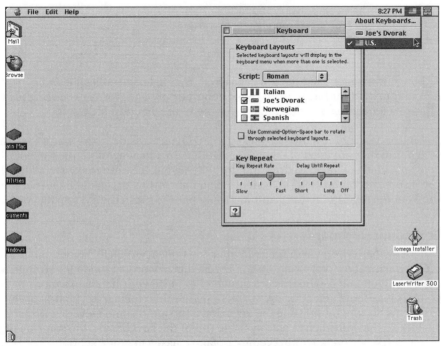

Figure 10-4: Changing the way your Mac interprets the layout of a keyboard

One popular keyboard layout you might want to switch to is the Dvorak layout, a 1936 efficiency expert's answer to the slow and somewhat injurious nature of the QWERTY layout. What the Dvorak keyboard layout does is change the way your keyboard's keys are interpreted by your Mac to match that shown in Figure 10-5. You don't have to buy a special keyboard to implement this layout, although you might find it handy to run to a crafts store and buy some alphabet stickers to put on your existing keyboard's keys.

On the CD-ROM

You can find Joe's Dvorak layout, a keyboard layout file for the Mac, on the CD-ROM included with this book. To install it, close all applications and then drag the file to the System Folder. Click OK to add it to the System file. You can then change to the layout in the Keyboard control panel.

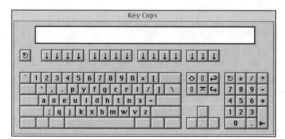

Figure 10-5: The Dvorak layout. Supposedly 70% of the letters you type won't require you to move your hands.

Although I've never used the Dvorak layout myself, I have colleagues who swear by it. And frankly, after hacking out these hundreds of pages for your reading pleasure, I think I'll look into something that gives my typing hands a little rest.

So how do you install a layout? All keyboard layouts reside in the Mac's System file, which is in the root level of the System Folder. To add a layout to the Keyboard control panel, you need to drag and drop the layout file onto the System file. This can also be accomplished (in System 7.5 and above) by dragging the layout file onto the System Folder, which will automatically put the file in the System file for you.

Ergonomic keyboards

Other keyboards you encounter will offer the typical QWERTY layout, but feature a more comfortable (or, to employ an overused buzzword, ergonomic) arrangement of keys. Ergonomic keyboards are designed to place your hands in a more comfortable, more scientifically correct posture than regular keyboards promote. Often this is done by splitting the keys down the middle and elevating the wrists slightly so that your hands curl over the top of the keyboard — the same position you may have been taught in typing or piano classes in grade school.

Of major concern is the possibility that the repetitive nature of typing and mousing (especially for the eight to ten hours a day that some of us spend doing it) will hurt us in the long run if not done correctly. My best advice to you is to try new keyboards, and don't be afraid to spend some money on the right one. Again, go with a store or mail-order house that offers a liberal return policy, and test the thing intensively for a few days before settling on it conclusively.

Other keyboards

There doesn't seem to be a particular shortage of keyboard solutions, although your selection may be limited to obvious choices in stores like CompUSA. Aside from Apple's basic-but-quality keyboards bundled with every Mac (such as the Apple Design Keyboard) and sold as replacements, third-party vendors step in with the occasional gadget or interesting add-on.

Adesso, Inc., for instance, offers not only ergonomic keyboards, but also models that enable you to use a trackpad or small joystick-like pointer (centered on the keyboard) for mousing tasks. Visioneer has, in the past, made a Mac keyboard that included a page scanner for quick document scanning tasks. Still other keyboards have been made for special purposes, including those suited for point-of-sale computers or single-handed operation. For Macs that lack them (such as those with classic form factors and PowerBooks), you can get add-on ADB keypads for entering numerical data.

Mousing

You probably don't need a reprise of the whole story of how Apple came to think of the computer mouse as an important component in computing, but suffice it to say that they did and it is. (Steve Jobs and other Apple employees gained access to Xerox's PARC laboratories, where mousing and graphical interfaces were being developed on computers that were destined to fail in the marketplace.) The mouse and similar devices are an important part of how users deal with computers, perhaps humanizing computers in a way that makes it easier to use them productively.

Not that the original mouse was, by any means, the end of the line. Although pointing devices remain basically subjective in their merits (you need to decide for yourself what you like the most), the standard Mac mouse has a few obvious drawbacks. For instance, it's not a good idea to grab and hold onto a small slab of anything for hours at a time (see Figure 10-6), because it'll cramp your hand.

Figure 10-6: An early Mac mouse (Mac Plus) offers a number of drawbacks, including sharp edges and a single button.

Although Apple has, over the years, made various improvements to the basic mouse included with every Mac, it certainly hasn't reached a satisfactory stopping point. Many third-party companies have stepped up to fill in some of the gaps, such as:

✦ **Size.** Some mouse manufacturers and ergonomics experts argue that a larger mouse is better than a smaller one, enabling you to drape your hand over the mouse and guide it instead of clamping down on a smaller mouse with your hand.

✦ **Shape.** Ergonomically shapped mice are also in vogue, offering shapes that work specifically for the left or right hand, supposedly to reduce stress on your fingers, wrist, and/or arm.

✦ **Buttons.** Although die-hard Mac users may argue that a one-button mouse offers a simpler, more elegant interface, it's also true that you can do a lot more with a multibutton programmable mouse. The Mac OS is even starting to support dual-button mice, in spite of the majority of Mac users having mice with one button. (The Mac OS enables you to hold down the Ctrl key while clicking the mouse button to access a second set of mouse button features.)

✦ **Wiring.** Although of dubious value, some users enjoy spending a little extra money to get a wireless mouse for their setup. Useful only in limited circumstances, these mice at least offer the benefit of enabling you to place them on a more comfortable surface.

The precision of a mouse or mousing device is measured in dots per inch (dpi). A typical mouse has a precision of 200 to 400 dpi — anything less than that is too little, and anything more than that is considered very precise. There are also three basic types of technology used to create mice, some more common than others:

✦ **Mechanical.** A mechanical mouse has a rubber ball that comes in contact with the surface and rolls along with your movements. The sensors inside the mouse in this case are mechanically — usually small rollers that detect the direction and speed of the ball, moving the mouse pointer accordingly.

✦ **Optomechanical.** This works the same way as a mechanical mouse — with a ball and sensors — except that the sensors are optical, using light to detect changes in direction and speed.

✦ **Optical.** Optical mice are more rare (and more expensive). These mice use only light to judge movements, usually reflected by a specially designed mouse pad. Optical mice tend to be more precise than others, and are used in computer-aided design and similar pursuits.

Trackballs and trackpads

Originally making their Mac debuts in PowerBooks, trackballs and trackpads have mutated into popular desktop alternatives to the mouse. (Actually, early non-Apple trackballs predated the PowerBook, although their popularity has grown in recent years.) Although some people swear by them and some people swear at them, trackballs get points for not forcing you to move your wrist in awkward directions or stretch your arm while trying to make things happen on the computer screen. Of course, the motions are still repetitive and the physical benefits are best left to scientists to determine. My only advice is to pick a device you enjoy using (see Figure 10-7).

Figure 10-7: Trackballs are my favorite for mousing, but only because I'd prefer to keep my hand close to the keyboard. I find mice to be more exact.

Trackpads are often found integrated with ergonomic keyboards like those offered by Macally and Adesso. You'll find some sold separately, though, including the Alps Desktop Glidepoint series made by Cirque (www.glidepoint.com). The MicroMac trackpad from Microspeed (www.microspeed.com), for instance, is smaller than a mouse, hooks up to a standard ADB port, and works as a direct replacement for the Mac mouse. (It also includes its own control panel for higher-precision control.)

Programmable mice

I've personally found a programmable mouse to be quite a useful add-on for my day-to-day computing. With four buttons on my personal trackball (a Kensington Turbo Mouse, although others are great, too), I can do an amazing number of things: a single press of a particular button can bring up an application swapping menu, or substitute for Ctrl-click or even a double-click. Silly as it may sound, you do a lot of double-clicking on a Mac, and I've found the added convenience of being able to use a single click instead is worthwhile after many hours of mousing.

Of course, you can create your own behaviors for each button — that's what programmable means. Options include *cursor focusing* (switching to a window by simply pointing at it), *snap to default* settings that automatically place the pointer at the default OK or Cancel button in a dialog box, and many others for the buttons and various button combinations (see Figure 10-8). One of my favorites: When I click the two bottom buttons on my Turbo Mouse, the pointer is constrained to the current axis, meaning it can only draw a straight line. That's perfect for some of the Web graphics work I do.

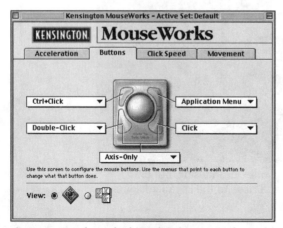

Figure 10-8: The only thing that bugs me about this software is the user has to decide which functions to use and which to pass on, because there are a limited number of buttons.

Digitizers

Often called *graphics tablets* (at least by me they are), *digitizers* are designed to use a pen-like device for input, translating that into a digital manipulation of the mouse pointer. This opens up a whole world of possibilities to the casual user, as well as providing a professional-level input device for artists and graphics professionals who need precision control over a mouse pointer.

Art isn't the only application for these tablets. Although they're great for drawing and painting, they can be used to substitute for a mouse in any application. Adding musical notation, controlling transitions in a multimedia presentation, or annotating a PowerPoint slide are all possibilities.

Most graphics tablets are pressure sensitive, meaning they only draw when you place the pen on the pad and begin to move it. Others have a powered pen that only writes when a button is held down or turned on. The technology you choose is up to you, along with extra features (such as more sophisticated pens and programmable buttons). You might also find some variance in resolution, although even low-end digitizers tend to offer thousands of lines of resolution per inch. From the low end (see Figure 10-9) to the very high end, digitizing products range from hundreds to thousands of dollars in price. For instance, the SummaGraphics line of digitizers (`www.calcomp.com`) includes a monster tablet capable of 10,000 lines per inch of resolution.

Figure 10-9: The CalComp UltraSlate (www.calcomp.com) is a small, consumer-oriented art pad that's a great substitute for the standard Mac mouse.

One important caveat: Not all graphics tablets can use ADB to connect to your Mac. Because the ADB port is limited in the amount of information it can transmit at one time, a highly sophisticated graphics tablet will bog down the interface. In those cases, most tablet manufacturers opt for a serial (modem/printer port) connection instead.

How sophisticated can they get? Wacom, makers of the popular ArtPad line of digitizers, goes so far as to blur the lines between digitizer and touch screen with one of their offerings, the PL-300 — an actual LCD screen that you can draw and mouse on directly.

Touch screens

Maybe you're already a multimedia professional or corporate IS type who knows very clearly that you want a touch screen for a kiosk, electronic map or for kids to use in schools. But, if you're a bit more like me, you're constantly just a little amazed that this stuff is available to the general consumer — and, intriguingly enough, at decent prices.

A touch screen can work a number of ways. The actual glass on a monitor can be made to sense touch or pressure, as can a glass or plastic overlay. In other cases the screen doesn't directly sense touch or pressure; sensors pinpoint the area someone touches on the screen, and the mouse pointer moves correspondingly.

Overwhelmingly, though, the affordable, consumer-level touch screens are those that simply overlay a store-bought monitor. One such device, from Edmark, is actually somewhat inexpensive, as it's designed more to appeal to parents and teachers than high-end corporate types (see Figure 10-10).

Figure 10-10: This consumer-level touchscreen is easy to add and a great choice for parents of smaller kids. (Photo courtesy Inc.)

Other touch screens are actual monitors, like those offered by PixelTouch (www.pixeltouch.com). These monitors range in size and technology, including both CRTs and LCD screens. They feature not only monitor connections, but also ADB connectors for transmitting the touch signals.

Other touch screen companies include the following:

✦ **ELO TouchSystems** (www.elotouch.com) makes a full range of touch screen CRTs and LCD solutions, including comprehensive support for Mac OS. Their Web site also features some other content, including tips for effective kiosk presentation.

✦ **TouchWindows** (`www.touchwindow.com`) offers a number of different touch screen products and add-ons.

✦ **KeyTec** makes the MagicTouch series (`www.magictouch.com`) of touch screen add-ons and monitors that support Mac as well as Amiga and Intel-compatible machines.

✦ **MouseTouch** (`www.mousetouch.com`) offers to integrate their system into your existing monitor, and they sell LCD touch screens.

✦ **Information Display Systems** (`www.idisplay.com`) features LCD touch screens for business and kiosks.

✦ **Troll Touch** (`www.trolltouch.com`) makes cross-platform CRTs, LCD screens, add-ons, and even screens for PowerBooks.

Special needs input/output

Not to be left behind are users who have special needs, whether physically challenged or recovering from injury, who still need to use their Mac on a regular basis. Products aimed at such users run the gamut from one-hand keyboards to head-mounted pointer controllers and speech technologies for the sight impaired.

Maltron keyboards (`www.maltron.com`), for instance, makes keyboarding products that run the gamut, from highly ergonomic keyboards designed for people suffering from repetitive strain injuries (RSI) to people with limited use of their hands. Single-finger or mouth-stick keyboards are also available from the company.

Companies that make special needs products include the following:

✦ **Alva Access Group** (`www.aagi.com`) makes the OutSpoken text-to-speech program and products for the visually impaired.

✦ **Duxbury Systems** (`world.std.com/~duxbury/products.html`) offers braille translation products for Macintosh and other platforms.

✦ **Dragon System's PowerSecretary** (`www.dragonsys.com`) allows for speech-to-text recognition for creating reports and memos.

✦ **R.J. Cooper and Associates** (`www.rjcooper.com`) creates software and hardware solutions for a variety of challenges, including keyboards and trackballs for individuals lacking fine motor skills.

✦ **Synapse Adaptive** (`www.synapseadaptive.com`) sells sophisticated adaptive products including the Synapse workstation, a speech-recognition computer that acts as a go-between for the user and a Macintosh or other computer. They also offer the Headmaster Plus, a hands-free pointing device that switches between Mac and PC compatibility.

Universal Serial Bus

An emerging standard seems bent on replacing the venerable ADB standard that's held sway over Mac peripherals for all these years — Universal Serial Bus (USB). The USB standard is similar to ADB in many respects, although it blurs the line between SCSI, serial connections, and ADB in an interesting way. The most important statistic, USB's 12 Mbps transfer speed, puts it right at about Ethernet speeds, with all the convenience of ADB.

USB will be a replacement for a number of different data ports you've gotten used to on your Mac, including the serial ports, ADB and, in some cases, SCSI. Although Ultra SCSI and Firewire aren't going away any time soon for high-end needs, USB promises to be quick and easy enough for other traditional SCSI devices, such as Zip drives and scanners.

The other advantage is USB is also an Intel-compatible standard, meaning a much larger market of peripherals is likely to appear sporting USB connectors. From there, all a vendor has to do is write Mac OS software drivers to make their USB peripherals compatible with the iMac and other Macs that will support USB in the future.

How USB works

In fact, USB may even be slightly more convenient than ADB. Aside from being much faster, USB also supports up to 127 devices, if you use a USB hub. On the iMac, the first Mac model to feature USB, the keyboard serves as a hub, enabling you to add other devices either directly to the machine or by way of the keyboard. This speed and convenience means USB can be used for peripherals other than input devices — printers, scanners, and even external storage devices are already planned for USB on Macs.

There are actually two different speed standards for USB, 1.5 Mbps and 12 Mbps, although both can operate through the same hub at the same time. This enables slightly less-expensive peripherals to use the slower speed for activities — such as mousing and keyboarding — that don't require much bandwidth.

It's also worth pointing out that each USB port on the iMac (and presumably on future Mac models that incorporate USB) each have full USB bandwidth (12Mbps) at their disposal. This means that even if you had several USB devices humming away on one port (for example, a scanner hooked up to the same port as your keyboard and mouse), you could use the other USB port for more heavy-duty requirements (such as an external removable media drive or a high-speed Internet connection), and still get full 12 Mbps speeds through that second port.

Although details aren't yet available at the time of writing, the expectation is the Mac OS will be updated to include a USB Manager, perhaps in the form of a control panel, that will feature basic device driver services for USB-based peripherals. This would mean you'd be able to hook up any PC-oriented keyboard or scanner and use it — at a very basic level — with your Mac by plugging it into the USB port and choosing one of the included drivers. Such a feature could apply to a number of scanners, modems, and even printers that are based on industry standards such as TWAIN, Hayes-compatibility, and Postscript, respectively.

In other cases, USB peripheral manufacturers may need to write Macintosh-specific drivers for their peripherals to work on Macs (or to ensure that their peripherals are full-featured beyond the basic USB Manager driver services). This additional work might keep some manufacturers from making their peripherals available to the Mac market. Some manufacturers will make the leap, however, seeing that it's much easier to tap into the Mac market by creating a software driver than by creating a hardware solution — such as different cabling for ADB, SCSI or the Mac's version of serial connections.

Hooking up USB devices

If your Mac model has USB ports, you should certainly consider using ADB if you have older devices, but I'd opt for USB peripherals whenever it's practical and affordable to do so. The connections are about the same — just plug in the device, load the Mac OS driver software, and start using the device.

USB features a four-pin connector that can only be inserted the correct way. There are different cables for high-speed USB than for low-speed USB, so you need to make sure you're using the right cable for your device (the peripheral likely comes with the correct cable, but you should take care when purchasing replacements). The USB cabling carries power to USB devices, so low-power devices don't need their own external power supply (higher-powered devices will still need external power). If you're hooking up a number of USB peripherals, a powered hub is recommended to service them all with USB-based power.

USB devices can't be daisy chained the way that ADB devices are — each device needs its own port. That means you either need to limit your USB upgrading to the number of ports you have available, or you need to add a USB hub that allows you to add more USB devices. On the iMac, for instance, the keyboard acts as a hub, because it has two additional USB ports — one for the mouse, and another for a second device. Taking into account the second port on the iMac's side, a total of two additional USB devices can be connected without the use of a special hub.

Indications are USB may be hot-swappable (meaning you don't have to turn the Mac off or put it to sleep to plug USB devices in) and reasonably free of voodoo. Unfortunately, there's not much I can say from personal experience, having only worked briefly with USB devices on an Intel-compatible PC (where they weren't yet working very well). It's just something we'll have to watch.

I'll try to keep up on the discussion regarding USB on the Mac-Upgrade Web site. Check in for details at www.mac-upgrade.com/.

Installing Input Devices

For the most part, Macintosh input devices use the ADB port on the back of your Mac's case to communicate with your Mac. Installing them is simple: Using the included cable or a standard ADB cable, you connect the device to the port. If you have more than one ADB device (and I know you do!), you'll want to daisy chain the devices by plugging the second one into an available ADB port on the first device. In some cases, you'll need to switch the order of devices if the first one doesn't offer a pass-through port.

In all cases, you'll want to power down your Mac first.

Here's the procedure for installing an ADB device:

1. Shut down your Mac.

2. Find the ADB port on the back of your Macintosh or on any of the ADB devices already plugged into the Mac. (The port should be labeled with the ADB icon. You may also find that some Mac monitors offer ADB ports. Usually these monitors need to be attached to the Mac's ADB port; additional ADB connectors are offered on the monitor standard for easier connection.)

3. Using an ADB cable, connect the new device to the available port.

4. Power up the Mac.

5. Install the software that came with the device. If it's a keyboard format, you'll want to select it in the Keyboard control panel (or in the menu bar menu created by the Keyboard control panel).

6. Test the device.

Remember to keep your ADB devices to a maximum of three or four; you may have trouble with that many if any of your devices is particularly sophisticated (for example, a digitizer or a touch screen.) If you notice sluggishness or if one of your devices isn't working properly, try disconnecting (after powering down your Mac) one or more of the additional devices, power back up, and see if that improves the device's response. You'll probably always need a keyboard connected, but you can leave the mouse disconnected for a while if you're using a touch screen, for instance.

Note

In its Tech Info Library, Apple makes a point of saying ADB ports are not designed for the repeated plugging and unplugging of peripherals. Although you're unlikely to damage the ports in any way, they weren't designed, for instance, to have the mouse plugged and unplugged on a daily basis.

Longer cables

If your keyboard mouse or other device doesn't extend far enough away from the computer, you may need to invest in an ADB extension cable. If you do, remember your 5 meter limit to the ADB chain and pick the peripheral that would add the least length to your chain while enabling you to connect the others.

An example is the AppleDesign Keyboard, which includes a hard-wired ADB cable. By attaching the extension to your trackball (assuming it features two ADB ports), and then attaching your keyboard to the trackball, you'll be adding less overall length to the ADB chain. This usually isn't a problem with two basic peripherals, but can cause degradation of the signal if you've installed more devices or if you're trying to get far away from the Mac.

For products that extend ADB and other Mac input cables by tens or hundreds of feet, check out products like the ex•tend•it series of stand-alone and rack-mounted devices from Gefen System (www.gefen.com). These devices enable you to move ADB devices hundreds of feet away and switch the same keyboard and mouse for use with many different Mac OS computers.

Intel-compatible peripherals

Want to plug standard Intel-compatible peripherals into your Mac? In many cases you can, with the right adapter. USR Systems (www.usr.com) offers their AppAdapter product, which enables Mac owners to plug in PS/2-style keyboards and mice, translating the PS/2 commands into Mac ADB data.

Summary

✦ Although it may one day be very common to use voice recognition to chat with our computers, most of us continue to communicate with our Macs by using pointing devices and keyboards. Within those categories, though, are plenty of different options.

✦ Before you can attach input devices, though, you'll need to know a little something about the Mac's Apple Desktop Bus — the technology used to connect input devices to the Mac. It's a flexible and easy-to-understand system, but it does offer the power user some limitations.

✦ Once you know how you'll be getting everything connected, take a look at the different devices you can use. Input devices range from standard and ergonomic keyboards to trackballs, touch screens, graphics tablets, and even input solutions for the physically challenged.

✦ Finally, you're ready to connect the devices. Above all else is the golden rule: Turn off your Mac before playing around with ADB devices, unless your Mac is specifically equipped with hot-swappable ADB ports (in which case it's just plug and go).

✦   ✦   ✦

Scanners and Digital Cameras

For some crazy, inexplicable reason, using a scanner is a lot of fun. Maybe it has something to do with the scanner letting you take real objects and interact with images of them on your computer screen. Maybe it's because scanners can make any of us feel like professional digital artists. Or, maybe scanners hold for humans the same fascination that copying machines do: You can make funny shadow scenes by pressing various parts of your body to the glass and hitting the "on" button.

Whatever the reasons, scanners are popular add-on accessories for Macintosh computers. They're made all the more popular and easy to add because of the Mac's built-in support for SCSI; nearly all Mac-compatible scanners are SCSI-based, with a few notable exceptions. Scanners also fare reasonably well at external ("regular") SCSI-1 speeds. You'll probably find that hooking up a scanner is simply a matter of plug and go.

Digital cameras offer even more fun. If you've never shot pictures without film, you're in for an interesting experience. And digital cameras have professional-level implications for all sorts of different applications, from shooting houses for your real estate Web site to shooting fashion for magazines and catalogs. Personally, I haven't picked up a regular camera in six months, although I've used my digital camera to create images that have appeared in all sorts of places: Web sites, multimedia databases, magazine stories, and, yes, this book. Digital cameras come in all shapes and sizes, and are certainly compelling add-ons for a number of different professional and amateur applications.

Let's begin by quickly discussing how a scanner works, and look at the different types and quality of scanners you'll encounter. You'll then see how to install a scanner. Also in this chapter I'll discuss how digital cameras create images, what the various features of these cameras are, and how you'll get the images into your Mac.

All About Scanners

Scanners create an image by passing a light along the surface of a piece of paper (or similar object) while *charged-coupled device* (CCD) sensors follow behind it, picking up the information and turning it into ones and zeros. The sensors determine how much lighter and darker parts of the image are in relation to each other, giving the scanner a sense of how dark a particular part of the image is.

Doing this, the scanner can create a *grayscale* scan, which results in a fairly true-to-life, non-color image. For even faster scanning, the scanner can simply determine which parts of the page are white, and which are not. This results in a true *black-and-white* scan, which might be useful for a page of text, a scan intended for faxing, or a line-art drawing — something that doesn't need the distinction of many different levels of gray (see Figure 11-1).

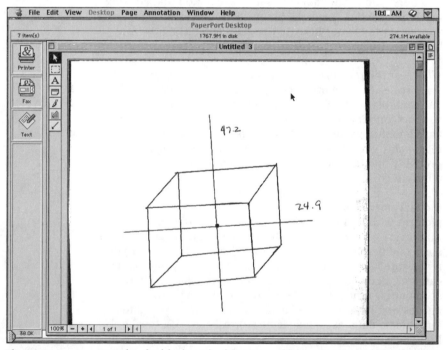

Figure 11-1: An example of a black-and-white scan of line art, using a Visioneer PaperPort scanner (www.visioneer.com)

Of course, you've probably heard that scanners can scan color images as well. How do they do that? Instead of emitting a white light and then judging the dark and light spots, the scanner emits colored light: red, green, and blue. (Some scanners use a filter over the sensor instead of a different colored light, but it's pretty much the same result.) The scanning software can then react to the different levels of intensity on the page to determine how much of a particular color is present. It then mixes the colors together and comes up with a final, full-color result.

Because color scanners use three colors, you'll often come across three-pass scanners. Each color gets its own chance to examine the image, whereupon the scanner software pieces everything together. This can take some time, but it gets good results. Of course, this also means it's very important to correctly align the document for each pass. If you move it slightly between passes, you'll end up with a patchwork final scan that probably will only somewhat resemble the original.

More recent scanners, however, turn the colored lights on and off quickly enough to accomplish all that data gathering in one pass of the scanner head. This makes it possible for scans to come out more quickly with the same amount of color information. It also requires that the scanner be fairly efficient in how it deals with data, because scanned images can take up megabytes of data at a time — a 24-bit (millions of colors) image scanned at 300 dpi for low-resolution printing can take up 3 megabytes of storage space or more. Images scanned at much higher resolutions for professional printing (for example, magazine advertisements or newspaper inserts) can take up many times that amount of storage space.

Types of scanners

Scanners come in a number of different shapes and sizes, each with its own target applications. Most often you'll see flatbed scanners, especially if you're wandering around the Macintosh aisles of your local computer store. However, you can run into a number of other types as well, including sheetfed scanners, handheld scanners, slide scanners, and other specialty devices. Here's a rundown of the different types of scanners available:

- ✦ **Flatbed scanners.** These are the most common variety of scanner, generally resembling the top portion of a copier machine. By lifting the lid, you reveal a glass surface onto which you place a document or similar item for scanning. Of the scanners normally reserved for consumers and professionals, flatbeds offer the best quality, the most color options, and the highest resolutions.

- ✦ **Handheld scanners.** You won't see many of these around anymore, as they were really an answer to the costliness of flatbed scanners in the past. The fact is, though, that a good flatbed scanner can be had for little over a hundred or so dollars these days, so cost-cutting options aren't as important. For the record, handheld scanners are usually about 4 inches wide and require that you roll them down the surface you're scanning. It's difficult to get a perfect scan, because you need to hold the scanner very steady and scan in a straight line.

- ✦ **Sheetfed scanners.** More common, although faltering somewhat, are sheetfed scanners. Although they made quite a splash in the mid-1990s, sheetfed scanners seem to have succumbed to the affordability of flatbeds as well. They're still a great idea for document management and modem-based faxing (I use one every day), if not great for high-end graphics use. Sheetfed scanners are usually small devices designed to sit behind your keyboard or in front of your monitor, and they resemble the tractor part of a typical fax machine. A sheet of paper can be fed in the front, then little motors pull it past the scanning sensors, finally spitting it out the other end. Most sheetfed scanners are grayscale scanners, although a few of them have climbed into the world of low-end color scans. They're also often serial-port scanners, requiring a connection through the modem or printer port on your Mac.

✦ **Photo scanners.** Although not yet terribly common, photo scanners are usually inexpensive, low-end devices that enable consumers to scan snapshot photographs into their Macs, and then add them to Web pages or desktop-publishing documents. These are typically all-in-one bundles that include easy image-editing software, and so on.

✦ **Slide scanners.** Almost in a class by themselves, slide scanners are used by imaging and publishing professionals to scan 35-millimeter slides into digital images that can be incorporated into the published page. These slides generally result in reasonable quality at an affordable price, allowing product and people photos to make it into high-end newsletters, newspapers, and other midrange applications. Slide scanners may diminish in importance as more publications and corporate media outlets begin to rely on digital images being passed back and forth over the Internet. For now, though, it's a simple matter to pop a slide into an overnight envelope and send it for publication the next day (see Figure 11-2). In addition, it results in an amazingly high-end image for creating color separations, film and otherwise publishing the image traditionally, as opposed to sending the image directly to a laser printer.

✦ **Drum scanners.** These sophisticated, expensive devices actually use scanning sensors different from most consumer-oriented scanners. The original document or image is placed on a fast, revolving drum that enables an intense light source to pass millimeters away from the original photo or document. The scanner can then bring more color detail and scanning information in front of a high-quality scanning sensor. The result is a professional-quality scan that's ready for use in a glossy magazine or a coffee table book.

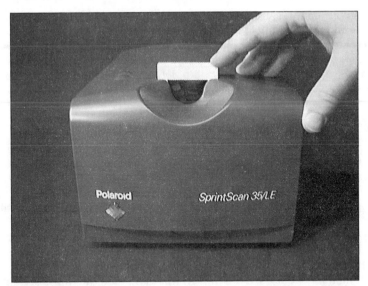

Figure 11-2: A slide scanner takes a standard 35-millimeter slide and outputs a digital image to the computer. Pictured is a Polaroid SprintScan 35LE (www.polaroid.com).

Scanner quality

The quality of a scanner is generally measured against a couple different statistics, including the resolution at which the scanner scans and the number of colors it's capable of seeing. Other technological issues — such as the number of passes the scanner makes and the quality of the sensors — are also important. Of course, the different types of scanners can also be compared for various advantages and disadvantages. In most cases you'll find that flatbed scanners offer the highest level of quality (at the consumer level) while offering the most flexibility. Slide and sheetfed scanners are designed for more specific tasks.

For starters, you should look closely at the scanning resolution offered by the scanner. Scanners are rated by the number of dots per inch (dpi) they use to convert documents into digital images. Inexpensive scanners scan at 300 dpi, whereas more expensive scanners can go to 1,400 dpi or higher. In many cases, more dots per inch results in higher-quality images, although it's a bit more complicated than that. Suffice it to say that a scanner that offers the ability to scan at higher resolutions gives you more flexibility for various tasks. Outside of a professional publishing setting, though, you're unlikely to scan images at resolutions higher than about 300 dpi (see the sidebar titled "Comparing resolutions: Dots versus pixels").

When shopping scanners, watch out for a number called *interpolated* resolution. This may be the reason that you're seeing a 1,200 or 1,600 dpi scanner available at a price that just doesn't seem to compute. Interpolated resolutions are those arrived at by sophisticated software routines that artificially multiply the number of dots per inch by assuming a linear relationship between two larger dots scanned at a lower actual resolution. Although this process can sometimes result in a more smoothly rendered image, it isn't really a substitute for actual high resolution — especially if you're scanning very detailed images and art.

Most inexpensive scanners work with *24-bit* color, meaning they can digitize as many as 16.7 million colors, which also happens to be about as many colors as the human eye can see. The 24 bits are divided three ways so that 8 bits are assigned to each red, blue and green value for a particular color. Because computers can use 8 bits to store number values between 0 and 255, there are 256 unique possible values for each of the three colors. Multiply those together — 256x256x256 — and you come up with the total number of RGB combinations — about 16.7 million.

More sophisticated scanners work at 30 or 36 bits per pixel, meaning they can distinguish billions of colors. Even though this is outside the range of human perception, these colors can be useful for setting off colors around them or offering very gradual transitions between two colors that humans can distinguish. Of course, this level of nuance is probably unnecessary for the typical home or small-business user who simply wants to scan images for a newsletter or Web site. But the high-end scanners are there if you need them.

Of course, other factors differentiate inexpensive scanners from those that offer higher quality. One of those is the dynamic range of the scanner. *Dynamic range* represents the breadth of tonal values that the scanner can register. This results in shading and low-contrast areas that scan at higher quality with more detail. By contrast, a scanner with a low dynamic range won't map colors as correctly, resulting in more washed-out results. Generally, dynamic range goes hand-in-hand with the number of colors (24-bit, 36-bit) the scanner works with. The additional colors, even if they aren't in the visible spectrum, add range to the image, giving it more clarity.

Scanner software

Other factors in comparing scanners include the quality of the components used, the type of light the scanner shines on your documents, and the overall packaging of the device. One of the most obvious differentiators in scanners designed for Mac users is the software package included; many scanners offer versions of Adobe Photoshop, the leader in image manipulation programs. Because Photoshop costs hundreds of dollars, a good deal can be had by buying it as part of a scanner bundle. But watch the fine print. Photoshop Lite Edition (LE) is one way that scanner companies include the software while lowering costs; however, the LE version, while useful, offers far fewer features.

Comparing resolutions: Dots versus pixels

Scanning resolutions, screen resolutions and printing resolutions—all of which tend to be measured in dots per inch—have very little in common with one another. For that reason, it's difficult to say to you, "Buy a 300 dpi scanner if you have a 300 dpi printer." Because there's no international standards body that defines what, exactly, a dot is in this context, dpi is only a relative term, not an absolute one. That makes it tough to choose a scanner.

For instance, a printer's dpi measure refers to a physical ink dot that's placed really close to a bunch of other ink dots. These dots, eventually, make up an image. The more dots per inch, the less jagged the printed text and images.

On a computer screen, dots per inch is a calculated number based on the size of your computer screen and the resolution your monitor is set to display. When you think about it, dots per inch is almost meaningless on a computer monitor. What's an inch on a computer monitor? A user can set different resolutions on a monitor, as well as use monitor controls to "squish" or otherwise distort the picture. Unless you adhere strictly to WYSIWYG resolution rules (which is nearly impossible, but discussed in Chapter 12 nonetheless) or you hold a ruler up to your computer monitor out of curiosity, inches are irrelevant.

The resolution of a scanned, digital image represents only the *size* of a displayed image, not the quality. When printed, a 300x300 image will often look better than a 200x200 image. On a computer screen, the 300x300 image is simply bigger than the 200x200 image.

So the question is what sort of scanner do you need to scan images that will print well? The answer: Less resolution than you think. You can't just compare resolutions, however. Instead, scanned resolution is more strongly related to the lines per inch (lpi) that your printer is capable of printing. Once you determine your printer's lpi (check the printer's documentation), the math is easy: Scan at 1.5 times the lpi rating for your printer. In most cases, this will translate to between 150 and 200 dpi scans for most inkjets and lasers. The only exception is black-and-white line art (text, clip art and drawn images), which should be scanned at the full resolution of the printer (300 dpi, 600 dpi, and so on), when possible.

If such low resolutions are recommended, why have high-end scanners at all? Those scanners are meant for professional color-separation work, usually. When outputting directly to a computer printer, the resolution of scanned images can be pretty low. But digital output intended for a print house needs to be much, much higher. You may also want to scan at higher resolutions for some of the latest, photo-realistic color and photo printers on the market today (check their documentation and Chapter 15 for details).

You should also take any other bundled software into consideration, as well as learning what image capturing software the scanner is compatible with. Specifically, you'll want to know if the scanner comes with any special optical character recognition (OCR) software—and if it's a fully enabled version—so you can scan text into your computer. You'll also want to know if any Photoshop-compatible plug-ins are available, or if the standard TWAIN plug-ins are completely supported. If you plan to use Photoshop often for your scans, it's certainly convenient to use a plug-in, which enables you to scan directly into Photoshop, instead of using an intermediary program that just scans and saves the images (see Figure 11-3). If you don't plan to use Photoshop (or if you don't have a copy and can't afford it), make sure your scanner offers a decent image-scanning program that also features editing and touchup tools.

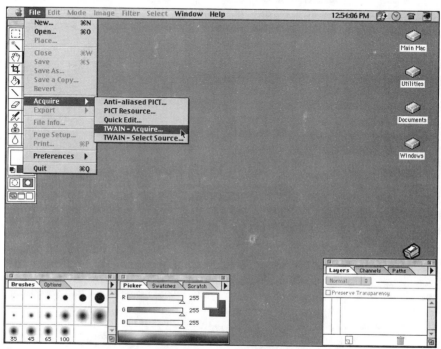

Figure 11-3: Using a plug-in you can scan directly into Adobe Photoshop, which enables you to manipulate and save the image directly.

So what's TWAIN? It stands for (believe it or not) Technology Without An Important Name, and, although the acronym is tongue-in-cheek, the standard itself is very interesting. In essence, any TWAIN-compatible scanner can be accessed using a TWAIN standard plug-in or software program. In Photoshop, for instance, a TWAIN-compatible plug-in is bundled with the program. This gives you access to your scanner, even if it doesn't have its own Photoshop plug-in, assuming the scanner itself is TWAIN compatible. Of course, TWAIN can't completely replace the scanner company's software, because the manufacturer is able to write much more sophisticated controls for image manipulation, batch scanning (scanning many documents at once), and any other advanced features.

Finally, don't forget about optical character recognition (OCR) software. This class of software can actually read scanned images, and then turn the text in the image into computer text that can be, for instance, loaded in a word processor or desktop publishing program. In essence, OCR replaces the need to retype documents. Instead, the software takes a scanned image, analyzes it against sophisticated algorithms, and outputs a text file that, if you're lucky, bears a striking resemblance to the original text (see Figure 11-4).

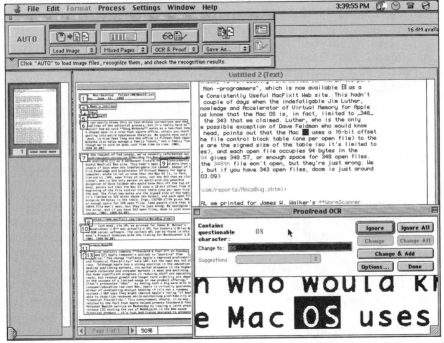

Figure 11-4: Most OCR programs do a pretty good job of character recognition, as long as the font in the original document is fairly standard, large enough, and easy to read.

Choosing a scanner

Resolution, color depth, quality, and software are all factors that should come together in your decision to purchase a scanner, although the most important issue to consider is purpose. How do you plan to use the scanner? Your answer will give you a much better idea of the scanner that's a good fit for your needs. Here are a few sample scenarios:

✦ *I'll be scanning text documents only, mostly for archiving and faxing.* In this case, low cost and convenience are probably primary. I personally use a scanner this way often, and I've found that a PaperPort or similar page scanner is often the best way to go. These scanners are simple to deal with, fire up immediately, and turn your computer into a full-featured plain-paper fax machine. If you have a choice, though, get a SCSI version so you're not struggling to find an open serial port whenever you go to use it.

✦ *I want basic scanning and color for my home/small-office Mac.* A 24-bit, 300-dpi scanner will work fine for this sort of application, as will some of the high-end page scanners. In fact, part of the consideration of choosing flatbed versus a page scanner is whether or not you'll be using the scanner as a copier replacement as well. If that's the case, a flatbed is easier to use for copying stapled reports, pages in books, and magazine stories. At the same time, advanced page scanners also feature enough color support and quality features for Web design and small-business newsletters.

✦ *I need good color for my creative business setting.* A 30-bit or 36-bit scanner with real resolutions of 600 dpi or greater may prove necessary for such a task. In reality, even these scanners are reasonably inexpensive, although you may find that additional capabilities (such as large format scans for oversized documents) and productivity add-ons (such as an automatic document feeder) boost that cost significantly.

✦ *I need the top of the line.* Consider some of the 36-bit scanners made by MicroTek, Agfa, and UMAX, among others. The optical resolutions can stretch to 1,000x2,000, with the capability of scanning both transparent and regular documents. Sizes tend to get larger, too, with support for full tabloid-size scanning. They can often be faster, making them worthwhile for larger workgroups that need to share the scanner.

✦ *I've got to scan some slides.* A dedicated 35-millimeter slide scanner is your best choice, with a transparency add-on as your second choice. Some higher-end scanners can pull off scanning both, although you're unlikely to get the same quality you get from slide scanners using a dual-pronged solution.

Table 11-1 points you to the Web sites of some popular scanner manufacturers that include Mac-compatible versions and bundles.

Table 11-1
Scanner Company Web Sites

Company	Web Sites	Type of Scanner
Agfa	www.agfa.com	Flatbed
Apple Imaging	imaging.apple.com	Flatbed
Epson	www.epson.com	Flatbed

Company	Web Sites	Type of Scanner
Hewlett-Packard	www.hp.com	Flatbed; page
Kodak	www.kodak.com	Slide/film
LaCie Ltd.	www.lacie.com	Flatbed
Linocolor	www.linocolor.com	Flatbed
MicroTek	www.microtek.com	Flatbed; page
Polaroid	www.polaroid.com	Slide/film; photo
UMAX	www.umax.com	Flatbed
Visioneer	www.visioneer.com	Page

Installing a scanner

For the most part, scanners work like any other SCSI device, except (perhaps) they're more widely reported to be picky about the SCSI chain than are some other devices. Not all scanners are trouble, but some certainly can be. If you're having trouble with a scanner, you'll need to go into SCSI-troubleshooting mode.

A few scanners offer serial port connections; usually these are the smaller page scanners that offer only black-and-white scanning capabilities. (You probably won't find such scanners new, but they're still available through many mail-order houses and ads in the back of Mac magazines.) Because of the increased amount of digital information that a color scanner has to provide, it's unlikely you'll find one that connects to the relatively slow serial port. (I wouldn't be surprised if USB versions of all sorts of scanners have started appearing on the marketplace, too, although I haven't seen any for Macs at the time of writing.)

After you've decided what SCSI ID number is available for your scanner (consult the Apple System Profiler if you're not sure what SCSI ID numbers are already taken), you're ready to add the scanner:

1. Shut down your Mac and ground yourself electrically.

2. Set the scanner up on a sturdy, level surface next to your Mac.

3. Find the special shipping pin that holds the scanner mechanism in place when the scanner is being transported. (Consult your scanner's manual for information on how to remove it.) Some scanners may ship without this pin, but it's important to know that; otherwise, you could ruin the scanner simply by turning it on if the pin is still in place.

4. On the back of the scanner, select a SCSI ID number for your scanner (see Figure 11-5).

Figure 11-5: As with many SCSI devices, scanners generally have a SCSI ID selector near their SCSI connectors.

5. Plug the scanner's SCSI cable into the scanner and into your Mac's SCSI port or into the last SCSI device in your SCSI chain. Unless the scanner is internally terminated (check your manual), you'll need to insert the SCSI terminator block into the other SCSI port on the scanner.

6. Plug the scanner's power cord in and turn it on. You should see the scanner's mechanism come to life.

7. Turn on your Mac. Install any software that came with the scanner, and then restart your Mac if the installed software requires it.

You're done. If you like, you can consult the Apple System Profiler to make sure the scanner appears as a SCSI device. Start up your scanner software (or Photoshop if the scanning software is a plug-in) and test your scanner.

For serial-port scanners, the process is even simpler. Just power down your Mac, plug the scanner into a free serial port (the printer or the modem port), plug the scanner into the wall-power socket, and then power up the Mac. Run the software installer that came with the scanner, and then restart the Mac if the installer requires it. When your Mac starts up again, you're ready to scan.

Note

With many page scanners, you simply insert a piece of paper and the scanner comes to life, scanning the page and loading the scanning software. The only thing that has to be "on" is the scanner software itself—usually a small application or a control panel (see Figure 11-6). The power to the scanner is managed internally, enabling it to spin down and consume very little energy while it waits for another document to scan.

Figure 11-6: The Visioneer PaperPort control panel determines whether or not the PaperPort should be on the alert, waiting patiently for a new document to scan (www.visioneer.com).

Digital Cameras

In a way, digital cameras are sort of upright scanners. Instead of scanning a single, small document or photo, however, digital cameras enable you to point and click at the world around you, turning an image in the lens into a computer image. They're nothing short of amazing, in certain respects, and I can easily foresee a day when most of our daily photography is done digitally.

In fact, not a lot about the camera has to change. For professional uses, digital camera backs can be attached to traditional camera mechanisms, allowing your trusty Nikon or Canon to take digital images instead of film ones. In other cases, the cameras are designed to be digital from the ground up — yet, they often have a tendency to mirror their film-based cousins in appearance and functionality (see Figure 11-7).

Figure 11-7: The Apple QuickTake 200 camera looks almost exactly like a typical point-and-shoot 35-mm camera. (Courtesy Apple Computer, Inc.)

Of course, the difference is the lack of film. Instead of stopping into the drug store to buy a few rolls of daytime or nighttime film, a digital camera stores images internally — usually on a small storage wafer, in hard-wired static RAM, or, in some cases, on a removable floppy disk.

How digital cameras work

In a way, digital cameras are video cameras that only have the internal electronics for taking still images instead of moving video images. Actually, many of the cameras can act as live video cameras as well — you just need to lug a VCR along with you. With video out ports (for RCA-style video adapters that plug directly into modern video equipment), you can use the viewfinder to frame a moving image and display it directly on a TV. Similarly, you can hook one of these cameras up to an AV port on your Mac, if it's so equipped.

However, these cameras are mostly for easy point-and-click shots. Via a regular camera lens, these cameras use digitizing sensors to store the image instead of the traditional exposure on chemically treated film. Usually, the sensors are an array of CCDs, similar to those used in consumer scanners. The image is also fed through to an LCD viewfinder (in most cases) that gives a fairly accurate rendering of the framed image. When you've got the shot you want, you press the camera's picture button, and the image that's on the viewfinder at that moment is saved to memory.

Like regular cameras, digital cameras use a lens, requiring you to adjust focus, macro settings (for extreme close-ups), and, often, aperture settings. In fact, many digital cameras don't even include a flash or additional lighting of any sort, because those cameras are capable of accurately rendering the amount of light in the room with little trouble. On some, a setting change brings more or less light into the camera, depending on the natural or other types of light that's in the room or outside.

After the shot is taken, the digital data is stored in the camera or on a removable storage medium. With no standards to go by, these storage options range from manufacturer to manufacturer. Sony, for instance, makes a series of cameras that save digital images directly to a standard 3.5-inch floppy disk. Apple opts for a tiny memory card that can be filled with images, removed, and replaced to extend the usefulness of the camera between download sessions with your Mac. Other cameras use slightly different methods. Some have only an internal storage option, relying on static RAM or a similar technology to store the images.

Note

Static RAM is a type of RAM that's designed to store data even when the device that holds the RAM is powered down. (In regular RAM, information is lost when you shut down your Mac.) This is usually accomplished by feeding the static RAM a small trickle of power — from a small battery, for example.

Shopping for a digital camera

Digital cameras come in many shapes and sizes, although three useful categories will jump out at you when you go shopping. On the low end are consumer-oriented cameras, designed to give you decent picture quality, but more of a point-and-shoot experience. These cameras range from $150 to $500 or so and, generally, rival the basic, fixed-focus 35-mm cameras you'd find in an electronics store for $35 to $50. Actually, I'm kidding—a bit. Although the picture quality will probably be similar to cheaper traditional cameras, almost any digital camera offers other interesting features, such as video output to TV devices and similar extras.

Higher-end digital cameras ($500 to $1,000) offer the hobbyist or professional more choices and features. These cameras still don't output high enough quality for many tasks—magazine print work, professional product shots, and similar pursuits—but they're a good solution for real-estate agents, brokers, attorneys, investigators, book authors, and anyone else who needs a convenient way to take good-quality archival photos. These cameras tend to offer more storage space for images, higher resolutions, zoom lenses, and more sophisticated focusing and light handling.

In the professional photography arena ($1,000 and up), digital cameras come in two types—really high-end all-in-one cameras and digital camera backs for traditional camera bodies. These expensive digital cameras tend to sport all sorts of goodies, including amazingly high resolutions, good storage, and professional touches such as very fast processing of images, higher-quality CCDs, and other elements that combine for better pictures. Where lower-end digital cameras are great for snapshots, these high-end cameras are expensive outfits designed for top-quality editorial and advertising needs.

No matter what the price range, you should ask some basic questions when comparing the quality and performance of digital cameras:

✦ **Resolution.** Lower-end cameras tend to shoot pictures designed more for computing applications than for printing, so their resolutions are smaller; 640x480 is a standard field of pixels for inexpensive cameras. Others offer better resolution, usually up to 1,024x768, or, in the case of digital camera backs, 1,012x 1268 resolution images with over a million pixels.

✦ **Color depth.** On the low end, you'll find cameras capable only of 8-bit color (256 colors), with thousands of colors becoming more commonplace. Like scanners, the higher-end cameras offer 24-bit, 30-bit, and even 36-bit color for displaying colors beyond the visible spectrum (although they still add to image quality).

✦ **Compression.** To get these large digital image files to fit into a finite amount of storage memory, most digital cameras use a compression scheme. These can certainly vary in quality, with some of the schemes introducing errors or *artifacts* within the image. Depending on the camera, you'll probably have a choice of compression schemes. Compression is the norm on the Web and in lower-end tasks, but a very sophisticated approach to compression is necessary for photographic-quality images for professional applications.

Note

On the World Wide Web, JPEG and GIF image file formats are the norm. Both are compressed formats, enabling them to transmit more quickly over a network. They also tend to be lower quality than either TIFF or EPS (Postscript) image files. So, if you're working with images destined for print, you'll probably want a camera that saves images in TIFF format. Low-end cameras often won't, opting instead for JPEG-compressed files. (Some PICT image files, by the way, are actually JPEG compressed, even if they're not in the JPEG format.)

✦ **Storage.** As mentioned earlier, these cameras rely on an internal storage mechanism for holding onto the images until they can be downloaded onto your Mac. One feature of the more expensive cameras is a unique or high-capacity approach to storage. If you can easily get additional storage modules, for instance, or if the storage inside the camera can hold many, many images, the camera might be worth the extra investment.

✦ **Interface.** Although most low-end digital cameras offer a serial cable interface, this can be an incredibly slow way to transfer images. (Not only slow, but many Mac-based transfer programs also tie up the computer while downloading the images, forcing you to find other things to do while the images are transferred. You may even find yourself — gulp — reading.) High-end cameras offer a SCSI interface instead, enabling images to be transferred much more quickly.

Other factors may influence your choice as well. Most cameras, like scanners, come with an image-editing program (most likely an Adobe product). If the camera you have your eye on also happens to offer a full version of Photoshop, it may be worth the price.

Similarly, different cameras offer extra features that may interest you. Zoom lenses are available in many midrange cameras, as are high-quality LCD screens, red-eye reduction, auto-flash capabilities, and rechargeable batteries. If you'll be using the camera as a presentation tool, you'll want to make sure it can be hooked directly to a TV through an RCA-style video cable. In some cases, you'll even find models that enable you to upload your own images to the camera, which can then be used as a hand-held, portable presentation device.

Also, if it's important to you, don't forget to check for pass-through video capabilities. Some low-cost cameras I've encountered (like the Apple QuickTake 200) do a better job of full-motion display than cameras costing hundreds more. Hook up the camera to a VCR, and you've got an instant (albeit heavy) camcorder!

Note   If you're into editing your images, don't forget to make sure your camera offers a Photoshop-compatible plug-in for downloading the images from the camera directly into a Photoshop-compatible image-editing program.

Using the camera with your Mac

Once you've shot your heart out with the digital camera, it's time to hook it up to your Mac and download the images to your computer. Most likely, you'll need to have installed the software (or Photoshop plug-in) that came with the camera. From there, the task is usually a simple one:

1. Shut down your Mac, and install the serial cable that came with your camera on the modem or printer port (whichever is free).

2. Attach the digital camera to the cable through the camera's interface port.

3. Restart the Mac.

4. Start up your image-retrieval software (if it's Apple's software, it's called Camera Access). You may have to tell the software what port you've plugged the camera into, although some of the retrieval programs can find the camera without help.

5. Choose the option in the software through which you can preview your images.

6. Select the images you want to download to your Mac. (You can usually hold down the Shift key or the ⌘ key while clicking multiple images to select more than one at a time.)

7. Invoke the download command in the image software. You may be asked to choose what folder to save the images in. Do so and click OK. (See Figure 11-8).

That's usually all there is to it. With most of the image-download programs, you'll have an option to delete all the images currently stored on the camera. This will clear them out so you can take more pictures, but be sure you've downloaded and saved onto your Mac all the images you wanted to keep.

Figure 11-8: In Apple's Camera Access, you choose each image you want, and then use the Save Selected to Disk option to download them from the camera.

If you're interested in downloading the images from the camera directly into Photoshop, you do that by invoking a Photoshop plug-in. In most cases, the plug-in you'll be using is actually an Export/Acquire plug-in, so that's how you'll install it:

1. Make sure Photoshop isn't running, and then copy the plug-in to the Export/Acquire folder that's inside the Photoshop folder on your hard drive.

2. Start Photoshop.

3. In Photoshop, choose Open, Acquire from the menu, and then choose the listing for your camera. This brings up the plug-in for your particular camera (see Figure 11-9).

In most cases, this plug-in will work a lot like the image-download program for your camera, although the plug-ins will sometimes have fewer capabilities — for example, only downloading one image at a time.

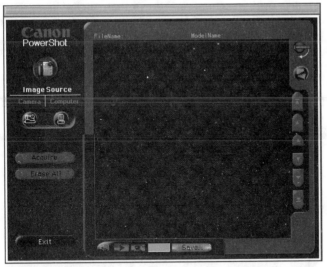

Figure 11-9: The Canon PowerShot has a Photoshop Acquire plug-in that offers full-featured access to the camera.

Summary

✦ Scanners and cameras are both great add-ons for Mac users at any level, whether you're just trying to dress up your small-business newsletter or you need to prepare images for magazine layouts. Scanners and cameras are also popular peripherals, resulting in widely varying feature sets, costs, and performance.

✦ Scanners use bright light and special sensors to create an image of an existing document and turn it into digital information that can be used on your computer. You can then use image-manipulation programs to change the scanned document or photo, or you can use an OCR program to recognize the text in the scanned document, enabling you to then paste the text into a word processing program for editing.

✦ A variety of scanners are available, and can be differentiated by the type of documents they scan, how they're inserted into the scanner, and what type of interface (serial or SCSI) the scanner uses. You'll also encounter some other factors, such as the number of colors the scanner recognizes, the scanner's top resolution (usually in dots per inch), and the document sizes the scanner can work with.

✦ Install a scanner the same as you would most other SCSI devices: After picking an available SCSI ID number, plug it into the SCSI port on the back of your Mac or into one of the other SCSI devices in your SCSI chain. You'll need to remove some shipping materials if the scanner is brand new, and then turn everything on, run the software, and test the equipment.

✦ Digital cameras are like upright scanners — they create digital images through a camera lens. From inexpensive to professional quality, digital cameras offer many different features and performance factors, including color depth, resolution, image storage, and image compression. You'll probably want to check out any additional features on the camera, such as zoom lenses and TV-video output.

✦ To hook up your digital camera, you'll probably attach it to a serial cable or, in some cases, to a SCSI device. You'll then run the camera's access program or a Photoshop plug-in.

✦   ✦   ✦

Monitors and Monitor Cards

I imagine that a lot of Mac users — especially those who've been at it for a number of years — describe themselves as visual people. The Mac OS interface plays to that sort of individual, offering lines, fonts, icons, and other elements that, for the most part, are carefully crafted to be aesthetically pleasing. It follows, then, that a very high-quality computer monitor can make your Mac experience even more pleasurable.

It also helps to have a nice monitor if you're going to be sitting in front of that computer for hours on end. I know I tend to harp on this, but I don't believe you should ever take the cheap way out when it comes to buying a monitor for your system. Unless your eyes aren't terribly important to you, or you'll only be using the computer rarely, it's of utmost importance to get a monitor that offers good color, flicker-free display, and crisp, clean text. I'm no doctor, but I can't imagine looking at a washed-out or blurry monitor could possibly do your eyes any good.

Fortunately, a lot of monitors designed to be Mac-compatible are of very high quality. These days, almost any computer monitor made can be fitted to work with a Mac, even if it adheres to the Intel-compatible monitor standards. So there's plenty of competition on the market to keep prices down.

In case you don't think you need a new monitor, you may want to look into improving your Mac's internal video hardware, whether that entails a simple upgrade to the video RAM or a wholesale installation of a new video card. New video can add more colors, better resolution, and even acceleration to your computing experience.

Finally, even if you have the monitor and video capability you need, you should *still* check out this chapter; you might learn something about screen resolution, built-in video, and even how to accelerate certain video tasks on certain Mac OS computers. Video hardware settings in the Mac OS monitor control panels can be confusing to some users, so I'll try to explain how it all works in this chapter, too.

Note   Remember, nearly every Mac has the ability to take advantage of the screen real estate offered by two or more monitors (as many, in fact, as you have video cards for). I'll discuss how to do this in more depth later in the chapter. Just remember, it's a great reason to shop for a new monitor and video card.

How Mac Monitors Work

It takes three different elements working together to create an image based on data from the Mac processor — the video interface circuitry, the software drivers in the Mac OS that control that circuitry, and a video display monitor. The video circuitry can be built into the Mac or supplied on an expansion card. The software is usually included with the Mac OS, although some video cards include extensions that must be installed as well. The display must be compatible with the Mac's RGB (DB15) output cabling, but the cabling can be easily adapted for use with a VGA (Intel-compatible standard, HD15) monitor.

When you're looking at video, then, both the circuitry and the monitor itself are important components that must work together to make images appear that human operators can interact with. This requires not only compatibility, but a special synchronization between the two elements to make sure everything works flawlessly.

Note   The Mac has a group of programming routines built into it, called QuickDraw, that controls the machine's graphical capabilities. Every program written for the Macintosh is required to deal with drawing to the screen on its own via QuickDraw, which helps by creating routines that make it easy to draw standard Mac OS elements such as text, shapes, graphics, and colors. QuickDraw is also part of the underlying printing architecture of the Mac OS, making it possible for Mac programs to communicate with printers.

Bitmapped images

Inside every Macintosh model is circuitry designed to paint the screen dot by dot; this circuitry determines what each dot should look like at a given moment of time, including whether it's on or off (on a black-and-white screen) or what intensity of red, green, and blue the dot will represent to form a particular color. (Actually, in a color monitor, each dot can only be one color, so the dot for each of the RGB colors are positioned closely together to create a single *pixel*—short for picture element—of the screen image. To the human eye, this results in a blending of the intensity of each dot to create a unique color.)

The process of creating and storing such an image is called *bitmapping*, wherein each bit, or pixel, of an image has its associated value stored in computer memory. This creates a map of the overall image that is then communicated to the monitor, which responds by turning on the dots at the light intensities necessary for the image. It does this by using an electron beam to draw each line of the screen, energizing a phosphorescent coating that glows as required.

It sounds complicated, but a typical Macintosh actually performs this task between 60 and 85 times per second, depending on the capabilities of the display and computer. This results in images that appear to move seamlessly, when, for instance, you drag a window or launch an application.

You may have heard of *interlacing* monitors, which were popular for a time in the Intel-compatible world (and can be used with some Mac models). These monitors work the same way a standard television does, by drawing every *other* line of the screen image, and then filling in the alternating lines on the second pass. This makes the monitor work less hard, enabling it to update each set of lines on alternating passes. It can result in an image that appears to flicker slightly, however, even though the image is being updated many times per second.

Note

You may hear people use the letters *CRT* and the word *monitor* interchangeably. CRT stands for *cathode ray tube*, the most common type of technology used for desktop monitors. Other technologies exist, though, and some of them—like LCD technologies used for years in Power Books —are beginning to encroach on traditional CRT turf. Apple has even begun to offer a model, the Apple Studio Display, that uses LCD technology—resulting in a very lightweight, thin display that, unfortunately, is also quite a bit more expensive than typical CRTs.

Refresh rate

The number of times a Mac's screen is redrawn per second is called the *refresh rate*, often measured in hertz (Hz). For the most part, individual monitors or displays are capable of a particular refresh rate, and they must be set to show images at that rate for the display to be useful. For instance, the original Mac classic form factor includes a black-and-white display with a fixed refresh rate of 60.15Hz, meaning the screen is updated approximately 60 times per second. The Mac OS won't allow you to change this setting, because the monitor will only synchronize with the Mac's video interface at that speed.

Most newer monitors are called *multisync* monitors because they're capable of synchronizing to different refresh rates and screen resolutions. In this case, you'll need to know the limits of your monitor yourself, as the Mac video software may allow you to exceed the maximum refresh rate at which your monitor can display an image. This can be potentially damaging to the monitor, so it isn't recommended — under *any* circumstances — that you run your video circuitry at a refresh rate higher than the monitor's specified limit. (Usually the Monitors or Monitors & Sound control panels will keep you from "overdriving" a monitor.)

Actually, two refresh numbers appear in the rating for most monitors, but only the vertical refresh rate is interesting; the horizontal refresh rate simply tells you, in kilohertz (KHz), how long it takes for each line to be drawn as the screen updates. Notice that KHz translates into *thousandths* of seconds, so the number, whether it's 30 or 70, represents a very fast rate, and therefore is rarely a selling point for an individual monitor.

Resolution

Another important factor in monitor and video-card purchases is the resolution supported. Resolution is measured by the number of pixels high and pixels wide at which the screen image is displayed. These pixels create the grid of bits that are turned on and off by the computer to create the bitmapped display.

On earlier monitors, the resolution is fixed by the monitor. The classic series of black-and-white Macs, for instance, offer a fixed resolution of 512 pixels by 384 pixels. Multisync monitors, however, offer a range of different resolutions that can be dialed up by the Mac OS and displayed on the screen. This enables you to change the number of pixels that appear on screen by changing a setting in the Monitors control panel (see Figure 12-1).

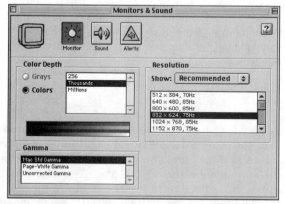

Figure 12-1: The Monitors control panel (or Monitors & Sound control panel in Mac OS 8 and above) enables you to change the resolution on multisync monitors.

Why switch resolutions? A few reasons exist, the most obvious one being that changing the resolution changes the size of the images on your screen. The lower the screen resolution, the bigger each pixel. Remember, a *pixel* isn't a fixed measurement. It's just a shorthand way to say "picture element." So, the fewer picture elements you have on a given screen, the larger the image.

That's why many game programs will switch the monitor to a resolution of 640x480 before beginning the game. Because games tend to be very demanding on your video hardware (what with many video effects, 3D images, and complex textures that need to change quickly), the game will default to a lower resolution setting so it has to change fewer pixels at one time, making its job easier.

But the size issue can involve more than simply choosing between bigger or smaller images for gaming, comfort, or whatever other reasons. Screen resolution also has a loose correlation to the concept of What-You-See-Is-What-You-Get (WYSIWYG, pronounced "wizzy-wig"). Given a particular monitor size, you can set the resolution so that the size of images and text on the screen corresponds almost exactly to the size the images and text will be once printed. For page layout tasks, this capability is crucial — and it's a standard that Macs have always aspired to.

At least, until recently. As the Mac and Intel-compatible worlds continue to converge, Macs have begun to work well with monitors that are standard in the Intel world, along with the set of resolution standards for those monitors. These are often close to the Mac standard resolutions, but not as precise when it comes to WYSIWYG. In fact, the sheer number of different monitors you can now hook up to your Mac makes WYSIWYG an impossible standard for monitors, because one so-called 17-inch monitor might actually show 15.3 inches of viewing area, whereas another might show 14.7 inches or 15.6 inches.

Note

There's another reason monitor resolutions have gotten a bit screwy recently: Fewer people care. At one point, Macs and their monitors were fixed at the magical WYSIWYG resolution because print publishing was such a primary function for Macs. The prevailing attitude in the Intel world, however (at least for Microsoft Windows users), has been that increased resolution gives you more screen real estate to work with, therefore it should be jacked up so you can see more of a word processing document or Web page than you would at a lower resolution. Neither approach is necessarily better than the other. Whichever you adopt depends on what your preferences are. You should consider how important true WYSIWYG is to you before choosing the resolution at which your Mac will run. It may not prove important to you at all.

The magic WYSIWYG number is 72 dots per inch. That's the point at which letters on the screen look just like letters on the printed page. You publishing types might notice something else about this magic number: It means each pixel corresponds to a *point* (a unit of measure used to gauge the size of typefaces), as there are also roughly 72 points per inch. At this resolution, increasing a font's point size by a single point (from an 11-point to a 12-point font, for instance) changes it by one pixel on the screen.

To get to this WYSIWYG nirvana, however, you either have to crunch some numbers or buy your monitors directly from a single company that still cares about such things. Not even Apple seems overly worried about it anymore, so you might want to just skip the math and go straight to Table 12-1, which shows you how to approximate the correct dpi.

If you do want to get an exact match, you determine the exact measurement for the height and length of the viewable area of your monitor in inches. You then multiple each by 72 dpi. That gives you the dimensions of pixels you should use for your screen size.

For instance, a 15-inch monitor with a diagonal viewable area of 13.9 inches would have a width of about 11.1 inches and a height of about 8.3 inches. Multiply 11.1 by 72 dpi, and you get 799 pixels. Multiple 8.3 by 72 dpi, and you get 598 pixels. So an ideal WYSIWYG resolution for this monitor would be 799x598. Look that up in your Monitors control panel, and you'll likely find a choice that's pretty close: 800x600 (see Figure 12-2).

Note

You kooky, nutball mathematicians are probably ahead of me on this one: You can use the Pythagorean theorem to find monitor dimensions if you need to. Remember that, in a right triangle, $A^2+B^2 = C^2$, where A and B are the height and width and C is the diagonal. (On the other hand, those of you who think I'm just showing off my firm grasp of geometry are probably right. It's the last level of math I grasped at all, firmly or otherwise.)

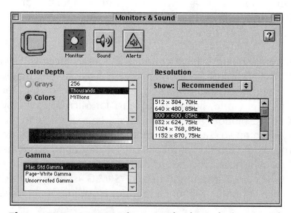

Figure 12-2: 800x600 is a standard resolution, good for a monitor that has a diagonal viewing area of approximately 14 inches.

Monitor manufacturers have a history of making monitor comparisons tough, because they've often measured the glass screen of their monitors instead of the viewable area, and then advertised the screen according to that higher resolution. Table 12-1 accounts for that, showing you the optimum viewable area for a particular resolution, along with the "marketing department" resolution it usually corresponds to.

Table 12-1
Ideal Monitor Resolutions and Viewable Areas

Resolution	Best for Viewable Areas of...	Marketed Resolution...
512x386	8.9 inches	9 inch
640x400	10.5 inches	12 inch
640x480	11.1 inches	14 inch
800x600	13.9 inches	15 inch
832x624	14.4 inches	16 to 17 inch
1024x768	17.8 inches	19 inch
1152x870	20.0 inches	21 inch
1280x1024	22.8 inches	24 inch

As viewable areas can vary dramatically, you'll find some exceptions to these rules. For instance, Apple has traditionally named their monitors in a way that's more accurate about their viewable areas. Apple marketed two popular monitors in the early 1990s as 16-inch and 20-inch monitors, even though they conformed to sizes that other manufacturers typically called 17-inch and 21-inch, respectively. These days you'll find monitors made by Apple that are called 20-inch monitors but have viewable areas of 19 inches. This makes them difficult to pin to a 72 dpi WYSIWYG resolution.

Indeed, with very large monitors the dpi is a little greater than 72 if you use 1152x870 or higher as your resolution, making the images on the screen slightly smaller than they'll print. The higher resolutions do, however, enable the monitor to display more information in the same amount of space.

Dot pitch

Two other things to consider when comparing monitors are the technology used to create the image and the dot pitch on color monitors. Let's take the second issue first.

Dot pitch is a measurement in millimeters of the distance between the red, green, and blue dots that make up a single pixel on a color monitor. In the case of a black-and-white monitor, there's exactly one dot per pixel, since it just needs to be on or off (or, in the case of a grayscale monitor, on or off at varying intensities). In the case of color, though, each pixel needs a different dot that represents a color of the RGB tandem. Taken together, these three basic colors (at various intensities) can create up to millions of unique colors.

However, each dot is a slight distance away from the other dots so that each of the three colors can be illuminated separately. This results in a *dot pitch* that can be measured and used to compare monitors.

You'll find a dot pitch of .28 mm on most modern, multisync monitors. That's certainly good enough. Quality doesn't really begin to disintegrate until you get over .40 mm, and such monitors are hard to find these days. Slightly older, very large monitors (like 21 inches and up) will often sport higher dot pitch numbers like .31 mm or .35 mm. These are fine, too, for a large monitor.

If you come across a dot pitch of .26 mm or lower, you're probably looking at a monitor based on Sony's Trinitron technology. Sony uses a different approach to the aperture grille (thin metal strips) that enables the pixels to shine through to the screen, resulting in a sharper image that almost always looks better than traditional CRT monitors (which use a fine mesh screen called a *shadow-mask* instead of an aperture grille)— at least, in my opinion.

Another important note: Your monitor doesn't even have to have a dot pitch. LCD-based screens are becoming more and more common for desktop systems. Once only found in laptop/portable computers, LCDs and similar technologies are being offered in stand-alone monitors that can be connected to nearly any Mac. Currently the prices on these monitors make them difficult to recommend, but those prices could change fast. If you see a good deal on an LCD screen, you might consider buying it. LCDs are generally easier to look at for long periods of time; they don't use an electron gun and don't have a refresh rate, so there's no chance of flicker. Although they're still more difficult to view from a sharp angle than conventional monitors, they consume less energy and less space on your desktop (see Figure 12-3).

Note   If you're in a situation where you're comparing CRTs and LCD screens, understand that the viewable area of an LCD screen is almost always the same (or very close to) its marketed dimensions. So, a 12-inch LCD screen is likely to offer almost the same viewable area as a 14-inch CRT monitor.

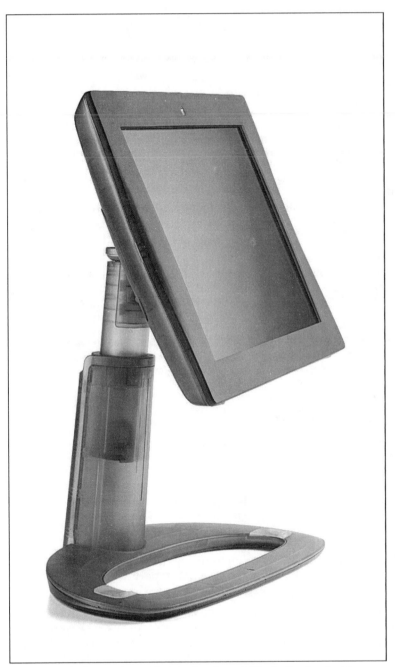

Figure 12-3: The Apple Studio Monitor is an LCD display for desktop computers. (Photo courtesy Apple Computer, Inc.)

Buying tips: Monitors

Once you've got the basics of monitor technology down, you might still be at a loss for exactly which model to choose. You'll want to look at these factors: cost, size, and clarity.

The best advice I can offer is to give yourself a break. Go into a monitor purchase with a willingness to shop a bit and some flexibility in your budget. I know from first-hand experience that it can be awful to look at a bad monitor for hours at a time. And, once you've committed to the monitor, any problems or shortcomings will become part of your daily life.

So, judge the quality and clarity of the monitor in a computer store before buying. Also, read the reviews in *Macworld* magazine and elsewhere. Put the monitors side by side for your own comparison if you feel it's necessary. (Tell the salesperson I told you it was okay for you to demand that they move monitors around on the shelf. This is an expensive purchase that shouldn't be treated lightly.)

The picture should look square—not curved or warped (check the monitor controls on the front to make sure the monitor settings aren't causing the problem before drawing conclusions). Straight lines on the screen should look straight. Colors should be vibrant, not washed out. Changing the brightness control shouldn't warp the image terribly or blur text on the screen. Play with the Monitors control panel to see if the monitor syncs well to other resolutions or if switching is difficult. Buy the largest monitor you can afford.

Remember, you can shop in the Intel-compatible parts of the computer stores, too; any VGA-compatible multisync monitor will work with your Mac and an RGB-to-VGA adapter.

Installing a monitor

Once you've chosen the monitor you want to use with your Mac, installing it should be a fairly simple matter. You just need to answer a few quick questions before you're ready to connect the cables:

✦ *Is this a multisync monitor?* Older Apple-branded monitors and a few others that are capable of connecting to Mac OS computers are not multisync, meaning they're only designed to accept one resolution and one refresh rate. (Such monitors include the Apple RGB series, Apple Color, Apple Color Plus, and Apple AudioVision 14.) If you have one of these monitors, you'll probably have to plug it directly into an Apple monitor port, which will enable it to sync properly with the Monitor control panel.

✦ *Is the monitor an Apple or Mac-only monitor?* If your monitor is nearly any Apple brand, or if it's a Mac-only monitor with cabling exclusively for Mac, then it uses an Apple RGB port adapter (see Figure 12-4). Otherwise, the monitor is probably a VGA-compatible monitor. (VGA is the Intel-compatible video standard.) In this case, you'll likely need a special adapter to plug the VGA monitor into the Apple RGB video port.

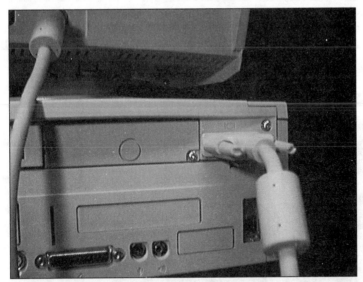

Figure 12-4: Apple monitors hook directly to the Apple RGB video port on most Macs.

✦ *Does your Mac have a nonstandard video port?* Some Macs — especially late-model Quadra AVs and early Power Macs — offered special video ports for AppleVision AV displays. (The connection enables both video and audio information to travel directly to the monitor.) Unfortunately, without an adapter these ports aren't compatible with any displays other than the AppleVision models. The adapter is included with these computer models, or you can buy such an adapter separately (see Figure 12-5).

✦ *Does this non-Apple monitor offer any sync limitations?* Depending on the age and capabilities of a VGA-compatible monitor, you may need a particular adapter that limits the resolution, color depth, or refresh rate to certain levels. Knowing the specifics will help you determine which adapter is necessary.

If you're planning to connect an Apple monitor and an Apple-branded Mac, you should have no trouble; just connect the monitor's video connector to the RGB port on the back of your Mac, as shown back in Figure 12-5. Tighten the monitor connector by turning the thumbscrews until they offer some resistance. (They don't need to be terribly tight, just secure.)

If you're attaching a standard VGA-compatible monitor to your Mac, most likely you'll need an adapter. Although many models exist (including some that may be made by your monitor's manufacturer for your particular monitor), the best adapters to buy are probably the universal models offered by Sony and a number of other manufacturers (see Figure 12-6). Using DIP switches, you can set up the monitor cable so that the adapter interprets the Mac's video signal in any resolution, color depth, and refresh rate your monitor supports. Adapters are also useful for multisync monitors, enabling you to hook up the monitor, and then choose from the many different resolutions the monitor supports.

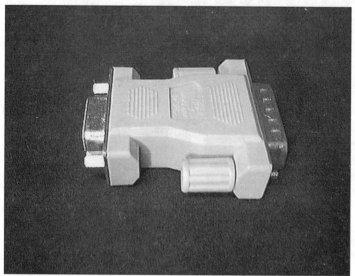

Figure 12-5: Certain Mac models require a special adapter cable for attaching regular Mac RGB monitors.

Figure 12-6: A universal RGB-to-VGA adapter for attaching VGA-standard monitors to Mac OS computers

If you happen to have a very new Mac or a Mac OS clone computer, or if you have an add-on video expansion card installed, check to make sure you don't already have a VGA port available. Modern Mac cards and video circuitry expansion cards often include both a RGB port and a VGA port. Unfortunately, you can usually only use one or the other of the ports if they're attached to the same expansion card.

Video Circuitry

The other part of the video equation is your Mac's video circuitry. It's important to know what sort of monitors your computer can support before you go shopping for one. Or, if you're just interested in using the monitor you already have, it's important to know the full capabilities of your Mac and whether you should add more video features via an upgrade card. For that, there's nothing like a chart.

Table 12-2 delves deep into the mysteries of built-in video, showing you the resolution and capabilities of built-in video for all of Apple's major Mac series, as well as some of the clones. Shown are the top resolutions, highest possible colors, and how the video can be upgraded. Note that the table tries to differentiate between upgrades that enable you to add VRAM to your existing setup and those that require you to replace the VRAM with either a new, high-capacity memory module or a replacement video expansion card.

Table 12-2
Mac Built-in Resolutions and Video Upgrades

Mac Model	Built-in?	Top Resolution	Top Color Depth	VRAM Upgrade?	Other Upgrades?
Mac classic models, Performa 200	Yes	512x384	Black and white	No	None (PDS in SE/30)
Mac Color Classic, Performa 250	256K	512x384	8-bit color	100 ns 256k	PDS slot
Mac Color Classic II, Performa 275	256K	512x384	8-bit	80 ns 256k	PDS slot
Mac II, IIx, cx, fx	None	N/A	N/A	N/A	Requires NuBus video card

(continued)

Table 12-2 (continued)

Mac Model	Built-in?	Top Resolution	Top Color Depth	VRAM Upgrade?	Other Upgrades?
Mac IIci, IIsi	1MB[2]	640x870	8-bit	No	NuBus
Mac IIvi, vx	512K	640x480	8-bit	100 ns 512K	NuBus
LC, LC II, Performa 4xx	256K	640x480	8-bit	100 ns 512K[1]	PDS
LC III, III +, P450, 46x	512K	832x624	16-bit	100 ns 256K	PDS
LC475, P47x	512K	1152x870	16-bit	2 80 ns 512K[1]	PDS
LC520, 550, P520, 550, 560	512K	640x480	8-bit	80 ns 256K	PDS
LC575, P57x	512K	640x480	8-bit	2 80 ns 512K[1]	PDS
LC580, P58x	1MB	640x480	16-bit	No	PDS
LC630, P63x, P640, Quadra 630	1MB	832x624	16-bit	No	PDS
MacTV	512K	640x480	8-bit	No	None
Quadra 605	512K	1152x870	16-bit	2 100 ns 512K[1]	PDS
Centris 610, Q610	512K	1152x870	16-bit	2 100 ns 256K	PDS
P600,870 1152x C650, Q6505	16-bit	2 80 ns	256K	12K	NuBus

Mac Model	Built-in?	Top Resolution	Top Color Depth	VRAM Upgrade?	Other Upgrades?
C660AV, Q660AV	1MB	1152x870	24-bit	No	NuBus
Q700	512K	1152x870	8-bit	6 100 ns 256K	NuBus
Q800	512K	1152x870	16-bit	2 80 ns 256K	NuBus
Q840AV	1MB	1152x870	24-bit	4 80 ns 256K	NuBus
Q900/950	1MB	1152x870	16-bit	4 80 ns 256K	NuBus
Power Macintosh 4400/160	1MB	1152x870	16-bit	4MB DRAM[1]	PCI
PM 4400/ 200	2MB	1280x1024	24-bit	4MB SGRAM[1]	PCI
P5200, 521x, 522x, 53x0, 54x0CD, PM 5200, 5300, 5400/1120	1MB	832x624	16-bit	No	PDS
P5260, 5270, 5280, PM 5260	1MB	640x480	16-bit	No	PDS
P5400/160, 5400/180, 5430, 5440, PM 5400/ 180, 5400/ 200	1MB	1024x768	16-bit	No	PDS
PM5500	2MB	1280x1024	24-bit	No	PCI
P611x, PM 6100	512K[2]	832x624	16-bit	No	PDS
PM 6100AV, 7100AV, 8100AV	2MB[2]	1152x870	24-bit	No	None
P62x0, 6310, 6320, PM 6200/750, 6300/12	1MB	832x624	16-bit	No	PDS

(continued)

Table 12-2 *(continued)*

Mac Model	Built-in?	Top Resolution	Top Color Depth	VRAM Upgrade?	Other Upgrades?
P6360, PM 6300	1MB	1024x768	16-bit	No	PDS
P6400, PM 6400	1MB	1024x768	16-bit	No	PCI
PM 6500	2MB	1280x1024	24-bit	No	PCI
PM 7100	1MB[3]	1152x870	16-bit	4 80 ns 256K	NuBus
PM 7200, 7215	1MB	1152x870	24-bit	3 70 ns 1MB	PCI
PM 7220	2MB	1280x1024	24-bit	4MB SGRAM[1]	PCI
PM 7300, 7500, 7600	2MB	1280x1024	24-bit	4MB VRAM[1]	PCI
PM 81xx	2MB[3]	1152x870	24-bit	4 80 ns 512K	NuBus
PM 8200	1MB	1152x870	24-bit	3MB VRAM	PCI
PM 85xx, 8600	2MB	1280x1024	24-bit	4MB VRAM[1]	PCI
PM 9500[4]	None	N/A	N/A	N/A	PCI
PM 9600	4MB	1280x1024	24-bit	No	PCI
PM 9600/3xx	8MB	1280x1024	24-bit	No	PCI
PM G3	2MB	1280x1024	32-bit	6MB SGRAM[1]	PCI
20th Anniversary	2MB	800x600	16-bit	No	PCI

Power Computing Systems

Mac Model	Built-in?	Top Resolution	Top Color Depth	VRAM Upgrade?	Other Upgrades?
Power 100/120	2MB	832x624	16-bit	No	NuBus
Power Base	2MB	1280x1024	24-bit	4MB DRAM[1]	PCI
Power Wave	2MB	1280x1024	24-bit	4MB[1]	PCI
Power Curve	1MB	1280x1024	24-bit	4MB VRAM[1]	PCI

Mac Model	Built-in?	Top Resolution	Top Color Depth	VRAM Upgrade?	Other Upgrades?
Power Center	1MB	1152x870	24-bit	4MB VRAM[1]	PCI
Power Center Pro	2MB	1280x1024	24-bit	4MB DRAM[1]	PCI
Power Tower Pro	4MB	1920x1080	24-bit	8MB[1]	PCI
Motorola Systems					
StarMax 3000[5]	1MB	1024x768	16-bit	4MB[1]	PCI
StarMax 4000	2MB	1280x1024	24-bit	4MB[1]	PCI
StarMax 5000[6]	2MB	1280x1024	24-bit	4MB[1]	PCI
UMAX Systems					
c500, c600	1MB	1024x768	16-bit	No	PCI
c600x/ 280	2MB[7]	1280x1024	24-bit	No	PCI
j700 series	2MB	1920x1080	24-bit	4MB[1]	PCI
j700/ 233	4MB	1920x1080	24-bit	No	PCI
s900 series	4MB	1920x1080	24-bit	8MB[1]	PCI
S900/233, S900/250, S900DP/250	8MB	1920x1080	24-bit	No	PCI

1 Upgrade replaces existing VRAM.

2 The Mac IIci, IIsi, and Power Macintosh 6100 use the system's regular system RAM memory for built-in video.

3 Power Macintosh 7100 and 8100 include both 1MB of dedicated VRAM and support the use of system DRAM for built-in video (dual-monitor capable).

4 Many Power Macintosh 9500 models were bundled with a 2MB video card expandable to 4MB of VRAM.

5 Some StarMax 3000/225MT and 3000/240MT models include 2MB or 4MB of VRAM standard.

6 StarMax 5000/300 features 4MB of VRAM standard.

7 c600x/280 features 1MB built-in VRAM and 2MB video card (dual-monitor capable).

Color depth

Let me quickly explain some of the numbers you're seeing in Table 12-2 — especially the spy-code-like references for color depth. *Color depth* refers to the number of colors that the Mac and display have to choose from for each pixel in an image. This number is generally expressed in terms of the number of data bits available for storing color values. Table 12-3 shows the typical color depths and the number of colors each includes.

Table 12-3 **Color Depths**	
Color Depth	*Number of Colors*
1-bit	Black and white
2-bit	4 colors
4-bit	16 colors
8-bit	256 colors
16-bit	Thousands of colors (32,768)
24-bit	Millions of colors

A 32-bit color depth also has "millions of colors," except that 8 bits of data are dedicated to the *alpha* channel, which enables a graphics system to define transparency and determine how the colors of the pixels will overlap one another (to show translucence). This extra 8-bits can also be used for other purposes, such as chroma key (transparency, like the blue screens used for movie effects) support. You may also think that 16-bit color should have 65,536 different values, not 32,768. The lower number is a result of the use of *signed* math, which enables low-level programming instructions to execute more quickly, but requires the 16th bit to hold the positive or negative sign (meaning only 15-bits' worth of colors can be used).

Although most modern Mac-compatible monitors can handle as many colors as you can throw at them, others — especially those built into older Mac models — are very limited (monochrome and black-and-white displays are especially hampered). Check your monitor's manual for more info, or look in your Monitors control panel — it will usually show you the limit to the number of colors your combination monitor and VRAM can display.

VRAM

Whether your Mac currently uses built-in video circuitry or video on an expansion card, there's RAM memory, often called video RAM or VRAM, on that card. Because each pixel of your bitmapped screen image must be stored in VRAM, the amount of VRAM your Mac has determines the combination of video resolution and the number of colors you can display on your monitor.

Some video cards feature upgradeable VRAM slots; they're almost always manufacturer-specific, so check your documentation. One megabyte of VRAM can display anywhere from a resolution of 640x480 and millions colors, up to a resolution of 1024x768 and 256 of colors. Beyond that, you'll need 2MB or more. Video cards (and Mac built-in video) tend to come with the following amounts of RAM: 256K, 512K, 1MB, 2MB, 4MB, and 6MB.

As you may have gathered from Table 12-2, the amount of VRAM you need depends on the maximum resolution and color depth at which you'd like to run your display. Fortunately, you can calculate the amount of VRAM needed for a particular resolution. Here's the formula:

Width x Height x Pixel depth/8 = RAM Needed

It's a simple matter of multiplying the resolution by the pixel depth divided by eight. So, consider the example of a standard 14" color display:

640 x 480 x 8bit/8 = 307,200 bytes

For the basic 256 colors at 640x480, you don't need more than about 300K, which in most cases would translate to 512K of VRAM. (VRAM amounts, like RAM numbers, are generally upgraded in increments of 256K, 512K, or 1MB.)

Often you can upgrade a Mac with 512K of VRAM to 1MB of VRAM. Why would you want to do this? To get 800x600 resolution at thousands of colors — perfect for driving a 15-inch monitor:

800 x 600 x 16bit/8 = 960,000 bytes

If you can, you might want to bump up to "true" color (24-bit color depth) and enough resolution to drive a 19-inch monitor. Here's the sort of setup that's fitting for a graphic designer or multimedia professional:

1028 x 764 x 24bit/8 = 2,359,296 bytes

That's over 2MB, which means you'd need at least 4MB of VRAM to run it. You may have that much if you have a reasonably new Mac (especially one that was originally a high-end system), or you may need to buy a video expansion card.

Adding VRAM

If you want more color and resolution, you should considering adding VRAM to your existing video circuitry. This is usually cheaper than a new video card, although it's important to note that VRAM won't speed up your Mac's display at all (like an accelerated video card will). It just adds more resolution and color choices.

Before you get started, you'll need to answer a few questions:

✦ *What sort of VRAM does your Mac support?* This refers to the actual type of memory module. Macs can vary from model to model—check your manual.

✦ *How much additional VRAM can you install?* Check Table 2-2 for this information.

✦ *Where are the VRAM sockets?* Consult your Mac's manual for help on this information.

Armed with these answers, you can install the new VRAM. Follow these steps:

1. Shut down your Mac, unplug it, and ground yourself from static discharge.

2. Locate the VRAM sockets on your Mac's logic board or video card.

3. Remove the VRAM that's currently in the VRAM socket, if necessary. (Some Macs enable you to add VRAM without removing the existing memory—check Table 12-2 and your Mac's manual.)

4. Install the new VRAM. (In some Macs, you'll simply add the VRAM to an open socket, as shown in Figure 12-7. In others, you'll add the VRAM just as you would a RAM SIMM, as described in Chapter 6.)

Figure 12-7: Adding VRAM to your Mac's logic board

5. Close everything up and start your Mac. To test the VRAM, open your Monitors (or Monitors & Sound) control panel. You should have new color depth and/or resolution options.

Choosing a card

As with most expansion cards, you'll want to focus primarily on the expansion capabilities of your Mac before you run out and purchase a new card. You've got to get the right expansion technology, or you won't be able to install it at all. Fortunately, as shown in Table 12-2, nearly all Macs have an upgrade path of some kind.

Aside from the interface the card uses, there are three reasons to purchase a video expansion card:

✦ **Increased capabilities.** If you know your monitor is capable of more colors or better resolution than your Mac can give you, you'll want to add a more powerful card. The card should be capable of displaying higher screen resolutions, higher refresh rates, and more colors per pixel than your Mac's current video. This usually means a card with more RAM (or a VRAM upgrade to your existing video).

✦ **Increased speed.** Video expansion cards can also offer an increase in speed by offloading some of the QuickDraw drawing tasks to a specialized processor on the card itself. In the case of basic video tasks, this acceleration is usually called QuickDraw acceleration, or 2D acceleration. You may also find cards that include 3D acceleration, which is discussed in more depth in Chapter 18.

✦ **More monitors.** If you want to add more monitors to your setup you can pretty much buy whatever video card you'd like — from a cheap one that just gets the job done to an expensive card with all the bells and whistles. If you're willing to dedicate the desk space to additional monitors, you'll never be wasting the video features built into your Mac. Plus, a video card for an additional monitor only needs to be as capable as the monitor you'll dedicate to it. You can run Mac monitors at different color depths, resolutions, and sizes, so whatever card you buy should work with any other video circuitry that's already in the Mac.

Once you've decided what the purpose for the card will be, you're ready to shop. There are three major factors to concern yourself with:

✦ **Expansion card technology.** It almost goes without saying — you'll need to get an expansion card that fits an available slot in your Mac. If you don't have a free slot, you may be in trouble. Your only choice, in that case, will be to add more VRAM if your Mac can handle more.

✦ **VRAM.** Buy a card with the most VRAM you can afford, up to a point. If you definitely won't be using the card for professional-level image-editing tasks, there's probably no reason to go over 4MB in VRAM, which gives you true color (24-bit) in most resolutions. Higher-end cards feature 32-bit color in all resolutions by boosting the VRAM to 6- or 8MB.

✦ **Acceleration.** One reason to choose an expansion card over a simple VRAM upgrade is to take advantage of the acceleration built into many of these cards. For daily duties, look for a card that accelerates 2D tasks. If you work with 3D objects, panoramas, or games, you may find that 3D acceleration is a nice touch — QuickDraw Rave acceleration should do the trick. (3D acceleration is discussed in more detail in Chapter 18.)

Installing the Card

As you might imagine, installing a video card isn't much different from installing any other sort of expansion card. If it varies at all, it will only be because video cards always feature an external video connector (and perhaps other ports) that enables the external monitor and similar devices to connect to the card.

Note Depending on the card and monitor, you might also find that you need an adapter to get them to talk to one another. Macadapter (www.macadapter.com/) manufacturers a few different types, as does Griffin Technologies (www.nashville.net/~griffin).

Card installation

Installing a video card is pretty much the same as any card installation:

1. Shut down your Mac, unplug it, and electrically ground yourself.

2. Open the Mac's case and locate an empty expansion slot. (Visually inspect it to ensure it's the right type of slot for your card.)

3. Remove the screw and metal dust plate that covers the hole in back of the case for the slot you'll be using.

4. Position the card so that its interface is directly over the slot. If it's a NuBus card, make sure the card's housing fits over the NuBus slot on the logic board. If it's a PDS or a PCI card, make sure the card's connector fits snugly in the slot (see Figure 12-8).

5. Press down lightly and uniformly on the top corners of the expansion card until it's firmly installed in the slot. Screw the card into the back of the case to secure it.

6. Attach the monitor cable in the back to the card. You may need to use an adapter for VGA-compatible monitors. Make sure you set the resolution and refresh rate to levels the monitor can support.

7. Try restarting your Mac and see if the card manages to drive the monitor, resulting in a picture. You may need to install a software driver or extension that enables you to control any acceleration capabilities the card offers. If you have trouble, make sure to check all connections between the card, the logic board, the monitor, and the monitor cable.

Figure 12-8: The MicroConversions 2124NB II card being installed in a Mac IIci. The NuBus card offers 2D acceleration and increased VRAM over a IIci's standard video, resulting in better video performance (www.microconversions.com).

Once the card is installed and working, you're ready to open up the Monitors (or Monitors & Sound) control panel and set the card up for optimal performance. In the control panel you can change the resolution, color depth, and refresh rate (assuming your monitor is a multisync model).

Setting up two (or more) monitors

If you now have two sets of video circuitry (two cards or one card and built-in video), you can also use the Monitors control panel to set up both monitors for use with the Mac. (Actually, if both monitors are correctly connected to their respective video ports, they should work immediately after you've started up the Mac — but there are still some things you'll need to tweak.) If both screens are active, their icons will appear in the control panel, with each screen numbered 1, 2, and so on. You can click and drag the mouse pointer on either of the screens to reposition it relative to the other one (see Figure 12-9). If you desire, you can arrange the screens so that dragging the pointer off the left side of the rightmost monitor's screen causes it, as logic would dictate, to appear on the right side of the leftmost monitor. Otherwise, things could get tricky.

To set the resolution of one of the monitors, double-click its screen in the control panel. That gives you access to resolution, color depth, and refresh rate settings (see Figure 12-9).

Note   The Monitors & Sound control panel in Mac OS versions after System 7.6 looks slightly different from the Monitors control panel shown in the picture, but the concepts and tools are similar. (In Monitors and Sound, choose the Arrange button to gain access to the two screens shown in Figure 12-9.)

Figure 12-9: If you've installed two monitors, you can use the Monitors control panel to position the screens relative to one another and change their characteristics.

You can also, in the Monitors or Monitors and Sound control panel, drag the menu bar from one of the screens to the other. Generally, the positioning of the menu bar determines which screen is the main screen, where new applications will launch and alert dialog boxes will most often appear.

Summary

✦ Monitors and monitor cards work together to display a bitmapped screen image that's created by your computer using Apple's built-in QuickDraw technology. The screen refreshes many times a minute to give you the impression that images on screen change instantly. The more quickly the screen refreshes, the more flicker-free the display. Fast refresh also makes higher demands on your video card and monitor, especially as the screen's resolution and color depth increase.

✦ Today there isn't much point in buying a monitor that doesn't offer multisync capabilities. But you'll also want to look at some other numbers, including dot pitch, refresh rate, and the top resolutions supported. Also, get the largest monitor you can afford.

✦ Part of buying a monitor includes understanding your Mac's built-in video capabilities. You can check the chart in this chapter, and then decide if you need to upgrade the VRAM or add a video expansion card. Adding VRAM gives you more color and resolution choices. Adding a video card can do that, as well as enabling you to add a second monitor and even speed the display of your Macs.

✦ Once you've made your decisions, it's time to install everything. VRAM can be a new experience, but installing video cards is about the same as adding any other expansion cards. When you go to attach the monitor, though, the issue is all about compatibility — you'll likely need a special adapter, which may take some detailed setup.

✦   ✦   ✦

Digital Video

If desktop publishing and Web publishing were the killer applications of the 1980s and 1990s for the Macintosh, digital video editing may be the killer Mac application for the beginning of the new century. Long dominated by high-end workstations and dedicated equipment, it's become very easy for even the hobbyist Mac owner to get involved with video editing. Solutions for creating QuickTime video that can be broadcast over the Web or included in multimedia presentations (kiosks, CD-ROMs, and so on) are incredibly affordable. But even higher-end systems for television-quality editing are in a price range that many small businesses and freelancers can afford.

For the most part, the digital video process can be broken down into three steps: First, you need to get the video into your Mac somehow. This usually involves hooking a video camera or VCR to a port on your Mac and running the tape. Your Mac, using video-capture software, records the images digitally. The quicker your computer, your hard drive, and the video capture circuitry's ability to digitize video, the better the video quality will be.

Your second step is to edit the video. Using QuickTime, video-editing software, and (sometimes) add-on input/output equipment, you can turn your Mac into a digital editing studio, adding fades, wipes, music, dialog, and anything else you can come up with.

Third, you need to get the video out of your Mac and back onto videotape, a TV screen, or some other analog medium. (Of course, you might also want to save your video to a CD-ROM drive or removable drive, but those are digital mediums and therefore don't require any special translation.) To put your digital images on TV, you need to hook one up to your computer — again, through special video ports on the back of your Mac.

In This Chapter

QuickTime and digital video

Chart: Does your Mac have built-in AV?

Adding video-in capabilities

Displaying your Mac's screen on a TV

Getting started with video

Some Macs have all these capabilities (maybe even including some related bundled software) built right in. Others, though, will require upgrading. Some of those upgrades, as you might have guessed, can include NuBus or PCI expansion cards. Others consist of hooking up external boxes to your existing video card. Whatever way you pursue it, though, you'll want to understand some of the basics of digital video so you'll know exactly what you need to get to upgrade effectively.

Note   If you're not interested in all this crazy digital video stuff, why not take the couch potato approach? There's also a quick discussion of TV tuner upgrades for Macs at the end of this chapter.

The Digital Video Basics

At its most basic, creating a digital video is like using your Mac as a video-recording device, enabling you to spool a camcorder video or similar video signal to your hard drive. The end result, in some cases, is very similar to videotape.

Delve a bit further, though, and you'll see that digitizing video is really a much different process. With tape, everything remains static and linear; if you want to get to a particular part of the video, you need to fast forward until you find it. If you want to add more video in the middle of a particular clip, you'll need to run the video out to another recording device, pause it at the right moment, and then start recording the new video. When it's done, you start up the original and finish the recording sequence. If you want the video to look really good, you'd better have some editing equipment and professional-level recording devices.

Digital video is different — it's what word processing is to typewriting. With digital video, the images have been transformed into an actual computer file that can be manipulated just like any other computer document. If you wanted to add more text in the middle of a word processing document, you'd just place the cursor in the document and start typing (or use the Cut and Paste commands to insert a chunk of text). The same possibilities apply for digital video. Using a movie editing program, you can find a particular moment in a video, and then cut and paste new digital footage into the movie (see Figure 13-1).

What you need

Nearly any owner of a modern Macintosh computer can play digital video clips directly on his or her desktop. In most cases, it's simply a matter of point-and-click. The Mac OS, with its QuickTime underpinnings, is able to arrange the video in a window and give you controls for playing the video on screen. The differences between older and newer Macs will sometimes shine through in these demonstrations, though. A number of factors can affect how well a digital movie plays:

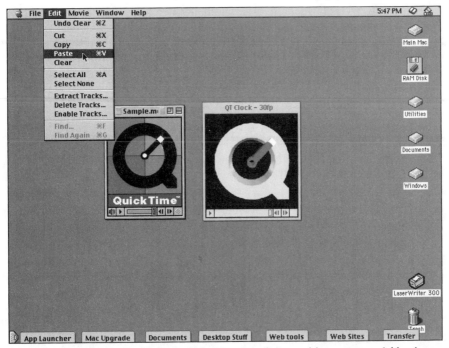

Figure 13-1: Even the most basic digital movie editor enables you to quickly piece two video clips together.

✦ **Processor speed.** A lot of things have to happen at once to get a digital movie to play back well, including synchronizing the audio to the video, playing each frame as it decompresses, and changing the pixels required to play the video in a larger window. The faster your processor, the smoother and larger your video will be.

✦ **Video cards.** Some video add-on cards are designed specifically to improve the quality of QuickTime and/or MPEG video formats. Other video cards simply accelerate the display overall, resulting in slightly better videos.

✦ **Hard drive.** The faster your hard drive (or other media on which the digital video is stored), the faster and more smoothly the video will play. A fast hard drive is required to get the data in the video to the system RAM quickly enough for the processor to display the video on screen.

✦ **RAM.** Digital videos tend to be huge documents, requiring a lot of RAM to play back. Often this can be compensated for by turning on Virtual Memory, but that tends to affect the quality of playback.

When it comes to recording and creating digital video, you'll need more hardware. Dedicated expansion cards and other add-on devices are often necessary for recording digital video to your hard drive so you can edit it. You'll then need still more hardware to get the image back out of your computer and onto a CD-ROM or a videotape, if that's your desire.

Here, then, are the basic necessities for creating quality digital video:

✦ **Fast processor, good video, fast hard drive, lots of RAM.** Everything you need for a good video playback machine is doubly important for a good video studio Mac. You'll need fast and wide *everything* to create and edit video smoothly and effectively.

✦ **Video inputs.** Your Mac needs special circuitry to accept video inputs from a VCR, camcorder, or similar device, and then translate that signal into a digital computer file that can be used by the computer and its editing software.

✦ **Digitizing software.** Although the basic software for digitizing and dealing with video is a portion of the Mac OS called QuickTime, you'll still need special software to access the routines in QuickTime responsible for digitizing the video. (You may also want to work in a format not supported by QuickTime.) This software has to be capable of accepting the video signal, compressing it (in most cases), and storing it in a movie file format on your hard drive (see Figure 13-2).

✦ **Editing software.** Again, basic tools are built into Apple's QuickTime MoviePlayer application. You can get more capabilities out of the Pro version of QuickTime, but you may want yet more sophisticated software for higher-end editing.

✦ **Output hardware.** Finally, you'll need some way to get the digital movie back out of your Mac so that people can enjoy it (or learn from it or otherwise appreciate it). To do this, you'll most likely want output hardware that enables you to send a computer signal back out to a TV or TV-like device, a VCR, or a camcorder for recording.

QuickTime

QuickTime, the multimedia portion of the Mac OS (and a prized add-on for Microsoft Windows), offers the infrastructure you need to begin digitizing and editing movies. Apple calls QuickTime a software architecture that includes a file format (the QuickTime Movie format), support for the translation and integration of other file formats, and services that can be referenced by programmers so that their applications have access to features offered within QuickTime. This means programs based on the QuickTime architecture can easily include a ton of tools that enable images, video, and audio to be synchronized, optimized, compressed, and otherwise manipulated to create digital video and multimedia files.

Figure 13-2: The Apple Video Player, which comes with AV-capable Macs, offers basic digitizing functions.

To applications programmers, the QuickTime format provides convenience: Programmers don't have to reinvent the wheel when they want to deal with digital movies. For instance, many Windows-based multimedia producers have used the Video for Windows (VfW) file format and infrastructure in the pass. If they wanted to, they could switch over to QuickTime by simply using programs based on the QuickTime architecture, even if they have a lot of files already in Video for Windows. Programmers of QuickTime-based tools can easily integrate support for the VfW file format into their programs, because QuickTime offers VfW translation ability directly.

Note

In fact, QuickTime is so universally accepted as a multimedia standard that it will eventually become the basis of the MPEG-4 standard, a wide-reaching standard destined to be the foundation for quite a bit of digital video in the near future.

To the rest of us nonprogrammers, however, QuickTime provides a multimedia document format. In other words, you can use QuickTime to create QuickTime audio and video documents (see Figure 13-3). These documents can then be read, understood, and displayed (or played) by programs that are capable of translating and working with the QuickTime format.

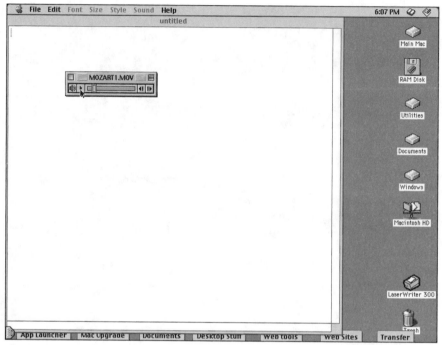

Figure 13-3: Notice there's no picture? That's because QuickTime is an audio document format, too, and this file is an audio-only QuickTime file. It's also being played in SimpleText, by the way.

In fact, many Mac OS applications and desktop accessories are capable of working with QuickTime. For example, SimpleText, the Mac OS basic text editor, can play QuickTime movies, as can the Scrapbook. Because QuickTime makes digital video tools so easy to integrate into applications, you'll probably be working with a tool that's tied pretty closely to QuickTime if you plan to work on a Mac to create or edit digital video. In that case, you'll want to know a bit about how QuickTime works together with other file formats and how it deals with digital data.

QuickTime is included when you install the Mac OS, but that doesn't always mean you have the latest version. Check `http://quicktime.apple.com` for upgrades, preview (beta) versions, and other QuickTime-related goodies.

Digital movies

QuickTime movies are a very sophisticated approach to the old flipcard animation system you may have once implemented in the corner of a textbook during a grade school lecture. With QuickTime, a series of digital images are arranged in a particular order so that, when displayed very quickly, they give the impression of fluid movement across the screen. This is the same basic concept that drives all motion-picture technology, whether it be the individual frames of a film strip, the cells of an animation, or the scan rate of a television set.

For QuickTime movies to be considered television quality, they must display about 30 frames per second so that motion feels very fluid and skips or jumps are imperceptible to the human eye. However, it's difficult for desktop computers to manage a full-screen, 30-frames-per-second data rate, considering the bottlenecks — RAM, hard drive speed, processors, and video subprocessors. All these factors have to come together in order to create a smooth digital movie.

QuickTime gives you the opportunity to do two things: First, you can use QuickTime-based tools to edit digital movies as you would other computer documents. You can edit each individual frame, if you wish, or use application tools to add different special effects over time. You can also add or delete individual frames or groups of frames.

QuickTime also gives you the ability to optimize your digital movies for whatever your ultimate output medium is. If you want to display the video on a television or record it to tape, you can tweak your QuickTime movie so that it will play at the full resolution for a television screen and at broadcast-quality speeds (assuming your Mac is powerful enough and you've added a few extras).

If you're creating video for the Internet, though, you'll jump through some different hoops: In this case, you're probably less interested in video quality and more in the speed at which the video can transfer. To optimize the video for speed, you can use special QuickTime routines to compress the file size of the movie.

Movie file formats

I've already mentioned that most Mac AV tools will enable you to save digital audio and video in the QuickTime format so that you can use those digital documents in many different applications. Aside from the QuickTime movie format, the QuickTime architecture will support a number of file formats, including the following:

✦ **AVI (Audio/Video Interleave).** This file format is most popular on the Windows platforms, where its use is encouraged by Microsoft. QuickTime 3.0 and above can read and write directly to this file format.

✦ **OpenDML.** The OpenDML format extends the AVI standard to include such features as the capacity to have really large files, the capability to focus on the number of fields-per-second displayed, and the addition of timecodes. QuickTime enables users to read and write to the OpenDML extensions to AVI.

✦ **OMF.** The Open Media Framework format was created by Avid, a leading developer of high-end, professional digital-video solutions. The format allows Avid products and other high-end digital-editing software to exchange files. QuickTime includes the capability to work with OMF documents, enabling a typical Mac to exchange files with more powerful workstation-level computers.

✦ **MPEG.** The Moving Picture Experts Group (MPEG) standard, one of the premier standards for digital video, is designed for the consumer market. MPEG provides low data rates (for transmission over the Internet or by CD-ROM) while maintaining high picture quality.

✦ **DVC.** New digital-only cameras use the standard DVC format for transmitting digital images between the camera and a computer. QuickTime can work directly with the stream of data that these cameras use to communicate, enabling QuickTime applications to work directly with video from these cameras.

QuickTime also enables you to deal with a number of audio formats, including Apple's own AIFF, Microsoft's WAV format, Sun Microsystem's AU files, and Sound Designer II documents, along with MPEG-2 audio files. In other words, you can take different input file formats and devices and bring them together in a QuickTime-enabled editor to create and edit a complete digital multimedia document. This includes audio and video clips you transfer over the Internet or similar networks, audio you record using your Mac, video you record using a camcorder and your Mac, and video you get from any other standard source.

Compression and codecs

If you've worked with regular image files much on your Mac, you know that they can often get rather large, requiring hundreds of kilobytes or even a few megabytes to store depending on their complexity.

To keep digital movies to a manageable size, various *codecs* (*c*ompressor/*dec*ompressor*s*) can be used. These codecs compress redundant data in most cases, making the file smaller for transmission and storage. Some of these compression schemes are *lossy*, however, meaning they introduce a level of inaccuracy into the color or pixel reproduction of the video. In other words, the smaller you want the file, the more likely it will result in a slightly lower image quality (see Figures 13-4 and 13-5).

Figure 13-4: Here's an uncompressed movie (file size approximately 3.3MB).

Figure 13-5: Here's the same movie heavily compressed (and much smaller at 2MB).

QuickTime offers you tons of codecs to choose from when you save your movie. Realize, though, that saving a digital movie can be quite a chore. The video-in software will give you a choice of codecs, quality schemes, colors, and the like. As the movie is saved, it will be compressed, and this feat sometimes takes minutes or hours to accomplish. To get the ideal compression for your particular QuickTime document, Apple offers a number of different codecs. Table 13-1 shows you some of the video-related codecs and their recommended usage.

Table 13-1
QuickTime Video Codecs

Codec Name	Use	Compression
Video	Provides fast compression, good for hard disk playback	10:1
Component Video	Produces high-quality, big files; good for TV-destined clips	2:1
Animation	Works with clips that have few color changes	2:1
Graphics	Provides slow decompression; good for 256-color graphics	2.5:1
Photo JPEG	Good for high-quality images	5:1 to 50:1
Cinepak	Good for CD-ROM–based movie playback	25:1
None	Provides best capture rates, but huge files	1:1
DV	Used with digital video cameras	1:1
H.263	Used for video conferencing	Varies
Sorensen	Used for Web-based, streaming video	Varies

If you have the QuickTime Pro package (available from Apple) or QuickTime 2.5 or above, you'll have some or all of these options available to you through the MoviePlayer application when you go to save a digital movie (see Figure 13-6). You may also see these options if you save a digitized movie using some other program, including Apple's Video Player and similar programs.

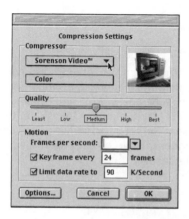

Figure 13-6: Choosing codecs and other settings for saving the movie file

Key frames and data rates

Once you've gotten through your choice of codec, you'll want to address a few other issues that have to do with QuickTime movies. One such issue is the *key frame rate*. Key frames are frames of a QuickTime movie that QuickTime uses as reference points. At each key frame, QuickTime considers the entire frame, showing it immediately in the movie-playing application. All subsequent frames are treated a bit differently, however. To speed things up a bit, QuickTime only compares the differences between subsequent frames and the current key frame until it reaches the next key frame. This process makes the movie a bit smaller for quick transfer, but it also can hurt the quality of the clip.

If you've created a clip for the Internet or another slow medium, setting the key frames fairly far apart (15 to 20 frames) makes some sense. In those cases, a key frame every two seconds or so is reasonable. If you'll be playing back the video from a much faster source, though, use a lower key frame rate.

Another issue is *data rate*. For some codecs, setting a specific data rate tells the QuickTime movie what its limitations are going to be as the movie is saved. For CD-ROM based movies, for instance, 200- or 250 kilobytes per second is recommended.

Video-in Hardware

Once you've got a basic grasp of how QuickTime works, you're ready to get some video into your Mac. To do this, you may need to buy some additional hardware, depending on your Mac model. In some cases, Macs come with built-in capabilities for accepting video feeds and turning them into digital images. In other cases, you'll have to opt for an expansion card.

To start, though, let's look at the basic issues that need to be addressed regardless of the video-in solution you're using.

Interface types

The key with any video-in solution is getting it to talk to your video source, whether that's a VCR, camcorder, or something more exotic. Therefore, you'll want to take a close look at the interface options you have for connecting the camera or similar device to your Mac. These tend to be as follows:

✦ **RCA video plugs.** These days the little yellow RCA video wires are vying for dominance over cable-TV coax wiring for attaching a composite video source (such as a standard VCR). If you've messed around behind your home-entertainment system, you know what I'm talking about. RCA plugs are male adapters with a small shield around their points. The video cable, almost invariably, is yellow, whereas the white and red cables are used to connect the left and right channels of audio, respectively.

✦ **S-video.** An S-video (or super video) connection achieves higher-quality output (especially to a VCR or TV) by splitting a video's signal into two parts — one for color, one for brightness. Television sets are designed to split the two values, but standard composite video sends them using the same signal. However, S-video connections require S-video–capable equipment. The S-video connector resembles a standard Din-8 or ADB port connector. Don't plug one into the other — take care that you only plug the S-video connector into the Mac's S-video port.

✦ **FireWire.** Although technically a new serial technology, FireWire (originally developed by Apple) is quickly becoming a popular interface for video cameras and equipment. Also known as IEEE 1394, this connection is another high-speed wonder that's also *isynchonous*, meaning it guarantees a particular data rate. This is perfect for video-in applications that require a reliable high-speed input option. Digital video cameras are required for this connection, because FireWire isn't really designed to digitizing video; it's designed to tranfer DV format files from a DV camera to your Mac. A FireWire adapter is a thin, flat, 6-pin serial connector, as shown in Figure 13-7.

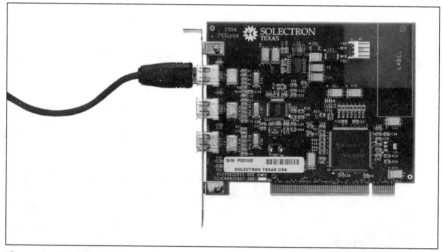

Figure 13-7: A FireWire connector is unlike any serial cable the Mac world has ever seen. (Photo courtesy Apple Computer, Inc.)

Your interface choices will be highly dependent on the sort of AV capabilities your Mac has. If you've got AV built-in, you're probably given a choice between RCA and S-video connectors. Some cards also offer both, although earlier cards might be limited to RCA-style connectors. A FireWire card is pretty much a stand-alone creature these days, so if you have FireWire built in, you probably know it. Otherwise, you'll need a PCI adapter card.

There's something else to consider, too. You need to make sure you have the right adapters, hardware settings, and other elements in place for dealing with the television standards to which your video equipment adheres. In the U.S. and most of North America, that's the National Television Standards Committee (NTSC, also called *RS-170a*) standard. In Europe and other places, the Phase Alternating Line (PAL) standard reigns supreme, and the SECAM (SEquential Couleur Avec Memoire) standard covers just about everywhere else. The differences include the number of lines of resolution and how often the picture is updated. What's important, though, is that you'll need the right adapter to accept a video source from a video component using one of these standards, and you'll need a video-out option that supports the correct standard if you plan to send QuickTime movies back out to a videotape or television.

Built-in AV

Before getting too far ahead, let's make sure you know exactly what capabilities are built into your Mac. If you've never really taken a hard look at the back of your Mac's case, you might be in for a shock. Table 13-2 shows the Apple Macintosh models that include video-in hardware.

Table 13-2 Macintosh Computer with Built-in AV Capabilities			
Computer	**Built-in AV Capability?**	**Includes Expansion Card?**	**Special Video Slot?**
LC 580, Performa 580 series			Yes
Quadra 660AV	Yes		
Quadra 840AV	Yes		
Performa/Quadra 630 series			Yes
Performa (and Power Macintosh) 5200, 5300, 5400, 5500 series		(Some models)	Yes
Performa (and Power Macintosh) 6200, 6300 6400 series		(Some models)	Yes
Power Mac 6100AV, 7100AV, 8100AV	Yes		

(continued)

Table 13-2 (continued)

Computer	Built-in AV Capability?	Includes Expansion Card?	Special Video Slot?
Power Mac 8500, 8600	Yes		
Power Mac G3 Minitower	Yes		

Video-in expansion cards

If your Mac didn't come with built-in AV features, you still have plenty of video-in upgrading options. Although some older Macs — say, pre-68040 Macs — aren't really ideal for video editing, a surprising number of aging Macs still are. (It's 3D rendering that will kill you if you don't have a high-end processor.) In fact, for years the Quadra 840AV — with its upgrade slots, high-end SCSI (for its time), and secondary digital signal processor — was a favorite digital editing platform even as newer Power Macs were rolling off the assembly lines.

As they say, it's all in the card(s). Many 68040 and early Power Macintosh models are capable of accepting NuBus cards with good video digitizing throughput that, these days, are even pretty affordable. If you've got PCI slots in your Mac, you're in great shape; the more capable PCI bus makes add-on video-in cards an easy alternative for the budding video editor. Plus, such upgrades often prove affordable.

If you have a Performa or all-in-one Power Macintosh computer (along with a few regular Quadra and Power Mac models), you may not have video-in built into your Mac, but you do have a different option. For a number of years, Apple built a special video slot into its consumer and education-market Macs. That slot enables you to add a specially designed video card — the Apple Video Card — that adds S-video and RCA inputs for video-in and video capture.

Note

Unfortunately, the Apple Video Card has been discontinued, and I'm not aware of a company that's stepped in to fill the void. To get the card, you'll need to comb the mail-order companies or check the usual used Mac parts message boards and gathering places.

If you don't own one of these Macs, your choices are only limited by the type of expansion bus you have and what you're willing to pay for the upgrade. Video-in cards exist for all sorts of budgets and technologies, including PCI video-in systems ranging in thousands of dollars for low-budget television or in-house video editing. Or, you can spend a few hundred dollars and grab a card that's capable of reasonable video-in performance, along with offering regular Mac video features, accelerated video features, and more (see Figure 13-8).

If you choose to go with FireWire, chances are you'll be forced to buy a PCI card; FireWire is a new enough technology that companies are unlikely to make NuBus versions of the cards (although anything is possible). You'll also need a FireWire-capable video camera or similar video equipment and special software, probably included with the FireWire card.

You'll also find that some solutions offer both video-in and video-out capabilities, while others require you to use a special converter to send video out to a television or video recorder.

Table 13-3 lists some companies that offer video-in add-ons and video-out expansion.

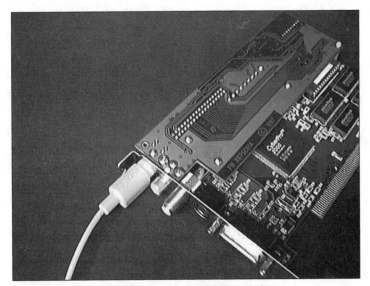

Figure 13-8: The Video Wizard by MicroConversions (www.microconversions.com) is an affordable, all-in-one card with Mac video features, video-in and video-out capability, and even a cable TV tuner feature that installs easily in a single PCI slot.

Table 13-3
Web Sites for Various Video-in and Video-out Add-on Manufacturers

Manufacturer	Products	Web Site
Apple Computer	FireWire, video-in	www.apple.com
Radius	FireWire, video-in	www.radius.com
Micro Conversions	Video-in, video-out	www.microconversions.com
Digital Vision	Video-in, video-out, SCSI solutions	www.digvis.com
Aver Media	TV-in, video-out	www.avermedia.com
Avid Technology	High-end digital editing systems	www.avid.com
Media 100	High-end digital editing systems	www.media100.com
ProMax	FireWire	www.promax.com
TrueVision	Video-in, video-out	www.truevision.com

Video out

As mentioned in the last section, you'll need to consider what sort of video-out capabilities are available to you if you plan to send video from your Mac to a television or video device. Although many video-in cards also feature this capability (offering RCA or S-video ports that head back out to your video equipment), other capture cards are only good for getting the video into your Mac — it's up to you to get it back out.

You may also find yourself in a situation where you'd like to display your Mac's video output to a TV or VCR. In that case, you'll need a special output device, called a *scan converter,* that converts the Mac's RGB signal into something a TV can understand — NTSC or PAL broadcast signals.

A scan converter is usually a box about the size of a paperback book or smaller. The box connects to your Mac's RGB (monitor) output port, converts the signal to an appropriate television video format (NTSC or PAL), and then sends the signal down the RCA or S-video cables to the video device.

Television-format output capabilities are built into most AV Macs and come with some Performa-style Macs in the form of the Apple Video System. If you suspect your Mac may have this capability built-in, check your Monitors or Monitors & Sound control panel for an option that enables you to display output on an NTSC or PAL source.

When looking for a video-out device, you should consider a few factors:

✦ **Resolution sync.** What resolutions is the device capable of rendering on the TV screen? You may find that 640x480 won't be adequate for your presentation (although much higher resolutions tend to render things difficult to read on screen). Make sure the device is compatible with a resolution and refresh rate that your Mac's video can sync to.

✦ **Underscan capabilities.** Televisions tend to overscan an image, causing the Mac desktop to be cut off by the edges of the television set's case. That gives you the largest possible picture, but it might also cut off parts of the menu bar and other screen elements. To compensate, the scan device should be able to underscan the image, displaying it entirely on the TV screen within a black border.

✦ **Quality of features.** Although these devices can be very difficult to test, they can also vary wildly in quality. If you're looking for high-end output, you'll need to shop carefully to see which will work for you. Some features can be gimmicky (screen freeze and pan-and-zoom for presentations) but others add picture quality and sharpness you might appreciate for video-out purposes.

Your Mac can likely get away with using a video-out device that's designed for an Intel-compatible PC, especially if you already have a VGA adapter for your Mac's RGB output. This can be great if you need to connect a PowerBook, for instance, to an existing overhead projection or presentation system. For video production work or an in-house system, however, you'll get better results from a video-out device that's designed to work specifically with the Mac's RGB output. You'll also have better image quality using S-video, although the quality increase isn't always noticeable.

DV/DVCAM

Although closely related to FireWire, as far as your Mac is concerned, digital video (DV) is an emerging standard in the world of video cameras that, for the first time, enables handheld cameras to record full-motion video directly to a digital format. This offers a number of improvements over analog tape–based systems, such as the following:

✦ *Data is transferred directly to your Mac.* Using FireWire as the high-speed intermediary, such DV cameras aren't really playing their images for your computer to digitize, as with regular videotape players and camcorders. Because the images are *already* digital, they're simply transferred to your Mac like any other computer file.

✦ *No generational loss.* Nothing is transmitted or copied (in the analog sense) in order to get the images into your Mac, so there's no quality loss due to cabling, connectors, and other variables.

✦ *Less expensive quality.* Although DV codecs are required for getting the images into your Mac, the quality of the digitized images you work with are more reliant on the camera instead of the main bottleneck — the video-in ports on your computer. Instead of paying for high-speed digitizing technology, more of your investment gets focused on the quality of the camera.

DV is just emerging as a broadcast and professional option, and, although consumer cameras are following suit quickly, it may be a little while before DV is pervasive. That said, it's a very interesting option for anyone who wants to make high-quality video presentations that are more easily transferred to the Mac and edited.

Getting Started with Video

If you have one of the Macs that sports built-in video or if you've already installed a digital video card, getting started with digital video is simple — you just plug the video cables into the back of the Mac and fire up a digitizing program. You'll first need to know a few things about your equipment, including whether or not you need to use S-video cables or RCA video cables (see Figure 13-9), and what sort of video standard your equipment uses (the US NTSC standard for video or the European PAL standard).

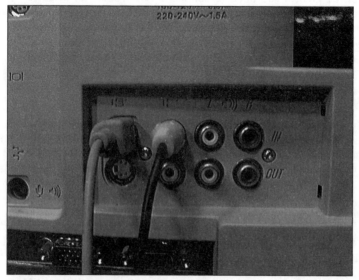

Figure 13-9: On the left is an S-video cable and connector; on the right, an RCA style cable and connector.

With the correct cabling installed on your video player or camcorder device, you're ready to attach the cables to your Mac's AV ports. If you're using RCA-style cables, simply plug the yellow video cable into the video-in port on the back of your Mac. (Some Macs only offer S-video ports, so an RCA video patch cable is usually included. You may need to plug that patch cable into the S-video port first, and then plug the RCA cable into that patch cable's adapter.)

If you're using S-video, you simply plug the S-video cable from the video device into the S-video–in port on the back of the Mac. With the cable attached, start up a video capture program on the Mac and test to see if any images appear. (Don't forget to turn on the video source.)

Note

> If you want to record both audio and video, you'll need to attach audio cables from the video source. Some Macs offer two channel audio-in, featuring red and white RCA connectors on the back panel of the Mac, usually near the RCA video connector. If your Mac doesn't have these, you'll need an adapter that will enable you to connect the RCA audio cables from your video source to the single RCA stereo miniplug connector that most Macs include.

With everything wired up, fire up your Mac and launch the Video Player (or similar) digitizing program. Turn on your video source and try to display an image (just point the camcorder at something or tap the Play button on a VCR). If everything works well, you can begin digitizing the video source.

From there it's pretty much up to you. With the movie digitized, it's become a computer document. You can use the QuickTime MoviePlayer or another program to edit the video, compress it (to make it better for playback on CD-ROMs or the Internet), and then save the final result. Once you are done, you can display your Mac's video on a TV screen or output it to a VCR (or other, more professional recording device), and then play the QuickTime movie. Save it to tape, if desired, and you'll have a complete, edited video.

Watching TV

So what about something basic and boring like watching a regular television program on your Mac? Well, you can do it with any AV model. If it can accept a digital-in signal, a Mac can accept a feed from a VCR or other cable tuner, acting just as if it were a television. Or, at least, almost like a television. Most Macs — even if they're digital video capable — don't include a TV *tuner* to enable them to translate antennae or cable-borne signals into TV pictures. Instead, AV-capable Macs are more like dumb TV screens that can show TV video as long as some other device does the interpreting.

If you'd like TV tuner capabilities for your Mac, that's another card. (Or similar add-on.) With the exception of the MacTV, the 20th Anniversary Mac, and a few high-end Performa models, no Mac has a dedicated TV tuner; some Performa-series logic boards include a slot for a special Apple TV/FM Tuner expansion card. As far as I know, only Apple has made that card for Performas and similar Power Macintosh machines (such as the all-in-one Power Macintosh 5500 series), and they don't make it anymore. However, you may still be able to find it through catalog dealers and on the used market.

Cross-Reference

Apple models that include a TV expansion slot are shown in Table 4-2 in Chapter 4.

For other Macs, a TV tuner can be added by inserting the right expansion card. Such an expansion card can be nothing more than a tuner, or it can be a rather advanced, full-fledged graphics subsystem. Check out ixMicro (www.ixmicro.com/), MicroConversions (www.microconversions.com/), and ATI Technologies (www.atitech.com/) for new, PCI-based TV tuners; other companies have made other cards that may still be in use.

With such a card installed in your Mac, you then hook up the cable coax connection just as you would connect your cable to a television set. (If you have a cable converter box, you may want to string it in between the cable input at the wall socket and your Mac.) Next, run the Video Player software (or the TV viewing program that came with your card) to view the TV signal and watch shows. With compatible Apple Performa models, you can even use the TV remote control to change channels!

Summary

✦ Most Macs can play digitized movies — digital video — without any extra hardware or software because QuickTime technology is built in. But it's also increasingly easier to make your own digital video. Digital video is becoming very inexpensive to experiment with and use for all sorts of business tasks. Of course, if you're already a video professional, you might want to look into Mac-based systems that could make your editing tasks easier and less expensive.

✦ On a Mac, it takes a couple different components to create a digital movie. First, you need AV hardware; it may be built into your Mac or you may have to buy an expansion card. Next, you'll need to know something about QuickTime, the Mac's built-in digital video technology. Finally, you'll need some software for getting the video into your Mac.

✦ Digital-video connections come in a few different flavors. If your Mac has built-in AV capabilities, you'll find RCA jacks and S-video ports on its back panel for easy connections to a video source. Other Macs will require an expansion card — like any other card, it'll be NuBus or PCI, whichever is appropriate for your Mac. (Some Macs have a dedicated video card option, too.) You might also be interested in FireWire, which enables you to hook up a high-speed serial port directly to the latest camcorders, and then just copy the digital movie to your Mac.

✦ Once you have everything hooked up, you're ready to digitize. Sync up your video source, and then hit record in your video player software. It's that simple.

✦ If you'd like to skip straight to the important stuff, you can add a cable tuner to many Mac models, giving you the ability to watch television or a video feed directly on your Mac's desktop.

✦   ✦   ✦

Sound, Speech, and MIDI

If you've never seen some of the old classic form factor Macs in their carry bags, you should try to catch a glimpse of one. It's quite a treat (okay, I'll go ahead and include a snapshot as Figure 14-1). Originally thought of as portable, those aging Macs offered you the chance to pick them up and lug them around—if not from the dorm to the library, at least from the dorm to back home for the holidays, I suppose.

When Apple introduced the Macintosh to the press back in 1984, Steve Jobs pulled the Mac out of just such a bag. He plugged it into the wall, started it up, and waited for it to take its cue. After the requisite smiley face, the first thing it did for the press was say, out loud, "Welcome to Macintosh. It sure is great to get out of that bag."

Sound has been part of the Macintosh experience ever since, with constantly advancing sound capabilities built into every subsequent Macintosh. Eventually, Macs would become the top platform for sound and multimedia production, with great tools and software applications for editing sound. The Mac would also be a musician's tool, supporting advanced MIDI capabilities and playback, through QuickTime MIDI and other technologies.

And the Mac has advanced its capabilities to deal with computer-generated speech, as well as to accept speech as a method for inputting data. The Mac OS has built-in options, and third-party programs extend this capability even further. I'll discuss speech separately a little later in the chapter.

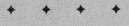

In This Chapter

Mac's sound capabilities

Buying and installing digital audio equiptment

Speech and speech recognition

Working with MIDI

Figure 14-1: A Mac SE and its carrying case

The Mac's Audio Capabilities

The audio capabilities of a typical Mac let you accomplish three things: You can record audio (get sound into your Mac), playback audio (get sound out of your Mac), and edit audio (rearrange sound on your Mac). All Macs have these capabilities built into them, with any AV Macintosh or Power Macintosh model giving you the highest level of stereo and quality sound available.

You also have two choices as to how the audio is going to be processed by your Mac.

One way to get audio into your Mac is to digitize it — record it to the Mac's hard drive. This is done in a way that's very similar to creating digital video. A sound source is connected to the audio input(s) on the back of the Macintosh, which takes very quick samples of the audio as it plays. These samples are digital — computer data — enabling them to be stored on the Mac's hard drive. And, just as with QuickTime movies, digital audio is simple to edit, manipulate, and play back through your Mac's speakers.

The other type of audio is more like a blend of a player piano script and the PostScript printing language. It's the Musical Instrument Digital Interface, or MIDI. *MIDI* is a computer language for controlling music synthesizers — for example, keyboards, drum machines, and electric pianos. That is, it can control pretty much anything that can accept a MIDI interface. Through this interface (a small box that plugs into your Mac's serial port), instructions are transmitted between the instrument and the Mac and back again. This allows notes played on the synthesizer to be stored as musical notation or otherwise represented in a Mac application. At the same time, storing these notes on your Mac means you can instruct a MIDI-capable synthesizer to play the song whenever you get the urge.

Technically, digital sound is not really too different from digital audio, but your Mac, depending on its age, may have the ability to read text aloud using Text-to-Speech technology. Some more powerful Macs can even recognize your speech as a method of input. It's still a young technology, but it's fun to play with, and it takes advantage of the built-in audio capabilities of AV and Power Macs.

Take a look at how each type of Mac sound works.

Digital audio

If you record something to a cassette tape, you're recording the entire audio source. It all gets laid right down on the magnetic tape. Digital audio, including audio CDs, doesn't quite work like that. Instead, digital audio works much the same way a movie camera does, by taking quick *samples* of the source and recording them. A typical film strip is composed of individual frames that run at about 24 frames per second to convince the human eye that the picture is moving. Similarly, a digital-audio recording samples the audio source many thousands of times per second to convince the ear that the digital recording is continuous.

In fact, the number of samples per second — or the *frequency* of the sample — is a very real test of the quality of a recording. The more samples, the better. Measured in kilohertz (KHz — corresponding to thousands of samples per second), the frequency is really a measure of the complexity of the sound, telling you the range of tonal information that's included in the sample. The lower the frequency, the less faithful the reproduction of the sound. An example might be a telephone call, which has an analog frequency of 4KHz. Although you can understand what is being said, the quality of a telephone call is really pretty bad. Think of something that someone has sung to you (or played a recording of) over the phone. (You know, back in high school.) Even a good singer who sings to you over the phone loses quite a bit of their quality.

In digital sampling, you double the frequency of an analog device, so an 8KHz digital sample would result in 4KHz analog telephone-quality. Audio CD quality is generally considered to be 44.1KHz, which translates into around 44,100 samples per second. This is actually ever so slightly outside the realm of human hearing. However, the highs and lows you can't hear affect the overall quality of the tones you do hear, because they help to complete one another. Audio still sounds pretty good at about 22KHz, where it's about at the quality of an FM radio broadcast. Audio 11KHz sounds like an AM radio signal.

The other thing that's important about a digital-sound sample is the bit depth at which it's sampled. Sound is usually sampled at either 8 bits or 16 bits, with the latter offering higher quality. The sound sample is *quantized*, meaning the sample must somehow be turned into a number. In an 8-bit sample, you've got 2^8 or 256 choices for the number. Because the number is not likely to fit neatly into one of 256 slots, it has to be mathematically rounded, which introduces errors. 8-bit samples are much smaller than 16-bit samples (in the amount of storage space they require), but they generate more random noise, often hissing. 16-bit samples offer 2^{16} or 65,536 choices. This makes for a much more accurate reading.

The third factor is called *channel depth*, which is an overly fancy way of factoring in whether or not the sample is in stereo. If it is, that takes twice as much storage space as a mono signal, because stereo requires separate right and left channels.

All taken together, the frequency, bit depth, and channel depth of a sample help to decide exactly how much disk space your digital recordings will take up. And that can be quite a bit. Table 14-1 quantifies the relationship between quality and storage space.

Table 14-1
Disk Space Consumed by Stereo Audio Samples

Sample rate	Quality	Space at 8 Bits	Space at 16 Bits	30 min recording (16-bit)
8KHz	Telephone	16KBps	32KBps	57.6MB
11KHz	AM Radio	22KBps	44KBps	79.2MB
22KHz	FM Radio	44KBps	88KBps	158.4MB
44KHz	Audio CD	88KBps	176KBps	316.8MB

Surprised at the sizes? If you've worked with digital audio samples in the past, you might think the table is running a tad high; after all, you've listened to long samples that didn't take up nearly that much space. In cases like that, you're probably dealing with a compressed audio file. Compression is common in the digital-audio world, and a number of compression schemes are very effective, resulting in high-quality sound that takes up a lot less disk space than an uncompressed file. Be aware, however, that as you record digital samples, you often can't compress them on the fly (at least, not without some quality issues). Instead, you'll have to record the full sample first, and then compress it. That can require even more disk space, at least temporarily while you work with the file.

I want to tell you more about compression schemes and which ones work best for most audio files, but first I need to tell you a little about file formats before we move on.

File formats

Just like any other pursuit on a computer, digital-audio creation generates computer files. And, like QuickTime and digital video, there are plenty of these formats. It seems that nearly every operating system — Mac OS, Windows, Solaris, SGI, Amiga — has its own audio scheme, along with a few other sound file formats designed to be cross-platform or used in a completely different technology (such as consumer electronics). These days, QuickTime helps the user with a lot of these formats, enabling import and export of sound data to a variety of formats, depending on the usage.

Here are a few of the more common sound file formats along with their origins and uses (note that sound on a Mac is usually governed by QuickTime, so I've included the formats that QuickTime deals with well):

✦ **AU.** Also know as the μ-law format, this popular sound file format is native to Sun and Next workstations. Seen as something of a lowest common denominator on the Web, AU can't reach beyond 8KHz in most cases (some alternative implementations sample at about 22KHz). The result is a telephone-quality sound file that's small, so it's popular on the Internet.

✦ **AIFF/AIFC.** Apple's own original file format — the Audio Interchange File Format — was good, but uncompressible in its first incarnation, so Apple extended the format with AIFC. These sounds can sample at the highest rates — stereo, 16-bit, 44.1KHz samples — but they require a lot of disk space to do it. Standard MACE compression of 3:1 or 6:1 isn't recommended by Apple anymore, so experiment with new QuickTime compression schemes, covered in the next section.

✦ **WAV.** The WAV format is native to Microsoft Windows and therefore popular. (WAV started its life before that, though, as a joint effort between Microsoft and IBM during the heyday of DOS.) It works pretty much as AIFC does, with a full range of sample rates and the ability to take on compression schemes. QuickTime translates existing WAV files and exports to WAV.

✦ **MPEG.** Popular as both a video and audio format, MPEG sets the standard for a number of applications — for example, CD-ROM video and high-quality, compressed audio. MPEG is all about quality compression. The MPEG Level II standard supported by QuickTime allows for compression of files by 6:1 or 7:1 without noticeable quality loss. The MPEG standard is determined by the Motion Picture Experts Group.

✦ **Sound Designer II.** In case you're curious, QuickTime natively supports the Sound Designer II format, enabling you to digitally swap files that are saved in the popular application format. Sound Designer II is a sound-editing application written by DigiDesign (www.digidesign.com).

Compression

Hand-in-hand with the audio file formats come various types of compression that can be used to make the sounds take up less storage space or transmit more quickly over mediums such as the Internet or a SCSI connection to your CD-ROM drive. Compression offers a trade-off between quality and size, enabling you to fit the audio sample to your needs. Fortunately, standards such as the MPEG compression schemes don't trade *much* quality for gains in storage compression.

There are many different compression schemes for audio, with some of those schemes designed for specific purposes — voice, music, Internet transmission, and video conferencing. QuickTime has opened up an entire world of these compression schemes, many of which can be used to compress the audio tracks of a QuickTime movie (even if a QuickTime file is audio-only, it's called a movie.)

For regular audio formats (those non-QuickTime formats discussed in the previous section), the compression schemes are a bit more limited. Over the years, a few have emerged as common, with some of them associated specifically with particular sound formats. These schemes tend to be designed to give general compression capabilities to a wide variety of sound file types and uses (as opposed to newer compression schemes designed specifically for the task at hand — for example, compression voice transmission versus music).

On the CD-ROM

You'll find a program like SoundApp (located on the CD-ROM that accompanies this book) very adept at translating between the audio file formats that are common to the Mac, as well as adding basic compression schemes to make the files smaller.

Let's take a look at some of the general purpose audio-compressor technologies you may run into:

✦ **μLaw.** Pronounced "mu-law" for μ, the Greek character *mu,* this compressor is typically applied to AU sound files, originally a Sun format. Compression is 2:1, and the compression takes place quickly — fast enough to happen immediately the sound is digitized.

✦ **MACE.** This Mac-based compression technology isn't really recommended by Apple anymore, even though it was an early favorite for developing QuickTime audio tracks. MACE works quickly and compresses well, but quality of the reproduction is low. The format only supports 8-bit samples, but can compress at 3:1 and 6:1 ratios.

✦ **IMA/ADPCM.** IMA supports 16-bit sounds only, but compresses them at 4:1 with decent quality. Good for compressing audio in an interim stage, for temporary hard-drive storage, or for compressing audio before committing it to tape. Compression takes place very quickly.

✦ **MPEG.** Like the file format, MPEG compression is popular for many consumer-oriented purposes such as CD-ROM audio for games or as part of an MPEG video track for computing. Other uses abound as well. Compression is really good, around 8:1 or more before quality degrades. MPEG is computer intensive during the compression stages and requires modern computers for playback, although audio doesn't demand as much as MPEG video. (Some Macs have even included hardware to accelerate MPEG playback.)

Those are some of the commonly distributed formats, although they're not the only ones. Some audio codecs are proprietary, designed specifically to be used with the encoder or server software created by the owner of the codec. Examples would be the Voxware codecs, RealAudio codecs, and others. You may find that QuickTime gives you access to these, if they're installed. You might enjoy trying them out.

> **Note**
>
> One major coup for QuickTime 3.0 when it came out was the inclusion of the Sorensen codecs for video and audio, both of which generate excellent quality with small file formats, making them great compressors for streaming audio and video over the Internet.

MIDI

Up until now I've been talking about using a computer as a digital recording device. Philosophically, there really isn't too much difference between recording digitally and recording to an analog source. Of course, it's convenient to record digitally, as it allows you to pick up bits of a recorded clip and drop them somewhere else for unprecedented control and speed in editing. But for the most part, the results are similar.

MIDI, in a way, really represents a leap forward in thinking. With MIDI, computers have a language that actually enables them to control electronic musical instruments. Your Mac can issue commands to synthesizers to turn on and off notes, adjust the volume, change modulation, and do a number of other things.

The short of it: MIDI controls more than one synthesizer from a single keyboard or computer. Using different *channels* to communicate over a chain of MIDI devices, you can pretty much create as large an orchestral sound as your budget can support. Music professionals, hobbyists, and music teachers can all benefit from a number of MIDI advantages, including the computer's ability to annotate music as it's played on the keyboard (see Figure 14-2).

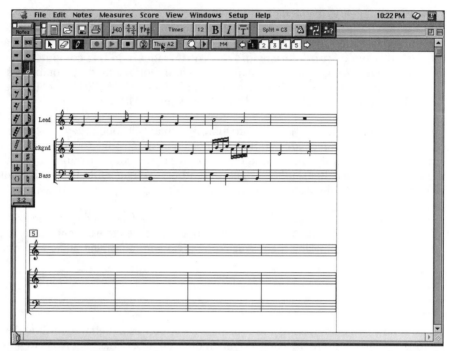

Figure 14-2: A MIDI annotation program diligently marking notes as they're played (Shown is Passport Designs' Encore.)

MIDI requires a few basic components. QuickTime is an integral part; in fact, you can work with and edit music on your Mac without having a synthesizer of any sort connected if you use the one that's built into QuickTime. This is a little limiting, because stand-alone synthesizers offer much better sound, but it does make it possible to turn your computer—even a PowerBook—into a musical synthesizer, using the computer keyboard for musical input.

In most cases you'll want to connect synthesizers to your Mac. The components for such a setup include the following:

✦ **MIDI interface.** This one is for your Mac. You'll need a MIDI converter box to communicate with MIDI devices through your Mac's serial port. These interfaces are often little boxes about the size of cassette tapes, although they can be much larger and more feature-laden.

✦ **MIDI-capable synthesizer.** Most folks will want a keyboard synthesizer as the anchor of their MIDI recording system, but plenty of options abound for synthesizers—drums, guitars, bass guitars, and generic-looking electronic boxes that make all sorts of noise. Most important will be MIDI connections—look for the 5-pin IN, OUT, and (often) THRU connectors on the back of the instrument.

✦ **MIDI-capable software.** Your Mac is not going to be much good if it doesn't have a software application to accept and interpret the MIDI data being sent from your synthesizers. Many of the software packages available are called *sequencers,* meaning they record the notes being played, and then enable you to rearrange them, layer them on top of other notes (for fuller-orchestral effects), and edit them. Other programs are for annotation, teaching music, and turning your Mac into a player-piano/music-automation system.

With these components in place, you're ready to start sending commands over the MIDI interface. You do this in one direction or the other: from the synthesizer to the computer or from the computer to the synthesizer, depending on what you're trying to do.

The MIDI language is fairly standard, although it can be augmented by commands for particular synthesizers or language sets created by certain manufacturers. Overall, though, the language is basically a series of commands sent out as bytes of data that are mostly notes to be played. There's other info, too, including what channel the commands are intended for and how long they should be played.

Each channel is technically a different instrument — if you have classic synthesizers at your disposal, they probably synthesize one sound at a time, such as a piano, a drum set, or something similar. Some modern instruments allow for a number of different instrument sounds to be played at once. These synthesizers can be assigned a number of different channels so that different data streams are all accepted by the same instrument. That's how you can use MIDI to command an entire rock band to play through a single keyboard synthesizer, for instance.

Note

When shopping for a MIDI-compatible synthesizer, you may come across some basic terms related to the size of the orchestra the keyboard is able to reproduce. *Polyphony* represents the number of discrete notes that can be played at once — 32 or 64 notes isn't unheard of. *Timbres* refers to the number of instruments that can be played simultaneously by the synthesizer, although you may find the synthesizer refers to timbres as channels or instruments. Sixteen separate instruments isn't uncommon, although some really good synthesizers are only capable of playing one instrument — that's very well reproduced — at a time.

Being able to assign all these different instruments to different channels could get confusing — confusing enough, in fact, that you might not ever be able to reproduce a MIDI song correctly on a different set of equipment, which would make MIDI less than worthwhile as a standard. So, another standard, General MIDI, governs the first 128 voices on any MIDI synthesizer that supports multiple voices. This makes it a simple matter for a MIDI file to specify the instrument, channel, and a particular quality for that instrument. That's part of what enables MIDI files to be saved and played on different computers or equipment.

General MIDI is split into the 16 different channels supported by MIDI, with one major instrument type assigned to each channel (except Channel 10, which is reserved for unique percussion instruments). The major instrument groups include the Piano, Chromatic Percussion, Organ, Guitar, Bass, Strings, Ensemble, Brass, Reed, Pipe, Synthetic Lead, Synthetic Pad, Synthetic Effects (FX), Ethnic, Percussive, and Sound Effects. Each of these main instruments offers eight sub-instruments, which results in the total of 128.

Of course, the quality of the sound isn't governed by the General MIDI specification, just the sound type that the synthesizer is supposed to make. So, your results may vary. Table 14-2 shows you the different General MIDI instruments.

Note   Aside from supporting the 128 General MIDI instruments, other criteria add up to making an instrument truly General MIDI compatible (as defined by the MIDI Manfacturer's Association — www.midi.org). The instrument must also support at least 24-voice polyphony, must support different instruments on all 16 channels, and must respond to certain basic General MIDI commands, such as fine tuning and pitch bend. If a keyboard qualifies, it can display a General MIDI logo.

Table 14-2 General MIDI Instruments	
Instrument	**Number**
Piano	**Channel 0**
Acoustic Grand Piano	1
Bright Acoustic Piano	2
Electric Grand Piano	3
Honky-tonk Piano	4
Electric Piano 1	5
Electric Piano 2	6
Harpsichord	7
Clavi	8
Chromatic Percussion	**Channel 1**
Celesta	9
Glockenspiel	10
Music Box	11

Instrument	Number
Vibraphone	12
Marimba	13
Xylophone	14
Tubular Bells	15
Dulcimer	16
Organ	**Channel 2**
Drawbar Organ	17
Percussive Organ	18
Rock Organ	19
Church Organ	20
Reed Organ	21
Accordion	22
Harmonica	23
Tango Accordion	24
Guitar	**Channel 3**
Acoustic Guitar (Nylon)	25
Acoustic Guitar (Steel)	26
Electric Guitar (Jazz)	27
Electric Guitar (Clean)	28
Electric Guitar (Muted)	29
Overdriven Guitar	30
Distortion Guitar	31
Guitar Harmonics	32
Bass	**Channel 4**
Acoustic Bass	33
Electric Bass (Finger)	34
Electric Bass (Pick)	35
Fretless Bass	36

(continued)

Table 14-2 *(continued)*

Instrument	Number
Slap Bass 1	37
Slap Bass 2	38
Synth Bass 1	39
Synth Bass 2	40
String	**Channel 5**
Violin	41
Viola	42
Cello	43
Contrabass	44
Tremolo Strings	45
Pizzicato Strings	46
Orchestral Harp	47
Timpani	48
Ensemble	**Channel 6**
String Ensemble 1	49
String Ensemble 2	50
Synth Strings 1	51
Synth Strings 2	52
Choir Aahs	53
Voice Oohs	54
Synth Voice	55
Orchestra Hit	56
Brass	**Channel 7**
Trumpet	57
Trombone	58
Tuba	59

Instrument	Number
Muted Trumpet	60
French Horn	61
Brass Section	62
SynthBrass 1	63
SynthBrass 2	64
Reed	**Channel 8**
Soprano Sax	65
Alto Sax	66
Tenor Sax	67
Baritone Sax	68
Oboe	69
English Horn	70
Bassoon	71
Clarinet	72
Pipe	**Channel 9**
Piccolo	73
Flute	74
Recorder	75
Pan Flute	76
Blown Bottle	77
Shakuhachi	78
Whistle	79
Ocarina	80
Synth Lead	**Channel 11**
Lead 1 (Square)	81
Lead 2 (Sawtooth)	82
Lead 3 (Calliope)	83
Lead 4 (Chiff)	84
Lead 5 (Charang)	85
Lead 6 (Voice)	86

(continued)

Table 14-2 *(continued)*	
Instrument	*Number*
Lead 7 (Fifths)	87
Lead 8 (Bass + Lead)	88
Synth Pad	**Channel 12**
Pad 1 (New Age)	89
Pad 2 (Warm)	90
Pad 3 (Polysynth)	91
Pad 4 (Choir)	92
Pad 5 (Bowed)	93
Pad 6 (Metallic)	94
Pad 7 (Halo)	95
Pad 8 (Sweep)	96
Synth Effects	**Channel 13**
FX 1 (Rain)	97
FX 2 (Soundtrack)	98
FX 3 (Crystal)	99
FX 4 (Atmosphere)	100
FX 5 (Brightness)	101
FX 6 (Goblins)	102
FX 7 (Echoes)	103
FX 8 (Sci-fi)	104
Ethnic	**Channel 14**
Sitar	105
Banjo	106
Shamisen	107
Koto	108
Kalimba	109
Bag pipe	110
Fiddle	111

Instrument	Number
Shanai	112
Percussive	**Channel 15**
Tinkle Bell	113
Agogo	114
Steel Drums	115
Woodblock	116
Taiko Drum	117
Melodic Tom	118
Synth Drum	119
Reverse Cymbal	120
Sound Effects	**Channel 16**
Guitar Fret Noise	121
Breath Noise	122
Seashore	123
Bird Tweet	124
Telephone Ring	125
Helicopter	126
Applause	127
Gunshot	128

The Standard MIDI File (SMF) is a third standard in the MIDI world, this one a file format. Like .DOC for Microsoft Word documents or .AIFC for compressible Mac audio files, .MID or .MIDI is a standard filename extension that suggests a universal MIDI file. In nearly all cases, something that's capable of playing MIDI files can deal with SMF. This includes MIDI sequencers, players, and even the Mac's MoviePlayer with QuickTime installed (see Figure 14-3).

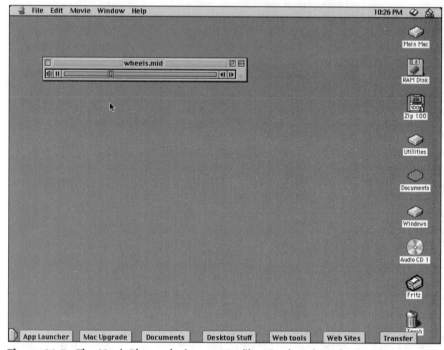

Figure 14-3: The MoviePlayer playing a MIDI file. It's played on the QuickTime General MIDI library, which gives pretty true sound through the Mac's speakers.

Speech technologies

As I mentioned before, speech technologies don't really require anything special to work, because they use the same basic sound hardware that's built into recent Macs. For speech recognition, that's any recent AV Macintosh or Power Macintosh (early Macs have Text-to-Speech capability, but not speech recognition, which debuted on the AV Macintosh series with the code name "Casper"). In fact, Macs that are equipped for speech recognition even come with a special microphone called the PlainTalk microphone, shown in Figure 14-4. (PlainTalk is Apple's name for the technology used for speech recognition.)

So, no particular hardware needs to be added. What's needed is software.

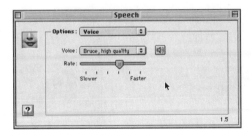

Figure 14-4: The Speech control panel gives you control over speech recognition and Text-to-Speech technology.

Speech technologies are handled by the Speech Manager, an add-on to the Mac OS that handles speech responsibilities. Head to the Apple menu and look for a control panel called Speech in Mac OS 7.6 and above. It's the center of operations for Text-to-Speech and speech recognition.

Cross-Reference

If you can't seem to find a Speech control panel, make sure the control panel is in the Control Panels folder in the System Folder and the extensions Speech Manager and Speech Recognition (if desired) are in the Extensions folder. Extension troubleshooting is discussed in Chapter 32.

The Speech control panel enables you to do a number of things. You can pick basic elements, such as what voice you want your Mac to use and whether or not you want the Mac to read all alert boxes. You can change the volume and rate of speech. (If you're looking at the control panel right now and you notice that you have at least this many options, you're enabled for Text-to-Speech technology.)

This technology allows your Mac to actually read the text it finds in enabled applications. One such application is Apple's shining centerpiece to new technologies — SimpleText. To get your Mac to read text to you, open a file in SimpleText and type something (or open an existing text document). In the SimpleText menu bar, select Sound, and then choose Speak All. Your Mac should start to talk to you.

You can also highlight text in SimpleText and choose Sound ➪ Speak Selection. This will cause your Mac to just read the highlight portion aloud (see Figure 14-5).

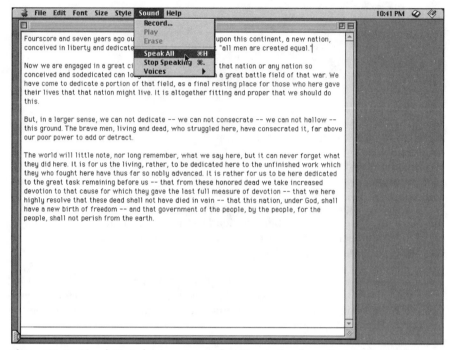

Figure 14-5: SimpleText showcases another Mac technology, Text-to-Speech.

With the Speech Recognition extension enabled, you can do even more. The Speech control panel now changes to offer a number of other options, including Speakable Items. Choosing this menu item from the Speech control panel, and then enabling Speakable Items, will bring to the screen a new little window—one that puts a face on your Mac (see Figure 14-6).

Now, with the PlainTalk microphone (or a compatible line-level mike) plugged into the sound-in port on the back of your Mac, you're ready to chat with it. You'll find a list of recognizable commands in the Speakable Items folder that's stored in the Apple Menu Items folder. (Access Speakable Items from the Apple menu.) You can add your own Speakable Items: Add aliases for programs you want to launch, and then say "Launch *name of program,*" and the Mac should recognize that command and execute it. In a similar way, you could store AppleScripts in the Speakable Items folder, making your Mac pretty much do anything you can think of.

The Speech control panel gives you some other customizations as well, including the opportunity to change the voice your Mac uses and to change how your Mac knows to respond to a spoken command—you can have your Mac ignore anything it hears until you say something specific, such as "Computer," or you hit a particular keystroke sequence.

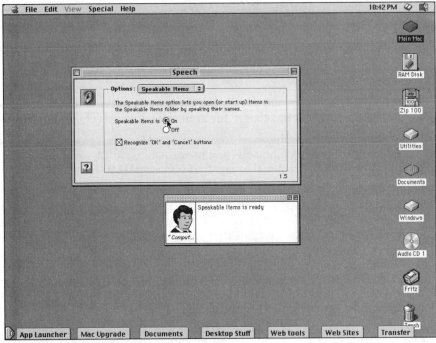

Figure 14-6: Enabling Speakable Items introduces a new element to your Mac's interface.

Add-ons exist for Apple's PlainTalk technology, including some products that build on the Mac's capabilities and take them further:

✦ **MacYack** (Scantron Quality Computers, www.lowtek.com/macyack) extends Text-to-Speech with additional voices, adds speech to most applications, and uses Text-to-Speech more often in the Mac OS.

✦ **Power Secretary** (Dragon Systems, www.dragonsys.com) adds full-fledged discrete voice recognition to a Mac OS system, so you can dictate typing and control the computer.

✦ **Write:Outloud and Co:Writer** (Don Johnston, www.execpc.com:80/~labres/dj.html). Write:Outloud is a word processor that reads text out loud as it's typed; Co:Writer is a text prediction program that predicts possible words to help typing/learning impaired users work more quickly.

✦ **JABRA earphone** (JABRA, www.jabra.com) is an earpiece/microphone combination that aids in speech recognition and other speech tasks, including using your Mac as a standard telephone or an Internet telephone.

✦ **MicNotepad Lite** (Nirvana Research, `www.moof.com/nirvana`) is a freeware application that records voice to your Mac, enabling you to use your Mac as a fairly sophisticated transcription device that runs in the background, slows down the recording to catch up with typing, and bookmarks certain passages. It doesn't use much speech technology, per se, but it's interesting nonetheless.

✦ **MacIRC** (Chris Bergmann, `www.macirc.com`) is an Internet Relay Chat client that speaks text as it appears in the application.

✦ **SurfTalk** (Digital Dreams, `www.surftalk.com`) is a background application that accepts speech commands and uses them to surf the Web in Netscape Navigator. The program makes any hyperlinks speakable and recognizes commands such as "Go back" and "Bookmark."

✦ **Plaintalk Plug-ins** (`speech.apple.com/plug`) is a page for links to speech-related plug-ins for Web browsers. They include plug-ins that will read Web pages to you as well as plug-ins that enable you to maneuver on the Web using speech commands.

Note

The PlainTalk microphone is different from the standard karaoke model — or even a higher-end type — that you'd buy in the local electronics store. That's because the microphone port on newer Macs is actually a line-level input, the same sort you'd use to connect a tape deck or CD player to your home receiver or amplifier. This means a device connected to that port needs to provide line-level input, and most microphones, aside from the special PlainTalk ones, don't. If you find one, though, feel free to plug it in and try it. Otherwise, you'll need to plug regular mikes into a mixing board or amplifier first.

Sound Hardware and Software

To get sounds in and out of your Mac — whether it's digital sound or MIDI sound — you'll need to hook some things up to your Mac. For digital audio, you may find a lot of what you need is built-in to your Mac, especially in later models. All AV Macintosh and Power Macintosh computers have 16-bit stereo-in and 16-bit stereo-out capabilities. But if your Mac is younger than that, or if you want more than just single stereo input, you'll need to go shopping for an expansion card. And you'll need software to do the actually digitizing, storing, and mixing of sounds.

As far as MIDI goes, you can consider a whole range of add-ons if you're interested in adding digital music to your Mac's repertoire. I'll show you many of the options, and how to install them, in this section.

Digital audio hardware

Since digital audio became a rage in the late 1980s and early 1990s, Macs have been on the scene with built-in capabilities that were certainly adequate for a lot of audio editing. With early adoption of CD technology players, SCSI for CD creation and a full range of digital audio capabilities built-in, the Mac has been ready for serious production for years. Early Macs, however, suffer from low-end audio capabilities (issues like 8-bit sound and mono inputs) that keep them from being more than just adequate for audio editing. To add good digital-audio capture capabilities, you'll need to add a sound card.

Better Audio

Newer Macs can suffer from sound that isn't the best, too. Only the 8500, 8600, and G3 Minitower series of Macs have sported RCA-style connectors for audio, for instance, with the rest of the stereo audio–capable Macs using a stereo miniplug. Although this isn't an awful solution, professionals may squirm at the ten or so decibels of noise that a miniplug can add to the mix. In general, a pro-level sound card can add better noise reduction, digital connectors (for downloading digital data directly from digital-audio sources such as DAT recorders), and on-board digital signal processors (DSP) for more advanced effects.

These cards install like any other NuBus or PCI cards and should be quickly recognized by your Macintosh. Only a handful of professional audio manufacturers make the cards, especially in the face of improved built-in capabilities in the latest Mac models. Companies making audio I/O cards include the following:

✦ **DigiDesign** (www.digidesign.com). This clear leader in the field of Mac audio products offers a few different cards that feature multiple audio connections, improved sound quality, and DSP functions. The AudioMedia II (NuBus) and III (PCI) cards are tops at improving on the Mac's basic internal sound capabilities.

✦ **Korg** (www.korg.com). Known for keyboards and other musical equipment, Korg also offers a fantastic PCI-based interface card for Macs that supports up to 12 different audio channels or separate tracks, including digital and analog connections.

✦ **Lucid Technologies** (www.lucidtechnologies.com). Offering digital-only PCI and NuBus solutions, Lucid cards can accept S/PDIF digital input or connect to rack-mount solutions that digitize multiple analog audio sources.

✦ **Emagic** (www.emagic.de). This company also provides audio cards that offer multiple inputs and outputs, enabling individual tracks to be recorded in audio software.

Note   You'll see the letters *S/PDIF* often in audio hardware literature. If you're unfamiliar with it, it's a popular digital-audio interface for high-end consumer and professional audio hardware such as DAT components.

Audio mixing

I personally can attest that any Power Mac is simple to hook up to a mixing board, for instance, which can allow you to do basic voice work or Internet radio broadcasts with little additional equipment (see Figure 14-7). Obviously, you could perform music editing and similar work with such a setup as well, using the Mac as little more than a digital tape recorder and editing base. For higher-end editing, though, you may find it even more fun to bring in each channel of audio separately, and then do all your editing in a digital-editing software application.

Figure 14-7: Basic audio mixing can be done using your Mac as a recording device and post-processor.

With a setup like this one, the mixing board preprocesses the signal, mixing it before it gets inside your Mac. The sounds are then recorded as a single *track* inside your computer, even if you have, say, multiple voices speaking and audio underneath it. All that is mixed in the mixing board, and then recorded to your computer as if it were simply a digital-audio tape machine. Of course, that's not completely accurate, because you can cut, paste, and otherwise edit the digital audio, even if it's premixed. You can also run special effects on the recorded track to give the entire recording reverb, echo, fade, or any other combination of effects.

For instance, I use this setup to record digital audio for Webcasting — talk shows over the World Wide Web. Usually, that means I just need to record a few voices and maybe a phone call — all of which is premixed by my Mackie (www.mackie.com) mixing board. I then record it to the Mac and edit out anything that doesn't sound good or isn't tight enough. For the final go-around, I record some music that I can use as an intro and outro to the piece, adding another track to the recording that I can match up with the first one. I piece the tracks all together so it fits nicely (see Figure 14-8), and save the entire file as a digital audio file — usually AIFC. The next step is to run the file through a compression program that's aimed at Web broadcasting (probably something from RealNetworks or using QuickTime Pro).

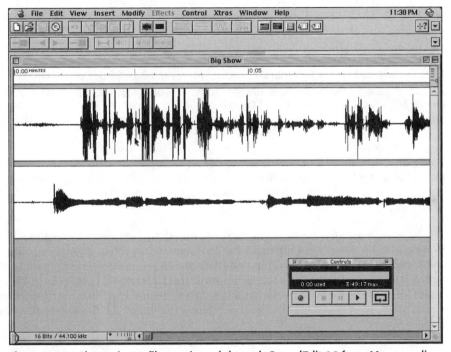

Figure 14-8: Shown is my file, as viewed through SoundEdit 16 from Macromedia. On top is the audio from the speaking part of the show; on bottom is audio I've added later.

Compared to most, my approach is very basic, and it betrays what little training I've had in radio production. For the most part, the level on the microphones, the quality of the phone call, and the overall feel of the show are accomplished manually in my studio, using dials and buttons on a mixing board. It's probably sufficient for what I'm trying to accomplish. But digital musicians and serious editors would look at my setup and scoff.

The reason? You can do all the mixing on screen if you have a powerful enough Mac and the right add-on hardware. Instead of using a mixing board and recording it all at once (flaws, miscues, and bad settings included), you can record raw audio for each of any number of sources — for example, a microphone, a phone line, an electric guitar. Using a virtual mixing board in software you can then process the audio and mix it all together without being forced to do anything over if it isn't set up correctly the first time. The mixing and production work take place at the same time, giving you much more flexibility.

As an example of the differences between the two approaches, let's say I have a talk show that also features a cohost. Doing it my way, the show is recorded through the mixing board into which we've both connected our microphones. There's only one recorded track that includes both our voices. So, if her mike is a bit louder than mine, or if we get a weird echo from her setup and none from mine, there's little I can do to process that out using the computer.

If we're each recording to separate tracks, however, I have more possibilities. I can bring her volume down some or use an audio editing program to process my voice a little bit to add the same echo. I can also edit her out when I didn't like an answer she gave, or use other controls to make it sound as though one of us is farther away from the other.

To do this, though, I can't have just a single audio input into the Mac. Instead, I've got to force the Mac to notice that it has a number of different audio sources connected to it, so that it will record each to its own track. That requires additional hardware.

The hardware usually comes in the form of something rack-mountable, the sort of thing you'd find in an ultra high-end stereo component system or, more likely, a radio station. These systems offer a number of different analog and digital inputs, which let you hook up many sources for multitrack recording (see Figure 14-9). The audio interface is then connected to a special expansion card that performs digital signal processing (DSP) tasks as well as feeding the channels of audio to the mixing application.

Figure 14-9: These rack-mount designs make it easy to add multiple analog tracks — just plug your equipment into the interface instead of into a mixing board. Now the raw audio can be edited completely digitally. (This one is from DigiDesign — www.digidesign.com.)

The implications of this are significant for professional-level audio editing. Even if you mix everything (voices, audio, effects) "live", you can drop out any component that you want to, rearrange them, or otherwise edit without affecting some other part of the session. For instance, you can cut four minutes from your cohost's diatribe without creating jerky cuts in the music that was in the background, because it's on a different track.

Beyond these solutions is where serious money is spent — digital editing workstations. Although you supply the Mac yourself, the rest of it comes along for the price tag. Often, digital-editing workstations include multiple NuBus or PCI cards, rack-mount hardware, and multitrack editing software. The names you hear in this arena include DigiDesign's ProTools series of workstations, which features the ProTools software for multitrack management. Sonic Solutions (www.sonic.com) offers a dizzying array of solutions as well, including digital-audio workstations, radio-station management suites, and editing studios for motion-picture audio. Another familiar name might be Avid Technology (www.avid.com), the parent company for DigiDesign and manufacturer of high-end audio/video workstations for integrating sound and video.

Audio software

Once you have the hardware and the equipment, you're ready to bring the audio into your Mac. You'll want an audio-editing program that can accept the audio feed, work with the audio, and output it in an acceptable way. If you'll be dealing with the audio from a poor Mac's point of view — one track at a time — you'll want to focus very closely on the editing software and its capabilities. Big-time users — those with multiple channels of audio coming into the computer at the same time — will need even heftier software for recording and mixing all those channels at once.

On the CD-ROM

At its most basic, audio needs to be digitized and saved to disk in a familiar audio format. Many applications are capable of doing this, including shareware and freeware programs such as SoundApp, which is included on the CD-ROM with this book.

Beyond these programs are professional-level sound-digitizing and editing packages that allow for multiple tracks, drag-and-drop editing, and adding effects. The most popular of these programs include DigiDesign's SoundDesigner II and Macromedia's SoundEdit 16 (www.macromedia.com). In fact, you may recall QuickTime's bow to SoundDesigner's popularity; QuickTime can read and work with SoundDesigner II files without translation. EMagic offers a few entries in this class, including Logic Audio Discovery. Opcode's AudioShop is also an option (www.opcode.com).

Finally, the upper crust of editing software includes audio-management systems and mixing environments — software designed to piece together four, eight, or more channels of audio that has been edited in SoundDesigner or SoundEdit. These programs are used in lieu of actual sound mixing boards to provide levels, effects, and other sequencing tasks to bring an entire production together. They're also offered by the usual suspects: DigiDesign's ProTools software, Macromedia's Deck II package, EMagic's Logic Audio. In this same vein, Opcode offers StudioVision, and Mark of the Unicorn (www.motu.com) offers Digital Performer, both of which integrate not only hard disk storage, digital audio, and mixing, but MIDI capabilities as well.

Note   You'll find that there's a thriving plug-in market for SoundDesigner and the like. These plug-ins tend to add effects, sound cleaning, and other interesting features that might address a need you have in the realm of professional audio. Although I'm loathe to recommend a particular store for your purchases, even as strictly an information source, Computers and Sound (www.computersandmusic.com) is one of the better sites I've found on the Web. Its strong leanings toward Mac solutions don't hurt, either.

MIDI stuff

MIDI hardware runs a similar gamut to digital-audio hardware; there's a MIDI solution for just about anything you're trying to do. At the most basic level, you need a MIDI translation device that gives your Mac the same MIDI ports that keyboards and other synthesizers already have built into them. The MIDI translator isn't a terribly unwieldy device, as its only function is to connect MIDI ports to your Mac via a serial connection (see Figure 14-10).

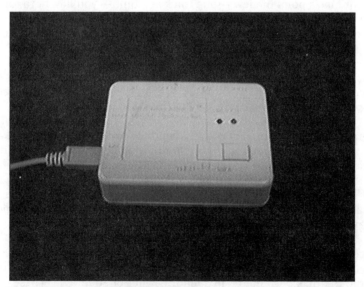

Figure 14-10: A basic MIDI translator from Opcode (www.opcode.com)

From there, MIDI equipment gets more and more advanced, offering higher-end sequencing, more connections for additional instruments, built-in clocks for synchronization, and other tidbits, such as rack-mount form factors and LED indicators. You'll find most MIDI hardware coming from two manufacturers: Opcode and Mark of the Unicorn, although patch cables and noncomputer MIDI hardware is made by a variety of musical-instrument manufacturers.

MIDI software varies in price and purpose as well, with the low end being notation software. These packages listen in on a MIDI-capable musical instrument while you play, and then translate your work to musical notation for editing or printing. The software will then, generally, play back the song using a MIDI device or MIDI library such as QuickTime's built-in MIDI voices.

Sequencing software allows you to play a MIDI instrument, record what you've done, edit it, and then add more and more tracks of MIDI instruments — up to the 16 channels that MIDI allows. You can then use sequencing software to play back all the MIDI commands at once, managing a studio full of instruments if you have them all hooked up to the Mac.

More and more common, too, are MIDI sequencing programs that have grown to include digital audio as well. These programs add digital and MIDI audio together, manage all the instruments and tracks, and then output to analog or digital sources, depending on your connections and capabilities. At the highest end you could easily integrate a MIDI orchestra of music with dialog from a motion picture and lay it all down on the QuickTime audio track of a digital movie.

Companies that make MIDI software include the following:

✦ **Coda Music Technology** (www.codamusic.com) makes a few notation programs, including Allegro and the high-end standard, Finale. Coda also makes other MIDI applications, including the Vivace Practice Studio, which accompanies a practicing musician with intelligent backup music, along with tuning help and other teaching tools.

✦ **Passport Designs** (www.passportdesigns.com) offers a variety of notation and other MIDI software packages, including both annotation and educational software.

✦ **Invision Interactive** (www.cybersound.com). The Cybersound Studio MIDI sequencing package is aimed at hobbyists and beginning musicians interested in writing their own songs.

✦ **Mark of the Unicorn** (www.motu.com) offers a full range of software MIDI solutions including Mosaic for music notation; FreeStyle for sequencing and notation; FreeMIDI, a freeware solution for controlling MIDI hardware; and Digital Performer, the high-end MIDI/Digital audio studio.

✦ **Opcode** (www.opcode.com). Aside from Studio Vision Pro, Opcode's MIDI/Digital audio studio, the company offers some MIDI-only solutions like MusicShop for sequencing and Overture for notation.

Summary

✦ You'll want to do basically three different things with audio on your Mac — digitize it for editing, record in the MIDI language for creating music, and use speech technology to talk to your Mac and have it talk back.

✦ You can use your Mac as a digital tape recording, taking thousands of audio *samples* per second, and then stringing them together into an audio file. The files are stored in various standard file formats, many of which are handled by QuickTime on a Mac. The audio files can then be edited like any other computer file, making it a simple matter to edit audio with no generational loss.

✦ MIDI works a different way — the Musical Instrument Digital Interface is a computer language that enables Macs to communicate with music synthesizers. With the right hardware and software, you can connect your Mac to a synthesizer, record songs in music notation, edit them, and play them back. Many instruments can be supported at once, allowing a Mac to control an entire band or orchestra's worth of sound.

✦ The Mac OS has speech technology built into it so that your Mac can speak the text it finds in word processors, dialog boxes and on the Web. You can also speak to your Mac, enabling it to respond to your voice commands the same way it might respond to mouse or keyboard directives.

✦ Although the expansion cards install the same way as any others, digital audio and MIDI hardware and software vary greatly in what they look like, what they do and how they do it. You can spend a few hundred bucks or thousands and thousands to outfit the perfect computer music studio for your needs.

✦   ✦   ✦

Printers and Print Sharing

It's amazing how many Mac owners I've talked to who feel their printing situation is good enough or adequate for their needs. Not that I'm saying it isn't necessarily true or that the key to happiness is buying a new printer. But I do know a lot of people who fool themselves into believing they're happy with their printers. The fact is many printers are too slow, offer low quality, and can seriously affect your quality of computing life. Sometimes it's time to upgrade sooner than you think.

That said, a printer decision is all about what you want to accomplish. There are plenty of trade-offs, such as cost for speed and speed for color. Knowing what you want out of your printer is a very important first step to buying one.

You'll also find there's another important step and a dilemma somewhat unique to Macintosh. You need to know what printer description technology you plan to use for your printing tasks. The two major choices — QuickDraw and PostScript — are often dictated by the type of printer you choose. (Inkjets are mostly QuickDraw-based, whereas most lasers use PostScript.) That isn't always the case, though, so you'll want to know what you're getting into before you buy.

Mac Printer Technology

Two basic issues need to be addressed before you run out and buy any printer, although a number of other factors will affect your decision, too. The first is the actual, physical mechanism used to create the image. The major types — inkjet, laser, and the occasional dot-matrix printer — employ different strategies for making text and images appear on the page.

You also must consider the software technology used. The Mac offers two general ways to get a printer and Mac to talk to one another. The first method is QuickDraw, the basic technology that's also used to draw images on the screen. The other is Adobe's PostScript technology, a cross-platform printer description language that is generally used for professional-level applications. Which option you choose depends somewhat on who you are and what you're trying to accomplish.

Printer issues

A huge part of being a printer (I say this for you Method actors out there) is getting text and images on a piece of paper. Different printers set out to accomplish this in various ways, resulting in a variety of speeds, color capabilities, print qualities, and a few other factors.

For most printers, speed is measured in pages per minute (ppm). The faster the page-per-minute rate, the faster a batch of printing gets done. Often, however, page-per-minute ratings from manufacturers don't take all factors that can affect speed into consideration, such as how long it takes a printer to warm up, or how long it takes for the printer to prepare each digital page for imaging. Printer speeds also vary (with some printers) based on how much of a given page is covered by text and images. If a high percentage of the page is to be covered, the page can take longer than the average ppm number given by the manufacturer.

Another measure specific to printers is resolution, measured in dots per inch (dpi), horizontally and vertically. The higher the resolution of a printer, the higher the cost of the printer in most cases, although higher-resolution printers are certainly becoming more affordable as the years pass. A resolution of 300x300, the norm for the first ten years of the Mac's existence, is the low end for inkjet and laser printers these days. Instead, higher resolutions — 600x600, 720x720, or 1200x600 — are becoming more popular, even for nonprofessional purposes.

The higher the resolution, the smaller each individual dot used to make up the lettering or parts of an image in your document. The end result is that higher-resolution printers can use all those extra dots to give the illusion of smoother curves and cleaner lines. That means text and images begin to look more as though they were professionally typeset (modern typesetters reach up to 5,000 dpi), and less as though they were computer generated.

Along with dpi comes another fairly important statistic — lines per inch (lpi). This is the measurement used when printing *halftone images* — the fake grayscale images that any black-and-white printer has to print to suggest the different shading in various parts of the image. The more lines per inch, the better the grayscale reproduction of photographic images. You'll also find that the lines per inch measure is closely related to the resolution for scanning images, as discussed in Chapter 11.

Choosing a printer

When you go to purchase a new printer, you'll stumble across a few other interesting issues to consider. You might want to concern yourself with the type of *consumables*, such as the type of ink and paper the printer uses. This depends on the technology behind the printer (a laser printer uses imaging toner like a copier does, whereas an inkjet printer uses ink), but that's not always the whole story. Some printers can use more expensive inks and toners. Others require special paper for optimum results. Some can use a variety of different consumables to cut down on costs.

You'll also want to know what add-ons the printer is capable of accepting. Can it be expanded with an Ethernet networking card? Can it be shared easily with a workgroup of users? Does it offer expandable RAM or font-storage features? Can you add a sheet feeder or an automatic envelope feeder?

You'll find that different types of printers are more likely to offer these features than others, but the high end of any printer segment should offer you a few extras. What exactly you need depends on your circumstances and how much convenience and efficiency you have to have from your printer. But first, you should understand the software technology behind printing to help you make the right choice.

Printing money: Cost per page

If you've thought it'd be a good idea to buy an inkjet printer because they're so much cheaper than laser printers, you may want to think again. Although you can certainly pay quite a bit of money for a laser printer, the up-front price is often not the only dollar amount you should concern yourself with. What may prove more important is your cost per page.

Everything about a laser printer seems more expensive. They are hundreds more dollars in the store. They use toner cartridges and consumables that cost twice or three times as much as inkjet cartridges. They have expensive add-ons and make you pay for things you don't need, such as networking capabilities.

If you decide on an inkjet, it's certainly not a bad choice, especially for home users and for Mac owners who need to proof their work in color (or print occasional color for home or small business use). In most other cases, though, it's better to buy a laser printer.

First, inkjet cartridges, at $20 to $30 a pop, seem cheaper than laser-printer toner cartridges — until you factor in the number of pages each type of cartridge is capable of producing. With inkjet cartridges, you'll average 500 to 1,000 pages of text and graphics. Toner cartridges are often rated at 5,000 or so pages; the Apple LaserWriter 12/640, for instance, can print 6,000 average pages, according to Apple's literature. By comparison, the Epson Color Stylus 800 inkjet printer boasts a cartridge life of 960 pages.

(continued)

(continued)

Consider the output cost of two theoretical printers. A $100 toner cartridge that prints 6,000 pages costs you $.02 per page. A $30 ink cartridge that prints 500 pages costs you $.06 per page. That's a difference of $40 per every 1,000 pages you print. To think of it another way you'd end up spending a total of $360 for ink cartridges to match the same output of one $100 toner cartridge.

Good inkjet paper tends to be more expensive, too, with higher-strength bonds recommended for holding the heavy inks. Some inkjet printers require special paper to achieve high-resolution results. Watch carefully for this requirement when you're shopping for an inkjet — don't get carried away by claims of 720 and 1440 dpi. They may require special paper that can be rather expensive.

If you'll be printing text and black-and-white images quite often, especially in an office setting, think twice before choosing the printer with the cheaper sticker price. If you plan to keep it for a while, check the prices charged for the printer's consumables and make sure you'll be getting a good deal over time.

Printer languages

Macintosh-based printers offer two major methods for getting text and images on the page: QuickDraw and PostScript. QuickDraw is the Mac OS's native way of doing things, whereas PostScript is a cross-platform solution developed and controlled by Adobe Systems. Both are adequate for most printing jobs, but PostScript is certainly considered the more professional of the two, as it is the language spoken by publishing, printing, and multimedia programs across a variety of computer platforms and solutions.

PostScript

PostScript is most accurately characterized as a printer description *language*. It provides a complete solution in many ways, from describing high-resolution graphics to creating resizable fonts and even controlling a printer's page breaks, test pages, and other features. In a way, PostScript is the older stepbrother to QuickDraw. Apple didn't invent PostScript (Adobe Systems, Inc., did), but it became a part of the Mac OS early on as the desktop-publishing revolution was just getting underway.

PostScript printers are often laser printers, although inkjets, dye-sublimation, and other printers (notably typesetters and digital-printing presses) can also be based on the PostScript description language. PostScript must be processed by a CPU, which is often built into the printer itself, increasing its cost and sophistication. PostScript requires printers to have their own RAM, own CPUs and, in some cases, their own hard drives (usually for storing fonts). These printers can be great performers, but PostScript is generally associated with a price premium over QuickDraw printers.

PostScript is pervasive; it's a font technology, a printer control technology, and a screen drawing technology — at least, for some OSes, such as NextStep and OpenStep. (It isn't clear that Display Postscript will be included in future Mac OS versions.) NextStep, and OpenStep after it (both from Steve Jobs' Next, Inc.), actually used PostScript to describe screen images as well as fonts and printers, resulting in amazing WYSIWYG (What You See Is What You Get) capability and reasonably inexpensive PostScript printers. (The lower cost was due to the Next printers not actually having to process the PostScript data. Instead, they acted like a QuickDraw printer on the Mac, simply receiving the raster file from the computer, which did all the imaging itself.)

QuickDraw

QuickDraw already is the Mac OS's screen description language, which would seem to make it a natural for the Mac's printing technology. It so happens, though, that QuickDraw isn't as robust as PostScript, as it was designed for the original Macs that were black and white (not grayscale), low-resolution, and generally unconcerned with the problems of modern publishing.

QuickDraw doesn't describe fonts and it doesn't control printers. Instead, the Mac OS is responsible for enabling printer drivers to access the printers, usually through the Chooser or similar options (like desktop printing) that printer manufacturers can take advantage of.

Likewise, QuickDraw offers no particularly advanced font technologies — at least, not natively. In Mac OS System 7.0 and above, Apple's answer to PostScript fonts — called TrueType and developed with Microsoft — very capably takes care of fonts, both on the screen and on the page, resulting in great output for QuickDraw-based printers. But early QuickDraw was limited to bitmapped fonts, which only work well at a few particular point sizes.

QuickDraw (especially when combined with TrueType) is certainly adequate for daily business and home printing tasks, and it's cheap to implement. Instead of dedicated languages and processors, your Mac is responsible for creating the QuickTime image and, just as it draws your Mac's screen, it "draws" the page to a printer driver. The driver software makes sure the page is formatted correctly for the printer, and then feeds the data to the printer.

You can probably see why QuickDraw printers are often cheaper than PostScript printers: PostScript printers require more horsepower (a processor and lot of RAM) to get things done. Many QuickDraw printers have no internal processors or RAM, because they rely on the Mac OS to create the image, even if it slows your Mac down a bit.

Printer types

Although in one respect, Mac printers can fall into one of two camps—QuickDraw or PostScript—they can also be categorized by the method they use to print text and images on paper. Some of these methods are old standards; others are less common, but perfectly acceptable, alternatives such as dye-sublimation, thermal wax transfer, and even techniques designed specifically for printing photos.

More than likely you'll pick something from the big two: laser or inkjet. And, although cost per page is an important issue, you'll also notice that the technologies, in some ways, are converging. Inkjet printers aren't as slow as they once were, and laser printers can print in color. Additionally, other types of printers offer an alternative to both that might fit more specialized needs.

Table 15-1 shows a number of manufacturers who make Mac-compatible printers for individual Macs and workgroups.

Table 15-1
Mac-compatible Printer Manufacturers

Manufacturer	Type of Printers	Technology	Web Site
Apple	Laser, inkjet	QuickDraw, PostScript	imaging.apple.com
Epson	Laser, inkjet	QuickDraw, PostScript	www.epson.com
GCC Tech	Laser	PostScript	www.gcctech.com
Canon	Inkjet	PostScript	www.canon.com
NEC	Laser	PostScript	www.nec.com
QMS	Laser, dye sublimination	PostScript	www.qms.com
ALPS Electric	Dye sublimation	PostScript	www.alpsusa.com
Tektronix	Inkjet, solid ink	PostScript	www.tektronix.com
Hewlett-Packard	Inkjet, laser	PostScript	www.hp.com

Laser printers

Sometimes called page printers, laser printers image an entire page internally before printing it, making them take a little longer than most inkjets to get started on a page. However, they move the page through more quickly once the process is underway. That process also explains some of the cost difference between lasers and inkjets. Page printers must have on-board processors and enough RAM to image an entire page, as well as hold the fonts required for the page.

Page printers don't necessary have to use a laser, either. Some printers in the past have used LEDs and LCDs to do the same thing a laser does: Charge particles on a rolling drum to get them to pick up toner that's transferred to paper. Otherwise, these technologies are very much like that of the laser printer.

Laser printers offer a number of advantages over other printer types, at least for black-and-white printing. Let's look at some of them:

✦ **Speed.** Laser printers are generally faster than any other type, offering the best speed for both individual and workgroup printing needs. Low-end laser printers offer speeds of 4 to 6 ppm, whereas high-speed lasers can print at 20 ppm or more.

✦ **High-capacity.** Laser printers offer bigger paper trays and longer-lasting consumables for everyday printing. They're good for networked workgroups and situations where many people need access to the same printer.

✦ **Flexibility.** Designed for office tasks, laser printers tend to offer the most peripherals — RAM upgrades, envelope feeders, and larger bins for paper. You can even find laser printers with copier-like qualities — sorters, staplers, and such.

Laser printers really don't offer many disadvantages over other printer types, unless your needs are more specialized. Laser printers print in black and white really well, but color laser printers are only just now becoming affordable for corporate installations. Inkjets and other printers rule, even in creative offices, where it's important to create color proofs of documents destined for color reproduction or full-fledged publishing. And, of course, there's the biggest hurdle to overcome: Laser printers tend to be a bit pricey in the beginning, especially considering that most of them are based on PostScript, which carries the baggage of a licensing fee from Adobe in addition to the requisite fonts, RAM, and processor.

In fact, laser printers tend to use quite a bit of RAM, considering they aren't full-fledged computers. Realize, though, that each pixel needs to be stored before the printer can start to create the image; the inner workings move along faster than the processor in most laser printers. This means the printer needs enough RAM to hold all the pixel information for a printed page. Remember that it can take a few megabytes of RAM to hold a screen image (as discussed in Chapter 12). Also note that screen images are usually only 72 to 75 dpi. A 600x600 dpi printout on an 8½"-by-11" piece of paper requires about 33.6 million dots (not accounting for margins and printer limitations). Assuming one bit per dot, it'd take about 4MB to store that many dots before the printer can get started printing.

Not that a printer necessarily needs that much RAM. Many modern laser printers use compression techniques to lower the amount of RAM required for storing a page. This makes a lot of sense, especially considering that the average printed page has only about 5 percent coverage of ink or toner. The rest of the white space could be subjected very easily to a basic compression scheme. Table 15-2 shows some typical RAM quantities for laser printers.

Note　Adding RAM to a printer can even speed it up a tad, especially if the printer is used to print a lot of PostScript fonts. Just having that extra bit of RAM tends to get many troubled workgroup printers up and running with fewer glitches and errors.

Table 15-2
Typical RAM Quantities in Laser Printers

Printer Specs	RAM
300x300	2MB (1MB compressed)
600x600	4MB
600x1200	8MB
1200x1200	12MB
Color 600x600	12–16MB
Workgroup 600x600	8–16MB

Now let's turn to the matter of how laser printers translate the image in RAM to something that can appear on paper. At the heart of a laser printer is the photoconductor drum, which is designed to spin around while holding an electric charge. The electric charge repels toner. The laser in a laser printer goes to work on the drum, drawing a bitmap of the page line by line. Wherever the laser hits the drum, it alters the charged state of the drum, so that those parts hit by the laser now attract toner. The toner is rolled onto the drum, which picks up toner where appropriate, and then the image is rolled onto paper. The paper is sent through a fusing roller, which heats the toner (formerly dry ink) and fuses it with the paper. (This explains why paper is always a tad warm when it comes out of a laser printer or a copier.)

The printer's toner is kept in a second, removable cartridge that can be replaced when the toner is depleted and the printer no longer prints reliably. Some earlier laser printers featured toner and drum assemblies that were installed separately or as kits, although more often today you simply change toner cartridges (see Figure 15-1). Printers do tend to have a limited lifespan, however, which can sometimes be extended by replacing internals such as the photoconductor drum.

Figure 15-1: The Personal LaserWriter 300 features a toner cartridge that's easily removed from the front of the printer.

For one-color printing, it's possible to change the toner cartridge to a different color ink, and then print. With two printing passes, you could also add *spot color* to your documents: Printing the black parts of the page first, replace the black cartridge with a color cartridge, and then refeed the page through the printer to print the color sections. To achieve full-color results, though, a color laser printer has to have four separate toner colors, each of which has to be rolled onto the drum. Each color is drawn on the drum separately while the paper spins on a special transfer drum, which rotates the page past the photoconductor drum four times. Once all the color has been transferred, the page is output.

The result? At the time of writing, color laser printers still haven't fallen to a reasonable technology price point as often happens in computing, and they still cost five to ten times as much as black-and-white laser printers. More manufacturers are making color laser printers these days, though, which bodes well for a less-expensive future for color printing.

Expert tip: Shipping laser printers

My sometimes writing partner, Dave Johnson, tells a personal anecdote about a sprawling laser-printer comparison article he did once for one of the larger Intel-compatible PC magazines. With some ten printers shipped to his house, he tested and judged them against one another. Then it came time to ship the printers to the photographers so that pictures of the printers could be included with the article.

"Remove the toner cartridge from a laser printer before shipping," Dave wisely offers. His information was garnered directly from personal experience.

It seems that two of the printers arrived at the photographer's studio "toner bombed"—covered in the black, staining soot of printer toner. Ruined, at least for the purposes of the photo shoot, they had to be returned to the vendors. (One of the two vendors decided the printer was a total write-off and didn't even bother to try to clean and fix it.)

To ship toner, first remove it from the printer, and then package it in its original shipping materials or a close facsimile. If you don't, you could risk ruining the entire printer.

Inkjet printers

While we're all waiting for the price of color laser printers to come down, inkjet printers are an inexpensive way to print both color and black-and-white documents.

Inkjet printers use tiny nozzles to spray wet ink onto the page as the printer pulls the paper along a paper path. The nozzles use a number of different proprietary technologies (such as Canon's BubbleJet technology) to bring the ink out of its storage well in exactly the correct quantities and in the right places. The nozzles and printhead work very quickly, though, resulting in speeds that vary from a typical 1 or 2 ppm all the way to 8 ppm and more on some very high-end inkjets.

The ink is held in special ink cartridges, or reservoirs, designed to force the ink to flow smoothly without air bubbles and other elements that could clog the nozzles, which are also part of the cartridge. The ink also needs to be a fairly special composition that dries quickly enough to keep from streaming down the page (a problem called *wicking*) or to otherwise streak as the print head moves quickly along. The spacing of the nozzles is an exact science, and it's that precision that enables the print head to move quickly along the page while maintaining a resolution of between 300 and 720 dpi in both horizontal and vertical directions, making the output of many inkjet printers competitive with that of standard laser printers.

Note

Although inkjet cartridge refill packages are popular ways to cut down on inkjet costs, it's important to note that, as stated above, the printer nozzles are replaced every time an old cartridge is replaced by a new one because they're built into the cartridge. When inkjet cartridges are refilled by hand, these nozzles aren't replaced, which can result in degraded quality over time.

Because inkjets use wet ink for printing (as opposed to a laser printer's dry toner), it's easier to build inkjets that can work with color. By mixing three or four colors together (usually the CMYK colors — cyan, magenta, yellow, and black), inkjet printers are capable of printing in full color with only minor technical tweaks; most of the color printing is actually done in software updates, not hardware changes. This results in color-proofing solutions that remain inexpensive because they still rely on QuickDraw and the Mac OS for most rendering tasks.

In fact, most inkjets printers are QuickDraw-based, and most of them do not have internal processors or RAM. Unlike laser printers, most inkjets printers do not render an entire page in the RAM that's installed in the printer itself; instead, the page is rendered by the Mac OS, and then transferred to the printer when it can handle the data. (Instead of megabytes of RAM, QuickDraw printers tend to have only a few kilobytes to serve as a buffer while parts of a page are printing.) When using an inkjet printer, you may notice that it can take some time for a printing task to relinquish control of your Mac, or the Mac runs a tad slower as the document prints in the background. This is because the Mac OS is performing the page description for the printer, instead of simply transferring data to it.

Color proofing printers

Some other printers are less common for office and home tasks, but worth the consideration nonetheless. Focusing on high-color output and proofing, both dye-sublimation and solid-ink printers offer slightly more expensive output and, usually, incredible results. Once only the domain of graphics professionals, both solid-ink and dye-sublimation techniques may be making comebacks as more practical alternatives to the more common printer types.

With dye sublimation, the printer melts ink from a ribbon onto special paper. The color is defused into the paper, and other colors can be melted directly on top of the first colors. This creates a continuous color image that mimics a photograph. In fact, one of the more popular uses of dye-sublimation printers is to create photographs — that is, to print images captured using digital photographs.

Solid-ink printers use dyed wax — sticks not completely unlike a child's crayons — that is melted into a glossy ink and then transferred to the page. The result is a very bright color image that doesn't necessarily require a special type of paper. These printers also tend to be very expensive, although a reasonable cost per page can make them useful for color-printing professionals and offices that need high-quality color proofing.

Dot-matrix printers

Once the prevailing printer technology, dot matrix now plays a bit role in the world of printing. Although dot-matrix printers are cheap and offer a very low cost per page, they also offer output quality that is considered inadequate for nearly any but the most informal of documents. With the low cost of getting a higher-quality inkjet printer, few folks opt for dot matrix these days (and you'll be hard pressed to find one new for Macs).

There's one good reason to keep a dot-matrix printer around. Dot-matrix printers form letters and other printed characters by forcing small pins (usually 9 or 24 of them) to strike a ribbon and create a character. Doing this very quickly, the printers are capable of a number of lines per second, resulting in perhaps a page per minute or so. What's operative, though, is the *striking* part. The pins actually physically hit the ribbon and the page to create their mark, making dot-matrix printers useful for printing on multipart, carbon-copy-based forms, such as purchase orders. Laser printers and inkjet printers can't help you in this department.

Specialty printers

A final category catches any other printers that slip through the cracks, especially those designed for a specific purpose, such as printing receipts for point-of-sale computers or printing shipping labels. Often such printers use a low-end inkjet technology, connect directly to your Mac, and have specialized application programs responsible for printing correctly to them. If you happen upon one, you'll have to decide on your own if it's a worthy purchase. Just be aware it might need to use the same port you've already dedicated to another, more traditional printer.

Installing Printers

Printers hook up to Macs in a few different ways. The most obvious connection — the printer port — can actually qualify as either a LocalTalk connection or a serial connection, depending on the printer. A laser printer that has its own processor and RAM, for instance, will almost always be connected to your Mac's printer port over a LocalTalk connection using a LocalTalk cable. This has its advantages, including making it a simple matter to add the printer to your entire workgroup without any special settings on the host Mac (assuming you use PhoneNet or a similar LocalTalk cabling scheme for your entire network, or you're using a software or hardware LocalTalk bridge — see Chapter 17).

However, there are other ways to connect printers. Here's the rundown:

✦ **Printer port.** Using either a LocalTalk cabling solution or an Imagewriter (standard serial) cable, printers can be attached directly to the printer port on a Mac. (QuickDraw printers can also be attached to the modem port, if necessary, although you can't use LocalTalk on the modem port.)

✦ **Ethernet.** Many PostScript printers designed for workgroups — or primarily designed to work with Microsoft Windows — offer a connection over Ethernet that enables Macs and Intel-compatible PCs to talk to the printer over a local network.

✦ **SCSI.** Some high-end color printers rely on SCSI instead of a slower serial/LocalTalk connection. SCSI printers tend to be a bit pricey, but are much quicker than equivalent serial-port printers.

Cabling

How a printer is installed can be traced directly to the printer language—PostScript or QuickDraw—that the printer uses. A QuickDraw printer doesn't have a processor, so it relies directly on a Mac to create the bitmapped image that's ultimately printed. This means the printer is unlikely to be connected to the Mac by anything other than a serial connection, because it's not capable of receiving printer commands directly.

Note

When installing any printer, check the manual and packaging carefully for any indication of shipping ties or stops that have been installed on the printer to keep it from moving in transit.

To hook up a QuickDraw printer to your Mac, follow these steps:

1. Shut down your Mac.

2. Plug the serial cable into the printer, and then plug the cable into the printer port on your Mac.

3. Restart your Mac.

A PostScript printer, on the other hand, has its own RAM and processor. That makes it a computer. In almost all cases, PostScript printers are actually connected to Macs as if over a network, even if there's only one Mac to connect to. Instead of using the printer port for a serial connection, a LocalTalk printer will use the port for a LocalTalk connection. This means any additional computers should also be able to access the printer with no problems. If an Ethernet connection is desired, it's just as easy to hook up.

If you want to hook up a LocalTalk printer, follow these steps:

1. Shut down your Mac.

2. Plug the LocalTalk cable into your Mac's printer port. If you'll be using the printer on a workgroup network, connect it to a PhoneNet adapter (or a similar transceiver), and then connect the transceiver to the network.

3. Restart the Mac.

An Ethernet connection may require a special card for the printer. If such a card is already installed, you should be able to plug the network cabling into the Ethernet port on your printer, and then plug the other end of the cable into your network's Ethernet hub.

Note   Some printers may require a special Ethernet transceiver. If you're using a 10Base2 (BNC, coax) cabling system, you may be able to daisy chain your printer to other Macs in the network instead of using an Ethernet hub.

If your printer offers a SCSI connector, check the manual for information on setting its SCSI ID number. Next, install the printer as you might any other SCSI device like a hard drive, Zip, or scanner. Find an available SCSI ID, shut down your Mac, and the printer to the daisy chain of peripherals. If it's the last device on the SCSI chain, add a SCSI terminator to the printer if it doesn't offer active or internal termination.

Driver software

Once you have your Mac turned back on, you should run any software included with the printer; this action installs the driver software that enables your Mac and printer to communicate. For LocalTalk printers, this will usually involve a completely new software driver that's placed in the Extensions folder in your Mac's System Folder. After the installer program is done and you've restarted your Mac, you can turn the printer on and bring up the Mac's Chooser. You'll then have a new option in the Chooser through which you set up the installed printer (see Figure 15-2).

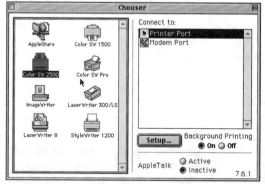

Figure 15-2: Choosing a printer driver in the Chooser

Click the printer driver's icon on the left-hand side of the Chooser and notice that the options on the right-hand side change to reflect the possible connections you can make to this printer. If you're using a LocalTalk or Ethernet connection, you should have AppleTalk turned on; if you're using a QuickDraw printer over the printer port, you'll need to turn AppleTalk off. (If you're using the modem port to talk to the printer, you can leave AppleTalk on.) Now choose the connection that you'd like to use for printing by clicking that connection's icon. Once you've done this, click the window's close box to put the change into effect.

If you're dealing with a PostScript printer, the process may be similar — running the installation software, restarting, and checking the Chooser for your printer driver. You may also find, however, that your PostScript printer doesn't have a driver. Like Apple-compatible laser printers, it may use the standard LaserWriter driver instead:

1. In the Chooser, select the LaserWriter driver. Any printers currently connected to your network are available in the right-hand side of the window.

2. If your printer shows up, choose it and click Create. (If your printer doesn't appear, make sure it's properly connected, AppleTalk is active, and the printer is turned on.)

3. Choose Auto Setup if possible. Otherwise, you may be forced to choose a PostScript Printer Description file. If you don't see your printer, use the dialog box to locate the appropriate PPD for your printer — it may be on a floppy disk or CD-ROM included with the printer.

4. You can then use the other LaserWriter options (Get Info, Configure, and so on) to alter the printer description if necessary. When you're done, choose OK.

5. Now, click the Chooser's close box to set your changes into motion. The Chooser will warn you that the printer has changed and that you need to choose Page Setup from any open applications. That's the first sign things are going well.

If you've got the printer set up and the driver activated, try printing. You should get instant feedback letting you know if your printer is humming along successfully or if you're running into trouble. With many printers, you can check the Print Monitor (in the Applications menu) for status on currently printing jobs, or double-click the desktop printer icon to get more info on the printer's status (see Figure 15-3).

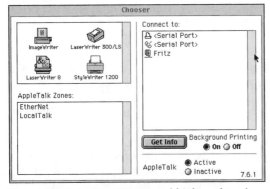

Figure 15-3: In Mac OS 7.6 and higher, choosing a new Apple-made or LaserWriter 8–based printer driver generally results in a new desktop printer icon. Double-click the icon for printing status or drag-and-drop files on the icon to print them.

Mac expert tips: LaserWriters, old and new

Looking for a used laser printer, trying to administer your new printer, or trying to get a non-Apple printer to fit in at the Club Macintosh? Mike Kent, system administrator and Mac author, has a few hints for you:

"For LaserWriters, administration is pretty simple. The Apple Printer Utility (included with your printer or available at Apple's Support Web site at `www.apple.com/support`) will make most of the adjustments needed, including turning off that wasted test page at boot up, or turning it on to see how many pages have been printed.

"Beyond that, be sure your Printer Descriptions folder in the Extensions folder contains descriptive files for your LaserWriter. This is the folder that the Setup button in the Chooser consults when setting up your printer. If you have a Hewlett-Packard LaserJet, for example, put the description files that came with that printer in the Printer Descriptions folder so output can be adjusted properly. You can save disk space by trashing all other files in the Printer Descriptions folder if you don't have those printers. Similarly, you can use the Extensions Manager to turn off printer drivers you don't need and thus keep them from appearing in the Chooser.

"If you're looking for a cheap printer for home use, a number of older LaserWriters are turning up in garage sales and the like. Often they are sold without the setup disks or they may have unusual settings, so Apple's Support Web site can be an invaluable resource. The Personal LaserWriter NT, for example, has a SCSI-like dial on the back that has nothing to do with SCSI, and a check of Apple's Tech Notes shows that the dial is instead used to set the type of network input, with '1' corresponding to AppleTalk."

You can even input the name of the printer and search just the subject lines of articles in the Tech Info Library (`http://til.info.apple.com/`) to get all articles related to your new, used printer.

Printer sharing

You may have noticed from the descriptions that only PostScript printers tend to set themselves up on the network using LocalTalk or Ethernet, thereby giving everyone in the workgroup access to the printer. But what if you got a great deal on a QuickDraw printer? Many of them can be shared, too, using Apple's Printer Share technology.

Apple's Printer Share basically enables other computers on your network to print to the printer as if they were accessing it from your computer. Their Mac turns the pages into bitmaps, prepares them for printing, and then sends the pages to your Mac, which manages them using the Printer Share software. As the pages arrive on your Mac, Printer Share passes them to the printer driver, which outputs them to the printer.

On Macs that use Mac OS 7.6 and above, Printer Share is built right into the Chooser (assuming it's installed in the Extensions folder):

1. Open the Chooser and select the QuickDraw printer.

2. On the right-hand side of the Chooser window, click the Setup button.

3. The Printer Share dialog box appears (on printers capable of printer sharing). Select the Share This Printer check box to activate printer sharing. You can enter a password to limit usage of the printer, as well as checking the Keep a Log check box to keep a log file of printer jobs completed by the printer.

4. Click OK when you're done configuring Printer Share.

5. Click the close box in the Chooser to effect the new settings.

Now other Macs on your network should be able to see the printer, even if they're not specifically logged into your computer. Likewise, they should be able to choose the printer in their own Chooser, just as if it were a QuickDraw printer connected to their system. The only major difference will be that the printer will appear on the list as a printer name and network icon instead of a printer or modem port icon (see Figure 15-4).

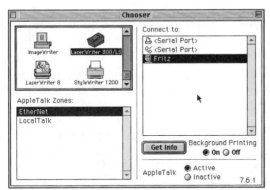

Figure 15-4: My QuickDraw-based Personal LaserWriter, as seen from another Mac on the network. Notice the printer is named ("Fritz") and it has a network icon next to it.

Note

Not all third-party QuickDraw printers support Printer Share, although some of them do. In cases where they don't, check to see if a networking-related printer driver is included with the printer. HP inkjets, for instance, often include a special AppleTalk version of the driver that will enable you to hook up an inkjet using LocalTalk cabling and then print to it over the network.

Printer Add-Ons and Software

A number of different utilities and software add-ons will enable you to do more with your current printer, or, in some cases, give you access to a new printer you might not have been able to use. Software can also be added, in many cases, to enhance your printer's printing capabilities.

Accessories

Printer hardware accessories are usually designed to increase the capabilities of the printer. You can add another tray for holding a different type of paper to many workgroup laser printers, for instance. A few common add-ons include the following:

✦ **Paper handling.** Paper trays, special feeders for envelopes, add-ons for printing to transparencies.

✦ **Duplex printing.** Special hardware add-ons designed to enable printing to both sides of a piece of paper.

✦ **Networking options.** Add an Ethernet card or a LocalTalk adapter to a printer to allow network printing.

✦ **RAM upgrades.** Add more RAM to support more complex pages or more fonts for printing. This is a good idea if you get frequent errors telling you that the printer can't handle the entire page you're sending.

✦ **SCSI hard drive.** Some fairly advanced workgroup printers have options for adding a dedicated hard drive to the printer for storing fonts and/or bitmapped pages for printing.

These add-ons are oftentimes proprietary in nature, meaning you'll need to consult the manufacturer to find out how you can add paper handling, duplex printing, and networking options. If your printer can handle a SCSI hard drive, you shouldn't have too much trouble installing it using hints from Chapter 7; the only main difference is you probably won't have a choice of SCSI IDs (check your manual), and you won't have much reason or opportunity to daisy chain devices to the printer (which wouldn't be useful anyway).

To add RAM, you'll want to consult the printer's documentation and shop around for RAM designed specifically for your printer. Apple, for instance, has used a number of different types of RAM modules for upgrading their laser printer over the years, including 30-pin modules, 72-pin modules, and special cards. Table 15-3 shows some of the memory options for Apple laser printers.

Table 15-3
Apple Laserwriter Memory

Printer	Min. RAM	Max. RAM	Slots	RAM Type	RAM Speed	Sizes
LaserWriter	1.5MB	1.5MB	N/A	N/A	N/A	N/A
LaserWriter Plus	1.5MB	1.5MB	N/A	N/A	N/A	N/A
LaserWriter IISC	1MB	1MB	N/A	N/A	N/A	N/A
LaserWriter IINT	2MB	2MB	N/A	N/A	N/A	N/A
LaserWriter IINTX	2MB	12MB	12	64-pin	120 ns	256K, 1MB
LaserWriter IIf	2MB	32MB	8	30-pin	80 ns	256K, 1MB, 4MB
LaserWriter IIg	5MB	32MB	8	30-pin	80 ns	256K, 1MB, 4MB
LaserWriter 8500	16MB	48MB	1	72-pin	80 ns	8MB,16MB, 32MB
LaserWriter Pro 600	8MB	32MB	2	72-pin	80 ns	4MB, 8MB, 16MB
LaserWriter Pro 630	8MB	32MB	2	72-pin	80 ns	4MB, 8MB, 16MB
LaserWriter Pro 810	8MB	32MB	3	Module	N/A	4MB, 8MB
LaserWriter 4/600PS	2MB	6MB	1	Card	N/A	2MB, 6MB
LaserWriter 16/600PS	8MB	32MB	2	72-pin	80 ns	4MB, 8MB, 16MB
LaserWriter Select 300	0.5MB	4.5MB	1	30-pin	80 ns	1MB, 4MB
LaserWriter Select 300	1.5MB	5.5MB	1	72-pin	100 ns	1MB, 4MB
LaserWriter Select 360	7MB	16MB	1	72-pin	80 ns	4MB, 16MB
Personal LaserWriter SC	1MB	1MB	N/A	N/A	N/A	N/A
Personal LaserWriter LS	512K	1MB	4	30-pin	100 ns	256K

(continued)

Printer	Min. RAM	Max. RAM	Slots	RAM Type	RAM Speed	Sizes
Table 15-3 *(continued)*						
Personal LaserWriter NT	2MB	8MB	2	30-pin	120 ns	1MB, 4MB
Personal LaserWriter NTR	3MB	4MB	1	72-pin	80 ns	1MB
Personal LaserWriter 300	512K	512K	N/A	N/A	N/A	N/A
Personal LaserWriter 320	2MB	8MB	1	card	N/A	2MB, 6MB
Color LaserWriter 12/600PS	12MB	40MB	2	72-pin	60 ns	1MB, 4MB, 16MB
Color LaserWriter 12/660PS	16MB	40MB	2	72-pin	60 ns	1MB, 4MB, 16MB

On the CD-ROM The Apple Spec Database, included on the CD-ROM, is great for getting information such as which type of RAM your Apple printer uses and how much you can upgrade.

It's certainly possible that you'll find a need to upgrade RAM. Over the years, more than a few laser printers have been sold with too little RAM—this occurred more often back when RAM was incredibly expensive. The RAM would be adequate, say, for printing a single-spaced text document with little or no graphics. Beyond that, the printer was overloaded. If you find yourself in a similar situation, add some RAM and consult Chapter 26 for information on troubleshooting printers.

Software

To improve your printing experience, aside from some basic advice (such as keep your printer drivers up-to-date by checking the manufacturer's Web site occasionally) there's other software you can add that'll often do the trick. This includes newer versions of the Mac OS; for instance, Mac OS 7.6 and up include features like desktop printing, built-in Printer Share for many QuickDraw printers, and a better functioning Chooser. If you've got a PostScript LaserWriter–compatible, you'll likely want to stay on top of the upgrades to the LaserWriter driver; Apple continuously improves the reliability and features of that driver.

On the CD-ROM

You might want to look into some other special software options. Adobe Type Manager (ATM) is an important addition for both PostScript and QuickDraw users. Included for free with the Adobe Acrobat PDF viewer (found on the CD-ROM that accompanies this book), ATM causes PostScript fonts to look smoother on your Mac's screen and on QuickDraw printers. This allows you to view PostScript fonts the way they'll appear on the page if you're printing to a PostScript printer. It also makes PostScript fonts behave when printed to a QuickDraw printer, resulting in better results and fewer jaggies.

Another software option is StyleScript, a printing utility from Infowave (www.infowave.com). This extension grabs print jobs before they reach the printer and implements PostScript in software, using your Mac's processor instead of a standard PostScript printer's processor. The result is PostScript-like output from a QuickDraw printer. The only price is the cost of the box and the time you have to wait for PowerPrint to let you have your Mac back after processing all those PostScript codes.

PC printers

Envy the myriad choices available to PC users for printing? Infowave — the StyleScript people — have a few hardware options to help solve that dilemma. The PowerPrint (see Figure 15-5) is a parallel-to-LocalTalk adapter that enables you to print from a Mac directly to an Intel-compatible PC printer. To do this, it has to offer certain software drivers (specifically to translate QuickDraw commands into PCL — Printer Control Language, the Intel-compatible PC standard originally created by Hewlett-Packard). Fortunately, it includes drivers for all sorts of printers, including various models from Brother, Canon, Epson, H-P, Okidata, Panasonic, and Ricoh.

Figure 15-5: The PowerPrint is a small box with software drivers that make printing to PC printers possible (www.infowave.net/).

The PowerPrint is such a good idea, in fact, that Apple has recently announced partnerships with Infowave and other printer manufacturers — Hewlett-Packard and Lexmark, for example — to bring more options to the Mac platform through the PowerPrint interface. This may prove to be an important development as Apple continues moving away from the printer business to focus on computing solutions; at the same time, a transition to USB may also require help from companies like Infowave.

A PowerPrint Pro version makes PC printers available on a Mac network and a PowerPlot interface device lets Macs print directly to Encad and Hewlett-Packard brand large-format plotters and printers.

Similar devices and software are available from the PhotoScript Group (`www.photoscript.com`), a company that specializes in hardware raster image processor (RIP) solutions that add PostScript capabilities to non-PostScript printers. These solutions act as the processing engine for creating PostScript output that can enhance the text and images printed to a QuickDraw printer, much the way StyleScript and PowerPrint do.

The major difference with PhotoScript is the extent to which their equipment is capable of doing this. PhotoScript actually off-loads the PostScript raster work to another computer, this one with a processor specifically designed for the task of creating the PostScript image. One obvious advantage is speed. Another is that the RIP can connect to the printer over LocalTalk or Ethernet and then output using SCSI or a standard parallel connection, thus obviating the need for a Mac-to-PC printer solution. The main disadvantage is price.

PhotoScript offers software-only versions as well, which enable you to use the RIP on your own Mac. Coupled with a LocalTalk-to-parallel adapter, you can get that same great PostScript-like output with a less hefty price tag.

Summary

✦ All printers have a few things in common: Their speed is measured in pages per minute, and their quality is measured in dots per inch. Lines per inch, an oft-overlooked statistic, is an important parameter to know in regard to your printer as well.

✦ Two printer languages are common in the Mac world: PostScript and QuickDraw. QuickDraw is the Mac's standard way of getting text and images on a page, as it simply uses built-in QuickDraw routines to "draw" a page onto paper. This process is handled completely by your Mac, so the printer doesn't need any special features. For PostScript, on the other hand, the printer needs RAM, its own processor, and (sometimes) a hard drive. PostScript is Adobe's printer description language, popular because it results in professional-quality output and works cross-platform.

✦ Aside from the printer languages used, there are other technical differentiators for printers, especially the way they print. Laser printers fuse toner to the page, inkjet printers drop ink on the paper, dye-sublimation printers melt ink from a ribbon onto the page, and solid-ink printers melt crayon-like wax melted onto the page. The venerable dot-matrix printer actually strikes a ribbon with small pins, much like a typewriter.

✦ Once you've got the printer, you may have a number of different options for connecting it. Printers are connected to Macs over networks (LocalTalk and Ethernet), directly over serial ports, and, occasionally, via a SCSI connection. You then need to work a little magic in the Mac's Chooser to get the Mac and printer to communicate.

✦ With your printer up and running, you may find that your printer needs to accessorize a bit to make it more presentable. Many laser and workgroup printers can accept add-ons like network cards, RAM, sheet feeders, and envelope trays. You can also add software and hardware to print PostScript-like output to QuickDraw printers or print from your Mac to Intel-compatible PC printers.

✦ ✦ ✦

Modems and Internet Access

Modems are a big part of the infrastructure of the Internet and a huge contributor to the sense of community that permeates the Mac world. Mac owners tend to be more connected than other computer users, with a larger percentage of Mac owners heading out on the Internet than the marketplace would seem to dictate. (Whereas Macs make up 7 to 10 percent of all computers, studies show they make up about 25 percent of Internet users.)

If you're not already connected, you've got to get on the Internet. And if you are connected, you probably want to go faster. You'll need to get some better equipment or take better advantage of the technology built into your Mac. Fortunately, these things aren't tough. Access to the online world can do amazing things for your Mac. Sure, you can waste time online. But at the same time, there's so much you can do, see, and learn, even if you don't have the world's most powerful Mac.

On the Internet, chat and video conferencing provide instant communications, and e-mail is at your disposal for rapid communications; Usenet newsgroups are full of people who share your interests and goals; mailing lists enable you to participate in discussions on thousands of topics; FTP lets you download tons of files for your Mac. The World Wide Web is a mixture of all these things. (This book, for instance, would be nearly impossible to complete without the reference points, company information Web sites, and communications made possible by the Internet.) To get started, though, you've got to have access.

The majority of folks get their access one of two ways: either with a direct connection to the Internet over an Ethernet network, or via a modem of some kind. For home access, modems remain the most likely way you'll get service, although folks in large metropolitan areas are starting to have other options. For the most part, though, if you want access and your company, school, apartment building, office park, or organization doesn't offer it, you'll need a modem. I'll talk about how to choose a modem, how to install it, and how to get your Mac online in this chapter.

Note   Part of what I mean by "Mac community" is played out in the book itself. In the early and middle stages of writing, I sent messages to the Evangelist, an Apple-sponsored mailing list that reaches tens of thousands of subscribers a day, most of whom are self-described Mac Evangelists, people interested in promoting the Mac and helping others find solutions that enable them to use Macs in their homes, offices, or schools. I asked these Mac Evangelists to submit personal anecdotes that related to upgrading and repairing Macs, and many of them eagerly obliged. Their stories, advice, and warnings appear in sidebars throughout the text. (Check the Preface for more info on this mailing list.)

How Modems Work

The word *modem* is really an acronym for modulate/demodulate, which describes what a standard modem does to send data over regular telephone lines. Because the telephone system is designed (in most cases) to transmit analog signals (sound waves), the modem's digital signals don't do it much good. So, modems change digital data into analog data (actually, audible tones) that can be transmitted over the phone lines, received by another modem, and translated back into digital form for use by the receiving computer.

In actual usage, the term *modem* gets tossed about a bit more than it should. Most people think of modems not as modulators/demodulators, but as little boxes that give them access to online services and the Internet. For instance, the terms *ISDN modem* and *cable modem* are inaccurate, as both of these types of connections are completely digital — no modulating or demodulating needs to happen. Although I talk about these sorts of so-called modems later in this chapter, be aware that the term only applies loosely.

In fact, cable and ISDN connections actually require *terminal adapter* (TA) devices, because both are networking technologies. The latter, ISDN, connects to the phone company's digital network, and the other, cable, connects to the cable company's digital network. Unfortunately, TA isn't nearly as cool a marketing term as modem, I'd guess.

Note   You may choose to believe that the word *modem* is a neologism (a made-up word), not a true acronym, because it uses more than the first letter of each word that it stands for. That's your prerogative, but don't write me to complain about it. *Webster's Tenth New Collegiate Dictionary* supports my usage, so I'll call modem and codec acronyms to my dying day!

Modem types

Modems for Macs are generally either internal expansion cards or external boxes connected to the Mac via a serial port (usually the modem port — the one with a telephone icon next to it). External modems are much more common for Macs than internal ones, with the exception of the PowerBook and Performa lines and the iMac, all of which often sport internal modems. Although both NuBus and PCI modems are relatively uncommon, modems have been made in the past for the communications slot featured in many Mac models (see Figure 16-1).

Note

There's another type of modem — one that's created entirely in software. When you use a GeoPort adapter pod or expansion card, the PowerPC processor (or the special digital signal processor in an AV Macintosh) to which the adapter is connected is actually the modem. The adapter is just there to enable the software modem to communicate over phone lines.

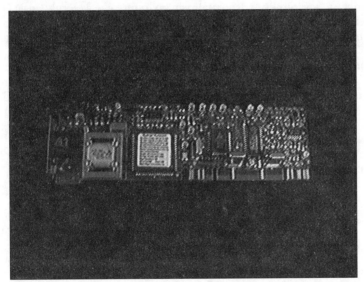

Figure 16-1: An internal modem pulled from a Performa's communications slot

Modems use a typical modular (RJ-11) phone jack to connect to a standard phone line. Most modems also offer a pass-through connector that will allow you to install a standard telephone by plugging the phone's line directly into the modem. External modems often use special serial cables, called *hardware handshake* cables, to connect to the Mac's modem port. In most cases, this cable is either permanently attached to the modem, or it's connected to the modem by a special 25-pin plug on one end and an 8-pin serial connector for the Mac on the other end.

With many Mac modems, the power supply is an important component. Certain models of Global Village modems (a popular manufacturer of Mac-compatible modems) won't work with other power adapters, for instance. Other modems must be plugged into the Mac's ADB port to receive power, and consequently offer a pass-through connector for mice, keyboards, and other devices.

Cross-Reference   Read the discussion on ADB in Chapter 10 before opting for a modem that requires use of the ADB port. It's possible that the addition of such a modem will overwhelm your ADB connections if you already have three or more devices attached.

Modem speed

As mentioned, regular analog modems change digital signals into analog signals. To do this, modem manufacturers have to agree to adhere to certain standards, most of which are set up and controlled by the International Telecommunications Union (ITU). These standards define the characteristics of communications that allow modems to connect at various speeds, usually given in bits per second (bps). Often a modem is referred to by its speed, for example, a 28.8 or 33.6 modem. These are standard modem speeds (in kilobits per second) governed by the ITU standards.

The earliest modem speeds were measured in *baud* rate — the number of signaling elements, or electrical changes, that occur in a second. This is different from the bps rates now used, because faster modems are able to communicate more and more bits per baud. A 300-baud modem, for instance, transferred 1 bit per baud, so its transfer rate was 300 bps. A 1,200 bps modem, might well have a baud rate of 600, but be capable of transmitting 2 bits per baud. The same with a 9,600 bps modem — it probably actually operates at 2,400 baud, but it can send 4 bits per baud, netting performance of 9,600 bits per second.

The bottom line: Avoid saying "baud" when you mean "bps." These days, the common measurement of modems is always bps or, even more likely, kilobits per second (Kbps). Table 16-1 shows you the common modem bps rates and their associated standards. Note that I've indicated in quotes how the standards are usually referred to in casual shorthand. (For instance, "thirty-three dot six" and "thirty-three six" are common ways to say "33.6" in conversation.)

Note   Note that *bis* is a French word that can be translated as "second" or "revision" in this context. In many cases, the *bis* refers to an update of the original standard that provides faster transmission rates (or some other feature, such as better compression).

Table 16-1
BPS Rates and Modem Standards

Standard	Bit Rate	Notes
Bell 103	300 bps	US standard only; "300 baud"
CCITT V.21	300 bps	
Bell 212A	1,200 bps	US standard only; "1200 bps"
ITU V.22	1,200 bps	
ITU V.22bis	2,400 bps	
ITU V.29	9,600 bps	
ITU V.32	9,600 bps	
ITU V.32bis	14,400 bps	"14.4"
USR V.terbo	19,200 bps	Proprietary US Robotics standard; "19.2"
ITU V.34	28,800 bps	"28.8"
ITU V.34bis	33,600 bps	"33.6"
USR X2	56,600 bps	Proprietary US Robotics standard
56KFlex	56,600 bps	Proprietary Rockwell standard
ITU V.90	56,600 bps	"56K"

To confuse things even further, a few different measurements of online speed are common, especially when you're *downloading* files — transferring data to your computer from a remote computer. In older programs for downloading, the speed might be measured in characters per second, which translates (roughly) into bytes per second.

These days, many programs will show you the *kilobytes* per second at which you're receiving a transmission over the Internet and online services. You'll probably notice that this number doesn't seem to bear much resemblance to your modem's stated speed. In fact, you'll almost never see speeds as fast as you might think they should be. That's because various factors influence the speed of your modem, such as the quality of your phone connection, the speed of your Internet provider's computers, traffic on the Internet, the speed of the remote computer, and so on. Ideally, you should get bytes-per-second rates that are exactly one-eighth of the bps rate of your modem (for example, 4,200 bytes per second for a 33.6 Kbps connection). With the parity bits and checksums used for error correction and modem negotiation, a more realistic ideal is a 1:10 ratio. But even that sort of throughput rarely happens under real-world conditions.

Compression and correction

Other factors also ultimately dictate the speed at which your modem is communicating. If you have a modem that transmits at a bit rate greater than 9,600 bps, for instance, it probably has additional modem protocols helping it along — in particular, error-correction and data-compression protocols.

Because a modem transmits audible signals (and, if you have any experience with a telephone, you know that a telephone line can add strange noises of its own), it's important for high-speed protocols to use a special scheme for ensuring that interference and noise aren't generating random errors in the data being sent. At very low rates, this can be easily accomplished with a *parity bit*, which is sent with the other bits in each character to make sure they arrive intact. A parity bit would be sent along with the other seven bits required to form each basic text character that the modem transmitted to a remote computer. If the parity bit uncovered something wrong after the transmission, an error message was generated, and the character re-sent as a result.

This doesn't work as well for higher speeds because of the whole bit/baud thing. If you lose one baud of data at 28,800 bps, you'll lose 12 bits of data (a 28.8 Kbps modem operates at 2,400 baud). If you lose 12 bits of data, you've lost the parity bit, which, by definition, means it can't check the rest of the data. Instead, a bigger-picture approach is taken to error correction: *Checksums* are used to succinctly describe larger amounts of data.

As with the modem communications standards, there are confusing names for error-correction standards as well. MNP-4 and V.42 are the commonly used standards that modems use to check for errors between them. MNP-10 is used for cellular-modem connections.

Related to those standards are the standards for data compression, which enables a given modem connection to transmit more data by compressing the redundant bits according to a designated standard. In most cases, the standards used are MNP-5 and V.42bis. These compression schemes sometimes add to the apparent bps rate of modems, and some connection programs will report the connections accordingly, claiming a 38 or 41 Kbps connection, for instance, using a 33.6 Kbps modem. These designations are spurious at best; compression relies completely on the compressibility of the data being sent.

In general, text is more compressible than binary data (images and programs). Data that's *already* compressed, like StuffIt or PKZip archives, are the least compressible of all.

Flow control

In communications parlance, a modem is often referred to as the Data Communications Equipment, or the DCE. Not to be outdone, your computer gets a name, too—the Data Terminal Equipment, or DTE. Data terminates at the computer, or the *terminal equipment*. This is important to know because the DCE/DTE connection is another critical piece of the modem-connection puzzle see Figure 16-2).

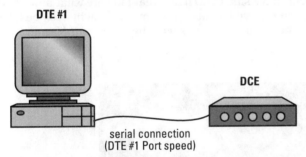

Figure 16-2: The connection between the DCE and DTE is usually via a serial cable on a Mac. Depending on the Mac, this can slow things down quite a bit.

Because the computer (DTE) and the modem (DCE) are often capable of communicating data at different speeds, they need some way to direct the traffic between them. This is done through *flow control* protocols. These protocols are designed to tell the device that's sending data when to send it and when to wait awhile. Early modem communications (as well as old-style teletype communications) used the *Xon/Xoff* protocol, which very simply sent a special byte of info to tell a component when to wait and when it was okay to transmit.

Since that time, things have gotten more complicated. For one thing, the connections between DTE and DCE have sped up considerably; to keep up with today's modems, the connection needs to be somewhere around 57,600 bps or faster. This is in stark contrast to older modem connections, where the serial port would top out at 9,600 bps. Back then, sending a "turn off" or "turn on" byte was fine. Now, though, something beyond software control is needed.

So, hardware flow control was introduced. Now the DCE and DTE send electrical signals to one another that are separate from the data stream, enabling them to communicate on what amounts to a direct communications line for managing the flow of data. When the modem is ready to receive data, for instance, it can send a Ready to Send (RTS) command to the computer. That means the modem is connected and ready to send data over phone lines. If the data is coming the other way, the computer can offer a Clear to Send (CTS) command, meaning the Mac is ready to accept data sent from the modem.

If you've ever had or worked with an external modem, you may have noticed your Mac and modem communicating at this level, even if you didn't really know what was going on. Often, modems have small LED lights that indicate what flow-control commands are being sent and received; lights on the modem might even be labeled "DSR," "DTR", and some of the other commands used between your Mac and modem (see Figure 16-3).

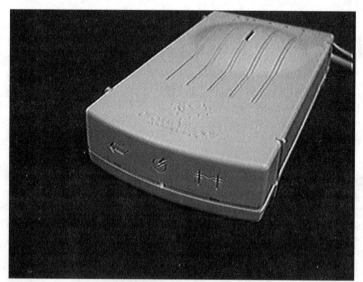

Figure 16-3: This Global Village modem includes LEDs for the current hardware flow-control commands.

You'll often find modem-related software includes these flow-control commands buried somewhere in their settings boxes. The latest modems pretty much set these things up automatically, but you'll occasionally find yourself needing to choose the flow control for your modem. In this case, what do you choose?

If the modem is a high-speed (9,600 bps or greater) modem, your choices for setup will usually be one of the following: CTS and RTS (DTR), CTS Only, RTS (DTR) only, and None. CTS and RTS is the way to go if possible. If you experience problems, though, a common setting for Mac modems is CTS only.

Port speeds

Hand-in-hand with flow control is another setting you'll want to pay attention to if you ever need to set up a modem manually—port speed. This is the speed at which the Mac's serial port can communicate with the external modem. Remember, we're still discussing that DTE/DCE connection. The port speed is a vital part of making sure the entire connection is fast enough for the data that's flowing through it. If it's not, the fastest modem available won't do you much good.

Port speed also goes together with compression technologies; remember, modems are able to compress data streams so that, say, a 28.8 Kbps connection actually nets a data rate of 57.6 Kbps or more (under favorable circumstances). In fact, a 28.8 connection could technically see compressed transmission rates of 115.2 Kbps or better, although it's rare, and there wouldn't be more than a burst of data at that speed.

Remember, though, that the amount of data being sent is the same—28.8 Kbps. Compression just fits more data in that space, by compressing the 57.6 kilobits so they fit into 28.8 kilobits' worth of space. Once that data arrives at the receiving modem, it's uncompressed.

That presents an interesting problem: How do you get the modem to transmit the uncompressed data—all 57.6 kilobits of it to the computer fast enough to avoid a traffic jam while another 28.8 Kbps stream of compressed data is coming into the modem and being decompressed? Suddenly you've got twice as much data coming out of the modem as you had going in (see Figure 16-4).

Note

The numbers representing compressed and uncompressed data in this section are theoretical and simplified for the sake of discussion. Normally a modem compresses data as it can, coming up with widely varying rates of compression depending on the data being compressed and other factors.

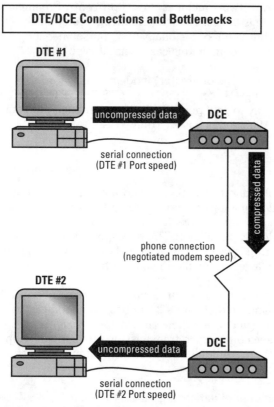

DTE/DCE Connections and Bottlenecks

DTE #1

uncompressed data

DCE

serial connection
(DTE #1 Port speed)

compressed data

phone connection
(negotiated modem speed)

DTE #2

uncompressed data

DCE

serial connection
(DTE #2 Port speed)

Figure 16-4: This diagram shows the dilemma that
can be created by modem-compression schemes.

The trick is to speed up the connection rate as well, which is accomplished by
setting the port speed at the highest point the Mac, the serial cable, and the modem
can handle. Table 16-2 shows the top port speeds for most Mac models. In general,
AV and Power Macs are capable of the fastest data rates (theoretically 230 Kbps),
although you're more likely to see good throughput at 115 to 130 Kbps. 68040 Macs
(and most PowerPC PowerBooks) support 57.6 Kbps port speeds; 68030 and earlier
Macs tend to support only 19.2 Kbps.

When you actually go to set a port speed, you want to choose something at the
upper limit of your Mac's port capabilities, even if your modem isn't as fast as the
port. That way, any compression taking place can be compensated for because
there's a wider pipeline for data that needs to be transmitted between the modem
and the Mac.

Table 16-2
Top Port Speeds for Mac Models

Model Range	Top Port Speed (bps)	Notes
Mac 128k, 512k	9,600	Doesn't support handshaking
68000, 68020, 68030	19,200	Varies by model; newer, faster models do better
68040	57,600	Slower 68040 models may top at 38,400
AV Macs, PowerPC-based Macs	230,000	Practical modem limit tends to be 115 Kbps
PowerBook 3400, G3	230,000	Practical modem limit tends to be 115 Kbps
Other PowerPC PowerBooks	57,600	
Earlier PowerBooks	19,200	

But where do you make these settings? Often, you won't have to. With modems that are reasonably good at self-configuration, you'll find it's often unnecessary to change the settings (the Global Village and Apple-branded modems, for instance, tend to take care of most of their own settings). Otherwise, your modem may have installed a control panel on your Mac that can be used to change settings. If this is the case, check that panel to see if you can alter the port speed. If not, you may be able to pick a port speed in your communications software.

Connection negotiation

With all these settings possible, it's a wonder that two modems can actually talk to one another, given the likelihood that they support different speeds, have different port settings, or implement compression in different ways. Two things prevent total chaos, however. First, the modem standards set by the ITA govern (for the most part) what and how modems should be able to communicate with one another. Second, modems themselves go through a basic negotiation ritual to determine which standard is best for them to use for communications.

If you've worked with a modem in the past, you might be familiar with the audible screeches they tend to make as they're connecting to other modems. Here's a quick look at what, exactly, is happening when two modems begin to chat:

1. Your modem (let's call it the *caller*) picks up the phone line and tests for a dial tone. If it finds one, it dials the number it's been assigned by a software program.

2. The answering modem picks up the line when it detects ringing. It then waits to hear if the caller is a modem.

3. When the caller modem detects that the line has been answered, it sends out a basic *carrier* signal designed to let the receiver know it is a modem.

4. The answering modem, recognizing the carrier, sends back its answer as a carrier, usually slightly higher in tone and continuous.

5. The answering modem then broadcasts all the communications protocols it knows. With any modem, the noise can be horrific; if you have a 56K modem, you know what an amazing cacophony it is capable of emitting.

6. The receiving modem broadcasts its protocols, too, and one by one the modems determine which protocols they support and which they don't. If they don't both support a particular protocol, a connection isn't established at that speed. Line noise can affect this; if you get bad noise at a time when 33.6 Kbps modems are trying to negotiate a 33.6 connection, they might decide that the most they can really support is 31 Kbps.

7. Once they decide on a top speed, it's reported to the respective computers as a connect, followed by the speed that was established. Usually the modems' speakers go quiet at this point, but they continue to negotiate things like compression and error correction. Once all this is established (usually in a matter of seconds, if that), the modems are ready to send data back and forth.

There's some logic to leaving the speaker on through this process: It lets you hear the connection and see how things are going between the two computers. If you get really used to listening to your modem, you may even find you're able to predict what sort of connection is being made by the sounds of the tones.

Cross-Reference   If you really want to turn the modem's speaker off, you can do that. If it's not an option in your Modem setup control panel or your communication program's preferences menu, check out the guide to the modem AT command set, discussed in Chapter 26.

Choosing and Connecting a Modem

It would seem the most important thing to consider when choosing a modem is speed. That's certainly true for the majority of modem users. It's nice to get the fastest connection possible for accessing online services and the Internet. "You can never be too thin, have too much RAM, or have enough bandwidth," the saying might go. (*Bandwidth*, incidentally, is one way of describing the capacity of a networking connection. The more bandwidth your connection has, the more data it can transmit at one time, resulting in data transmissions that are completed more quickly.)

Table 16-3 lists popular Mac modem manufacturers.

Table 16-3 Mac-Compatible Modem Manufacturers	
Name	**Web Site**
Global Village	www.globalvillage.com
Supra	www.diamondmm.com
3Com/USRobotics	www.3com.com
Best Data	www.bestdata.com
Hayes Communications	www.hayes.com
Boca Research	www.bocaresearch.com

Modem choices

Aside from speed, however, you may find a few other factors go into your modem decision. Modems can come with different sets of features that focus on telephony capabilities, voicemail, fax capabilities, and so on. You might also find modems that support software upgradeability, enabling you to move up to the latest modem transmission standards as they're agreed upon. In most cases, such modems are *flash* upgradeable, meaning they have special nonvolatile memory that can be erased and rewritten by a special software program.

Note

Although most people have no argument with buying upgradeable modems, one line of thinking suggests you stay away from modems that require the use of a control panel for day-to-day operation. This makes some sense, although it's a clear trade-off. If you have a modem that doesn't require a special control panel, you won't have to install or configure any software just to get it to work; instead, the software you use for the modem, like a PPP control panel or the AOL client software, can be completely responsible for the modem configuration. A modem that *does* have its own control panel, though, makes it easy to change basic settings that might otherwise be buried in AT command set codes, but the extension can cause conflicts. And you can't operate the modem at all if you start up your Mac with extensions turned off.

Internal or external

One of the first decisions to make is whether or not you want an internal or external modem. Most Macs offer better support for external modems, with the exception of the internal modem port supported in the Power Macintosh 5200, 5300, 5400 series, most Performa models from the Performa 630 through the Performa/Power Mac 6500 series and many PowerBooks. In other cases, you really have very little choice for internal modems.

406 Part II ✦ **Performing the Upgrade**

Most of the models just described (aside from the PowerBooks) offer a special Apple *communications slot* (or comm slot) that can accept an internal expansion card. These slots require cards made especially for them. Even though most of the communications slots are based on PCI technology, they aren't true PCI cards, and only communications slot–compatible cards will work correctly.

The most fun part of shopping for comm-slot modems is that they're pretty tough to find. Having been discontinued by both Apple and Global Village (who made many of the comm-slot modems for Apple), they're really only available on the used market. You can have some luck posting a *WTB* (want to buy) message in some of the usual online places, though.

Another thing to note: In many Macs that feature communications slots, that slot is the *only* way you can get Ethernet connectivity for that Mac. (And, fortunately, comm-slot Ethernet cards are easier to find.) If you expect to use the Mac at any point on an Ethernet network, you're probably better off with an external modem so that the comm-slot remains available for the networking card.

The other thing I don't like much about comm-slot modems is that they don't have any lights. An external modem gives you much more feedback, allowing you to see immediately what's going on with the modem, if it's still connected, and other little tidbits. Plus, external modems are simple to install, uninstall, and trade with neighbors.

Add-ons

Smart people have told me in the past that their best advice is to buy a modem that's really well designed for *being a modem*, and let something else handle speakerphone, answering machine, or voicemail duties. There's probably some logic to this — the more things a modem does, the more things that can go wrong. Often, modems are using complicated software programs to perform functions that telephones and voicemail systems can manage without the threat of crashing.

That said, nearly any modem is going to be capable of dealing with faxes and, if you expect to use that ability, it's nice to get good fax software as well as a deal on optical character-recognition software, if it's included. If you do plan to use your Mac as communications central for your home or small office, you might consider some of the other possibilities:

✦ **Speakerphone.** Some modems use their own microphone and speaker for the connection, whereas others use the Mac's PlainTalk microphone (on AV and Power Macintoshes) and the Mac's speakers. Note, however, that nearly any modem has a pass-through port to which you can plug a telephone set. Not only can you answer calls when they come in, but you can have your modem dial out for you (from a personal information manager program, for instance).

✦ **Voicemail/answering machine.** If your answering machine is on the fritz and you don't want to spend the $5 a month for the phone company's voicemail, certain modems will have your Mac take messages for you. If you do get this feature, remember it's usually only implemented in software. That means you've got to leave your Mac on all the time to take messages.

✦ **Caller ID.** This is a handy feature you might as well turn on if your modem allows it. Usually a simple software add-on, this enables your modem to translate Caller ID signals to let you know who's calling.

The problem with most of these add-ons, aside from the fact that they require you to keep your Mac powered all the time, is that they require you to hook your modem up to your main voice line instead of a secondary line that's only for data. To get these benefits, then, you need to be someone who only occasionally uses the modem for, say, connecting to other modems.

Faxing

It's tough these days to buy a modem that doesn't come with the capability for communicating directly with facsimile machines, and it's a nice feature. This is especially so if, as discussed in the previous section, you have at least two phone lines, so that one can be dedicated to the modem (as a data-out and fax-in line) and one can be reserved for voice calls.

Different modems support different faxing capabilities, although all typically support 9,600 bps Group 3 faxing, the basic standard for most of the industry. This enables your modem to generally communicate with any fax machine, whether a modem or a stand-alone machine, without trouble.

You may also find that your modem supports 14.4 Kbps or higher speeds for faxing. Although few stand-alone machines support these speeds, some of the newer ones do. This can also be useful in instances where you want to fax a document from one computer to another. (Although I'm sort of knocking my head against a wall to come up with a really good reason for you to do that. You might as well e-mail the document as an attachment. Here's the only reason I can come up with: Use it as a "poor man's scanner". Fax a document to another computer so you have a graphical image to work with. Of course, you could just take a screen shot of the original document using ⌘-Shift-3, so that's still not much of a reason. Go ahead and ignore me. I'm just chattering.)

Probably the most important component for faxing is fax software. Some are certainly better than others. Global Village fax and the fax software that comes with Apple-included modems is generally well integrated with the Mac OS, going so far as to enable you to hold down the Option key while pulling down the File menu to find that the Print command has been replaced by a Fax command. (The Print command resurfaces when you access the menu without holding down Option.) Similarly, some software packages add a special Fax command to the File menu and/or a special icon on the menu bar.

In any case, faxing is usually handled with a driver in the Chooser, a virtual printer driver that prints pages to your modem so that they might be faxed. If you need to send a fax and other commands aren't working, you'll usually have luck by selecting the fax printer driver in the Chooser as your default printer (see Figure 16-5).

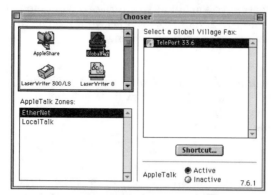

Figure 16-5: Click the fax driver in the Chooser to "print" pages directly to your fax/modem.

Flash-upgradeable

If you have the choice, you really can't go too wrong by choosing a software-upgradeable modem. These modems have their command codes and programming in a stable but rewritable form of static RAM. This is sometimes called *firmware* because it's not hardwired into the modem, but it's not quite as easy to change as a typical software driver, either.

Different manufacturers have different processes for upgrading modems via firmware additions. Usually, you'll find the firmware upgrades and instructions posted on the modem manufacturer's Web site or available from their customer-support lines. After downloading the firmware upgrade, you may be asked to restart with Extensions off (hold down the Shift key as your Mac boots up) or to simply turn off AppleTalk and disconnect devices from your serial ports. Next, run the update software. It (and any README text files that accompany the update) will guide you through the process.

The end result can be pretty incredible. Although some firmware upgrades don't do much more than fix bugs, many of them are designed to upgrade the modem to a higher-level modem protocol—that means faster speeds. The latest round of upgrades has been for 33.6 Kbps modems, many of which can be upgraded to 56 Kbps speeds. Now, many of these same modems (or newer 56 Kbps modems) can be firmware upgraded from their original 56 Kbps standards (either USR's X2 or Rockwell's 56KFlex) to the v.90 universal 56 Kbps standard.

If you have the opportunity to buy one of these modems, snatch it up; it might even be worth paying a few more dollars than for a modem that isn't upgradeable.

GeoPort Telecom Adapter

Many Power Macintosh (and AV Macintosh) users have one other option that hasn't yet been touched on much: You can get online without a modem at all. How's that? Using the GeoPort technology built into a Power Mac's serial ports, the PowerPC chip (or DSP chip in an AV Mac) can be made to *emulate* a modem using nothing more than software. In other words, no physical modem and special communications chips are required; instead, the Mac does all the converting, compression and sending of data on its own.

This is actually conceivable for just about any computer, but Apple decided to do this because of the advanced capabilities of the GeoPort serial ports when combined with the power of the PowerPC processor. It was also to be quite the boon for Mac users, because they wouldn't ever have to buy a new modem, just upgrade the software to faster speeds.

It hasn't exactly taken off. Although the GeoPort/modem approach has met with some success and was a popular way for Apple to add modem capabilities to PowerPC Performas for a while, three problems have hindered adoption of the GeoPort approach: First, you have to buy a GeoPort Telecom Adapter, which enables your Mac to communicate directly with phone lines (see Figure 16-6). These tend to run about $100 — cheaper than many modems, but not by too much.

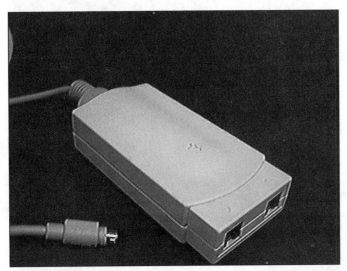

Figure 16-6: The Telecom Adapter isn't an actual modem, but it is required for your Mac to use the GeoPort to emulate modem functions.

The second problem is that Apple has been slow to release upgrades to the GeoPort software (the Apple Telecom software) that made it work as a faster modem. The GeoPort software tends to be months, if not years, behind modem standards. By the time Apple writes the software to catch up to modems, the price of those modems is very competitive.

Lastly, the Telecom software has become more of a drain on the PowerPC as the software's modem speeds and functionality has improved. That is, running at higher modem speeds seems to slow down a PowerPC chip considerably; a GeoPort solution running at 14.4 Kbps leaves the system sprightly and responsive, but a GeoPort modem emulator running at 33.6 Kbps can make the overall system seem slow (depending on the processing speed of the Mac, although reasonably powerful PowerPC 603e and 604e-based Macs get sluggish in my experience).

That is unfortunate, because the GeoPort offers a number of other advantages, including advanced voicemail functions, great built-in fax software, and a number of other features. Included with the Apple Telecom software is Apple Phone, a very cool little program designed to help you manage telephony (voicemail, faxing) on your Mac (see Figure 16-7).

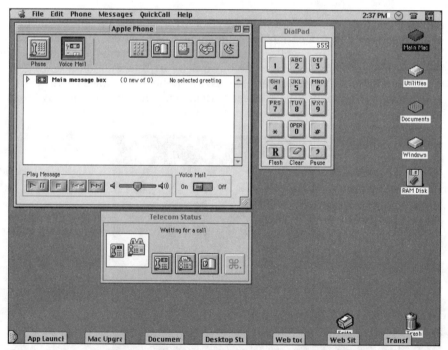

Figure 16-7: Apple Phone software, included with the GeoPort Telecom software, helps you manage your phone from your Mac.

If you like the idea of the GeoPort, you can certainly try it. The GeoPort adapter is still available from Apple retailers in some quantity, although Apple has stated in its Tech Notes that the company won't be upgrading the Telecom software past the version included with Mac OS 8.0. This is a good indication that Apple is moving away from the GeoPort approach. In fact, even though the Power Macintosh G3 machines include GeoPort technology (GeoPort is also the reason that Power Mac serial ports can transmit at 230 Kbps), they don't support the Telecom Adapter, presumably to save costs.

Tip

If you already have an Internet connection via Ethernet, for instance, you could always use a GeoPort adapter as an advanced telephony device for managing your voice phone and outgoing faxes. It's a little cheaper than a regular modem and offers very capable software for those tasks.

Got a 6300, 6400, 6500? You may have a GeoPort

In the Performa 6300, 6400, and 6500 series of Macs, Apple did something interesting—it shipped different modems with different Mac models. One of those models is a GeoPort adapter that happens to be built as an expansion card instead of an external GeoPort adapter. The net result is your internal "modem" is really using the PowerPC's processor to handle communications duties, which can often slow down the system.

Here's how you can figure out if you have a GeoPort modem. Go into ClarisWorks and open a new communications session. In the window, type ATI1 and press the Return key. If the number returned by the modem is a 0, you have a GeoPort Telecom Adapter. (A Global Village 28.8 modem will return the number 240, and a 14.4 Kbps Global Village modem will return 255.)

I got a Performa 6400 a little while back for the office. The first thing I did with it was rip the GeoPort adapter out of the communications slot. They can be very frustrating little buggers. On that particular machine, modem communications slowed the processor so severely that it was a horribly unpleasant experience to surf the Web.

If you don't have the budget to buy an external modem for your GeoPort adapter, a few tricks are available for speeding it up. First, make sure you have the latest version of the Telecom software that is included on the CD-ROM for Mac OS 8.0 and above or can be downloaded from Apple's support library. Second, make sure you've got plenty of RAM in your system, and add a cache RAM SIMM if you can afford it—these 603e-based Performas and Power Macs get a good boost from a cache RAM chip anyway.

The only other option is to try backing the GeoPort down in speed a little bit, settling for 28.8 connections instead of 33.6. Reports have it that the entire system reacts a little more quickly at that transmission speed.

Installing a modem

Once you've decided on a modem, you're ready to install it. In most cases, the modem is the easy part — it's installing all the software to run it that's more challenging. You'll have to install the correct modem driver to get your Mac to recognize it. Next you have to install software to use the Mac for various activities: Internet access, online services, or modem-to-modem communications.

Note   Whatever sort of modem you have and however it's installed, there's one precaution you should take in every instance — use a surge protector on the phone lines connected to your computer. If you have a modern surge protector (not just a power strip) it should feature phone jacks for protecting your twisted-pair phone cable. It's very important that you do this. In my experience, more damage is done to ports, modems, and Mac internals from surges over phone lines than from surges over regular power lines. It's that important.

Internal modems

Installing an internal modem is very similar to installing any other expansion card — the only difference is you'll most likely need to install the card in the special communications slot in your Mac. If you're not sure which it is, consult your Mac's manual. Figure 16-8 shows you what the slot looks like in a Performa 6200–series Macintosh. The slot is usually quite a bit smaller than other upgrade slots and should be clearly labeled as a communications slot or a modem slot on most Mac logic boards.

Of course, before you go looking for it you should shut down your Mac, ground yourself and unplug the computer. Open your Mac (or pull the logic board out to access it) and locate the communications slot. Once you find it, plug the card into the slot so the phone connectors are available through the back panel of the computer (you may need to remove a small piece of plastic to open a hole in the case for the connector). If everything looks well seated, close up the computer and turn your Mac back on.

After the Mac has started up, run any software that came with the modem; if it's a GeoPort adapter, run the Apple Telecom software included on the Mac OS 8.0 or above CD-ROM. (Otherwise, most comm-slot modems were made by Global Village and require Global Village's Teleport software to work correctly.) You may have to restart after installing the software.

With the software installed, you'll probably have a new control panel that controls the modem — either a Teleport control panel (for a Global Village modem) or an Express Modem control panel (for GeoPort modems). Use that control panel to alter any settings you feel are appropriate for your setup.

Figure 16-8: Installing a comm-slot modem is like installing a PCI or NuBus card, only it requires cards that will fit in this special slot.

You'll notice something else, too. In the Chooser, the modem port is no longer a choice. Unfortunately, you still can't use the modem port for another device, even though you're not using it for a modem anymore. It's locked up together with the communications slot, rendering it useless for other devices.

External modems and GeoPort adapters

You'll generally install an external modem on the modem port, if it's free. If it isn't, you can install a modem on the printer port, but you'll have to make sure AppleTalk is off, and that means you'll be cut off from any opportunity for LocalTalk networking. (If you're using a different sort of hardware for your network, you can leave AppleTalk on and make sure that LocalTalk isn't selected in the AppleTalk or Network control panel.) Using the printer port also means that certain modem-based software programs may be confused because your modem isn't on the modem port. (Few program will mind, but some older programs may have trouble with this setup.) Also, modem software tends to default to the modem port, so you may have to change that setting in most of your modem programs.

To install the modem, shut down your Mac, and then plug the modem's cable into the serial port on the back of your Mac. Plug the modem's power supply into a wall socket or surge protector, and then turn on the modem (if necessary). Restart your Mac.

When the Mac has restarted, install any software that was included with your Mac. Once it's installed, you may have to restart your computer. From now on, you should have a new control panel for your modem, in most cases. In others, you may have communications software or something similar that sets up your modem.

If you've installed a GeoPort adapter, you'll need to install the latest version of the Apple Telecom software you can find, probably the version included with your latest Mac OS CD-ROM. Or you can download the software from Apple's support site at `www.apple.com/support`. The Telecom software installs a control panel called Apple Express Modem (or just Express Modem) in your Mac's Control Panels folder.

High-speed Connections

Modems aren't the only way to connect to the Internet and online services; they're just the cheapest and most convenient choice for many users because all they rely on is a regular telephone line. The connections are low-speed at best, however, even with the most advanced modems.

To get yourself a faster connection, you generally have to turn to a new type of connection technology—preferably something that acts a whole lot like a regular computer network, transmitting data over lines of higher quality than the typical copper phone lines installed by the telephone company when your home, apartment, or office building was built.

Most of these high-speed connections are actually basic networking schemes. Using some sort of network adapter, you hook up to a larger, regional network. This network, in turn, is connected to the Internet. Here are the sort of technologies I mean:

- ✦ **Integrated Services Digital Network (ISDN).** This is a digital telephone service, a concept pioneered by the phone companies in the 1960s and then promptly forgotten—for all practical purposes. A desire for higher-speed access to the Internet has generated interest in this technology again, but it's only taken off in the urban centers of the largest U.S. cities (and a few others around the world, I'm told). It's a consideration for small business and home office use, although other technologies may soon eclipse it. It's expensive to implement, because standard phone wiring can't be used; the phone company has to dig up streets and change your home or business wiring to make it all work.

- ✦ **Cable data connections.** It just so happens that the TV cable connection running into many homes is a whole lot like computer-networking cable. (At least, it's a lot like one of the types of networking cable, called coax, thinnet, or 10Base2.) Repurposed for Internet access, the connection that your cable company can provide you fast connections to the Internet at a pretty reasonable price.

✦ **Satellite connections.** Using satellite dishes a lot like the 18-inch minidishes used for TV programming, satellite service providers can give you fairly high-speed access to the Internet. Unfortunately, the transmission only goes in one direction. You can't beam data back up to the satellite yourself, so you have to use a modem connection to send data.

✦ **Digital Subscriber Line (DSL).** This is another phone company technology, only it uses regular phone lines. By using the high-frequency parts of a phone connection (outside of human hearing), DSL achieves high data rates while maintaining voice communications. DSL is coming on quick and strong in a number of locales. If you have the opportunity, a DSL connection might be a great idea for your Mac, especially if it has Ethernet built in.

✦ **T-1 line.** Using fiber optic cable, a T-1 line is the preferred way to get entire buildings or companies online at once. The T-1 handles 1.5 megabits per second. These leased phone lines are a tad expensive, although you can often find *shared T-1* access that enables you to use part of the T-1 line for lower fees.

✦ **T-3 line.** Currently the backbone of the Internet, T-3 lines are rarely used for direct, individual Internet access. They transfer about 45 megabits per second. Higher-capacity lines beyond T-3 are starting to be added to the Internet infrastructure, whereas T-3 lines are occasionally used to serve data to and from typical big-city Internet service providers.

You can choose a good number of high-speed technologies. But how likely are you to get a faster connection? A lot depends on where you live. If you live close to a large city, near a major street, and within the service area of a progressive phone, cable or utility company, you may have a chance. Rural dwellers will have less luck, although some technologies may still become available to you over time.

I'll talk in more depth about ISDN, DSL, and cable modems because, at the time of writing, these three technologies are thriving options for many Mac users. (If you're lucky enough to have access to a T-1 line for Internet connections, you can learn more about connecting to one of those in Chapter 17 — T1 and Ethernet go hand-in-hand.) Satellite access is still on the horizon for Mac owners; the only viable satellite solutions currently use ISA expansion cards, an aging Intel-compatible PC-only technology.

ISDN

At one point, *Integrated Services Digital Network* (ISDN) was the next step for our telephone infrastructure. The phone company decided that the copper wiring and mechanical switches, as well as other aspects of our aging telephone network should be overhauled, allowing for a more feature-rich phone service that would be easier to run and allow more people to have access to it. (World Fair–style video phones may have been largely anticipated.) It wasn't seen as an opportunity to create a huge distributed network of PCs; when it was first conceived in the 1960s, there weren't any PCs.

Since that time, the phone companies have broken up, PCs have used modem technology as a mobile means of connecting to one another, and trends toward smaller offices, telecommuting, and working on the weekends have all contributed to demand for such a network to be instituted for dial-up data, instead of just feature-rich voice or teleconferencing communications. Many regional phone companies have pushed ahead with the massive infrastructure change that ISDN requires, although progress hasn't been as universal among the Baby Bell companies. At the same time, the world hasn't waited for phone companies to get their act together, instead creating new and innovated technologies — for example, Caller ID, 56K transmissions, DSL — that can exist over the old copper wires that most of us have running into our house.

Now, ISDN is at an interesting crossroads. In the urban centers of many larger cities, you can switch your house or office over to ISDN service completely, or you can just add an additional ISDN line. If you switch completely, it means you've got to do some radical purchasing, too, as ISDN only works with special digital phones (not regular analog phones). It also means a couple of other annoyances — such as all your phones having to have power to them to operate. Lose the lights, and the phones go with them.

Is this a great idea? That remains to be seen. Current phone service for voice communications is pretty adequate, and other competitors — such as satellite and cellular communications — may end up taking a load off of land lines in the near future. At the same time, DSL technology promises to use existing phone lines, but at a different frequency from voice communications, meaning it will be possible to overlay an entire nation's worth of digital data without tying up the phone lines the way we do now. And people really like the idea that their phones work even when their electricity does not, so they may be unlikely to make a wholesale change to ISDN for regular phone communications. The lack of such a comfort as phones that work during bad storms would not necessarily be seen as progress.

The switch to digital phone technology may continue behind the scenes, much as it is now, with the phone companies transparently updating their own equipment for higher speeds and more bandwidth, while leaving our phone lines relatively alone. That might also play out if some other sort of high-speed access becomes the dominant one.

How ISDN works

Of course, all this talk of the future isn't all that useful if you're sick of watching Netscape Navigator spin its icon. If you live in an area that offers ISDN, it is an interesting solution to higher speed Internet access — and one that works both *downstream*, for receiving data quickly from the Internet, and *upstream*, for sending data to the Internet (as in running your own Web server computer). For most people, the upper limit of an ISDN connection (especially using off-the-shelf computer peripherals) is about 128 Kbps, or a little over twice the speed of a 56 Kbps modem. There are, however, other advantages over modems, including the following:

✦ **Latency.** Overall, a modem has to "think" about a connection more than a networking technology such as ISDN does. With all the compression, error correction, line noise, and other issues, modems tend to waste micro- and nanoseconds transferring data, checking it, and uploading it to your Mac. Over time, this lag builds up to something noticeable.

✦ **Negotiation.** Most ISDN connections take about three seconds to initiate and begin transmitting. For 56 Kbps and other high-speed modems, this negotiation process can take 30 to 45 seconds or longer. That means ISDN connections seem quicker for intermittent surfers and can be cheaper for by-the-minute Internet services.

✦ **Reliability.** Because line noise isn't a factor for the completely digital connection, ISDN gives you a high-speed connection every time, instead of the shoot-and-miss process for analog modems.

✦ **Flexibility.** Because an ISDN line is "smarter" than a regular telephone line, the ISDN line can scale your Internet connection from 128 Kbps to 64 Kbps, for instance, to allow a voice call to ring through on your telephone set. It can also give you more information about incoming calls and reroute them more intelligently so that faxes, for instance, always get picked up by a computer or ISDN fax machine.

Unless ways to overlay these features on regular phone lines continue to be discovered, ISDN could easily be the phone technology of the future. Currently, though, most people focus on using ISDN for high-speed Internet connection if they worry about it at all. In addition, because it's not yet a completely accepted technology, it can be quite a headache to have installed. You need new wiring, new service, and, most likely, a new billing scheme from the phone company.

In exchange, you get higher-bandwidth *channels* coming into your house that offer interesting features and high-speed data. In essence, you become a network node on your phone company's network, almost as if their Ethernet or LocalTalk cabling was stretching over telephone poles and under streets to reach from their offices to your home or business.

Most phone companies offer *Basic Rate* access, which gives you three channels — two full 64 Kbps channels (A and B) for data and voice, and a D channel that's used for sending data about incoming calls and otherwise controlling the other two channels. Your ISDN equipment can then either link these two channels together for data service, or selectively use them for voice calls and data calls at the same time.

Another level of service, called *Primary Rate*, is designed more for larger businesses, enabling many, many channels to be typed together to create high-bandwidth solutions for voice and data in an office situation. Primary Rate service is generally charged on a channel-per-channel basis so that companies can gain T-1 level access or higher, depending on their locations' needs.

Note

You may also find that your phone company offers single channel service, designed for people who want to use the connection almost exclusively for online access. This gets you one 64 Kbps channel, making it faster than the fastest modem, with the same inherent latency and negotiation advantages.

Getting ISDN

If you're interested in ISDN for your home or office, call the phone company and find out if they offer ISDN in your area. If they do, you'll want to ask them how they bill for ISDN; some companies bill by the minute, whereas others offer a flat rate. If your phone company bills by the minute, take a hard look at the numbers before choosing the service. You may find some other method of high-speed access is more price competitive.

If you are interested in ISDN, you'll have to sign up for installation. Reportedly, that takes a few days or weeks, no matter where you live in the U.S. Californians probably fare the best in their larger cities, but the accepted truth is that it takes longer to get ISDN than it does to get a regular phone line. The phone company may need to dig up your street to get it to you — and, at the very least, they'll need to replace the wiring near your house and often inside as well.

Next, you'll need some equipment for your computer. Remember that an ISDN connection is a connection to the phone company's network. That means you'll need to terminate the networking connection on your end, just as with the LocalTalk or Ethernet connections discussed in Chapter 17. So, a *terminal adapter* or *TA-1* is required for an ISDN connection. You'll then need an ISDN network adapter (either an expansion card or a modem) for your Mac. This plugs into the terminal adapter, allowing it to translate the network feed into data your Mac can use.

As you read early on in this chapter, some devices called modems aren't really modems, because they don't modulate/demodulate. An ISDN modem is the perfect example of this. It isn't a modem, it's just an all-in-one ISDN box that fills the same need as a regular modem — it allows access to the Internet. But ISDN modems are cute, and they offer most of the advantages of an ISDN connection without some of the headaches, including an integrated adapter and TA-1 in a single box.

Armed with an ISDN line and an adapter, you're ready to get connected. You'll need to connect the adapter to your Mac's serial port (if it's external) or install it in a NuBus or PCI slot. Next, follow the instructions for installing the adapter's software carefully. Hooking the ISDN adapter up can be a rather complex process, requiring quite a bit of help from your phone company.

You can also add ISDN to your local area network. Using a special ISDN router, you can add the full bandwidth of an ISDN connection to your small office network, allowing everyone access to e-mail and Web surfing. ISDN can also be connected to a Web server computer, enabling a small business to have reasonable all-around access to the Internet for the cost of a few modems and the access. (I'll discuss this sort of access more in Chapter 17.)

Table 16-4 shows some manufacturers of ISDN connections and solutions. Note that Sagem offers a GeoPort adapter for ISDN, which is a little cheaper than a full-fledged ISDN all-in-one modem.

	Table 16-4	
	ISDN Solutions for Macs	
Manufacturer	*Solution Type*	*Web Site*
3Com	Modems, network	www.3com.com
Netopia	Modems, network	www.netopia.com
Motorola	Modems	www.bitsurfer.com
Sagem	Cards, modems, GeoPort	www.sagem.com
US Robotics	Modems	www.3com.com
Zyxel	Modems	www.zyxel.com

Note

If you're considering an external ISDN adapter, remember the modem port limitations on pre-PowerMacs. The GeoPort in AV and Power Macs is capable of up to 230 Kbps, so it shouldn't be limiting to an ISDN connection. Quadra and older Macs, however, are limited to 57.6 Kbps connections and may have trouble reaching high speeds with external ISDN adapters that use more than one ISDN channel. Opt for an internal card (assuming you can find one that supports Nu Bus), which shouldn't suffer the same setbacks.

DSL

When I first wrote this chapter, I decided that digital subscribe line (DSL) technology wouldn't be discussed in much depth, as it seemed more of a development for the future. In the time it took for the chapter to be returned to me for a second look, I'd decided that DSL was happening much faster than I'd initially thought, and the time had come to discuss it. That's how quickly things are moving in this industry. This fervor makes sense, however.

Unlike ISDN, which requires you to have your phone lines and phone equipment switched over, DSL technologies work over your existing phone lines, using high-frequency tones on your lines that won't interrupt regular phone service. Instead, data just hums along as if your phone line were a high-speed network connection, while your phones work as usual.

How it works

DSL is often called xDSL because there are so many other related and somewhat interchangeable technologies. (They're all also sometimes called ADSL, just as a convenient way to confuse matters.) If you're really interested, Table 16-5 gives you some indication of the different types.

The xDSL technology works by using the higher end of the frequency spectrum on a regular twisted-pair copper line for data transmission. You get regular telephone service between 0KHz and 4KHz on the line. But data can fill the void between 4kHz and 2.2mHz on your regular telephone line, allowing you to connect to an ISP or a corporate xDSL dial-up. This line then provides transmission of data at varying rates, depending on the technologies used and the conditions of the line, as well as the type of subscriber loop (telephone network connection to your nearest telephone company's office) and the conditions on the line.

So what's up with this upstream/downstream stuff? With many Internet connectivity options, the speeds at which you can receive data at your Mac (or your LAN) are much faster than the speeds at which you can send data back to your ISP. So, the downstream numbers represent the speeds at which you'll be able to download data; upstream numbers tell you how fast you'll be able to upload data. This is particularly interesting if you plan to run an Internet server computer over your DSL line; if the upstream numbers are too slow, your Internet visitors may not have an optimum experience.

Table 16-5
Different Types of DSL Technologies

Acronym	Name	Description	Throughput (Downstream/ Upstream)
ADSL	Asymmetrical DSL	Catch-all name	1.5–6 Mbps/64–384 Kbps
HDSL	High-speed DSL	Higher speeds for upstream	128 Kbps–1.5 Mbps
SDSL	Single-line DSL	Like HDSL, but only uses one wire pair	128 Kbps–1.5 Mbps
VDSL	Very high-speed DSL	High-speed, but must be very close to telephone company	51 Mbps/1.6–2.3 Mbps
RADSL	Rate-adaptive DSL	Likely deployment candidate, adapting speeds for line conditions	256 Kbps–6.1 Mbps/256 Kbps–1.5 Mbps

xDSL connections are subject to the same conditions modem connections are — noise on the line, poor installations, unshielded cabling, and even weather will ultimately affect the speed and quality of your connections.

The xDSL technologies have an advantage over most ISDN connections, however, in that they're usually continuous connections that require no special phone-call style negotiation. (You may find your phone company offers a bandwidth-on-demand system that works a little differently.) This adds to the lack-of-latency advantage ISDN has over regular modems: With xDSL, it doesn't take any noticeable delay before you start downloading data after a few minutes of idle time; with a modem it can take a full minute and with ISDN it can take a few seconds. Eventually, this adds up. It also means that phone companies and ISPs may be more likely to offer flat-rate services for xDSL, because you can't easily log off.

xDSL connects to your Mac — or to a workgroup of Macs — via an Ethernet connection. That means, for the most part, that xDSL connection hardware doesn't need to be Mac-specific. Instead, the equipment acts as an Internet router through which you can access the Internet over an existing Ethernet connection or by connecting your Mac directly to the Ethernet port on the router.

From there, the options abound. You may need a special *splitter* to use the same phone line for voice and data communications, or you may not. Your router may be in the form of an ADSL "modem" (like ISDN, it's not really a modem — just a convenient little box) that you can hook an analog phone directly to for voice communications. You may also find that the modem is designed to dial up your phone company or ISP for bandwidth-on-demand service.

Note

If you've ever wondered why Apple's iMac model — specifically designed for home users — shipped with an Ethernet port for networking, you may be seeing your answer right here. xDSL may prove to be a killer Internet technology for a lot of small offices and households currently hampered by slow modem connections. It's not a boom for absolutely everyone, but it has potential.

How to get service

Your local phone company probably controls xDSL service in your area, so that's where you should go to learn about service. In my experience, xDSL service is coming on like gangbusters, with local telephone companies seeing this as a profit-center they never really believed ISDN was. So, it seems phone companies are rolling it out more quickly.

That's not to say you'll necessarily see it in rural areas anytime soon. The current xDSL technologies tend to be limited most severely by the distance your particular local loop covers. If you're more than a few miles from your telephone company's physical switch, you'll have trouble getting this first round of service.

If you live in a large or medium-sized city, though, you should have better luck. In most cases you'll need both the xDSL service (which will require an installation fee and an additional monthly or by-the-minute charge) and ISP service to get connected to the Internet. You may find that your phone company offers both and/or that the ISP service isn't much more expensive than regular modem-based service.

You'll also need a router of some sort, whether it's an enclosed modem-style box for an individual connection or a networking contraption designed to serve a larger office workgroup. (Note that even minimal xDSL service has the potential to serve as a quality Internet connection for five to ten Macs in a small office.) You'll plug the router into your Mac's Ethernet port (or into your workgroup's hub), and then set up your Mac's TCP control panel according to your phone company's and/or ISP's instructions. (In some cases, you may need to use the PPP control panel, too.) That's it—you're on the Internet.

Netspeed (www.netspeed.com), a division of Cisco Solutions (www.cisco.com), is an important early player in xDSL access, as are most of the local telephone companies. For more information of xDSL, check out the Telechoice xDSL Report at www.xdsl.com/.

Cable

Offering up to two megabits per second, the cable companies have a couple of advantages in the race to provide people high-speed Internet access in their homes and offices. First, cable is already pretty pervasive. Having control over a line coming into your home is a critical advantage—a lot of Internet providers have to convince you to use some other mechanism for using their services (such as satellite receivers, wireless boxes, or a new type of wiring). Because cable is often already wired through the neighborhood—and uses a type of cabling that offers more bandwidth than telephone lines—it's certainly worth considering.

Cable has one serious drawback: It's currently a *downstream-only* technology. That is, cable companies and cable wiring are only designed to send signals to your TV, but aren't designed to accept anything back from your home. Internet connectivity is a two-way street, however, so cable companies will either need to figure out how to offer upstream access or require you to use a phone line to send commands while receiving higher-speed feeds along the cable wiring. (In some cases they already are coming up with solutions, so consult your cable company before taking my word for it. Newer cable technologies are beginning to appear that enable you to upload over the cable connection, albeit at slower speeds than the downstream technology.)

Even if it's downstream only, the connection should be pretty fast, as cable has the potential to offer 2 Mbps of bandwidth. This bandwidth will need to be shared among households or businesses in a particular node of the cable company's network, so realistic bandwidth will probably be closer to 200 to 300 Kbps for a typical cable connection. That's still great speed, however, offering some of the same lack-of-latency and negotiation advantages as ISDN and xDSL.

As the cable companies ramp up their offerings, it's likely that a number of methods for getting connected will emerge, although the Mac compatibility is currently suspect. The only indicators available are cable access trials going on around the country. Although many of the solutions don't currently involve Mac solutions, at least one impressive offering does — the CYBERsurfer from Motorola (see Figure 16-9). This cable "modem" is an all-in-one solution that cable companies can opt to use for cross-platform connectivity capabilities.

Figure 16-9: The Motorola CYBERSurfer comes in versions for both Macs and Intel-compatible PCs, making it a likely candidate for cable companies to adopt. (Courtesy Motorola Corp.)

The Massachusetts Institute of Technology is keeping track of cable modem technologies at `rpcp.mit.edu/~gingold/cable/` and the @Home network seems to be leading the charge into cable-based future at `www.home.net`.

Setting Up Internet Access

Once you've chosen your Internet technology and your hardware, you're ready to set up Internet access. Entire magazine articles and book chapters (in really good books by famous Mac-loving authors) are devoted to helping you choose a service provider, so I'll skip that here. Once you've got a service provider, though, you're ready to head into the Mac OS to set up your Internet access — and that is something I can help you with.

If you've got Mac OS 8.0 or above, you probably don't even need to bother with this section if you don't want to. Instead, look on your Mac's hard drive for a folder called Internet, open it, and look for the Internet Setup Assistant. Run the assistant to set up all the Internet preferences and addresses you'll need to get online.

If you're going to forge ahead on your own, you'll need to gather some pretty specific information, and then head into the Mac OS to change the appropriate control panel settings. You also need to know a little about the technology the Internet uses.

TCP/IP

Transmission Control Protocol/Internet Protocol (TCP/IP) is the AppleTalk of the Internet. It's simply a protocol used by the networking hardware attached to computers sending data to one another on the Internet. The data packets need to know where to go and how to get there so that an e-mail message I send from Colorado, for instance, ends up in your e-mail program's inbox somewhere in Peoria or wherever the heck you live.

TCP/IP is also the name of a control panel on your Macintosh that gives you access to a TCP/IP network—in most cases, the Internet. (Other networks can use the TCP/IP protocol, too, to transfer information between a more limited number of computers. These are usually called *intranets*, because they use the Internet protocols, but are limited in scope.) The TCP/IP control panel is the Internet interface for Open Transport, the Mac's all-inclusive networking infrastructure which allows for different types of access, like AppleTalk, TCP/IP, and others. (Older Macs may still use the MacTCP control panel, which instead layers TCP connectivity on top of older versions of the Mac OS.)

Your Mac knows intrinsically how to get on the Internet and talk to other computers in the Internet language. But it doesn't really know *how* it's going to connect and what its address will be until you step in and tell it. You also need some other (slightly more esoteric) numbers to round out your Mac's ability to access Internet protocols. Figure 16-10 shows the TCP/IP control panel.

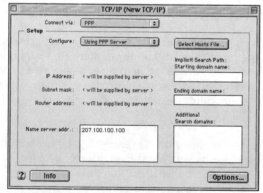

Figure 16-10: The TCP/IP control panel gives you access to the intricacies of the Transmission Control Protocol for Internet access.

Here are what things mean in the TCP/IP control panel (these are also the questions you'll need to ask your ISP, in most cases):

✦ **Connect via.** Through this pull-down menu you select the method you're going to use for connecting to the Internet. If you've got an Ethernet card designed for shared T-1 access, choose Ethernet. If you'll be using a modem or ISDN dial-up, choose PPP or the method recommended by your equipment manufacturer. (Using 802.3 is recommended for most standard Ethernet networks.)

✦ **Configure.** This menu determines how your Internet address and other information will be entered. If you have a PPP dial-up connection without a fixed IP address, you'll probably choose the option Using PPP server. Your service provider should be able to help you choose the appropriate option if you're using a nonstandard connection.

✦ **IP address.** This is your Mac's physical address on the Internet. Using this address, which is made up of four groups of digits separated by periods, anyone can gain access to anything that's *served* by your Mac — data that's explicitly made available. That includes Web servers, FTP (file transfer) servers, and even AppleTalk servers (if you intend to allow people to access your computer over the Internet using AppleTalk Remote Access software). If you're dialing an ISP over a modem, this address may be dynamically assigned to you, meaning you don't have to enter it yourself.

✦ **Subnet mask.** This mask is used for Macs behind firewalls or otherwise using internal IP addresses that aren't individually visible on the Internet. In this case your Mac is connected to a subnet, and gains access to the Internet through another computer in your local network.

✦ **Router address.** This is the IP address of the router that gives your particular Mac its gateway to the Internet.

✦ **Name server address.** Internet addresses are, at their lowest level, numbers like 255.255.255.255. (Actually, they're binary numbers like 11111111. 11111111.11111111.11111111 as far as the computers are concerned, even though they're translated into decimal numbers, like 256, for us — but don't tell non-techy people you know that. They'll think there's something wrong with you.) Because people like addresses such as "www.apple.com" much more than they like "255.255.255.255", name-server computers (called *DNS servers*) exist to match these names with their associated IP addresses. Your local Internet service provider probably has a DNS server or two; you enter those computer's numbered addresses here.

Note

If, for some unfathomable reason, you'd prefer to use a Hosts file instead of a name server, you can select that with the Use Hosts file button, which brings up an Open dialog box to help you locate the file. This is a text file that lists the domain name associated with a particular IP address. Your Internet provider should offer a name server to do this for you (because keeping up a Hosts file yourself — with hundreds of domains being added daily — could be tedious), but you may have need to use a Hosts file on some remote island or something. (If you use one, write me and let me know why.) You'll only use the other search-path parameters if you understand the whole Hosts file things.

Close the dialog box, and your setting should take. If you're using a direct connection (Ethernet or related), you're done. If you're creating a dialup connection, you'll need to set up PPP, too.

PPP

The *Point-to-Point Protocol* (PPP) is a common method for establishing a TCP/IP network connection over a phone line. TCP/IP is designed for direct connections — it's only a transmission protocol, relying on the Mac's underlying network infrastructure to actually talk to your Ethernet card, for instance. But even your Mac doesn't know how to create a TCP/IP connection using a modem. So, PPP must be added to the mix.

PPP is also a control panel in the Control Panels folder on your Mac. Open it up and you'll see some basic options (see Figure 16-11).

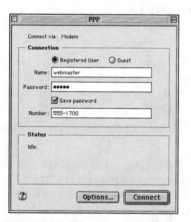

Figure 16-11: The PPP control panel enables you to hook up to a TCP/IP network (usually the Internet) over a phone line.

In the PPP control panel, you enter the username and password for your PPP account (your ISP will assign these to you). You also enter the phone number your modem is supposed to dial to access the ISP's modem pool for gaining access to the Internet. Click the Options button, and you'll get a few options regarding *how* your modem is dialed (whether it auto-redials, dials when you launch a Web browser, and so on).

After setting up PPP, you need to set up your modem — with PPP control panel active, pull down the PPP menu and choose Modem. This opens the Modem control panel (which you can also access from the Apple menu or through other conventional means). In the Modem control panel, you should select the modem model you're using for this dial-up connection.

But what if your modem doesn't show up? You then need to add an Open Transport PPP script (OT/PPP) for your modem. The manufacturer should provide the script. (Call their customer service department or check their Web site.) To install the script, drag it to the Modem Scripts folder, in the Extensions folder, which in turn is stored in the System Folder.

With all this set up, head back to the PPP control panel and click Connect. You should hear your modem wind up, dial and connect to an answering modem at your ISP's site. Soon, you'll have an active TCP/IP connection. Fire up a Web browser or e-mail program and test it.

Telephony

Outside of modems and their faxing capabilities, you may also want your Mac taking over even more of your phone-related duties, whether that's creative handling of Caller ID information, paging, or just plain voicemail. A number of solutions exist, even though you don't hear much about them, that can help you in a home or small office environment to manage your phone like you manage data.

There are two sides to adding telephony features and management to your Mac — hardware and software. You may already have the hardware you need, although some unique solutions exist. The software, however, is where the power really kicks in.

Hardware solutions

Many telephony software solutions on the Mac make use of PowerPC-based Macs and the GeoPort Telecom Adapter. As mentioned earlier, the Telecom Adapter does more than simply act as a modem; it basically allows your Mac to interface with the telephone. In fact, it doesn't have to act as a modem at all. Instead, it can act as a telephony device designed for voicemail or other pursuits. The GeoPort Telecom Adapter hooks up to the modem port on your Mac in the same way any external modem does.

The YoYo from Big Island Software (www.bigisland.com) is a personal favorite of mine, although indications are that further development may have been discontinued. The YoYo is a small white box that, once connected to your ADB port for power, acts as a pass-through for your phone line and phone extension.

Features of the YoYo include the following:

✦ The hardware features an LCD indicator that blinks to tell you when you have a voicemail message. If you have voicemail through your phone company, a stuttered dial tone is usually the indication that you have a message. YoYo listens for this dial tone, and flashes its light when detecting it.

✦ The hardware is also capable of recognizing Caller ID information and paging a predetermined pager number as calls come in, even if the Mac isn't turned on. The Caller ID phone number appears on the recipient's pager along with a code denoting that the page was sent by YoYo. For YoYo owners, it's like having mobile Caller ID. When the Mac is turned on, Caller ID information is displayed on screen and can be announced with audio cues or spoken text (if Speech Technologies are enabled for your Mac).

✦ A combination of the software and hardware enables you to set certain times when the YoYo's extension phone won't ring, so you'll be undisturbed, at least in that room.

✦ The combination also helps you track and log incoming and outgoing calls based partly on Caller ID information. This can be very helpful to professionals and small business people who bill by the hour.

Other telephony software can make use of voicemail-capable modems and other particular models. It's possible that some of these companies will soon make use of PCI cards that exist for Windows (and wouldn't need more than driver software to work on Mac PCI-based machines), but I haven't seen any concrete indicators as of this writing.

Software

More important than how your Mac gets connected to a phone line is how the software handles its duties. In most cases, the software is designed to offer a more sophisticated approach to single-line voicemail handling, although some versions may offer multiline voicemail solutions in the future. Here are some different software programs that handle telephony:

✦ **MegaPhone** (Bing Software, `www.bingsoftware.com/`) is telephony management software for the home and small office, giving you conferencing features, call scheduling, call logging in a contact database, and voicemail, all based around a GeoPort Adapter or a voicemail-enabled modem.

✦ **PhonePro** (Bing Software) is even more extensive, allowing you to use a Mac-based network in your office to take voicemail messages and pop them up on the correct desktop, offer fax-back services, route calls to the correct extension, create a voicemail hierarchy, and automatically dial the recipient's pager when a voicemail message is left.

✦ **PhoneMaker** (MicroMat, www.micromat.com) is a similar, full-fledged telephony product that's actually a visual telephony programming tool. It allows you to create voicemail systems for your office. Implement phone mail, auto-attendant, call-processing, fax-on-demand or integrated voice response.

✦ **MacComCenter** (Smith Micro, www.smithmicro.com) is another more basic fax and voice application for personal or small office use, including voicemail, Caller ID, and paging capabilities.

Summary

✦ Modems are far and away the most popular method for getting on the Internet and signing onto online services, although they can also be used for voicemail, as a speakerphone, or to communicate with fax machines. In any case, choosing the right modem for your particular needs takes some consideration of the different types of modems and the varying features they offer.

✦ In many cases you'll install a modem using the external modem port on your Mac, simply plugging it in, and then installing any software that came with the modem. If you have an internal communications slot, however, you may opt to install the modem internally, which will require opening your Mac's case or pulling out the logic board. You'll then need to configure it to work correctly over phone lines.

✦ If you want higher speed access to the Internet, you'll find that more and more options are popping up. ISDN is a reasonably popular way to double or triple modem speeds, with xDSL technologies coming on strong in the high-speed arena. If it's offered in your area, cable-based Internet connections may also be a popular alternative, through which you can use your TV's cable connection for high-speed Internet downloads.

✦ Once you have a connection — whatever it is — you'll need to set up your Mac's system software to properly deal with the Internet. In a way, it's a basic networking connection (just to a very large network). You'll use the TCP/IP and PPP control panels, in most cases, along with some important numbers and other information you'll need to get from your ISP or system administrator.

✦   ✦   ✦

Networking

T he Mac's built-in and easy-to-add networking features have made it a connected machine from very early in its existence. Ever since somebody came up with a really good use for Macs — desktop publishing — Mac owners have been using LocalTalk and AppleTalk to connect their computers to share files and offer laser printing to the entire office. Although local networking has been around as long as UNIX (and even longer with mainframe-type sharing of data and applications) the Mac did a lot to popularize the idea of the *local area network* (LAN), or small workgroups sharing files and print jobs over a limited amount of space. LocalTalk, the Mac's first networking hardware standard, remains among the simplest to implement and manage.

In contrast to the Mac, other computing platforms initially made networking tough to master. Novell and Microsoft offer extensive training courses for network administrators designed to teach them all the nuances of a new network operating system and a long laundry list of codes and keys to passwords, security, permissions, and drivers. You also needed to know quite a bit about designing a network topology, keeping track of cable lengths, and installing devices like hubs and routers.

Mac networks can get almost this complicated, these days; some university campuses and professional creative agencies have extensive Mac networks that need to be closely managed. But, by and large, everything is a little easier for Mac workgroups, even when using technology originally developed for other platforms, such as Ethernet networking and TCP/IP protocols.

Depending on your level of interest, Mac networking is completely flexible for the task at hand. If you want to connect two machines for basic file sharing and print sharing, that's easily done. If you want to connect 30 machines and a high-end laser printer for the same tasks, this can also be accomplished. Want to actually control the screen of another Mac or Windows PC from across the room, the building, or over the Internet? You can do that, too, with the right tools.

In This Chapter

How networking works

Networking Macs together

Adding PCs to your network

Remote networking

Adding the Internet to your network

In this chapter, you'll start by looking at the basics of Macintosh networking and networking protocols. You'll then learn how to create a network, install networking hardware, and even add Intel-compatible PCs to the mix. Later, I'll talk about other cool productivity tricks such as adding Internet access, remote networking, and more.

Mac Networking Technologies

In networking, you have three major issues to worry about. One is the type of hardware being used to connect the computers. This includes expansion cards, cabling, connectors, and terminators, but depends mostly on the overall technology that's used for the hardware. In the Mac's case, that's generally one of two *cabling schemes*: Ethernet or LocalTalk. A third scheme, Token Ring, is based on a proprietary IBM standard that had a brief flare of popularity, but is no longer widely used. You're unlikely to find Token Ring hardware for Macs any more, although you'll occasionally come across odds and ends for upgrading purposes.

The second issue you need to worry about is the networking protocol — the software commands — used to route data from one place to another. It's interesting to note that, in spite of a mouthful of confusing names, the topology of a network and the networking protocol being used are really unrelated. In general, you can use any topology (for example, Ethernet) with any networking protocol (for example, AppleTalk) that the Mac supports. In fact, Open Transport, the Mac's underlying networking technology, makes this even easier.

For most folks, the networking protocol choices will be threefold: AppleTalk, TCP/IP, or Novell NetWare. (The Point-to-Point Protocol can also be included in this list, although it's usually simply used to create a network connection for one of the other protocols over phone lines or other networking options such as ISDN.) Even more generally, AppleTalk will be your most likely choice for workgroup settings, as it's the protocol around which Macintosh networking has been built. If your workgroup is primarily Mac-based, you'll probably use AppleTalk to connect the Macs, and then use other protocols to add Intel-compatible PCs or applications for accessing Novell and Windows NT server computers. If your office has mostly Intel-compatible PCs, your Mac is going to have to be a better citizen than usual, most likely running NetWare for speaking to DOS-based network servers, or AppleTalk for accessing a Windows NT server that's friendly to Macs.

The third issue? The *topology* of your network, or the pattern in which your network is laid out, is an important consideration. In a *bus* topology, each computer is connected to the next in turn, with the cable ending on each end of the network, usually with hardware terminators. This topology is most common for LocalTalk connections. In a *ring (or token ring)* configuration, the network loops back on itself, and the last computer is connected to the first computer to complete the loop. In a *star* topology, the network is served by a hardware *hub* that has a length of networking cable running out to each individual computer. This is how most Ethernet networks are wired together.

LocalTalk

LocalTalk is a networking architecture that's built into every Mac. It is easy to use and fairly flexible. It's also pretty slow. At a maximum speed of about 230 Kbps, LocalTalk is designed more for occasional file and print sharing in very small offices. A 1MB file, for instance, takes about 30 seconds to transfer over a LocalTalk network, making it the wrong solution for large workgroups of designers and artists.

LocalTalk is a fine idea for a smaller office or organization, though, especially if it deals with smaller documents and has few workstations. In fact, as discussed in Chapter 15, you'll often have reason to create a LocalTalk network of only two computers — a Mac and a PostScript printer. Remember, however, that LocalTalk has limitations; without a repeater or hub (devices that will boost the LocalTalk signal), you're limited to 32 devices and 1,800 feet of cabling.

LocalTalk uses the Mac's printer port as a networking interface, requiring a special *transceiver* to chain the Macs in the workgroup together. The transceiver is a small box with two LocalTalk ports on it and a serial cable for connecting to the printer port. The two LocalTalk ports enable one LocalTalk cable to come in from the previous transceiver in the chain and another cable to head out to the next Mac in the chain.

It's somewhat rare to have a hub or other networking device at the center of your LocalTalk network; instead, like a SCSI chain, Macs are all connected to one other to create a LocalTalk connection. At the last Mac on either end of the LocalTalk chain, a terminator is installed in the open LocalTalk port on the first and last transceiver to signify the end of the network. (As noted earlier, this is a bus topology.)

LocalTalk connections are usually accomplished using one of two types of cable — either standard LocalTalk cabling or PhoneNet cabling. A LocalTalk cable looks a lot like a typical Mac serial cable, except it only has 3-pin connectors, and it's only designed to connect between LocalTalk transceivers. The transceivers, in turn, connect to the Mac via a typical serial cable connector (as shown in Figure 17-1).

Note   You'll also occasionally find a third type of network "wiring" — an IRTalk transceiver that enables your Mac to communicate with the network using its wireless infrared (IR) port, as appears on many newer PowerBooks. Farallon (www.farallon.com/) makes the AirDock transceivers for this purpose.

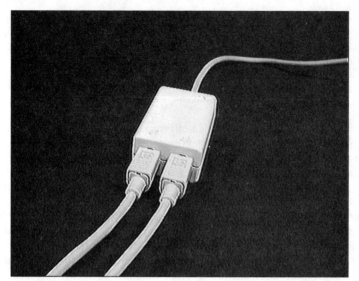

Figure 17-1: LocalTalk transceiver and LocalTalk cabling

The problem with the typical LocalTalk connectors and cabling is they tend to come unattached pretty easily — a circumstance that can be frustrating if you're managing more than one or two computers. The solution to this problem was created in the late 1980s by the networking solutions company, Farallon. Called PhoneNet, this LocalTalk cabling solution uses regular phone wire (with RJ-11 connectors) to connect between special PhoneNet transceivers. Not only is this a bit less expensive and easier to string than the thicker, heavier LocalTalk cable, but PhoneNet connectors tend to lock together and stay connected. One disadvantage: PhoneNet limits your network to about 24 devices.

PhoneNet is probably more common than regular LocalTalk cabling, and it's now made by a number of manufacturers. Even Apple has sold PhoneNet cabling and transceivers. Figure 17-2 shows a PhoneNet connector.

Note   Some phone wiring (the jacks and wiring in the walls of your home or office) is actually capable of handling two lines over a single connector; all you need is a Line 1/Line 2 modular adapter. If your home or office is wired in this manner, and you're not using that second line, you can use the phone wiring for PhoneNet connections, too, because these connections use phone wiring and RJ-11 connectors. Instantly, your office or home is wired for a network.

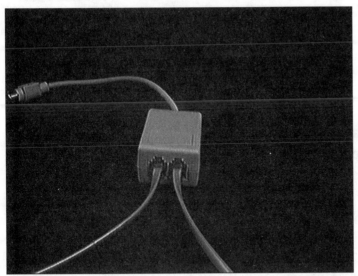

Figure 17-2: PhoneNet wiring is a little easier to install, and the connectors tend to stay firmly in place.

Ethernet

The standard on many computing platforms, Ethernet is easily the most popular way to network computers together. Ethernet is inexpensive to add to a computer, it's fast (either 10 Mbps or 100 Mbps, depending on the network's equipment) and it's well supported by networking protocols. Perhaps best of all, Ethernet is built into many popular Mac models (see Table 17-1).

Table 17-1		
Ethernet Options for Major Mac Models		
Model	*Ethernet Connector*	*Ethernet Upgrade Options*
Classic Macs (Mac SE and newer)	N/A	PDS card
Mac II series	N/A	NuBus card
LC series	N/A	PDS card
Performa series	N/A	PDS or comm slot card
Performa 5400, Power Mac 5400, 5500, 4400	10BaseT	Comm slot
Performa 6110 series	AAUI	NuBus

(continued)

	Table 17-1 *(continued)*	
Model	*Ethernet Connector*	*Ethernet Upgrade Options*
Centris/Quadra	AAUI	NuBus
Quadra 605	N/A	N/A
Quadra 630	N/A	Comm Slot
Power Mac (NuBus)	AAUI	NuBus
Power Mac 6500, 7200, 7300, 7600, 8600, 9600	10BaseT/AAUI	PCI
Power Mac G3	10BaseT	PCI
Power Computing	10BaseT	PCI
Motorola StarMax 3000, 4000	N/A (optional)	PCI
StarMax 5000	10BaseT	PCI
UMAX (J & S models)	10BaseT	PCI

Macs that offer a 10BaseT port can accept a 10BaseT connector directly into the back panel of the Macintosh. Those Macs that offer an Apple Attachment Unit Interface (AAUI) transceiver option can use an external transceiver device to add either 10BaseT or 10Base2 (different types of Ethernet cabling) connections. Those that offer no standard connection can have Ethernet added via an expansion card.

Standard Ethernet offers theoretical transmission limits of about 10 Mbps, although real-world results are generally much lower than this. A 100 Mbps standard is starting to catch on with users and administrators, resulting in a proliferation of 100 Mbps Ethernet adapters, hubs, and other equipment. Although you still aren't likely to reach such speeds (because of slowdowns in the OS, among other things), you will see an impressive increase in performance as a result of moving up to 100 Mbps equipment.

Note

If your Mac doesn't offer an internal Ethernet solution, you can add Ethernet with a SCSI-to-Ethernet adapter. Both Dayna Communications (www.dayna.com/) and Sonic Systems (www.sonicsys.com/) offer solutions for connecting to an Ethernet network using your Mac's built-in SCSI port.

Expert tip: Comm slot defined

If you have a Performa, Power Macintosh all-in-one, or another similar Mac model, you may have a communications slot ("comm slot") port available in your Mac for conveniently adding Ethernet capabilities or certain modem models. The problem is knowing which comm slot you have. If you're scratching your head over how to distinguish the original comm slot from comm slot II, Rick Voelker, owner of Voelker Research (www.voekler.com/) in Colorado Springs has the answer:

"Here's my official definition: A comm slot is a slot in which internal cards can be installed, typically communications products such as modems or Ethernet cards. Comm slot II is the same as above, except it's the slot found in PCI Macs, including the Power Macintosh 5260 and up. They're not interchangeable.

"So, how can you be totally sure which slot you have? If you don't trust the definition given above, check the Apple Tech Info Library (http://til.info.apple.com/) for a spec sheet on the particular Mac you are researching. It will tell you which your model has.

"How do you know which kind of card you are ordering? The spec sheet for the card is the ultimate identifier. Typically, a card will be described as a 'CS' or 'CSII' in the description."

Ethernet cabling

So, for an Ethernet network, you need the Ethernet circuitry — either built-in or on an expansion card — and some cabling. Two major types of Ethernet cabling are common: 10Base2 and 10BaseT.

10Base2 cabling is also called thinnet, coax, or BNC (the connector is actually a BNC connector, but often you'll hear the cabling referred to by its connector type). This is usually black or gray cabling that looks a lot like the cable used to connect a TV to cable television input or, sometimes, a VCR. 10Base2 cabling connects to a BNC connector or a 10Base2-compatible Ethernet transceiver or card: The transceiver features a small, round post that can accept a connection from the BNC connector (see Figure 17-3).

Although 10Base2 is the less popular (these days) of the two types of Ethernet cabling, it does offer one major advantage: Like LocalTalk, 10Base2 cabling can be used to daisy chain Macs into a long line of networked computers in a bus topology. 10Base2 doesn't require any other hardware — such as a networking hub — to operate. Most 10Base2 transceivers offer two BNC connectors, one for the cable coming in and one for the cable going out. This enables you to connect to the next Mac downstream or add a terminator if you've reached the end of the networking line.

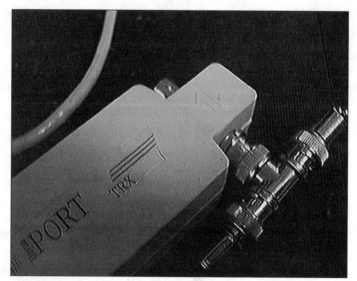

Figure 17-3: 10Base2 cabling and connector

This is good, hearty cable that's recommended for a number of installations — especially industrial environments, factory floors, and anywhere where you need sturdy cable that's resistant to electrical noise. A daisy-chain network of 10Base2 cabling can only stretch about 600 feet before problems creep in or you're forced to add a hub or network switch.

10BaseT is a bit easier to work with, although it does require a special hub to connect more than two computers to one another. 10BaseT is also commonly called *twisted pair* and sometimes referred to by its connector type, *RJ45*. 10BaseT wiring is very much like typical phone wiring (which is also referred to as twisted pair). They are two different types of cable, though. Visually, the thickness and connector are different; the 10BaseT connector is larger, and the cable overall is thicker. Regular phone cable uses an RJ11 connector, whereas Ethernet cabling uses an RJ45 connector.

The hub in a 10BaseT connection is a small box into which you hook a number of RJ45 connectors so that they can talk to one another. With the hub at the center, then, this configuration is often referred to as a *star topology* because each connection branches away from the center like the points on a star.

There are a couple of advantages to 10BaseT that deserve to be looked at:

✦ *Fault-tolerant.* Because 10BaseT Ethernet requires a hub, each individual workstation is isolated. If there's a problem with one of the lines, it won't bring down the entire network like a 10Base2-based topology can (and often does). Usually a 10BaseT network can keep running if one of the client computers starts having trouble.

✦ *Easy to troubleshoot.* For pretty much that same reason, 10BaseT is easier to troubleshoot. On a 10Base2 bus, a network problem can be the result of a disconnect on any one of the lines strung between the computers, or a problem with the Ethernet connection itself. Unfortunately, nothing points you to the specific computer that's causing the trouble. (In some cases you'll notice that downstream network connections are failing while upstream connections aren't, suggesting which Mac is the source of the break in the cabling. In other cases, this won't be as obvious.) With 10BaseT, a computer that's having network trouble *is* the problem computer, as it's only connected to the hub, not to a string of other computers.

✦ *Easy to move.* When you work with 10Base2, you need to focus on how long each segment of cable is, where the next computer is, and how you're going to get the cable to it. With 10BaseT, you can move a computer, and then plug it back into the hub without worrying about where it is in relation to the other computers.

Of course, if you have your heart set on using 10Base2, you can get hubs for it, too, although they're not as common.

Hubs and switches

So what, exactly, are these hubs? Hubs are boxes that offer ports for Ethernet cabling and indicators that tell you (at a basic level) what's going on with your data. Hubs range from low-end, small-business-oriented models that have a few ports to those with many ports and modular designs destined to be linked together. Although hubs generally use 10BaseT connections for most of the Ethernet cabling, you'll often find they offer a BNC connector for a coax cable that can link hubs together.

Hubs come in different shapes, sizes, and levels of technical prowess. If you're shopping for a small business hub, a basic *passive* hub should work fine for ten or fewer nodes. Here's how the different types of hubs, scaled upward in capabilities, compare:

✦ **Passive hubs.** These hubs connect Ethernet cabling to form a star topology, but don't do anything particularly special to the data packets as they pass through. Often, data packets are replicated onto every port in the hub and sent to all the linked computers, where the packets are ignored by nodes for which the data was not intended (see Figure 17-4).

✦ **Managed hubs.** This type of hub enables an administrator to talk to it through a software interface, picking and choosing different behaviors for each port. The administrator can turn on and off certain ports, tunnel direct connections between certain ports, and manage the flow of data.

✦ **Switched hubs.** Also just called *switches*, these hubs actually take note of the data that's being transmitted and move it to the proper port. This results in a more expensive hub that's capable of much more efficient networking. An example is a switched hub with a 100 Mbps connection to a server and switched 10 Mbps connections to each Mac. If there are ten Macs on the switch, each could theoretically receive 10-Mbps streams of data simultaneously. What's better, all the data will be relevant, because it's addressed to that particular port.

Figure 17-4: This little passive hub is easy to set up for a smaller workgroup. Just plug it in and add Ethernet connections.

If you'll be using an all-Ethernet network to get your Macs working together, a hub is definitely the right way to go, and you can change or add hubs as you upgrade the network. It's certainly not as tough to buy a hub as it might seem — for basic uses a passive hub is fine. Once your network grows larger or you identify bottlenecks (for example, a creative workgroup might need better bandwidth for transferring digital images than the accounting department, which has low-bandwidth needs), you can add managed and switched hubs.

Look for a manufacturer that offers an easy-to-grasp modular approach to adding hubs, as well as one that can help you understand and add other technologies, like routers for Internet access or bridges for crossing over to another network topology.

What's a router and a bridge, anyway?

For the record, I don't consider myself particularly slow. But this router thing has been driving me nuts for as long as I've been involved in computing. What is a router? Why would you need a router? I asked and read and wondered, and still couldn't quite figure it out. After years of pounding my head against the wall, I think I've finally hit on the simplistic, understandable answer to what a router does.

In a nutshell, a router is smart hardware designed to filter data coming from one network and forward it to another network. Like a bridge, a router has the potential to take data from one network architecture and move it onto another network architecture. (A bridge might be used to get a LocalTalk and an Ethernet network to share AppleTalk data packets.) The router is smarter than a bridge, though, because it can tell what a data packet is for and send it along in the right direction.

If you're a business and educational user or administrator, you'll want to know if you need a router for Internet access. The answer is yes, you do need that router . . . at least somewhere—if not your office, then in your building, your company, or your ISP. After all, you've got to grab the data packets of the Internet backbone and direct them toward your organization somehow. (I'll discuss Internet access for LANs later in the chapter.)

Otherwise, you only require routers when data packets need to find their way efficiently around larger networks—such as those on large school campuses or in corporations and organizations. At that point, routers become part of a larger scheme of inter-networking—taking smaller LAN networks (or workgroups) and getting them to talk together in a Wide Area Network (WAN, or internet). Somehow the data has to know when to jump off the local network in search of its destination on another network. That's what a router is for.

Open Transport

If you've got a PowerPC or 68040-based Macintosh with Mac OS 7.6 or higher, you're running Open Transport. (You can get Open Transport to run on Macs running Mac OS 7.5 or higher, but you'll need to download it from Apple's Support site at www.apple.com/support/.) Open Transport is the basic networking technology found in the lowest levels of the Mac OS; all other networking is based on Open Transport.

It may help to think of Open Transport as the QuickTime-like technology of Mac networking. Remember how QuickTime is able to take many types of files and file formats and then bring them all together on a Mac to create a single multimedia movie? That's sort of what Open Transport does for Macs in reverse; it speaks a single networking language to the Mac OS, but then uses different networking protocols—AppleTalk, TCP/IP—to talk to the outside world. This approach not only makes the Mac multilingual for flexibility on the Internet, it also makes it easier to set up networking service on your Mac without getting a master's degree on the subject.

From your Mac's viewpoint, Open Transport is a series of shared libraries stored in the Extensions folder providing programmers access to the AppleTalk and TCP/IP. On most modern Macs, you'll need to have these libraries (and other Open Transport files) installed properly for networking to work.

AppleTalk

AppleTalk is far and away the most popular networking protocol language for Macintosh computers and workgroups. Although AppleTalk was and is a proprietary Apple-owned standard, Apple has made AppleTalk's inner workings available for public consumption, enabling other manufacturers to write to its specifications. As a result, AppleTalk services appear in a wide range of products, including AppleTalk networking services built into Windows NT servers, AppleTalk software for Windows 95 desktops, Novell network software for Macs, and even AppleTalk connectivity for UNIX and other platforms.

Types of AppleTalk networks

Originally conceived as a *client/server* protocol, AppleTalk in the beginning was configured so that one computer acted as a conduit for most of the communication. On that server computer, shared files were stored and accessed by the individual client Macs used by the rest of the workgroup. The server computer was also responsible for handling the printer services for each Mac. When a Mac wanted to print, it asked the print server to put its print request in a queue.

The server software for a client/server AppleTalk network is called AppleShare (just to keep things perfectly clear) and must be purchased from Apple or Apple retailers. The AppleShare IP server software runs on one particular Mac in the office, which serves files and allows access to the printer as needed. The latest versions of AppleShare IP feature Web, FTP, and Internet e-mail servers as well.

With the appearance of Mac System 7.0 (Mac OS 7.0 in today's parlance), that client/server requirement changed somewhat. Although large offices and workgroups that require strong printing capabilities will often use AppleShare, a new level of networking, called *peer-to-peer* networking, was included in the System software. Also known as Personal File Sharing, this system allows Macs to talk to one another without using a server computer as a go-between. In essence, every Mac on the network is both a server and a client, enabling network users to log into one another's computers and share files in that way (see Figure 17-5).

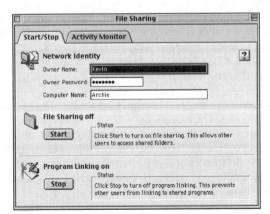

Figure 17-5: With only a few Macs in our office, I can use Personal File Sharing to share files with one or more of them.

Along with this capability came Printer Sharing, a technology that allows an individual Mac to share its direct-connected printer with the rest of the AppleTalk network. With Printer Sharing turned on, the shared printer simply shows up in the Chooser on any Macs that are part of the network.

Note

> The current AppleTalk implementation is actually called *AppleTalk Phase 2* because it extends the original AppleTalk specification conceived for the original Mac models. Through Phase 2, more Macs can be connected to a particular network at once, and data can be routed from one smaller network to another so that a number of different networks can communicate with one another.

AppleTalk addresses

AppleTalk is a *packet*-based networking protocol that sends data between computers in the form of individual electronic messages. Large files will be broken down into smaller packets, each of which has both an originating and destination address. The packets manage to find their way to a specific computer because each node (Mac, PC, laser printer, and so on) on an AppleTalk network is given an address, or a series of numbers that uniquely identify it on the network. These addresses are assigned dynamically, meaning no individual has to sit at a particular Mac and assign the addresses to each computer. Instead, Macs assign themselves the addresses when they first sign onto the network.

When a Mac becomes active on a network, it chooses a networking number and polls the other computers to find out if that number is already taken. If it's not, the Mac assigns itself the number; if it is, it starts the process of choosing and polling all over again.

The AppleTalk addressing scheme consists of three different numbers: a network number, a node number and a socket number. These three numbers uniquely identify not only each Mac, PC, and printer on a given AppleTalk network, but also each network. That makes it possible for the networks to communicate with one another, usually through special hardware called *routers*.

Because Mac designers and programmers rarely like to have users looking at raw numbers and bizarre addressing schemes, they came up with the concept of AppleTalk *zones*. A zone is really just a network with a particular network number. In general, these zones are separated by router hardware, which enables them to communicate with one another, but still maintain a certain separation. For example, say a systems administrator in a company was trying to decide how to implement a computer network. This would give everybody the ability to exchange e-mail messages and files. However, there might not be much point in having a situation where someone in the accounting department accidentally prints documents to the creative department's printers. So, the system administrator might want to assign the various departments to separate zones to keep users in one zone from seeing the printer servers of another zone in their Mac's Chooser (unless those users specifically choose that other zone). The system administrator could even restrict users from accessing a particular zone, or require a password for a new zone, just so that everything remains orderly.

Signing on

To activate AppleTalk services for your Mac, you first need to be properly configured on the network using either LocalTalk or Ethernet hardware and cabling. You then use the AppleTalk control panel (in Mac OS 7.6 and later) to choose which cabling will be used for your AppleTalk connection (see Figure 17-6). After choosing a topology, the Mac will check to make sure everything is in working order. It'll then turn on AppleTalk networking for you.

Note   Earlier versions of the Mac OS rely on a control panel called Network, which does basically the same thing as the AppleTalk control panel, but looks more like the Chooser (it has icons you click instead of a pull-down menu).

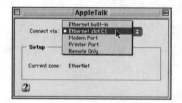

Figure 17-6: Use the AppleTalk control panel to choose your networking topology.

If you've already visited the AppleTalk control panel in the past, your main base of operations for AppleTalk networking will be the Chooser. In the Chooser, you can turn AppleTalk on and off, and you can click the AppleShare icon to see what file volumes are available to you (if you're using AppleShare client/server software) or what other Macs can be accessed (if you're on the Personal File Sharing peer-to-peer approach).

You can also choose the AppleTalk zone in which you'd like to look for servers and file volumes, and you can enter an IP address for accessing an AppleShare IP server over the Internet (see Figure 17-7).

Figure 17-7: The Chooser is at the heart of most Mac networking decisions.

To access a particular hard drive from the Chooser, start by clicking the AppleShare icon, and then double-clicking the volume or computer name that appears in the right-hand window. The Mac responds with a dialog box that asks you to enter your name and password. If you pass muster, the drives are mounted, and they appear on your desktop.

File sharing

What if you want to set up your computer as a server? This is especially important in a peer-to-peer network, where people want to access different folders and drives from different people's Macs. To do that, you need to turn on Personal File Sharing.

Head to the Control Panels entry in your Apple menu (or the Control Panels folder in your System Folder), and you'll find the File Sharing control panel. Open it to reveal settings for file sharing.

File sharing is pretty straightforward. You need to give the Mac an owner's name, a password, and a computer name—the name that will appear in the Choosers of other Macs on the network. Next, hit the Start button to start up file sharing. After a few moments, file sharing is active (see Figure 17-8).

Note   The File Sharing control panel also includes a control for Program Linking, through which you access certain types of programs and documents on another computer on the network. You might use this to get data from a word processing document on another computer to insert into a spreadsheet, for instance, or for remote shutdown of a computer. Programs have to be specifically designed to use Program Linking. If the programs are designed to use it, though, Program Linking needs to be turned on in the File Sharing control panel.

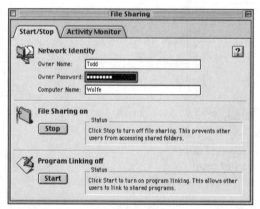

Figure 17-8: The File Sharing control panel gives you control over whether or not your hard drive is available over an AppleTalk network.

You still have to do a few more things to finish the setup, though. AppleTalk relies on the Sharing setting to set permission for who can access files and folders across the network. You need to head over to the folder that you want shared, highlight it, and then choose File ⇨ Sharing from the Finder's menu. In the Sharing Setup dialog box, you can set the permission from each individual user or group of users to whom you want to grant access to this drive. The various permission levels include the following:

✦ **Read access.** The user can copy the file to their own hard drive or load it in its associated application, but the user can't overwrite the file on your hard drive. He or she also can't save new files in the folder.

✦ **Write access.** The user can copy a file to your hard drive, but he or she can't examine the contents (the filenames) of the folder. Apple calls this a *drop box* because it allows users to drop off files for you to examine and use, and he or she can't see what anyone else has dropped in the directory.

✦ **Read and Write access.** In this case, the user has full use of the directory just as if they were using the same physical Mac to access it. He or she can view, load, and replace files on the drive.

✦ **None.** This option dictates that the user or group in question has no rights for viewing, write to, or overwriting the contents of a folder.

Of course, you'll need to set up the users and groups, which is accomplished through another control panel called, remarkably enough, Users and Groups. In this control panel, you create new users who are allowed access to your Mac, assigning them names and passwords. You can then attach them to groups of individuals who have the same permissions to access folders and files on your hard drive. You can limit a certain group to the Documents folder, for instance, or only give them access to one of your hard drives (if you have more than one). Figure 17-9 shows the Users and Groups control panel.

Figure 17-9: Create new users and groups in this control panel, and then head out in the Finder to set the permissions for folders and drives in the Finder.

AppleShare IP

If you plan to run a larger workgroup of Macs, AppleShare IP may be more your speed. This is the client/server solution to networking with Macs. It runs on top of the Mac OS, but turns a Mac into a complete workgroup server solution — basically taking over the computer (in most cases) and centralizing many of the networking issues and tasks that are usually distributed among many computers using a typical file sharing setup.

The most recent versions of AppleShare IP offer a number of different servers in one package, including the following:

✦ **File server.** Create a shared directory of files and folders where the entire network can store and retrieve data.

✦ **Printer server.** Manage one or more network printers for an entire workgroup, including queuing print jobs and assigning priorities.

✦ **Web server.** Built into AppleShare IP is the ability to serve Web pages over the Internet. The server features a special folder for Web pages, Common Gateway Interface (CGI) scripts for interactive pages, and tools for logging Web activity.

✦ **E-mail server.** This component enables access to both internal and Internet-based e-mail for the workgroup. If an Internet domain name has been assigned to the server computer, it can be used to create and manage unique Internet e-mail addresses, such as "bob@yourcompany.com", that can be assigned to each member of the workgroup.

✦ **FTP server.** Allows users on the Internet to upload and download files from your AppleShare server.

AppleShare IP offers other interesting features, such as network management tools for the network administrator to use that are also pretty simple to master because they're based on familiar concepts like the Users and Groups control panel. AppleShare IP also features an extensible architecture that allows the network to expand as your needs grow. You can add an armload of third-party options for everything from managing traffic on the network to logging Web hits and adding Windows 95 clients to your network.

Web

AppleShare IP is a complete set of protocols, add-ons, and applications for a Mac server that can't be done justice here. Visit www.apple.com/appleshareip for information on the server software, performance statistics, add-ons, third-party software, and other information.

Evangelista tip: Server misconceptions

Think you want to move up to an AppleShare network, but afraid you can't afford a big and fast enough server computer? Scott Barber of SOHO Macintosh News and Tips (www.mac-times.com/soho/) sees things a bit differently:

"One of the common misconceptions that IS managers face is that to have an office file server a monstrous 256MB Apple Workgroup G3 server with a 40GB RAID hard drive is the minimum. Fortunately, this is not the case; a computer needs only a 10MHz bus to transfer data at full 10BaseT Ethernet speeds, and file serving only requires one dedicated process.

"Given that 68000 and 68030 machines don't multitask well but perform single tasks with ease, assigning one of these machines the task of being a file server requires only adequate hard drive and memory. Often these slow machines can handle file serving for 10 to 20 networked machines just as quickly as a G3 server could, especially for the small business office. Other services, such as Web serving, e-mail, and peripheral servers and bridges, are just as simple and efficient. Creating servers for small LANs, or home offices, is as easy as opening your closet and powering up your old Mac II."

NetWare for Mac

Novell's NetWare remains the standard means for networking in many businesses and organizations around the world, especially those that have standardized on DOS and Windows network-server solutions. NetWare is actually an operating system all to itself, focused on serving files, serving applications, and handling printers. The Mac can hook up to a server running NetWare using a special client add-on (NetWare for Macintosh) offered for free by Novell from its Web site (www.novell.com).

The software makes it possible for Mac users to browse NetWare file volumes, copy data from them, write data to them, and print to Novell print queues. NetWare services are added to your Chooser, allowing you to choose NetWare volumes and print queues.

Interestingly, one aspect of the NetWare client tends to get around more than many others, even on home and small-office machines—the MacIPX control panel. In fact, if you're much of a gamer, you may not be surprised; MacIPX is a popular way to add networkability to a Mac game, especially if it's capable of interoperating with the Intel-compatible version of the same game. Because IPX is a popular networking standard in the DOS/Windows world, it's popular for head-to-head gaming, too.

Setting Up the Network

Designing a network can require a little forethought and planning to make sure everything goes smoothly; this is especially true if you'll be using either a LocalTalk or a 10Base2 Ethernet network. In these cases, where you're installing a network without a hub, it's important to take a close look at how your office (or home) is laid out, how far away from one another the computers are, and how much cable length you've taken up.

Note   Remember, LocalTalk limits you to about 32 devices (24 with PhoneNet cabling) and 1,800 feet of cable. 10Base2 can connect an unlimited number of devices (theoretically) but can only stretch about 600 feet without a hub or switch.

The other major consideration is speed. In fact, the whole LocalTalk versus Ethernet decision is a speed and convenience tradeoff. LocalTalk is less expensive to implement, works well with most Apple-brand printers, and enables you to network just about anything Mac-related for the cost of a transceiver and some phone cord. In some ways, it may be the perfect solution for a home business or small business.

But Ethernet is much, much faster, providing speed that could seriously affect your productivity if you're working with large files, printing graphical layouts, or otherwise taxing your network. And, if you have Ethernet built into your Macs already, the cost of the transceivers and cabling is only about double that of LocalTalk cabling for speeds that feel much closer to instantaneous. Of course, you'll have to buy Ethernet adapters for anything that doesn't already have some sort of Ethernet capability, or you'll have to invest in upgrade cards for almost any system if you're interested in taking advantage of 100 Mbps Ethernet connections.

So, the choice is yours. Just remember to consider everything you need to invest in LocalTalk (transceivers, cabling, and so on) before choosing it over Ethernet. You may have to make a bigger investment in Ethernet, but you'll only have to make it once.

Note   Most of the system software required to use built-in Ethernet solutions — such as LocalTalk, Ethernet (EtherTalk on older systems), and file sharing extensions — is installed when you run the Easy Setup option in your Mac OS installer program. But, for various reasons, you may not have all the software you need installed anymore. If you suspect you're missing some important networking extensions, check Chapter 27 for hints and help.

Installing a LocalTalk network

If you're going to be working with LocalTalk, it's easy enough to get started setting up the network. First, take a good look around the office, measuring the distances between each Mac so you can get the right number and lengths of cabling. Count to see how many transceivers you're going to need — one for each Mac. Don't forget to make sure you have transceivers for your printers, if they'll be used on the network. Also, you'll need LocalTalk terminators, one for each end of the chain of LocalTalk connectors.

So where do you get all this stuff? A number of companies have dedicated themselves to LocalTalk solutions, including those shown in Table 17-2.

Note   Want a quick and simple LocalTalk connection between two Macs? You won't get optimum performance with this setup, but you can transfer files by simply connecting a serial cable to each of the Macs' printer ports, and then turn on AppleTalk and file sharing. Now, log into one or the other of the computers, and transfer everything you need. It's a simple way to synchronize a PowerBook and a desktop — or transfer old data to a new Mac — but it only works for two machines at one time.

Table 17-2
LocalTalk Cabling and Solutions Manufacturers

Company	Products	Web site
Farallon	Transceivers, hubs, routers	www.farallon.com
Netspan	Hubs, routers	www.netspan.com
Transware	Routers, sharing solutions	www.transware.com
Webster Computer	Routers, hubs	www.webstercc.com
Sonic Systems	Routers, bridges	www.sonicsys.com
Dayna Communcations	Transceivers, hubs, bridges	www.dayna.com

Basic installation

Here's how to install a LocalTalk transceiver and cabling on a Mac:

1. Shut down the Mac and ground yourself.

2. Plug the transceiver into the printer port.

3. Plug the LocalTalk or PhoneNet cabling into one of the transceiver ports (it doesn't matter which).

4. If this is the end of the network, plug a terminator into the other port. If the network continues on, plug the next length of LocalTalk or PhoneNet cabling into the transceiver.

5. Turn the Mac back on.

Do this for the rest of your network, making sure you're always continuing a chain of wiring from Mac to Mac and not doubling back or leaving any Macs out the loop. (I have seen both happen, even in carefully planned networks.) Next, you're ready to set up each Mac on the network.

To set up the software for network access in Mac OS 7.6 and above, follow these steps:

1. Open the AppleTalk control panel.

2. If AppleTalk isn't already turned on (in the Chooser), the Mac will ask you if you want it turned on. Choose OK.

3. In the AppleTalk control panel, choose Printer Port (assuming that's the port you used) from the Connect via: menu.

4. Close the control panel.

You should be up and running on the network. If you have other Macs connected (and they have file sharing turned on), you can open the Chooser and click the AppleShare icon to see if they show up. If they do, you've successfully connected.

Note   If you're using a Mac OS version before 7.6, you'll find the choice for LocalTalk in the Network control panel. You may need to restart your Mac for the change in network cabling to take effect. You may also need to manually turn on AppleTalk in the Chooser.

LocalTalk hubs

Although they're not as popular or easy to find as Ethernet hubs, LocalTalk hubs can be useful for networks that require a lot of distance between Macs, or any LocalTalk network where you're sick of cables coming loose and network services becoming unavailable to your workgroup. A LocalTalk hub acts as a go-between for each Mac, centralizing control of the network in one unit with diagnostic capabilities and tools to help you manage individual connections. Using a star configuration, this cuts out the possibility that any single dropped connection or bad wire could bring down the rest of the network.

This does two things: First, it sets you up for managing larger LocalTalk networks more efficiently so you can find breaks in the system and add new Macs to the network quickly and easily. The hub will also manage traffic for you more efficiently, gathering data packets and sending them to the right Mac, instead of sending them down a long cable and through many connections before the packets find the right Mac. It also cuts down on collisions and slowdowns caused by data meeting in the middle and being rerouted by each Mac.

If you're managing a large number of LocalTalk-networked computers, you don't have to hook them all up to a hub; you can use a hub to centralize connections for smaller networks of 10 to 15 Macs. That way the router can manage traffic between the different daisy-chained networks. This makes a large LocalTalk network work well without requiring expensive hubs that connect every single Mac. It also cuts down on the number of Macs that can be affected by a cabling problem.

LocalTalk bridges

So what happens if you're heavily invested in LocalTalk transceivers and connectors, but you need access to an Ethernet network, either for your newer Mac or to access the Internet? In that case, you need a LocalTalk bridge — a hardware or software solution that connects Ethernet and LocalTalk. Because both types of network architectures can handle AppleTalk, you've already got that part covered. Now you just need to translate LocalTalk into Ethernet.

Using hardware, you just hook your last LocalTalk connection into the bridge and do the same with your Ethernet connection. (If you're using an Ethernet hub, you just connect an Ethernet cable between the hub and the bridge as if the bridge were another Mac.) Some of these bridges can handle three or more LocalTalk networks, connecting them all to an Ethernet network (providing TCP/IP services, for instance, if your office building is wired for Internet access).

Other bridges are small devices, perhaps designed to accept one LocalTalk connection on one side and an Ethernet connection on the other side. Don't let this simplicity fool you, though. The microBridge from Sonic Systems, for instance, allows a 12-node LocalTalk network to connect to an Ethernet network using the tiny device (see Figure 17-10). The Tribestar IP from Zoom Telephonics, Inc. (www.zoomtel.com/) is an interesting hybrid; it's actually a switching hub between LocalTalk and Ethernet, essentially bridging the networks by turning up to eight LocalTalk connections into a virtual Ethernet connection. With smart packet switching, it can increase the speeds of the LocalTalk to Ethernet connection.

You'll also find bridges on the user market that were manufactured by Adaptec (www.adaptec.com) and Cayman Systems (www.cayman.com), among other companies.

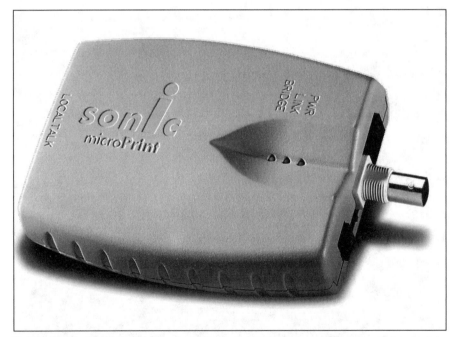

Figure 17-10: The microBridge from Sonic Systems (www.sonicsys.com) connects a small LocalTalk workgroup — or a collection of eMate computers — to an Ethernet network.

The last type of bridge is implemented completely in software. For some time Apple has offered the Apple LocalTalk Bridge, through which a single Macintosh (even an aging classic Mac or Mac II) can act as a bridge between Ethernet and LocalTalk, accepting connections from both and translated between the two. The Apple LaserWriter Bridge also enables LocalTalk to Ethernet connections, but only for LaserWriter printers. (The Apple Internet Router, part of the Apple Internet Gateway package, can bridge Ethernet and LocalTalk.) Other packages from manufacturers such as Sonic Systems and Vicom Technology (www.vicomtech.com) do much the same thing (see Figure 17-11).

Figure 17-11: Bridge software, also from Sonic Systems, allows a Mac to act as a LocalTalk-to-Ethernet bridge.

Note

Don't let the terminology fool you. Remember that a router, in some cases, can act as a more intelligent bridge. Routers are designed to move data packets to a new network, but they can also be used to move those data packets to a new network architecture, too.

Installing an Ethernet network

With Ethernet, things can be a bit more complex. First, you'll need to decide what type of cabling you're going to use: 10Base2 (coax) or 10BaseT (twisted-pair). Next, you'll need to find out what Ethernet capabilities your Macs have, what capabilities need to be added, and what cable lengths you need for the Ethernet cabling. If you're using 10Base2, you'll need to focus on the daisy-chain aspects of networking—how close are the computers, what's the logical order, and so on. With 10BaseT, you'll need to get a hub.

Note

There is one exception to the rule that 10BaseT cabling needs a hub: Etherwave transceivers from Farallon (www.farallon.com). These transceivers attach to the AAUI Ethernet port and use 10BaseT wiring, but they each have two ports that enable you to daisy-chain the connections between Macs instead of using a central hub. They're more expensive than standard transceivers, because they act as mini-repeaters that boost a twisted-pair signal well enough for it to work without a hub.

If you're using built-in Ethernet that includes a 10BaseT connector, or you're using an Ethernet add-on card that uses either 10Base2 or 10Base2, all you need to do is connect the wiring properly:

✦ With a 10BaseT connection you simply plug the RJ45 plug into the transceiver, card, or built-in 10BaseT port.

✦ For a 10Base2 connection, you'll need to push the BNC connector onto one of the two posts extending from the transceiver or card. Once the connector is fitted over the post, twist it clockwise to lock it onto the connection. If this is the end of the network, attach a BNC terminator to the other post. If the network continues on, connect another length of cable to the other post.

Many Macs with built-in Ethernet require a transceiver to connect them to a network (Apple calls the port that accepts a transceiver the AAUI port). Transceivers are available for both coax and twisted-pair cabling. With the right transceiver in hand, you can add that Mac to the network:

1. Shut down the Mac and electrically ground yourself.

2. Attach the transceiver to the AAUI port. To do this, line the transceiver's AAUI adapter up with the port, and then squeeze the sides. Push the adapter onto the port and release the sides to lock it into place.

3. Attach the cabling to the transceiver as discussed above.

4. Restart your Mac.

If you're ready to set this Mac up on the network (if it's plugged into the 10BaseT hub or your 10Base2 network is completely set up with terminators on either end), you can start up AppleTalk:

1. Open the AppleTalk control panel.

2. If AppleTalk isn't already turned on (in the Chooser), the Mac will ask you if you want it turned on. Choose OK.

3. In the AppleTalk control panel, choose Ethernet from the Connect via: menu.

4. Close the control panel.

You may have an entry that's slightly different from "Ethernet" such as "Ethernet (C1)" or something similar, especially if you've installed an Ethernet card or your Mac came preconfigured with an Ethernet card. In that case, choose that entry. (If you have two entries, you may have both built-in Ethernet and an Ethernet card. Choose the one you've attached to the network.)

Note

If you're using a Mac OS version before 7.6, you'll find the choice for Ethernet or EtherTalk in the Network control panel. You may need to restart your Mac for the change in network cabling to take effect. You may also need to manually turn on AppleTalk in the Chooser.

Expert tip: Don't put a filing cabinet on your cabling

IS professional Jim Cox from Vancouver, BC, Canada used a little networking troubleshooting savvy to track down a rather unique problem with a Macintosh network. Although you may not have the same exact experience, hopefully there's something to learn in here:

"A few years ago, I was the IS director of what the editor of *Health Care Magazine* called 'the only all-Mac hospital on the face of the planet, maybe in the universe.' It was an old building, and we were constructing a new one so it was not worth installing the network inside the walls. We just used surface mount outlet boxes and built AppleTalk backbones by running a cable from box to box and office to office along the base of the wall. A rearrangement of one secretary's office resulted in the wall box being moved and about 10 feet of slack in the cable. The maintenance guys just coiled up the cable and stuffed it behind her filing cabinet.

(continued)

(continued)

"Some months later, I started getting complaints from users that their Macs would sometimes drop off the network for a few seconds up to several minutes. Because the fault was so intermittent, we were never able to track it down. Then one day, we got a rash of complaints. We started checking and discovered that everyone upstream from that secretary was okay and everyone downstream was dead. When we went to her office we found her with her filing cabinet open doing a major reorganization. As we were tracing the wiring, she closed the drawer and a user immediately reported that she was back online. We discovered that every time we opened the drawer the network died and when we closed it the network sprang to life again. Magic?

"What had happened was that over the months, the filing cabinet had been moved a bit and was now resting on top of the network cable. It had apparently broken a wire inside the cable. If the drawer was closed, the pressure caused the wire ends to connect. With it open, they would disconnect. We removed the cable from under the file cabinet, spliced out the excess and the network ran on blissfully until the building was retired.

"The moral of the story: Take care of your cables."

Installing the hub

With most Ethernet hubs, there really isn't much to the installation process. In most cases, you can simply plug the hub into the wall, and then start using the ports on the front to attach 10BaseT connections coming from your Macs. If you're connecting hubs to one another (to connect to other Ethernet networks or to your organization's Internet connection), you can use the uplink port on the hub, if you see one. Otherwise, any of the ports should work fine.

Ethernet switches work pretty much the same way. Plug them in, turn them on, and connect the Ethernet cables to them. Some of the popular small office switches, however, may feature different ports for different tasks — for example, an uplink port reserved for connecting to another hub or switch and fast Ethernet ports for 100 Mbps connections (see Figure 17-12).

With wiring connected to the ports, you should begin to see activity. Each port will often have its own LEDs; one might tell you that a successful connection is in place, whereas another tells you specifically when it's sending packets. You may also have indicators that show wiring errors, collisions, and slowdowns on the network.

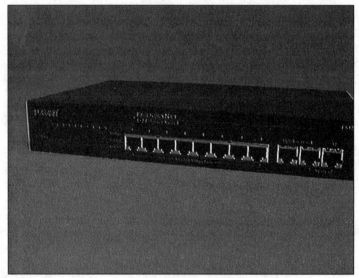

Figure 17-12: The Asante FriendlyNet switch enables my network nodes to access the hub at 10 Mbps each, while the switch itself is accessing the building's Internet router at 100 Mbps (www.asante.com).

Adding a PC to the network

I've seen figures that state as many as 80 percent of networked computers in the world (UNIX, Mac, PC, workstations, minicomputers, mainframes) are using Ethernet. That's a pretty pervasive standard, as well as being a convenient one. It means that accessing an Intel-compatible PC over a typical Mac-oriented Ethernet network is nothing more than a matter of software. And, often enough, software problems are easy to overcome.

In fact, hubs, routers, and switches usually don't care what sort of computer you're running. In many cases, they don't care what sort of data you're using (some do — especially routers). So, it's easy enough to take a PC and hook it up to your Ethernet hub, and then add the right software to enable it to access the network.

The software you need adds AppleTalk services to a Windows or Windows 95 PC — one such program is called COPStalk from COPS, Inc. (www.copstalk.com). This software allows a PC to connect to an AppleShare server or computer with AppleTalk Personal File Sharing. The drives and printers available on an AppleTalk network are then made available to the Windows machine through the File Manager or Windows Explorer.

COPS, Inc., also offers LocalTalk cards for PCs, which enable the PC to communicate with an Apple LocalTalk network or connect directly to LocalTalk printers. The cards can also be used by Novell network or Windows NT server computers to provide services to Mac LocalTalk networks.

PC MACLAN from Miramar Systems (www.miramarsys.com) offers a similar product that provides bidirectional support for Windows/Mac OS networking. The software gives AppleTalk services to Windows that work in both directions; Macs see the Windows machine as part of the AppleTalk network, just as the Windows machine can see the Mac networking. It actually installs on the Windows machine, giving it a newly found ability to access AppleTalk networks. Nothing has to change on your Mac machines to get them to work with the Intel-compatible PC.

Hooking a Mac into a PC network

Although MACLAN and COPStalk both offer solutions that hook PCs up to Mac networks, you'll need a different program to get your Mac to act as a node on a Windows 95 peer-to-peer network. Called DAVE (from Thursby Software Systems, www.thursby.com), this program runs on the Mac and gives it Windows-like networking services and protocols. As such, it ends up working very much like PC MACLAN, except it runs on the Mac, giving it Windows networking..

DAVE works by encapsulating NetBIOS commands (a typical PC networking protocol) inside TCP/IP packets so that the Mac can read and write to PC file services. The Mac ends up looking exactly like a PC to the Windows network, and can be centrally managed by Windows-based networking administration software. This software also makes it simple to add the DAVE-enhanced Mac to Windows peer-to-peer setups in smaller networks.

If you have a Novell-based client/server network of PCs, you can install Novell NetWare for Macintosh. This client software gives you access to a Novell NetWare network served on an Intel-compatible PC.

The last choice is to install Microsoft's Macintosh Services for Windows NT. If your company or organization is using Windows NT as a server, the Mac can be integrated with that server so that file and printer services appear in the Chooser. Windows NT can also be used as an Internet router (in software) to route TCP/IP over an AppleTalk network.

Accessing the network remotely

One other interesting capability is offered by some Apple networking tools. Apple Remote Access, a software package from Apple, allows Macs to log into an AppleTalk network via modem or over the Internet. This basically creates the same network that would be available over Ethernet or LocalTalk, but uses a phone line or TCP/IP connection instead.

Apple Remote Access requires two components: the Apple Remote Access server and the Apple Remote Access client. The client is installed with Mac OS 7.6 or above (in most cases — you can install it manually from the System CD if necessary) and runs on the PowerBook or other Mac that you're going to use from a remote location. The server software has to be purchased from Apple directly or from an Apple retailer, and is installed on a server computer that's part of the physical AppleTalk network. The server also needs a modem attached for receiving the incoming call from the client computer.

Apple offers two versions of the ARA server product:

✦ **Apple Remote Access Personal server** is reasonably inexpensive and provides one single connection to an AppleTalk network via modem or Internet.

✦ **Apple Remote Access Multiport server** enables up to 16 dial-up connections to access a local area network at a time.

With the server software installed and ready to answer a particular modem, you can set up the client software on your remote computer through the Remote Access Setup control panel, telling it how to dial out, what number to use, and what port the modem is attached to. (In version 3.0 of the client and above, you can also choose to use a PPP connection to access the remote AppleTalk network via the Internet.) Figure 17-13 shows the Remote Access Setup control panel.

Figure 17-13: Use the Remote Access client to dial in over phone lines to an AppleTalk network.

Now, to access the server, you load the Remote Access Client, a program you'll likely find on your hard drive in a folder called Remote Access Client. Double-click the client to start it up, and then create a profile for the network you're going to access by entering your user name, password, and the phone number for the remote computer. When you're ready to dial out, click the Connect button. If all goes well, you'll connect to the remote server.

Depending on which server you've used (and whether the remote computer is on an AppleTalk network with other servers), you'll have access to the files on the remote computer as if you logged into it over a regular AppleTalk network. If you'll also need to access other machines on the network, head back to the Chooser and choose the AppleTalk icon. On the right-hand side of the Chooser window, any servers on the remote network should be visible, and you can now log in to any of them.

Peripheral sharing

You can use some third-party add-ons to share other items over a printer besides printers and files, including scanners, modems, and pretty much any device that's connected to a port on one of the host Macs. One of the main purveyors of such solutions is Stalker Software (www.stalker.com/), a company well-known for its Communigate server solutions for Web, e-mail, and other LAN-to-Internet pursuits.

For peripheral sharing, Stalker offers several specific solutions:

✦ **LineShare.** This serial port sharing software makes all your serial devices (modems and printers) available over the network. Through a single control panel your Mac can be both a server and a client, making it simple for other Macs to use peripherals connected to your Mac.

✦ **ScanShare and SCSIShare.** This software makes local scanners available to the rest of your network. Scanshare works with Apple-specific scanners, and SCSIShare works with other scanners.

Internet and Intranets

Although AppleTalk is easily the most prevalent networking protocol on Macs, TCP/IP has certainly given AppleTalk a run for its money in recent years. The TCP/IP protocol has a few things going for it, not the least of which is that the Internet is based on it. UNIX-based networking is based on TCP/IP, too, and as the UNIX underpinnings of OpenStep slowly make their way into the next-generation Mac OS (perhaps through the Mac OS X [ten] edition — the Mac OS version that melds Mac OS 8.x and the new Apple OS code-named "Rhapsody"), TCP/IP will become even more important down the road.

TCP/IP services have been available to Macs for a long time, however, first offering built-in access to the Internet with Mac OS 7.5, then called "System 7.5". (It was actually available before, but not as part of the OS.) The MacTCP control panel used at that time is now called *classic networking* because it wasn't based on Open Transport.

These days the MacTCP control panel has been replaced with the TCP/IP control panel, suggesting the new priority level placed on TCP/IP; it's now an integral part of the Mac OS. As such, it's probably important for many Mac networks out there, too.

With TCP/IP and a LAN, you can do one of two things. The first is to offer Internet access to everyone on the network. Even reasonably inexpensive options abound for doing this, including options you might want to consider for a small office or offices in your home.

The other thing you can do is use TCP/IP internally to build an *intranet*, a closed network that uses TCP/IP and Internet-type tools (such as Web servers) to communicate company or organizational information to employees and other participants. An intranet is a great way to share ideas between larger workgroups of people, including features such as chat rooms, Web pages, documents for downloading (HR forms, for instance), and other goodies.

Internet access

If you've got a single Mac, you'll likely opt for a modem, ISDN, ADSL, or cable solution like those discussed back in Chapter 16. But for a LAN, you'll find very quickly that you can run into problems with a system like this. For one, you may need to have dozens of dial-up accounts and modems as well as install extra phone lines if everyone is expected to get on the Internet in this way.

At some point, the better plan is to simply add TCP/IP services to your LAN. This can be accomplished in a number of ways. They pretty much all rely on an Internet router solution, but the router can take on many shapes and sizes.

Building-level Internet

Here is a great example of how easy adding Internet services can sometimes be. In the basement of the building where I rent my office space, an Internet Service Provider (ISP) has installed a router that's designed to bring T-1 (high-speed fiber optic) access into the building through a line that's running down the street from an MCI T-3 (even higher-speed fiber optic) backbone connection about three blocks away. That ISP rents me as many IP addresses as I need to get my computers on the Internet. I don't need too many, so it ends up being a good deal.

I then hook my Ethernet switch up to the building's Ethernet network, input the IP address and the ISP's router address into my TCP/IP control panel, and tell the AppleTalk control panel that I want to use Ethernet for networking. Now my Macs are networked through the switch, using AppleTalk, at the same time that they all have access to the building's Ethernet network. Using individual IP addresses, each of the computers can directly access the Internet, thanks to the router provided by the ISP.

Two problems are immediately apparent in this setup, both dealing with security. Because each of my Macs is available on the Internet, it's possible for others to link directly to my machines and, if they are able, log in using AppleTalk (over TCP/IP, presumably using AppleTalk Remote Access). They could also conceivably log into the Macs using TCP/IP, but because the Mac isn't providing any particular file services to TCP/IP, the infiltrator won't get much further than being able to tell that the Mac is active on the Internet.

Any Macs (or AppleTalk-enabled Windows PCs) could conceivably access your network if they're also wired into the building. Without the proper security measures, they may easily be able to access your data. In my building, the top floor houses a local weekly newspaper that uses Macintoshes for much of their production work. The first day I set up my network for Internet access using the building's Ethernet connections, I was able to log directly into that paper's server and had access to nearly everything they'd stored there. (I've since consulted with them to fix this oversight.)

Otherwise, this is the easy way to add Internet to a Mac-based LAN. With IPs assigned and TCP/IP control panels active and properly filled in, my entire office surfs and sends mail at a gleeful fraction of 1.5 Mbps. The same could easily be done for a larger business or organization that can afford a dedicated T-1 connection for its own buildings. Get somebody to install a router for your LAN, and you'll have high-speed Internet available to all your Macs.

Note   Some security risks result from putting your Mac on the Internet or a building-wide network, including incorrectly setting the privileges for file sharing and Web sharing. Setting up file sharing and Sharing privileges is discussed in more depth in Chapter 27.

Internet gateways

A Macintosh, UNIX machine, or Windows NT server can often act as an Internet router of its own, using two Ethernet connections to accept a T1 connection on one end and use the other card to wire it to a network of Macs (or other computers). Although it often makes sense to use a hardware router designed to do the same thing, employing a computer can make sense in some circumstances, too.

Note   The combination of hardware and software to translate and route network data is often called a *gateway*, perhaps to differentiate the concept from hardware *routers*, which are physical boxes that sit between networks, moving packets back and forth.

One such software router is the Apple IP Gateway, a product that enables LocalTalk networks to access Internet resources. Running on a server that's attached to Ethernet and LocalTalk, the Gateway acts in conjunction with the Apple Internet Router to route TCP/IP protocol packets from the incoming Ethernet connection to the computers on the LocalTalk network.

Another interesting solution is the Vicom Internet Gateway (www.vicomtech.com), a software gateway that gives three, five, or an unlimited number of Macs on your network Internet access through a single Internet account connection. The Vicom Internet Gateway runs on a Mac that has a connection to an ISDN modem or a cable-modem connection, or is connected to a physical Internet router. The Gateway then acts as a firewall, an access shield, and a transparent gateway for Macs connected to it that access Internet resources.

Note

A similar gateway product, IPNetRouter, was in alpha testing during the writing of this book. Created by Sustainable Softworks (www.sustworks.com), it promises to be a low-cost solution to routing IP data from dial-up and ISDN accounts to Macs attached via network cabling. It uses a technology called IP Masquerading to offer multiple Macs the opportunity to use a single IP account.

Other software routers tend to be part of larger non-Macintosh server bundles designed to offer Internet service to AppleTalk-based networks. Windows NT, for instance, provides AppleTalk IP services that will route TCP/IP packets from the server to the AppleTalk network, when necessary. Although Ethernet-based Macs are generally capable of dealing with TCP/IP without help, the Windows NT gateway makes the process more efficient by routing TCP/IP packets addressed specifically to those Macs.

How do you access the Internet using one account and stay secure?

It may seem like two different problems, but it really isn't. Here's a situation typical of school networks, although you may feel the same way about your small-business network: You'd like to use a single Internet account to access the Internet, but you want the whole network to have access. You'd also like to keep your data secure, and you'd like to filter the sites that your users see. Can it be done?

Products like the Vicom Internet Gateway are designed to do just that. They offer access to a single account for multiple Macs using something called a Dynamic Host Configuration Protocol (DHCP) server. This allows a number of Macs to use internal IP addresses to communicate amongst themselves, but use a single external IP for transactions on the Internet. That's the first thing to look for.

The second thing you'll need is *firewall* support. This can be done through a software gateway or a hardware firewall router. In essence, a firewall lets TCP/IP data get out from your network, but it will only allow certain data back in. That, in theory, keeps people from crawling around in your computers. Firewalls can also guard against other sorts of Internet hacking, such as denial-of-service attacks. (That's when a hacker tries to catch your Web server, mail server, or other Internet server in an endless loop of meaningless data, making it impossible for the server to handle normal data.)

(continued)

(continued)

The third thing to look for is filtering technology. You can use gateway software that gives you control over the domains, types of search queries and other information regarding the sites visited by your users to keep a list of sites or keywords that should be disallowed in searches or attempts to link to the sites. This keeps employees from surfing aimlessly and kids from seeing things they shouldn't—at least, that's the theory.

SOHO routers

If you're setting up Internet access for a multinational corporation, you'll probably need a resource other than this book to set up a router for your T-1 or T-3 connections. That's inter-networking, after all, which is pretty much platform independent. You'll need to set up an industrial-strength router for the task and begin the process of configuring it.

For SOHO (small office, home office) networks, however, routers exist that make more sense. Specifically designed to send TCP/IP packets across your AppleTalk network, these routers usually hook up to the Internet over phone, ISDN, or other high-speed lines, and then route the TCP/IP data to your LAN (see Figure 17-14).

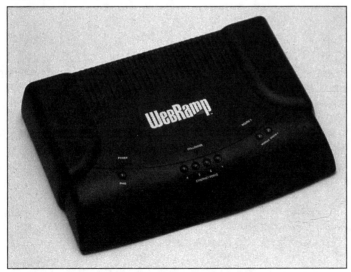

Figure 17-14: The WebRamp M3t Internet router (www.webramp.com) bonds two phone connections together to offer higher-speed Internet access to your small LAN. (Photo courtesy Ramp Networks.)

Some of these routers connect to two or more dial-up PPP Internet accounts, and then use both together to offer access to the entire office LAN. Others use ISDN, ADSL or similar technologies, but share that bandwidth with every machine attached over networking cable to the router. Most of these products also feature DHCP support, enabling multiple internal IPs to be assigned while using only one (or two) Internet accounts and IPs for accessing the outside world.

Table 17-3 includes Mac-friendly companies that offer Internet routers for home or small businesses.

Table 17-3
Internet router manufacturers

Company	Connection Technology	Web Site
Sonic Systems	ISDN, modem, leased line	www.sonicsys.com
Netopia	ISDN, T-1, leased line	www.netopia.com
Ramp Networks	ISDN, modem	www.webramp.com
One World Systems	Modem	www.oneworldsystems.com
Sustainable Softworks	ISDN, modem (software only)	www.sustworks.com

Summary

✦ Macs support three basic networking protocols and three basic networking cabling specifications, although two of each are more common. You'll find both AppleTalk and TCP/IP widely used on Mac networks, although clients exist for the Novell NetWare standard IPX protocol. You'll also find Macs connected to each other using LocalTalk and Ethernet cabling, although the IBM standard, Token Ring, was in vogue for a while.

✦ To set up a Mac network, you'll need to decide first on the network technology you're going to use — LocalTalk or Ethernet — and then you'll have to decide on the type of wiring. LocalTalk networks can use either LocalTalk or PhoneNet cabling; Ethernet networks use 10Base2 or 10BaseT. With those decisions out of the way, you'll need to access your Macs' capabilities for networking, add new cards if necessary, and then wire the Macs all together. Finally, configure AppleTalk and start networking.

✦ If you want to add Intel-compatible PCs to your network, you'll need to use compatible cabling and software. Adding Ethernet to PCs is easy, because it's the same technology PCs use to network to each other. Adding LocalTalk is a bit tougher, but not impossible. After the Macs and PCs are wired together, you add the special software drives to enable PCs to communicate in AppleTalk or Macs to communicate in PC networking protocols — whichever seems more appropriate.

✦ Apple has also come up with some interesting ways to access your Mac — or a whole AppleTalk network — from a remote location. Using Apple Remote Access, you can dial in to your Mac and access anything on its hard drive or on the AppleTalk network. All you need is a modem and software.

✦ If you've got a network up and running, you'd probably like to add Internet access to the network. That's easy to do, too, with a number of different options. If you have accounts for everybody, you can attach yourself directly to the Internet using a router or a direct Ethernet hookup to your ISP. If you'd like to use one account for many different users, you'll need gateway software.

✦ With the right hardware, you can even hook up a small business or home network to the Internet. All you need is an Internet router and one or two Internet accounts. The special router will tie together two different modem connections, a single high-bandwidth ISDN, or cable connection, giving everyone reasonable speed for their Internet connection over your network.

✦   ✦   ✦

Multimedia and Gaming

◆   ◆   ◆   ◆

In This Chapter

3D technologies

3D accelerator cards

Installing an
accelerator card

Joysticks and
controllers

◆   ◆   ◆   ◆

I t could easily be argued that the topics of gaming and
professional multimedia production don't belong together.
At one end of the spectrum you have artists and animators
spending thousands of dollars on equipment that can help
them render 3D objects, get those objects moving around the
screen, and output them to film, video, or CD-ROM. At the
other end are people clambering into the computer store to
plop down $50 for the latest shoot-'em-up. Funny thing is, both
require powerful computers and attention to the same
technology.

On the Macintosh, those gaming and multimedia capabilities
have a lot to do with a technology I've already discussed at
some length in other chapters — QuickDraw. Specifically,
QuickDraw 3D. To get 3D objects rendering and moving
quickly around the screen, you can accelerate the
programming interfaces provided by Apple for creating these
objects — routines found in the technologies that draw to the
screen, QuickDraw and QuickDraw 3D.

There are other important technologies, too: QuickTime,
QuickTime VR (for creating 3D virtual reality panoramas), and
other programming helpers Apple has written called Game
Sprockets. These programmer's shortcuts, in turn, have
brought about some other hardware to look into — game
controllers. From humble beginnings as add-ons for the
computer mouse, the joysticks, flight controllers, and steering
wheels for Mac gaming — or other simulations — have come a
long way.

Accelerating 3D

Think for a moment about the dimensions displayed on a computer monitor. Obviously, because there's no *actual* depth to the screen (it's flat), anything you're seeing on screen is in two dimensions (width and height), just as objects are two dimensional in a canvas painting. Of course, the images can be arranged in such a way as to suggest that they have depth, whether you're playing a first-person shooter game or you're looking at a classic acrylic of a French country road. The perspective created can give you a sense of depth that suggests three dimensions.

But rendering this sort of perspective on a computer screen can give mere mortals fits of anxiety. QuickDraw, the technology responsible for drawing a Mac's screen, just wants to worry about the colors and brightness of the various pixels that make up the bitmapped screen image. QuickDraw doesn't really care what those pixels represent, and it doesn't want to worry about that sort of thing. So, although some rules and limitations for graphics are built-in, just exactly what is displayed on your screen is completely up to the programmer.

Over the years, Apple has written software routines for programmers that make up the Macintosh Toolbox and associated technologies. One of the things they've focused on are tools that help programmers draw windows, buttons, icons, and text on the screen—all the sorts of things you often expect to see in a Mac program. With these tools, programmers don't have to write such detailed instructions for their programs as the following: "Start at the pixel 2,10 and draw a line 100 pixels down, take a right turn and draw the line 200 pixels long, and then draw the line up and to the left. In the middle, color it gray, put scroll bars at the bottom and to the right, and put a close box at the top left." Programmers can instead focus on creating the unique parts of the program by calling routines that are more like this: "Draw a standard window on the screen and position it in the standard place for a new document."

QuickDraw 3D

Once Apple got all those basic routines out of the way (of course, those things are constantly being upgraded with newer versions of QuickDraw and new routines like the Appearance Manager), Apple's programmers turned their attention to more complex routines, such as those that make up QuickDraw 3D. QuickDraw 3D's routines make it much, much easier for programmers to incorporate 3D graphics and rendering capabilities into their programs (see Figure 18-1).

Figure 18-1: QuickDraw 3D makes it possible for a fairly simple program to display and manipulate basic objects that appear to be three dimensional.

QuickDraw 3D encompasses several components — the programmer's application programming interfaces (APIs), a special file format called 3-D MetaFile (3DMF), and a rendering engine, called Render Acceleration Virtual Engine (RAVE). These all go together to make QuickDraw 3D the unique entity that it is, offering an entire layer of 3D capabilities to the Mac OS.

QuickDraw 3D offers some interesting compatibility statistics: It only runs on PowerPC-based Macintosh computers and requires at minimum a Pentium in its Windows incarnation. The Mac version is also optimized for either 16-bit or 32-bit color depths, meaning it actually runs faster with your monitor set to use thousands of colors instead of 256 colors, according to Apple. If you're working with QuickDraw 3D, then, you'd be advised to set your monitor accordingly (see Chapter 12 for more on setting color depths).

APIs and file format

You've already seen that the QuickDraw 3D APIs are simple programming routines that applications can use to more easily add 3D capabilities to their programs.

These APIs include the ability to create various polygons quickly, shape and bend them in different ways, and render them at certain levels of shading or detail, depending on how quickly a task needs to be done. (The more complexly rendered an object is, the better and more realistic it looks. The better it looks, the longer it took to render it.) These APIs are also uniquely extensible, enabling a program, for instance, to add a different type of polygon that the QuickDraw 3D people hadn't added to the base code. That polygon definition is then available for use with any program that implements QuickDraw 3D.

Somewhat separate from this is the 3DMF format, a file format that's a lot like the other types of Mac files I've mentioned (for example, word processing, sound, movies). The 3DMF file format completely defines a 3D object, including the geometry of the object's structure, the way the shape is rendered, and other multimedia elements that might be related to it, such as sounds. This enables programs to share files that include all of this information, as opposed to some of the other file formats in the 3D world, such as the XDF format. XDF is widely supported for transferring files between different 3D applications, but it includes no information on *how* a particular object is rendered.

3DMF has also been tapped to be the basis for the Virtual Reality Modeling Language (VRML) 2.0 binary file format. VRML is the standard for 3D worlds on the Internet, and Apple's 3DMF will be the building block for VRML's binary file format. (VRML can be described using either a text file of commands that humans can read and understand or a binary file to be read by VRML applications only.)

QuickDraw 3D RAVE

Although QuickDraw 3D is certainly a leap forward for standardizing 3D on the Mac platform (it also works with Windows, where QuickDraw 3D code sits on top of Microsoft's Direct3D technology), it's more a standard for programmers and software developers than users. But both can benefit from knowing a little something about QuickDraw 3D RAVE.

Called an acceleration virtual engine, RAVE does something very interesting as a plug-in to the Mac OS: It manages the acceleration of drawing functions for 3D applications. In other words, a programmer can write an application using QuickDraw 3D, which sits on top of the QuickDraw 3D RAVE layer. When the application needs something drawn on the screen, the RAVE layer will intercept the command and manage it most efficiently — using the processor, a plug-in accelerator card, or software to draw the image.

This allows for two things: First, programmers can write their own drawing engines (or driver software) that meet certain minimum requirements imposed by the RAVE specifications, in essence enabling programmers to draw more quickly to the screen or support special capabilities. RAVE also gives programmers a certain level of distance from the Mac's hardware, enabling them to write to QuickDraw 3D or another 3D API, including the popular OpenGL standard developed by Silicon Graphics, and used on other UNIX-based, and Windows-based machines.

As mentioned, this allows those programs to work with QuickDraw 3D RAVE accelerator cards, even if the programs weren't originally written to work with the specific card. Instead of requiring special support for each individual accelerator card, the RAVE layer handles all that for the programmer.

RAVE, then, is a popular way to incorporate accelerated 3D into a variety of 3D pursuits on Macs. If you're a professional 3D artist, you might be using a RAVE-based accelerator card to support your complex rendering tasks, even for jobs like creating digital images for incorporation into motion pictures. If you're a multimedia gamer, you might be using RAVE, too, to accelerate the more basic, but breakneck, 3D rendering that's required for a good action game.

Voodoo graphics

The antithesis of RAVE acceleration is Voodoo acceleration, named for the Voodoo 3D chipset created by 3Dfx, Inc (www.3dfx.com/). To work with Voodoo, game programmers have to add commands from 3Dfx's Glide API to their games. This enables the program to speak directly to an accelerator card that's designed to boost the speed in typical 3D gaming functions. Everything that RAVE stands against — proprietary design, board-specific drivers for applications — is what the Voodoo approach is all about. The result: Amazingly fast and crisp 3D for gaming.

Note

You'll sometimes see Voodoo, 3Dfx, or Glide listed as the type of acceleration sup-ported by a particular game — these all refer to the same thing (for practical pur-poses). To play games that support any of the Voodoo specification, you need a 3D accelerator expansion card with a Voodoo chipset.

For most modern games, the 3D function calls don't really have to be that advanced; games don't require the shading, perfect shapes, smooth curves, and photorealistic quality of the most complicated rendering being done for print and film. Not that gamers and game designers don't appreciate these qualities. It's just that there's a trade-off between gaming performance and the richness of the graphics. So, games are designed to make the most impact with less emphasis on the highest levels of 3D sophistication.

Ultimately, this means you can be more specific about the 3D needs that a game has. Although RAVE is designed to accelerate all 3D in a very general way, other technologies can be designed specifically to accelerate the way a game treats 3D, making consistent, smooth-flowing, moving 3D its top priority.

Voodoo graphics is a specification and technology built and maintained by 3Dfx, Inc., which in turn licenses what it develops to card manufacturers like TechWorks, maker of the Mac Power3D accelerator card (see Figure 18-2). 3Dfx also offers the technology in the form of software development kits for game designers and other programmers, enabling them to easily incorporate Voodoo.

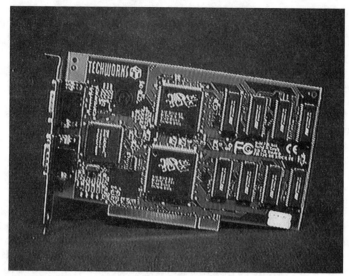

Figure 18-2: The TechWorks Power3D card is the first to allow Mac games to use Voodoo technology for 3D acceleration.

When compared to RAVE acceleration, the Voodoo technology is a one-trick pony; it only kicks in when a Voodoo-enabled game is running, and it only works for 3D acceleration — 2D graphics tasks continue to be handled by a regular video card. So, unlike RAVE technology, it can't be repurposed to some other 3D task, such as creating 3D objects for print or multimedia presentations. And it won't accelerate the editing or manipulation of regular QuickDraw 3D objects in Mac applications.

However, the results can be pretty astounding compared to regular Mac rendering or even RAVE accelerated 3D video. That makes Voodoo technology an enticing prospect for gamers who really enjoy good graphics.

Note

Interestingly, TechWorks has worked with Connectix and Insignia — the makers of VirtualPC and SoftWindows, respectively — to give Intel-compatible PC emulators the capability of using the Power3D card as if it were also part of the emulated PC. (Learn more about PC emulators in Chapter 19.) That means these emulators can render PC-based games at higher rates of speed and better quality, opening up a large selection of PC games to Mac owners.

3D Accelerator cards

If you're interested in Voodoo-based cards, your choices for Mac-specific ones are almost completely limited to the Power3D card from TechWorks (www.techworks. com). This card is a PCI expansion card that connects to your original video circuitry using a special cable, which is included. Although it's currently the only stand-alone Voodoo accelerator specifically for Macs, its popularity suggests that others may appear on the market soon, so keep on the lookout. (Note, by the way, that all accelerator cards require PCI-based Power Macs, with the exception of some early QuickDraw 3D RAVE accelerators that can work with NuBus-based Power Macs.)

The Power3D card actually supports gaming-specific RAVE acceleration, too, so it's recommended for games that offer either RAVE or 3Dfx compatibility.

Another card, the Mac Picasso 540 from Village Tronics (www.villagetronics.com), offers Voodoo support through an add-on 3D accelerator card that complements the basic 2D video card. The whole package is a bit more expensive than the Power3D, but it offers 3D in a window (not just for full-screen gaming) and other more general 3D acceleration. All-in-all it's a powerful solution, but the price may make it overkill for someone who's only interested in gaming acceleration.

Fortunately, you also have the choice of using an Intel-compatible PC-oriented card, if you so desire, thanks to an adapter and driver software from Griffin Technology (www.nashville.net/~griffin). The adapter is promised to work with nearly any Mac and monitor combination, but stop by the Web site to be sure.

At the time of writing, a new 3Dfx card has been announced for Macs that supports the Voodoo 2 chipset from Micro Conversions (www.microconversions.com). Another interesting move is support for the acceleration of yet another 3D standard, OpenGL. OpenGL may become more popular in Mac gaming (and in professional multimedia) as a result, although that remains to be seen. The first of these cards is the Vision 3D, offered by Mactell (www.mactell.com).

Installing the Power3D

The Power3D is a fairly unique add-on for Mac video, because it doesn't actually take over the 2D video functions as well as 3D rendering — so, your original video circuitry and connections will stay, too. As the card has to turn on and off depending on the application (when a Voodoo-enabled game is running, the 2D video circuitry is interrupted by the Power3D card), it has to have a way to control the Mac's video. It does that by intercepting the signal via a cable connected to the Mac's video circuitry. You then connect your monitor to the Techworks card.

To install a Power3D card, follow these steps:

1. Shut down your Mac, ground yourself, and unplug the Mac from your surge protector or wall socket.

2. Open the Mac's case and locate an available PCI expansion slot.

3. Install the Power3D card in that slot.

4. On the back of your Macintosh, remove the monitor's cable from your Mac's video port (or the video port on your video expansion card, if one is present). Plug the cable that Techworks includes with the Power3D into the video port, and then plug the other end of the cable into the video-in port on the Power3D card.

5. Connect your monitor to the Power3D card's VGA-out port. (You may need to use the included Mac-video-to-VGA adapter).

6. With everything reassembled, plug in your Mac and start it up.

7. Run the Power3D software installer. After restarting your Mac, you should be ready to use the card. Install and play one of the included Voodoo-compatible games (or any others you have on hand).

Notice that the Power3D card — with its VGA-out port — is directly compatible with many third party monitors, but requires an adapter to work with Apple displays. However, the cable that is installed between your Mac's video port and the Power3D is an RGB-to-VGA adapter. You'll need to call Techworks to request a different adapter if your video card happens to have only a VGA (HD15) port, because the cable assumes that your Mac has an RGB (DB15) port for video.

Also realize that the Power3D card may not work with non-multisync monitors (like the Apple 12" and 13" color monitors) and it doesn't support resolutions lower than 640x480. The adapter that's included generally won't cause trouble with multisync monitors, but you may find that using another RGB-to-VGA adapter (one with selectable resolution settings, for instance) improves your monitor's ability to change resolutions and color depths.

Choosing a RAVE card

RAVE-compatible accelerators are a much more open market, offering a wide range of capabilities, features, and prices. The most basic RAVE cards are usually 3D accelerators combined with 2D video card circuitry — which may also offer regular QuickDraw acceleration for drawing windows, icons, and other 2D tasks. This makes the low-end RAVE video cards a nice addition to modern Macs, giving them the ability to speed up all sorts of computer video tasks.

Apple made the earliest of these cards, the Apple QuickDraw 3D Accelerator (which can still be found occasionally on store shelves, although it's been discontinued). Other companies in this space include ATI Technologies and IXMicro.

High-end cards are designed for professional applications, and the cards themselves require more advanced chipsets, more RAM, and broader feature sets. Many of these cards tout advantages like Gourand shading, parity with QuickDraw 3D textures, and z-buffering (a process by which data regarding the perspective of a 3D image is buffered so it plays back smoothly when animated). Table 18-1 shows the major vendors of QuickDraw acceleration cards.

Table 18-1
QuickDraw 3D Accelerator Manufacturers

Manufacturer	Web Site
ATI Technologies	www.ati.com
Matrox Graphics	www.matrox.com
IXMicro	www.ixmicro.com
Number Nine	www.nine.com

As an added bonus, you'll find that most of these cards also accelerate QuickTime playback, giving you full-screen video capabilities. Some also specifically offer MPEG acceleration, which usually means you get crisp, full-screen playback of movies in the popular MPEG video format (see Chapter 13 for more on video formats).

Installing a Rave video card

Unlike the Voodoo variety, 3D-accelerated RAVE-compatible cards tend to offer a built-in alter-ego: a mild-mannered 2D video card. Therefore, installation doesn't require the extra cabling that Voodoo cards do, as all video functions are built into the single card. The card installs like any other expansion card, with the exception of the software drivers. Here's how to install the typical video card:

1. Shut down your Mac and electrically ground yourself. Unplug the Mac from its surge protector or wall socket.

2. Open the Mac's case and locate an empty expansion slot. (Visually inspect it to ensure it's the right type of slot for your video card.)

3. Remove the screw and metal dust plate that covers the hole in back of the case for the slot you'll be using.

4. Position the card so that the card's interface is directly over the slot. Press down lightly and uniformly on the top corners of the expansion card until it's firmly installed in the slot.

5. Attach a monitor's cable to the RGB port on the back of the card. You may need to use a multisync adapter if your monitor has a VGA connector, although many accelerated video cards offer both RGB and VGA connectors (see Figure 18-3).

6. Turn on your computer and monitor. You may need to install special software for your accelerated video card: Do so and restart your Mac. You should then be able to adjust how your monitor displays the Mac's graphics using the Monitors (or Monitors & Sound) control panel.

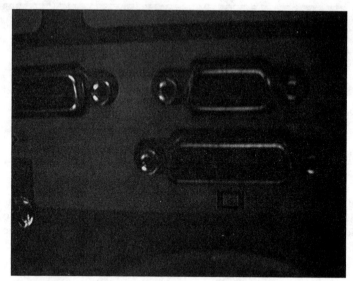

Figure 18-3: It's very possible your video cards offers two port choices — standard Mac RGB or Intel-compatible VGA.

The software you install will likely appear where it should on your Mac, although you may have to manually drag system extensions to the System Folder in some cases. To accelerate graphics in games and multimedia, the card is likely to install a number of QuickTime extensions, too, such as QuickTime RAVE. Note very carefully that the card doesn't install *older* versions of these QuickTime files — a somewhat common occurrence. (Chapter 31 offers specific tips on how to track newly installed files.)

If your Mac has built-in video or a video card that you're not replacing with your new RAVE-compatible one, don't forget that it should still be fully functional and useful, because nearly any Mac can handle multiple monitors for output. Hook up another monitor to your original video circuitry and run them side by side, if you like. Just don't forget to use the RAVE-compatible screen and video circuitry when you want to work with accelerated 3D.

Mac Gaming

Apple made a big commitment to game developers in 1997, with a renewed commitment vocalized by Apple's management since then, in relation to Apple's push back into consumer markets with the iMac and its siblings. Although Apple has historically had a love/hate relationship with games (spurning the notion that the Mac is a "toy" computer — a moniker it received shortly after introduction in 1984) these days Apple seems more at ease with game developers and encourages their proliferation. After all, the Intel-compatible PC world is filled to the brim with games, yet those Windows machines are still seen as a major standard in the business world.

Part of that commitment to gaming can be seen in some interesting new system software that Apple wrote to help game producers — Apple Game Sprockets. These OS add-ons enable game developers to focus more on painting graphics, creating monsters, and building storylines, because they're able to call on Apple standardized routines for things like controlling the action and creating advanced sound and images.

At the same time, this approach to gaming (and its constantly increasing popularity on Macs) has spawned the next generation of control devices for playing games, from steering wheels to weapons control systems (WCS) that emulate the F-16 fighter jet. There probably hasn't been a better time than now to get involved in computer gaming on the Macintosh.

Game Sprockets

As a typical user, you probably won't have to deal much with the Game Sprockets. After all, they're simply extensions (actually, shared libraries) that games can install in your System Folder. Of course, you'll need to know they exist and figure out how to troubleshoot them if you have problems with a game (you can find a discussion of this in Chapter 28).

But if you'd like to know what these sprockets actually do, here's a quick overview. Aimed at game designers who want to design for the Mac's advanced interface but are also interested in getting the games quickly to market, the sprockets take some of the Mac's best features and make it easy for the game developer to add them.

Here are the current Game Sprockets and what, exactly, they do:

✦ **SoundSprocket.** Gives the programmer easy access to routines for traditional sound functions as well as new 3D sound technologies developed by Apple. The 3D sound approach enables the programmer to immerse gamers in a virtual world where sounds travel around the central characters as they move through a gaming environment. Doppler effects, distancing, and spatial location are all made possible.

✦ **DrawSprocket.** Helps developers to create smoother display of images on screen, using a technology called *double-* or *triple-buffering*. This means the Mac renders images ahead of time, putting them in a buffer (reserved portion of memory) until they're needed. The DrawSprocket can automatically use special hardware or just software to render the scenes. The DrawSprocket also has access to screen sizing and resolution and color depth options, and it works with QuickTime for some animation functions.

✦ **NetSprocket.** Provides a standardized mechanism for adding Internet and local network connections to your game for head-to-head and teamwork-style game choices. It allows the developer to use Open Transport protocols and to create groups of gamers for connected play.

✦ **InputSprocket.** Offers the developer a standard way to accept input from a variety of devices. This creates a quick-and-useful standard for writing input device drivers — small bits of software that describe the joystick's capabilities to the InputSprocket. With all this in force, it's possible for very advanced controller options to be used by games without too much specialized programming.

This is just a bit of brute-force programming Apple has done to help game developers along, though it's also a smart way to get programmers to support other Apple technologies — QuickDraw 3D, QuickTime, and QuickTime VR, for instance; this in turn results in games that offer Apple and Mac-specific advantages. Because many games use programming code originally developed for Intel-compatible or set-top box players, having these specialized sprockets makes it easier for cross-platform-oriented companies to add special Mac features to their games.

Game controllers

Although game controllers were around well before Apple's Game Sprockets technology, the offerings seem to have been enhanced somewhat by the availability of simple work-arounds such as the InputSprocket. Early Mac controllers tended to be very much like a Mac's mouse — using ADB connections to generate movements that the Mac would interpret as mouse movements, even if the device was a joystick or other contraption (see Figure 18-4).

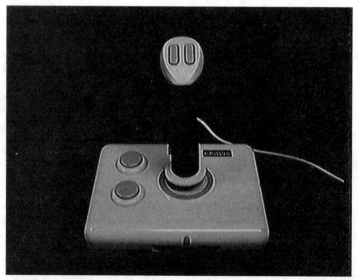

Figure 18-4: The venerable MouseStick II from Advanced Gravis (www.gravis.com) is still popular, even though it sends only mouse-like signals to the Mac.

These days, though, some of that has changed. Although unique controllers are considerably more popular in the Intel-compatible world (where such PCs have had a standard joystick port for years), the Mac has its share of interesting devices for enhanced gaming. Table 18-2 lists some popular Mac-compatible game controller manufacturers.

Table 18-2 Mac Game Controller Companies		
Manufacturer	**Devices**	**Web Site**
MacAlly	Joysticks, gamepads	www.macally.com
Gravis	Joysticks, gamepads	www.gravis.com
ThrustMaster	Steering, flight controllers	www.thrustmaster.com
Microsoft	Joystick	www.microsoft.com/sidewinder/
CH Products	Joysticks, flight controllers	www.chproducts.com
Suncom	Joysticks	www.suncominc.com

In general, you'll come across three classes of controller. Some offer different levels of specialization, but most can be categorized as joysticks, gamepads, and flight controllers.

Note   If the current crop of Mac game controllers aren't enough to satisfy you, perhaps a joystick adapter is the appropriate solution. The Choicestick adapter from Kernel Productions (www.kernel.com) promises to enable you to use any number of joysticks and controllers from Atari, PC, Playstation, and Sega Genesis machines. And how about joysticks for the iMac and future USB-based Macs? CH Products has already announced their intention to build USB joysticks, with others sure to follow. Plus, USB won't be Mac-specific, so other controller companies focused on the Intel-compatible world may find themselves writing Mac driver software for their USB joysticks, too.

Joysticks

These are probably the oldest form of game input for computers and gaming devices, modeled on the controllers used for early standup arcade games, which in turn modeled their controllers (presumably) on input controllers used in robotics and military applications.

Originally, Mac joysticks simply offered a different way to give mouse input, and hence rarely required any additional extensions or settings to work properly. As more sophisticated ideas and technologies have become popular, however, joysticks have added functions. In some cases, joysticks offer more precise movements, programmable buttons, and, occasionally, *force feedback*. This technology actually causes the joystick to react to events in the game with shudders and shimmies.

Figure 18-5 shows a joystick modeled on a fighter aircraft's controller.

Figure 18-5: The Fighter Stick from CH Products is a serious joystick.

Gamepads

Joining us from the world of set-top game machines is the gamepad, a small, handheld device used as a rocker control; individual buttons provide movement control. These controllers often feature a number of buttons, some of which can be programmed for a particular game. Gamepads encourage you to use both hands completely while playing, making them less than ideal for games that require keyboard input, but really useful for games that don't. Some models are easy to switch from right-handed play to left-handed play (that is, you can configure the button functions to suit whichever hand is dominant), offering a clear advantage over many joysticks. Figure 18-6 shows a gamepad.

Flight (driving) controllers

Serious and often more expensive than your average joystick or gamepad, these controls tend to offer very specific shapes and designs. Playing off the popularity of flight and driving simulator software, both CH Products and Thrustmaster offer very sophisticated knock-offs of real-world controls.

Both companies include joysticks and yokes fashioned after real-life fighter planes and other aircraft, as well as rudder pedals, throttle controllers, and weapons systems that round out the realism. With all of these controllers at hand, you probably will have spent a few hundred dollars — but, with the right software (and maybe a 3D accelerator) you'll have a full-fledged simulation cockpit (see Figure 18-7).

Figure 18-6: The CH Gamepad from CH Products is an example of a gamepad controller.

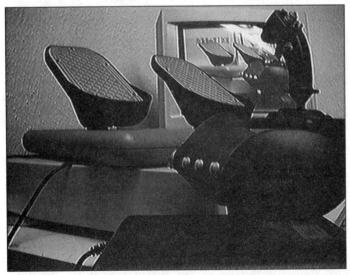

Figure 18-7: With all these controllers you can put together a fairly convincing flight simulator for your home or office.

Note   Your cockpit doesn't have to be all fun and games, either. Realistic flight models exist in a number of cross-country and general aviation simulations for the Mac, some of which use these controllers for more realistic input.

Summary

✦ The force behind a lot of Mac multimedia development is QuickDraw 3D, a Mac OS technology that programmers and artists can use to render complex 3D objects, landscapes, and other vistas for film or print. It's also the basic engine that drives a lot of Mac gaming, along with QuickTime technologies.

✦ You can get better 3D performance from your Mac — and sometimes better overall video — by adding a QuickDraw 3D accelerator card. Various levels exist to help different sorts of users.

✦ If your needs are more gaming oriented, a Voodoo graphics add-on card is another option. This works in conjunction with your existing Mac video circuitry to create incredible 3D performance in games, but at a very affordable price.

✦ In fact, gaming is a strong theme for Apple these days, with the release of Game Sprockets, a set of programmers tools that enable game developers to add special Mac-only sound, input device, and Internet tools to their games.

✦ Game Sprockets and some other factors have led to newer and more exciting game controllers, including joysticks, gamepads, and amazing flight and driving controllers that turn your Mac into an arcade-style simulator.

✦   ✦   ✦

Dealing with DOS and Windows PCs

A lot of people use the Mac because they want to, in spite of some pressure to join the majority and use the same computing platform — the Intel/Windows combination — that most of the rest of the world has decided to use. In many cases, you'll find that, even within your organization or your company, or among your colleagues, having a Mac stands out from the norm.

Perhaps because of the Mac's uniqueness, the burden of proof tends to fall on our shoulders. Whether it's remaining compatible with DOS floppies, working with their removable media, translating Windows file formats, or even running the occasional Windows program, the Mac has had to be the more flexible of the two platforms.

Fortunately, the Mac does a pretty good job. If you have a reason to use just about any file format, disk, or even a program from the Windows/Intel (Wintel) world, you'll probably be able to. And you might even impress your Windows-using friends along the way.

When I say your Mac can work well with the Wintel world, what do I mean? Here are all the choices you have to help your Mac be a good citizen:

✦ You can use your Macintosh to read PC floppy disks, Zip disks, and other removable media.

✦ Your Mac can read Windows (and DOS) file formats and convert them for use on the Mac.

✦ Mac applications can export most files in a Windows-compatible format.

✦ Macs can run Windows programs in software.

✦ You can install an expansion card in many Macs that enable them to run Windows and DOS programs on an actual Intel (or Intel-compatible) processor.

✦ You can use Intel-compatible peripherals such as keyboards, mice and — in some cases — modems and other serial devices.

Sharing DOS Files

The easy way to get along with your DOS or Windows-touting counterparts is to be able to work with just about any file that comes your way. With a well-equipped Mac, you can do just that. This used to require separate control panels for your Mac that had to be store bought, but these days most of the software you need to be compatible is sold as part of the Mac OS; if you've upgraded to Mac OS 7.6 or above, you should have the basic tools for reading DOS-formatted floppy disks, formatting DOS floppies, reading DOS-formatted removable media (most of it), and translating files to and from Windows application formats.

By the way, I talk about *DOS* or *MS-DOS* (Microsoft Disk Operating System) formatting because floppies and media used on Windows and Intel-compatible machines are formatted to be backward compatible with nearly all Windows and DOS versions, even if the floppies themselves are used in Windows 95 or Windows 98 machines. The same is somewhat true for Mac disks; in most cases, disks aren't formatted for a particular Mac OS version — they work with all versions.

Because Windows, in a matter of speaking, is simply a new version of DOS, the file format hasn't changed. The only major difference is that Windows 95 and above can use long (255-character) filenames, whereas DOS can only handle eight-character names with three-letter extensions (known as the 8.3 convention). Before Mac OS 8.1, the Mac OS could also only handle the 8.3 version of DOS filenames when using DOS-formatted media. The latest OS versions, however, now handle Windows' longer names.

Note   Actually, even if you have an older version of the Mac OS, you can still work with files that are named using the newer long filename convention for Windows 95 or Windows 98 — you just won't see those long filenames. Because it has to continue to be backward compatible with DOS, the Windows long-filename scheme also includes short (8.3) filenames that are saved as part of the disk's information about its files. So, if a DOS-based or older Mac OS–based computer tries to view the directory of files, that OS sees the shorter names it's expecting to see.

Reading DOS media

If you're working in an office or organization where you often receive DOS floppy disks, you may already know that you can read the floppy simply by inserting it in the floppy drive of any Mac (in the Mac II series and up) that's running Mac OS 7.5 or above.

Two elements come together to enable this to happen. First, Macs newer than a Mac II feature what Apple calls a SuperDrive floppy mechanism — a high-density (1.44MB) floppy drive that offers the ability to read variously formatted disks. That includes DOS formats, Mac formats, and even ProDOS, the Apple II disk format.

The second factor is PC Exchange, a control panel included with the Mac OS 7.5 and above. (It was available separately for earlier Mac OS versions.) This control panel makes it possible for the SuperDrive to read and write to DOS-formatted floppies, as well as being responsible for mapping DOS/Windows *file extensions*, the three-letter system DOS uses to relate programs and their associated documents. Using the control panel, you can tell your Mac which of your Macintosh applications should be used to open a particular DOS document.

In Mac OS versions before Mac OS 8.1, other DOS-formatted media could be read as well, including CD-ROM drives, Zip drives, and Jaz drives. The Mac wasn't always reliably reading Zip and larger removable media drives that were DOS-formatted, however, so Mac OS 8.1 included an upgraded version of PC Exchange. Now, not only can it read removable media more reliably, but it also supports the Windows 95/98 long filename system.

As you may know, the PC Exchange control panel also makes it possible to format a floppy disk in DOS format so you can exchange it with DOS/Windows users. To do so, just insert the floppy in the Mac's floppy drive. If the disk is unformatted, you'll be asked if you want to format the disk — choose DOS 1.4 from the Format menu. If the disk is already formatted, you'll get the same choices by selecting the disk's icon in the Finder and choosing Special ➪ Erase Disk.

Translating DOS file formats

Even after you've gotten the DOS floppy mounted on your desktop and the DOS/Windows files copied onto your hard drive, you've still got to do something with the files. As with Macintosh programs, DOS and Windows applications tend to have their own file formats, even for new versions of the same program. Microsoft Word documents, for instance, might be in Microsoft Word for DOS 1.0 format, Microsoft Word for Windows 6.0 format, or even Word 97 (for Windows 95) format. Each of these formats requires a particular filter to properly load a file into a Macintosh word processing document.

You'll find that some Macintosh applications have the built-in ability to read DOS and Windows files — especially if the files are made by the same company. For instance, Microsoft Word 6.0 for Mac can read Microsoft Word 6.0 for Windows and Microsoft Word for DOS file formats, whereas Word 98 for Mac can read those formats as well as the Word 97 format. (It can also translate Rich Text Format and MS Works documents, both of which are also Microsoft file formats.) In these cases and in others, Microsoft makes these translators available from within the program or as add-ons (often free) available on upgrade CD-ROMs and via the Microsoft Web site (www.microsoft.com/macoffice).

These capabilities are far from universal, however. To add system-level translation of file formats for nearly any of your Mac applications, a system software add-on is required. The most popular, MacLinksPlus from Dataviz (www.dataviz.com), is not only commonly used, but included with Mac OS 7.6 and above.

Indications are that these translators may not be included with Mac OS 8.5 and higher, in which case I highly recommend installing them from an older installation disc and/or contacting Dataviz for a new version.

What MacLinksPlus does is append the File Open and Save As dialog boxes with a number of different translators that support DOS/Windows file formats from many different manufacturers. Not all Mac applications support MacLinksPlus, but a good number of them do. ClarisWorks and AppleWorks, for instance, get quite a boost from adding MacLinksPlus, as shown in Figure 19-1. (Certain versions of ClarisWorks and ClarisWorks Office include a version of MacLinksPlus, just in case you haven't upgraded your Mac OS recently.)

Dataviz also makes translators that work the other way — Mac files to DOS/Windows formats — for the lonely PC user in a sea of Macintosh-based colleagues. The program ConversionPlus is available for Windows and Windows 95/98 users, and Dataviz makes other programs for more specific uses. The company also offers upgrades to the version of MacLinksPlus offered with the Mac OS. The upgrades generally feature bug fixes along with more and newer translators for programs that have come on the market since the latest Mac OS release.

DOS file archives

DOS file archives are the third link in the chain — especially if you'll be transferring documents over the Internet. *Archives* are files or groups of files that have been compressed into a single, much smaller file that can be used to store or transmit the files over phone lines. (Actually, not all archives consist of compressed files, as archives can also be used to simply group files together in one file. That said, most of the Mac and DOS archive formats are also designed for compression.) Compression schemes look for redundancies in the file data (whether it's a binary file — like an image or program — or a text file) and compress the files based on sophisticated algorithms. The result is a file that takes up less disk space and transfers more quickly over modem or Internet connections. Once a file is compressed, however, it can't be used until it's decompressed by a utility that understands its archive format.

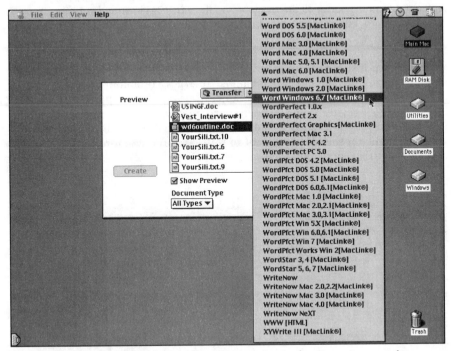

Figure 19-1: MacLinksPlus adds quite a few entries to the Open As menu in a ClarisWorks dialog box.

Macs and Intel-compatible PCs have traditionally used different archive formats. On the Macintosh, the overwhelming favorite is the StuffIt format, created by Aladdin Systems (www.aladdinsys.com), makers of StuffIt Expander and StuffIt Deluxe. Another favorite is Compact Pro, maintained by Cyclos (www.cyclos.com), although it's more popular for creating professional installer programs than it is for day-to-day use between Mac users. (StuffIt files are much more the standard, at least for individual use. Other programs, including StuffIt InstallerMaker and MindVision VISE, are also popular for creating professional installations for programs and applications.)

On the Intel-compatible side, PKZip, created and maintained by PKWARE, Inc. (www.pkware.com), dominates for archiving. Unfortunately, StuffIt and PKZip aren't compatible with one another, so special utilities are required for either the Mac or the PC to read the other's archives.

Again, the translation tasks usually fall to the Mac owner. Because you can't rely on an Intel-compatible PC user to have StuffIt Expander on hand (although Aladdin Systems makes a Windows-compatible version of the program), it's important to create PKZip-compatible archives for them to use. To do that, you'll need ZipIt, a shareware program by Tom Brown.

On the CD-ROM

ZipIt and StuffIt Expander all are available on the CD-ROM included with this book. ZipIt is a shareware program that you should pay for if you enjoy using it; StuffIt Expander is freeware from Aladdin Systems.

With ZipIt, for instance, both creating and using PKZip-compatible archives is simple. From ZipIt's file menu you can use the New command to create a new archive in PKZip format, and then add files you want to compress inside the archive by choosing Zip ➪ Add from the menu bar. If you want to extract files from an existing archive, you can open the archive through ZipIt's File ➪ Open command, and then highlight the files you want to return to an uncompressed state and choose Zip ➪ Extract from the menu bar (see Figure 19-2).

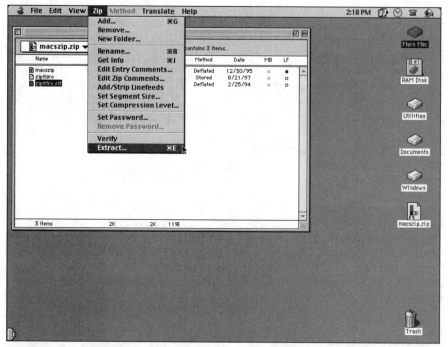

Figure 19-2: The ZipIt compression/decompression utility makes it easy to deal with PC files.

One word of caution: ZipIt has a habit of saving files in a MacBinary format by default when you go to create an archive of compressed Mac documents. However, MacBinary files tend to confuse Intel-compatible PCs — MacBinary is really only useful if you're sending files to other Mac users in an archive using PKZip format. In the Preferences (File ➪ Preferences ➪ General), find the Use MacBinary entry and choose the When Necessary or Never button. Choose Never if you'll only be sending PKZip files to Intel-compatible PC users. (Realize, though, that you may lose Mac-specific information when you send a file this way; this method is best used when you're sending cross-platform documents like graphics files or word processing documents. If you're sending a Mac application or file that isn't going to be used on the PC, just archived there, as on an FTP server, you'll want to leave it in MacBinary format.)

If you don't plan to create PKZip-compatible archives, you don't have to get ZipIt. StuffIt Expander can decompress PKZip-compatible archives, but only if you have the optional DropStuff with Expander Enhancer shareware program from Aladdin. This add-on to StuffIt Expander enables you to decompress all sorts of archives, including CompactPro, PKZip, and UNIX *zip* and *tar* archive and compression formats.

E-mail attachments

Here's another place where you can run into trouble trying to translate files between PC and Mac formats — attachments to e-mail messages. For documents, programs, and compressed archives to be sent through the Internet e-mail system, they have to be *encoded*, or translated using special utility programs. The reason for this is pretty simple — the Internet e-mail protocols are generally only capable of sending text messages, not binary (computer data) files. So, binary files must go through a process where they're translated into a text-based code, and then transmitted. When they arrive at the receiving computer, the encoded file can be turned back into a binary file for use on that computer.

That's where the trouble starts. Macs tend to use a different text-encoding scheme — called BinHex — than do PCs. (MacBinary is another format for Mac text encoding, although it's a bit less popular.) In many cases, the e-mail application itself does the encoding, and many PC e-mail programs aren't designed to translate BinHex. Instead, they'll need you to send your files in a format the DOS/Windows e-mail application can understand and translate.

The most common format for PCs is called MIME, or Base64 in your e-mail program — in some Mac applications it's also called AppleSingle. (Actually, these are all slightly different formats, but they fall under the heading of "MIME-compliant," which makes them easiest to use in a cross-platform situation.) If you are sending an e-mail attachment to a PC user, choose whichever of these options is available in your e-mail program; in most cases, you don't need a new utility program to send an attachment that PC users can work with. Figure 19-3 shows Claris Emailer translating an e-mail attachment into Base64.

Note   You probably shouldn't allow your e-mail program to automatically compress files it's sending to PCs, since it'll most likely use the StuffIt file format. Instead, compress the files into PKZip archives ahead of time, before adding it to the e-mail as an attachment.

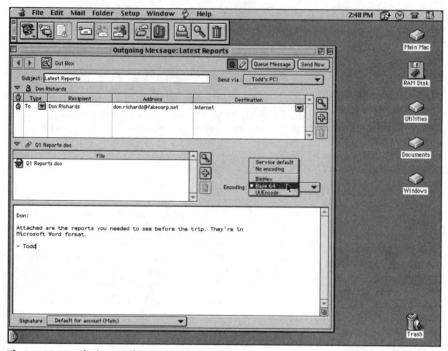

Figure 19-3: Claris Emailer makes it simple to encode files for transfer over the Internet to Intel-compatible PC users.

If you receive an e-mail attachment from a PC user, you'll find that most of the more recent Mac e-mail clients handle Base64 and other MIME-compliant attachments with grace. Usually you simply save the attachment or double-click it in the e-mail program to use it. But if you ever do have a MIME file slip through the cracks, you can use StuffIt Expander 4.5 or above (you'll need DropStuff with Expander Enhancer) to translate the MIME file. Just drag the encoded MIME document onto the StuffIt Expander icon (or load it in StuffIt Deluxe, if you've purchased a recent version of that program).

StuffIt will even handle the uuencode/uudecode format for attachments, which is a UNIX standard for encoding files for Internet transfers (Windows and other platforms have tools to deal with this type of attachment). You should consider sending attachments as uuencode/uudecode if your recipient is a UNIX user.

Running DOS and Windows Programs

Because about 90 percent of the personal computers on the planet use DOS and Windows as the operating system, there's a lot of software written for them. As a Mac user myself for years, I've rarely pined for a program for my Mac (other than some games) that was only written for an Intel-compatible PC. Of course, some of these programs are in demand among computer users — and you'll often find them lurking more in the business-management arena than anywhere else.

Most often you'll find that such programs are *vertical market* applications — that is, written specifically for a particular type of business or to solve a particular industrial problem — designed to run exclusively for Windows or DOS. In those cases, it's often important to be able to run the application, even if you'd like to use a Macintosh.

Short of having the program rewritten (or writing a compatible program yourself, if you're a Mac-savvy programmer), there are two basic types of solutions for running Windows programs: hardware and software. On the hardware side, your options depend on the Mac you own. Certain models can accept a *PC compatibility* expansion card that enables you to actually start up and run the DOS and/or Windows operating systems on a second processor installed inside your Mac. You can then run most DOS/Windows programs unaltered.

On the software side, a number of Windows and Intel-compatible PC *emulator* programs can actually run as Macintosh applications, but they imitate a Windows environment to enable Windows programs to run. These emulators can take over your floppy and CD-ROM drives and even print directly to Macintosh printers.

PC compatibility hardware

PC Compatibility Cards is the name that Apple has given in the past to a class of expansion cards that adds PC functionality to certain Macintosh models. Other vendors make or have made these cards, too. One of those companies, Orange Micro (www.orangemicro.com), continues to make a variety of these cards for various Mac models. Another of the companies, Reply Corporation, has since sold its technology to Radius Corp. (www.reply.radius.com), which has repackaged the cards as the Radius Detente series of cards.

With PC-compatibility expansion cards, the Mac OS does some fancy footwork to enable you to run programs in both an Intel-compatible and a Mac environment simultaneously (usually you hit a hot-key sequence to change from one environment to another). The major advantage to this approach is the expansion card features an actual Intel-compatible processor chip on it, along with video circuitry and other components. In some cases, you can even upgrade the card by adding extra RAM to it.

Adding an expansion board is generally the best way to get fast PC performance. Because you're running the DOS or Windows programs on an actual Intel-compatible processor, there's no translation or emulation that has to take place. The expansion card treats your Mac's monitor as if it were a PC monitor and your hard drive as if it were a PC hard drive (at least, part of it). So the performance relies completely on the processor that's installed on the card (and factors such as the Windows version you use and how much additional RAM you install on the card).

Note   There's some question as to why Apple called some of its products "DOS-compatibility cards" and others "PC Compatibility Cards." The easy answer: Apple calls the cards DOS-Compatible if they're designed for a particular Macintosh model, because the model is called DOS compatible (the Power Macintosh 6100/60 DOS Compatible is an example). The PC-compatible moniker is reserved for cards that can work in more than one Macintosh model. (Heck, it's not a great reason, but it's something to hold on to.)

PC-compatible issues

There's no question that the engineering feat that enables an Intel (or Intel-compatible) 486 or Pentium processor to run inside a Mac and access most of the Mac's internal (and many external) devices is nothing short of amazing. Still, there have been some hurdles to overcome, and not all Macs have done so completely. In most cases, though, these shortcomings shouldn't affect your ability to use the compatibility features in most business scenarios.

One of the major issues is ports. The Mac's ports can be remapped and used by DOS or Windows when the compatibility card is operating, but only with limited success. With serial ports, connecting to a Mac modem from the PC side can be problematic at best. In general, Wintel software isn't able to get the feedback it requires through the Mac's serial port, which reacts a little differently than a PC's serial port. The result is you can't get CTS/RTS-type flow control to activate, meaning you're generally limited to connection speeds of 9,600 bps or less.

As far as parallel ports are concerned, the Mac doesn't use any such technology at all, so it's impossible to repurpose some port on the Mac and use it for printing to PC-oriented printers or some other parallel device.

Orange Micro's PC Compatibility Cards (see Figure 19-4) get around this by including the port technology on the card itself. Many recent Orange Micro cards come with cabling that you hook up to a single port on the card. The individual cables sprout from this port like spaghetti, enabling you to hook up all sorts of devices — PC serial and parallel periperals, a second monitor, PC game controllers, and more.

Apple and Reply have used a different solution in the past — an add-on card for serial and parallel ports. These cards can generally be found on the used market or in select retail/mail-order warehouses. Check the major catalogs and contact Radius' customer service people for other options.

Figure 19-4: Orange Micro is currently the only manufacturer of new PC upgrade cards, offering a range of sizes and speeds for different Power Mac models (www.orangemicro.com).

The other major problem you encounter with PC Compatibility Cards is that most of them don't include 32-bit driver software for the Windows 95/98 environment. Instead, those operating systems are forced to drop into a special compatibility mode reserved for older (16-bit) driver software. In the world of actual Windows PCs, this 16-bit compatibility mode is reserved for older components such as CD-ROM drives and video cards sold with aging 386 and 486 systems. And, in many cases, even the drivers for that old equipment have been upgraded to be compatible.

The Windows 95/98 environment is slowed somewhat by being forced into a compatibility mode, but there's more fallout. Advanced graphical games often use the DirectX graphics architecture written by Microsoft for game developers (similar to Apple's QuickDraw 3D and associated technologies discussed in Chapter 13). Unfortunately, DirectX won't work reliably with 16-bit driver code as part of the mix. PC owners generally have to upgrade their systems to be 32-bit clean before their highest-end games will run correctly—if at all.

If you have a PC Compatibility Card from Apple or Reply/Radius, you're faced with the same problem. But Apple and Radius have made no move to upgrade the drivers to 32-bit, and it doesn't seem they will anytime soon. So, you'll be unable to take advantage of DirectX in Windows.

Orange Micro owners get a better answer — as of this writing, Orange Micro has released testing drivers for its OrangePC line of cards. If you don't get the 32-bit drivers with your new card, you should head over to www.orangemicro.com to download and install the new drivers.

Note

Reports have it that Orange Micro is also working with Apple to write 32-bit drivers that would be available from Orange Micro to expand the capabilities of Apple's (and potentially Reply's) PC Compatibility Cards. Check Orange Micro's Web site for updates or confirmations on this rumor.

Finally, Orange Micro comes through with more support than Reply and Apple when it comes to cards that can run multiple operating systems. In most cases, Apple and Reply cards are limited to running DOS and the various flavors of Windows 3.1, 95, and (with limited success) 98; running IBM OS/2 and Windows NT, for instance, isn't possible. The OrangePC line of cards, however, does support Windows 98, Windows NT, and OS/2.

Macs and PC Compatibility Cards

Unfortunately, not all Macs can accept a PC Compatibility Card. Although nearly any PCI-based Macintosh can accept one of the cards from Apple, Reply, Orange Micro, or Radius, others have been specifically designed for particular Apple Macintosh brands. Table 19-1 shows those systems that could accept (or came with) PC Compatibility Cards.

Table 19-1 DOS-Compatible Macs from Apple	
Model	*Type of Intel-compatible Processor*
Quadra 610	486-level processor
Quadra 630, LC 630, Performa 630, 640	486-level processor
Power Macintosh 6100, Performa 6110 series	486-level processor
Power Macintosh 4400, 7220	Cyrix P166 processor
Power Macintosh 7200, 7300	Pentium 166 processor

Note that the Cyrix-based PC Compatibility Card has unique power requirements that prevent it from working in other Macs. The true Intel Pentium card designed for the 7200/7300 series, however, can work in many Macs (Power Mac 7500, 7600, 8500, 8600, 9500, 9600) and is reported to also work well in PCI-based Mac OS clones. Apple made and sold this PC Compatibility Card separately for Macs that could handle PCI expansion cards.

If you have one of the earlier Macs designed for a particular type of PC Compatibility Card, you'll need to shop a bit on the used market to see if you can find the board made particularly for your Mac. Figure 19-5, for instance, shows a PC Compatibility Card being installed in a Power Macintosh 6100.

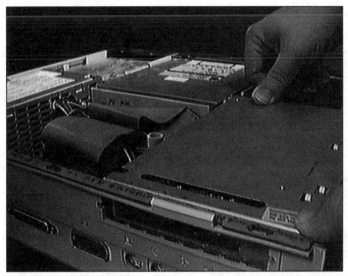

Figure 19-5: This DOS compatibility card was designed specifically to fit the PDS slot that's particular to a Power Macintosh 6100.

Other Macs can accept the Orange Micro and Reply series of cards. Reply actually made some of the Apple PC Compatibility cards, but has been making them for other Mac models for quite some time. Radius cards are available for Macs with LC PDS slots, PDS slots in NuBus PowerMacintosh computers, and PCI-based Pentium class cards (both 7" and 12" PCI cards. Table 19-2 shows the Radius line and associated Macs.

Most of these cards feature 1MB of VRAM to connect the PC to a monitor as well as SoundBlaster 16 support, options for add-ons like actual Intel-compatible serial and parallel ports, and support for Ethernet through the Mac's Ethernet connection. In fact, some models can actually run two separate IP addresses, one each for the Mac and PC processors. Not all these models are still generally available through retail outlets, but you should have some luck finding one on the used market.

Table 19-2
Radius/Reply PC-compatibility Cards

Model	Processor	Mac Supported
PDS 5x86/133	AMD 586-133	Power Mac 7100, 8100
LC PDS 5x86/133	AMD 586-133	Performa and Power Mac 5200, 5260, 5300, 6200, 6300 series
Detente AX 586/133	AMD 586-133	Power Macintosh 5400, 5500, 6360, 6400, 7200, 7300, 7500, 7600, 8500, 9500 and 9600 series computers and Mac clones with 7″ PCI slots
Detente MX PCI	Various Pentium	Power Macintosh 7200, 7300, 7500, 7600, 8500, 9500 and 9600 series computers and Mac compatibles with 12″ PCI slots

Finally, the Orange Micro cards tend to be the most comprehensive solutions to DOS-compatibility technology. Many of their cards have worked in a variety of Mac models, usually based only on whether the card supported NuBus or PCI expansion and whether the model supported a long expansion card; if the card fits in the chassis, it should be able to work. Orange Micro cards have traditionally included more support for Mac models by focusing on using the standard expansion buses (NuBus and PCI) instead of PDS slots. The latest versions of Orange Micro's cards use more powerful Pentium processors than the Apple and Reply cards, and are being actively updated and marketed, especially in the face of stiff competition from the software-only emulation companies discussed later in this chapter.

Installing a PC Compatibility Card

For the most part, these cards are installed like any other expansion cards: Turn off the power, ground yourself, find the available slot, and install it so the ports are accessible through the back of your machine. One important caveat: Many of the older cards are based on PDS slots, not NuBus or PCI, so you'll need to have the PDS slot available in your Mac.

With the card installed, your next step is likely to be connecting a web of cabling to the card. Most of the Apple and Reply cards come with cables that connect a unique 26-pin port to the Mac's video, with a pass-through connector for your monitor (and one for a PC game controller). This is the cabling that makes it possible for you to switch between the PC and Mac environments using the same monitor.

Note

If you want to use two monitors (one each for the PC and Mac environments), you still need to connect this special cable to the PC Card's port, but connect the RGB-out cable directly to the second monitor (you may need to use an RGB-to-VGA adapter). This enables you to use the PC's internal video and PC game connector.

Here's how to connect the PC-to-RGB cable:

1. Connect the PC's cabling connector to the port on the expansion card.

2. Connect the RGB connector to your Mac's RGB port.

3. Hook up the remaining RGB-out connector, which is designed for your monitor, to your Mac's monitor. You may need to attach an RGB-to-VGA adapter if your monitor only has a VGA connector.

If this is the only cabling your card came with, it should also have a game connector for use with PC joysticks and game controllers. You can connect this directly to a controller or use a Y-connector — from the PC-side of your local computer store — and connect two game controllers. (Some game controllers are too sophisticated to share the port. Check the documentation that comes with the game controller.)

Note

Other cards, such as the OrangePC series from Orange Micro, include cabling for a number of different ports and connections such as PC serial and parallel connections. These cabling solutions generally connect to the PC Compatibility Card with a single port, with the cables themselves branching out for different purposes.

Your next step is to install the software that came with the card. This generally consists of drivers for the Mac environment that enable you to activate the card (look for a disk or CD-ROM that says it's for the Mac OS). Once you have these installed, you'll restart your Mac to activate the control panel. Next, you can access the appropriate control panel, called PC Setup. The control panel gives you a number of options (shown in Figure 19-6).

Figure 19-6: The PC Setup control panel enables you to control the PC environment.

The PC Compatibility Card will need a number of settings initiated before it can boot for the first time. Most importantly, it needs to know what to use as a hard drive for the system. Because your Mac's hard drive is already formatted for the Mac file system (HFS or HFS+), the PC can't use it directly for storing files; the PC uses a different sort of drive format (FAT or FAT32). The PC Card works around this by creating a new sort of Macintosh file, called a *drive container*. The PC Setup control panel (for Apple's PC Cards) tricks the card into believing that the container file is actually an entire hard drive formatted for its use.

Note   In fact, because this is a DOS volume that's saved as a *disk image* — a special file that acts like a disk — on your Mac, you can mount it when the PC Compatibility Card isn't running. Just double-click the file and it will appear on your desktop, just as would a floppy or removable media disk.

The PC Setup control panel enables you to choose the setup file you want to use for the C drive (the main hard drive), the D drive, and other subsidiary drives. (You can pretty much create as many drives as the control panel — and the free space on your hard drive — will support.) You also choose a configuration for your video display (so the Mac knows how to display the PC screen) and how much of the Mac's system RAM you want to share with the card if you haven't installed a SIMM on the card. (The capability to share RAM depends on the sort of PC Compatibility Card you install. Some share RAM, some don't.)

With all those choices made, your next step will be to insert a disk in the Mac's floppy drive. The disk will need to be able to boot the PC system (the first disk for DOS or Windows should work) so that you can install software for the PC to use. Start up the PC and switch to it to watch it begin the boot-up process. Once it's booted successfully, you'll need to install an operating system, along with video and sound drivers and any other system software that was included with the card. (Most PC Compatibility Cards include software that can share data between the Mac's and PC's clipboards for supporting the Copy and Paste commands across both platforms.)

Note   Reply has its own control panel, called Detente, and Orange Micro supplies OrangePCi, an application (instead of a control panel) for controlling the PC environment. You'll need to install these and use them for setting up the PC environment, but they're very similar to the Apple versions.

Upgrading a PC Compatibility Card

You should generally be able to tell by looking at a PC Compatibility Card what can be upgraded and what can't. A few manufacturer-specific things can be added to your Mac that work with the card — such as the serial/parallel card that Apple and Reply have offered in the past. But some other upgrades happen right on the card itself.

The most obvious of these is RAM. Most of the PC Compatibility Cards made support a single SIMM upgrade through which you can add between 4- and 64MB of RAM to your card. (Newer Orange Micro cards can support up to 256MB of RAM on a single DIMM.) It's definitely recommended that you add RAM. With additional RAM, both the card itself and the PC operating system will run more efficiently. Recommended minimums are 8MB for DOS and Windows 3.1 and 16MB for Windows 95. More than that is necessary if you'll be using graphical programs or games, or if you plan to have more than one program open in Windows at a time.

Some of the later PCI cards from Apple and Reply offer a VRAM upgrade from the paltry 512K included with the card to 1MB or more for better color depth and higher resolutions in the Windows environment. Consult your manual for specifics on the type of VRAM required — it may be a bit tough to come by. (Reply/Radius sells a VRAM upgrade direct from their price list.)

It seems that only cards built earlier — the DOS and Mac cards for Quadra/Centris and Power Macintosh 6100 machines — have a socketed Intel processors. (Other PC Compatibility Cards have soldered processors.) This means that cards can be upgraded with processors that fit that processor socket. Originally shipped with 486-level processors, those cards can be upgraded to Pentium-level performance.

Although you may have luck finding your own AMD or Cyrix processor with a 486-compatible pinout (and I'd be interested to hear if you have any success doing so), Reply/Radius offers their own 100MHz 586 (Pentium-level) upgrade complete with installation instructions and some software upgrades (if necessary). Check out their Web site for details.

PC emulator software

While hardware companies have been hard at work for years trying to solve the running-Windows-on-Macs dilemma, software-emulation technology was pretty quiet until recently. SoftWindows — and SoftPC before it — were the only solutions for emulating DOS and Windows on a Mac so you could run applications for those operating systems. Of course, some of this was a question of logistics, because the original SoftPC versions were designed to run on 68040 processors, which didn't quite have enough power for high-speed emulation.

With the advent and popularity of the PowerPC processor, that's changed somewhat. The first generation of Power Macs made it possible to run Windows and even Windows 95 (if somewhat slowly). The second and third generations of PowerPC processors — especially the G3 and above — offered a lot of power to burn for emulation. Under the right circumstances, these emulation programs can rival the power of still-current, full-featured Pentium-class computers. For the first time, Mac users are even playing PC games and multimedia titles using software emulation.

So you can see where software emulation could be a boon for office users, too, especially if you have a particular program written only for DOS or Windows that you have to use as part of your job description. These emulation tools are making it possible for Macs to stay in office settings and offer their unique advantages while still supporting basic tasks that require DOS or Windows.

Types of emulation

There's a pretty big difference between emulating and *porting* an operating system. When you port an operating system, you actually design it so it can run on a certain type of hardware, like the PowerPC processor. In fact, the Mac OS is a great example of both porting and emulating an operating system. For the Mac OS to run on the PowerPC, a new port of the original OS had to be written, as the original Mac OS was designed to run on the Motorola 68000 family of processors. Because the Mac OS was ported to PowerPC, older programs couldn't even be run on the PowerPC version of the Mac OS. Instead, only new programs could be compiled in PowerPC computer language compilers, and then run on the new processor.

That should have made all those older programs break when they were run on the PowerPC version of the Mac OS — they would have crashed or refused to run in the first place. But that wasn't really the experience awaiting Mac users. The reason: The Mac OS for PowerPC was also able to emulate the older Mac OS for Motorola 68000 processors. This enabled the older programs to run right along with the newer programs that had been compiled specifically for PowerPC. And, because the PowerPC was much faster than the 68000 series, older programs didn't seem to slow down too much, even though they were running in emulation.

So running emulation programs such as Insignia's SoftWindows and Connectix Virtual PC isn't really the same as running Windows or DOS directly on a Mac. The difference is emulated operating systems are always wrapped in a layer of *native* code — instructions that know how to talk directly to the processor and hardware. On a Power Mac, those instructions are part of the Mac OS for PowerPC. Even Mac OS for 68000 series Macs can't talk directly to the processor, because it's being emulated.

The same goes for SoftWindows, which runs on top of the Mac OS, translating Windows-type commands into commands that the Mac OS can recognize. The difference would be the same as if Microsoft wrote Windows NT for PowerPC, for instance. (Actually, Microsoft was trying to do this at one time, but abandoned the attempt even as it neared completion.) In that case, programs written for Windows NT for Intel processors would have to be recompiled, but would probably run just fine. Plus, the PowerPC version of Windows NT would be talking to the PowerPC processor directly instead of through a Mac OS intermediary.

SoftWindows and Virtual PC are alike in this respect: Both work as emulators, bathed in Mac OS instructions that help them communicate with a PowerPC processor. In other ways, though, they're very different. SoftWindows, for instance, takes the approach of emulating Windows 95 (or Windows 3.1 in some versions), enabling you to run Windows programs on top of the Mac OS (see Figure 19-7).

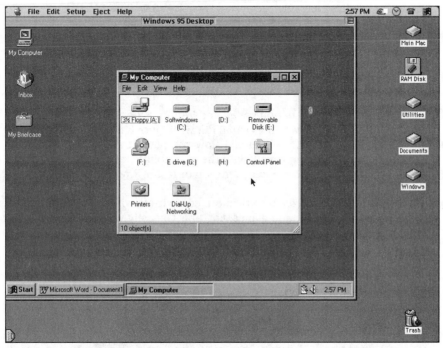

Figure 19-7: SoftWindows 95 emulates Windows 95 so you can run most Windows 95 applications in an application on top of the Mac OS.

Virtual PC, on the other hand, emulates an actual Pentium MMX-class PC, right down to the processor, video card and other hardware. That means any compatible operating system can run in Virtual PC, including OpenStep, OS/2, Linux, and others. It also means Virtual PC offers more support for more games than require regular DOS; because Virtual PC emulates PC hardware, any sort of configuration is possible. This approach became popular enough with the release of Virtual PC that Insignia developed with their own competitor, RealPC, which is marketed as an inexpensive emulator that enables you to play DOS games (or load Windows, if you buy a separate copy from Microsoft). Table 19-3 shows a breakdown of the PC emulation programs for Mac OS.

Company	Product	Features
	Table 19-3	
	PC Emulators for the Mac OS	
Insignia	SoftWindows	Emulates Windows 3.1 on Macs and Power Macs
Insignia	SoftWindows 95	Emulates Windows 95 on Power Macs
Insignia	RealPC	Emulates a Pentium PC on a Power Mac (DOS-only)
Connectix	VirtualPC	Emulates a Pentium PC, comes in Windows, Win95, and DOS versions

In general, the lead in emulation speed and Windows performance go back and forth between SoftWindows and Virtual PC, with innovations and improvements coming from both camps. Both remain slow compared to hardware solutions, but their speed is certainly improving with the availability of faster and faster Power Macs. (Both also require second-generation or faster PowerPC processors.)

Virtual PC is better if you want to be more compatible with PC operating systems, more flexible with drivers and games, and able to easily upgrade (to, for instance, Windows 98 or Window NT) using the same emulation base. SoftWindows is better if you know your main concern is running Windows programs—specifically, business applications. SoftWindows is a tad friendly because it's only designed to run Windows on top of the Mac OS. That makes it a bit easier to set up for activities such as Internet access and networking.

Note   If your primary motivation is gaming, you'll be interested to note that both Connectix and Insignia have rolled support for the Voodoo chipset (offered by the Techworks Power3D card, as discussed in Chapter 18) into their products. That means 3DFX-optimized games running in SoftWindows, RealPC, or Virtual PC can take advantage of the 3D acceleration offered by a Mac-based VooDoo card.

Installing emulation software

Installation of most of these emulation products is simple—you just insert the CD-ROM or disk and double-click the installer program. With SoftWindows, you simply follow the installer's instructions through to the end, and then start running the program. You'll be asked to provide some information, such as set the size of the hard drive, how much RAM you want SoftWindows to use, and other factors.

By default, Virtual PC will also install the OS that came with your particular version—different Virtual PC versions come with DOS, Windows 3.1, or Windows 95/98—which will appear when you start up the PC emulation program. Once that's done, you're free to reboot the machine and install some other OS (see Figure 19-8).

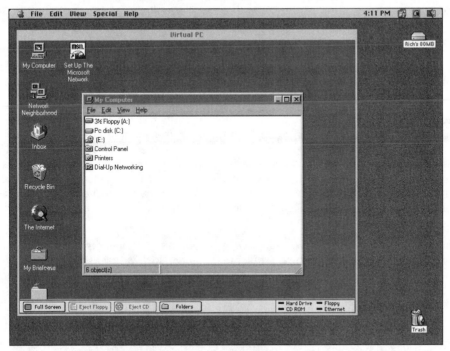

Figure 19-8: Virtual PC includes controls outside the application window for you to manipulate the program as if it were a hardware PC.

Both emulators offer controls and settings you can use to make them work better for you. Sometimes you can hand over more system RAM to make the emulation program faster, use fewer colors or an optimum desktop position, or even set preferences for using the floppy drive and CD-ROM drive for PC-formatted disks.

Sharing DOS and Windows Programs

One of the best ways to run Windows programs on your Mac desktop might be to forego the extra cards and emulators and buy yourself a full-fledged PC. If you connect the PC to your Mac network (or set up the PC so you can dial in to it with a modem), you can use a program called Timbuktu from Farallon (www.farallon.com) to access the PC.

Advanced tip: Run without the Finder

After the problem of sluggish Virtual PC sessions was bandied about on the Evangelist site and elsewhere for a while, someone finally hit on a solution: Quit the Finder first. This works well for at least two different scenarios: You want to play games, or you need to run a Windows (or DOS) program that requires the Mac OS to be locked out.

Steve Wozniak, cofounder of Apple Computer (and often lovingly referred to as "Woz"), wrote to the Evangelist with an example of the latter scenario, the lock-out situation: His son, going into finals in college, was supposed to use a special software program for his testing. The program works in Windows, effectively locking out anything but the test's basic word processing capabilities. This system made things easier on the teacher — who didn't have to read anyone's handwriting — but made it hard to switch to another program and consult notes or a cheat sheet. It also made it tough for PowerBook owners like Woz's son, as the program wasn't written for Macs.

The solution suggested to Steve and others goes like this: The Finder is simply a program. With the correct preparation, you can quit the Finder and load Virtual PC (or SoftWindows), giving it complete control over your Mac (or almost complete control). This gives teachers a lock-out while boosting the performance of Virtual PC and other emulation programs quite a bit.

There are a couple of approaches to doing this, but here is my favorite. First, you want to create an AppleScript that will quit the Finder and load Virtual PC (or SoftWindows). In the Script Editor program (look in your Apple Extras folder), create this very simple script:

```
Tell application  Finder
  quit
end tell
tell application  Virtual PC
  activate
end tell
```

Now, save that compiled script as something like "Boot VPC" and store it in the Startup Items (disabled) folder. (When you run the script for the first time, it may ask you to locate Virtual PC. You can run the script from the editor once, just to get that out of the way. You can also save the script as run-only if you'd like it to avoid the Script Editor when the script launches.)

Next, open the Extensions Manager and create a new, minimal set of System Extensions. (Make sure Extensions Manager is one of them.) Save the set as "Boot VPC" or something similar, and make sure you turn on the Boot VPC AppleScript as a Startup Item for that set of extensions. Check your other sets to make sure Boot VPC wasn't accidentally turned on in those other sets.

Finally, choose the set in Extension Manager and restart your Mac. It should boot up with minimal extensions, and instead of seeing the Finder, you should see Virtual PC or SoftWindows. With any luck, things will even run a bit faster. (See the included CD-ROM for FindKiller and FinderReset, AppleScripts that also can be used to quit and restart the Finder.)

Screen sharing

Timbuktu is a screen-sharing program through which you can view and control a Mac, Windows, or DOS session over a network or modem connection. The other computer's screen appears in a window on your own desktop, enabling you to do just about anything you could be doing if you were sitting in front of the machine itself (see Figure 19-9).

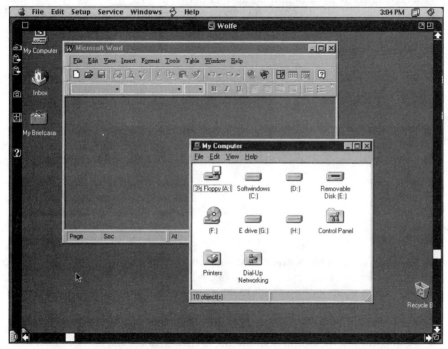

Figure 19-9: Timbuktu enables you to control distant computers, whether they're Macs or PCs.

The first downside to this is the speed of the Windows environment is still subject to the speed of your network, but only for the purposes of displaying the screen. Most of the processing happens on the actual Intel-compatible computer, making it a fairly simple matter for you to use both the Windows machine and your Mac at the same time, because Timbuktu doesn't take up too much processing power.

The other problem is programs can't do anything weird when it comes to the way they draw to the screen, so you'll find that some games, DOS programs, and other nonstandard implementation may not work in a Timbuktu window.

Screen swapping

The other solution to using an actual PC means you'll *really* be physically using an Intel-compatible machine (instead of accessing it over a network), but you'll use the same monitor and keyboard for both your PC and your Mac. A couple of solutions exist to enable you to use the same keyboard and monitor to control two or more computers:

✦ The Omniview from Belkin Components (www.belkin.com) gives you control over four or six PCs from one keyboard and monitor, and, with a special Mac adapter, allows you to control a mix of PCs and Macs. You control the Mac with a PS/2-style keyboard.

✦ Network Technologies (www.networktechinc.com) offers a rather sophisticated switcher that controls Macs, PCs, Sun workstations, and other minicomputers. Called the ST-4UX, this switcher enables you to use Mac, PC, or Sun keyboards and mice, too.

✦ Raritan Computer (www.raritan.com) offers the Master Console, through which you can control from 2 to 64 different computers via one keyboard and monitor. A Mac adapter called the Guardian enables you to control both Macs and PCs.

Summary

✦ The Mac OS and Macintosh hardware are made to help you work with DOS files, disks and removable media. Because Macs are the smaller market, it's generally incumbent on them to do a good job of supporting Windows and Intel standards, and they do.

✦ With built-in and add-on software utilities, you can work with just about any PC file format, including documents, archives, and even compressed files.

✦ If you need to run DOS and Windows programs, you also have a couple of options. The faster choice is a PC-compatibility expansion card that actually places an Intel-compatible processor inside your Mac. You can then use the same monitor and keyboard to run DOS and Windows programs on your Mac's screen.

✦ You can also opt for software emulation. SoftWindows and Virtual PC are two software products that offer Windows compatibility without requiring a dedicated processor. They can be a bit slow compared to actual Pentium-based processing, but they do take advantage of the growing speed of G3 processors and beyond (someday, the emulators may even be faster than Pentium-based cards and computers). Virtual PC has the additional advantage of being capable of running any operating system that a typical hardware PC can.

✦ If you've got a real Intel-compatible PC, you can share its screen over a network and control it using a software program called Timbuktu. Or, if the machine is sitting on your desk and you just want to be able to switch your keyboard, mouse, and monitor back and forth between Macs and PCs, you can do that with switch boxes from a number of different companies.

✦　　✦　　✦

PowerBooks

You'll probably think I'm silly, but I'm still amazed every time I see a PowerBook light up and start computing. It looks just like regular computer! In most cases, PowerBooks are eight pounds or less, feature a good keyboard, a way to mouse around, plenty of ports, internal expansion, and a glow-in-the-dark screen — all the same stuff you can get on a desktop computer. And, these days, PowerBooks are even as powerful as regular desktop computers.

PowerBooks are a tad more limited; specifically, they have fewer ports and usually very few internal upgrading options. When put up against comparable desktop computers, PowerBooks usually have slightly smaller hard drives, slightly slower video, and can generally accept a little less RAM. Up until very recently, you probably wouldn't have bought a PowerBook if your primary work centered around working with Photoshop, QuarkXPress, or 3D animation. You still might not buy a PowerBook for those tasks, but that scenario is becoming much more likely.

Of course, if you already have a PowerBook, you know all this. What you're probably more interested in doing is getting that PowerBook to do more stuff for you: compute better, faster or communicate with more peripherals. Chances are, you can get all that accomplished.

In this chapter, I'll take you on a whirlwind tour through the various accessories and add-ons you can come across for your PowerBook. If you've got a PowerBook already or you're thinking about getting one, you'll enjoy this chapter, which shows you how to upgrade them and what's possible with a souped-up PowerBook.

Upgrading Your PowerBook

You'll find that PowerBooks and PowerBook upgrades are often more expensive than upgrades for desktop Macs. Part of that is because so much design work goes into each PowerBook—somehow, everything has to fit, spin, avoid catching on fire, and continue to compute in that little box. Usually that means using cutting-edge, miniaturized technologies that are beyond the typical components you'll find in desktop computers—both in technology and in price.

It also means that the upgrades tend to be a bit more proprietary. RAM, for instance, often has to be designed not only for PowerBooks, but often the RAM has to be made just for a particular PowerBook model. As that's the case, the RAM can't benefit from the economies of scale that usually affect desktop RAM prices; because desktop Macs share RAM designs even with Intel-compatible PCs, a lot of the same RAM can be manufactured and sold, keeping the price reasonable.

You'll still find PowerBook RAM modules at a decent price, but don't be surprised if that price doubles the price of regular RAM. It's just going to cost a tad more. The same is true of other components, such as processor upgrades, new hard drives, and internal modems or networking solutions.

Other than the price, though, you'll find that PowerBook upgrades come in two basic categories—blissfully easy and somewhat messy. Certain models—PowerBook 5300, 1400, 2400, 3400, G3, or higher—include PC Card slots (also called PCMCIA slots) that make adding a number of different upgrades (RAM, modems, Ethernet, hard drives) pretty easy to do. In most cases, you stick the card in and add the functionality. (These cards are discussed in detail in the next section of this chapter.)

If you won't be upgrading using a PC Card, things can get a bit messier. You'll have to open the PowerBook's case, which can be quite a study in engineering itself. Next, you'll need to get the right parts and install them correctly. First things first, though. Table 20-1 shows the PowerBook chart for internal upgrades (there's another one later in this chapter for port info and external upgrades).

Table 20-1 PowerBook Internal Upgrades					
Model #	*Processor*	*Megahertz*	*Processor Upgrade?*	*Form Factor*	*Slots*
100	68000	16	No	PB 100	Modem
140	68030	16	No	PB 140	Modem
145/145B	68030	25	No	PB 140	Modem
150	68030	33	No	PB 140	Modem
160	68030	25	No	PB 140	Modem

Model #	Processor	Megahertz	Processor Upgrade?	Form Factor	Slots
165	68030	33	No	PB 140	Modem
165c	68030 (w/FPU)	33	No	PB 140	Modem
170	68030 (w/FPU)	25	No	PB 140	Modem
180/180c	68030 (w/FPU)	33	No	PB 140	Modem
190/66	68LC040	66	Logic board to 5300	PB 5300	Two Type II PC Card
Duo 210	68030	25	Logic board to 2300	PB Duo	Modem, dock
Duo 230	68030	33	Logic board to 2300	PB Duo	Modem, dock
Duo 250	68030	33	Logic board to 2300	PB Duo	Modem, dock
Duo 270c	68030 (w/FPU)	33	Logic board to 2300	PB Duo	Modem, dock
Duo 280/c	68LC040	66	Logic board to 2300	PB Duo	Modem, dock
Duo 2300	PPC 603e	100	No	PB Duo	Modem, dock
520/520c	68LC040	50	Card to PPC	PB 500	Modem, PC cage[1]
540/540c	68LC040	66	Card to PPC	PB 500	Modem, PC cage[1]
550c	68040	66	Card to PPC	PB 500	Modem, PC cage[1]
1400	PPC 603e	117/133/ 166	Third-party card	PB 1400	Two Type II PC Cards, comm[2]
2400c	PP C 603e	180/250	Third-party card	PB 2400	Two Type II PC Cards
3400c	PPC 603e	180/200/ 240	No	PB 3400	Two Type II PC Cards
5300	PPC 603e	100/117	No	PB 5300	Two Type II PC Cards

(continued)

Table 20-1 *(continued)*					
Model #	**Processor**	**Megahertz**	**Processor Upgrade?**	**Form Factor**	**Slots**
G3 (3500)	PPC 750	250	No	PB 3400	Two Type II PC Cards
G3 (BTO)	PPC 750	225, 250, 292	No	PB G3	Two Type II PC Cards

1 The 500 series can accept a PCMCIA card cage as a substitute for one of its two battery-expansion bays. It can then access PC Card upgrades.

2 The communications slot on the 1400 can accept an Apple video-out card or an Ethernet card.

Although there's a rumor that upgrade cards may become available for the PowerBook 3400 and 5300 series, they're not available as of the writing of this book. The PowerBook 1400 series can accept upgrade cards that extend them to 183MHz 603e processors, or they can accept a G3 upgrade card, which has been announced by NewerTech (and some other companies). Check NewerTech's Web site (www.newertech.com) and this book's Web site for continued reports.

Notice that two versions of the PowerBook G3 are listed. The original PowerBook G3 was based on the PowerBook 3400 form factor and is sometimes referred to as the 3500 series. The second PowerBook G3 series are the first models available under the Apple Store *build-to-order* system: This means Apple doesn't necessarily sell them in standard configurations, but can add or subtract components according to individual orders as the machines are being built. There is an expectation that these G3 models will be processor upgradeable, but nothing has been announced.

Note

Although there's no official kit (or official support) for it, you can swap the logic boards in earlier PowerBooks to increase the speed. In the PowerBooks that use the PowerBook 140 form factor, it's possible to swap logic boards to add life to an aging machine. That's beyond the scope of the book, if only because it's tough to come up with a great reason to do it; with today's modern software, there's little advantage to moving from a 25MHz 68030 to a 33MHz 68030. And to do it, you'll probably have to buy the faster PowerBook anyway. Therefore, unless it's got a bad screen or other trouble, there's not too much point in trying to upgrade one machine's logic board for the other's. Just use the better machine. If you need a replacement logic board, though, try DT&T Service at www.dttservice.com/Powerbook.html on the Web along with the usual used market suspects.

Opening your PowerBook

We're fortunate in this respect: Apple has used basically nine different PowerBook form factors over the life of the portable's line, so it's pretty easy to pin down the specifics of each. What governs how you'll open yours is the form factor of the machine, as detailed in Table 20-1. The text that follows will include a quick discussion of what's required to get a particular PowerBook model opened, along with a photo of the PowerBook being opened.

Note

Apple is a little wishy-washy about whether they really want you opening your PowerBook to add RAM. They make it easy to do, with diagrams all over the place and tantalizing references to all the upgrades you can add to the PowerBook, but then they tell you that they'd prefer you consult an Apple Authorized Dealer for installation. What should you do? If you're under warranty, I'd recommend reading the arranty and your manual to see if opening your PowerBook voids the warranty. If it doesn't, upgrade away. If upgrading will void your warranty, then do so at your own risk.

PowerBook 100

Models include: PowerBook 100

The PowerBook 100 requires a T10 Torx screwdriver to remove its screws. Here's how to open the PowerBook and expose its memory upgrade slot (the only upgrade possible with this model) (refer also to Figure 20-1):

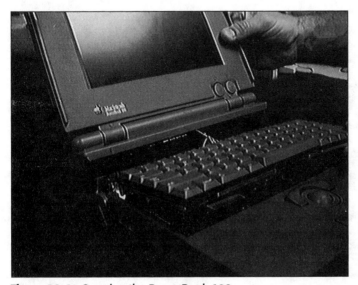

Figure 20-1: Opening the PowerBook 100

1. Shut down the PowerBook, and remove all cords and cables to external peripherals. Ground yourself.

2. Remove the main battery (slide the battery door to the right, and then pull the battery out of the computer). Also, take out the backup batteries in the rear compartment of the PowerBook 100.

3. Remove the three rubber pads on the underside of the PowerBook. You'll find screws underneath the pads. Remove the screws.

4. With the machine right-side up, open the display. Lift the display and pull it off the base, but don't disconnect it from the rest of the machine.

5. Lift the keyboard up off the computer and lay it down on the display panel. Don't disconnect it from the rest of the PowerBook.

To put the PowerBook back together, replace the keyboard first, and then the screen. Next, reinstall the screws on the bottom of the PowerBook. If everything seems solid, hook up the battery and power cable, start up the Mac, and test it.

PowerBook 140 form factor

Models include: PowerBook 140, 145, 145B, 150, 160, 165, 165c, 170, 180, 180c

The PowerBook 140 form factor requires both a T8 and a T10 Torx screwdriver to remove its screws. Here's how to open the PowerBook and expose its memory-upgrade slot (see also Figure 20-2):

Figure 20-2: Opening the PowerBook 140 series of PowerBooks

1. Shut down the PowerBook, and remove all cords and cables to external peripherals. Ground yourself.

2. Remove the main battery by sliding the battery door to the right, and then pulling the battery out of the computer.

3. On the underside of the PowerBook, remove the four recessed screws using the T10 Torx screwdriver.

4. Open the rear access door and remove the T8 Torx screw next to the SCSI port.

5. With the PowerBook upside down and the rear facing you, lift the bottom of the PowerBook until you see a cable connecting the two halves of the PowerBook. While holding the casing open, disconnect the cable from the section you're lifting (the PowerBook's true bottom).

6. Continue to lift until the section you're lifting separates from the keyboard section of the PowerBook. Rotate and flip the section you're lifting so that it lies exposed on the table.

To put this type of PowerBook form factor back together, place the bottom section of the PowerBook back on the upside-down top section, aligning the tabs on the front edge of the PowerBook (the front edge is where the screen latch is). With the tabs aligned, lower the bottom section until it's close enough to plug the cable into, and then connect the cable. Lower the casing the rest of the way, and reinstall all the screws. If everything looks good, turn the PowerBook over, replace the battery and power, and start up the Mac to test it.

PowerBook Duo form factor

Models include: PowerBook Duo 210, 230, 250, 270c, 280, 280c, 2300

Mac Evangelista tip: Your PowerBook screws

Mac Evangelista Lisa Devlin notes that her PowerBook has often been accused of having a screw loose. This seems to be particularly true as a PowerBook ages:

"Models with keyboard screws, that is, the 140–180 series, should be checked at least once a year, and more often if the PowerBook is used heavily or if you're a violent typist. If the screws are not tightened regularly, they can wiggle loose and damage other parts of the PowerBook, including the logic board and disk drive."

The PowerBook Duo form factor requires a T8 Torx screwdriver to remove its screws. Here's how to open the PowerBook and expose its memory-upgrade slot (refer also to Figure 20-3):

Figure 20-3: Opening the PowerBook Duo series of PowerBooks

1. Shut down the PowerBook, and remove all cords and cables to external peripherals. Ground yourself.

2. Remove the main battery by sliding the battery door to the right, and then pulling the battery out of the computer.

3. On the underside of the PowerBook, remove the three keyboard screws using the T8 Torx screwdriver. (Don't remove the fourth screw, which is closest to the front of the machine.)

4. With the PowerBook right-side up, open the screen. Now place your hand on the PowerBook's keyboard (it's been loosened and will fall out). Lift the back of the PowerBook so that you rotate the PowerBook toward its front, causing the keyboard to fall into your hand.

5. Don't remove or damage the cables that connect the keyboard to the computer. Gently put the PowerBook back upright and lay the keyboard down on the front wrist-rest section of the PowerBook.

Putting these PowerBook Duos back together is pretty easy. Just gently place the keyboard back in its place, close the screen, and turn the Duo over. Replace the keyboard screws. If everything looks good, add the battery and power supply, and start up the Mac to test it.

PowerBook 500 form factor

Models include: PowerBook 520, 520c, 540, 540c, 550

The PowerBook 500 form factor requires a T8 Torx screwdriver to remove its screws. Here's how to open the PowerBook and expose its memory-upgrade and processor-card upgrade slot (see Figure 20-4):

Figure 20-4: Opening the PowerBook 500 series of PowerBooks

1. Shut down the PowerBook, and remove all cords and cables to external peripherals. Ground yourself.

2. Remove the battery or both batteries, if installed. Remove the PCMCIA cage (PC Card cage) if it's installed. (Remove these by sliding the grooved slider toward the front of the PowerBook, and then pop the battery out.)

3. On the underside of the PowerBook, remove the two (most deeply recessed) keyboard screws using the T8 Torx screwdriver. Don't remove the other screws.

4. Open the rear access door and remove the two T8 Torx screws located on either side of the serial number label.

5. With the PowerBook right-side up, open the screen. Lift the keyboard up from the PowerBook, but don't disconnect its cables. Place it on the front wrist-rest of the PowerBook.

6. Push slightly forward and pull up on the plastic strip near the screen's hinge to remove it.

7. Remove the three heat-shield screws. (One screw is located beneath where the plastic strip was installed.)

8. Remove the heat shield. If you're upgrading RAM, remove the plastic holder that sits over the RAM slot.

When you put the PowerBook 500 form factor back together, you'll need to take care, especially around the RAM module, which can be delicate. Slide the plastic holder over the RAM module (if you've installed one) and replace it in its original position. Next, replace the heat shield and its three screws. (This is a delicate process, so be patient. The heat shield can be difficult to get back in place.) Replace the plastic strip and then the keyboard. Close the screen. Replace the screws on the back of the PowerBook, and then the screws on the bottom.

If everything looks good, add the battery and power supply, start up the Mac, and test it.

Mac Evangelista tip: Upgrading 500 series

Mac Evangelista Philip Accas has a love-hate relationship with his PowerBook 500 series machines. Apparently he loves to upgrade them, but hates some of the pain that comes with the process. (As you can tell, PowerBook 500 upgrades can be a little tricky; I certainly recommend you have a dealer look at the PowerBook for you if any of this seems confusing or tough to accomplish.) Here are some tips he's gleaned from his 500 series experiences:

"To add RAM or other components to a 500 series PowerBook, you must first remove the keyboard and the little plastic strip immediately behind it that screws into the back of the PowerBook, behind the flip-down door. This strip needs to come out because it covers the last screw you need to unscrew to remove the cover, allowing you to access the CPU/RAM.

"Tip 1 is this: Make sure something about 2-inches high (a hardback book, for example) is behind the PowerBook, bend the screen back until it just about touches this support, and then loosen both screen hinge screws about two turns. This gives you enough room to easily extract (and replace) the plastic strip without removing the screen completely.

(continued)

(continued)

"After getting inside the PowerBook, you still have to remove the perforated metal piece that covers the CPU daughterboard/RAM/modem area. Two of the screws thread into a thin plastic support that 'clips' around the RAM module. Once you've removed the screws, you'll need to extract the screwholder to access the RAM module. Unfortunately, that screwholder can be tough to get out.

"So, Tip 2 is this: Bend out a side panel—the one that separates the RAM/CPU middle section from the floppy and hard drive sections—and its restraining tab slightly. Move the plastic screwholder towards the back of the PowerBook just a bit; this should free one side of the plastic screwholder. Bend the other metal side panel out, and with your other hand, slip the plastic screwholder off the RAM card entirely. You should now be able to pull the RAM straight up using a chip-puller. You'll also be able to get to the CPU daughtercard.

"To reinstall, slip the plastic piece onto the RAM module first, and then bend a metal side panel (with the restraining tabs) out slightly, inserting one side of the screwholder under the metal tab. Bend the other metal side/tab out and, with your other hand, position the RAM module and screwholder right above the RAM connection socket. Press straight down until it clicks, and release the second side; both metal tabs should be holding the plastic screwholder down and in place—a little wiggling may be necessary to achieve this."

PowerBook 5300 form factor

Models include: PowerBook 190, 190cs, 5300 series

The PowerBook 5300 form factor requires a T8 Torx screwdriver to remove its screws. Here's how to open the PowerBook and expose its memory upgrade slot (refer to Figure 20-5):

1. Shut down the PowerBook, and remove all cords and cables to external peripherals. Ground yourself.

2. Remove the main battery.

3. On the underside of the PowerBook, remove the three recessed keyboard screws using the T8 Torx screwdriver.

4. With the PowerBook right-side up, gently open the screen to a wide angle. Now, place your hand on the PowerBook's keyboard (it's been loosened and will fall out). Lift the back of the PowerBook so that you rotate the PowerBook toward its front, causing the keyboard to fall into your hand.

5. Don't remove or damage the cables that connect the keyboard to the computer. Gently put the PowerBook back upright and lay the keyboard down very gently on the bottom half of the screen, with keycaps facing up. (You may want to place a clean, dry towel over the screen to protect it.)

Figure 20-5: Opening the PowerBook 5300 series of PowerBooks

Putting the PowerBook 5300 form factor back together is pretty easy. Just gently place the keyboard back in place, close the screen, and turn the 5300 over. Replace the keyboard screws. If everything looks good, add the battery and power supply and start up the Mac to test it.

PowerBook 1400 form factor

Models include: PowerBook 1400 series

The PowerBook 1400 series is fairly simple to open for upgrading: It requires only a small Phillips-head screwdriver to remove its screws. Here's how to open the PowerBook and expose its memory and internal upgrade slot (see Figure 20-6):

1. Shut down the PowerBook, and remove all cords and cables to external peripherals. Ground yourself.

2. Remove the main battery. (Push the release on the bottom of the battery to pop it out of the left-front bay.)

3. Gently open the screen wide. Slide the speaker grille above the keyboard slightly to the left, and then pull up on the grille. (It may take a little power to release the grille.)

4. Place your finger under the metal guard at the top edge of the keyboard (it's actually part of the keyboard). Lift up on the keyboard until it comes free. (This will take some maneuvering, but not much strength.) Place the keyboard upside down on the wrist rest. Don't disconnect its cable.

5. Remove the five or six screws from the heat shield that's exposed when you remove the grille. Lift the heat shield out of the PowerBook.

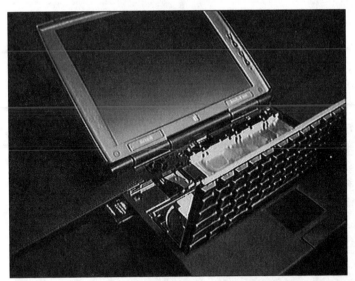

Figure 20-6: Opening the PowerBook 1400 series of PowerBooks

To put the PowerBook 1400 back together, just reverse the process. Screw the metal heat shield back into place (the longer screws go in the rearmost holes). Place the keyboard gently back into place, and then cover its top with the speaker grille (begin with the grille slightly offset to the left), sliding it to the right to secure it. If everything looks good, replace the battery and/or power supply, start up the Mac, and test it.

Note   If you're installing an internal expansion card, you'll need to pop off the plastic cover for the internal expansion port (on the back of the PowerBook) using a flathead screwdriver. Once the card is installed, you'll need to screw the expansion card into the PowerBook from the rear, using the connector holes on either side of the port opening.

PowerBook 2400 form factor

Models include: PowerBook 2400 series

The PowerBook 2400 series is very difficult to open for upgrading—so much so, in fact, that I'll go along with a number of other experts and recommend against trying to upgrade it yourself. Although Apple recommends against upgrading any PowerBook, its engineers make some of them pretty easy to get into. The PowerBook 2400 is a wonderful example of an instance in which that's *not* the case.

Although the PowerBook 2400 does take fairly standard RAM modules (making that part of the upgrade enticing), I'd say that the chance of marring the plastic or losing a screw is too high, especially compared to other PowerBook models. In most cases I'd recommend handing this one over to an authorized service center.

If you're still interested, though, here's the process you have to go through to open a PowerBook 2400 (see also Figure 20-7). You'll need a small flathead screwdriver and a small Phillips-head screwdriver:

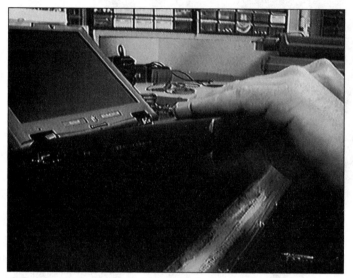

Figure 20-7: Opening the PowerBook 2400 series of PowerBooks

1. Shut down the PowerBook, and remove all cords and cables to external peripherals. Ground yourself.

2. Remove the main battery.

3. Locate the two small screw covers on each side of the screen bezel at the top of the keyboard. Remove the covers by prying them up with a flathead screwdriver with a very thin blade, and remove the two screws found under those covers using a small Phillips-head screwdriver.

4. Remove the bezel itself using a flathead screwdriver to release the two tabs holding the bezel in place. One tab is located over the F3 key; the other is over the F12 key.

5. Using your index fingers, slide the top section of the PowerBook gently away from the screen. You should only slide it back far enough to expose the ribbon cable that's connecting the top section to the logic board.

6. Remove the ribbon cable connecting this top section to the logic board. A small flathead screwdriver can be used to release the two small tabs that fasten the ribbon to the logic board. Remove the top section.

7. The keyboard has six screws, which need to be removed. There are three gold screws along the top and three black screws along the bottom of the keyboard. Remove them with the Phillips-head screwdriver.

8. Flip the keyboard up so that it rests against the bottom of the PowerBook's screen. (You may want to use a soft towel between the two to keep the screen safe.) Do not disconnect the ribbon cables for the keyboard.

9. To access the RAM upgrade slots, locate the metal heat shield that covers the RAM slot found near the lower-left corner of the PowerBook. Remove the two screws on the left side of the heat shield, and then remove the shield.

A bit tricky, eh? To put it back together, reverse the process. Note that there are quite a few screws to keep track of; try to keep the colors of the screws right and put them back in the holes they came from. You should also decide *before* continuing whether or not it's going to be too much of a sleight-of-hand maneuver for you to plug the top section of the PowerBook back into the logic board with the benefit of only a screwdriver and some ingenuity. If that's too much pressure, abort the mission and take the PowerBook to an authorized service center for a quick upgrade.

PowerBook 3400 form factor

Models include: PowerBook 3400 series, G3 (3500)

The PowerBook 3400 form factor requires a T8 Torx screwdriver to remove its screws. Here's how to open the PowerBook and expose its memory upgrade slot (see also Figure 20-8):

1. Shut down the PowerBook, and remove all cords and cables to external peripherals. Ground yourself.

2. Remove the main battery. (A slider on the bottom of the PowerBook will release the battery.)

3. On the underside of the PowerBook, completely loosen the three recessed keyboard screws using the T8 Torx screwdriver. Turn the PowerBook over so that the screws fall out.

4. With the PowerBook right side up, gently open the screen to a wide angle. Now lift up very slightly (no more than 1/4-inch) on both the right and left side of the front end of the keyboard.

5. Pull the keyboard very slightly toward the front of the PowerBook until the small tabs on the back edge of the keyboard come free from the case.

6. Don't remove or damage the cables that connect the keyboard to the computer. Very gently place the keyboard down on the bottom half of the screen with keycaps facing up. (It's recommended that you place a clean, dry towel over the screen to protect it.)

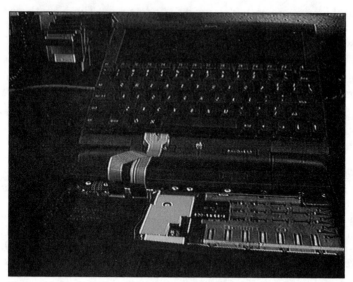

Figure 20-8: Opening the PowerBook 3400 series of PowerBooks

Note

If the PowerBook has been plugged in and/or turned on recently, make sure you avoid touching the heat sink, the metal section located in the center of the exposed area in the PowerBook. It can get very hot.

Putting the PowerBook 3400 form factor back together is pretty easy. Just gently place the keyboard back in the case, making sure to angle it in carefully to fit the tabs into the back of the keyboard opening in the case. Lower the keyboard into its slot. Close the screen and turn the PowerBook over. Replace the keyboard screws.

If everything looks good, add the battery and/or power cable, start up the Mac, and test it.

PowerBook G3 form factor

Models include: PowerBook G3 (BTO) series

The PowerBook G3 BTO series is very simple to open for upgrading — all it requires is a Phillips-head screwdriver. Here's the procedure (also refer to Figure 20-9):

1. Unplug the PowerBook, ground yourself, and pull the front-mounted expansion bay release levers toward you to release the battery and/or devices that are in the expansion bays. Remove those devices.

2. Reach into the device bays and pull back the spring-loaded tabs to release the PowerBook's keyboard.

3. Remove the two Phillips-head screws that secure the heat shield. Remove the heat shield to gain access to the RAM upgrade slots and processor daughtercard.

Figure 20-9: Opening the PowerBook G3 Build-to-Order series

Simply reverse the process to put the PowerBook back together — screw on the heat shield and snap the keyboard back into place.

Upgrading RAM

Aside from getting the PowerBook open, you'll also need to explore the various requirements for the RAM in your particular PowerBook. I've got another chart for you in this section to help explain these requirements.

In just about every case you'll have one available slot for upgrading; fortunately, PowerBook RAM modules can be installed one module at a time. (Makes sense, eh?) In the PowerBook 1400, unlike most others, you can stack memory modules on top of one another, which enables you to add two modules to the one slot. In the G3 (BTO) series, the PowerBook has two available SO-DIMM slots. The base RAM is installed in one of those slots and the other is available for upgrading.

If your Mac is currently showing more RAM in the About this Computer dialog box than the model's base amount listed in Table 20-2, then you probably already have an upgrade module installed in the Mac. In that case, you'll have to replace the existing module (unless it's in a PowerBook 1400), so make sure you buy a module with a much higher capacity than the module that's currently in the upgrade slot — otherwise the upgrade won't be very much use. For instance, if you have a Duo 210 with a total of 8MB of RAM, the upgrade slot is taken by a 4MB module. You'll want to get a larger module (at least 8MB) to make up for replacement of the 4MB module.

Table 20-2
PowerBook RAM Upgrades

Model	Base RAM	Max. RAM	Type	Speed	Module Sizes
100/140/145	2MB	8MB	PB100	100 ns	2-, 4-, 6MB
145B	4MB	8MB	PB100	100 ns	2-, 4MB
150	4MB	40MB	Duo	70 ns	4-, 8-, 2-, 36MB
160/165/165c 180/180c	4MB	14MB	PB100	85 ns	2-, 4-, 10MB
170	2MB	8MB	PB100	100 ns	2-, 4-, 6MB
190/190cs	4MB[1]	36MB[1]	PB5300	70 ns	4–32MB
Duo 210, 230, 250	4MB	24MB	Duo	70 ns	4–20MB
Duo 270c	4MB	32MB	Duo	70 ns	4–28MB
Duo 280/280c	4MB	40MB	Duo	70 ns	4–36MB
500 series	4MB[2]	36M[2]	PB500	70 ns	4-, 8-, 12-, 20-, 32MB
1400 series	16MB[3]	64MB[3]	PB1400	70 ns	8–24MB
Duo 2300	8MB	56MB	Duo	70 ns	4–48MB
2400 series	16MB	144MB	SO-DIMM	60 ns	16–128MB
3400 series	16MB	144MB	PB3400	60 ns	4–128MB
5300 series	8MB[4]	64MB	PB5300	70 ns	8–64MB
G3 (3500)	32MB	160MB	PB G3	60 ns	4–128MB
G3 (BTO)	32MB[5]	192MB	SO-DIMM	N/A	16–128MB

1 Some later model 190 series PowerBooks came with 8MB of base RAM, increasing the maximum to 40MB.

2 Installing a PowerPC upgrade card in a PowerBook 500 series raises the base RAM to 8MB (because 8MB of RAM is soldered on the card, but the 4MB on the logic board is disabled), resulting in a new maximum of 40MB of RAM.

3 Early 1400cs/117 models came with 12MB of base RAM, reducing its maximum to 60MB.

4 Later models of the 5300c and 5300cs came with 16MB of base RAM. The 5300ce came with 16MB of base RAM and a 16MB upgrade in the available RAM slot.

5 At the time of writing, some build-to-order G3 models include 64MB of RAM installed in one of the two available SO-DIMM slots.

With the exception of the G3 BTO and 2400 series of PowerBooks, which use *small outline* DIMMs (SO DIMMS) — a smaller version of standard DIMMs that have become popular for notebook computer memory — every single one of these PowerBooks requires a special type of RAM module designed to fit their respective form factors. When shopping for RAM, make sure you get the right type.

In general, you'll need to be careful with these RAM modules, as they often have fragile connectors and pins that can be quite different from desktop RAM modules. You should also be very sensitive to the possibility of static electricity discharge when working inside a PowerBook — wear a grounding strap before adding RAM. Remember, PowerBook logic boards and components tend to be much more expensive that desktop logic boards.

Cross-Reference

To learn more about RAM in general, see the desktop RAM discussion in Chapter 6. If you're interested in upgrading your PowerBook soon, you should also immediately download the Apple Memory Guide PDF (Adobe Portable Document Format) from Apple's Support Web site (www.apple.com/support), which includes not only memory requirements but diagrams and instructions for installing RAM in various PowerBook models.

Internal slots

Not all PowerBooks have internal slots (see Table 20-1 to see if yours does), and those that do can usually only accept very specific add-ons. The PowerBook 1400 has exactly three upgrade cards that can be added to its internal slot: a video-out card from Apple, an Ethernet card from Focus Enhancements (www.focusinfo.com), and a 16-bit video-out card available from Newer Technology (www.newertech.com). Figure 20-10 shows a PowerBook 1400 being upgraded with the Apple video-out card.

With other models, such as the PowerBook 500 series, only the PowerPort Mercury 19.2 modem from Global Village was ever made available for internal upgrading. The Duo series could also be upgraded with a special Global Village Mercury modem. The PowerBook 100 series can be upgraded by a number of different PowerPort modems designed specifically for that PowerBook 100 series. Apple and Supra (www.diamondmm.com) also made internal modems for the PowerBook 100 series, including a Supra modem that runs at 33.6 Kbps.

Figure 20-10: The PowerBook 1400's internal slot is right next to the RAM upgrade slot so that its port can line up with the others on the back of the notebook.

Unfortunately, none of these modems remains available for retail sale. If you're interested in an internal modem for a non-PowerPC PowerBook, you'll need to shop the used market.

Note

Aside from the used Mac and PowerBook Usenet newsgroups (comp.sys.mac.forsale, comp.sys.mac.wanted, comp.forsale.computers.mac) **and your local classifieds, you may have luck finding PowerBook parts at** www.sirius.com/~exupery/forsale.html **or** www.macresq.com.

Most of these internal slots include an internal connector and an external port on the back of the PowerBook. You'll usually need to pry a plastic cover off that back port opening, and secure the card to the back of the PowerBook once it's been installed. The cards themselves are considerably smaller than NuBus or PCI cards and tend to use a miniaturized, completely nonstandard connnector between the card and the logic board. The connectors are apt to be delicate, so be very careful when you're installing internal PowerBook components (see Figure 20-11).

Along with the cards, you'll likely need a software extension and other driver software that lets the PowerBook know that it's been enhanced. Those drivers should come on a floppy disk or two included with the upgrade card. Install those after you've installed the card and sealed up the Mac.

Figure 20-11: Here's the available slot in a PowerBook 140 form factor.

Note

Again, Apple doesn't really encourage upgrading your own PowerBook, and may not pay for repairs if something goes wrong, even if the PowerBook is under warranty. Consult your manual if you're concerned that you may not be able to perform the upgrade yourself. Such service shouldn't be too expensive.

Processor upgrades

There isn't a slot in processor-upgradeable PowerBooks for the small daughtercard that boosts its processing speed. In most cases, you just replace the PowerBook's original processor, often using a small card that includes the new processor and any other components it needs to function, such as cache RAM. (The exception to this rule is the G3 BTO series, which does put its processor on a daughtercard but which, according to Apple, is officially non-upgradeable, as mentioned below.)

Installing a processor upgrade is a very delicate operation in many cases, requiring patience and close adherence to the instructions that come with the upgrade. In particular, you should be very careful when pulling processor chips and plugging chips into processor sockets. These chips feature hundreds of tiny pins that can bend or break very easily. If that happens, you may have lost a single component worth hundreds of dollars.

The upgradeable PowerBooks include the PowerBook 500 series, PowerBook 1400, PowerBook 2400 and the G3 BTO series, although Apple officially says the BTO series isn't upgradeable.

Note

Apple presumably doesn't certify their systems as upgradeable these days because they lost a lawsuit a few years back, requiring them to provide a special upgrade because the company had advertised some Performa models as "upgradeable." Be that as it may, the G3 BTO series is built around a removable daughtercard that will likely entice some company to build an upgrade for faster processors in the future.

Table 20-3 shows the potential upgrades.

Table 20-3 Processor Upgradeable PowerBooks		
PowerBook Model	**Upgrade(s)**	**Company**
500 series	PowerPC 603e/100	Apple
	PowerPC 603e/167	Newer Technology
	PowerPC 603e/183	Newer Technology
1400 series	PowerPC 603e/183	Newer Technology
	PowerPC G3/216	Newer Technology
	PowerPC G3/250	Newer Technology
2400 series	PowerPC G3/240	Newer Technology

Evangelista tip: Speed up more than the CPU

It isn't tough to find people who were pleased that they could bump up the speed on their PowerBooks from earlier PowerPC processors into the realm of G3 speeds. But Dr. Ronald D. Leppke found even more to be pleased about:

"In the general area of PowerBook upgrades, I am just delighted with the NUpowr G3 upgrade from Newer for my PowerBook 1400. I have the 250MHz version, which is very fast, as expected.

"What surprised me, however, was an improvement in download speeds. Because I am connected via a cable modem, I was already seeing 115 Kbps download speeds. But, after the upgrade, I watched as large files downloaded to my PowerBook in seconds, with an indicated speed as high as 263 Kbps. Productivity per hour has just taken a very significant jump."

Adding a hard drive

Adding a hard drive to your PowerBook certainly isn't impossible, although it involves some minor surgery. Aside from getting your Mac opened up and ready for upgrading, you'll also need to get the old hard drive out of there and get a new one to put in its place. Probably most important is buying the right upgrade drive for the task.

The type of drive you need for your PowerBook depends on the model of the PowerBook you want and how large a hard drive you feel you need. If you have a PowerBook in the 100 series (aside from the 150), a 500 series PowerBook, or a Duo model (with the exception of a Duo 2300 originally equipped with a 1.1GB drive), you've got a SCSI internal drive, so you'll need a SCSI replacement.

The best bet you have for buying one of these drives is buying a true, 2.5-inch SCSI drive with Apple ROMs built in. (You don't have to buy an Apple ROM drive, although such drives are easier to work with, especially when upgrading the Mac OS and troubleshooting system software. Other SCSI drives will work, but they require third-party driver software such as FWB Toolkit.) In general, you should have luck finding drives in 800MB, 1.0GB and 1.2GB capacities that have SCSI interfaces and Apple ROMs, as well as smaller drives such as those that came in older PowerBook models. PowerBook Duo models require a drive that's 17 mm in height. Most other PowerBook models require a hard drive that's 19 mm in height.

You may occasionally find a repurposed IDE drive that's been given a SCSI interface; although I won't tell you to stay away from these drives (especially if you get good instructions for installing the drive and a liberal return policy) I will say you'll probably see a performance hit as a result of using one of these drives. That's usually a trade-off people are willing to make because of the potential to put a high-capacity drive (1- or 2GB in some cases) in their aging PowerBook.

Most other PowerBooks — the 150, 190, 5300-series, 1400-series, 3400, 2400, and G3 models — all include IDE drives. (The Duo 2300 with a 1.1GB drive also shipped with an internal IDE interface.) In most cases, these drives can be upgraded with most off-the-shelf 2.5" IDE-compatible drives, although in some cases (such as the 1400 series) you'll specifically need a "thin" 2.5" IDE drive.

This is actually really good news; large-capacity IDE drives are very affordable, even in 2.5-inch capacities, because many of them are made for Intel-compatible notebooks as well as for PowerBooks. Very few other notebook computers used 2.5-inch SCSI drives, making them more difficult to come by.

Mac Components Engineered (www.powerbook1.com) is an excellent resource for getting information about and buying replacement hard drives for PowerBook computers. Although I haven't used them myself, I've heard excellent things about their ability to help with installation instructions and kits to get the job done. Another resource that seems to be good is Other World Computing (www.macsales.com).

If you buy a new IDE drive for your PowerBook, it'll need to be, physically, an exact replacement for your existing drive, including the screws and mounting brackets. If you can't get the drive to fit in the PowerBook, you may want to consult the dealer or return it for one that will fit in your particular PowerBook. While installing, make sure you hang onto all the screws you removed to get the original drive out, because you'll need them for the new drive. (The PowerBook 2400, according to Apple and Mac Components Engineered, features some 20-plus screws to remove the internal drive. It's recommended that you have that particular Mac serviced if you'd like a replacement hard drive.)

Once you have the drive installed in your PowerBook, boot from a floppy or a System CD-ROM to format the disk with Drive Setup. (If you order a drive from a Mac-centric dealer, it may come preformatted for use on a Mac.) You'll then need to install the Mac OS on the drive to use it as the startup disk. Drive Setup can format and deal with many different IDE drives, although the brand names (IBM, Toshiba, Hitachi) might be the smarter choices.

Screen upgrades and replacements

Many PowerBook models can actually have their screens updated to show more colors or be a little larger, especially if the PowerBook in question shares its heritage with a more advanced model (such as the PowerBook Duo 230 and Duo 270c, for instance).

You'll also want to swap the screen if it shows any dead pixels (pixels that always glow while when the screen is turned on) or stuck pixels (which are always black when the screen is on). Stuck pixels are especially disconcerting, because they drain power. (A black, gray, or colored pixel requires power, because it's "on," whereas a white pixel doesn't draw power.) Backlighting needs to be turned on on many recent models for these errors to appear.

If your PowerBook is still under warranty, you should consult Apple to see if the company will replace the screen. Reports have it that Apple often will replace these screens if the problem is a manufacturing or packaging defect.

Apple rarely recommends replacing these screens on your own, and I pretty much have to agree. The screen bezels, plastics, and components are complicated, easy to break, and rather expensive. Screens also need to be handled in a completely static-free environment and need to be carefully placed and installed. A number of companies and authorized Apple dealers will swap screens for you at a reasonable cost, so I'd recommend looking into those services.

Note

MacResQ (www.macresq.com) offers screen replacement and service, as does DT&T service (www.dttservice.com). Likewise, most authorized Apple dealers should be able to replace a PowerBook screen or send it to Apple for service.

Table 20-4 shows you the PowerBook models that can be upgraded to a new screen, according to Apple. (Most PowerBook screens can be directly replaced if necessary, but only certain models can be upgraded to better screens.)

Table 20-4		
Apple-Recommended PowerBook Screen Upgrades		
PowerBook Model	**Upgrade**	**Makes It a . . .**
PowerBook 190/190cs	10.4" Active Matrix	PowerBook 5300c[1]
PowerBook Duo 230	Active Matrix; Color Active Matrix	PowerBook Duo 250; PowerBookDuo 270c
PowerBook 5300	10.4" Active Matrix	PowerBook 5300c
PowerBook 5300cs	10.4" Active Matrix	PowerBook 5300c

Docks, Bays, and Slots

The next type of upgrade focuses on stuff you plug your PowerBook into (or plug into your PowerBook) to give it desktop-like capabilities. That includes CD-ROM drives, hard drives, Zip drives, and other upgrades.

Docks are designed so that certain Mac models (mostly PowerBook Duos) can make one quick port connection and immediately access an array of external peripherals, such as additional hard drives, modems, full-size keyboards, mice, and even an external monitor or two. The Apple Duo Docks, specifically designed for this task, are a great example. Like a video cassette, the closed Duo slides right into the Duo Dock, which otherwise resembles a full-sized Mac. Now the Duo is ready to be connected to a slew of desktop peripherals, including internal drives, SCSI devices, or external serial devices. Other docks made by third-party vendors slide onto the back of various PowerBook models.

Bays are something relatively new, starting with the PowerBook 1400 series and moving up through the line of newer PowerBooks. These expansion holes in the PowerBook enable you to swap out different components — floppy drive, DVD-ROM drive, Zip drive — to keep from being locked into using specific external peripherals. Instead, you can plug in a CD-ROM drive and take it with you on the plane for reference while you write a report, or swap to a Zip drive in the hotel room if you're planning to share data with colleagues at your next meeting.

PCMCIA (or PC Card) slots have been available on Macs since the Powerbook 190 and 5300 series, although it was possible to add PC Cards even before that; the PowerBook 500 series was capable of adding PC Card support through an add-on "cage" that fit in one of its expansion bays (which also double as battery bays). These cards make it easy to add modems, Ethernet support, multimedia features, and even miniature hard drives (although they often offer a lot of storage) to your PowerBook.

Docks

The Duo Dock isn't available new anymore, which almost makes sense. After all, PowerBook Duos aren't available new, either. The PowerBook 2400, the logical successor to the PowerBook Duo line, is a little more self-sufficient than previous Duos and can't work with the Duo Dock. Although most PowerBooks (including the 2400) have ports on the back of the machine for a variety of connections, PowerBook Duos were built with one special Dock connector and, in some cases, a port for a telephone wire connector to enable use of the internal modem on the road. To use removable media, connect to a network, or work with different input devices, you had to connect through the Dock.

You can still find Duos and Duo Docks on the used market, making it possible to upgrade the Duo Dock to take care of your external expansion needs. Duo Docks include an RGB port for external monitors, a SCSI port for external drives, internal space for SCSI hard drives, and ADB ports for external keyboards and mice. On top of that, Duo Docks generally have one or two NuBus slots you can use for expansion cards that are accessible from the Duo when it's plugged into the Dock.

The Apple-branded Docks weren't the only ones made for the Duo series; you'll find *minidocks*, usually adapters that plugged into the Duo to give it regular PowerBook-style ports, available from a number of vendors.

These mini-docks are such a good idea that some of them have been created for other PowerBook models, too. One of the popular models, Bookendz models from Newer Technology (www.newertech.com), is available for a number of newer PowerBook models; you can slide the PowerBook into the dock, which then automatically connects it to your external devices for use at your desk (see Figure 20-12).

With most docks, you put your PowerBook to sleep, and then insert it into the dock and tap the full-size keyboard to wake it again. (You may also need to install special software on the PowerBook to get certain things to work correctly.) With the all-inclusive Duo Docks, you need to shut down the Mac before it can be docked. If you try to insert it when the PowerBook is asleep, it will be ejected; if you insert it while the PowerBook is on, the PowerBook will likely crash.

Figure 20-12: The Bookendz port replicator makes it possible to dock many popular PowerBook models.

The AirDock, from Farallon (www.farallon.com), is a slightly different animal. Designed to work with PowerBooks that feature an IrDA port, the AirDock integrates a PowerBook into your network by simply placing the PowerBook close enough to the AirDock.

Apple also made a Duo Floppy Adapter, which allows Duos to connect directly to an HDI-20 interface for a floppy drive, just like the drive designed to work with the PowerBook 100.

Bays

The PowerBook 1400, 190/5300, 3400, G3 (3400 series) and G3 BTO series of PowerBooks (so far) all feature expansion bays that enable you to swap between different peripherals — mostly different types of storage devices. The majority of these devices — floppy, CD-ROM and DVD drives — are made by Apple. A couple of other options are made by VST Technologies (www.vsttech.com) including a Zip drive and hard-drive solution for the bays of most modern PowerBooks.

One unique use of the bays in 3400, G3 (3500), and G3 BTO machines is an adapter that allows the PowerBook to communicate with three PCI expansion cards. The expansion chassis looks like a miniature external computer case, and it's made by Magma (www.magma.com).

In general, you simply use the device that is in the PowerBook's bay (or bays) as you would any other storage device. Its icon appears on the desktop (or appears when you insert media) and allows you to open it as you would any drive.

What's different is that you can swap these expansion bay devices for other devices. Although many of the PowerBook models do this differently, there is one important rule. When you get ready to swap, make sure the drive isn't in use, files or applications on the drive aren't open or being accessed, and any removable media (floppy disk, CD-ROM, Zip disk) has been ejected before swapping. If you don't do this, the PowerBook will probably complain with an error message. Or, you could cause a crash and a loss of data.

The expansion bays in the PowerBook 1400 are *sleep-swappable*, meaning you don't have to shut down the Mac to swap the expansion bays, but you do need to put the PowerBook to sleep. You can do that using the Special ⇨ Sleep command. The 5300 and 190 models are also sleep-swappable in practice, although Apple officially recommends that you shut these models down before swapping expansion bay devices.

Newer PowerBooks feature *hot-swappable* expansion bays, meaning you don't have to shut the PowerBook or put it to sleep before parts get swapped (see Figure 20-13). When you're done swapping, you touch a key to wake the PowerBook back up.

Note

Don't swap expansion bay devices as the PowerBook is starting up or shutting down. You should install them only when the PowerBook is in Sleep mode (for the PowerBook 1400) or shut down completely (for the PowerBook 190/5300) or when the PowerBook is on but there are no media in the drive and/or files being used on it. Also, be aware that some third-party expansion modules may not be hot-swappable or may require special treatment when being swapped.

Check your PowerBook's documentation to learn exactly how to remove the expansion bay device once the correct state of power and sleep has been achieved. Generally, it's done by releasing a catch on the bottom of the drive, and then smoothly sliding the device out of the bay. Adding a device is the opposite: Line it up carefully, and then slide it in smoothly and easily until it clicks into place. Make sure the device is secure in the bay; if it's loose at all, it won't work correctly.

Figure 20-13: Swapping drives in an expansion bay

PC Cards

If you'd like a quick and easy way to add capabilities to your PowerBook, you should probably opt for a PC Card. They're easily the most convenient method of upgrading a PowerBook computer — at least, for models in the 190/5300, 1400, 2400, 3400/3500, and G3 series. Earlier models can't accept PC Cards, with the exception of the 500 series, which can accept the cards only if it has a special add-on cage installed in one of its expansion bays.

Note
> You can't buy the PowerBook 500 series PCMCIA card cage new these days, but if you're shopping for a used version, be warned that only the Revision C model will work with a PowerBook 500 that's been upgraded to PowerPC.

PC Cards are popular in the world of Intel-compatible notebook computers, too, so you'll find that a lot more of them are manufactured than are PowerBook-only solutions, such as expansion bay drives. And, in many cases, PC Cards designed for Intel-compatible PCs can also be used with Macs, especially if the manufacturer provides driver software to make the transition possible. (The G3 BTO series is the first PowerBook to be compatible with the Cardbus interface, a higher-speed PC Card interface that is popular on Intel-compatible notebooks.)

So just what are these cards? Also called PCMCIA cards (an acronym so unwieldy that it's recently been dropped), PC Cards are about the size of a credit card, usually a bit thicker, with a 68-pin connector on one end. On the other end, you may have a number of different connectors, although, in most cases, you connect some sort of cable to the card (at least, if it's designed to interface with something). Figure 20-14 shows a PC Card modem.

Figure 20-14: A PC Card modem, complete with interface cable for connecting to the phone line

PC Cards can perform a number of different functions. They're most popular for add-on modems and Ethernet capabilities (especially for non-PowerBooks) although a number of other applications exist. PC Cards can be video-out cards, video-in cards (especially when designed for particular video cameras), sound cards, static RAM storage cards (for storing a few megabytes or data in high-speed but non-volatile RAM) and hard-drive cards. Table 20-5 shows some vendors of Mac compatible PC Cards.

Note

Apple warns that any PC Cards you attempt to use should be specifically Macintosh compatible. Otherwise, you could damage the card, your PowerBook or data stored on either.

Table 20-5
PC Card Vendors for Macintosh

Vendor	Type(s) of Card	Web Site
3Com	Modem, combo	www.3Com.com/
Dayna Communications	Combo, modem, Ethernet, ISDN	www.dayna.com/
Farallon	Ethernet, combo	www.farallon.com/
Fujitsu	Storage	www.fpca.com/
Global Village	Modem, combo	www.globalvillage.com/
Motorola	Modem	www.mot.com/
TDK	Modem	www.tdk.com/
Viking Components	Modem, storage	www.vikingmem.com/
Zoom Telephonics	Modem, combo	www.zoomtelephonics.com/

Using a PC Card is easy. With the Mac either on or off (not in Sleep mode), plug a compatible card into one of the PC Card slots. Make sure you've lined the card up level with the slot; it's easy to get a little out of alignment, and if you force the card, you may damage something.

You should use a smooth motion (you'll encounter a little resistance) until you hear and/or feel the card click into place. After a few seconds (if the PowerBook is turned on) you'll see an icon pop representing the card on screen, as shown in Figure 20-15.

If the card is designed for storage, then you can double-click it and begin to use it as you would any other removable storage device. You may be asked by the PowerBook to format the device before using it. If it's an ATA/IDE (rotating hard disk) device, you can format it using the Special ⇨ Erase Disk command. You can choose to format it as a DOS or Macintosh volume.

Other PC Card storage devices often come preformatted for DOS/Windows machines. Assuming the card doesn't use some special compression scheme, you should be able to use the DOS-formatted card on your Mac if PC Exchange is active. If you want to reformat the device for Macintosh use, you'll need to disable PC Exchange and restart the Mac. Now, when you enter the card in the PC Card slot, the Mac will ask you if you'd like to erase it and format it in Macintosh format. Choose to do so.

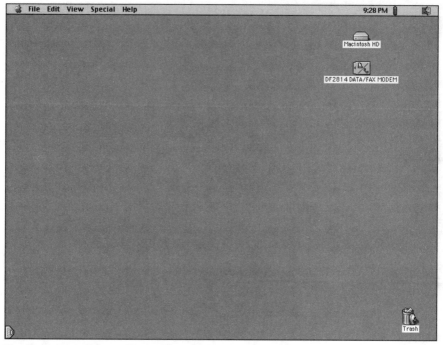

Figure 20-15: An icon appears that represents the card.

Note

You can't use your PowerBook to erase and reformat a Mac-formatted PC Card into a PC-compatible format. You'll have to use an Intel-compatible PC with a PC Card interface to format the card for use with PCs.

If the card is for some other function, you'll likely need to install the configuration software that came with the card before you can start using it.

If the card is a modem, you'll need to configure your modem software to work with it. In most cases, you'll be able to choose the type of modem you're using and how the card is connected (choose the Upper PC Card slot or Lower PC Card slot entry, as opposed to the modem or printer port). Figure 20-16 shows a modem being set up in the Modem control panel to use Open Transport PPP for an Internet connection.

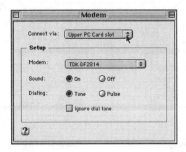

Figure 20-16: Setting up a PC Card modem

If you need to eject a PC Card device, make sure it's not in use anymore, select the card's icon, and choose File ⇨ Put Away from the Finder menu, or drag the icon to the Trash. The PC Card should pop right out. If the PowerBook is powered off, push the button next to the card slot to release the card. Don't remove cards while the PowerBook is asleep — you'll just confuse it.

External Ports and Peripherals

Aside from the Duo series, nearly all PowerBooks feature a full complement of ports on the back for hooking up to external devices, as described in Table 20-6. All PowerBooks through the PowerBook G3 BTO series (aside from Duos) support external SCSI, for instance, as do nearly all Macs and Power Macs. Most PowerBooks also feature serial connectors, ADB ports, sound-in and sound-out ports, and some feature Ethernet connectors.

Mac Evangelista tip: When in Rome . . .

Mac Evangelista Doug Holmes tells me that his consulting work often takes him abroad. While traveling, he needs to access his e-mail regularly. Unfortunately, every country requires a different converter cable to connect your modem's RJ-11 connector to their phone lines. But he's discovered a tip that might be useful for you, too:

"Most telephone-related office equipment (for example, fax machines and answering machines) is made in the Far East, and most of it has a female RJ-11 receptacle on the back or bottom. So, look around and see if you can find a device that has one of these ports on it. Next, ask permission to hook up your PowerBook here.

"How to hook it up? All these machines have a 'localized cable' that has a male RJ-11 on one end, to connect into the device, and a male local plug to mate with the local wall socket, on the other end. Hence, my solution is to unplug the cable at the device, and insert this male RJ-11 plug into the modem of my PowerBook. This has saved me several times, in different countries, in both hotels and office buildings."

Table 20-6
PowerBook external expansion ports

Model	Sound	Mic Port In/Out	Ethernet	Video	Printer	Modem	ADB
100	No/ mono	No	No	No	Yes	No	Yes
140/ 145B	Mono/ mono	Omni	No	No	Yes	Yes	Yes
150	No/ mono	No	No	No	Yes	No	No
160/165/ 165c	Mono/ stereo	Omni	No	Mini-15	Yes	Yes	Yes
170	Mono/ mono	Omni	No	No	Yes	Yes	Yes
180/ 180c	Mono/ stereo	Omni	No	Mini-15	Yes	Yes	Yes
190/ 190cs	Stereo/ stereo	No	No	Option	Yes	No	Yes
Duo series	Mono/ mono	No	No	No	Yes	No	No
500 series	Stereo/ stereo	Line in	AAUI	Mini-15	Yes	No	Yes
1400 series	Stereo/ stereo	Line in	No	Option	Yes	No	Yes
5300 series	Stereo/ stereo	Line in	No	Mini-15	Yes	No	Yes
2400 series	Stereo/ stereo	Plaintalk	No	VGA	Yes	No	Yes
3400 series	Stereo/ stereo	Plaintalk	10BaseT	VGA (1,3)	Yes	No	Yes
G3 (3500)	Stereo/ stereo[2]	Plaintalk	10BaseT[3]	VGA	Yes	No	Yes
G3 (BTO)	Stereo/ stereo	Plaintalk	10BaseT	VGA[4]	Yes	No	Yes

1 10BaseT is optional on the PowerBook 3400/180.

2 The G3 (3500) includes a special headphone jack.

3 Connector is shared for modem and 10BaseT connection; both can be used together if you install the included adapter.

4 G3 BTO series includes an S-video out port (for connecting directly to TV devices) on configurations that include the 13.3- and 14.1-inch displays.

You'll notice that some of the PowerBooks feature a mini-15 connector for video-out; this requires a special adapter, included with the PowerBook, that converts it for use with an Apple RGB monitor connector. VGA adapters can also be connected to the RGB port on this mini-15 converter to make it work with projection systems.

The PlainTalk microphone is a special microphone designed to work with a PowerPC-based Mac's line-in audio input. Unlike most microphones, the PlainTalk microphone enables you to record voice over a line-level input. Other microphones require an amplifier to work correctly with the audio input ports on these Macs. A connection from a receiver or mixing board, however, will work just fine.

The PowerBook 500 series requires an AAUI transceiver, but can be configured to connect to either a 10Base2 or 10BaseT network. Other PowerBooks can connect directly to 10BaseT cabling.

Note

Older PowerBooks have no Ethernet built-in and no way to add it — except through a SCSI adapter. Because all PowerBooks (except Duos, which can accept an Ethernet card through their Docks) have SCSI, you can use a SCSI-to-Ethernet adapter, such as the one sold by Dayna Communications (www.dayna.com).

SCSI

Although it's not mentioned in Table 20-5, all PowerBooks, except the Duo series, feature an HDI-30 SCSI connector. To actually hook something up to this port requires an adapter, either a SCSI Dock adapter that connects that adapter's HDI-30 port to a 25pin SCSI adapter (that can then be used to accept a typical SCSI cable) or a specially designed cable that allows you to connect the PowerBook directly to a SCSI peripheral. Or, if you don't use one of the standard cables, a SCSI Doc adapter can be useful for PowerBook SCSI connections — both for SCSI disk mode and for regular SCSI connections. You use a switch to change between the two, as shown in Figure 20-17.

Apple actually makes a few very specific cables for hooking up PowerBooks and SCSI devices:

✦ **HDI-30 SCSI System cable** (Apple part no. M2538) is designed to begin a SCSI chain by adapting the HDI-30 port to a Centronics SCSI interface. The cable is light gray with 29 pins (a pin appears to be missing).

✦ **SCSI Peripheral cable** (Apple part no. M0207) is for connecting two different SCSI peripherals together, but can be used (with a special SCSI Dock adapter) to connect to the PowerBook's HDI-30 port.

✦ **SCSI Disk Adapter cable** (Apple part no. M3927) is for use with the PowerBook when you want it to operate in SCSI disk mode. This cable is dark gray and has a full 30 pins.

Figure 20-17: SCSI adapter and cable for PowerBook SCSI connections

Note SCSI cables and docks are also made by Interex (www.interex.com/), **APS Technologies** (www.apstech.com/), **and** TechCessories (www.techcessories.com/). If you don't have any cabling solution, I'd recommend a SCSI Dock, which usually allows you to switch between regular SCSI operation and SCSI disk mode.

In PowerBooks that use an internal IDE bus for the hard drive and CD-ROM drive (if one is present), all SCSI ID numbers (0 through 6) are available to external devices. (As with desktop Macs, SCSI ID number 7 is reserved for the PowerBook itself.) These IDE-based PowerBooks include the 150, 190, 5300, 1400, 2400, 3400, G3 3500, and G3 BTO. In earlier Macs, the SCSI ID 0 is taken by the external SCSI hard drive.

Not all PowerBooks have included internal SCSI terminators in the past. Check your PowerBook's manual for information on whether or not you need a terminator at the SCSI port itself before you connect to a SCSI chain of external devices. In many cases, you'll need to add an external terminator *before* the first SCSI device, especially if you're only connecting one device in a Mac with a SCSI drive. If your Mac has an IDE drive, you'll likely need an initial terminator for the SCSI chain. More recent PowerBooks don't require the initial terminator, including the PowerBook G3 3500 series. (Oddly, the very similar PowerBook 3400 series *does* require an initial terminator.)

Note If your PowerBook crashes when you turn off the external SCSI device, this is a good sign that you need termination between the device and the PowerBook. When termination is lost (after the SCSI device is powered down), the PowerBook's SCSI chain loses integrity and crashes the PowerBook. An additional pass-through terminator — or a SCSI Doc device from APS Technologies (www.apstech.com/) — will solve this problem.

Otherwise, dealing with SCSI devices works pretty much the same way as described in Chapter 7. The only caveat is SCSI Disk Mode, which allows the PowerBook to act as an additional external hard drive when connected to a desktop Mac. SCSI Disk Mode is discussed later in this chapter.

Modem/Printer

Many PowerBook models only include one serial port — a modem/printer port — that gives you access to an external serial device. The thinking seems to be that these same Macs generally have some other expansion options, such as space for an internal modem or a PC Card modem, so that you're free to use the modem/printer port just for printing.

The modem/printer port is also a LocalTalk port and, in the case of the PowerBook 3400 and G3 (3500), a GeoPort. Because it can do so many things, it's sometimes important to fool the port into being either a modem port or a printer port. Trouble can arise when it believes it's both or otherwise gets confused.

If you plan to install an external modem using the port, for instance, you should do the following:

1. Power down the PowerBook and the modem. (You may be able to do this with your PowerBook in Sleep mode — check the documentation.)

2. Connect the modem's serial cable to the modem/printer port.

3. Turn on the modem and the PowerBook, in that order.

4. Once the PowerBook starts up, open the Chooser and turn off AppleTalk, if it's on. (If you're using Ethernet for your network, you don't have to turn off AppleTalk.)

5. Choose a printer other than a serial printer — a LaserWriter, for instance — that would likely be connected over a network.

6. In the Network or AppleTalk control panel, choose something other than LocalTalk or Modem/Printer for the interface (this can slow down external modems). Ethernet is fine, if you're already using it for a network connection.

7. In the Modem control panel (if you'll be using PPP) or in your modem application, choose the Modem/Printer port for your connection. If that's not an option, choose Modem.

The modem should work. Try dialing out to test it. If you have trouble, check your PowerBook's manual for setup advice and consult Chapter 29. With some PowerBook models, you may need to open the PowerBook Setup control panel and choose Normal for the Modem's compatibility mode. (This mode makes the modem work better with certain Communications Toolbox programs.)

For a printer, the requirements are less stringent. Make sure you're not using the port as a LocalTalk port (if your printer is a direct-connect QuickDraw printer) in the Network or AppleTalk control panel. Next, make sure you don't have a modem program or control panel that's set to use the modem/printer port. Now connect the printer as you would to any Mac, as discussed in Chapter 15.

You may occasionally come across a peripheral that specifically requires either the printer or the modem port to work correctly. If it requires the modem port, set it up as if it were a modem (turning off AppleTalk and any LocalTalk connections in the Chooser and Network/AppleTalk control panels). If it requires a printer port, you may need to turn off AppleTalk.

If the serial device has its own control panel that polls the port for information, make sure AppleTalk is turned off (or that a networking scheme other than LocalTalk is selected in the Network/AppleTalk control panels) and restart with the device connected to the modem/printer port if you have trouble getting it to be recognized. It may also be important to set the internal modem to Normal in the PowerBook Setup control panel.

Video

Although many PowerBooks have internal video or will allow internal video to be added (see the section on internal slots earlier in this chapter), some PowerBook models treat video differently from others. In earlier models with two video-out ports, the connector is a mini-15 plug, which requires a special adapter (see Figure 20-18).

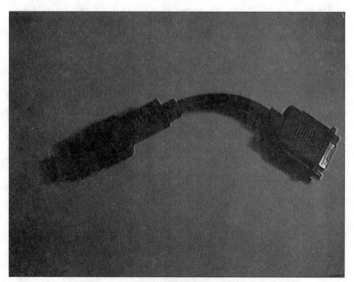

Figure 20-18: To connect an external monitor to earlier PowerBooks, you needed an adapter.

The adapter connects directly to Apple-branded monitors with RGB connectors; for other monitors, you'll need a VGA adapter, as described in Chapter 12. Later PowerBook models have incorporated a direct VGA-out adapter that connects to most non-Apple video displays and projection systems. Additionally, the PowerBook G3 BTO series includes an S-video–out port in some configurations that allows you to show the PowerBook's screen on a TV (or a TV-like device or projection system).

There are two modes of video for working with an external monitor, and which you use depends both on what your PowerBook supports and what settings you've assigned it. Dual-monitor support means you can use the PowerBook's screen and an external monitor the same way you can use two video interfaces and monitors on a Mac — side-by-side to increase the size of your desktop screen.

If your PowerBook supports this, it'll most likely be the default mode when you connect the monitor and awaken or start up the PowerBook. (You should put PowerBooks to sleep before adding an external monitor.) If you're using Mac OS 7.6 or above, you'll use the Monitors & Sound control panel to set up the monitors. You should have two control panels — one on the external monitor and one on the PowerBook. The main Monitors & Sound control panel will feature new options, including an Arranging button (see Figure 20-19).

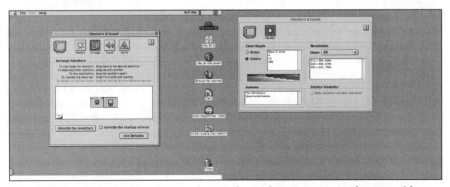

Figure 20-19: The Monitors & Sound control panel on a PowerBook 1400 with a video-out card and external monitor.

This allows you to set and arrange monitors just as you can with other Mac dual-monitor systems, as described in Chapter 12.

The other video mode for a second monitor is called *mirroring* and it means simply that the monitor and the PowerBook screen show the same thing. This is the only mode that some PowerBooks (such as the 3400 and G3 3500 series) offer, whereas it's an option on other monitors.

If you're using the Monitors & Sound control panel, you can choose to set up mirroring by selecting a Simulscan resolution from the Monitor screen in the control panel. (If you don't see a Simulscan resolution, choose the Show pull-down menu and select Simulscan.)

If you're using a PowerBook that supports dual-monitor display, you'll need to change the mode to mirroring via the PowerBook Display control panel.

Note   If you hook your PowerBook up to a monitor that is limited to a resolution lower than the PowerBook's built-in resolution, you'll notice that the PowerBook screen shrinks a bit to accurately represent the shared resolution. An 800x600 PowerBook 1400 screen, for instance, will become smaller to represent the 640x480 screen required to display a mirrored image on an Apple High-Resolution RGB Color Monitor.

SCSI Disk Mode

SCSI Disk Mode is a system that's built into the Mac's ROM modules, enabling you to turn your PowerBook into a (rather expensive) external SCSI device for another Mac. In essence it operates exactly like an external hard drive, appearing on the desktop of the Mac to which it's connected. You can then quickly transfer documents and other files back and forth between the two computers.

You enter SCSI Disk Mode by starting the PowerBook with a SCSI Disk Mode cable (or a SCSI docking adapter) plugged into the SCSI connector on one end and a desktop Mac's SCSI connector on the other. (Actually, you could use two PowerBooks, in which case the host PowerBook should be using a SCSI System cable.) Every time the PowerBook starts up, the ROM code routinely checks for the presence of the SCSI Disk Mode adapter. If it doesn't find the adapter, the PowerBook's SCSI ID number is set to 7, which is standard for the CPU in typical SCSI chains.

If the SCSI Disk Mode cable is found, the ROM checks the battery's remaining power to see if the PowerBook has enough energy stored to enter SCSI Disk Mode. The ROM then changes the hard disk's address to the ID number that you've previously chosen in the PowerBook Setup control panel (see Figure 20-20). This value has been stored in PRAM. Instead of starting up the Mac as normal, the ROM just performs a few basic housekeeping chores: It turns on minimal backlighting, spins up the hard drive, and places the Disk Modem ID number on the screen, animating it to prevent burn-in (or just to be entertaining, I guess).

Note   The PowerBook 140, 145, 145B, 150, and 170 models do not support SCSI Disk Mode. PowerBook Duo models require a mini-SCSI dock or other Duo Dock to work in SCSI Disk Mode, but otherwise they support it.

Figure 20-20: Setting the SCSI ID the PowerBook will use when it's in SCSI Disk Mode

Although the only thing you really need to do is connect the appropriate Disk Mode cable or adapter to make SCSI Disk Mode work, there are a few caveats to getting it to work correctly for the first time:

✦ Make sure you set the SCSI ID for the PowerBook (in the PowerBook Setup control panel) according to the SCSI chain in the host Macintosh, not the SCSI chain for the PowerBook itself. That is, if you set the SCSI ID to 2, make sure this is a valid ID number on the host Mac.

✦ Only connect the SCSI Disk Mode adapter when the PowerBook has been completely powered down (using the Special ⇨ Shut Down command). The ROM-based commands necessary to enter SCSI Disk Mode are executed only at startup. If you connect the Disk Mode adapter while the PowerBook is in Sleep mode, the SCSI bus will potentially have two devices with SCSI ID 0, which could cause data loss or corrupt files.

✦ The host Mac and the PowerBook can't have hard drives with the exact same name. If they're both called Macintosh HD, for instance, change one of them before activating SCSI Disk Mode.

✦ The host Mac needs to be powered down, too, and should remain that way until SCSI Disk Mode is completely active on the PowerBook. Otherwise, it may not recognize the drive.

✦ The PowerBook needs to be properly terminated in the scheme of the host Mac's SCSI chain, just as does any SCSI device. In most cases, because the PowerBook only has one SCSI connector, you'll want it to be the last SCSI device in the host Mac's chain. A pass-through terminator should actually be applied before the connection to the PowerBook, in this case.

With those precautions in place, you're ready to start up SCSI Disk Mode and access your PowerBook as if it were a regular external hard drive on the host Mac's SCSI chain. Here's the basic procedure:

1. Assuming you've already set the SCSI ID for the PowerBook in the PowerBook Setup (or PB Setup) control panel, shut down the PowerBook. With both Macs powered down, connect the cables and appropriate terminators.

2. Touch the PowerBook's power key to start it up. After a moment you'll hear the startup tone, the PowerBook's hard drive begins to spin and the screen flickers. Wait until you see the SCSI symbol and a SCSI ID number on the screen. It's now fully initialized in SCSI Disk Mode.

3. Power up the desktop system. Once the host Mac has completely started up, you'll see the PowerBook's hard drive icon on the host Mac's desktop. Work with it as you would any hard drive icon.

4. To exit SCSI Disk Mode, power down the host Mac. Now, press the PowerBooks power button to shut down the PowerBook. If you want to use the PowerBook normally, just remove the SCSI Disk Mode adapter and start up the PowerBook. The next time you turn on the PowerBook, it will start up as usual.

Note

PowerBooks 500 and 5300/190 series can have a particular problem when being shut down after operating in SCSI Disk Mode that keeps the PowerBook from restarting without a Power Manager restart (see Chapter 29). To work around the problem, you should shut down the PowerBook by highlighting the PowerBook computer's hard drive in the Finder on the desktop of the host Mac, and then selecting File ⇨ Put Away to unmount the drive. Now press and hold the Power key on the PowerBook for three seconds, and then release it.

Note

While in SCSI Disk Mode with a Macintosh IIfx, remember to use the black terminator between the Disk Mode adapter and the SCSI system cable. With other desktop Macintosh models, use the standard gray terminator.

Summary

✦ If you want to upgrade your PowerBook's insides, you'll need to know which form factor your PowerBook fits into and how, exactly, to pop it open. There are nine different form factors for PowerBooks (at the time of writing), and they all offer slightly different ways to get inside the machine. Some are easier than others.

✦ If you want to add internal cards or processor upgrades, you'll need to know if your particular PowerBook model can handle it. Nearly every PowerBook has room for some sort of internal upgrade, whether it's a processor upgrade, an internal modem, or better video.

✦ The other thing you'll want to add is RAM. In almost all instances, you'll need to buy RAM that is specially designed for your particular PowerBook model (see Table 20-1). The best advice I can give for the actual upgrade is to download the Apple Memory Guide PDF document for diagrams and instructions for installation.

✦ Externally, your PowerBook likely has a full complement of ports although, again, each PowerBook is slightly different. Once you figure out your machine's unique gifts, you can add SCSI devices, video-out capability (for dual-monitor usage and monitor mirroring), modems, printers, and even Ethernet networks.

✦ Finally, you may find it compelling to hook up your PowerBook to a desktop Macintosh in SCSI Disk Mode. This built-in feature enables the PowerBook to act as an external SCSI device on the SCSI chain of the host Mac. The PowerBook's drive icon appears on the host Mac's desktop where files can be swapped, saved, and backed up just as though the PowerBook were simply another drive.

✦   ✦   ✦

Troubleshoot
and Repair

Part III begins with a discussion of troubleshooting in general — specifically, deciding if the problem is likely in your Mac's hardware or in its software. If you have a software-only problem, you'll probably find the solution in Part IV. In the remaining Part III chapters, hardware and software/hardware integration issues are discussed — anything from hard drive and scanner problems to downed networks and troubled PowerBooks. This part also includes chapters on major troubleshooting issues, such as what to do when the Sad Mac icon appears, or when you have trouble with the logic board, power supply, and system memory.

P A R T

In This Part

Troubleshooting Basics: What's the Problem?

A big part of being a computing consultant, technical representative, or repair specialist isn't necessarily knowing, off the top of your head, what the correct order number is for the plastic facing on an external SCSI drive enclosure. In fact, you might not even need to know such a thing exists, as long as you know where to find it in a catalog or technical reference.

What's more important is being able to reason out the basic trouble that the computer is having — determining whether it's a software problem or a hardware one, what the most likely culprit is, and how to fix it. Secondary to this is knowing how to identify a problem and circumvent it in the short term so that it can be fixed once the computer's user is off their deadline and, preferably, busy somewhere else. That's when a Mac troubleshooter is really going to get some work done.

If you've ever watched a TV doctor drama — or if you're an actual doctor — you know exactly what I'm getting at. Whenever anything is broken, mechanical or biological, there's a pretty logical course of action you can apply toward fixing it. Troubleshooting a Macintosh isn't tough to do — it isn't brain surgery. It just uses the same diagnostic process that leads up to brain surgery.

There are three parts to understanding troubleshooting: You need to know what types of Mac problems are possible, you need to know the typical indicators for various types of problems, and you need to know how to isolate the problem so that you can focus on it more closely. I like to wrap all of this up under the heading, "The Troubleshooting Scientific Method." In fact, we can steal from the actual Scientific Method to determine how to go about diagnosing Mac problems.

From there you can decide if your Mac just requires a little digital therapy that you can perform in the ER or if you're going to have to send your Mac up to surgery and call in a professional.

The Troubleshooting Scientific Method

You may remember this one from grade school (if you're like me), or you may remember it from yesterday when you applied it to the solution of real-world problems (if you're a useful person, unlike me). The Scientific Method, for the most part, is just as applicable to computing as it is anywhere else. It's definitely a great place to start troubleshooting a hardware or software problem.

So how does it apply to computing? Here's a quick overview and how you can use the Scientific Method for Mac troubleshooting:

✦ *Observe the problem.* Probably the most important step in computer troubleshooting is witnessing the actual problem. Part of this step is determining whether the problem is reproducible. If you can figure out what makes a problem happen over and over again, you're on your way to a solution.

✦ *Hypothesize a solution.* This is the heart of troubleshooting — narrow things down. Once you can reproduce a problem, you can start to decide what parts of the computer may be affected and why. You can move from a larger system — the Mac — to a smaller system — the video subsystem — and make a best guess at what's causing the problem.

✦ *Experiment.* With a possible solution at hand, test that solution to see if it's the right one. Specifically, you can test things by removing the problem from your Mac (for instance, removing a possibly errant system extension or removing a device from the SCSI chain), or you can test by replacing the problem device (for instance, try printing to a different printer).

✦ *Form a conclusion.* If your experiments prove fruitful, you can make a decision about what the problem is and then do something about it. That could mean digging through a manual for the correct setting in a control panel, removing the peripheral completely in favor of a new one, or deciding that it's time to call an authorized service center.

The bottom line to applying the Scientific Method to Mac troubleshooting is this: It's really not that tough to find and fix the majority of nonfatal errors you'll encounter with your computers. It can take some time, but you don't need to know the inner workings of computer processors or how data flows around on your Mac's circuit board. If you've got a hardware problem that needs to be looked at by a professional, at least you can get to the point where you're making that determination in a knowledgeable way.

Anyone can do this sort of troubleshooting — just stop when you're done getting your hands dirty. You'll be happier walking into a service center and saying, "I think there's something wrong with the on-board video or video connector," than you would be saying, "I can't see anything on screen!" You might even find that taking your Mac in for major surgery is cheaper after you've done a bit of diagnosis on your own, because the repair shop won't waste billable hours trying to find a problem you can point out directly.

Note

I've been told by Mac repair professionals to warn you not to be too adamant that your Mac's problem lies in a particular area, although it can be helpful if you tell them very specific symptoms and alert them to reproducible problems. After they've put your Mac through their diagnostic routine, they may find that the problem is more complex or more simple than you'd envisioned.

Observation: Hardware versus software

The first step in troubleshooting is observing the problem and determining which direction you should start out in — looking at either hardware or software. A couple of obvious indicators can often suggest whether one or the other is at fault. The trick is to step back from the problem for a moment and look at what the symptoms of the problem are, and then determine whether they fall under the broad problem categories of user, software, or hardware problems. Once you've figured out which category most likely applies to your problem, you can begin to isolate the problem. But you'll have to observe the problem, first.

Is there a problem?

It's not uncommon for a problem to just go away — maybe because it wasn't a problem in the first place. It's even more likely that what you're experiencing isn't a serious problem with hardware or software — the source of the problem may be a cable you swore you plugged in (but didn't), a bad setting on your monitor, or a paper jam in your printer. These are the day-to-day occurrences that often make a call to the help desk seem necessary, but actually fall under the heading, "User error."

Obviously people are smarter than computers, and computers aren't always designed right by the smart people that build them. But people are also much more at the whim of their perceptions than are computers. Even Mac experts get confused about things and have to stand back looking puzzled for a while. For example, my main Mac features three or four devices dangling off a manual serial switch box. If I want to print, I better not have the dial set to my page scanner. Still, it happens to me almost daily. (That doesn't surprise people who know me well.)

The first thing you need to ask yourself when observing the problem is whether or not there really is a problem — that is, did something happen as a result of an error, a bug, or a defect? Did anything break? Or is something just not set or configured correctly?

The most important thing to remember about the observation problem is to sit back and think clearly about what could be causing the problem. Leave the room if necessary. Most of all, take a page from the Hippocratic Oath and *do no harm*. Before diving into the System Folder to look for a more complicated answer or deleting files you intend to restore from a backup, make sure you've completely and correctly diagnosed the problem.

Note

This might be a good time to remind you to think of the *order* of the Scientific Method of troubleshooting. Don't just delete files, even if you're sure you have a backup and you know you could easily restore them. You should begin to diagnose the problem well before you start trying to fix it. Once you do get to the experimentation stage, try things like moving files to a temporary folder (for instance, move system extensions or the System file to the Extensions Disabled folder or the desktop instead of throwing those files immediately in the Trash). And always test your backups first to make sure you really have replacements for files you decide need to be dumped.

Software problems

You're much more likely to have software problems than hardware ones, and they're usually less expensive to fix. However, software problems are more often of the variety that causes you to pull out your hair. The solution to software problems can sometimes be buried behind the obvious — somewhere deep in the System Folder, for instance — where you hadn't planned to go. Software problems can also, ultimately, be the fault of the company or programmers who created a particular application. And even if you can't really blame *them* (maybe they have a small firm and can't afford months of software testing to find possible conflicts with every known Mac program), you may still need their help for a solution. Bug fixes generally have to be offered by the programmers and publishers of the software that needs them.

Software problems tend to result from one of three things:

✦ **Bugs.** Bugs are problem areas in applications or the System software that cause errors to occur; for example, bugs can be the source of a program's failing to release a communications port, writing data to the wrong parts of memory, or simply not performing a function correctly.

✦ **Conflicts.** Conflicts may result from bugs, but don't necessarily occur when the program or code is executed by itself. Instead, conflicts occur between specific programs and system software fragments. An example would be a conflict between Netscape Navigator 4.05 and Open Transport 1.1 that results in unexplained crashes not seen when Navigator runs with Open Transport 1.3 or higher. (This is an actual conflict, in fact, reported by Netscape in their release notes.)

✦ **Corruption.** Corruption occurs when an important system or setup file — for example, the preferences file, the desktop database file, or something similar, or a low-level hard drive management file — gets overwritten with either bad or nonsensical information. This often happens as programs or the entire computer crashes with files open and being accessed — sometimes bits of data are written to those files that weren't supposed to be. In that case, the next time the file is accessed it may give bad information to an application or an OS, resulting in a crash.

You can actually make some interesting generalizations about these conflicts that might offer clues as to what's going wrong in a problematic Mac. Each of these can occur under certain circumstances (although are by no means limited or likely said circumstances).

Bugs, for instance, will usually crop up in earlier versions of software — including major revisions of existing programs. This is a gross generalization, but you will often find, for instance, that the 4.05 or 4.1 version of an application is more stable than the 4.0 or 4.01 version. In general, this is the reason for such numbering schemes; it indicates to you exactly what sort of revisions have been done to a program. A major revision warrants a whole-number increase, whereas minor new features will usually bump the number by a tenth (from 3.0 to 3.1, for instance) and bug fixes are bumped by one hundredth (from 2.03 to 2.04, for example).

Of course, that's not to say that a bug-fix release will be perfect. It's completely reasonable that a bug-fix release could actually contain new bugs. Still, if there's an apparent bug in one of your applications, head to the software publishers site and find out if they've released a bug fix. A quick upgrade may solve your problems.

On a Macintosh, conflicts tend to occur on two different levels. The first is very similar to the example cited earlier — Netscape having a "known issue" with Open Transport. These known issues tend to be incompatibilities that either the publisher fixes to work around a mistake Apple has made, or the publisher simply recommends you don't use a particular feature or extension when working with their application. This isn't limited to Apple's system software either; applications can often have conflicts with third-party system extensions designed to enhance the Mac OS. (For instance, SpeedDoubler and RAMDoubler, from Connectix, are two programs that often have to be upgraded to avoid conflicts with applications.)

Note For both conflicts and bugs, you'll find information usually on the installation CD or disk, or in the folder for the program in question once it's been installed. Look for a file named Read Me or Release Notes for information about bugs, conflicts, and fixes.

The other sort of conflict is an extension-to-extension conflict. Some extensions simply don't get along, causing crashes or bizarre behavior for the entire system — not just a particular application. Some of these are known conflicts, some aren't. In any case, such a conflict can be tough to diagnose and even tougher to determine the exact cause of: Symptoms of extension conflicts include a Mac that won't start up correctly or a Mac that has multiple crashes in many different programs. A great clue is sudden catastrophic crashes that result right after you've installed a new application or utility.

Note Don't forget that applications can add system extensions to your System Folder without you even knowing it's happening. That's why extension-to-extension conflicts can arise even after you've simply installed a new application program.

Cross-Reference Extension conflicts are discussed at length in Chapter 32.

Corruption usually happens in one of three different places on your Mac's hard drive—preferences files stored in the Preferences folder in your Macintosh, the System file in your System Folder, or the desktop database files that are hidden in the root directory of your hard drive.

The first two can happen quite often, especially if you're experiencing crashes while some activity is taking place, whether it be something as innocuous as surfing the Web in a Web browser program or something as critical as running a disk-fixing utility on your hard drive. But no matter how important or unimportant that activity may be, nearly any crash has the potential to bring down your system through corruption of data.

When this happens the solution is generally to throw the corrupted file in the Trash and start working again from a new copy. Usually this isn't tough to do and it isn't catastrophic; you can easily restore preference files and the System file without too much heartache. Rebuilding the desktop database isn't much tougher. You can use either a keystroke sequence (⌘-Option) as your Mac starts up, or you can use a software program to help you get the job done (see Figure 21-1).

Figure 21-1: TechTool from Micromat (www.micromat.com) is great for deleting and rebuilding the desktop files— even in its freeware version.

Is it starting to sound as though your Mac has a System software problem? Mac OS troubleshooting takes up the whole last section of the book, starting with Chapter 30. If it's software that's specific to a particular hardware device, I'll be covering software drivers for hardware over the next eight chapters.

Aside from my site for this book (www.mac-upgrade.com/), if you're looking for help for specific bugs and software glitches, let me recommend MacFixIt at www.macfixit.com, where Ted Landau (author, humanitarian) offers news and searchable tips about problem software.

Hardware problems

Thankfully, hardware problems are considerably more rare than software problems. I say thankfully for two reasons: First, it's tougher to fix a hardware problem on your own; if you really have a bad printer or a bad monitor, you're unlikely to have the skills required for fixing them to manufacturer's specifications. Second, hardware problems that can be fixed by a specialist tend to be rather expensive.

The hardware problems you can fix will often be configuration issues. The main indicator that you've got a hardware problem is simple: Something seems broken. Not that it necessarily *is* broken, just that it *seems* broken. You've got all the right software loaded, everything is plugged in and running okay, and you've triple-checked the order in which you've connected things — and still, it doesn't work. That's a clue that you've got a hardware problem.

But there are other clues that hardware is the issue. Start by taking a look at the three basic types of hardware problems:

✦ *Misconfigured or wrongly installed.* Something doesn't seem to be turning on or working correctly. This could be something as simple as an incorrectly inserted power cable, a loosely installed expansion card, or an overloaded ADB interface. Usually this points toward human error, but ignorance is certainly a reasonable defense in many of these cases.

✦ *It's cracked or broken.* If you can't get a floppy disk in the drive, if your printer won't move paper past the roller, or the hard drive makes horrific noise when it's powered up, that's a good sign that something is broken. Things can break as the result of electrical surges, being dropped, wearing out, or being defective in the first place. If there's no "sign of life" in a component, it's either not getting power from its power cable or power supply, it needs to be reset — or it's broken.

✦ *Voodoo.* In Mac circles it's perfectly acceptable to talk about the voodoo involved in certain hardware pursuits — specifically, you can talk about SCSI voodoo, ADB voodoo, and networking voodoo. In these cases, sometimes things work and sometimes they don't. Most of these technologies are a boon to upgraders, allowing for untold goodies to be added to your Mac without repercussion. Unfortunately, things don't always work out that way and problems that arise surrounding these expansion technologies can sometimes only be described as, well, weird.

Obviously, some of these things are tough to fix for people who aren't certified technicians. If a piece of hardware is broken, it's broken; some components, like a computer's power supply, aren't even considered worth fixing by the manufacturer. In other cases, you'll need to take into consideration things such as whether the warranty will be voided if you remove or explore something while looking for a problem.

> In fact, a good general rule is this: the only case you'll need to take off is your Mac's case. Once you've gotten inside the case, you're troubleshooting at the component level, which is about as far as a noncertified technician should go. That means, in a nutshell, don't take the case off anything else – a monitor, a hard drive, a CD-ROM drive, or a power supply. Most "no user-serviceable parts" warnings really do mean it. Obeying them has just as much to do with your safety, in many cases, as it has to do with the complexity of the component or your warranty.

You can usually have good luck with fixing physical configuration, component-level troubleshooting, and dealing with voodoo. If a SCSI chain needs a terminator, a CD-ROM drive needs to be plugged into the IDE interface, or the PRAM battery has gone dead on the logic board, these are all things you might want to try to fix. At the very least you should try to diagnose them – you might give your service dealer a head start on figuring out what's wrong with your system.

> I'll probably emphasize this a couple of times, but you should never trust a cable. When you're troubleshooting to see if a problem is a physical one, always swap cables around to see if one or more of them might be the problem. This is especially true for both ADB connections and SCSI.

Hypothesize and experiment

Once you know whether you have a hardware or software problem on your hands, you're ready to move on to creating a hypothesis and experimenting to see if that hypothesis plays out. Put even more simply, you need to isolate the problem.

Experimentation in computer troubleshooting usually comes down to a question of isolation. Where is the problem, what's causing it, and is it getting a reaction out of anything in particular? That's why it's important to be able to duplicate a problem, or to at least know that there's a trend starting to form. Once you can begin to isolate the problem, you're that much closer to the solution.

> It may be a tough one to pull off, but the best way to start isolating a problem is to document the problem. For instance, just knowing that your Mac keeps crashing (or, if you're a system administrator, hearing the same thing from one of your network's users) doesn't help much in getting at the problem. Keep a notepad and pen next to the computer. Next time it happens, jot down what you were doing. Experience the problem a few more times, always taking notes, and you'll likely start to see a pattern.

There are a couple of specific steps you can take to isolate the problem. Ultimately, you want to determine what subsystem is affected and what might be the cause of the problem, especially if you can narrow it down to a conflict. (Again, check Chapter 30 for tips on isolating system software conflicts.)

Take a look at some common scenarios to see how you might narrow down the problem.

Note

This actually leads me to an important issue — manuals. You should organize them and put them all somewhere on a little shelf space that's dedicated to your Mac(s). You may not be the type to read all those manuals, but one day you'll really appreciate knowing exactly where they are.

Does my Mac have a startup problem?

If your Mac is offering you an error message as it starts up, it's trying to tell you that something basic has failed in such a way that it can't go on. Certain internal tests take place before the Mac can move on to loading the full Mac OS. If any of those fail, a tell-tale error message appears. Likewise, other typical problems can happen at startup that might be indicators of fixable problems.

Here are some of those messages and indicators and a brief explanation:

✦ *Nothing on screen, but my Mac makes odd sounds.* These are sound codes that tell you about different problems your Mac is experiencing in the startup phase. See Chapter 22 for details.

✦ *A Sad Mac icon appears.* Something is wrong with the Mac internally — either the hard drive isn't connected properly, there's a RAM-related error, or something is wrong on the logic board. Consult Chapter 22 for more on the Sad Mac icon.

✦ *A blinking disk icon appears.* The Mac passed all its internal tests, but it can't find the correct startup disk where the Mac OS System file is stored. See Chapter 23 for troubleshooting advice.

✦ *The Mac starts up, but the mouse pointer won't move.* You may have a keyboard or ADB problem. See Chapter 24.

✦ *The monitor's video isn't working correctly — the picture is an odd shape, color, or size.* You may be having trouble with the monitor startup or with the logic board battery. There could also be a monitor failure or a video circuitry problem. See Chapter 25.

Is it completely dead?

Whether it's a monitor, port, modem, or internal hard drive, the first question you should ask yourself about hardware is whether or not your Mac is completely dead by way of some act of nature, the electric company, or blind luck.

✦ Is the dead hardware an external drive or device? Make sure the power cable or supply is plugged into a wall socket or power strip. If it's plugged into a power strip, make sure the power strip is turned on. If it's a wall socket, make sure the wall socket is working. Are other devices plugged into this outlet working? Check the power cables and interface cables where they connect to the peripheral. Unplug them and plug them back in to make sure they're seated correctly. If your peripheral has a power switch, make sure it's turned on correctly. If the peripheral doesn't power on, try a different power cable. **If power is working but the device isn't, the problem could be with the device's power supply.**

✦ If it's an internal drive, make sure its ribbon cable and power connector are both secure. Also make sure the power cable and ribbon cable are connected to the power supply and logic board, respectively. Power the Mac on and watch and listen to see if the internal drive starts up and makes any noise. Power down the Mac, switch the power cable to a new, identical power cable, and turn the Mac on again. Try other cabling configurations, and try to use cables inside the machine that you know work with other devices. **If the drive doesn't spin up with working power applied, either the ribbon cable is defective or the drive is.**

✦ Is the Mac not coming on? Make sure the Mac itself is plugged in, the Mac's power cable is plugged into the wall, and the Mac powers on correctly. If it doesn't turn on, try a different power cable, a different wall socket, or a different socket in the power strip. (You might also try a completely different power strip.) Pick up the Mac and carry it to another part of the room or building. With nothing attached to it, plug it into the wall. Plug in a keyboard if necessary and try to turn the Mac on. Hit the reset or programmer's reset button if your Mac has one. Listen to see if the fan is turning (in the back of the machine) when power is applied. Take off the case and try pressing the reset or front-mounted power switch (on some models) manually. Look for a red button on the logic board and press it to reset. Apply power again, and listen and watch for any activity. **If nothing happens, the Mac's power supply might be bad. It may also be having logic board trouble.**

✦ Is there nothing on the screen? Check the monitor's power cable, connection to the outlet, and connection to the Mac's video out port. Switch power cables with the Mac or a similar device to test the monitor. Unplug the monitor from the Mac and try to power it on without having it connected to video circuitry. Does the LED light up? If you move the brightness knob from one lock all the way to the other lock, does it change the look of the screen? How about contrast? Pick up your monitor, take it across the room or building, and try the power there. Any better? **If you get no reaction from the monitor, it may need professional servicing.**

Is the I/O port/cable/controller bad?

If you can get the device to power up, but it doesn't seem to be talking to your Mac, you probably have some sort of input/output problem. These can be a bit tough to pinpoint, as both software drivers (in the form of extensions and control panels) and bad hardware can create these problems.

✦ Does the external drive or device light up, make noise, get slightly warm, or otherwise show signs of life, but still not seem to want to work with your Mac? Make sure any interface cables between the peripheral and the Mac are plugged into the correct ports securely. ADB and serial ports can look similar. ADB and S-video connectors can fit into one another's ports. LocalTalk and serial cabling can look similar. Some serial cables, even if they seem identical to others, don't work correctly for different peripherals. If you can, try the questionable interface cables on other devices and see if they work using those cables. Remove the drive or device from your system, boot the Mac, and see if you still have problems (or if any error messages appear relating to the device). **If there are no signs of communication, either the cable is bad, the port is bad, or the software drivers are set incorrectly.**

✦ Is it SCSI or ADB? If it's SCSI, the cable might be too long, the SCSI chain might not be correctly terminated, or the cable itself might be low-quality, cracked, or bad. You may also have too many devices (on an ADB port), or the devices may be assigned to the wrong SCSI ID addresses. Try plugging the device in (ADB or SCSI) by itself and see if things improve. If they don't, try different cables while the device is plugged in by itself. Try different SCSI IDs and different termination settings. Use the Apple System Profiler or SCSIProbe to see if the device can be recognized. Also try plugging in all the other devices without the problem device and see if things improve or if there are still problems. **If a device doesn't work by itself and all other devices work fine without it, the problem might lie in that particular device or the software setup.**

✦ Is it the port? Try another device on that port to see if it works. (For instance, try another modem on the same port as a defective modem or try connecting your printer to that port and printing.) Check the settings and control panels governing that port. Use a port utility (like the shareware program Reset Serial Port available from www.macdownload.com) or the device's control panel software to reset the port, and try the defective device and other devices again. If the other devices work, try a different cable with the defective device. **If it still doesn't work with a new cable or two, but other devices work on the port, the device may be defective. Or, it could be a software setup problem.**

Of course, nearly every device is different — that's why there are still eight more chapters in this section of the book. Generally speaking, you should be able to troubleshoot most devices at this level, but some Mac peripherals and drives will simply have a few extra trouble spots that will (hopefully) be covered in the coming chapters.

Is it a software driver?

One of the places where devices can vary widely is in the driver software that they use. You may need to read the device's manual to truly gain an understanding of how the device's control panels and extensions work. They can certainly be a source of trouble.

✦ Are the software drivers set correctly? Start up your Mac and bring up the Extension Manager (hold down the spacebar as the Mac begins its startup cycle). When the Extensions Manager appears, choose to start with extensions off or only with the Mac OS base extensions. Next, manually activate the extension(s) or control panel(s) necessary for the device. When the Mac has completely started up, go to the control panel for your device and set it correctly, according to its manual. **If the device works, the problem may be a conflict with other device drivers. If it doesn't work, you may be missing software components.**

✦ Reinstall the software drivers from the original diskettes or CD-ROM. Start up the Mac again with all extensions active and try the device. If it doesn't work, drop back to the previous bullet point's advice. If that works, you may still have a device driver conflict. Check the device manufacturer's Web site for updated driver software. **If the device still doesn't work, it may be defective.**

Conclusion: What to do next

If you've gotten through all these different questions and they haven't hit on the likely source of the problem, it looks like the problem is isolated to the device or component that seems to be failing. For instance, if the modem isn't working but you've checked the power, port, cable, and software, there's a good chance the problem lies with the modem. Same for a printer, networking device, scanner, CD-ROM drive, or other component. In your scientific opinion, that may be the most obvious conclusion.

Of course, it may not yet be time to throw the component out yet. If it's dead and nothing seems to revive it, take the component to a repair shop to find out the prognosis. If you're lucky, computer surgery may help. If the component is simply giving you fits, and you can confidently say that it's the component's fault and not a software glitch or an I/O problem, you're ready to move on to the chapter that covers that specific component and troubleshoot from there.

Note   The rest of the chapters in this section of the book features a wide variety of ways to troubleshoot particular components, including the software drivers and conflicts that can arise with some hardware. Also check the Apple Tech Info Library (www.info.apple.com/til) and the Mac-Upgrade.Com site (www.mac-upgrade.com) for updates.

Evangelista tip: The Coke fix

I have two favorite troubleshooting tips that, I'll admit, I don't always follow myself. But they're really clever little bits, the sort of thing that can make you tons of money on the lecture circuit. So, I'll offer them here for your perusal.

Based on the popular advice for getting dressed in party regala — "Back up and take off one accessory" — my advice is this: If you're having trouble figuring out what's causing a problem, back up and take a good look at the problem. Think about it as a series of logical steps, and see which one you may have missed. Many, many problems grow from a user error or oversight of the real problem because somebody plunged in, got frustrated, and took things to greater depths more quickly.

My other advice is to take a break or a walk, if necessary. Get away, clear your head, and come back to the problem. If you're like Evangelista Doug Dickeson, (self-described "Mac geek and guitar freak" from Lincoln, NE) you may find the problem solves itself:

"I started repairing and configuring Apple equipment in 1980, predating the Macintosh by some four years. Another technician and I discovered 'zapping PRAM' by accident, way before it was common practice.

"We'd both been working on a nonfunctioning Mac Plus, and had tried everything we could think of: different system, different drives, reseating RAM, praying, and so on.

"We pulled out the battery to make sure it was functioning and it tested OK. We threw up our hands in disgust and said, 'Let's go get a Coke.'

"After about five minutes we came back, plugged the battery back in, and tried to startup once more. We were stunned when it came up and smiled at us! We then decided that the proper way to fix a Mac with these symptoms was to pull out the battery and go get a Coke. We named it the 'Coke fix' — later learning other less pernicious methods of clearing parameter RAM, or PRAM."

Summary

✦ The key to successful troubleshooting is following the old Scientific Method: observe, hypothesize, test, and conclude. The ultimate goal in any Mac troubleshooting is to eliminate the parts of the system that are working correctly so you can get to the root of problems affecting your system. This way, even if you take the machine to a service center, you'll have a much better idea of what the problem is, potentially saving money and time.

✦ Mac problems are more often software-related than hardware-related, and that's good, because hardware problems tend to cost more money. Unfortunately, software problems tend to be more obscure. You'll want to do what you can to eliminate software as a possible problem area first, and then move on to hardware troubleshooting. You should also make sure there is no human-error element to the problem.

✦ Once you know you have a problem, you need to begin asking questions about it to see if you can narrow it down to subsystems within your Mac. This is the hypothesize-and-test portion of the Scientific Method — take an educated guess at what might be wrong, and then test to see if that's really the problem. You usually do that by isolating part of the system and testing it on its own.

✦ Once you think you've found the problem, you'll need to come to some conclusion as to what to do. If the repair or replacement is within your skills — and/or if you find an answer in this book or through a company's tech support machine — you can conclude that fixing the problem component will solve the problem. You may also, in some instances, need to conclude that it's time to take the Mac into an authorized service center for repairs.

✦   ✦   ✦

Startup Problems, Memory, and Ports

Sometimes the things that make Macs go — or go faster — can bring them to a screeching halt. This is certainly no more evident than when a component of the processing subsystem — RAM, the processor, the logic board, or the power supply — starts to fail or give you fits. These aren't always the most obvious problems to troubleshoot, either, because they're not always tied to an immediate failure. Instead, many RAM or processing problems will show themselves only in roundabout ways, such as frequent, odd crashing, sudden slowdowns, and unexplainable freezes. It is possible to narrow a problem down to the logic board and/or RAM, however.

The most immediate problem you can have with a Mac, though, is when it simply won't power on. In those cases, you can do a certain number of things to test the system and see what, exactly, the problem is. From there, you can decide if you need to take the machine in for repairs.

When the Mac Won't Start Up

There are probably few problems more annoying or disturbing (especially if you paid for your Mac yourself) than a startup problem. These problems, as outlined in Chapter 21, are those that stop you in your tracks before you're able to get started with the Mac. The machine has detected a problem very early in the boot sequence, probably as a result of special diagnostic tests that go on right when your Mac gets power. These tests, administered by the Startup Manager (programming code stored in the Mac's ROM chips), determine whether the system is healthy enough to begin loading the Mac OS from the hard drive, ultimately resulting in the loading and relinquishing of the Finder to the user. If the Mac doesn't get far enough into this process, the user can have almost no control, making it difficult to troubleshoot problems.

The first indicator of the type of startup problem you're having is how far you get in the startup sequence. The sequence is pretty straightforward, offering a few hurdles that the Mac has to overcome before it can start loading the Mac OS and enable the user to control the computer. These fail-safes keep you from doing more damage to a fragile system, but the fail-safes themselves are a bit obscure. You'll need to watch closely if you're having trouble.

Power-on

Obviously, the first thing a Mac needs to do is to power on correctly. When you hit the power key on a Mac's keyboard (or the Power button on some pizza-box-style Macs or the power switch on the back of many all-in-one Mac models), power is sent to the logic board, which begins the standard power-on process. At this point, you should hear the fan start up and the power supply come on (usually this brings with it a quiet humming sound that gradually gets higher in pitch, like a jet engine starting or the Frankenstein monster first coming to life). If the fan isn't spinning, shut the Mac down immediately.

Next, power flows to the Mac's ROM chips, which begins the power-on diagnostic. The Start Manager is invoked, testing the components on the logic board. It continues the testing by sending out simple electronic commands to most of the machine — CPU, drives, ports, and NuBus and/or PCI slots — to see that everything is working properly. Next, it tests RAM.

If there's a problem with RAM — or any of these early steps — that's when you'll likely see a Sad Mac icon or you'll hear the death chimes (sounds that aren't like the typical Mac startup sound). Your Mac won't go any further than this until you do something about the problem that caused the Sad Mac to surface.

Much of the troubleshooting discussed about powering on a Mac covers what to do if nothing happens and the power supply fan doesn't start turning. However, what if the power supply fan doesn't turn, but other things (such as the Mac starting up or the monitor coming to life) do happen? Turn the Mac off immediately and have it serviced. The lack of air circulation inside a Mac could cause a heat-related failure that could affect very valuable internals.

Troubleshooting power

Symptom: You turn the Mac on and nothing happens, including no sounds being made and the fan in the back not turning.

Let's start at the beginning: What do you do if the Mac doesn't seem to power on? If you hit the power key and absolutely nothing happens, it's time to dig a little deeper. Here are some steps to try:

✦ *Check the power cable for the Mac.* Make sure the power cable is the same cable that came with the Mac and that it's attached correctly. Test the connections, and then try powering on again. If that doesn't work, try plugging the power cable into another device that you know does work. Usually Mac monitors and Macs share the same sort of power cable; plug the cable into the monitor and see if it turns on (it probably won't light up, because it's not attached to a Mac, but if it has power LED [a small light on the front], this can give an indication as to whether the monitor is getting power). **If the power cable works, the problem is somewhere in the Mac's case.**

✦ *Hit all the reset buttons you can find.* Check the manual for the reset buttons on your Mac — some models have more than one reset button, power rocker switch, or power button. In fact, your Mac may need to have a button pressed or a power switch on before it'll start from the keyboard. (Certain Macs, such as the Power Macintosh 6100, don't start from the keyboard at all.) Some Macs even have a small, red reset button on the logic board that needs to be pressed sometimes after you've swapped components. **If the reset buttons still don't work, the problem may be with the power supply — or it could be the keyboard or ADB port.**

✦ *Test the keyboard.* If you can, plug in a different keyboard, or try to start up with the ADB cable plugged into a different ADB port on the keyboard (some keyboards give you no option). Also try starting with fewer ADB components and/or plug your keyboard into the second ADB port, if your Mac offers one. **If you still can't get the Mac to start, the problem may lie with a battery or the power supply.**

✦ *Change the PRAM battery.* These batteries (discussed a bit later in more detail) are located on the Mac logic board and designed to keep a tiny trickle of power headed to a small portion of RAM called Parameter RAM. This RAM holds such settings as the time, date, colors, and state of AppleTalk from session-to-session. If the battery dies, your Mac's ability to power up may be affected. This is more likely to happen on systems three years old or older, but the battery could be defective in most any Mac. Replace the battery (any Mac store and most computer stores should be able to get you the correct PRAM battery). I'll discuss how to replace it later in this chapter in the section "Troubleshooting PRAM." **If replacing the battery doesn't fix things, you likely have a power supply problem.**

In most cases, the power supply should fire up and spin the fan, even if you're having trouble with the Mac's logic board. Assuming you believe the keyboard, ADB cabling, and ADB ports to be operational, it's likely your power supply has died. If that's the case, you can consider replacing it and testing again.

Replacing the power supply

I need to make a couple of points up front. The power supply is not user-serviceable, so don't open it or unscrew it. In fact, most Mac repair shops toss out power supplies (or ship them back to the manufacturer) instead of opening them. They're more toss-and-replace components than they are serviceable.

Also, Apple doesn't recommend users replace power supplies on their own, and doesn't condone the practice. In many cases, it may void your warranty if your machine is new. In fact, if your Mac is still under warranty, I recommend vigorously that you take the machine into an authorized service center and have them look at the power supply and other components; for one thing, it'll probably be cheaper, as Apple will often replace defective parts such as power supplies for free (see your Mac's own warranty for specific details).

However, if you have an aging Mac that seems to have suffered from a power spike, or you believe its power supply or power supply fan has gone through old age, one option is to replace the power supply. It isn't impossible, but it'll take some keen observation and a little time.

You'll also need to get your hands on the correct power supply. Not only will the power supply need to be rated the same as your current Mac's power supply, but you'll need to get one that fits your particular Mac's case. The best plan is to find a Mac component supplier that offers power supplies designed specifically for your brand and model of Macintosh. Such vendors are listed in the back of Mac magazines and on the Web.

You'll find that power supplies are only available for modular Macs and Macs built around industry standard form factors like most Power Macs and Mac clones. Generally, that excludes all-in-one Macs and many Performas that feature pull-out logic boards for upgrading. These Macs should always be professionally serviced.

Once you've got a replacement power supply, you're ready to switch it for the old one. To start, follow these steps:

1. Shut down your Mac, ground yourself, and unplug the power supply from the wall socket or surge protector. *Make doubly sure it's unplugged!*

2. Examine the power supply carefully. It's the metallic box with all the warnings plastered on it (see Figure 22-1). What you're looking for are the mounting screws that hold the power supply into the Mac's chassis. These are different from the screws that hold the power supply together — avoid confusing the two.

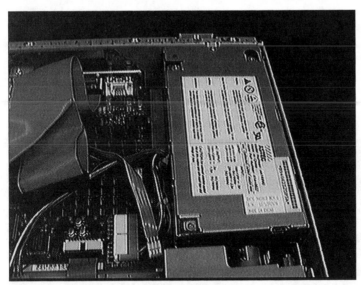

Figure 22-1: The power supply usually sits in a corner of the machine, parceling its power connectors to internal devices. It's important to note which screws attach it to the Mac's chassis and which are part of the power supply itself.

3. Unplug the power supply's power connectors from the internal drives in the Mac. You'll also want to unplug the power supply's power connectors from the Mac's logic board. When doing this, make careful note of their orientation — specifically, which goes on which side and in what direction. You'll need to plug the new supply's connectors in the same, exact way. Compare the old connectors to the new connectors and label the new ones (using masking tape), if possible.

Note

Some Macs use a specially designed connector to plug the power supply directly into the logic board instead of using power cables. If your power supply doesn't have cabling connecting it to the logic board, you might find that the power supply plug is under the power supply, attached to the logic board (see Figure 22-2).

4. Unscrew the retaining screws that mount the power supply to the Mac's chassis. Hang onto the screws.

5. Pull the power supply from the chassis. If you have trouble removing it, make sure you didn't miss one or more of the retaining screws. You may also find that some Mac models have plastic tabs that retain the power supply. Look for a tab (sometimes part of the internal drive assembly) that releases the power supply.

6. Position the new power supply so that the retaining screws can be used to mount the supply to the Mac's chassis. Screw in the retaining screws.

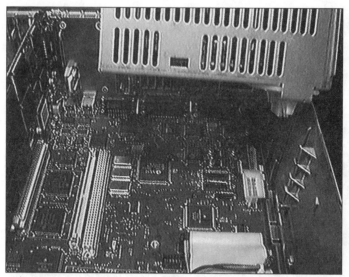

Figure 22-2: Some older Mac power supplies plug directly into a special socket on the logic board.

7. Reconnect the power supply's power connectors to the Mac's logic board. Take care that they're installed correctly (see Figure 22-3).

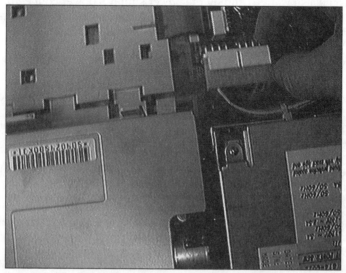

Figure 22-3: When installing a new power supply make sure the power connectors for the logic board are properly aligned.

8. Reconnect the power connectors to the Mac's internal drives.

8. Reconnect the power connectors to the Mac's internal drives.

With all this accomplished, you can seal your Mac back up (or partially so), reconnect a keyboard and monitor, and then plug the Mac's power cord from a wall socket or surge protector into the Mac's power supply. (You may need to use a reset or power switch before the keyboard power key is operational.) If the power supply spins up and the fan begins working, you may have solved your problems.

Troubleshooting Death Chimes

Symptom: The Mac starts up and power seems to be fine, but it chimes four times, eight times, or makes a sound like the Twilight Zone theme, a car crash, or breaking glass instead of (or just after) the typical Mac startup sound.

For the most part, the only clear generalization you can make about hearing strange sounds from your Mac at startup is that it's not happy about something. Even Apple's Tech Info Library is less than helpful on some of these matters, suggesting the same thing I just said — if you hear the tones, there's a problem. Mac models tend to vary in what these sounds are, how they vary, and what they indicate. Although the sounds are sometimes suggestive of a hardware problem, they also sometimes mean a software problem, depending on the Macintosh or Power Macintosh model you have.

Evangelista tip: Jump-start your Mac

Standard warning — this tip may be something that no one should try. I haven't even tested it myself, so I can't vouch for its usefulness or veracity. But it does sound like a good idea if you've decide that a $150 Mac II is worth the risks involved. Don't try this at home — I won't be responsible for the consequences.

That said, Etienne Michaud from Montreal, Quebec had this to say about jump-starting a Mac:

"Those old Mac IIs might be starting to be a bit tired after so many (computer) years of duty. When you run into a unit that won't start up anymore, you might want to try jump-starting it, just like a car on a cold day. Typically, the Mac will gradually refuse to cold boot before going completely deaf to the power key over a period of time.

"Take a battery pack with 3 AA batteries and connect one wire to the power supply casing and the other one to the closest pin (when you are standing in front of the Mac) that goes from the power supply to the motherboard.

"You should hear the startup chime. If not, you've most likely just toasted your Mac. . .or it had a problem that had nothing to do with the power supply.

"Now, don't shut down that Mac anymore. Leave it on as a mail server, DNS, router, or something like that. Macs never die."

The only real advice I can give you is this: If the sound is something weird, it probably suggests that something went wrong with the startup process. If you recently made a change to your Mac — for example, adding RAM, adding a hard drive, or adding an expansion card — you might not have installed the component in question correctly or it may be defective. There could be a software problem, but software problems are generally supposed to give other indications.

If the sounds are a series of tones, that's a little more helpful. Four tones, according to Apple, is cause for concern over the hard drive. Try booting with a Disk Tools disk, a Zip disk (or other removable disk), an external hard drive, or from a CD-ROM that includes a valid System Folder (see the section "Startup key commands" and Chapter 23 for more on booting from other drives in your system). If you're hearing eight tones, that's often a memory problem. Check to make sure your memory is properly installed. If it is and the tones persist, try troubleshooting memory.

Troubleshooting Sad Macs

Symptom: The Mac powers up and gives the standard startup sound, but a sad Mac face appears on the screen instead of a happy one.

The Sad Mac can be interpreted as meaning the Mac isn't "happy." It certainly doesn't look happy. Actually the Sad Mac icon tends to give you a better indication of what may be the problem in your system. The first thing to concern yourself with is exactly *when* the Sad Mac icon appears.

If the Sad Mac appears after the Happy Mac or Welcome to Macintosh screens, the problem is almost certainly with your software. In this case, you should troubleshoot the startup drive and Mac OS system software — consult Chapters 23 and 30 for starters.

As mentioned earlier, the Mac tests the logic board components, ROM, ports, and system RAM rather early in the process. The Sad Mac can appear in response to these tests, but if it does, it'll appear quickly — within seconds of turning the Mac on. In this case, you almost certainly have a hardware problem of some sort.

On Macs newer than the Mac Plus and other classic Macs, the Sad Mac icon is generally accompanied by an error code; the codes, in hexadecimal, give an error number that can sometimes be used to track down the problem. These codes are usually two 8-bit hex numbers in two rows under the Sad Mac icon, as in the following:

xxxxyyyy

zzzzzzzz

In general, experience and Mac experts agree that the first line of codes is where the action is — that's what you want to focus on for troubleshooting help. In fact, you can focus in even more: The first four numbers of the first line (*xxxx*) can be ignored, says Apple. What you should focus on are the second four numbers, represented by *yyyy*.

What do they mean? Consult Table 22-1 for a quick rundown.

Table 22-1	
Common Sad Mac Codes	
Code Number yyyy	**Trouble Spot**
0001	Macintosh ROM
0002, 0003, 0004, 0005	Bad or incorrectly installed RAM module
0008	ADB problem (Check your ADB ports, devices, or have ADB serviced.)
000A	Defective NuBus card or slot (Remove it or have the Mac serviced.)
000B	Defective SCSI controller
000E	Bad memory module or system bus problem
000F	Software problem

The errors to hope for, obviously, are poorly seated RAM modules or a single defective NuBus card — these are problems that you should be able to troubleshoot on your own. Otherwise, software problems generally mean there's something wrong with the organization of files on the hard drive. The Start Manager can't find a drive to start from or a System Folder to hand things off to. (See "Trouble with RAM" later in this chapter.)

System Startup

Once the Start Manager has successfully completed the startup task, memory is allocated for the Mac OS, portions of which are already available from the ROM chips. The Mac OS is transferred from the ROM chips into this part of RAM, and then the Start Manager goes on its quest for a *startup disk* to finish the task of loading the Mac OS into memory. A startup disk is a hard disk, removable media disk, or a CD-ROM that includes a valid System Folder. You can choose the specific startup disk you'd like to use through the Startup Disk control panel or by holding down certain keys as the Mac starts up, usually just after the Mac startup chime. (These keys are discussed in the next section.)

The Start Manager begins by polling the floppy drive to see if a floppy disk containing a System Folder has been inserted. Next, the Start Manager checks PRAM for a setting put in place by the Startup control panel (see Figure 22-4). If you've specified a particular hard drive (or other volume) for startup, the Start Manager will find that information stored in the PRAM.

Figure 22-4: The Startup control panel is used to tell the Mac what disk to employ as a startup disk at the next restart. This information is stored in PRAM after the Mac is shut down.

If the Start Manager can't find a valid System Folder on that particular drive, it'll start searching the SCSI chain in descending order — the device as SCSI ID number 6 gets checked, and then the one at number 5, and so on. The Happy Mac icon appears when the Start Manager finds a System Folder.

If the Start Manager doesn't find a valid System Folder, you'll likely get one of two errors: a blinking X icon or a blinking ? icon. Both mean that the Mac couldn't find a valid System Folder, but under different circumstances. (See Chapter 23 for advice on troubleshooting a startup disk problem.)

As this is happening, it's actually possible for you to use the keyboard to send commands that will interrupt this process, and then begin it again with new instructions. Using a *keyboard command* — a sequence of keys on the keyboard that are held down at the same time — you can guide the Mac along so that it does what you want it to do during the startup phase.

Startup key commands

Most of these key commands are used to alter the Mac's startup behavior, especially when you're having trouble or operating under special circumstances. If you find you're using keyboard commands with every startup, you may need to look more closely into your configuration. All keys should be pressed at the same time, usually before you hear the Mac's startup sound. Each should also be held for a certain duration, as noted.

Table 22-2 shows you some common keyboard commands to use as your Mac starts up.

Table 22-2
Startup Keyboard Commands

Command	Key Sequence	Until
Bypass internal drive	⌘-Option-Shift-Delete	Happy Mac appears
Boot from a CD-ROM	"C" key	Happy Mac appears
Rebuild the desktop	⌘-Option	Rebuild Desktop dialog appears
Zap PRAM	⌘-Option-P-R	Two or more startup tones have played
Start with extensions off	Shift	Welcome to Macintosh screen appears
Bypass Startup Items	Shift	(After Welcome screen) Finder appears
Open Extension Manager	Space	Extension Manager opens

Each of these startup command sequences is useful for different things, some of them being fairly straightforward, whereas others take a bit of explaining. For instance, the commands for bypassing the internal drive or booting from a CD-ROM enable you to choose a different drive to start up the Mac OS from, even if you didn't specify a new startup disk in the Startup control panel before restarting.

Rebuilding the desktop is a process that can solve a number of system software problems. It's discussed in detail in Chapter 31.

Starting with the extensions off lets you start up with a clean, basic Mac OS without any additional extensions, control panels, or startup items loaded. Starting up the Extension Manager gives you an opportunity to change the system extensions, control panels, and startup items folder. Bypassing Startup Items enables you to load a full complement of extensions and control panels while keeping any applications in the Startup Items folder from executing.

Zapping Parameter RAM, though, stands alone as a somewhat unique solution to many different Mac startup issues.

Parameter RAM

As mentioned, Parameter RAM is a portion of RAM that's kept active by a small battery that's mounted on the logic board. This RAM holds key information about your Mac that's required for starting it up and remembering certain settings after the Mac is powered down.

This is, in fact, its main purpose for being. As you've seen, the Mac goes through quite a few machinations before it begins to look for a startup drive. Because it can't access information stored on a hard drive until it knows where to find one, and regular RAM gets wiped out whenever the Mac loses power, shuts down, or restarts, the Mac needs somewhere else to store small, vital tidbits of information. That place is PRAM.

The tidbits stored in PRAM are things such as the settings in the Monitors control panel, the AppleTalk control panel, the General Settings control panel, the Startup Disk control panel, and the Time and Date control panel.

Unfortunately, PRAM can occasionally get corrupted, causing unforeseen errors. Some of those errors will make sense now that you know what's stored in PRAM— settings in control panels. If you're getting odd errors involving startup disks, control panels, time, dates, or AppleTalk, it's possibly a problem with PRAM. In fact, there are tons of reasons to *zap PRAM*, a process that resets PRAM to its factory default values:

✦ **Strange settings.** The date and time are set to odd times, the color scheme on your Mac is wrong, or your monitor starts up in the wrong resolution or in grayscale.

✦ **A port seems "jammed."** You can't seem to get anything to work on an external SCSI connection, you can't get a modem to dial out using a serial port connection, or your Mac refuses to send print jobs (or sends bizarre characters) to the printer.

✦ **Startup disk trouble.** You've gotten a startup error (Sad Mac, blinking disk icon) and can't get around it using the "C" key to boot from a CD-ROM or ⌘-Option-Shift-Delete to boot from a secondary drive.

Other symptoms could have something to do with corrupt PRAM, but aren't necessarily always PRAM-related at face value—issues such as a monitor screen not coming on, seemingly random error messages, and troubles with sound. You'll also find that resetting parameter RAM doesn't always do the trick; sometimes these symptoms are actually the result of PRAM resetting itself, usually because the PRAM battery is dying.

Zapping PRAM

Zapping PRAM is just an energetic way of saying you wipe the PRAM clean of its current values, returning it to its original factory settings. The process of zapping PRAM will root out any corruption in that special area of memory, usually getting rid of whatever was causing the trouble and enabling the Mac to once again boot safely. That isn't always the case, though, as PRAM isn't always responsible for your problems. Still, it can overcome some mysterious issues.

Zapping PRAM also deletes some settings you probably liked having in your system — like the correct time, the state of AppleScript, and so on. Once you zap PRAM, you'll need to reset those control panels manually. It can be something of a pain, but it's also something you should do instantly. The reason: If you forget you've reset PRAM, you may start to notice other errors — your network no longer functioning normally, for example — that could easily persuade you that other demons have inhabited your Mac. To avoid that, it's important to hit all the control panels after zapping PRAM.

There are two generally accepted ways to go about zapping PRAM. The completely free method for zapping PRAM is as follows:

1. Restart your Macintosh.

2. Immediately after hearing the Macintosh chime for startup, hold down the keys ⌘-Option-P-R.

3. Continue to hold the keys down until you hear the Mac startup chime two more times.

4. Release the keys.

Your Mac should begin to start up as it normally would, except you'll likely notice a few differences. Your Mac may start up in a grayscale mode, and it might start with a lower screen resolution, making everything on the screen seem bigger than normal. Once the Finder loads, you might notice other odd behaviors, such as the clock being set to an odd time.

Note   Notice I mentioned allowing the Mac to chime two times after you've begun zapping; the actual recommended number varies widely among Mac users and administrators. Apple's official stance is two chimes, but opinions range from a single restart tone to eight restart tones. My suggestion: Restart twice. If you don't think that did everything to PRAM that it should have, zap it a couple more times, or switch to TechTool.

The other way to reset PRAM is to use a third-party tool to do it. By far the favorite in this category is the freeware version of TechTool from Micromat (www.micromat.com). One of its options enables you not only to reset PRAM in a tried and tested manner, but also to avoid cycling through the PRAM reset tones multiple times.

On the   TechTool, available on the CD-ROM included with this book, enables you not only to zap
CD-ROM   PRAM, but also to save and restore PRAM settings. This can be useful if you've recently zapped PRAM, and then reset all the important settings — you can actually make a copy of the PRAM settings before any corruption gets a chance to set in (see Figure 22-5).

Figure 22-5: TechTool enables you to save, zap, and restore PRAM settings.

The latest version of TechTool will correctly zap PRAM and the NVRAM (nonvolatile video RAM) existant on PCI systems. But if you're zapping by hand, you'll have to be careful to do it exactly right. NVRAM can also get corrupted and is worth clearing at the same time you clear PRAM. Here's the drill:

1. Instead of restarting the Mac, shut it all the way down.

2. Start up the Mac from cold, and immediately hold down ⌘-Option-P-R.

3. Wait for two chimes, and then release the keys.

What's stored in NVRAM is reset separately from what's stored in PRAM. You'll have to get to the keys very quickly after starting up to reset the NVRAM, and then the process becomes the same.

Apple also recommends a slightly different course of action for PowerBook owners when it comes to PRAM. See Chapter 29 for details.

PRAM battery

The PRAM battery is the power source that maintains these settings after your Macintosh has been powered down. Generally speaking, the PRAM battery, usually a small lithium battery, either cylindrical or boxy (see Figure 22-6), is user-serviceable. It's expected to last about five years, but can go more quickly, especially if your Mac sits idle quite a bit of the time (or if it sat on the shelf for a while before you bought it). Two years isn't unheard of, but many people end up replacing the battery in three to four years.

Figure 22-6: Typical PRAM battery sizes

Indications that the battery has gone bad can range from machine to machine, but there are some basic similarities. Essentially, the machine acts as if PRAM has been zapped, even if all you've done is start it up recently. This includes resetting the internal date to either 1904 or 1956, losing time on the clock, and changing your AppleTalk setting. This can also be seen in changes to color depth, resolution, or the inability of video to appear after a power on. Others report even more catastrophic consequences, such as a Mac that appears completely dead.

These batteries come in two basic voltages — 3.6 volts (the cylindrical one) and 4.5 volts (the boxy one). There have actually been only a couple of Apple part numbers used to reference these batteries: The 3.6 volt battery used in most Macs is part number 742-0011, whereas the 4.5 volt battery used in the all-in-one Performa 500 series along with Performa, LC, and Mac/Power Mac models 630-6400 is part number 922-0750.

Later Mac models (7100 and above) tend to use a second cylindrical battery, part number 922-1262. The clone machines tend to use their own batteries, too; you'll want to investigate by reading your Mac clone's manual or opening the machine and locating the batteries.

These batteries aren't completely unheard of outside of the Macintosh world. If you remove the battery and take it to a computer or electronics store, they'll likely be able to get you a replacement. Obviously, you'll have the least trouble with an Apple branded battery.

Removing these batteries is fairly simple, although getting to them is not in all cases. Consult your manual. You may need to remove drive cages, power supplies, or other internal parts before you can expose the PRAM battery. (Fortunately, you'll only have to do this every three years or so.)

Once you find the battery, removing it depends on the battery type. For the cylindrical batteries, you remove the plastic battery guard from the logic board by grasping it and pulling straight up. (You might need to pull a bit harder than you'd imagine.) Next, you pry it out of its battery slot (a positive/negative battery bed typical of consumer electronics). Replace it with the new battery as you would any AA or AAA-type battery, aligning the positive and negative sides correctly. Replace the battery guard by lining it up, pressing the far sides slightly inward and pushing it back down into place (see Figure 22-7).

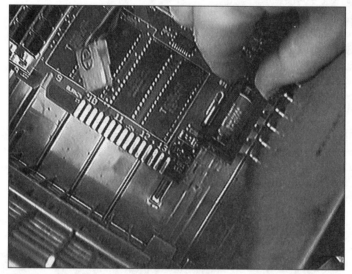

Figure 22-7: The typical battery setup in most Mac models.

If your Mac features the 4.5 volt battery, you'll remove it by removing its wiring connector from the logic board. (Note the position of the connector so you can replace the new battery's connector correctly.) Next, detach the battery from its velcro-style attachment to the motherboard. Reverse the process to replace the battery.

Evangelista tips: PRAM battery issues

More so than just about any other troubleshooting issue, Evangelistas have spoken out about their PRAM batteries. When I first started with Macs, PRAM was hardly even mentioned except in *Mac Secrets* — it didn't seem like the root of so much evil.

Of course, since that time, many more millions of Mac owners have bought Macs — especially Quadras, Centrises, and Performas. And those Macs have started to get a little gray at the temples. As they push three to five years of age, the PRAM battery starts to go.

Technical editor Dennis Sellers noted this first situation to me: There's a nonstandard PRAM-related item involving the PowerMac 5400 and others that include the Apple TV/FM Tuner and a remote control. Occasionally the machine will start up from the remote control, but from then on will not respond to the remote at all. One way to remedy this is to power the machine all the way down and unplug the power cable for a couple of minutes. Plug it back in, turn the rocker (or pushbutton) back to the "on" position, and you should once again have the use of the remote control.

Here are more of the best tips sent to me from Evangelistas who've lived through the death of a PRAM battery. See how your experiences relate to theirs:

"A while back when I was the primary support person for hundreds of Macs in the field, I started replacing a large number of Quadra 605 Macs which, for some reason, would not start up and would produce no video. I would get them in, swap out a power supply, and they would work. I couldn't figure out any other reason for the change in behavior, and I was looking at replacing about two dozen power supplies. Then one time I swapped out the lithium battery and the system worked. After some investigation, I determined that in any Mac that turns on via a power switch rather than the power key on the keyboard, one symptom of a dead battery is that you will get no video. This was at odds with systems that start via the keyboard since then you will usually get video, but the system will forget the time and date, and so on. This one had me going for quite a while so you might want to warn owners of Centris/Quadra 605/610 and PowerMac 6100s of this fact." — Rick Emery

"With some Power Macs, when the lithium battery dies, it seems as though your computer does, too. What do you do if you need to access an important file ASAP, but you can't get past that blank screen? Well, first turn your computer on for a few seconds. Let the blank screen stay on for about 10 seconds. Then turn off the computer, wait about 5 seconds, and turn it back on. With any bit of luck, after a few seconds of warming up your computer will have a normal startup." — David Lublin

"My first Mac was a Performa 450 (which is equivalent to an LC III). One day, when I turned on my Mac, it made the normal startup chime and then . . . did nothing! No Happy Mac, no Sad Mac, no blinking floppy, no error codes, not even a gray screen — just nothing! At first I thought my monitor was broken or unplugged, but (after repeated attempts at booting) I noticed that there was no hard disk activity. Mysterious.

"I scoured all my Mac books and magazines to no avail. None of them mentioned anything like this. About two months after the trouble started, I finally found the cause: The PRAM battery was dead (and I mean DEAD — it didn't even twitch the needle on my multimeter). A replacement (about $10) brought my Quadra back to life, and then I had two working Macs." — Bill Smith

Post-PRAM zapping

Once you've replaced a battery or zapped PRAM, you should make a point of immediately resetting most of the settings that got zapped so you don't mistake zapped behavior for other problems. One of the better ways to do this is using TechTool, which can restore PRAM settings from a saved copy.

Here are the control panels you should visit after a PRAM reset:

✦ Startup Disk

✦ Time and Date

✦ Monitor (or Monitors & Sound)

✦ General Controls

✦ Desktop Pattern

✦ Chooser (for AppleTalk settings)

✦ AppleTalk (or Network)

You may encounter others, depending on your Mac model and OS version. In any case, when you zap PRAM remember that you'll probably find bizarre setting choices for the next few hours or days of use.

Trouble with RAM

Early failures in the startup process can often be a sign of poorly installed RAM, especially if you've recently installed new RAM modules or if you've been inside your Mac doing other things. Because RAM is solid state, it's usually either good or bad when it comes off the assembly line. It rarely fails of its own volition, but it is very susceptible to power surges and *extremely* sensitive to static electricity discharge. You should always be electrically grounded and handle RAM carefully when working with it.

Startup RAM problems

Here are some troubleshooting approaches to try if you get a RAM error code, a Sad Mac or an error tone:

✦ *Check the RAM module.* It's not impossible to install some RAM modules backward, although it certainly isn't encouraged. You might also have installed the module in its slot without making perfect contact between the modules pins and the RAM socket. If part of the module is sticking up out of the slot or the small metal (or plastic) hooks that keep the module in place aren't properly secured, this could cause some errors.

✦ *Check the RAM placement.* Read your Mac's manual carefully to determine which RAM slots are best for the configuration of RAM you have. You may, for instance, need to group like RAM modules together. You should also try a different RAM slot on the off chance that the one you're using is bad.

✦ *Check the number of modules.* In many Macs, it's important to upgrade RAM using more than one module at a time. If you insert just one module, you may see no suggestion of that RAM in the About This Macintosh (or About This Computer) window, or you might get errors such as a Sad Mac icon. Check your manual and Chapter 8 carefully to see if you need a particular number of RAM modules to upgrade at one time.

✦ *Try the module in another computer.* If you're fortunate enough to have another, compatible computer lying around, insert the module in that computer and see if it results in an error. If it does, the module is very likely bad. If it doesn't, there could be something wrong with your Mac's logic board or another RAM module in your Mac.

If you suspect that a RAM module is bad, you can always just take it (instead of your entire computer) to a service center to have it checked. They should be able to test the module to see if it needs to be replaced.

Other RAM trouble

Although most of your memory woes will probably occur at startup, there are other times that RAM can be a problem. A poorly seated RAM module can get by the Startup Manager and result in bizarre system errors and crashes, much the same way a dirty or dusty Mac interior can sometimes affect the performance of RAM. You can clean a RAM module if necessary; usually blowing on it very lightly and placing it between your hands and a soft, lint-free cloth should clean it well enough.

You might also be able to install a RAM module, and then not see it in the Finder when you choose About This Computer from the Apple menu. This could be a result of the module not being seated, not being fully compatible with your system, or not being installed in pairs, if that's necessary for your Mac model (see your manual and Chapter 8).

On older Mac systems, you may not be able to see all the memory your Mac has installed if you haven't turned on 32-bit addressing in the Memory control panel Do this and restart your Mac again. Check the About This Computer (or About his Macintosh) item in the Apple menu and you should see the memory appear.

If you install more RAM than your Mac is rated to accept, it may cut off at the maximum level governed by ROM code and not make the extra RAM available. It may also result in crashes and system errors. More recent Macs (7300, 8600, 9600, G3 series) tend to be limited only by the number of DIMM module slots and the current RAM technology that's available. For instance, two new memory modules that offered, say, 512MB of memory each could theoretically be used to upgrade a Macintosh G3 to 1GB of RAM if they fit in the slots, even though the G3 is only rated for 384MB of RAM. However, Apple may not have tested that higher configuration of RAM, and therefore the company may not guarantee it'll work correctly.

Other times, it's certainly possible for you to simply get a RAM module that's slightly less compatible with your Mac than others, due to the workmanship, the connectors, and, often, the speed. You should only add RAM that has the same speed rating — the speed recommended for your Mac — in nanoseconds (ns). The best rule of thumb is to follow this for *all* RAM upgrades inside your Mac, even if your Mac specifically matches RAM in *banks*. If 70 ns RAM is recommended for your Mac model, choose 70 ns for all your RAM modules.

Note This may be overkill, but it's often recommended that the best way to keep from having the most mysterious, circuit-level incompatibilities is to buy RAM from the same manufacturer. That won't guarantee flawless operation, but it certainly can't hurt — unless you are forced to pay a premium for the identical modules, I suppose.

Cache RAM

There's another type of RAM to talk about — cache RAM — that's known to cause more than a few headaches. You'll find that cache RAM can be at fault in the case of sudden, dramatic slow downs, or even crashes, suggesting the RAM has gone bad or was installed incorrectly. (Installing and working with cache RAM is discussed back in Chapter 6.)

On 68040 Macs, a special cache was added to the logic board to speed up many programs. Unfortunately, not all Mac programs were compatible with that cache. So, a control panel is added to the machine when you install a Mac OS version that supports the 68040, called Cache Switch. The control panel gives you the option of shutting off the 68040's cache if you think there's a chance the cache is causing problems with older applications.

The Performa 5400 and 6400 series of Macs, including some Mac OS clone computers based on the same logic board (a PCI-based logic board that doesn't offer daughtercard upgradeability) had a problem with Mac OS 7.6.1, which would sometimes disable the level 2 cache. A fix (54xx/64xx L2 Cache Reset) has been added to subsequent Mac OS versions and can be downloaded from the Apple Support Web site.

Power Macintosh 7500 machines had a known problem with Apple and third-party cache RAM modules. If you install a cache RAM module in one of these machines and it fails to start up, you should contact Apple or the vendor for assistance.

Ports

One of the reasons Apple recommends that you plug and unplug devices from the ports with the Mac's power off is there is often a trickle of power that's exchanged through devices that use the Mac's ADB, serial, and parallel ports. Sometimes that electricity is a very real part of the ports operation; at other times there's simply a fear of static electricity discharge or the possibility that you'll plug the wrong cable into the wrong port, resulting in an electrical short or similar problem.

So, the first trick is to make a habit of shutting down your Mac before swapping cables. Also, make another habit of checking the port's label before plugging something into it — even if you feel as though you know the ports like you know your own name. Check the cable in your hand, and then check the port. Make sure you're not plugging the wrong cable into the wrong port, which can be not only pointless but damaging.

With serial devices, you should make very sure that the device is grounded. I have seen modem ports rendered useless because a modem attached to the port got hit by an electrical surge. What's worse is modem surges are often received from the *phone line*, not the power supply. Make sure you run your modem's phone connections through a surge protector — many have RJ-11 ports specifically for this purpose.

Ports will occasionally get left hanging by software or hardware; they can require resetting like any other software/hardware device on a Macintosh. Apple doesn't provide a utility for this, but the freeware Reset Serial Port program can be used to close a serial port that's been left open by a terminal program or PPP dialup connector. If this doesn't work, restarting the Mac will often reset the port, and reports have it that zapping the PRAM may do the same. (See Chapter 26 for help troubleshooting serial devices such as modems and printers.)

Resetting PRAM can also affect problems with microphone and speaker ports, as well as clear up some SCSI port blockage. (SCSI is covered more thoroughly in Chapter 23.)

Heat Trouble

A faulty power supply in your Mac can create some weird — and some not so weird — problems. Not-so-weird problems are things like the Mac not turning on, the Mac suddenly losing power, or the Mac smoking and cracking. These could all be attributed to the power supply.

Evangelista tips: Ports and port connectors

Here are a few more tips from Evangelistas, these relating directly to problems with ports:

"Most of the support stuff I do is for friends and colleagues who are less than fully literate with computers. One of the more common problems I see with peripherals is the 'bent plug pin,' where someone has tried to jam in a serial (or similar) cable and has bent a pin in the process.

"My solution (which I've never seen written up anywhere, even though I can't believe it because it's so simple) is to use a mechanical pencil with the lead pulled out. I believe a 0.7mm pencil works best. It leaves just enough play to straighten out small kinks, and a good enough grab to gently bend the entire pin back into place." — Bob Boyle

"While I was working as a service repair tech in Cincinnati, a guy called up and asked if I could come over right away to fix his problem. He explained that he just moved his computer to a different location in the same office and he could not print. He was desperate and did not want to 'troubleshoot' over the phone because he needed something printed right away.

"I asked him if he could see the printer in the Chooser. He couldn't. Then I asked him if he was using serial cable or phone line to connect the printer to the computer. He was using phone cable. I told him to unplug all the connections and put it back together. Still nothing showed up in the Chooser. '*Just come over and look at it,*' he says. I suggested one last thing: 'There are two places to plug in the AppleTalk box in the back of the computer. Is your printer plugged into the printer port?'

"Turns out it wasn't. The conversation lasted about four minutes. It would have cost him $140.00 if I had gone right away to his office instead." — J. Brian Rowe, Mac Consultant, Cincinnati

"Label your power bricks (external power supplies). Under the typical table we can find power bricks for a Zip drive, speakers, modem, printer, camera, printing hub, and so on. They all seem to be the same — that is, they all have the same tip. But are they?

"It turns out that if you plug a 12V AC supply (like the StyleWriter power brick) into a device that wants regulated 5V DC (like the Sonic EtherPrint2), you will smoke the device. How does anyone know this, but from personal experience? Ouch.

"I now label all my power bricks with my little Pocket LabelMaker." — Allan M. Schwartz, www.concentric.net/~Ams

"Never connect a monitor (15-pin) to an AAUI Ethernet port! Unless, of course, you're curious about how much smoke can be generated." — Mark Marinello

Often enough, though, the power supply will decide to be more devious than this, causing only intermittent problems. Some of these can be related to the power supply itself; in my experience, a faulty power supply is capable of causing trouble that looked a whole lot like a heavily corrupted hard drive, whereas other problems created by the power supply can seem heat related.

The case can contribute to this as well. Your Mac's case was built to move air through the Mac and dissipate heat through its industrial design, which is why it's important to run your Mac with the case assembled unless you're troubleshooting a particular problem. That's also why you should clean the case of dust and lint, as well as clean the power supply fan and keep your Mac's insides from getting too cluttered by wayward cables and, sometimes, expansion cards that are too hot.

The power supply

Heat is a big problem when it comes to your Mac. Many Mac models will shut themselves down if they reach a certain temperature. Sometimes heat will cause such things as random crashing (especially if the processor or RAM gets too hot), file corruption, and spontaneous rebooting. Hard drives and other storage devices can seem to fail, perhaps because either the drive mechanism or the SCSI interface is too hot. If heat is the problem, it will very often create symptoms that you feel certain have to do with something else.

First and foremost, make sure your power supply fan is working. Listen carefully for the hum — if you can, train yourself to listen for it as your Mac starts up and occasionally while you're working. If problems set in 15 to 30 minutes after you start working, immediately inspect the fan. Make sure it's turning, that it spins at a healthy pace, and that it's not blocked with hair, grime, or dust. Also, make sure it's not blocked by a wall, desk leg, trash can, or something else that may be affecting its ability to move air into the case.

Note

If you have a Power Macintosh 7300, 7500, or 7600 (and possibly similar, newer models), don't be surprised to hear the fan changing speeds — it's actually designed to vary its speeds depending on the cooling needs of the Mac's components.

Even when you aren't having trouble, clean the power supply fan regularly. Try to pull as much blockage out of the fan as possible (you may want to ground yourself and unplug the Mac first) before attacking it with compressed air. Remember, if you blow the dust *into* the machine, you may not be helping matters as much. Small vacuums made for personal computers can be even more effective.

The case

Similarly, dust and lint inside the case can cause problems, mostly by blocking airflow and causing heat to build up inside the case. (I've heard stories of enough dust building up inside a case for a small electrical charge to arc inside it and fry some components, but such tales may be apocryphal.) In any case, cleaning inside is a good idea.

With yourself grounded and the Mac unplugged, you can use compressed air or a small computer vacuum (the better choice), although I'd encourage you to use a dry rag to get most of the dust out of the case before resorting to gimmicks. Avoid spraying compressed air directly on circuit boards (especially at close distances) and focus very closely on the air-intake ducts and any other holes in the case, like drive bays and floppy openings. Focus your cleaning on the inside of the case itself and not just components.

While you're in there, you should also make sure that the processor fan is connected correctly (if you have one) and that its power connector is snugly installed.

Airflow is also an argument against positioning your Mac's case in any way other than its original design—for instance, by turning a Mac II style case on its side to make it look like a minitower. This could cause airflow and heat problems. (Fortunately, we all feel less compelled to do this with modern models because it becomes tough to use the CD-ROM drive.)

Summary

✦ When a Macintosh won't power on, it may seem as if there's nothing you can do but take it to the shop. That's not completely true, however. Power-on problems aren't completely unknown, and they don't always happen for the reasons you may think. It's important to carefully troubleshoot a machine that won't seem to turn on—the problem could be a simple matter of configuration.

✦ Parameter RAM, or PRAM, can be the source of many problems. Designed to hold settings from the time you shut the Mac down until the time you start the Mac back up again, PRAM has a tendency to get a little scrambled when your Mac encounters other problems. That can lead to some bizarre behavior that's otherwise a bit tough to trace to its source.

✦ RAM and cache RAM can cause their share of headaches as well. And, again, because this is part of the processor subsystems, the errors can sometimes be less than helpful in pointing out the problem; it just feels as though your Mac is crashing sporadically or having trouble completing basic tasks. Such problems could be due to an unseated RAM module, a problem with your cache settings, or even a slight defect that causes incompatibilities.

✦ Ports don't usually cause too much trauma on their own, but plugging the wrong thing into the wrong port is one way to cause trouble in a hurry. Aside from that, ports usually respond to application or system errors. Sometimes a port gets left "open," other times they seem generally inaccessible. You can usually fix this, though.

✦   ✦   ✦

Storage Devices, SCSI, and File Recovery

When it comes to storage devices, there are plenty of problems to go around. It really isn't a question of whether a hard drive or the hard drive's file system is going to fail, it's a questions of *when*. The physical hard drive has a limited lifespan to begin with, and then you start throwing it all these files. Those files have the potential to get corrupted, overwritten, misplaced, or, in certain circumstances, confused.

The problem is your Mac pretty much relies on its hard drive to get started and keep going. The Mac is built on the assumption the hard drive won't fail and software problems on the hard drive won't become severe enough that they affect the Mac's ability to start itself up. But both hardware and software problems can contribute to other problems with your Mac — including problems so severe that you can't use the Mac at all.

Most of the time, the fix is a software-related one: maintenance. If you keep your desktop files rebuilt, defragment your hard drive, and run a disk doctor program on a regular basis, you're much less likely to encounter problems. (Creating such a routine and troubleshooting other software and system software issues is discussed in the last part of this book.)

But even if you're adamant about maintenance, you can still encounter a storage problem that brings your Mac to its knees. When that happens, the first thing to determine is whether the problem lies with the software (corruption, conflict, or bugs) or the hardware. You do that by following certain troubleshooting steps in response to error messages that the Mac offers as guidance. This chapter covers those steps.

I'll also talk about some other nitty-gritty issues involving storage devices, including the low-level driver software used to get the hard drive to talk to your Mac. In addition, I want to quickly cover formatting and partitioning a drive, because there's important new technology you should know about Mac drives. None of this stuff is really that complicated, even if it seems intimidating at the outset. Hard drive maintenance and recovery are things that nearly any Mac user can pull off.

Cross-Reference
Backup solutions, software, and strategies (the three S's) are covered in Chapter 9; hard drive installation is covered in Chapter 7.

Startup Issues

First things first — what's the most traumatic thing that can happen to a Mac user?

It's probably the appearance of a Sad Mac icon or a Mac that won't power on at all. These can be pretty disconcerting. But a startup problem with a hard drive ranks really high up there on the list. This error occurs as the Mac starts up, usually right after the startup tone. When one of these errors pops up, it stops the system cold.

A hard drive startup problem manifests itself as a blinking "X" or a blinking "?", usually on top of a little disk icon. These problems really aren't as scary as they might seem, even if they do portend the possibility you'll be messing around with your Mac — instead of working on it productively — for the next few minutes or more.

Troubleshooting when the "X" icon appears

Symptom: The Mac starts up, chimes, and then displays a blinking "X" icon.

The blinking "X" simply means the Mac couldn't find a valid System Folder on the disk that's currently inserted in the floppy drive. Most of the time, you probably didn't mean to have the floppy in there and didn't want the system to boot from it anyway. If that's the case, just wait a few moments; the disk will be ejected, and the Mac will continue to look for a valid System Folder.

If you did want to boot from the floppy, you'll need to check the floppy after the Mac has booted (or use another Mac) to make sure a System Folder has been placed on the floppy and that the System Folder has been *blessed* (that is, that the System Folder contains a System file). (See Chapter 33 for how to create a System startup floppy.)

There may also be something wrong with the floppy disk itself. Try using another startup floppy and/or use Norton Utilities or Tech Tool Pro to troubleshoot the bad floppy disk.

Troubleshooting when the "?" icon appears

Symptom: The Mac starts up, chimes, and then displays a blinking "?" icon.

This problem can have more far-reaching consequences. At its most basic, it's telling you that the Mac has searched everywhere it knows to look, but can't find a startup disk with a valid System Folder.

There can be many causes for a blinking "?" icon. Usually they have something to do with the hard drive you're trying to use as a startup drive: It's either not properly connected, it's not functioning correctly, or software has been corrupted on the drive. (Another cause for a "?" is a faulty logic board, something observed especially in the Mac II series, although I've also personally seen it happen in the Quadra series — and any Mac model is susceptible. If your problem doesn't seem related to your hard drive, troubleshoot the logic board in Chapter 22, or consult an Apple authorized service center.)

Note

If you have a late-model PowerPC Performa or some Power Macintosh models with IDE drives, the blinking "?" icon could be the result of a known issue with versions of Drive Setup that predate Drive Setup 1.3.1. Upgrade to version 1.3.1, 1.4, or later to solve this problem (download these from Apple's Support Web site). With the latest Drive Setup installed, select Functions ⇨ Update Driver.

Why "?" appears

Most of the time, a blinking "?" issue is related to something you've recently done or changed. It suggests that the System Folder on your Mac's startup drive (and any others attached) can't be found. If you've been doing some spring cleaning on your hard drive, physically installed another drive, or added some new software, you may have inadvertently done something to trigger this response from the Mac.

Here are some of the typical causes for a blinking "?":

✦ *The Mac OS system software is missing or damaged.* Actually, the real problem is the Mac's Start Manager can't find a *blessed* System Folder — that is, a System Folder with a valid System file in it. This can be the result of file corruption, a physically damaged hard drive, a user mistake, or a momentary glitch.

✦ *Parameter RAM is corrupted.* PRAM tells the Mac which of your drives the currently selected Startup disk is supposed to be. If that information (or similar data in PRAM) becomes corrupted, it can confuse the Mac into believing it can't find a blessed System Folder.

✦ *There is a SCSI problem.* As detailed in Chapter 22, the Start Manager will usually take a look at PRAM to determine which drive is supposed to be the startup drive. If that one can't be found, the SCSI chain will be searched (from high SCSI ID to low SCSI ID) for a drive with a valid System Folder on it. It there's a SCSI configuration problem or conflict, this process can easily be thwarted.

✦ *The drive is misconfigured.* This can often have something to do with the drive's driver software, especially in instances where a drive is incorrectly updated with a driver that's not designed for the drive or not designed for the current Mac OS that's being run on the machine.

✦ *The drive is damaged.* If the drive has "died" or has other physical problems (including severe file damage or physical damage to the internal drive mechanisms), that might manifest itself as a blinking "?" issue.

Occasionally an extension conflict can cause a "?" problem, as can bugs in the Mac OS. If your Mac has been working normally, however, you're unlikely to suddenly encounter this trouble unless something has very recently changed—you zapped PRAM or installed new software. If that is the case, you've got a good idea of what caused the problem. Whatever you just did is the likely culprit.

Evangelista tip: Sometimes it's the drive

Sometimes you'll have a problem that's a mysterious configuration issue—and sometimes it's just a bad drive. Don't rule out the possibility that the hardware is a lemon. Hard drives (and other computer components) are defective more often than anyone would like to admit.

But the best way to get that drive replaced, especially if it's under an Apple warranty, is by testing it yourself. This tip, from Mac Evangelista Hunt Sidway of Louisville, KY, explains how:

"I once spent months with the defective hard disk in my Power Mac 7300, during which time I stumbled onto a quick way to determine if one's hard disk is defective: Back up the drive (if you can) and test it.

"Start up from your Mac OS CD-ROM. Rather than use Disk First Aid, go to Drive Setup, and in the menu bar, under Functions, select Test Disk. This performs a low-level, block-by-block test of the actual disk itself, and is the best and most thorough way to test for a hardware or firmware problem versus a software or extension problem. It can take 45 minutes or more for 2GB and larger disks, so plan on being unproductive for a while. [Note: These tests destroy all data on the drive.]

"When I ran the test, it could never even complete—not even once!

(continued)

(continued)

"Each time, the test would abort before completion, giving me a message that the test had quit due to unrecoverable disk errors. I tried one last test, just out of curiosity, and came up with a sound principle for testing a suspect disk: I ran a low-level format with write-to-zeros, in Disk First Aid. (That took 50 minutes.)

"Then, before installing any software, I ran the Test Disk function in Drive Setup. As I expected, the test quit with the same ominous message. That left no questions for Apple tech support. It had to be replaced.

"System freeze-ups? Think you might have a hard drive problem? Even if the problem is intermittent, don't waste a lot of time. Back up your data if you can, do the low-level format with write-to-zeros, and then run Test Disk. That will give you a clear indicator of a bad drive, which might help you get a new drive more quickly from Apple."

Note: See the section of this chapter called "There's no drive icon" for information on which version of Drive Setup you should use. Also realize that these tests all destroy data on the drive, so a good backup is a must.

What to do about the blinking "?" icon

First, make sure you've waited long enough. Sometimes a blinking "?" icon will show up while the Mac is still trying to find other drives on the SCSI chain or waiting for a bootable CD-ROM drive to spin up. In fact, you can get a quick blinking "?" for no other reason than having a bad setting in the Startup Disk control panel. If you get a blinking "?", wait. If it resolves itself, check the Startup Disk control panel and make sure the control panel is set to the correct startup disk — usually your Mac's main internal drive.

The next quick fix when you have a blinking "?" is to try zapping PRAM. It's not really harmful to do this, and it sometimes will cause a blinking "?" to simply disappear. PRAM holds settings related to the startup disk that could get corrupted. Even if you do recover in this way and your Mac starts up correctly, it would be a good idea to run Norton or TechTool to make sure there's nothing else wrong with the startup drive as a result.

Chapter 22 covers zapping PRAM and related issues. Working with disk fix utilities is covered later in the chapter in the section "Recovering Files and Folders."

If both waiting and zapping PRAM fail, the next step is get your Mac to boot in some other way. You need to bring the Mac OS up so you can troubleshoot the problem and find the source. Your best bet is to start the Mac from a Mac OS CD-ROM, using the Mac's internal CD-ROM drive. (If you don't have a CD-ROM drive, you can also boot from a floppy. See the sidebar "Creating a boot disk" for recommendations on creating a boot floppy.)

To boot from a Mac OS CD-ROM, follow these steps:

1. Place the Mac OS CD-ROM in the CD-ROM drive.
2. Restart the Macintosh. (Push the CD-ROM back into the drive if the tray auto-ejects.)

If all goes well, the Mac should find and boot from the CD-ROM on its own. (It may display the blinking "?" for a moment before finding the CD-ROM drive.) If it doesn't, try restarting the Mac, and hold down the C key or ⌘-Option-Shift-Del until "?" disappears and/or the Welcome to Mac OS screen appears. Note that you need to start with a Mac OS 8.1 or higher CD-ROM if your hard drive is formatted in HFS Plus. Otherwise, you won't see the contents of the drive.

This should allow you to circumvent problems with the System software, trouble with the internal drive and, perhaps, trouble with PRAM. It won't help you get around some SCSI problems, however. If you have termination or configuration issues on the SCSI chain, this could be affecting your CD-ROM drive as well as your internal drives.

Note

If you're dealing with a Mac OS clone computer, you might be best off booting from the *original* system CD-ROM that came with the computer. The System Folder on that CD should be best designed to interact with all the hardware in your system. Also, clone users should note that the C key won't work for non-Apple CD-ROM drives. Instead, hold down ⌘-Option-Shift-Delete to boot from the CD-ROM drive. Again, if you've upgraded your hard drive to HFS Plus, you may not be able to see the contents of your hard drive unless you boot up with a CD designed for Mac OS 8.1 or higher.

If your Mac still offers a blinking "?" after you've put a bootable CD in the CD-ROM drive (and waited patiently), then there might be something wrong with the SCSI chain. If you've recently installed an internal disk drive, you should go back and check your SCSI termination according to instructions in Chapter 7; you may have terminated the internal chain twice or otherwise terminated it incorrectly. There may also be something else wrong with the drive installation.

If you haven't changed anything inside your Mac, there might be a problem with your external SCSI chain. The best way to troubleshoot this is to simply disconnect the device that's attached directly to your Mac's SCSI port. This way, all SCSI devices are disconnected from the machine. Now you can try booting again first without the CD (boot from the internal drive) and then with the CD-ROM. If you have luck getting your system to come up, the problem is likely a SCSI configuration issue.

If your Mac still doesn't find its CD-ROM drive, though (or if you don't have any external SCSI devices), your next step is to boot from a floppy. You'll need to have already created a special boot floppy (the process is described in the sidebar that follows). With it in hand, restart your Mac. Insert the floppy right after the Mac restarts, and then wait. The Mac should boot from the floppy drive. It actually looks for a System Folder in the floppy drive before looking anywhere else, including the officially chosen startup drive in the Startup control panel.

From the floppy, you may be able to access the drive, run Disk Tools, or use the Apple System Profiler to check the SCSI chain. At the very least, you should be able to boot your Mac, check the drives, and load control panels for your CD-ROM drive and the startup drive, which may help you restart your Mac with more success (see Figure 23-1).

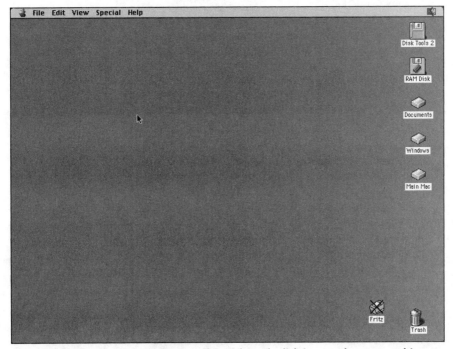

Figure 23-1: Booted from a floppy—the Disk Tools disk is now the startup drive, enabling me to troubleshoot my main hard drive.

Creating a boot disk

I haven't encountered a problem in a while that required a boot disk; I think the last time I couldn't get the Mac OS to boot from a CD-ROM in a crisis was 1993. Still, it never hurts to have a boot disk hanging around just in case the time comes when you need it (or if you have a Mac that doesn't include a CD-ROM drive). I also encourage boot disks for Mac clone users who don't have Apple CD-ROM drives. Some of the characteristic Apple CD-ROM drive behavior is hard-coded on the Apple CD-ROM's ROM chips, and clone vendors tend to use third-party CD-ROM drives. They may not always act as expected.

If you have your original Macintosh software, it should have shipped with a disk called Disk Tools. (Mac OS 8.0 and above sometimes include two disks.) This disk can be used to boot a troubled Mac, plus it contains the Disk Tools software on it to allow you to troubleshoot the internal hard drive of that Mac. If you don't have the Disk Tools disk, you can create one from a Mac OS CD-ROM.

To create a boot disk:

1. Insert your Mac OS CD-ROM.

2. Locate and open the folder Disk Tools. (This may be at the root level of the CD, or it may be buried in another folder such as Disk Images or Install Images.)

3. In the Disk Tools folder, double-click the icon Make Disk Tools floppies. Apple's Disk Copy utility opens.

4. When prompted, insert a blank floppy disk for Disk Copy to use as the new Disk Tools floppy.

5. Confirm that you want the disk created.

Once the disk has been created, you should test it by trying to start up from the floppy. (Restart and stick it in your floppy drive.) If the Make Disk Tools floppies program had you create two Disk Tools disks, you'll find out which one is for your computer at this point.

Label the disk(s) and store it somewhere safe and convenient. You'll be able to use this disk in the most extreme emergency—when you can't get your hard drive, CD-ROM drive, or removable media drive to boot the Mac.

If you've got a third-party CD-ROM drive, you need to take one more step to be able to access the CD-ROM drive once you've booted from the floppy. Drag the CD-ROM Toolkit extension into the Extensions folder in the System Folder on the Disk Tools floppy disk. If there isn't enough room, consider deleting the Drive Setup Lite Program, as the plan will be to boot from the floppy, and then fire up a CD-ROM such as the Mac OS system CD, Hard Drive Toolkit, Norton Utilities, TechTool Pro or something similar.

If you've successfully started up your Mac, wait patiently until the Finder has loaded. Now you'll need to check things out to see what the extent of the damage is. If you can't find your Mac's internal drive (the icon doesn't appear on the screen), you may have a SCSI conflict, a bad hard disk driver, or damaged hardware. If you do see your drive's icon, you should move on to troubleshooting a system software problem.

Note

If you can't even get your Mac to boot from a floppy, make sure you're using a floppy that includes a reasonably current version of the Mac OS. Some newer Macs will not boot using much older Mac OS versions. If this still doesn't help, you've likely got a hardware problem. Try the troubleshooting procedures for when a Sad Mac icon appears (in Chapter 22) and/or take your Mac to an authorized service center for repairs.

No drive icon

If you've booted from a floppy or CD-ROM and you don't see your hard drive's icon, it might have suffered some file damage and needs some help mounting. Try running Disk First Aid. If the drive appears in the window, select the drive's icon, and then click the Repair icon. This should mount the drive. From here, follow Disk First Aid's instructions for repairing the drive.

If Disk First Aid doesn't see the drive, try running Drive Setup or Apple HD SC Setup (whichever is appropriate — consult the following note) and see if the drive appears in its list. If it does, select it and choose Functions ⇨ Mount Volumes from the menu. (You can also try this in a program such as FWB Hard Disk Toolkit, Silverlining or SCSIProbe. It's probably best to use the software that was employed to format your drive in the first place.) If all goes well, this will mount the drive. It may still be in a fragile state, but at least it's been found and mounted.

Note

If the drive still doesn't appear, it's either damaged or you have SCSI trouble. One test is whether or not *other* drives appear. Do they? If not, the SCSI chain needs troubleshooting. If they do, check the connections for the troubled drive very carefully. (Check the SCSI troubleshooting section later in this chapter for more.)

Your next step should be to run Disk First Aid on the newly mounted drive. Select the problem volume and choose the Repair option. After getting feedback from the program, you may find that things have been fixed or that it recommends running a more intensive disk fix program. If it does, use Norton Utilities or TechTool Pro to fix the drive.

After you've been through all this, the moment of truth comes when you reboot the Mac and see if the problem persists. You can try rebooting the volume itself (use the Startup Disk control panel to set the drive as the startup disk), or reboot to the floppy drive or CD-ROM. If you try the latter, check to see if the volume appears once the Finder has loaded. If it does, you should test to see if it'll boot on its own. If it still can't boot on its own, the problem has likely become a system software issue (see the next section).

If the drive has disappeared again, this may suggest a problem with the hard disk's driver software. If this is an Apple-branded hard drive (if it came with an Apple Macintosh computer), run the Apple Drive Setup utility. Select the drive and mount it if necessary. Next, choose Functions ➪ Update Driver from the menu. Drive Setup may mount the drive itself after this. Restart the computer and see if the drive will mount correctly.

Note

Apple offers two major utilities for testing, initializing, and mounting hard drives. Drive Setup is used by all Power Macintosh computers and any 68040-level Macs that feature internal IDE hard drives. The Apple HD SC Setup utility is used for all other Macs. (For more information, see the section on formatting hard drives later in this chapter.)

If the drive is a non-Apple drive, follow instructions for the drive regarding the installation or updating of the disk driver. In many cases, you'll use Silverlining or the FWB Hard Drive Toolkit to update the driver.

System software problem

If you were able to boot immediately from either a CD-ROM or a floppy disk, and you've ruled out a SCSI conflict as described previously, then you may be having trouble with the system software itself. In general, each Mac drive should have one System Folder, and that System Folder needs to be properly "blessed," so that it has an active, working System file inside it.

Here's the procedure for testing your System Folder:

1. Open the problem hard drive.

2. Locate the System Folder and open it.

3. Locate the System file. If it doesn't appear in the folder, use the Mac's Find command to locate the System file. If you still can't find the System file, you should reinstall the Mac OS (see Chapter 33).

4. Double-click the System file. If it doesn't open correctly, you should perform a clean install of the Mac OS (or a replacement installation, as described in Chapter 33).

5. If the System file opens correctly, it should be working. Close the System file.

You're on your way to ruling out trouble with the System file. Your next step is to determine if the System Folder has somehow lost its blessed status. The first indicator of this is a System Folder icon that doesn't include a small classic Mac icon as part of the folder (see Figure 23-2).

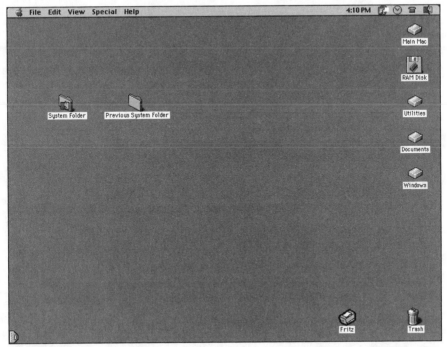

Figure 23-2: On the left, a blessed System Folder; on the right, a System Folder that lost its blessing.

If your System Folder isn't blessed, make sure there isn't a second System Folder on the hard drive. If there is, having two active System Folders on a single startup disk can confuse the Mac. Take the System file from one of the System Folders and drag it to another directory (the Fonts subdirectory in that particular System Folder is always a fine choice). You should also rename the folder to Previous System Folder or something similar to de-frock the System Folder.

If the only System Folder on your drive isn't blessed, it may simply need to be re-blessed:

1. Drag and drop the System file onto the Fonts directory icon (you can also drag it to the Mac's desktop).

2. Close the System Folder.

3. Reopen the System Folder and drag the System file back into the folder.

4. Close the System Folder again.

Take a look at the System Folder's icon now. Does it show the little Mac? If so, the folder has been successfully re-blessed. Restart your Mac to see if the System Folder takes hold and the Mac is able to restart from the drive. If it is, you should still run some check-up maintenance on the drive (see Chapter 31 for help in maintaining drives). If it's not, try a clean reinstall (or a replacement installation) as outlined in Chapter 33.

SCSI Trouble

Old Mac hands call the haze of trouble surrounding SCSI problems *SCSI voodoo*. In a way, some of the issues that can crop up when you're using SCSI devices can seem a bit weird, counterintuitive or just plain wrong. More than one Mac repair expert has given me the advice, "If it doesn't work the way Apple or the manual says it should, try it the exact opposite way." The heck with theory, I guess.

SCSI probably creates fewer problems in the aggregate these days. Some of the early confusion and glitches in self- and active-termination schemes have been worked out, and many SCSI devices these days rely on a more standard system for assigning and working with SCSI ID numbers. All the devices I've tested during the writing phase of this book, for instance, worked fine with one another — not a single complaint. I even had trouble *purposefully* getting SCSI connections to fail.

That doesn't mean the problems don't exist, however. Although many SCSI issues can be chalked up to configuration, the world of SCSI has a history of gray areas and things to watch out for. There are some new twists, too, such as Apple's dual-bus system for many of the latest Power Macs and the inclusion of ultra-SCSI options on the build-to-order G3 (and higher) Mac models.

SCSI symptoms

Hopefully, SCSI-related problems will crop up soon after you change something that is associated with SCSI — that's a telltale sign. Sure, it's not always that easy, but it often is. If you've changed a device's SCSI ID number, added a device, powered down part of the chain or moved a terminator, that's your first clue as to what's going wrong.

But the mysteries of SCSI run much deeper. Under some circumstances, the following can all be symptoms of a SCSI problem:

✦ Apparently random crashes in the Finder or in applications

✦ System freezes, especially when saving, scanning, or accessing another of the SCSI devices

✦ Appearing and disappearing drives and icons

✦ Read/write errors from hard drives and removable media

✦ Removable media that won't mount

✦ System crash or freeze shortly after mounting a device

✦ System crash or freeze shortly after startup

Although all of these problems can't necessarily be attributed to SCSI in every case, these are common symptoms that can help you narrow things down to SCSI problems.

Fortunately, really only a finite number of things can be wrong with a SCSI device or setup: configuration problems, cabling and termination, problematic hardware, or bad hardware. Take a look at each in turn.

SCSI configuration

Here's where you're going to have a lot of trouble with SCSI devices. If you have more than two or three external drives, scanners, and other devices, it's certainly possible that you simply made a mistake when connecting them, whether you loop a cable back on itself, forget to terminate something, or use the same SCSI ID for two different devices. (In fact, this should be a mantra for you: "No two IDs are the same. No two IDs are the same." It's the single most common problem in SCSI configuration aside from, perhaps, not turning the SCSI device on.)

Take a step back and consider your situation carefully. Ponder the possibilities. The common SCSI problems are as follows:

✦ SCSI cable not connected

✦ SCSI terminator not properly installed

✦ Same SCSI ID assigned to two different devices (including the typically reserved internal SCSI ID numbers such as 0, 3, 7)

✦ SCSI device not plugged in

✦ SCSI device not turned on

I introduced myself to a whole new world a few years ago when I decided to use an external hard drive as the startup disk on one of my Power Mac systems. I don't know how many times my heart seized up when I saw a blinking "?" as the Mac started up. "The drive? All my data?! What's wrong?!" I'd think. Then I'd gather my wits and throw the power switch on the drive, followed by a quick reboot of the Mac.

SCSI utilities

If it seems your problems are more complicated than simple configuration issues, you might find it helpful to use a SCSI utility application to determine what's connected to your Mac, to mount those devices and to perform some minor configuration miracles when necessary. Although you can use the Apple System Profiler to check SCSI ID numbers, you'll probably have more luck using SCSIProbe (see Figure 23-3) to mount and control SCSI devices. You may also have luck with hard drive utilities such as Drive Setup, Silverlining, and FWB Hard Drive Toolkit.

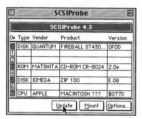

Figure 23-3: SCSIProbe, a freeware program from Robert Polic, enables you to review, test, mount and update SCSI configurations.

SCSIProbe allows you to see all the current SCSI ID assignments in your system and both SCSI buses if you have two (click the small 0 or 1 in the top-left corner to change buses). It also shows devices that are on the bus but not mounted. If a device doesn't appear in the display, click the Update button to search for other devices (this works in similar utilities, as well). If you'd like the device to then be mounted, you can select it and click the mount button.

Remember, only drives, removable media, CD-ROM, DVD, and similar devices are mounted. SCSI scanners, cameras, Ethernet adapters, and other devices usually aren't mounted on the desktop.

One thing to remember, though, is that it's not completely out of the realm of the possible for these utilities to lie. The Mac can often convince these utilities that everything is just fine, even if you purposely set out to confuse things (like setting identical SCSI ID numbers for different devices). So, you'll need to be diligent about double-checking SCSI configuration. One trick is to make sure you're turning your Mac completely off, not restarting the Mac, before you expect it to recognize a new ID assignment.

Cables, termination, and hardware

The key to troubleshooting SCSI is in isolating the problem. The best way to do that is to remove all SCSI devices from the chain, and take each SCSI device, one at a time, and attempt to add it to the Mac again. This can tell you not only which devices are causing trouble, but whether or not the problem has something to do with the cabling. The process may take a few minutes, but I promise it's less tedious and frustrating to do it this way at the outset.

If SCSI is causing consternation on your system, do the following:

1. Shut down the Mac. Detach all external SCSI devices.

2. Restart the Mac. Test your internal SCSI devices using SCSIProbe or a similar software SCSI utility. Test by trying to reproduce the problem you were having. Do any of the problems seem to occur as a result of having no external SCSI devices installed? If you get any of the same symptoms, it's possible that something is wrong with the internal SCSI bus. Check it for proper connections and termination.

3. Shut down the Macintosh. Reinstall one of the SCSI devices, giving it proper termination.

4. Restart the Mac and test the new device. Check its status in SCSIProbe and attempt to use the device directly. If you have trouble, you may have isolated it to the cabling, a problem with your terminator, internal termination problems, or the device itself.

5. Shut down the Macintosh. If the first device worked fine, add a second device to it with the proper SCSI ID number, cabling, and termination (don't forget to remove the termination from the first device). If the first device didn't work correctly, remove it before installing the second device.

6. Restart the Mac and test. If everything continues to work, keep testing until you've got a working SCSI chain up and running. If things don't work, try to isolate the device, cable, terminator, or combination that's causing trouble.

When you do come across a device that isn't working, it's probably best to pull it out of the chain and test the rest of the chain to ensure the problem you isolated is the only problem you're having. You can then troubleshoot that particular device.

If there's nothing wrong with the device itself (it seems to boot up, spin, blink, and all those sorts of things), it's time to suspect a bit of SCSI voodoo. What you do next is somewhat less than rational: You try everything. Specifically, add the device to the chain (or test it on its own) and try these things:

✦ Give the drive a different SCSI ID number than the one you've been trying. If you have two SCSI buses, choose an ID number that's not being used on *either* of the buses. You should also try giving it a *higher* SCSI ID number, because the SCSI bus gives higher numbers priority over lower numbers.

✦ Try a new SCSI cable.

✦ Try a new SCSI terminator.

✦ Put the problem device between two devices that aren't giving you any trouble. Install it with proper cabling and termination.

As a last ditch effort, try the following:

✦ Zap PRAM.

✦ Choose a different disk as the startup disk, even if that's not really the problem.

✦ Unterminate the device, even if logic dictates that it should be terminated.

✦ Try a different type of terminator, such as a pass-through terminator that terminates the chain *before* it reaches the device.

Note

Check Apple Tech Info Library (`www.apple.com/support`) for specific information about your particular Mac system. You'll find that in the Quadra and early Power Macintosh series of Macs, Apple experimented a bit with different types of active termination and dual-bus configurations. These can get a bit mind-boggling, but a search entry such as "Quadra 950, SCSI" or "4400, SCSI" should net you hits about your particular machine (substitute your Mac's model number).

Evangelista tips: SCSI voodoo

There's still a little oddity in the world of SCSI. For instance, Apple Tech Notes point out the Quadra 950 has two SCSI buses, but only one set of SCSI IDs—numbers 0 through 6 (the Mac is preassigned number 7). The Mac IIfx is the oddest SCSI machine Apple ever unleashed. Externally, it requires a different terminator (200 ohm instead of 100 ohm) from any other Mac. Internally, some IIfx machines have a SCSI filter that altered the capacitance of the SCSI bus (later IIfx models didn't require this). Check out these other voodoo submissions from Evangelistas:

" I have a (fairly specific) tip on installing the UMAX Astra 1200S scanner on Power Macs with two SCSI buses: Make sure the SCSI ID of the scanner is unique on both the internal and external SCSI buses, or the software won't be able to recognize it." — Andy Hendrickson, Mac Software Engineer (*Note: an update to the software may have solved this problem since this writing, but similar problems abound for older scanner and other SCSI device drivers that assume Macs have one SCSI bus.*)

"The termination rules are somewhat complicated on the 8100 (series). If you're using the external SCSI port for drives or a CD, you must have the internal SCSI ribbon-cable terminator installed. Because this was a new scheme for Apple with this series, some dealer techs who install a new internal drive for you may not know the severity of removing the internal terminator (as everything works fine in the shop without any external devices attached). I believe they think the internal terminator is like your appendix. If you have trouble with any and all of your external devices, check your Mac's documentation for information on internal termination. If you've ever had your Mac in to a dealer, go back and ask for another internal terminator. They'll have several in their parts box." — John Brassfield, Newcastle, CA

(continued)

(continued)

"If you're having trouble with a device installed on the SCSI bus, it could well be a cable. I have evaluated seven cables (25-pin SCSI to Centronics 50-pin) and only two of them work properly! My test: Use the device, in my case a Jaz drive, as you normally would, and time the different tasks with each cable installed. The worst cables have the slowest data transfer rates and take the longest. Or they fail, with error messages." — Bob Patterson, Port St. Lucie, FL

"One day I started up my PowerMac 6500/225 and the power came on, and then it just sat there like a sack of potatoes. Several more attempts failed to produce a Happy Mac. Two minutes of fretting and several expletives later, I started to unhook my external devices to see if they were my problem. One by one, I started pulling items off the end of the SCSI chain. Nothing. Then, like magic, my Mac restarted — after I had pulled the last device off. I then spent another 20 to 30 minutes playing mix and match trying to find a combination or even a singular SCSI device that worked. No joy.

"Just for giggles, I powered down my Mac (grounded myself) and popped the logic board out of the back of the case to see if anything was burnt or broken. I located the SCSI connector and followed the traces back to the controller chip. As I did so, I noticed a small, golden, metallic flake laying across two traces, just back from where the connector was soldered to the motherboard. 'There is no way that this is going to work,' I thought, 'but I'm going to do it anyway.' Out came the can of compressed air. I blew off the flake, and then proceeded to clean off the rest of the motherboard. Even after only six months of use, the fan and CPU were covered with a layer of gunk. I pushed the motherboard back into its socket, reconnected the SCSI chain in its original configuration, and then hit the power button and waited for the Happy Mac to show his mug. Sure enough, all was right with the world once again. One dinky metal flake had caused all my grief." — Eric Wesselman, Vancouver, WA

"Macs seem to like consistency. Try to always set your internal CD-ROM drive to SCSI ID 3, your scanner to SCSI ID 5, and your external hard drive (or removable media drive) to SCSI ID 2 or 4. These are what the Apple-brand devices are generally preset to." — Peter Trzcinski

All About Disk Drives

For the most part, this section discusses the behind-the-scenes, low-level functions that govern the birth, daily life, and rebirth of hard drive mechanisms — although a lot of this applies to removable media as well. If you ever find yourself in a situation where you need to (or want to) start over with a new lease on your Mac (at least, as far as software goes) you can reformat your hard drive and start over with clean magnetic plates on which to stream your bits of data.

As mentioned earlier, the Mac world is divided into different camps when it comes to the tool you'll use for managing your hard drive. With an Apple-branded hard drive, you'll use Drive Setup, if you have a Power Macintosh or a 68040-based Performa (or LC equivalent) with an IDE hard drive. Other Macs use the HD SC Setup utility in some cases.

If you have a third-party drive, you likely use one of two programs. FWB's Hard Drive Toolkit is a popular alternative, as is Silverlining, the driver software for LaCie-manufactured drives, shown in Figure 23-4. (LaCie makes drives that are often OEMed by other computer companies, and then packaged in their own branded external-drive enclosure. Apple has even OEMed some of these external drives in the past.)

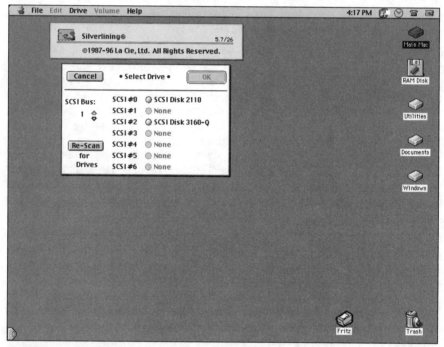

Figure 23-4: Silverlining is hard disk driver and management software for LaCie-manufactured drives.

Whichever you have, you may at some point need to use it to change settings, update a driver, or even format the drive. One of the tricks to doing this successfully is using the most recent version you can get your hands on when it comes time to do an upgrade or troubleshoot. The other thing that's important is not to use the wrong utility on the wrong drive.

Drivers and mounting

You've already seen in this chapter that updating the hard disk driver software is one way to fix problems with blinking "?" icons, freezes on startup, and other niggling problems. In fact, updating that hard disk driver is so encouraged by Apple that the company has rolled driver updating into the automated installation process for Mac OS system software. Although you can still choose not to update the drive, by default Apple will install a new driver for Apple-branded drives if one exists.

So, you should occasionally stop by the Web sites of your hard drive manufacturer(s) and see if they've come out with any add-ons or updates to your hard disk management software and/or hard disk driver software. If they have, download the patch and apply the changes. (Actually, you don't have to do this if nothing seems particularly wrong. Read the Read Me file or release notes that come with the update to see what exactly it fixes.)

In most cases, updating the driver is simply a matter of loading the hard disk management software, and then invoking the Update Driver command, as in Figure 23-5. This updates the small piece of software that loads as the Mac OS first starts up, telling the Mac how to access the drive. This driver can conceivably get corrupted (especially if a power surge or sudden crash brings the Mac down at a moment when the hard drive is working), resulting in blinking "?" Sad Mac icon errors.

You can also often use the hard drive management software to mount drives not currently on the desktop. A drive may not be mounted yet because there's a problem with it, it started up slowly as the Mac began its startup process, or it was turned on after the Mac had already polled the SCSI chain for hard drives. Whatever the reason, you can use the drive-management software to highlight the drive (you may need to invoke an Update command to get it to find the unmounted drive) and choose the Mount command or button.

The driver management software will often have other settings and utilities, including settings to change cache characteristics (whether or not the hard drive uses a built-in scheme to cache data in high-speed RAM to speed up operations), power down at a certain time, or even change the SCSI ID number in software.

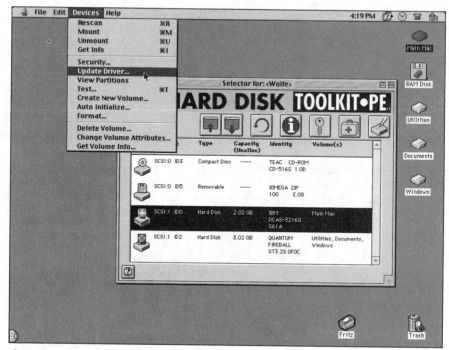

Figure 23-5: Your hard disk management software — or a recent update to the original software — should offer an Update Driver command.

Testing

Your driver management software will give you some other options, too. These can be useful in the troubleshooting process, although you need to be careful when you're dealing with these aspects of your hard drive management software; you usually only get asked twice if you really want to format your drive. Formatting a drive, partitioning a drive, and performing certain low-level integrity tests will destroy the data on the drive.

Note

If you can, back up your drive before performing any sort of hard drive tests, formatting, or partitioning. Even if the test says it will maintain your data, a recent backup is advisable. Such tests are an inopportune time for a crash, bug or power surge. (And the occurrence of such a hiccup is dictated by Murphy's Law.)

Formatting a drive should not be an early consideration in the troubleshooting process. Generally, your hard drive and Mac OS are not so completely mixed up that formatting the drive is necessary. And, in the off chance that you have a low-level virus on your hard drive, sometimes formatting won't eradicate it. (See Chapters 30 and 31 for more on viruses.)

If you do suspect that the hard drive has physical imperfections or other problems (perhaps excessive heat has been a problem or there seem to be a high number of read/write errors), it's possible that a low-level test will help you determine the condition of your drive. Explore the options in your drive-management software. Some tests are simply read/write tests that can tell you if the drive needs alignment or similar services. Others test the integrity of the actual media.

If you have gotten to the point where you'd prefer to reformat your drive, you should also think carefully about the ways you'd like it formatted and partitioned. See the section "Formatting and partitioning" later in this chapter for more on formatting and partitioning a drive.

Removable media

Removable media drives can be a special case. In general, they're a lot like hard drives in that they have their own driver software (usually in the form of an Extension in your System Folder) and they mount if present when the Mac OS is starting up. They also mount when inserted, though, tapping into the Mac ability to do this on the fly (the same way floppy disks do).

Special drivers

What's different about a lot of removable media is they tend to include the driver software for their operation on the media itself. This usually works okay, allowing the disk to mount on its own or, in a crunch, allowing it to be mounted by a tool such as SCSIProbe or the removable drive's own management software. A conflict can occur, however, when the two drivers aren't the same version or offer some incompatibility. Usually, things are fine if the drive in the System Folder is newer than the media's driver, but the opposite isn't always true.

In this case, the best rule is to probably go ahead and update whichever version of the drive is older — the one in the System Folder or the one on the media. You may need to download an update for your removable drive's management software, but once you do that, updating the media and/or the extension should be no trouble.

If you use an Iomega Zip or Jaz drive, you may encounter a similar problem; if the Mac OS starts up while a cartridge is in the drive, the Mac will use the cartridge's driver instead of the driver in the System Folder. If this driver is older, it can interfere with the operation of different cartridges that might be formatted to work with a newer driver. The best solution to this dilemma is to update the drivers on all your Zip/Jaz or similar cartridges — especially if you're the sort of admirable, well-organized person who could pull off something like that.

My solution is to simply eject Zip and Jaz cartridges whenever I'm not using the drive so the cartridge isn't in there to foul things up in the first place. (This system has the added benefit of not slowing down your Mac by spinning the drive at odd intervals as the Mac OS is wont to do if a cartridge is mounted.) Some older removable media drives *like* to be inserted when the Mac starts up, though, so you'll need to experiment with your own to see which is best.

Note You can often set a removable drive to automatically eject its media at shut down — or not — through its control panel (see next section).

Other removable media issues

Some removable media devices will include a control panel through which you can change certain settings relating to the drive and its performance. These settings can include behaviors — such as ejecting at shutdown — or dictate when some activity should occur — such as when the drive should lower its power consumption (see Figure 23-6).

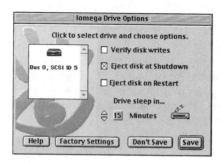

Figure 23-6: The Iomega Drive Options management control panel

Although removable media drives can often be formatted using the Mac's Special ⇨ Erase Disk command, you may have better luck with any utilities that are included with the drive. In general, these utilities will augment the capabilities of a typical Mac format, including options such as formats that also verify the integrity of the media.

Note You may also be able to format removable media in the Macintosh Extended Format (HFS Plus), which may enable you to store more on a given cartridge. Remember, though, that using HFS Plus will make the cartridge incompatible with any other Macs running Mac OS 8.0 or lower (HFS Plus was introduced in Mac OS 8.1).

In Mac OS 8.1, PC Exchange was updated to more readily recognize and mount DOS-formatted media in many removable media drives. (It also supports long Windows 95 file name conventions in PC Exchange 2.2.)

If you have trouble with this feature, though (or if you have an earlier version), one way to get PC-formatted media to work with your drive is to head over to the PC Exchange control panel *before* you insert the DOS-formatted media. Choose the Options button and click the removable drive once. Click OK and PC Exchange will keep the DOS-formatted drive from loading its own driver so that it doesn't cause trouble with the Mac OS.

Formatting and partitioning

To be used with a Macintosh, a hard drive needs to have a low-level format that governs how files are saved and tracked on the drive. In most cases, you'll want to do this using a native Macintosh format, although the Mac is certainly capable of dealing with drives in other formats, including DOS and Apple II's ProDOS. And, you can always run a different operating system on your Mac, such as Linux, BeOS or other UNIX variants, which may also require a different hard drive format.

For the Mac OS, though, your main drive will need to be formatted in a native Mac OS format — that's either the Mac OS Standard format (known as Hierarchical File System or HFS) or the Mac OS Extended format (known as HFS Plus). Doing this at its most basic is simple: Use the Special ➪ Erase Disk command to reformat an existing hard disk or removable media cartridge. This erases all previous information from the disk, giving you a chance to start over.

Formatting a hard disk or large removable disk is usually a more arduous process, however. If you've already been using the disk, you'll likely want to back up the data on that disk before reformatting, because a reformat causes all data on the drive to be almost irretrievably lost. You'll also need to decide what formatting scheme you want to use and whether or not you want to partition the drive.

HFS and HFS Plus

The HFS Plus format was introduced with Mac OS 8.1, providing some newer, more modern features and extending the capabilities of the Mac OS when dealing with files. It's also not backwards compatible, so you must be running Mac OS 8.1 or greater to use HFS Plus.

HFS Plus improves on some of the limitations of HFS, including a limit to the number of storage elements that HFS can track, a change in the naming scheme for files (HFS Plus builds on the Unicode scheme that allows for longer filenames), and the number of files that can be stored on a hard drive at any particular moment.

The biggest problem with HFS is that regardless of the hard drive's size, it is limited to a total of 65,536 storage elements that could be tracked at one time. The file system creates *allocation blocks* based on this number, so the entire drive is divided into equal allocation blocks that are then used for storing files. The problem is the larger the drive, the larger the minimum allocation block, which means that any file, no matter how small, fills that allocation block. Even if the file is one letter saved in a SimpleText document, it will take the entire allocation block.

In fact, you can calculate this effect. Here's how:

1. Because there are 2,000 logical blocks (512K blocks) in 1MB of space, you multiply the size of the drive in megabytes by 2,000.

2. Divide that number by 65,536 — the maximum number of allocation blocks under HFS.

3. Round this number up to a whole number and multiply it by 512. The result is the amount of space (in bytes) in each allocation block.

Take, for example, a 2GB (2,048MB) hard drive:

2048 x 2000 / 65536 = 62.5 (rounded to) 63 x 512 = 32,256 (bytes) ~ 32K

So, the minimum allocation block on a 2GB hard drive is 32K. That means any small file requires 32K for storing; it also means that any larger file that spills over into a new allocation block takes up that whole 32K block, even if only to store one more kilobyte of data.

Prior to HFS Plus, the best way to deal with this issue was to partition your hard drives so that you were working with more, but smaller, virtual drives (called *volumes*). When a partition was created, HFS was capable of assigning a whole new set of allocation block numbers for tracking files on that partition. So, making the allocation block sizes on the whole drive (now divided into two or more volumes) smaller wasted less space, and this usually led to users dividing larger hard drives into three, four, or more volumes to get optimum storage capabilities.

HFS Plus circumvents this problem by assigning very specific allocation block sizes instead of allowing them to grow according to size. (This is accomplished by using much more than 65,000 block numbers.) HFS Plus assigns allocation block sizes as shown in Table 23-1.

Table 23-1
HFS Plus Allocation Block Sizes

Volume Size	Default Allocation Block
256MB or smaller	512 bytes
256–512MB	1024 bytes
512–1GB	2048 bytes
Over 1GB	4096 bytes

So, the maximum allocation block is 4K on larger hard drives, a number that strikes a balance between file size and performance. (Moving around a *bunch* of 512 byte blocks on a larger drive could cause a performance bottleneck, so a compromise is in order.)

Note

The other advantages of HFS Plus (such as longer filenames) weren't yet implemented in Mac OS 8.1, and are likely intended to make an appearance in Mac OS X. At the time of writing, the main benefit is an increase in the number of files allowed on a hard drive and the additional space gained by using smaller allocation blocks.

Should you choose HFS Plus?

Although the possibilities of HFS Plus are certainly enticing, there are a few reasons to avoid using it. Aside from it's being a reasonably new technology (which means it lacks support or some major utilities, may not work with every application or file, and could have bugs or cause conflict), HFS Plus is also not backward compatible. That means there are some instances when you won't be able to use it. For instance, no Mac running Mac OS 8.0 or earlier can see an HFS Plus volume. The Mac must be running at least Mac OS 8.1 to see the HFS Plus volume. If you try to view an HFS Plus volume with an older version of the Mac OS, a single file called "Where_have_all_my_files_gone" appears on the desktop, explaining that the current machine can't view an HFS Plus volume.

So, before deciding to upgrade to HFS Plus, you'll need to consider all the different ways that an older Mac might try to access your HFS Plus-enabled Mac:

✦ *Over a network.* If your Mac is connected to a file sharing network, Macs using Mac OS 8.0 or below won't be able to access your drive.

✦ *In SCSI Disk mode.* If you connect an HFS Plus–formatted PowerBook to a Mac that is using Mac OS 8.0 in SCSI Disk mode, the desktop Mac won't be able to read the file.

✦ *On removable media.* A removable media cartridge formatted with HFS Plus will only work with Mac OS 8.1 or above.

The other thing you should consider before upgrading to HFS Plus is whether all your major utilities and applications will move forward. You may need new versions of your hard disk drivers and configuration software, new disk doctor programs, and new versions of password protection programs (even the PowerBook Security software needs to be updated), and some low-level control panels and/or extensions may not work correctly. HFS Plus also can't be used on any volume smaller than 32MB, including floppy disks.

One possible solution: Partition your hard drive and format a smaller chunk (of a few hundred megabytes, perhaps) in regular HFS. That will enable you to boot this Mac from an older Mac OS startup floppy or CD-ROM version in a crunch, and then you'll be able to run a disk doctor utility on that partition to get it up and running. You can format the rest of the drive (the remaining partition) in HFS Plus to get all the benefits of the new file system.

Note

If your Mac is reasonably isolated from older Macs and you won't be having much trouble with your applications, you can either reformat the drive as an HFS Plus volume (after backing up all your data) or you can use a utility like Alsoft's PlusMaximizer (www.Alsoft.com/) to switch to HFS Plus without reformatting. Alsoft offers other utilities, too, for upgrading to HFS Plus.

Formatting

Whether you've decided to go with HFS Plus or not, you may be interested in formatting your hard drive. It's certainly a great way to optimize the hard drive, especially after catastrophic system software problems, after cleaning off a virus, or when you've simply decided that it's time to start over with a fresh, clean drive. It's even the first step toward changing your drive's partitioning scheme, in most cases.

Formatting is really quite easy. Just make sure you have a good backup of the data on the drive, because formatting will destroy all data on the drive. Select the drive in the Finder and choose Special ➪ Erase Disk from the menu bar. After choosing the type of format you want (you may have no choice or a choice between Mac OS Standard and Mac OS Extended — HFS Plus — formats) click OK when you're asked if you're sure that you want to delete all the files on your drive.

Only click OK if you *really are sure* you want to delete all the files on the drive.

The Mac then takes over and formats the drive for you. When it relinquishes control, you'll have a clean, new drive in the format of your choice.

Of course, you can also choose to format a drive using a drive utility such as Apple's Drive Setup or third-party kits such as FWB Hard Disk Toolkit and Silverlining. The advantage of these utilities is you can update the hard disk driver, run certain tests and then partition the drive, if you'd like.

Note

Don't forget to upgrade to the latest version of your hard disk management tool if you use one. Silverlining is maintained at www.lacie.com/ and FWB Hard Disk Toolkit is maintained at www.fwb.com/.

Partitioning

As discussed earlier, there are a lot of reasons to format in HFS, instead of HFS Plus, although you may cringe at losing some of the features you'd get if you used the Plus scheme. To get around one problem HFS has — the tendency for large drives to eat up a lot of extra space when saving files — partition the drive.

Actually, both HFS and HFS Plus support partitioning of the drive into virtual drives, so that a 4GB hard disk, for instance, would show up as two different hard disks in the Finder, each of which could be 2GB in size. (Or, it could be four disks of 1GB each, or any combination, such as one 3.5GB disk and one 512MB disk.) This can simply be an issue of convenience; perhaps you'd like a separate drive icon for storing your documents so that you can then easily back them up.

However, the limitation in HFS causes a lot of disk space waste on larger (1GB+) drives. So, standard practice is to partition a large physical hard drive into several smaller logical volumes, which can hold small files more efficiently if you're using HFS.

Most drive utilities will also allow you to partition the drive with a special command (check the menu bar for partitioning tools). You'll then be able to choose the size for each partition, along with the type of file system you want put on that drive. In some cases, a partitioning tool will only be able to work with Mac OS Standard or Mac OS Extended formats; in other cases you can partition using various UNIX file formats, Apple II, and other interesting choices.

The result after partitioning? You'll have as many drive icons in the Finder as you have Mac OS formatted volumes. (If you want to then format the partitions into different file systems, you're free to do that, too.)

Mac Evangelista tip: Partition tuning

According to Mac Evangelista Gerald Wilson, there's more to partitioning an HFS drive than just picking a smallish size. If you can make the allocation block size an exact binary number (2-, 4-, 8-, or 16K), you'll get better performance from your drive volumes. Here's the chart:

Allocation Block (K)	Min. Partition Size (K)	Max Partition Size (K)
1/2 (512 bytes)	0	32,767
1	32,768	65,535
2	98,304	131,071
4	229,376	262,143
8	491,520	524,287
16	1,015,808	1,048,575

So, choose a size with the partition size range to get the best allocation block size for optimum performance. Says Gerald:

(continued)

(continued)

"You may need to experiment with your disk formatter to ensure you're hitting the correct range. Remember: One byte over or under for the allocation block and the disk is untuned and less efficient. Don't worry too much if you have an untuned disk that you can't easily rebuild. The effect is minor (at most a 20 percent disk speed improvement) and won't benefit all users or all applications. But if you've got a new disk which you need to partition, why not tune the partition sizes as you go?"

"Users doing media work (audio, video) need to stream huge amounts of data to and from disk. For them, a large extent size can be more efficient. If you're that sort of user, disk tuning will still help, but you probably need to set up one physical volume as your system disk with smallish partitions, and another volume as your A/V disk tuned to suit very large files."

Disk Fixing and File Recovery

I've mentioned that corruption can hit places like PRAM, the System file, and other parts of the Mac OS. But corruption and other factors can affect your regular files, causing trouble with your day-to-day work. The best way to keep this from happening is to maintain your file system regularly using some of the recommendations you'll find in Chapter 31. In cases of emergency, however, you'll want to step up the fight.

Most of the time, you'll follow a process of hard disk fixing and file recovery. If you're having a traumatic problem with the drive, you'll start as outlined earlier in this chapter — with Disk First Aid and Drive Setup. Once you've moved on from those tools, your next step is to get a commercial troubleshooter and run it to get things not just patched up, but back in full working order. In the Mac world, that means one of two products: Symantec's Norton Utilities (www.norton.com) or Micromat's TechTool Pro (www.micromat.com). Each offers tools to help you work through disk and file recovery issues.

Norton Utilities

Norton Utilities feature a number of different tools for recovery, including the Norton Disk Doctor, Volume Recover, and UnErase. These features enable you to choose a particular hard drive in your Mac system, mount it if necessary, and then perform a variety of tests on the files, directory structure, and the media. In many cases, Norton can dig deep into the bits and bytes of a drive to recover items that have been scrambled, deleted, or otherwise lost.

Most of the fixing and recovery takes place in Norton Disk Doctor, which is a generalized troubleshooting and repair tool for hard disks, removable media, and floppy disks. If you are having any sort of problem that can't be repaired by Disk First Aid, you should run Norton Disk Doctor to check the drive in question. (Figure 23-7 shows Norton Disk Doctor.)

Note   At the time of writing, Norton Utilities was still incompatible with the HFS Plus format for hard drives. Versions before Norton Utilities 4.0 are not compatible with HFS Plus. If you do accidentally use an older version of Norton Utilities with an HFS Plus volume, you can run Apple's Disk First Aid 8.2 or higher to recover from some problems, or try contacting Symantec's customer service or visit their Web site (www.symantec.com/) for information on recovering from this problem.

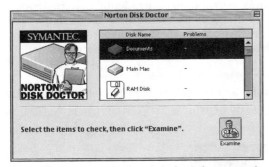

Figure 23-7: Examining a disk that's been causing a bit of trouble recently

Disk Doctor really works a little like a physical doctor. It has the responsibility of diagnosing the problem before it can fix anything on its own. For very complex problems, Disk Doctor can call in "specialists." Both Norton Unerase and Norton Volume Recover work in conjunction with Disk Doctor to solve more specialized problems.

So what does Disk Doctor look at? Here are the basics it cycles through to diagnose the problems with your drive:

✦ **Initial checks.** Disk Doctor begins by running tests that help it determine what type of media it's working with and how it tends to be used by the Mac.

✦ **Bad blocks.** It then checks the media's surface for damaged areas. Bad blocks are usually mapped out by the disk's directory so that data elements are not written to those blocks. Accidentally writing to such blocks generates errors and, occasionally, unrecoverable files.

✦ **Disk information.** Verifies that the disk is structured the way it's supposed to be.

✦ **Directory contents.** Checks and verifies that the disk's directory is structured logically and the directory's records are in order.

✦ **Missing files.** Checks for files that are listed in the directory but are missing, damaged, or cross-linked (two files sharing one block).

✦ **Analyzes files.** Checks for files that aren't following Mac conventions, and finds those that might be conflicting with one another or with system software.

One of the ways that Norton works is to ask you to run parts of it before any trouble starts, allowing it to take inventory of your system and determine what's changed through problematic writes, corruption, or accidental deletes. Using a program called FileSaver, Norton Utilities can track this information in the background while it also constantly tests your drives whenever your Mac encounters an idle period. This helps alert you to problems before they get out of control.

If you have Norton Utilities, consider activating FileSaver if you haven't already. Figure 23-8 shows the FileSaver control panel.

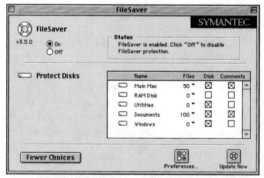

Figure 23-8: The FileSaver control panel allows Norton Utilities to constantly monitor your Mac.

TechTool Pro

Micromat made a big splash with their release of TechTool Pro 2, a product that adds to the value of the original TechTool and TechTool Pro, offering a suite of utilities that have a strong understanding of how Macs work. Even the freeware TechTool program is indispensable to Mac owners, what with its intelligent handling of basics such as zapping PRAM and rebuilding the desktop. TechTool Pro 2 covers many more bases, including file and volume recovery, along with support for HFS Plus.

TechTool Pro started life as more of a diagnostic tool, providing users with comprehensive access to information about the internals of their Macs—information about the SCSI chain, ADB, serial ports, the CPU, audio inputs/outputs, and so on. In my opinion, some of the information it can give is amazing (the manufacturer and type of RAM installed in your Mac, for instance.) If you intend to troubleshoot Macs at almost any level—from beginner to hobbyist to professional—you'll likely find TechTool Pro 2 of use to you, even if you prefer some of the tools in Norton Utilities (see Figure 23-9).

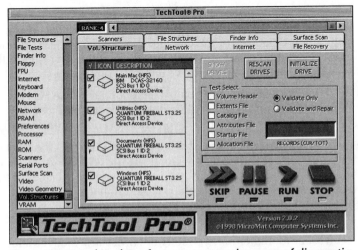

Figure 23-9: TechTool Pro features an amazing array of diagnostic and repair tools for Mac troubleshooting.

In addition to those abilities, TechTool Pro includes support for Mac OS 8.1 and above and the HFS Plus file system format. TechTool Pro 2 also now features file-recovery tools such as the following:

✦ Disk Structure Repair

✦ File Repair

✦ File Recovery

✦ Volume Recovery

✦ Block Scan

Like Norton Utilities, TechTool Pro 2 features the Protection control panel, which monitors your system and saves information about it to aid in file and volume recovery tasks in the future.

Note What if your drive is waterlogged, run over, or otherwise destroyed? You may still be able to get data off the drive, but you'll need to call in the highest echelon of low-level drive experts. Companies such as DriveSavers (`www.drivesavers.com`) specialize in dressing up in clean-room outfits, peeling apart the layers of physical hard disks, and recovering data from their innards. I hear it's costly, but your data may be worth more than a new car—or even the price of a new computer—to you.

Summary

✦ Startup problems can be caused by a number of different hard disk-related problems, including problems with the configuration of software, corruption in parameter RAM, or trouble with the hard drive. You can troubleshoot these successfully, but you'll have to get the drive mounted on the desktop first.

✦ SCSI voodoo is a term affectionately given to the tendency of the SCSI bus to succumb to odd problems that can be difficult to track down. Only a diligent approach to SCSI troubleshooting will get you back up and running quickly.

✦ Being able to work with your Mac's hard drive at a lower level—the level of driver software, formatting and manually mounting the drives—is important for the skilled Mac troubleshooter. Knowing how all this works can even help you make sense of some typical Mac problems. Additionally, at this level removable drives will tend to throw some interesting twists your way.

✦ If file or volume recovery is necessary, it's time to call in a pro—Norton Utilities or TechTool Pro. Either of these software Swiss army knives should be able to help you recover data, programs, and anything else that's been affected by a catastrophic drive failure (as long as the drive still operates).

✦   ✦   ✦

Input Devices and Scanners

✦ ✦ ✦ ✦

In This Chapter

ADB issues

Keyboards and mice

Scanner care

Troubleshooting SCSI and serial scanners

✦ ✦ ✦ ✦

I t's easy to let trouble with an input device fool you. The Mac on which I spend most of my time is sitting on top of a desk with one of those keyboard trays. (If you haven't tried one, you should consider it. Sitting with your elbows at 90-degree angles and your wrists slightly above the keyboard can be much more comfortable, and it may be better for you ergonomically.) Because my Mac is a minitower design, the keyboard ends up being quite a length away from the back of the Mac, so I got a little cable extender.

I must kick that thing out of its connector at least once a week. Usually I'm typing or mousing at the time, and my mouse pointer freezes immediately. After some words that probably wouldn't even pass the Fox censors, I usually figure out that the keyboard is unhooked right after giving my Mac the three-finger salute (Option-⌘-Power reboots most Mac models after a freeze, but not if the keyboard isn't connected). It's then that I peer under the desk at the real culprit: my right foot.

Of course, this is probably the least problematic input issue one could experience on a Mac. But the results can sure seem dire if you don't diagnose this one correctly. The same can be said for most problems that affect your Mac's input devices — as the basic method for communication between you and your Mac, a busted keyboard or problem mouse can cause not only frustration but, as in my case, miscommunication.

Note

So far, I haven't gotten much of a chance to play with USB devices and check around for troubleshooting help, because, at the time of writing, no one in the Mac world is yet using USB devices, and little information is available on the state of USB troubleshooting. It is a topic I intend to follow very closely, however, as it should have far-reaching consequences in the world of Mac upgrading. Check `www.mac-upgrade.com/` for special reports and tracking of USB issues.

The ADB Bus

The Apple Desktop Bus is certainly a convenient and clever way for adding input devices, especially with its no-hassle extensibility. But it has its limitations, as you might expect from any computing technology that's over 15 years old.

What can go wrong with the ADB? Let's take a look at some of the possibilities:

✦ *Overloading.* ADB can get overloaded with peripherals, all of which require a bit of power from the bus to operate. Use up this power, and you can get intermittent or completely unreliable feedback from ADB devices.

✦ *Overcabled.* There's a limit to how far an ADB chain can be extended before errors creep in.

✦ *Shorts.* ADB can (occasionally) experience an electrical short, especially if you connect a bad cable.

✦ *Mistaken installation.* The ADB port looks frighteningly similar to a number of other ports on the back of a Macintosh, and it's certainly possible to plug cabling into the wrong one, causing all sorts of problems.

ADB by the numbers

If you're concerned that you may have too many ADB devices hooked up to your Mac, I'm not going to tell you that you're wrong. You'll have to figure it out for yourself. Here's the skinny on how much power can be drawn from the bus and other significant statistics:

✦ The ADB bus can only handle about 500 milliamperes of power consumption. Keyboards tend to consume 85 to 100 milliamperes. Other devices may consume more or less. Be particularly wary of devices that use a pass-through ADB connector to use the ADB port only for power — modems tend to do this, as do some other devices.

✦ Three to four simple devices is about all the ADB chain can handle. Any more than that, and errors or poor response characteristics may creep in. Also, be wary of complicated input devices — such as digitizing tablets — which may limit you to two or three devices, tops.

✦ Five meters is the limit to the length of a typical chain of ADB devices. If you need to be further away from the Mac than that, you'll want to look into devices that boost the ADB signal, some of which are discussed in Chapter 10. Individual cables of six feet or more can sometimes cause intermittent problems.

Troubleshooting ADB

If you're having trouble with your ADB connections or devices, you should take the time to troubleshoot things carefully. It's important to know if you have an ADB device that's failing or if the ADB chain itself is the problem. Generally, symptoms of both types of failures can be quite similar.

The first thing to look at is the connection itself. Make sure you've got ADB cabling hooked up to the ADB ports on the back of your Mac. Apple warns of a scenario in which users with Macs that feature S-video ports will accidentally plug their ADB chain into the S-video port. The S-video port is designed to accept 7-pin connectors, but an ADB cable will fit in that port. However it's certainly not a good idea to actually plug the ADB into that port—at best, the device won't work, and at worst the device or port will be damaged.

Isolating an ADB problem generally means isolating each individual ADB device and seeing if it works correctly with your Mac. You can then test for conflicts that arise from using the devices together. If you think you're experiencing a recurring error that you might be able to reproduce, try this:

1. Shut down your Mac.

2. Unplug all the ADB devices you have connected to your Mac except the keyboard and your mousing device.

3. Restart the Mac. Try to reproduce the error.

4. If you don't get an error, shut the Mac back down.

5. If one of your other ADB devices is a mousing device (for example, a graphics tablet), uninstall the mouse and plug the new device into the keyboard.

6. Restart and test for the error.

If you don't get past the first step (keyboard and mouse together), it's either your mouse, your keyboard, or the ADB cable between your Mac and keyboard that is causing the problem. You should plug the mouse directly into the ADB port, and then restart the Mac. If you can mouse around and select things with no trouble, shut down and try the keyboard and mouse combination, this time with a new ADB keyboard connected to the mouse. The problem's not with the keyboard's cable, it might be with the keyboard. Take the keyboard to a Mac service center and have it looked at.

If your Mac passes the first test, continue to do this until you isolate the device that caused the error. If none of your mousing devices seem to be having any troubles or are causing a conflict, try adding all your ADB devices one by one, restarting every time to check the new chain. If you don't encounter any problems, you may have fixed things just by switching them around a bit. If you do have problems, suspect devices that use the ADB port only for power; remove those from the chain and see if your other ADB devices don't get along a bit better.

Expert tip: Could it be the cable?

It may not seem likely that an ADB cable could be bad, but it does happen. And, it can result in some unexpected results. This tip comes Guido Körber, vice president for products of Fesh!, a German manufacturer of ADB devices and Mac software:

"There is a nice trick [older, 68000-series] Macs play on you when there is a short circuit on the ADB. If the Power-On and the Ground line of the ADB are shorted, the self-powering models do not shut down. Instead, they put up the old 'You can now safely switch off your Mac' message.

"Since Apple tests the motherboards completely, you will never find a problem there. But you cannot rely on ADB device manufacturers testing the Power-On line if it is not used by the device (for instance, a trackball doesn't use the Power-On line). We are manufacturing ADB devices and we've had a few customers with the problem. It is solved by disconnecting the offending device or cable."

Other ADB advice

This tendency for ADB to get overwhelmed by devices and be a little sensitive to cable lengths can result in some voodoo-like symptoms. Apple has offered, in various Tech Notes, advice that doesn't always necessarily make sense, but might work if the logical approaches to troubleshooting ADB fail. Other experts have contributed their two cents to this list as well.

You might notice some of these troubleshooting tips are familiar:

✦ *Restart your computer.* Sometimes just clearing out RAM and starting again fresh can help get rid of input device trouble.

✦ *Zap the PRAM.* It may help, it may not.

✦ *Troubleshoot extensions.* Specifically, check with the manufacturer of your input device to see if it requires an extension or control-panel conflict and see if there are any known conflicts. If not, consult Chapter 32 for information on troubleshooting inside the System Folder.

✦ *Reinstall your driver software.* You may also want to delete the preferences file associated with your input device, if there is one. (Chapter 31 discusses the Preferences folder.)

✦ *Try a different or shorter ADB cable.* You might also try configuring without any ADB extension cable you might be using.

Keyboards and Mice

Over time, mice and keyboards can wear out, and they certainly deserve proper maintenance — but you're probably going to ruin them long before their natural lifespan has run its course. It seems to be a fact of life that, eventually, somebody is going to drench the keyboard in a sticky, sweet liquid or gooey substance. (If you have children, at least you can blame it on them.)

Take a quick look at what you can do to bring keyboards and mice back from the "great beyond" in times of crisis. Actually, keyboards and mice can pretty much just be cleaned; there aren't many other repairs or fixes to concern yourself with in this case (unless you accidentally set the keyboard to a foreign language keyset, as described back in Chapter 10). If you're noticing erratic behavior that you can't very well attribute to an ADB problem, you might just need to clean your input devices up a little and make them presentable.

Mac expert tip: The doorbell syndrome

Don Miller of 5-Minute Mac Consulting in Pittsburg, PA, has coined the phrase "doorbell syndrome," which he says is his name for problems that are generated when a user hits the mouse button over and over again. In his experience, the occasional client will click a mouse (or trackball) button, see nothing happen on the screen, and then respond by clicking the mouse button *much harder*. This is rarely helpful, but it does tend to damage input devices. (Don mentioned that "elevator button syndrome" would be an equally applicable name.) Here's his story:

"One day, I was called to a client's office to fix a Mac that had the flashing disk icon at startup. I tried every disk trick I know, but nothing helped. Even my portable hard drive, loaded with universal system software and repair utilities, failed to get rid of the flashing disk icon. The Mac obviously was not finding a boot drive anywhere. Even a bootable disk was refused. But nothing appeared to be wrong.

"Then I took the opposite approach by asking myself, 'What could I do to prevent a Mac from recognizing the startup drive?' Well, if you hold down the mouse button you can make the Mac bypass the internal drive at startup, I thought.

"Sure enough, after disconnecting the mouse (actually, my client used a trackball) the Mac started perfectly. The problem, as I discovered later, was one too many hits on the mouse button. It was broken and permanently 'pressed.' As a result, the Mac was made to refuse *any* startup drive."

Mice

Your mouse will probably let you know when it needs to be cleaned or looked at. If you're using a smooth, firm surface as a mouse pad, but experiencing less-than-ideal mouse behavior, it's probably time for a cleaning.

To clean your Mac's mouse:

1. Shut down the Mac, unplug the mouse, and turn it over.

2. The mouse ball is sealed inside the bottom of the mouse behind a dial that you can turn to remove. You'll generally turn an Apple mouse's dial counterclockwise to loosen it, as shown in Figure 24-1. (If you have trouble using your fingers, fit a pen, key, or small screwdriver in the open slot and push the dial so that it turns counterclockwise. The plastic is very soft, though, and will probably scar from the experience.)

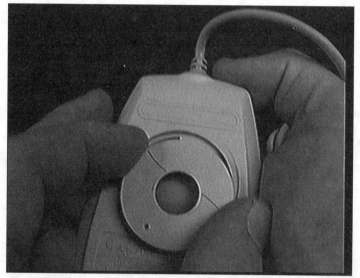

Figure 24-1: Turn the dial on the mouse counter-clockwise to open it.

3. Turn the mouse back over and roll the mouse ball into your hand. Rinse the ball with soap and water to clean the ball, and then set it aside until it dries completely.

4. Using a cotton swab and some rubbing alcohol, clean the wire rollers inside the mouse, again waiting until it dries completely.

5. Place the ball back in the mouse and replace the dial, turning it clockwise until it locks.

The mouse isn't the only thing you may need to clean. If your mouse continues to act erratic or becomes dirty again very quickly, you may need to examine your mousepad. If your mousepad has been treated in any way like the pads in my office generally are, it may be due for a scrubbing, too. Many of them can be cleaned with soap and water under the faucet, as long as you're very careful to dry the pad completely — perhaps overnight in a dish rack or all day in the sun.

Needless to say, you should replace your mousepad occasionally, and clean it immediately after something is spilled on it. Don't drag your mouse over a wet, sticky, or otherwise compromised mousepad. Also, it isn't a good idea to substitute newspaper, printer paper, mystery novels, or anything else for a mousepad, because paper fibers and other little bits can build up inside the mouse. Get a good quality mousepad, and then give yourself another one every birthday or so.

Note

If you continue to have trouble with your mouse, examine the rollers on the inside of the mouse very carefully. Sometimes hair, fabric fibers, or something else can jam the little rollers, causing them to stop rolling. Tweezers or a toothpick may help you get the offending item away from the roller. Be careful, though. If you bend the wire that attaches to the roller, you've probably ruined the mouse.

Your mouse trouble could also be caused by software, especially if you're experiencing something like a mouse pointer that seems to have a mind of its own: The pointer jumps around, it slides across the screen on its own, or something similar. Usually, this is a conflict — probably between similar control panels. If you have an errant mouse pointer, make sure its control panel is properly configured (if it has its own special control panel). You should also check the control panels for your joysticks, trackballs, control pads, or anything else you might have on your system.

Also, make sure you're not leaning on one of the buttons or using the controller incorrectly. Some people have trouble adjusting to a graphics pad or touchpad (such as those on newer Powerbooks) where tapping different parts of the pad may suddenly move the cursor. If you're accidentally touching a touchpad in two places, you may be contributing to the mouse pointer's erratic behavior.

Note

If your mouse or trackball is a Kensington model that uses the popular MouseWorks software, you may find its necessary to set some of its hidden options, including a few to keep your trackball from interfering with other ADB devices. To get to these hidden commands, hold down the Option key while accessing the Option ⇨ Compatibility Options command in the menu bar. The most likely reason to access these options is if your Kensington product is interfering with another ADB device by trying to use the same ADB ID number.

Trackballs

Trackballs can often be cleaned the exact same way as mice — at least, internally. You can swab the rollers with cotton swaps and rubbing alcohol. For the ball, you can use tap water and, if necessary, a mild detergent. Dry the ball completely with a lint-free towel. You might want to wait a while before plugging everything back in to allow the parts to air dry further.

Note

Kensington (www.kensington.com/), popular manufacturer of ADB peripherals, has an entire line of cleaning supplies — cleaning wipes, lint-free cloths — for mice and trackballs. They may be overkill, but perhaps they're a decent idea for an office environment or as small gifts to computing enthusiasts.

If you have trouble getting a ball out of trackball housing, turn it over (with your hand under it to catch the ball). If it doesn't fall out, look for a release button on the bottom of the housing.

Graphics tablets

Graphics tablets are slightly odd creatures, if only for the amount of data they can generate for a basic input device. That can make them problematic as ADB devices, because they need to be "good citizens," especially if you're using the tablet along with a mouse, keyboard, and any other ADB devices. Usually, graphics tablets scale back their capabilities a little bit so that they only work as quickly as the Mac can handle, but this can sometimes result in stalls or short changeovers when you move between a graphics tablet and a mouse. If you experience a short wait, don't immediately assume your Mac has crashed or frozen. Instead, wait a moment to see if the mouse or keyboard was just trying to catch up with the tablet.

If staggered input or short lock-ups happen repeatedly, troubleshoot by removing the tablet and testing to see if the problem recurs. If it doesn't, you might try using the graphics tablet as your only mouse-like input device, and get a couple of the other ones off the ADB bus.

Because the graphics tablet does have to coexist on these buses, it's important to keep its driver up-to-date. Check the manufacturer's Web site for updated drivers, especially if you're having trouble after a Mac OS upgrade.

Because most graphics tablets require a control panel and/or extension, you can expect trouble with these if you're having trouble getting the tablet to work or if your Mac freezes or crashes when using the tablet. Wacom lists some known issues on its Web site (www.wacom.com), including problems with some files included with Apple Remote Access (for ADB tablets) and conflicts with Global Village software and other fax programs (for serial tablets). A number of problems can crop up if you're trying to share a serial port between a tablet and a modem, because the modem's software will sometimes keep the tablet from working correctly. In general, if a serial tablet is being shared on a modem port, the other device's drivers need to be completely disabled before you can switch to the tablet.

Some early graphics tablets may not work correctly when plugged into GeoPort-style serial ports on Power Macintosh machines (CalComp makes a point of this on their site — www.calcomp.com). If you have trouble with a graphics tablet not enabling you to cover the entire screen, the problem may be with the preferences file for the tablet becoming corrupt (assuming you haven't very recently changed the resolution of your Mac's screen — if that's the case, restart your Mac). If you suspect the preferences file, remove it from the Preferences folder and restart your Mac to see if the tablet begins to behave.

Keyboards

If your keyboard has received a bad spill, you probably shouldn't spend forever trying to clean it. It can be very difficult to get a Mac's keyboard back in working order, especially because there are certainly some powered electronics inside a typical Mac keyboard. That said, keyboards tend to cost between $30 and $150 dollars, so it might be worth a little effort before you throw in the towel (so to speak) and buy a new keyboard.

To clean a keyboard spill:

1. Shut down the Mac and unplug the keyboard.

2. Dry the outside of the keyboard with a dry towel or sponge. If you spilled a sticky liquid, use a damp rag to clean as much of the exterior as you can.

3. Turn your keyboard upside down and shake it to remove any excess liquid. You can also use compressed air to blow liquid out from between the keys.

4. If you need to, unscrew the small screws from the back of the keyboard and remove the back plastic. You might be able to coerce more liquid out of the keyboard and clean some parts, but avoid touching the circuit board. Even a slight static discharge can kill the keyboard.

5. If you have a hair dryer, you might use it to dry the keyboard, especially if you spilled water or another non-sticky drink.

6. Let the keyboard dry for at least a day. Then plug it in, turn on your Mac, and test it.

If keys are sticking you may need to take the keyboard apart to clean it effectively. (Try compressed air first, but don't get too close to components with compressed air, which tends to be cold and can cause condensation. Not that that's the worst of your problems right now.) You can remove the keys from most keyboards, but only with a keycap removal tool from a specialty computer store. (I've also heard of people building their own keycap removal tools, as in the sidebar, but do so at your own risk.) Remove only the keys you need to clean under and don't try for the spacebar. Also, don't forget the order of the keys on the keyboard. Seriously. This one happens all the time. Heck, I sure couldn't close my eyes and tell you the order of every single one of the keys on a QWERTY layout.

A keyboard can survive a regular (annual or so) cleaning if you have the desire to do it. Shut down the Mac and unplug the keyboard, and then gently wipe the keys with a nearly dry rag (a little rubbing alcohol may help). Use compressed air or — better yet a small computing vaccum cleaner — to clean between the keys.

Mac Evangelista tip: Keyboard CPR

If your keyboard is on its last legs and your only other option is buying a new one, maybe you can kill an hour or so trying to fix it. First, think how proud you'll be of yourself if it works. And, even more importantly, think how proud you'll be of yourself if you actually get all the keys put back in the right order!

Rich Barron, Macknowledgist to the Stars, is back with more time-grabbing tips on getting the most out of a keyboard that's already on its last legs. If you've got sticky keys on an aging keyboard, you need to clean and lubricate the keys somehow. Here's how:

"I'm sure that someone sells a gadget for pulling the caps (that's what the letters are called) off of a keyboard switch, but my personal favorite is just to use two paper clips. Shut down your Mac and unplug the keyboard and move it to a good place to work. Take the rounded end of the paper clip and push it down between the bad cap and one of its neighbors. then slide it so that the rounded portion of the paper clip is under a corner of the bad cap. Now take the other paper clip and do the same for the opposite corner of the same bad cap. Take one paper clip in each hand (hold the keyboard down with your third hand) and lift straight up! Don't rotate your hands or go at an angle or you may snap the little stem that connects the keycap to the keyswitch underneath.

"You might want to wipe some of that grime out of there now that you have access to it before you lubricate the key switch. Compressed air works, as does a dry cloth or paper towel. Try not to touch any metal contacts or leads when the keyboard is open — there is a computer chip under the spacebar that could get zapped from a little bit of static electricity, so be careful.

"Take a spray lubricant (like WD-40) with an extension tube and spray a tiny amount of lubricant into the area where the little plunger goes down into the keyswitch. Wipe up any excess spray and then work the keyswitch up and down with your finger until you feel it loosen up a little or stop sticking down. It should happen fairly soon (20 to 40 presses), otherwise give it another slight spray with the lubricant.

"When you are done and satisfied with your work, just press the key caps straight down onto the keyswitch until it clicks into place. Make sure you get them in the right order, or you'll have to pull them off again."

Scanner Troubleshooting

A lot of scanner trouble is really SCSI trouble; getting some scanners up and running on the SCSI bus can be the biggest pain you ever have with the scanner. And what's most difficult about scanner SCSI problems is that they don't always act the way you'd expect a SCSI problem to act, because scanners (unlike hard drives and removable media) don't get mounted on the desktop. Generally, you have to go looking a little harder.

The other major problem you'll encounter is the scanner software. Scanner software is not all made the same, and some of it can be cobbled together hurriedly so that the scanner gets out the door quickly. This is especially true of some scanners that might, in the interest of economy, be offered for both Windows and Macintosh users. In this case the driver software can sometimes suffer. Bad driver software can lead to crashes, freezes, or other bizarre behavior (like missing scanners) that can frustrate you to no end.

First, though, you'll probably find it's a good idea to clean and care for your scanner on a fairly regular basis to ensure the most crisp, clean scans you can get. And there are a couple things you should consider if you're packing and unpacking the scanner — *before* you first take the scanner out of the box.

Installing and cleaning

You should follow the instructions very carefully when it comes to unpacking and installing a scanner. In some cases, it's possible to ruin a scanner if you simply rip it out of the box, set it up, and turn it on.

A shipped scanner is often *locked* in some way such that the scanner head can't move around during the shipping process. It could be locked using a setting, a lever, a pin, or a few other items. If your scanner is likely to suffer from the following, warnings will probably be plastered all over the scanner, so take notice of them. The point is, because the locking mechanism is designed to keep the scanner head from moving, it's a very bad idea to leave it installed when you start up the scanner and try to use it. That moves the scan head mechanically, which could cause damage depending on the scanner and the method used to lock the scan head.

You may also find that you need to clean the glass scanning bed occasionally to get the best scanning results. This is especially true if you're beginning to see small smudges or dots appear in your scans that can't readily be explained otherwise.

To clean the scanner's glass, use a damp, soft cloth and wipe the surface of the bed. Don't use spray cleaning solutions (or plain water) directly on the glass, because the force of the spray can cause the liquid to enter the scanner through gaps at the edges of the glass. If you prefer, prepackaged wipes and towels recommended for cleaning scanners can be found in most computer stores.

You may also find that dust accumulates inside the scanner on the underside of the glass. You can remove the glass to clean it, but try to do so only according to the manufacturer's instructions. Cleaning the inside may void your warranty. Plus, cracking or breaking the scanner's glass can result in expensive repairs that require you to ship the scanner back to the manufacturer.

Configuration

Scanners and SCSI configuration can be a little tricky, and often more of a pain than setting up SCSI storage devices, for two reasons: First, you're reliant on tools such as the freeware program SCSIProbe to tell you a scanner is detected and connected; scanners don't mount on the Mac's desktop, so there's one less indicator that everything is humming along. Second, you're reliant on the software that comes with your scanner. Although it may be possible that you can use other driver software and software for scanning, if the scanner is giving you trouble, the software won't always make things simple to troubleshoot.

SCSI issues

Scanner troubleshooting starts out, though, with observation and testing steps that are like any other SCSI issues. Your first goal in troubleshooting any scanner issue is getting the scanner to appear in SCSIProbe or a similar SCSI management program. If you don't see it there, you're not going to be able to get your scanning software to recognize it. So, start with checking recognition — fire up a SCSI probe program and see if the scanner is there (see Figure 24-2).

Figure 24-2: SCSIProbe recognizes my scanner, along with other SCSI devices.

If you can't seem to get your Mac to recognize the scanner, it could be due to a number of problems:

✦ **Power and cabling.** Make sure the scanner is plugged in and turned on, and all its cables are securely connected within the SCSI chain. Take special notice of the SCSI cabling: Some scanners may use a pass-through SCSI terminator that seems counterintuitive, for instance. Other scanners (such as the Apple OneScanner 600/27) don't require external termination. If your scanner didn't come with a terminator, or if you suspect a termination issue, consult your scanner's manual for details. You may have a scanner that needs to be turned on (and completely warmed up) before you start up your Mac. Otherwise, the scanner may not be properly set up on the SCSI bus, necessitating a restart of the Mac before it can be used.

✦ **SCSI ID.** Make sure the SCSI ID number is unique on your SCSI chain and that it was assigned correctly to the scanner at startup. You should be able the check that this is a SCSI management program; most of the time scanners are easily recognized by SCSIProbe. Don't forget that some scanners are particularly susceptible to problems on Macs with two SCSI buses. Choose an ID that is free on *both* SCSI buses if you're having a problem.

✦ **SCSI issues.** Test carefully to make sure there aren't any other SCSI annoyances on your SCSI bus, even if SCSIProbe does recognize the scanner. Specifically, look for termination issues, other SCSI devices that aren't appearing, or any potential SCSI ID conflicts.

✦ **Software.** Check your scanner's manual to make sure you're installing all the required software. In some cases this may include a System extension or control panel. For other scanners, there may be nothing more than a Photoshop plug-in and a physical SCSI setting that's required.

If you can't identify your problem as fitting one of these basic categories, or if the problem feels like SCSI voodoo, you should try some of the more basic SCSI troubleshooting methods, including restarting your Mac, reinstalling the scanner's software, trying a different SCSI cable, and zapping PRAM.

If all else fails, remove all devices from the SCSI chain and test them individually, starting with the scanner. If you identify a conflict (or if every other device but the scanner appears on the SCSI bus and can be configured), then you can approach the vendor's customer support personnel or a local computer shop with a general idea of the problem.

Note   Specific problems have been reported with some scanners and Macs that include internal IDE drives, most of which have been addressed by Mac OS updates. If you feel this may be part of your problem (for instance, your Mac freezes when a scanner is attached and you happen to know your Mac has an IDE drive), check Apple's Tech Info Library for specifics on the related issues and upgrades available.

Scanner software

Once you're able to move suspicion beyond the SCSI chain, you'll want to take a troubleshooting look at the software that runs your scanner. You may find that you have a number of different components to that software, including extensions, control panels, and scanning applications. But scanners vary wildly, and your scanner could come bundled with very few pieces of software — perhaps a PhotoShop plug-in and a light-edition copy of PhotoShop or a similar program.

In any case, there are a couple of caveats related directly to scanners and their driver software that you might look into:

✦ *Scanner drivers can be old.* Check the manufacturer's Web site or customer-service line to make sure there aren't any bug fixes, updates, or new software releases you should be aware of. This is especially true if you're using a newer version of the Mac OS and/or a Macintosh model that hadn't been released when the scanner first came into service.

✦ *Scanners may require system extensions.* Check your manual to see if the proper system extensions are installed in your System folder. If not, you may need to reinstall the software.

✦ *System extensions may be in conflict.* If everything seems to be correctly installed, you may be having an extension-level conflict. In this case, the scanner extension may have a conflict with some other extension in your System folder. For more on troubleshooting an extension conflict, consult Chapter 32.

✦ *Scanner, Photoshop preferences could be corrupted.* Some scanner manufacturers suggest that problems that occur *after* an initial scan (even after many scans) may be the result of corrupted files in the System Folder. If you find odd-sounding files in the System Folder that have "Preview" in the name, you might want to drag those to the Trash. Likewise, you can delete the preferences files (in the Preferences folder) for Photoshop or the scanner's own software if you have reason to believe the problem is in the software's setup, not in the SCSI chain or a hardware problem (for instance, if the program or Mac consistently and repeatedly crashes or freezes in the middle of a scan).

One general word of caution: If you're using PhotoDeluxe or Photoshop and a plug-in for your scanning, realize that the plug-ins are only registered as the application starts up; you can't move the plug-in to the Plug-in folder (in the application's folder) and then immediately use the scanner — you'll need to restart the application. In some cases, you may need to restart the Mac immediately after installing the plug-in or installing other software.

Serial scanners

If you have a scanner that communicates serially with your Mac (usually these are page scanners such as those made by Visioneer or older hand scanners), your problems will usually be somewhat more limited in nature. Like modems, serial scanners usually only have a few things go wrong — extensions, cabling, and power. If it isn't one of these three, there's a good chance the problem is hardware related. Before you leap to conclusions, check the following:

✦ *Is the scanner plugged in and turned on?* As usual, check power before doing anything else.

✦ *Is the scanner's serial cable plugged into the Mac and the device? If it's switched, is the switch set correctly?* If you have a modem, a serial scanner, and a printer, you may also have a switch box or a port extender. Both are popular add-ons, but you'll need to make sure they're correctly set if you expect the scanner to work.

✦ *Is the scanner's software active?* PaperPort and similar scanners have a control panel that needs to be turned on so that the scanner automatically senses an inserted page when you feed it to be scanned.

✦ *Are you using the right cable?* Serial scanners can occasionally require a special cable that can't be swapped for any typical Mac serial cable. If the scanner seems completely deaf to your Mac, make sure you're using the cable that came with the scanner.

Summary

✦ If you've got a problem with the input devices connected to your Macintosh, you might need to look into the possibility that ADB voodoo is affecting your machine. Although not as prevalent as SCSI, there are some problems that you should be aware of related to the length and the number of devices on an ADB chain .

✦ Once you've eliminated ADB as a suspect, you can troubleshoot the individual devices. Although a broken mouse or keyboard will usually stay broken (requiring that you buy and install a new one), there are methods for saving and salvaging input devices that simply need a good cleaning.

✦ Problems with scanners can often be traced to the SCSI bus or similar SCSI issues. In fact, scanners can be difficult to troubleshoot because they are SCSI devices that don't get mounted on the desktop, like hard drives and removable drives do.

✦   ✦   ✦

Monitors, Video, and Sound

Trouble with your monitor ranks up there as one of the most frustrating problems you might need to deal with on a Mac—especially if you're only having minor trouble. Because the monitor is a window into your machine, it's certainly ideal for that view to be as crisp and clean as possible. This is doubly so for professionals who spend hours in front of their Macs everyday, and triply so for graphics and multimedia creators who need every conceivable advantage to put together their creations.

But along with keeping your monitor in great shape comes troubleshooting video problems, getting all your video card's features to work, and making sure you're getting the most of your video settings. On top of that, if your Mac offers advanced AV capabilities, you'll want to work out any glitches in that system before you take on Hollywood.

Finally, all Macs have audio capabilities, but they've been known to cause some trouble, too. The last part of this chapter will look at how to troubleshoot microphones, CD sound, and even the occasional problem with a recorded audio sample.

Troubleshooting Monitors and Video

Most of the time your monitor will just work for you; when it doesn't, you'll probably begin by troubleshooting issues elsewhere, such as problems with the Mac's logic board or power supply. If those efforts prove fruitless, however, and you find there's a good chance it's the video subsystem (the monitor, cabling, video circuitry, and VRAM) that's causing you trouble, you'll need to move your troubleshooting efforts in this direction.

As usual, the point is to isolate the problem. With the video subsystem the problem can be in several different areas — power, cabling, the monitor's internals or the video circuitry. You can also have trouble with the software that drives the monitor, specifically the settings in the Monitors & Sound control panel. If you have a non-Apple video adapter, you may also have a control panel and/or extensions that need to load properly for your monitor to work.

Caution

I won't be discussing anything that requires you to open a monitor and troubleshoot the innards of a CRT. Only trained, qualified monitor technicians should work on monitors, because monitors are able to hold a very strong electrical charge (on the order of 30,000 volts) even when they've been unplugged for days. *Do not open your monitor to service it.*

When you get no picture

To begin, take a look at the troubleshooting steps for a Mac that isn't displaying anything on the screen. If you're troubleshooting at this point, I'll assume you've looked at the power supply and related troubleshooting discussion in Chapter 22. Realize that the monitor can often be affected by problems other than those with the video subsystem. For instance, a monitor may appear to be blank — and not responding to keyboard input or other things you do with the Mac — because the Mac has crashed while it was in a low-energy Sleep mode (see Figure 25-1).

This problem occurs more commonly with newer Macs that support the Energy Star system, which enables the Macintosh to automatically blank the screen after a certain amount of time. If the Mac crashes (due to some other software problem, often unrelated) while the screen is blanked, it may seem as if there's something wrong with the monitor. Instead, you simply need to restart the Mac.

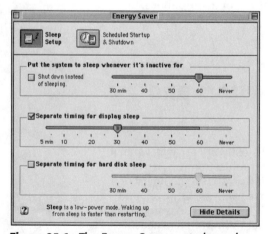

Figure 25-1: The Energy Saver control panel enables your Mac to automatically turn off an Energy Star-compliant monitor.

If you've isolated the video subsystem as the problem, you should begin to isolate the problem by looking into the following issues:

✦ *Power.* Check the monitor's power cable to make sure it's plugged into both the monitor and the wall socket or your surge protector (or, with certain Apple models, make sure the monitor is plugged into the socket on the back of your Mac). Check that the monitor is turned on; when you hit the power switch you'll probably hear a quick click, pop, or electronic hum that suggests the monitor is receiving power. Check any LED indicators on the front of the monitor to make sure the monitor is on and receiving power.

✦ *Cables.* Check the video cable between the monitor and the Mac — if this cable is stretched, pinched, or pulled out from either end, you'll be unlikely to see images on the screen. The same problem is true if the pins for the video connector are bent or the video connect is only partly installed in the Mac's video port.

✦ *Settings.* Check the brightness setting on the monitor and make sure it's dialed up far enough. Play with the contrast, too, to make sure you're able to see anything that might be there on the screen. If your monitor has a reset button, you might use it, as well, just in case the factory resets are necessary for solving some settings problems.

✦ *Reset the Mac.* If you continue to have trouble with the monitor but you hear the Mac starting up (maybe you hear the drive whirring and the startup chime), try restarting the Mac to see if you get a picture the second time around, especially if there was something wrong with the cabling for the Mac.

✦ *Zap PRAM.* Monitor resolution settings are stored in PRAM. If you accidentally set the monitor resolution to something that the monitor can't handle and then restart the machine, you might be stuck with a monitor that won't come up or a monitor that gives a bizarre flickering picture. If you restart the Mac and hold down ⌘-Option-P-R until you hear two more restart sounds, you'll reset the Mac to its lowest monitor resolution setting.

If none of these steps seem to solve the problem, you should test to see if the monitor is broken. If you suspect it isn't able to turn on and get power, you should test it in two ways: First, try different power cables to connect the monitor to the wall socket or surge protector. If none of the cables work, try picking the monitor up and moving it across the room (or into another room) where you have a different electrical outlet. Test the monitor with multiple cables on that new outlet. If you still don't get power (the monitor's LED doesn't glow), you'll need to take the monitor into a service shop for repairs.

If your monitor does seem to turn on, you've got a problem with the cabling or video circuitry. The best way to test this is to try the monitor and its cable by connecting it to another Mac's video connector to see if a picture shows up on the screen. (Shut down the second Mac, install the monitor in question, and restart the Mac to see if it is accepting a video signal.) If you don't get a signal, you might suspect the monitor's cable.

If you do get a signal on the monitor when it's plugged in elsewhere, your problem is either with your Mac's video port, video card, video circuitry, or VRAM. These are difficult to test on their own, especially if you're using a Mac's built-in circuitry instead of a video card. If you've recently installed any video-related upgrades, check to make sure you've seated them correctly and used the correct upgrade parts for your particular Mac model.

Otherwise, take the system to an authorized service dealer.

Note   According to Apple, a 6100, 600, or 400 series Macintosh will offer no video if the PRAM battery is dead, so you should replace the battery if everything seems to be working except the video.

When the picture is wavy or splotchy

Monitors are magnetic devices, with the electron guns in a typical CRT creating a powerful magnetic field. This magnetic field can build over time, creating problems that result in splotches of color, unfocused spots on the screen, and wavy areas on the screen.

These same phenomena, especially occurring at the very edges of the screen, can sometimes be attributed to magnetic devices that have been placed near the monitor — in particular, unshielded speakers. Because speakers use electro-magnets to create sound, they can also create a magnetic field that can distort a monitor. Most computer speakers are purposefully *shielded* to keep this from happening, but home-audio speakers often aren't. Similarly, the cheaper the computer speakers, the less likely they are to provide impressive magnetic shielding.

So, the first step to combat splotches or a wavy picture is to move speakers, stereo equipment and other electronics away from the computer screen. If you have more than one monitor on your desk, they can affect one another in this way as well. Although the Mac OS encourages many of us to use more than one monitor because it has this capability built in, the monitors are both magnetic devices. If they're poorly shielded, they can create disturbances on each other's screens. The best plan in this case is to try moving the monitors so their front edges are touching (that way the multiple monitor approach is still workable) but the backs of the monitors angle away from one other. If this doesn't work, you may need to move the monitors physically further away from one another and live with a gap between the two. (You can also place a large, heavy-duty, nonferrous cookie sheet between the two monitors to see if that cuts down on interference.)

You can encounter other external magnetic problems, too, caused by the proximity of electrical closets, stereo equipment, or other devices to your desk and computer. In fact, you can even encounter a magnetic problem related to your monitor's position relative to the Earth's magnetic poles. Believe it or not, monitors are calibrated so they sometimes work best when they're facing a particular compass direction, such as east-west or north-south. If you have distortion problems that can't be explained by electronic devices, see if you get better results by turning the monitor 90 degrees in one direction or the other.

Once you've eliminated external magnetic sources, you can turn to the internals of the monitor. To remove a built-up magnetic charge, a process of *degaussing* the monitor is required. In older monitors, this usually requires a trip to a service center — a strong oscillating magnet is passed near the monitor to cancel out built-up magnetic fields.

Newer monitors tend to include a built-in degauss feature. In fact, many higher-end monitors degauss as they're turned on. To test this feature in your monitor, turn its power switch off and on quickly. (This is best tested with the Mac on and displaying the Mac OS desktop.) As the screen comes back on, if the picture shudders or waves for a few seconds, then it's being degaussed. If this doesn't happen, look for a degauss button located near the rest of the monitor controls.

If your monitor has neither of these features, you may need to take it in to a service center to have it manually degaussed. Check your manual for degaussing advice and read on for troubleshooting tips to similar problems.

Other display movement

If your problem is a display that bounces and waves when you change the color settings in your Monitors & Sound control panel, you probably have a Mac RGB monitor and a Power Macintosh computer. According to Apple, nothing is damaged — it's a purely cosmetic problem.

Does your monitor strobe or seem to pulsate? This can be a result of a combination of factors, one of which is fluorescent lighting. The overhead lighting in many corporate offices will not always agree with some monitors, especially those that are incapable of higher refresh rates. If you can, try adjusting your monitor to a setting that includes a higher refresh rate.

If you can't change the refresh rate, try using the monitor in different lighting and see if that changes things; you can even shine light from a standard light bulb or a halogen bulb on your workspace (but not directly in front of or behind the screen) to try to counteract the fluorescent lighting. For some monitors you can get hoods that go over the top of the monitor and keep light from shining directly on the screen.

You may, ultimately, need to get your hands on a new monitor for this particular Mac, unless you can move or change the lighting.

When the picture is blurry

With color monitors, there are three very small dots (red, green and blue) that make up a single pixel, or picture element. The dot pitch between these dots can cause a picture to be sharper — the smaller the distance between the dots, the more distinct the resulting screen image.

However, over time or in reaction to other circumstances, another factor, called *convergence*, can affect the focus and quality of the screen image. As the CRT's electron beam sweeps back and forth across the dots to illuminate them, the convergence settings determine the exact aim of the beam. When it misses its mark, even slightly, the result is generally a slight blooming or rainbow effect, along with a perceived focus problem.

If your monitor enables you to resize your screen to the edges, you may find that your monitor has a convergence problem that you really can't do much about. The farther away from the center the beam hits, the more likely it is to create a blurry picture. That's why the factory settings on monitors often don't take the image to the edge of the screen.

Some monitors have external convergence controls for setting the convergence focus on your screen. These are especially useful if you notice a rainbow effect somewhere on the screen other than at the very edges of the display. (If the distortion is at the edges, you should probably resize the screen image so that it takes up slightly less of the display.) You'll need to consult your manual and adjust the convergence by trial and error.

Other monitors have controls more generally called *focus;* in many cases, this is a small screw that turns in one direction or the other to affect picture quality. Using a long, thin screwdriver, you'll turn this screw to change the focus. Location of the screw varies by monitor, but it's often located on one side or the other of the monitor in a recessed hole.

If you can't find an external focus control, it's likely that the focus and/or convergence controls are internal, in which case you'll likely need to take it in to a qualified service center for adjustment.

Note   Murphy's Law pretty much dictates that working with focus or convergence controls yourself will result in a picture that's worse than when you started. (At least, that's always the case for me.) If you like, play with the focus yourself. But a poorly focused monitor is a great excuse to take the monitor in to an authorized service center for a complete diagnostic session.

When the colors are bad

The colors may be off on your monitor for a number of reasons. The first issue is whether the problem is with the way the colors look on screen or a distinct difference between the monitor's colors and printed, color output. In the latter case, the problem most likely lies with the printer's settings or the Mac's ColorSync settings. (Consult Chapter 26 for more on those issues.)

If the problem is with the colors you're seeing on screen, available to you are some quick fixes and some more mechanical fixes. At issue is the fact that the typical computer screen is actually governed by two different sets of controls — a bad idea for something as elusive as color. Yet, it's important for the Mac's internals to believe they're displaying a certain quality of color, even if the monitor is incapable of producing those colors.

Note

Multiscan monitors can use the Monitors or Monitors & Sound control panel, or the control strip to switch quickly between different color depths. Some older or highly graphical programs may not adjust well to the color shift, however. If you have a problem application, try shutting it down and restarting the program after you've set the new color depth. If the application still misbehaves, it may be exhibiting a bug; look for an update to the program. You can also try restart the Mac, just in case that cures some ills.

Gamma correction

Internally, the Mac has software settings that dictate the colors. In the Monitors & Sound control panel (or the Monitors control panel with most pre-Mac OS 7.6 machines), you'll find *gamma* settings. These settings determine what your Mac uses as a reference for the brightness of colors. The purpose of these gamma settings is to smooth out a curve of brightness that, due to a limitation in monitor technology, results from the way monitors interpret the video-input signal as brightness.

When the monitor receives a signal from the video input, it doesn't translate that signal's value — say, 0.7 — directly into a corresponding brightness. Instead, it increases that value to the power of 2.5. (That's just how monitors work.) Because the values are all numbers between 0 and 1, raising them to a certain power results in them being slightly smaller than before ($0.7^{2.5} = .41$), but at varying levels, so that the values ultimately define a curve (see Figure 25-2).

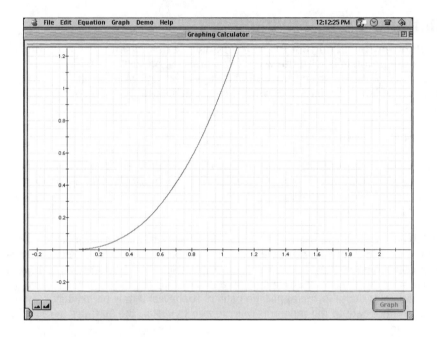

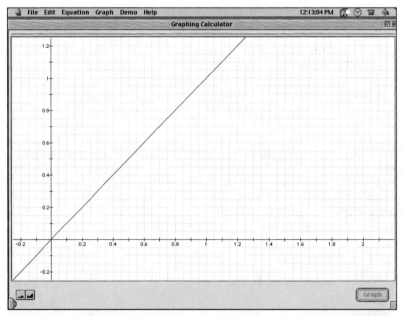

Figure 25-2A, 2B: On the top: uncorrected brightness values; on the bottom: theoretical linear brightness values.

But all this is only mildly interesting. What we find is that, by gamma correcting the values before they're received by the monitor, those values can then be translated in such a way as to mitigate this problem, resulting in brightness levels that are truer once they appear on the monitor. So, built into the Monitors & Sound control panel are two or three gamma settings: Mac Standard, Page White, and Uncorrected. Page White isn't terribly useful, having originally been designed for Macintosh RGB Color Display (it changes the temperature of certain colors as well as gamma correcting). If your monitor is set to Page White, you'll likely get odd results from your images.

Using an Uncorrected gamma means you stick with the original overall gamma of 2.5 for the Mac, which produces a fairly dark picture. This is useful, however. Many Intel-compatible PCs work with an uncorrected gamma, so you may find that switching between Mac Standard Gamma and Uncorrected helps you create Web images that will work on both platforms.

The Macintosh Standard Gamma does the best job of correcting for the inherent flaw in monitor brightness relationships, but it's still not a complete solution. Once corrected, your Mac system has a gamma of 1.8 (ideal gamma would be 1.0) instead of 2.5. This makes for a much truer image on your monitor screen, although images still display a little less brightly than they should (see Figure 25-3).

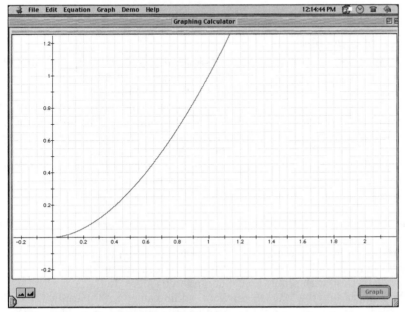

Figure 25-3: These brightness values are more accurate, showing less of a curve.

To compensate for this, applications that deal heavily in imaging will generally further the gamma correction on the order of 1.8, so as to bring the total gamma of the system to 1.0. You can see this phenomenon (most likely) in the standard settings for Monitor Setup in a program such as Adobe Photoshop.

Blurred, faded colors

If you have a particular color that's giving you trouble, especially white, something may be wrong with the way you've set up your monitor. The Earth's magnetic field can affect the way colors are displayed and the clarity of images. Monitors are generally calibrated to be facing a certain compass direction (either east-west or north-south) and placing the monitor at an odd angle can sometimes result in poorer picture quality. (This is more likely on larger monitors, incidentally.)

If you suspect this might be the case, turn the monitor 45 degrees or more and take another look at the monitor's image. If the picture improves, you can simply leave the display facing its current direction, or you can adjust the convergence settings (if your monitor has external convergence controls) with the monitor back in its original orientation.

You can also sometimes solve these problems with frequent degaussing and gamma correction. Symptoms are similar to magnetic field problems, so make sure you're not confusing this with a problem related to unshielded speakers or electronics located nearby.

Too much of one color

Because the monitor connection requires separate signals for red, green and blue, you'll sometimes see a picture that's predominantly one of those colors. Usually that means the monitor isn't properly attached to the video port on the back of your Mac. This is often true if the port itself is a bit unsteady; either the port is part of an expansion card that isn't firmly seated or the port itself has become dislodged from the Mac's case. (These ports are usually held in place using the same screw posts that you screw the monitor's connector into. Try tightening the posts with a vise or pliers before connecting your monitor's cable, just to make sure the port is secure.) Trouble with one color can also be a sign of a bad cable or monitor connection.

If the color is green, you may be having trouble with an older Mac that sends "sync-on-green" signals — the information the monitor needs to sync with the Mac is sent along with the green color data. Most VGA monitors aren't designed for sync-on-green without an adapter, and some of these monitors just aren't as compatible as others when dealing with older (Mac II and related) Macs. In that case, the solutions is upgrading the Mac OS software, adding an adapter (Griffin Technology [www.griffintechnology.com/] is one place to start) and/or adding the Color Monitor System extension. (Consult Apple's Support site at www.apple.com/support on the Web.)

Adjusting brightness and contrast

One of the easiest ways to get the color right on your monitor (at least, as right as the color is going to get on your monitor) is to adjust the brightness and contrast correctly. I've never been able to figure this one out on my TV at home. (Actually, all my troubles stem from the universal remote control.) Fortunately, with monitors, you can follow a quick little step-by-step to get the best results. (In Mac OS 8.5 and above you can use the special calibration tool in the Monitors and Sounds control panel for this adjustment.)

Here's how to adjust your screen for the best color:

1. Place an image on the screen that you can use as a reference. Some adjusters prefer to use a grayscale image (one with various levels of gray, black, and white), whereas others prefer a color image. If you use a color image, it should be one composed of colors that you know well.

2. Turn the brightness and contrast of your monitor all the way down.

3. Turn the contrast up until you see the complete image displaying strong blacks and/or rich colors.

4. Turn the brightness up until any white in the image is a comfortable but pure white. Check it against a piece of bright white paper, if possible (hold the paper up to the screen).

5. Adjust to taste, but back off of the brightness if you feel the whiteness of the screen makes you uncomfortable. Also note that increasing contrast will sometimes offer richer colors.

If you find that you're at the 100 percent mark on either of your dials, back off a bit. If you keep a monitor at its brightest settings, it will wear out more quickly over time. If you notice an older monitor losing some of its brightness, try bumping up the contrast before bumping up the brightness. Be a little stingy with brightness to keep your monitor around longer.

Glare and positioning

Different monitors will reflect light differently back at the user — and, generally speaking, the older and less expensive the monitor, the more it will reflect light in an unsatisfactory way. The result is glare that makes the images on screen more difficult to look at for long periods of time.

Some monitors simply offer a bad glare problem regardless of how you position the screen. In those cases you should consult the manufacturer to see if a glare filter is available for the monitor, or you can shop for a third-party glare filter that fits over the monitor and mutes harsh glare from the monitor's glass.

If you think the problem might be in positioning, though, you can take these steps:

✦ *Tilt the screen downward.* The proper way to do this is to make sure your eyes are aligned with the top of the screen when you're sitting comfortably in front of the monitor. (The monitor is positioned incorrectly if you have to physically look up or down at the monitor.) While you're looking straight at the screen, reach out and tilt it very slightly downward. This may reduce glare from overhead lighting. (If this forces you to look downward at the screen, you should raise the entire monitor a few inches.)

✦ *Choose window location carefully.* You should never place a monitor so that a window is directly behind it. Even though such placement might allow you to look out the window while working, the competing light sources — the window and your monitor — will force your eyes to adjust constantly between brightness levels. And if you place a window in front of the monitor (that is, the window is behind you when you compute), you're inviting harsh glare. Instead, place the monitor at a 90 degree angle to the window.

To promote comfortable viewing, the monitor should always be directly in front of you (not to one side, even though some computer desks are designed like that) and at eye level. If you have to lower or raise your neck to look at the monitor, you should move it. If you're like me, you give your monitor plenty of attentive hours during the day already. No point in allowing it to give you back and neck problems so you have to think about it at night, too.

When the screen doesn't synchronize

Ideally, your Mac and your multisync monitor will always get along. The Mac can generally recognize what resolutions your monitor can synchronize with and will only offer you those choices in the Monitors & Sound control panel. However, trouble can kick in for a variety of reasons; for instance, when you switch or unhook your monitor while the Mac is still turned on, when you switch settings on a universal VGA adapter, or when, for some reason, your Mac allows you to choose a resolution that your monitor can't handle.

If your Mac's monitor looks like a de-tuned television set, with the screen flickering at odd angles and appearing to roll over constantly, you've got a sync problem. (This is also sometimes characterized as a screen full of garbage or snow. You can usually make out a few desktop-like images, but they flicker by too quickly.) For some reason, the Mac has set the video's resolution at a setting that the monitor can't or won't accept. In this case, there are a few things to consider:

✦ *Is everything plugged in?* Monitors and video cards will sometimes act odd if the monitor isn't completely plugged into the video connection on the back of your Macintosh.

✦ *Is it really a multisync monitor?* Even if the Monitors & Sound control panel is confused enough to allow you to change the resolution, the monitor attached to your Mac may not necessarily be capable of higher resolutions. Try syncing to a lower resolution.

✦ *Was the monitor present at startup?* The Mac tries to set the monitor to the last known resolution choice (stored in PRAM) and sense the monitor's reaction as the Mac starts up. If you attach a monitor to the Mac after it's started up, you may have trouble getting the two to sync. Restart the Mac with the monitor attached.

✦ *Is your adapter set correctly?* Most sync problems come from setting an RGB-to-VGA adapter incorrectly. The Macintosh is sensing the adapter, not the monitor itself, so the adapter must be set to the appropriate codes for your particular monitor. Try using adapter settings for a more basic monitor (640x480 at 60Hz, for instance) if you have trouble with other settings.

Whenever changing resolutions, it's important to check your monitor's documentation for information on the various resolutions it can accept. It can be damaging to drive some monitors at refresh rates that they can't handle, for instance, and you'll get less-than-stellar results when you change to a resolution the Mac can't support.

Usually, you can wait a few seconds after setting the resolution for your Mac. If you don't click the mouse to accept the new resolution, the old resolution setting will be retrieved and the monitor will sync back to its original setting. This is designed specifically to help users who accidentally set the video to a resolution that the monitor can't handle.

If you still have a sync problem, try forcing the Mac to restart (if you can't choose the Restart command, hit the Ctrl-⌘-Power keys or press the restart switch on your Mac). If your Mac has a main Power button or switch, cycle the power to the Mac. It should restart and sync correctly. If it doesn't, detach the monitor and restart once more. Next, reattach the monitor and restart once again.

If the monitor still doesn't sync, you can try restarting the Mac yet again, this time zapping PRAM. That removes the previous monitor setting, reverting to the factory default — usually the lowest resolution setting your Mac is designed to display. (Of course, it resets all those other PRAM settings, too, which is annoying.)

If the monitor doesn't sync to the basic default resolution, you either have an improperly installed adapter on the cable, the monitor is bad, or the Mac was never designed to work with that particular monitor in the first place.

Note

If you don't see the resolution you'd like to choose for your monitor in the Monitors & Sound or Monitors control panel, you may still be able to locate it. (Just be sure your monitor will actually support the resolution.) In the Monitors & Sound control panel, choose Show All from the pull-down menu above the resolution settings. In the Monitors control panel, hold down the option key while double-clicking the screen that represents the monitor you'd like to change.

Old Macs and multisync monitors

Much older Macintosh models don't often support multisync monitors. Some machines in the Mac II series, for instance, were designed specifically to work with the Apple 13" RGB display. Others in the Performa series were designed to work with the Apple Basic Color Display.

Many of these Macs, however, can be coaxed into running at 832x624 resolution, even if resolutions can't be changed on the fly. A special adapter is available that allows these monitors to sync up at that resolution on a multiscan monitor:

✦ PowerBook 180, 180c, 160, 165, 165c, 500 series, MiniDock

✦ Macintosh LC III, Performa 450, 460, 466, 467

✦ Macs that include the Display Card 4/8, 8/24 and 8/24GC

Earlier Macs only support 640x460 resolutions and require an adapter to show an image on a multisync monitor. They include the following:

✦ Macintosh LC, LC II

✦ Performa 400 series, 600/600CD

✦ Macintosh IIvx, IIvi

Most other Macs can sync with RGB-based multisync monitors without a special adapter (although they require an adapter to work with VGA-based multisync monitors). These multisync-ready Macs include the following:

✦ Quadra/Cetris series

✦ Performa 475/476, LC 475

✦ Performa/LC 630 series

✦ Power Macintosh (including PowerPC Performa models)

✦ Macintosh Display Card 8/24AC

✦ All Mac OS clone machines

Energy saving and burn in

Monitors aren't likely to *burn in* these days; older CRTs used to burn unchanging text into the phosphors of the screen over time, a phenomenon that can still be seen in some old ATM machines and CRTs used as dumb terminals in libraries or universities. Eventually, it became popular to use a screen saver to keep the screen active so the phosphors couldn't burn.

Because it doesn't happen anymore with modern, color monitors, screen savers are really more for show and play. The odd screen saver will also offer a modicum of security, requiring a password, for instance, to get back to the Mac's desktop. This isn't overwhelmingly secure since, in most cases, a determined snoop could get past a basic screen saver, but it provides casual protection.

The way to save the screen and a bit of energy, though, is to do one of two things. You can turn the monitor off when it's not in use. Monitors eat a ton of electricity compared to the rest of your computer. Although leaving your Mac on 24/7 probably won't dissipate the Earth's natural resources at a significant pace (the Mac's power supply draws the equivalent of a couple of light bulbs), leaving a monitor on all the time has a much more dramatic effect.

You can also use the Energy Saver control panel to force your monitor to shut down automatically, but only if the monitor is Energy Star compliant. Older monitors need to be shut down manually. In fact, with the wrong monitor, the Energy Star control panel can sometimes cause the Mac to freeze, requiring a hard restart. If that's the case, try upgrading to the latest Mac OS or turn off the control panel and shut the monitor off manually.

Note   Conventional wisdom suggests it's okay to turn your monitor on and off a number of times during the day — it's made to withstand quite a few switches over its lifetime. The debate rages on over the actual Mac itself; it's not a good idea to turn a computer on and off more than once or twice daily, because the logic board is much more fragile and susceptible to the whims of electricity. Plus, the monitor uses a lot of power compared to other computer components. The next most energy hungry component, the hard drive, can be spun down using the Energy Star control panel, too. Of course, printers (especially laser printers) can eat up a lot of energy. Check your current printer's documentation to see if it offers any energy-saving capabilities. If you have the opportunity to purchase a new printer, make sure it's the type that powers itself down when idle. Many newer Stylewriter and Laserwriter printers do this, as do others well integrated with the Mac.

Apple monitors

Recent Apple monitor models have become increasingly attached to their software drivers, as well as integrating with ADB and the sound capabilities of your Mac. If you have an AppleVision or ColorSync monitor, you should take some additional steps when troubleshooting the machine.

Here are some of the hot spots regarding these monitors and what you can do about them:

✦ These monitors need to be connected to the built-in video port on 68040- or PowerPC-based Macs.

✦ If you get a green power light, but a blank screen try starting up with extensions off (hold down the Shift key as the Mac starts up). If this works, head to the Preferences folder in the System Folder and throw away the display preferences file.

✦ If starting with extensions off doesn't work, start up and hold down ⌘-Option-A-V. Once the Mac is started up, trash the display preferences file.

✦ Some problems, including crashes at startup and blank screens, can be solved by reinstalling the AppleVision software. You should also try zapping PRAM as an interim step. As a last resort, you can reinstall Mac OS 8 or higher and/or the AppleVision software.

✦ If you have blurry video problems, try using the monitor without hooking into the ADB port to see if the problem is an ADB issue. You can also start up and hold down ⌘-Option-A-V to reset the monitor and see if the video gets any better. Odd, erratic, or bad ADB devices can often cause problems that are mistakenly attributed to the monitor.

✦ If you suspect the Mac itself isn't starting up properly, unplug the audio cable from the back of the Mac to see if the internal speaker is playing the startup (and/or any error) chimes.

Apple's Tech Info library offers extensive information on the AppleVision and ColorSync series of monitors, including setup and troubleshooting tips beyond these. If you have one of these monitors, recognize that it's a complex component in an intelligent system that includes your video, ADB, and sound capabilities. This makes troubleshooting a bit tougher, so you'll need to pay careful attention to isolate problems.

Mac Evangelista tips: VRAM and Mac video

Gerald Wilson knows his VRAM and Mac models. Check out these tips for optimizing video output using certain aging Mac machines:

"On a Mac IIsi, the built-in video is driven from the main memory, rather than from specialized video RAM. The IIsi memory is logically divided into two banks. Bank A is the fixed 1MB on the logic board. Bank B is the four extra SIMM slots which take 1MB, 2MB or 4MB SIMMs. The screen buffer is allocated from Bank A.

"When you use a IIsi, you find that it seems to run much faster in black-and-white than in full color. In full color, the screen access hardware uses around half the clock cycles available for the Bank A memory just to refresh the screen, whereas in black-and-white it uses a small fraction of them. If vital parts of the system are loaded into Bank A (and they are!), the Mac can now run at only half-speed.

(continued)

(continued)

"To avoid this effect use this trick. Assign larger-than-usual cache sizes to use up the rest of Bank A, and hence push all System code up into Bank B. Either set the Disk cache (in the Memory control panel) to a high value like 768K, or set Adobe Type Manager's buffer to a high value. This way you can accelerate your Mac almost to full black-and-white speed while still enjoying color. (The Mac IIci has an identical architecture for built-in video. However, IIcis are often fitted with level 2 cache, which alleviates this problem.)

"The built-in video for early Quadras (700 and 900) can't drive the 19" resolution of 1,024x768 pixels. However, if you fit the machines with Apple's PowerPC upgrade card in the PDS slot, the enhanced ROM for PowerPC knows about this extra resolution, and you will find that when run in PowerPC mode the machine can drive a multiscan display at 1,024x768. (Getting the upgrade card may be a bigger problem, though.)

"The efficiency of built-in video varies from model to model. On early Quadras (Q700, Q900, Q950), 24-bit color is much slower than 8-bit color. On later Quadras (Q610, Q650), which lack 24-bit color, 8-bit and 16-bit color have about the same speed. On PCI PowerMacs (7200, 7500) 16-bit and 24-bit color are significantly faster for 3D work and motion-video work than 8-bit color. These variations depend on the built-in-video architecture, and whether it is tuned more for color-mapped (8-bit and lower) or for RGB (16-bit and higher) displays. Experiment with your own machine to find out how it works best."

Cleaning monitors

Although it might seem as though glass cleaner and a good towel are all you need, you should be a tad careful around computer monitors when it comes to getting them clean. Note that the procedure is a little different if your monitor uses LCD technology instead of a CRT—whether it's a PowerBook or a stand-alone flat screen.

Here are some tips regarding monitor cleanliness:

✦ Power down the monitor before cleaning it.

✦ Don't use regular, chemical glass cleaner because, in some cases, it can remove an antiglare coating that's been put on the monitor. (Check your monitor's documentation for details.) Don't use any abrasives.

✦ An antistatic cleaner (you can get them especially designed for monitors) is fine for use, but don't spray it or any liquid directly on the screen, because that can allow liquid to leak into the case. Spray the liquid on your cloth, and then clean.

✦ You can rub the monitor screen with a used antistatic dryer sheet for good cleaning results.

✦ A sponge or soft cloth that's barely wet can be used to clean the outside of the monitor. Take special care not to drip in through air vents or other open parts of the case, although cleaning those parts of the case (with a vacuum or cloth) to remove dust is a good idea.

✦ If your monitor is an LCD screen instead of a CRT, be extra careful, because the LCD screen's front is made of plastic, which could more easily be scratched or marred. Use a very soft towel and very little liquid. Don't use cleaners — instead, use a little rubbing alcohol (perhaps mixed with water) to clean the screen. Don't spray directly on the screen, but spray small amounts of liquid on your cloth.

Troubleshooting Digital Video and Audio

Apple is now including AV digitizing capabilities in their latest Power Macintosh models, giving you not only the time-honored capability of adding digital audio to your work, but also the capability of easily digitizing a video source as well. In early Power Macs, this capability was evidenced by two S-Video ports and some adapter cables that Apple included to allow you to use composite (RCA-style jacks) inputs and outputs. Lately, Apple has been including both composite jacks and S-video ports on their high-end Power Macs.

These recent additions are creating a couple of new problems that weren't an issue a few years back — how to get all these connections working correctly, how to get the Mac's video to look good on a TV set, and how to keep good quality sound coming into the Mac.

In most cases, none of this is particularly difficult to figure out, especially when you begin to isolate the problem — AV issues are fairly easily to isolate because they're very specialized. From there you can move on to some of the more common fixes for AV problems.

Digital video

In my experience, the problems you're going to run up against in working with digital video come from two sources: cabling and software. You need to have the right software to get everything to work together happily, and that includes a slew of Mac OS extensions that need to be present for best results. You need to have the codecs, the QuickTime extensions, and all the various bits of interface code for dealing with your divergent video and audio sources. And, above all else, you'll need to have the Monitors & Sound control panel set correctly.

What problems are common? Take a look at some of the general issues you may encounter in your efforts to create digital video:

✦ *Composite cabling.* RCA-jacks and composite cables vary enormously in quality. I've had entire projects come to a screeching halt because of a failure in one of the little yellow-jacked cables that are included with an AV Mac or a video-input expansion card. In most cases I've found it's useful to toss those cables immediately (or store them as an emergency backup) and head out to Radio Shack for higher-gauge, higher-quality cabling. You don't necessarily need gold-plated connectors, but you might ask for what the experts use in their media setups. These are analog cables, so there's no real theoretical limit to their length, although quality will degrade with very long cables. Depending on the cable's quality, 50 to 100 feet is a general maximum.

✦ *S-video cabling.* Don't confuse S-video with something else—for instance, an ADB or Mac serial port. Force one of these cables hard enough into an S-video port and you'll likely do some damage. Also, if you're getting no picture or black-and-white images, try switching the in and out S-video cables. Early Power Macs feature an S-video adapter used for hooking up RCA composite cabling—not the most reliable setup. If you can, use S-video directly to and from your camera and TV.

✦ *HDI-45 connector.* On early AV Power Macs (6100, 7100, 8100) the HDI connector is only recommended for use if you already have a monitor plugged into the AV card. If you don't have a monitor connected to the AV card, you may experience an odd ghosting problem that forces you to constantly switch settings in the Monitors & Sound control panel. (In fact, you can accidentally mess things up so as to make video capture difficult or impossible. This problem often manifests itself as a disappearing Video Monitor—or FusionMonitor—window.) If you have an AppleVision monitor, Apple actually recommends that you get an adapter and hook it up to the RGB port on the AV card, even though it means you can't use the HDI-45 connector for the HDI-45 port.

✦ *VRAM relationship.* Digitizing video inputs require a certain amount of video RAM to digitize video; this is especially true when working with early Power Macintosh AV machines. If the Mac can't digitize at the current bit depth, this probably means you've run out of VRAM. Back down to a color depth of 256 (8-bit) or thousands of colors (16-bit) and try again. (On Quadra AV Macs, 256 colors is the practical limit without a VRAM upgrade.)

✦ *Speed.* A number of things can affect digitizing speed on a Power Macintosh, including the amount of RAM dedicated to the digitizing program, the number of background applications running, the Mac OS extensions active, and hardware issues such as the speed of the SCSI bus and drive to which the data is being sent. For older Power Macs, the video connector used can also affect speed—using the 6100/7100/8100's RGB connector results in 15 to 20 times better digitizing speeds than using the HDI-45 connector.

✦ *QuickTime.* The QuickTime software is a major component of any digital video–editing setup, so it's important to keep up-to-date with the software. A full installation of the latest QuickTime distribution should solve most of your Mac OS extension dilemmas. Beware older games and multimedia applications that attempt to overwrite newer QuickTime components.

Note

If you're having trouble getting good throughput when digitizing audio or video, you may want to try "running lean" when you're actually going through the process of digitizing. To do this, pare down to a minimum necessary set of extensions, and turn off any extension that might affect hard driver performance — such as File Sharing, Web Sharing, Fax Receiving, and Remote Access serving. Check your digitizing software's documentation for hints and recommendations regarding the use of Virtual Memory and disk cache settings in the Memory control panel.

Audio issues

The sounds coming out of your Mac are not only entertaining at times, but often necessary for diagnostic and daily computing reasons. Whether you're not hearing your alert sounds, or you're not having luck trying to record audio, you'll find that audio problems tend to be similar to video issues: They revolve around control-panel settings and cabling problems.

No sound

If you're just not hearing what you think you should, try to isolate the problem to either software or hardware. Remember that the least common denominator is having nothing plugged into your audio-out port in that case, the Mac will use its internal speaker. If you still hear nothing, you've probably got a software problem.

Check the following when you hear nothing:

✦ *Cabling.* Are your speakers plugged into the wall socket and the audio-out port (not the audio-in or microphone port), and are they turned on? If you don't have external speakers but your Mac has a monitor with speakers, make sure the HDI-45 plug is connected (for AppleVision monitors) or a cable is connected between the audio-out port and the monitor's audio-in jack.

✦ *Power.* Macs require powered speakers for external sound (the internal sound requires nothing special), so make sure your speakers are a powered variety. (Some older Intel-compatible speakers and speakers for some portable stereos are not powered.) Make sure the batteries in the speakers are fresh or the speakers are plugged into a wall socket.

✦ *External volume controls.* If your Mac has an external volume control, you may have inadvertently set it to its lowest setting (or it may have reset that way for some reason). Try tapping it slowly to increase the volume. Tapping quickly can cause some Macs (using certain Mac OS versions) to freeze unexpectedly.

✦ *Control panels.* If you generally use the Control Strip, Audio CD Player, Video Player, or similar program to change volume in Mac OS 8 or above, you may notice on occasion that changing the volume has no effect on the sound — that's likely because the computer system volume has been set (or reset) to Mute. Open the Monitors & Sound control panel and choose the sound icon. Notice the different types of volume you have at your disposal. Click the Mute button for the master volume level and slide the slider to change the master volume level.

✦ *Sound source.* If you're having trouble hearing input from the CD-ROM drive, a line-level device, or a microphone, you may have the Sound Monitoring Source setting incorrect in the Monitors & Sound control panel. Check to see which device is currently selected.

✦ *CD audio.* If you can't hear an audio CD, check first that the appropriate sound monitoring source is checked. If the CD-ROM drive has been installed since the Mac was new, it's possible that the internal audio cable wasn't installed correctly. (There's a small four-wire cable that connects the internal CD-ROM drive to the internal audio-in plug on the logic board.) You won't be able to hear the audio from a CD over a network or through an external CD-ROM drive unless you're close enough to the drive to use headphones.

If you suspect hardware, unplug it all from the Mac (both audio-in and audio-out ports) and head to the Monitors & Sound control panel. Make sure the computer system volume is at about half and that it isn't muted. Now select the Alerts icon and double-click one of the alerts to test for sound. If you still don't hear anything, restart and try again.

Evangelista tip: Other sound interference

Sometimes sound settings on a Mac seem to be less than intuitive, especially if you're dealing with a program designed specifically to work with sound. Apple's engineers updated the Sound control panel in early Mac OS releases to the Monitors & Sound control panel because they felt it gave a more uniform interface for dealing with sound issues. Most Mac users just find the new tools a bit confusing.

Plus, there's the problem of older programs that rely on the old Sound control panel. My copy of SoundEdit 16, for instance, allows access to the Sound control panel from a menu item. This enables me to change sounds settings from within the program — or it used to. The reality is that these days the sound setttings need to be correct in the Monitors & Sound control panel before launching SoundEdit 16. (If you have similar troubles, try quitting the application, setting the sound values and restarting the application.)

Evangelista Nancy L. Spoolman wrote with this interesting tidbit, reminding me of a tried-and-true troubleshooting technique: When it doesn't seem to make sense, turn off Virtual Memory and trash the related preferences file. She says:

(continued)

(continued)

"I like to fiddle with movies, and for the past five years have taken movies of our district picnics, and so on. I decided to put them into a slide show and hoped (when finished) to record to video, with music. Anyone who works with graphics soon realizes their program memory runs out quickly. Working with PowerPoint, I increased the application memory and added more pictures until I had to increase it again and again. At 120 slides (two pictures per slide) I had to turn on Virtual Memory.

"Two weeks later I decided I needed to get that movie done and uploaded to my Web site. I'd already turned off Virtual Memory a week ago. I brought up Avid VideoShop, put movie clips in the sequencer, and played them back. To my dismay there was no sound! I looked at the Recording menu on the menu bar and noticed the Sound option was grayed out. I recalled this happening before, but could not for the life of me remember what it was that I did. I tried rebooting. Still the same. I was dejected. I decided to sleep on it.

"The following morning I began to put clips back in the sequencer, clicking on this and that, when suddenly Avid VideoShop quit unexpectedly with a 'Type 1' error. I decided to not restart the computer as suggested and brought Avid Video up again. It indicated to me that the preferences could have been corrupted when it unexpectedly quit. Of course! I clicked the Continue button, and immediately checked recording on the menu bar and there that beautiful Sound item was once more available! My mind flashed back to another time this happened. The culprit was Virtual Memory, which had corrupted my preferences. When the application quit and I told it to continue, I got my sound back. Am I happy or what?"

Bad sound

If you've got static, strange sounds, or an overall sense that things aren't good (especially while wearing headphones connected to your Mac), you may have a problem with sound output. Most of these are settings problems; unless you've blown a speaker in your high-end array of powered sound demons, you've probably got a slider setting wrong in the Monitors & Sound control panel.

Usually you'll have trouble with sound when you're playing sound samples; this can include games or multimedia titles that are playing the samples for you. In general, you want your sound output settings to be the same as the settings used to record a particular sample. This helps to keep the sound or sample from sounding tinny, or thin, as if it's being played over an AM radio or a telephone. You can set the sound output quality in the Monitors & Sound control panel, as shown in Figure 25-4. Usually the highest available number is the best setting, although you may want to set the output quality lower if you're using it to test the quality at that level — for instance, if you want to hear what an 11KHz sample might sound like over a Web audio connection.

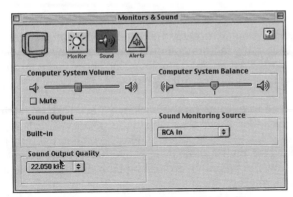

Figure 25-4: Setting the sound output quality

If you're getting static when you play back a sound, you may be playing a 16-bit sample at 8 bits, or your Mac may not be capable of playing 16-bit samples. The first Macs with 16-bit audio-out capabilities were the Quadra AV Macintoshes. Nearly all Power Macintosh models have 16-bit, 44KHz audio-out, but earlier 68000 series Macs only had 8-bit audio-out. The result is static.

Particular Macs also present some interesting sound output problems. Performa models with a subwoofer offer a separate volume control for the subwoofer, which can be left on sometimes, even if you're using headphones. Try switching the headphones from the monitor to the headphone jack on the front of the Mac itself.

If you have a weird effect in your headphones, you may have the SRS Surround Sound option still turned on in the Monitors & Sounds control panel. (Only certain Performa models and their Power Macintosh progeny, such as the Power Mac 5400 and the Power Mac 6500 series, have surround sound. Oh —and the iMac.) Another possible setting is in the Sounds control panel (if you have a separate version of the control panel). Check the SoundSprocket control panel for settings to align the stereo effects more precisely.

If you hear only very deep, difficult-to-hear sounds, you may have only the subwoofer on in your system, with the rest of the sound turned down. Check your settings in the Monitors & Sound control panel. The subwoofer is meant to add deep, bassline sounds, not act as a speaker on its own.

Note

Like any sound system, it's ill advised to set your sound volumes so that computer speakers and subwoofers are driven at their highest gains. Above about 80 percent of maximum, you'll introduce unappealing distortion anyway. You may also find that settings below 20 percent introduce distortion, so you'll want to set your sound at a reasonable middle level if you plan to work with sound in any professional or semi-professional capacity.

Sound recording

If you're trying to record sounds, you may not get the results you want the first couple of times out. It's true that many factors go into a good recording, and you'll need to experiment a bit to get the best sound from your Mac and your recording equipment. Here are some common audio-recording issues:

✦ Remember that the inputs and outputs on the back of a Macintosh are all line-level connections. To hear a Mac signal through standard stereo speakers, you'll need to connect the Mac to an amplifier. Similarly, you can't simply plug a microphone directly into the microphone jack; you either need to send the microphone through a powered mixing board or amplifier or you need to use the special Apple Plaintalk microphone.

✦ To get stereo audio input for the Macintosh AV and most Power Macintosh computers, you need a stereo Y-adapter to connect two RCA-style plugs to the 3.5 mm stereo minijack (indicated by the microphone icon) on the rear of the Macintosh. The latest Power Macintosh models that feature video inputs also include RCA-style audio plugs for stereo audio input.

✦ If you try to record but get no recorded sound, try to reset the Sound Monitoring Source option in the Monitors & Sound control panel. If this doesn't work and you're trying to record from the microphone, mute the Mac's internal speaker.

✦ When you're recording, record at the sample rate at which the sample will ultimately be played. One mistake is to create a high-end sound sample, such as a 16-bit, 22KHz sound, and then *downsample,* or reduce the quality, to 8-bit, 11KHz or something similar. This process generally introduces more static and noise than does recording directly to the lower sample rate.

✦ For quality audio that is to be recorded to cassette tape, VHS, CD-R, or digital audio tape, 16-bit samples are the bare minimum. From there, 11KHz is AM quality, 22KHz is FM quality, and 44KHz is CD quality. Eight-bit samples are generally too noisy for anything other than Web broadcast or swapping between computers. If you find that your recordings seem noisy or full of static, check to make sure you're recording 16-bit samples.

Summary

✦ Video problems are generally pretty easy to trace, with most of them related to cabling or power problems. Check all your connections carefully. If the monitor is getting power but not a picture, it doesn't necessarily mean something is broken; there's a good chance the problem concerns either an adapter issue or a software issue. There's certainly a bit of voodoo involved in setting up monitors, especially because Macs try to auto-sense a monitor's capabilities and adjust accordingly.

✦ Monitors can vary in quality and degrade over time. You can also hit the wrong button or knob and throw the whole thing out of whack. If you're getting a picture, but it's not a great picture, you'll need to do some fiddling with the controls to get it in shape, especially if you plan to use the monitor a lot.

✦ Macs with video-input capabilities sometimes experience unique problems associated with video. Most troubling is the introduction of new types of ports and cabling; you'll want to be careful as you get used to the different types of connections used for regular and digital video production.

✦ Audio production capabilities have been common on Macs for a while, but recent changes in the OS coupled with classic sound editing problems can make it seem as though things aren't working as well as they should. Beware multiple settings. The number of different ways to change volumes in software and hardware may result in your not hearing a thing even if the volume is turned all the way up.

✦   ✦   ✦

Printers and Modems

Are you wondering why modems and printers are grouped together in this troubleshooting chapter? Well, it's not only because they both usually have something to do with the serial port, although that's a good reason. It's actually because, in my unscientific opinion, printers and modems are the two devices most likely to fail when you're working toward a deadline. You've got to get a project out the door, a report finished, or an invoice sent off, and your printer or modem won't work correctly or at all. That's why I thought it'd be convenient to have them both here, in the same chapter.

It's too bad these problems can't happen when you're bored on a Friday afternoon (or, maybe they do, and you can't tell because you're not using your printer or modem). But whenever the trouble first starts, there are usually a few quick ways to identify the problem and get back up and running. Once you've got things working, you should go back and look into the whole process, just to make sure there isn't a more permanent fix.

In this chapter I'll discuss printer problems — trouble with printing, printer driver issues, and some basic printer networking problems — and modem problems — involving both faxing and Internet access. This chapter also includes information about the Hayes AT command set that can help you dig deeper into your modem's configuration, just in case you want to.

Printing Problems

Mac-based printers, especially PostScript printers, are really their own little computers, requiring complex and sometimes delicate relationships between hardware and software to work properly. (I suppose I could start every section of this book with "*X* is a delicate combination of hardware and software" but, aside from networking, this may be more true of printers than nearly any other peripheral.)

That means you'll have the occasional weird problem with printers. Surprisingly, printer drivers aren't nearly as advanced as they might be; certain printer drivers based on the LaserWriter 8 driver offer some interesting options, but the system for printing to PostScript printers has remained remarkably the same over the past ten years. This can make it easier on printer manufacturers and system administrators who are forced to update printer drivers less frequently, but it can make it tougher to find a problem that's buried somewhere between the Mac and its printer.

You should, of course, start at the beginning. If you can't get your printer to print at all, you probably have either a software problem or a configuration problem. Once you eliminate problems with the physical configuration, you can move on to troubleshooting the Chooser, System Folder, and printer drivers to see if the problem is lurking somewhere in those places.

Printer won't print

More than likely this is a software problem. In the modern Mac OS, a few hurdles need to be overcome before a printer and a Mac will communicate with one another; the correct printing extensions need to be loaded, printer drivers need to be present, and the Chooser needs to be properly configured. Of course, you should make sure the power and cabling are all set up correctly, too.

It's unlikely that you'll have mysterious printing problems, assuming all your printing extensions and software are turned on according to the instructions in Chapter 15. At a bare minimum, you need a printer driver loaded (in the Extensions folder when the Mac starts up), and you need to have that printer chosen in the Chooser. If the printer is connected using Ethernet or LocalTalk cabling, you'll want to have AppleTalk turned on in the Chooser (and the cabling type selected in the AppleTalk or Network control panel) as well.

With that much set up, at a minimum you'll receive an error message that gives you a decent idea of what the printer's complaints are. From there, you can troubleshoot the particular error message to see what you should do.

Note   Trial-and-error troubleshooting is the most frustrating type: Plug in the device, test it, plug it somewhere else, test it. It's important to walk away and take a break occasionally when things aren't working. Keep focused on eliminating the possibilities and identifying the problem. It may help to closely document everything you do with a pencil and notepad. Sometimes there's a mystical, magical combination that will work, so pay attention to what you're doing—you may want to do it again at some point in the future.

Error: Printer can't be found

You could get a variety of slightly different error messages depending on what extension is handling your print job (the Print Monitor, Desktop Print Monitor), or if background printing has been turned off. In any case, the error messages are all trying to say pretty much the same thing: The printer can't be found.

Probably the first thing is to check the printer's power and try printing again. If you didn't turn the printer on quickly enough and/or allow it to warm up, you may get this message. Laser printers especially can take a minute or two to warm up. If you chose the Print command soon after (or just before) powering up the printer, the Mac OS may have caught the printer when it was not quite awake.

Here's a quick rundown of the things to check if you receive either no error message or a "Printer can't be found" message, and the problem isn't a warm-up issue:

✦ *Is everything plugged in?* Check to make sure your printer is getting power from the wall socket or surge protector and that your printer is properly connected via LocalTalk, Ethernet, or directly to the printer port. Make sure you're using the same port you've selected in the Chooser. Check Chapter 15 if you're not sure how your printer should be connected to your Mac or network. If you have a serial switch box, make sure it's correctly dialed so that the printer is active. Also, make sure you're using LocalTalk cabling for LocalTalk connections and a printer cable for a QuickDraw printer.

✦ *Is everything turned on?* Make sure the printer is turned on, if necessary. If you have a switch box for your printer port, make sure it's correctly cabled and switched for using the printer. If your printer is jammed or has an error, fix the problem and reset the printer or cycle the printer's power. PostScript printers can crash, so it's always an okay idea to switch the power off and on to reset a printer if it seems to be causing trouble.

✦ *Is the printer configured correctly?* On non-Apple printers especially, you'll probably be able to choose a mode for the printer, particularly if the printer can switch between networking architectures or protocols, or if the printer can switch between PostScript and PCL compatibility. Make sure the printer is on the same page (so to speak) as the rest of your setup. Usually you'll make these choices either with dials and settings on the back of the printer or with an LCD screen and buttons on the front of the printer.

✦ *Is the Chooser correctly configured?* First, make sure your printer appears in the Chooser. If it doesn't, check the Extensions Manager to ensure the printer driver is included in the Extensions folder at startup. If your printer is there, click it to make sure it's selected, and then check to see if the correct port or connection is selected on the right-hand side. If you have a LaserWriter or compatible printer, make sure the LaserWriter driver is selected on the left side of the Chooser and that the printer's name appears on the right side. Select the printer name, if you haven't already. If the printer is connected via AppleTalk, check that AppleTalk is active in the Chooser.

✦ *Is the desktop printer working correctly?* If the desktop printer isn't highlighted with a thick, black border, it's not the currently selected printer. Select it in the Chooser, or delete the desktop printer icon and create a new one.

✦ *Are the necessary extensions present?* In the Extensions Manager, check that your printer driver is selected to load, as well as the Desktop Printing Extension and the Print Monitor (both are necessary if you're using Mac OS 7.6 and above and an Apple printer). If your printer has its own Print Monitor (such as the HP Print Monitor), make sure it is selected to load in the Extensions Manager.

The "Printer can't be found" error message usually suggests some fundamental problem, such as the printer driver is missing or the Mac is simply confused by your request to print because no printer is correctly assigned — the Chooser is misconfigured in some way. You may have inadvertently chosen the modem instead of the printer port in the Chooser, for instance. This may also suggest that the printer is turned off or not wired correctly. Check all of these things. If you can get to the point where you've selected the printer in the Chooser and were able to activate it without incident, you've succeeded.

How do you know if you've successfully chosen the printer? You will see the "Change Page Setup" message as you leave the Chooser (see Figure 26-1). This is the key to love and happiness in your printer relationship; if you see this message, you will most likely be able to print.

Figure 26-1: If you've successfully chosen the printer, this message will appear after you close the Chooser's window.

If you aren't able to select the printer in the Chooser successfully, you may have a corrupted printer driver or corrupted PRAM settings. Here are a few more desperate measures to try:

1. Try resetting PRAM first. That may enable you to choose the printer in the Chooser.

2. If zapping PRAM doesn't work, try reinstalling your printer's driver software from the Mac OS CD or from floppies you received with the printer.

3. If you have a QuickDraw printer, strip down your connections so that the printer is the only serial device connected to the Mac (remove other port connections, switch boxes, and so on), and test the printer again.

4. For a LocalTalk printer, check for proper connections, LocalTalk termination, networking problems, printer driver trouble or Chooser misconfiguration. Try another printer cable or LocalTalk transceiver.

5. If the printer is connected via Ethernet, troubleshoot your Ethernet network as described in Chapter 27.

6. If this still doesn't help, you may need to clean install the Mac OS, install your printer drivers, and try printing again.

Other suggestions include making sure you have the latest version of the printer driver necessary for your printer; visit the manufacturer's Web site to find out. The printer driver may also be corrupt, requiring that you copy a new version to the Extensions folder.

You can also try to set up and print to another printer (which proves the serial port is functional) and/or print to the problem printer using a different serial port (which proves the printer works). If you don't seem to be having any trouble with the printer or the port, you can trace the problem back to a software issue and dive into your System Folder to find the problem.

Note

In past Mac OS versions, it was possible to load QuickDraw GX when installing the operating system, which would force you to use only QuickDraw GX printers in the Chooser. If you can't seem to find the printer drivers you've installed for your printer (or can only find drivers that have "GX" in the name), you'll need to uninstall QuickDraw GX. You can use your Mac OS installation CD to selectively uninstall QuickDraw GX (see Chapter 33 for more on selective uninstalls).

Error: Printer port is in use

A "Port is in use" message suggests you've either attempted to print to a port that is being used by your modem, scanner, or a similar device, or you've tried to print to a crashed printer port or a connection that, through a switch box, isn't designed for a printer.

Here are the steps for dealing with this problem:

1. If you have a switch box, that's the place to start — switch to the printer's setting and try again. (With some printers you may need to restart your Mac.)

2. Next, check the Chooser. It's possible you've either chosen the wrong printer driver or your printer driver is set up to print to the wrong port. Check to see if you need to set the printer back to the printer port.

3. You may also have AppleTalk active and LocalTalk chosen as your networking architecture in the AppleTalk or Network control panel while trying to connect to a QuickDraw printer. (PowerBooks behave slightly differently — see Chapter 29 for a discussion of printer/modem port issues on a

PowerBook.) With AppleTalk and LocalTalk active, you can't connect to the Printer port directly, so your printer driver will default to the Modem port. Turn off AppleTalk, and then point your printer driver back at the Printer port. (If you have a QuickDraw printer, you'll encounter this problem whenever you zap PRAM or remove the PRAM battery.)

4. If you use a Teleport, GeoPort or any other modem that requires a control panel, check to make sure it isn't active on the port you're trying to print to. Check other control panels for serial devices such as fax controllers, scanner software, and other software drivers to make sure they aren't set to control the wrong port (see Figure 26-2).

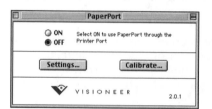

Figure 26-2: The PaperPort is an example of a control panel that can take over the serial port without evidence of that fact in the Chooser.

5. Make sure you don't have any docking software for personal digital assistants (such as a Newton or Palm Pilot) or classroom docking (for an eMate) running on that port. You may need to shut down the docking server software or a LocalTalk server if one is running.

6. If you've had trouble with the printer just before receiving the error message, it's possible the printer driver or part of the Mac OS has crashed, effectively hanging the port itself. In this case, you should try restarting the Mac to clear the port. If this doesn't work you may need to use a program like Reset Serial Port (on the included CD-ROM) or you might need to zap PRAM.

7. If all this fails, test the printer on the Modem port and see if it works. If it does, there's a chance the Printer port is bad; after you've managed to print a test page to the other port, try to switch back to the Printer port. Don't forget to test with another cable or set of cables, too.

You might also try a clean install of the OS and a minimum configuration designed to test the printing subsystem only. Load nothing but Apple extensions and any others necessary for your printer, and then try again to print. If it works, troubleshoot your initial set of extensions.

If you get all the way through these steps (and the previous section's steps), you may feel confident that you can attribute the problem to a bad serial port. Although it's rare, plugging and unplugging the printer while the Mac is powered could cause this to happen, as could plugging in a cable that isn't designed for the port. The port could also go due to an electricity surge, static electricity discharge, or some other freakish and unfortunate series of events.

Note

We're focused on the printer port right in this section, but surges through a modem due to an unprotected phone line connection (many surge protectors will also protect phone cabling) can easily burn out a modem and any serial port to which it was connected. If you're trying to use the modem port for printing, or you have reason to believe a modem was connected to the port you're trying to use and was affected by an electrical surge, the port may be broken, resulting in the error message.

PostScript errors

PostScript errors appear to be caused by only a few different factors most of the time: corruption, bugs, or conflicts. (These are the problems that typically affict all software, as discussed in Chapter 30.) Corrupt documents and corrupt fonts can cause trouble, bugs in the printer driver can cause PostScript errors, and conflicts between applications and the version of PostScript in your printer can cause problems.

Here are a few common reasons you'll get PostScript errors:

✦ A "Time out" error message may result if you send multiple copies of a document to print in the background, especially if the documents are complex. Try printing them one at a time or turn off background printing (printing will then take over the Mac's interface until the printer is done).

✦ A PostScript error will occur if you create a PostScript document (print to file), and then try to print that document on a less sophisticated printer. (This can also be true of Adobe Acrobat PDF files and similar documents generated at the level 2 standard.) For instance, some modern printers use PostScript level 2 or 3 instructions that an older, PostScript level 1 printer can't handle.

✦ Too many options selected, pages set too wide or tall, or other problems in the Page Setup dialog box (such as odd or unsupported paper sizes) can result in PostScript errors.

✦ Allowing unlimited downloadable fonts either in an application's Page Setup, in the printer's PPD file (in the Chooser, when setting up the printer), or in the Apple Printer Utility can cause PostScript errors, as can using many different fonts in a particular document.

✦ A corrupt font can cause errors — PostScript or otherwise — that you may be able to pin down (especially if you notice which documents generate errors, and what font they have in common).

If you've recently changed something on your Mac (such as the Mac OS version, your printer driver, or the fonts you use) or if you're printing a particularly complex document, you may run into one of the leading causes of PostScript errors — lack of RAM. If you get a PostScript error and half a printed sheet, for instance, too little RAM is a good bet.

You might also need more RAM if you're experiencing a rash of tiny PostScript problems, especially if you've begun printing more complex documents, changed your printer driver, or installed a newer version of the Mac OS. It's not uncommon to need a RAM upgrade after a few years of service, especially if your particular printer model was a little stingy on RAM in the first place. (Check your printer documentation first and make sure it can accept more memory. You should also check to see if the printer has any special memory compression schemes that need to be enabled. If these become disabled, it could cause errors.) You should add RAM or print less complex documents with fewer images, graphics, and/or fonts.

For more on PostScript, see Adobe's PostScript pages at `www.adobe.com/ prodindex/postscript/main.html`. For help with PostScript errors, try `http://ds.dial.pipex.com/quite/errors.htm` from Quite Software.

Freezes and crashes

You may find that your Mac consistently freezes or crashes when you go to print a document. Generally, this is a sign of corruption somewhere in the system. The first thing to check is whether the trouble stems from a corrupt document, a problem with background printing or a corrupt preferences file.

Here are some of the symptoms to look out for:

✦ **Corrupt document.** When printing, you get an error message, but the message also tells you to try again. If the error message pops back up almost immediately, the document may be corrupt. This can also be indicated by a document that sits in the queue for a long time when it's supposed to be printed or a document that can't be removed from the queue for some reason. To get rid of a problem document, open the PrintMonitor Documents folder in the System Folder and drag the document to the Trash. (If you're using a desktop printer icon, you can double-click it, and then drag the document from the queue to the Trash.)

✦ **Background printing.** If your Mac crashes in response to a movement of the mouse or a stroke of the keyboard while printing in the background, you may have some sort of background printing conflict. Isolate this problem by turning background printing off in the Chooser and trying to print again. (If there is another crash, it's likely a corrupt document.) If you have no trouble with regular printing, there's a background printing problem. First, check to make sure your hard drive hasn't filled up. (Background printing requires that the file be saved to the hard drive, and then fed to the printer.) Also, try increasing PrintMonitor's memory using the Get Info command. If all else fails, try a clean install of the Mac OS or a selective install of the PrintMonitor.

✦ **Preferences file.** Although corruption in a preferences file can manifest itself in many ways, the most likely manifestation is the most bizarre — the printer tries to print in odd ways, selections in the Print dialog don't seem to stay current, or the printer crashes regardless of whether or not background printing is turned on. The fix is to delete the Printer Prefs file or folder from the Preferences folder. If your printer is a non-Apple printer and/or an inkjet, the preferences file may have a different name (usually similar to the printer's name).

Other things can affect these seemingly random crashes and freezes, including trouble with the desktop file, corruption or fragmentation on the drive, and a lack of Mac OS system RAM (or a fragmentation of RAM resulting from running the Mac for a long time without a restart). You can also suspect the printer's driver if it's aging or the printer's RAM, especially if the problems occur with more complex pages.

Desktop printing issues

With Mac OS 7.6 desktop printing became popular and, in Mac 8.0 and above, desktop printers became even more closely integrated with the Mac OS. If you're using these versions of the OS, it's very common to see people bypassing the Chooser altogether in favor of desktop printers. However, with this newfound popularity have come some headaches that might still not be completely resolved. Desktop printing is certainly convenient, and it offers a more useful and interesting metaphor than the Chooser does. But it can cause some trouble, too, by introducing another layer of complexity.

Note

At the time of writing, desktop printing is limited to PostScript printers that use the LaserWriter driver and Stylewriter inkjets. At some point in the future, third-party printers should work as desktop printers.

Problems creating a desktop printer icon

Creating a desktop printer icon is fairly simple in most cases: You need to have the Desktop Printing extensions (Desktop Print Spooler and Desktop PrintMonitor) active, and then you simply choose a printer in the Chooser. If everything goes well, the Mac will automatically create a desktop printer icon for the printer — in Mac OS 8 and above, a desktop printer icon is required unless desktop printing is inactive.

You should also be able to throw away the icon at any time; just drag it to the Trash. The OS will automatically create a new printer icon for the desktop. If you have trouble with this process, it could be a sign that the desktop printer is corrupted or some other part of the system has gotten clogged. Indicators include the following:

✦ Nothing happens when you choose the Print command in your applications.

✦ The printer queue seems to hang or causes the machine to freeze when trying to print a document.

✦ Crashes, errors, or freezes occur when you drag a document to the desktop printer icon.

✦ Error messages are generated by printing, including a message that says a document "Isn't a valid print file."

✦ "Printer not found" message appears.

✦ Desktop printer icon appears as a regular folder icon on the desktop.

✦ After choosing a printer in the Chooser, a desktop printer icon isn't created.

Isolate desktop printing

The errors just listed point to a couple possible problems — usually corruption in the printer preferences, a corrupt desktop printer or a document that is hanging the print queue. (After a system crash, a document may be only half printed, thus causing problems.) The key to pinpointing a desktop printing error is to successfully print without desktop printing active. If that works, you've narrowed down the problem.

Here's how to isolate desktop printing:

1. Open the Extensions Manager (if you were forced to restart the Mac, hold down the spacebar to open the Extensions Manager before the Mac OS starts up). In the Extensions Manager, disable Desktop PrintMonitor and Desktop Print Spooler. (If you're using Mac OS 7.x, you'll need to turn off the Desktop Printing Extension, too.)

2. Start the Mac up as normal.

3. In the Chooser, make sure the correct printer is chosen.

4. Print a test document.

If this works, there's a good chance the desktop printing preferences are corrupt, an unprinted document is hanging the desktop printing software or something has become misconfigured.

Desktop printer solutions

Desktop printer corruption generally manifests itself as a printer that just won't print; there are no error messages and no indication of printing. Everything is configured correctly, the wiring is good, and the Chooser is happy, but the document disappears out of the desktop printer's window without a trace. (You may occasionally get an error message that says "Desktop printer unknown error - 192 at 18" or another one in plainer language that suggests you have a corrupt document blocking the queue.)

If you suspect a corrupt desktop printer, the easiest thing to try is to dump the desktop printer icon in the Trash. If desktop printing has been reactivated, the Mac will create another icon, and you can try to print again. If not, then you can reactivate desktop printing and create a new printer as outlined previously.

If your problems are more grave, you may need to jump into your system and delete some potentially corrupt preferences files and the print queue. Note that desktop printing should be disabled for this to work. Here's what to get rid of:

1. Drag all your desktop printers to the Trash.

2. Open the Preferences folder in your System Folder and trash the Printing Prefs folder. (You might want to take a look inside the folder before trashing it; it contains some templates and watermark files that you might want to hold onto. Of course, you can reinstall these by reinstalling desktop printing from your Mac OS CD.)

3. In the System Folder, locate the PrintMonitor Documents folder and drag it to the Trash.

4. If you're working with Mac OS 8, you should head to the Extensions Disabled folder and invoke the Get Info command on the Desktop PrintMonitor icon. Add 100 kilobytes to the minimum and preferred sizes boxes. (In later versions of the OS, this shouldn't be a problem.)

5. Go into the Extensions Manager and check the Desktop PrintMonitor and Desktop Print Spooler extensions so that they'll load.

6. Restart and hold down ⌘-Option until the Mac starts up and rebuilds the desktop file.

Now restart the Mac with the Desktop Printing extension enabled. When your Mac's desktop appears, the desktop printer icon may be created for you. (If it isn't, go into the Chooser and choose the printer you'd like to use. When you close the Chooser, it'll create the desktop icon.) Print as usual.

If you continue to have problems, you should suspect that there's something wrong with the Mac OS itself. You might try a quick upgrade of your current OS or look for new printer drivers — check your printer manufacturer's Web site and the Apple Tech Info library (http://til.info.apple.com/) for more advice. (You might try searching with the text "Desktop Print".) If necessary, a clean installation of the OS may prove helpful.

There are some known issues with desktop printing, including various problems with Quickdraw GX and some specific Apple printers (especially those based on Hewlett-Packard technology, such as the Color Stylewriter 4100 and 4500). Desktop printing requires the Shared Library Manager to work correctly, and it won't work at all if Extensions have been disabled.

Note

Desktop printing is helpful and convenient, but I wouldn't hesitate to disable it if you need to print immediately and you're up against a deadline. You can print through the Chooser as normal, and then fix desktop printing later.

The endless loop Error

In Mac OS 8.0 (and perhaps earlier—Apple isn't too clear in this case), it's possible for a bug in desktop printing to create an endless loop error. Your desktop printer tells you it's trying to print an invalid printer file, and recommends that you drag the file to your desktop. When you do, it copies the file back to its queue and complains again.

This is what's happened: Desktop printing has accidentally mistaken the hidden directory on your hard drive called Desktop folder for the hidden directory on your hard drive designed to hold desktop printing queued documents. Desktop printing works by constantly monitoring a particular hidden folder on your drive. When it erroneously decides that the Desktop folder is the desktop printing folder, suddenly it sees a bunch of files on the desktop that seem to be destined for printing.

This is a tough error to deal with. According to Apple's Tech Info Library, here's the solution:

1. Restart the Mac using the Disk Tools floppy. You can't start up with a CD-ROM, because that automatically locks the Desktop folder.

2. Make a new folder in your Mac's main hard drive window.

3. Drag all the icons that are on your desktop (except for the hard drive, floppy disk, and T icons) into this new folder.

4. Restart the Macintosh with the hard drive as the startup disk.

5. Go to the Chooser from the Apple menu and select another printer. It does not matter which printer you choose, as you are simply choosing another printer to force the Macintosh to create another desktop printer.

This should create a new desktop printer and put things back on track.

LaserWriter issues

For most of your PostScript printing you'll use the LaserWriter 8 printer driver that Apple includes with the Mac OS, even if your printer isn't Apple-branded. Instead of using a separate driver, different PostScript printers use a special PostScript Printer Description (PPD) file that enables the Mac to differentiate any special capabilities of the printer. It's a little bit of a hack job (it doesn't quite make sense for non-Apple printers to use a driver called the LaserWriter driver), but it works well most of the time.

You will, however, encounter a couple of problems specific to the LaserWriter driver. The LaserWriter preferences file can become corrupt, resulting in troubles such as PostScript errors, inability to pick the right paper size, and some other seemingly bizarre problems. In this case, you should remove both the LaserWriter 8.x Prefs file and the Parsed PPDs folder from the Printing Prefs folder in the Preferences folder. (If you find a preference file for an older version of LaserWriter 8, you can delete that one as well.)

If you receive Type 15 errors with a desktop printer and the LaserWriter driver, it's possible that you've disabled the AppleScript and Finder Scripting extensions, which are necessary for proper operation. Reinstall them from your Mac OS CD or re-enable them in the Extensions Manager. You may also need to drag your desktop printer icons to the Trash to reinitialize them.

Check your Read Me files (regarding the Mac OS, Mac OS Printing, and the LaserWriter driver) as well as search the Apple Tech Info Library (http://til.info.apple.com/) if you believe you're having trouble with the LaserWriter driver. There are a number of known issues involving applications and specific printer models that can be fixed or worked around.

Printer maintenance

The printer hardware itself needs a little care to keep it working at its best. Aside from drivers, queues, and errors, you'll also want to look at some of the physical components of printing, including paper, toner, and rollers.

Here are some hints for keeping printers working:

✦ You can clean the outside of a printer with basic detergent and water and a lightly moistened cloth (you should power the printer down and unplug it, just to be safe), but don't use an ammonia-based cleaning product.

✦ Be careful what you put in a laser printer. Don't print to non-laser label sheets, envelopes, stickers, name tags, or other sheet-fed items that use glues. The laser printer heats up toner and paper, causing normal label products to melt or leave glue on the inside of the printer.

✦ Only print on overhead slides designed for a laser printer. Regular acetate slides will melt inside the printer mechanism.

✦ Laser printers are usually designed to print to at least 20-lb bonds, preferably paper designed for laser printers (or copiers, in many cases). Avoid incredibly inexpensive paper that may be too fine and dusty. The pick-up gear can attract dust from cheap paper, which, eventually affects the paper's path through the printer (or the printer may not pick up the paper well or at all, just spinning and complaining of paper jams).

✦ The rollers in your printer can be refurbished if you've had your printer for a while and it doesn't pull paper through well or reliably. Have the printer serviced.

✦ Adhere closely to atmospheric and temperature requirements for LaserWriter printers. Humidity and temperature can affect print quality and reliability. In really dry climates, it's important to have your printer serviced and cleaned regularly; look inside the printer to see if toner is flying around inside. Pages may end up gray or blotched with toner as a result.

✦ Color LaserWriters can exhibit a purple haze that results from colored toners spraying and collecting inside the printer. Have the printer cleaned and serviced.

✦ Color output problems? You may not have ColorSync correctly configured (assuming you're using a ColorSync-capable printer). Open the ColorSync control panel and indicate what sort of monitor you're using. If yours isn't listed, check your monitor manufacturer's Web site or customer service center for a ColorSync profile. (ColorSync profiles are stored in the Colorsync Profiles folder in your Mac's Preferences folder.)

✦ Duplex (two-sided) printing (and printing to paper that already has a laser-printed side) can be tough on laser printers, because the toner that's already on the page can cause trouble with the paper path and can flake or dust off. Consider alternatives to duplex printing or weigh the advantages (saved paper) with the potential need to have the printer serviced more quickly. You should also get an opinion on this matter from the manufacturer or your printer's manual, if it concerns you. (I would encourage you to have used recycled white paper, however, even if you decide not to duplex print.)

✦ With inkjet printers, don't power down with the switch on your surge protector or other power strip. Instead, shut the Mac and printer down as normal. Inkjet printers have to go through a purge-and-store routine (where it cleans out the inkjet cartridge and moves it to a storage position) when cycling through the power-down phase. If you pull the plug on it, it won't go through this routine.

Troubleshooting printer output

If you think your laser printer isn't giving you the output you deserve, you should analyze its printed pages to determine what might be wrong. In general, only two problems occur with laser printers: an excess of toner and an absence of toner. If your page is generally lighter than normal (and no setting has been changed in your Page Setup dialog box or in setup options for your printer using the Chooser or the printer's own controls), it's possible that you're simply running out of toner. If you pull the toner cartridge and shake it gently from side to side, and then print with better results, that's a definite warning sign; you'll be needing new toner soon.

(continued)

(continued)

If extra markings are showing up on your page, you should determine if those markings are horizontal or vertical. Vertical problems (for instance, an unbroken line that runs down the entire front of the page) suggest there's something in the paper's path that's blocking the output or creating trouble. (You can try opening the printer to see if some sort of blockage is causing trouble.) Horizontal problems (like dots, splotches or lines that recur every few inches) suggest something wrong with an internal element — the toner cartridge, the fuser roller. You can troubleshoot this by trying another toner cartridge (although this may be an expensive choice) or by having the printer looked at by a technician.

Font troubles

Fonts are the files on your Mac that describe the appearance of text in your applications (on the screen) and to your printer. Times, Helvetica, Garamond, and others are all fonts that need to be described so that both the Mac's screen and any attached printers know what they're supposed to look like. So, small font files are kept in the Fonts folder in your Mac's System Folder to tell it how to create certain characters in certain styles.

Your Mac can use three different types of fonts to generate text and symbols on the printed page — bitmap fonts, TrueType fonts, and PostScript fonts. These three types behave in slightly different ways, resulting in differences between how they look on screen and how they print. If you're having trouble with jagged fonts (either on screen or when printed), you'll want to take a closer look at your fonts.

Here's a quick discussion of the different types of fonts:

✦ **Bitmapped fonts.** These are the original fonts used on the Macintosh, and they are considered rather limited these days. The exact nature of the font is described in this sort of font file, meaning you need to have a different font file for every different size of a bitmapped font. A font family of bitmapped fonts would feature the one font in many different sizes. If you choose a bitmapped font in a size for which you don't have an exact font description, the result will be jagged. Bitmapped fonts aren't used much for printing anymore and should be avoided, although they're sometimes used to create the text you see on screen.

✦ **PostScript fonts.** These were the original *outline* fonts, a technology that enables a font to be scaled by the computer to look good at the point size you choose for the font. Instead of simply consulting a bitmap image of the font, a PostScript font includes a mathematical description of the font that can then be scaled as needed. PostScript fonts are sometimes called *printer fonts* because they're really designed to describe output on a printer, not on screen. Originally, bitmapped fonts were used as a stand-in for PostScript fonts when displayed on screen; these days, Adobe Type Manager (a control panel for your Mac) is responsible for generating good-looking screen fonts from the PostScript printer description fonts on your hard drive.

Adobe Type Manager is included with Adobe Acrobat, which can be installed from the CD-ROM included with this book.

✦ **TrueType fonts.** This technology (codeveloped by Apple and Microsoft) was Apple's answer to PostScript when it became clear in the mid-to-late 1980s that PostScript was a huge hit among Macintosh professionals. TrueType is an outline font technology, but it's also a hybrid font technology that works both for screen fonts and printer fonts. This makes TrueType very easy to work with, because no special control panels, extra bitmapped fonts, or other workarounds are necessary — you just drop the font file in the Font folder and get to work. By this same token TrueType fonts enable QuickDraw printers to work, as a QuickDraw printer won't natively support PostScript.

When you look at a standard Mac font-size menu, you may notice something interesting that you hadn't before — some of the font sizes are outlines, and some of them are in regular black text. The outlined fonts are those for which your Mac can display an accurate point size; the others will appear jagged on screen. If every font size is outlined, you've got a TrueType font selected. If it's PostScript and you have ATM active, you may see some point sizes that aren't outlined, but they'll still look okay on screen.

It's possible for a font to become corrupt and cause problems for your Mac. Check Chapter 32 for a discussion of corrupt fonts.

Font doesn't appear in menus

If you've recently added fonts to your Mac, regardless of the type, they won't show up in your application's Fonts menu until you've restarted the application. (In fact, it's best to add fonts while no other applications are running. And if you have an extensions or font management program, you should probably restart your Mac after installing new fonts.) All you need to do is quit any open applications and restart them to see the new fonts. You'll also find that you can't move fonts out of the Fonts folder until you've quit all applications and are running just the Finder.

If you shut everything down and your Mac still won't let you move fonts around, you may need to startup your Mac and hold down the Shift key to disable extensions (or hold down the Shift key after the extensions have loaded to disable Startup Items). There may be a background application running that's confusing the Mac. Or, the Mac might just need to be restarted before it will release the Font folder to you.

You may be over your limit and have too many fonts in your Fonts folder (you're only allowed 128 fonts and font suitcases, not including PostScript fonts). If this is the case, some of the fonts will drop out of your Fonts menu. You can get around this limitation by grouping like fonts together in font suitcases.

To create a suitcase, make a duplicate of an existing suitcase in the Fonts menu (suitcases have icons that look just like — what else? — suitcases). Rename it "master" and double-click it to open it. Now, clear out this duplicate suitcase of all its fonts. Close it up and store it in a safe place on your hard drive; you'll want to use it as a template for creating suitcases in the Fonts folder.

To clean up the Font folder, create a new, empty suitcase (by creating a duplicate of your master suitcase) and drag it to the Fonts folder. Give the suitcase a name for the particular font family you're going to group together — "Times," for instance. Now, just drag all the bitmapped or TrueType fonts that you want to include in this suitcase onto the suitcase icon, and they'll be stored in the suitcase just as if it were a subfolder. The difference is, all the included fonts are still available to your applications (you may need to restart your Mac before it will recognize the new font folder).

So suitcases help you get beyond the 128 font limit, but they're also useful for managing your fonts. You can use a font management program, such as Suitcase from Symantec (www.symantec.com/) or MasterJuggler from Alsoft (www.alsoft.com) to swap your font suitcases in and out, depending on the application you plan to use. If you have many, many fonts, you can use suitcases to group together the fonts you use for a particular application (your memo fonts versus your artistic fonts) and have them put in the Fonts folder by your font management program only when it's necessary for you to use them. This speeds up the system overall as well as the launching of individual applications. It may even help your Font menu to appear more quickly in your applications.

Note

Rearranging your fonts into suitcases is also an opportunity for a similar housekeeping chore — deciding which bitmapped fonts to keep. (These fonts usually include a number at the end suggesting their point size — Times 12.) You can get rid of any of them for which you have corresponding TrueType fonts. If you use PostScript, you need one bitmapped font in the same family for use by ATM; otherwise, getting rid of them all should not be a problem. If you're nervous, just move them out of your Font folder and into another folder on your Mac for a while. If nothing bad results, toss them in the Trash.

One other reason why you may not be seeing your fonts is they've been stored in a subfolder of the Fonts menu instead of a font suitcase. Fonts and font suitcases should be stored directly in the Fonts folder, not elsewhere in the System Folder.

Jagged font appearance

If your font appears jagged on the screen, you should check to see if you're using a bitmapped font (you can look up the font name in the Fonts folder), which, in most cases, you simply shouldn't do. Choose a TrueType or PostScript font instead, because a jagged bitmapped font will look bad when printed. In fact, a good way to test this is to go ahead and print; if the output is jagged, you're using a bitmapped font. Choose a different font.

But what if the font looks jagged on screen but prints beautifully? In that case, you're using a PostScript font and ATM isn't turned on (or you don't have ATM). With PostScript fonts, the associated bitmapped font is used on screen, even if you don't have the exact point size of the bitmapped font in question. The Mac will just scale the bitmapped font to fit, making things look jagged. Remember, though, that the bitmapped font is just a stand-in for the PostScript font, which will describe very accurately what you want to a PostScript printer. The result will be a good-looking printed font. To work around this you can do one of two things: install ATM or install a TrueType version of the font.

TrueType fonts will never give you either problem—both the screen version and the printed version will look fine. And, TrueType fonts can offer another benefit. If you have a TrueType font installed that's part of the same family as a bitmapped font or a PostScript font (for example, Times), you'll never run into jagged text.

The reason is simple: The Mac tends to gravitate toward the best looking output in both circumstances. When the Mac wants to display a font on screen, it will look for the right size bitmapped font. If it doesn't find it, though, it'll display a matching TrueType font. (If it doesn't find a TrueType font and ATM isn't active, only then will it try to resize a bitmapped font.)

The same sort of thing is true for printing fonts. If you have a PostScript printer, the printer will try to print a built-in PostScript font first. If it doesn't have the font that you're requesting built in (most of these printers have about 35 common fonts built into them), the printer will download the PostScript font from your Font directory. If it can't find a PostScript font, it'll load a TrueType font in the family you've requested. Only after all these other attempts fail will the printer print a bitmapped font. If the printer is a QuickDraw printer, it'll try to print TrueType fonts, and then PostScript fonts (generated by ATM), and then it'll give up and use a bitmapped font.

Note   Note that, aside from making PostScript fonts look good on screen, ATM can also be used to print PostScript fonts to a QuickDraw printer. (The printer doesn't natively support PostScript, only TrueType, but ATM can generate a TrueType-compatible font.)

Wrong font

There are a few other issues that might crop up with your fonts. Most of these have to do with missing fonts or missing parts of a font family that should be stored in your Fonts folder. If you can, try reinstalling your fonts when things otherwise seem confusing or contradictory. Here are some basic font problems:

✦ *Displayed font is wrong.* Usually this happens when you load a document that you've received from someone else or off the Internet; the document's author used a font you don't have on your Mac. Your best bet is to either find and install that font (you may have to buy it) or reformat the document with a new font. If you *do* have that font on your system, just reformat the document using that font. Sometimes the font's ID number can change (from Mac to Mac), causing your application to believe that you don't have the necessary font. If you're using Adobe Acrobat or a similar document viewer, it's probably set to substitute a reasonably similar font. If it looks good enough, stick with it.

✦ *Printed font is wrong.* This can be a little more ominous. If you use a PostScript printer, make sure the printer isn't set up so that fonts can be substituted (usually an option in the PPD setup window or using the Apple Printer Utility). You may also not have enough memory in your printer. If neither of these seems accurate, the font file itself may be corrupt; try reinstalling the font.

Modem Troubleshooting

In Chapter 16, I discussed how modems work and what you need to do to install one. I also walked you through some of the basics of setting up an Internet connection. Configuration is a big part of most troubleshooting when it comes to getting online. Aside from determining that a modem has been struck by an electrical surge, you should find that your modem works just fine most of the time.

There are some exceptions to that, however. One really good thing to know about your modem is how much of it exists as a physical device and how much of it is implemented in software. It may sound like a silly thing to know, but GeoPort adapters, Global Village modems, and some internal Apple modems have come to rely highly on software compared to some other models, and this can make a strong difference in the way you troubleshoot the device. This also presents something of a Catch-22. A good Apple modem is a great device to have in your system, because it integrates so well with the rest of the machine. A third-party modem (such as many Boca Research, Motorola, USRobotics, and Supra modems) is more likely to rely on hardware for all its operations, making it a lot easier to troubleshoot.

In this section you'll take a look at both types of modems, along with some troubleshooting for a GeoPort device. I'll then discuss some common problems with Internet connections.

Modem doesn't work

The first thing you want to isolate with a modem is whether or not it's in fighting shape. I warned you in Chapter 16, and I'll warn you again: Surge-protect your modem. And don't just plug the modem's power cable into a power strip. You need to protect the modem from the phone line, which also has power coursing through it that can surge. Many surge protectors are designed to protect from phone line surges as well as regular power spikes. I've only ever had one problem that I suspected was due to a power spike, but I've lost more than my share of modems to phone-line surges. It does happen.

So, before you go rooting through the software configuration of your modem, you need to make sure it can turn on and seems to be responding to hails. If you're getting power, you should check that the modem is being recognized by its setup software or that it can otherwise be reached by communications software. From

that point, you can decide if the modem just needs to be reconfigured or if
something worse has happened.

Note

If you have a Performa or "consumer" Power Macintosh model (5300, 5400, 6400,
6500), realize that it may have a modem preinstalled in the internal communications
slot. If this is the case, you can't install an external modem by connecting it to the
Modem port until that internal modem is removed. You can, however, install an external modem if that port is filled with an Ethernet card.

External modem

Plug in the modem and turn it on. If it's getting power, you should see an indicator
light to that effect. If not, check the power connections. Some modems are powered
by the ADB port on your Mac; make sure that port is functional and that it isn't
overloaded with ADB devices. If your modem fails to show a power indicator, try
plugging it into a different wall socket or somewhere else in the building. If there's
still no life, the modem is probably dead or broken — take it in for repairs or
replacement.

Some modems have a control panel that's used to help identify the modem to the
Macintosh, as in Figure 26-3. (This is especially true of Apple and Global Village
modems.) If you get an indicator light, but you're having trouble getting that
control panel to recognize the modem, you'll want to try and rule out a problem
with the port.

Figure 26-3: Global Village Teleport modems
must be recognized by their control panel
before they'll function properly.

To do this, begin by resetting the control panel (or click to cycle the Modem On/Off
setting in the panel) to see if it is able to detect the modem. Make sure the control
panel is set to look at the correct serial port. If not, try to change the control panel
to recognize that serial port. If you can't investigate why that serial port is being
used by another device, check your control panels, PDA docking devices, Newton
servers, and other potential conflicts.

If you can't find a conflict, try resetting the port by restarting your Mac or using the Reset Serial Port program. Zapping PRAM may also be necessary to reset the port.

If you're able to set the software to the correct port, but it still won't recognize the modem, turn the modem off, wait a few seconds and turn the modem on again. If the modem gets its power from the ADB port, you might need to shut the Mac all the way down (not just restart), and then restart using the Power key or switch on the Mac. That should reset ADB devices, including the modem.

If you still can't get the control panel to recognize the modem, try shutting down your Mac and placing the modem on the other serial port. Next, make sure no devices conflict (you've probably chosen the printer port, so make sure no printers or scanners expect to use the printer port), and try to set the modem up to work on the printer port. If it works, there might be a problem with your modem port. If it doesn't work, there may be a problem with the modem or the cable you're using to connect the modem to the Mac; try another cable before giving up on the modem.

Note

If the modem is specifically a Global Village Teleport modem, the problem may be the power supply you used to plug the modem in. I don't know if this happens for other modems, manufacturers, or models, but when I upgraded once from a Global Village Teleport Internet Edition 33.6 modem to a Teleport X2 56 Kbps modem, I failed to use the power supply included with the new modem. (I plugged it in using the 33.6's supply, because it was already so conveniently plugged in under my desk.) After an hour on the phone with a friendly tech support representative, she recommended that I switch the power supply. I did so, reset the Teleport control panel and the modem popped right up. And, it hasn't given me trouble since.

Internal modem

A nonworking internal modem can be a bit tougher to troubleshoot. In most cases, the problem is one of configuration; internal modems are either Apple-branded or from Global Village. They always require a control panel to function correctly, and those control panels are usually the source of any trouble.

The only exception would be a modem that has been hit by a phone-line surge or has failed for some other reason, perhaps a manufacturing defect or a power surge that hit the entire system. If you suspect such a possibility, you'll need to take the modem to an authorized service center.

Otherwise, you can troubleshoot an internal modem through its control panel:

✦ Quit any communications programs that may be interfering with the internal modem, including a PPP connection or an America Online session.

✦ Make sure the control panel is installed and that the modem is turned on in the control panel.

✦ Click the reset button in the control panel, if there is one.

✦ Shut the Mac all the way down, and then restart and try again to reconfigure the modem through the control panel.

✦ Zap PRAM.

If after trying any of these actions the control panel tells you the modem is working, you can move on to the section "Connection trouble." Otherwise, you should shut down the Mac and examine the card to make sure it's set correctly on the logic board. If it is, move on to troubleshooting extension conflicts, as there may be a conflict with your modem's control panel. Finally, you can try a clean install of the Mac OS, reinstall the modem software, and see if that helps.

Connection trouble

If you're getting a response from your modem (it lights up, the control panel recognizes the modem, and so on) you may still be encountering difficulty getting the modem to connect with another modem. This can be somewhat difficult to troubleshoot, because a seemingly functional modem on your end shouldn't have too much trouble dealing with other modems. Be aware, though, that two factors can affect any modem connection: phone line quality and slight incompatibilities between modems. Either of these can make a particular modem connection impossible to complete, no matter what attempts you make to fix things.

But you can try anyway. If you're having trouble getting a modem to connect, the issue is likely in software. If your modem has its own control panel, for instance, settings in that control panel may need to be tweaked to complete the connection. It's also important to realize that individual communications programs — such as America Online, a terminal emulator, or your fax modem software — can be responsible for storing modem settings as well. Unfortunately, the integration of the modem into the Mac OS hasn't been a smooth ride characterized by complete control by Apple; instead, applications have historically been responsible for dealing with modems on their own, so a few different systems have emerged.

These days, newer software have more central settings than they can deal with, and there's even a Modem control panel that's used by the Mac OS's Open Transport software to allow for PPP connections to the Internet. If you're able to use Open Transport with your Mac, you'll find that these connections are fairly simple to troubleshoot. Otherwise, you'll need to look at your communications applications individually.

Wiring and indicators

The first problems to check are the physical connections and indicator lights. If your external modem has lights glowing on the front, do they indicate that there's activity? If your modem has transmit/receive lights (labeled TX/RX or with an arrow icon) and they're blinking or lit, the modem may believe it's communicating when it's not. Reset the modem, reset the Mac, check the serial cable connection or try another cable. If these fail to turn the lights on (or if the lights are on after the modem's power has been cycled and with the modem disconnected from the Mac), suspect a hardware problem.

If the on-hook light (labeled "OH", or with a telephone or telephone poles icon) is lit, there may be a problem with the phone wiring, the serial cable, or the modem itself. Reset the modem and check the cabling. Reset the computer. If all these fail, suspect the modem.

Modem settings

If your problem doesn't involve a hardware issue, you should start looking for an option to change the settings for your modem. In most cases, you won't need to get too deep into the codes that govern a modem's setup; you'll likely be able to find a modem-configuration profile that matches the modem brand and model that you're using. If you can't find an exact duplicate, check your modem's manual — it will likely list alternatives.

Two important examples of potentially problematic modem settings come to mind: those for America Online and for Open Transport PPP. Both install on your Mac with a slew of modem configuration profiles that match particular modem models. If you're having trouble getting your modem to connect, check for one of these profiles to ensure it's properly set (see Figure 26-4).

Note

As something of an aside, if you're an AOL user and you have another Internet service provider, you can use AOL over a TCP/IP connection (instead of over a modem connection), enabling you to run other Internet applications at the same time. This will especially speed up your AOL experience if you have high-speed Internet access through an ADSL, cable, ISDN, or T-1 connection. It can also be a workaround if you can get your ISP connection to work, but your modem refused to dial out or connect directly to AOL.

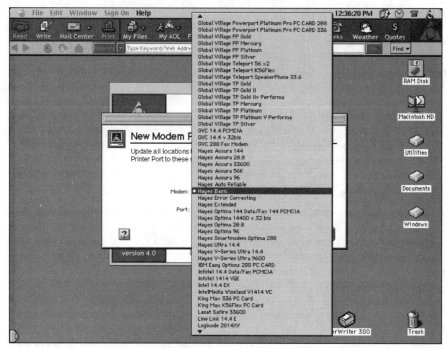

Figure 26-4: Setting modem profiles in America Online's client software.

If your modem doesn't enable you to choose a predesigned modem profile, you may need to dip into the underlying configuration language for the modem. In most cases, this language conforms to the *Hayes AT command set* standard, which is used by most modems to enable the user to manually communicate settings. If your communications program offers an option to enter a *configuration string,* it is most likely looking for a string of AT commands.

Although it might be mildly amusing to learn the AT command structure, you'll likely find the required configuration string in your modem's manual. In fact, the factory default settings for nearly all modems is a very simple string:

```
AT&F1
```

This will set the modem to the number one set of factory recommendations. You may find that your manual allows for a few different default configurations, such as AT&F2, and so on. In any case, a problem modem can often be fixed by simply entering the preceding line as your configuration string. If you need to get a bit more specialized, though, you can, as shown in the next section.

The AT command set

Although the AT command set is reasonably standard, you'll find that the command set has been altered and extended; the necessities have changed over the 15 or more years that the set has existed as a popular way to deal with modems. For the most part, though, you can hold on to a couple of truisms.

The command set is usually used to offer a command or a series of commands to the modem. Most of these are configuration settings, although a certain number of them are used to actually control the modem. (In fact, your communications program is using these commands behind the scenes.) In many instances, you'll use the command set to create a single string of commands that make up the configuration string. You'll enter this string in the modem preferences portion of your communications program.

However, these commands can also be used in a terminal application to directly control the modem. (Examples of terminal applications are zTerm, Microphone, White Knight, the communications module in ClarisWorks, and the terminal window option in your PPP dialer.) These commands begin with the letters *AT* (which puts the modem in attention mode) and end with the command, usually another series of letters. Here are some commands you might find useful (after any command, you'll hit the Return key to invoke it):

ATDT   Picks up the connection and dials the telephone using tones (usually followed by numbers, as in ATDT5551212). You could also use ATDP for pulse (rotary) dialing. Use the comma modifier (ATDT9,5551212) to introduce a pause when dialing, or a W modifier (ATDT9W5551212) to force the modem to wait for a dial tone before continuing to dial.

ATH   Hangs up the connection.

ATZ   Resets the modem or modem card.

ATA   Enters auto-answer mode.

+++   Serves as an escape sequence, enabling you to bring the modem from a communications mode into a command mode again so that AT commands will be recognized.

A typical configuration string begins with an AT command, followed by a string of other commands. Note that some commands have an ampersand (&) or percent mark (%) before them. An example of a configuration string might be as follows:

```
AT&F1M0&K4X1W2
```

In this case, the configuration string is telling the modem to initiate the first factory default settings, but turn the speaker off (M0), enable Xon/Xoff flow control (&K4), disable dial tone and busy signal detection (X1), and enable CONNECT messages based on the modem-to-modem speed. These are standard commands that might help you get a least-common-denominator connection if you're having tons of trouble getting two modems to talk — across an international long-distance phone connection, for instance. Check your modem's manual for suggestions on adding AT commands to the factory default.

Some common AT command parameters include the following (note that the x in each represents a number, usually between 0 and 4, with some exceptions depending on the number of options in each parameter):

Qx	Returns result codes (0); Doesn't return result codes (1); Returns codes when in originate mode only (2)
Vx	Returns short result codes (0); Returns long result codes (1)
Wx	Does not return negotation progress (CONNECT) messages (0); Returns progress messages that show the computer-to-modem speed (1); Returns progress messages that show the modem-to-modem speed (2)
Xx	No busy or dial tone detection (0); Returns CONNECT message, no busy or dial tone detection (1); Modem waits for dial tone, no busy detection (2); Modem detects busy tone, doesn't wait for dial tone (3); Modem gives call progress, detects busy tone, dial tone and connection speeds (4)
Mx	Disables speaker (0); Speaker on until connect (1); Speaker always on (2); Speaker on after carrier detected (3)
&Kx	Disables flow control (0); Enables RTS/CTS hardware flow control (3); Enables Xon/Xoff flow control (4)
&Qx	No error correction (0); Selects v.42 error correction (5); Selects MNP error correction (8)
&Ax	Connects as answering modem when auto-answering (0); Connects as originating modem with auto-answering (1)
&Cx	Forces modem carrier detect on at all times (0); Causes modem to track actual state of carrier detect (1); Forces carrier detect on except at disconnect (2)
&Fx	Enables Hayes compatible settings (0); Enables IBM-compatible settings (1); Enables Mac software handshake settings (2); Enables Mac hardware handshake settings (3)
Ox	Returns to online mode from command mode (0); Returns to online mode and retrain (1); Returns to online mode and negotiate the rate (2)

To a certain degree, it's up to you and your modem's manual to decipher the exact meaning of some of these commands and determine what they're going to do for you. Your manual may also have a more extensive reference and/or your modem may support many more commands than these; this is only a subset of commands that make sense *to me*. Your mileage may vary—in fact, your modem may not support every number of each of these commands, or it may offer more options for one or more of the commands.

If you have a very specialized program or modem-based task and you need help setting your modem's internals, the AT command set a good place to start.

Dial tone

Modems are designed to detect the dial tone on the line before dialing, saving you from the confusion of waiting for the modem to connect when it's actually dialing on a dead line—or, to keep you from being intrusive if you accidentally dial the modem when somebody else is talking on an extension.

This results in one common error: The modem can't find a dial tone. To test this problem, check to see if there really is a dial tone; plug a phone into the modem, if necessary, or pick up another extension on that same line. If you don't hear a dial tone, inspect your phones to make sure one of them hasn't been left off the hook. If you do hear a dial tone, it's possible that your modem needs to be reset or more drastic action needs to take place.

To reset the modem, choose the Reset command in the modem's control panel. If that doesn't work or if your modem doesn't include a control panel, simply turn the modem itself off and on again. If the modem doesn't have its own independent power switch, you may need to shut the Mac all the way down, and then start up again from the Power switch or key.

If resetting and/or restarting doesn't solve the problem, you may be having some trouble with the phone wiring that's connected to the modem or in your house. Try connecting the modem to the phone connector in your wall using a different RJ-11 phone cable. You might also try connecting the modem directly to the wall plug if you've had other devices on that same line in the past. Sending the signal through many different devices and connectors may be creating some interference for the modem.

If rearranging the devices doesn't help, you could have less-than-perfect wiring in your home, office, or neighborhood. If that's the case, the best solution is to try and turn off the requirement for a dial tone before the modem connects. This setting is often in the communications program's Preferences or Settings dialog box. For Open Transport PPP connections, the setting is in the Modem control panel (see Figure 26-5).

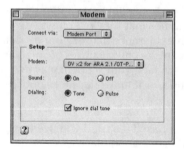

Figure 26-5: The Modem control panel has an option that forces the modem to dial without checking for a dial tone.

Note that stutter dial tones and other tone-related features that the phone company may implement can interfere with a modem's ability to recognize the dial tone. If that's the case, your only option is to turn off dial tone checking. You can do this through the modem's software or using the Xx AT command in the modem's configuration string. (See the AT command set section earlier in this chapter.)

Busy signal

Some modems will report that they've received a busy signal, even if what they're really hearing is just an odd sort of ringing sound. This can be especially true on international long-distance calls or particularly noisy phone lines. If that's the case, your only option is to dig into the AT command set and invoke the Xx command; although some programs do, most Mac modem software doesn't include a "Don't detect busy signal" option.

Manual dial/answering

If you simply can't seem to convince your modem to dial the right sequence of numbers or pause for the correct amount of time, you might consider invoking the manual dial options in your communications software — if the software allows it. For PPP connections, this can often be accomplished by opening the options for a particular dial up connection and choosing the Terminal Window option. You can then dial using the AT command ATDT, followed up by the appropriate numbers and commas for pauses.

To answer an incoming call, you can choose the Answer command in your modem software or enter ATA in a terminal window.

Other communications programs — especially fax programs — will enable you to actually dial the number using a telephone set, and then click the button in the program to finish the connection. Likewise, you'll often be able to choose a manual receive command when someone dials your computer with fax-modem software or a fax machine.

Problems during the call

Once the call is negotiated, you'll likely have a smooth connection. But be aware of a few caveats that can reset your connection or otherwise interrupt your modem sessions:

✦ **Call waiting.** If you dial out with a modem on a line that has call waiting active, you may be disconnected when the signal tone plays on the line to indicate a call. Because you can't answer the call anyway, it's recommended that you disconnect your call-waiting service when you plan to call out using the modem. Usually there's a code that the phone company provides for temporarily disconnecting this service. In many areas in the US, the code is *70. So, you can enter the dialing command: ATDT*70, *phone number* to disconnect call waiting and dial the number.

✦ **Noisy line.** If you pick up a regular handset and hear static or noise on the phone line, there's very little chance that you'll get a good data connection. You should have the line tested by the phone company and your internal phone wiring check by a professional. (If you have a long extension cord or many different adapters and couplers on the line, you might test right at the wall socket itself — even with a regular phone and a short cord — to see if it's an internal wiring issue.)

✦ **Latency, typing problems.** If your communications software is text-based, you may have trouble typing or sending data occasionally. This can sometimes be a problem or slowdown with the connection, although it may also be an issue with your OS. If you experience these same slowdowns in word processing programs, for instance, suspect a slight extensions conflict, too little RAM allocated to your applications, or a poorly maintained, fragmented hard drive.

✦ **Excessive errors.** If your communications software is slowed down because it's dealing with many errors during a file transfer, check the line for indications of noise. If the line seems okay, check your software for the proper settings for your particular modem and Mac (taking into account the flow-control settings, discussed in Chapter 16). Finally, try connecting to the other modem at a lower bps rate.

Don't forget to check your modem's manual, where you'll likely find more troubleshooting hints specific to your particular modem brand and its internal commands and characteristics.

Summary

✦ Printing problems often boil down to a few key error messages that you can troubleshoot. The printer needs to be connected properly and the Chooser needs to be configured with care, but that won't necessarily stop problems from occurring. You could have a corrupt document or preferences file causing trouble or a conflict between serial devices, drivers, and/or system software components.

✦ PostScript and desktop printing can cause their own sets of errors and problems. PostScript problems can very often be fixed with minor changes to your document or the Page Setup dialog box, or by adding RAM to your printer (or turning on additional features in your printer). Desktop printing problems tend to be corruption issues, especially if a system crash occurs while you're printing a document in the background.

✦ Printers themselves need some care, including cleanings, good supplies, and the occasional check-up from a professional. And, fonts can give you some trouble when you're trying to get your printouts to look good.

✦ Modem trouble often centers on either a configuration problem (which can get somewhat complicated, depending on the modem) or trouble with your phone lines. Many different issues can be overcome for successful modem communications, including noisy lines, weird dial tones, call-waiting and other annoyances. And you can do these things yourself — getting nearly any modem application to work correctly, to boot — with a little knowledge of the Hayes AT command set.

✦   ✦   ✦

Networking Issues

If you've already begun adding a network to your office or have been in the process of upgrading—perhaps with some help from Chapter 17—you're fully aware that networking is about snaking a lot of cable around furniture, through walls, and into the back of Macs. This can certainly be cause for headaches, even without throwing failure and misconfiguration into the mix.

You will occasionally encounter a failure in your network— whether it's a software glitch, a problem with cabling, or an issue with an Ethernet add-on. To be prepared for this, the best approach is to be organized (and, as always, to have a good backup system).

If you're lucky, most of the problems you encounter when troubleshooting a network will be due to configuration problems, such as AppleTalk not being set up properly, Ethernet cards not chosen in the appropriate control panels, and so on. However, don't rule out the possibility that the cabling could be giving you trouble (keep your receipts) or that your problem potentially lies with the hardware, such as transceivers or network interface cards.

Troubleshooting Your Network

If you're responsible for a network in a company or organization, it's probably not a bad idea to have a schematic of your network, geeky as that may sound. If you can get a copy of your building's blueprints, so much the better. Regardless, you should sketch out the offices and detail each connection. A few things are really useful to know:

✦ How long is each length of cabling?

✦ Where is the cabling? In the roof, the wall, under the carpet?

✦ In what order are the daisy-chained Macs connected?

✦ What port is each Mac wired to on your hub?

✦ How does each Mac connect to the network? Via expansion card, transceiver, built-in port, or other method?

✦ What version of AppleTalk and/or Open Transport does each Mac have?

✦ Any other special characteristics? Shared QuickDraw printers, AppleTalk zones, special privileges, any others?

You'll find that tracking your network connections and assets like this will probably be a big help, especially if you track things in pencil. You might also want to keep a log of exactly what you do whenever you're forced to add something or troubleshoot the network. In my experience, it's very easy to forget exactly how or why you did something, even if it was only a few days or weeks ago.

This level of organization will also help you combat networking voodoo, as it gives you a quick-and-easy way to check the overall length of your network cabling, account for missed connections, or know exactly what you're looking for when you examine the hub's flashing lights. Having this information at your fingertips will likely help you get the network up and running as quickly as possible after a problem hits.

Thus prepared, you can jump into the world of network troubleshooting.

Note

The different networking architectures are explained in Chapter 17. In this chapter, you'll notice that troubleshooting the hardware in a LocalTalk and a 10Base2 Ethernet network are similar, because both chain computers together to create a bus topology, or a long network all continuing a single data line. Their hardware, software, and performance characteristics are completely different, though, so their troubleshooting isn't always similar.

Can't connect a Mac

If you're having trouble getting a single Mac connected to your network, you should check the hardware first, and then suspect the software. In most of these cases, it's an issue of misconfiguration. Occasionally, hardware is to blame. Your first step will be to check the hardware connections and make sure the network is laid out and connected properly. You can then test the software side. If you get error messages, chase those down to their software or hardware origins and act accordingly.

Evangelista tip: The right mindset

As I've said, some of troubleshooting is more about the process — how you go about identifying the problem — than it is knowing a bunch of facts about Macs. Your first step is to try some basic first aid troubleshooting techniques to figure out the problem. Then you can jump into the reference books and Web sites to learn about known fixes. I think system administrator Mike Kent agrees, judging by this tip:

"Recently one of my users had a really weird problem. On bootup, his Mac attempted to log into another Mac, and it crashed whether the operation was canceled or the password was entered and OK clicked. It booted okay if extensions were disabled, but then there was no access to the network volume or anything else.

"His Mac didn't have the capacity or the correct copy of Open Transport to handle the log in, apparently, so enabling only a basic set of networking extensions in Extensions Manager got us to the desktop, where the remote volume could be accessed in the Chooser and his choice to automatically log onto the remote Mac could be undone. I run into lots of stuff like this, and it's mainly a matter of figuring out how to attack the problem."

Check hardware

You'll begin by checking the connections at your problematic Mac and, in some cases, elsewhere on your network:

1. Check the connection between the Mac and the transceiver. Make sure it's completely and securely connected.

2. Check the cabling at the transceiver. If this is a LocalTalk or 10Base2 connection, make sure the incoming cable connector is coming from the previous computer in your daisy chain and the outgoing connector is the right cable for the subsequent computer. It's possible to loop the connection back on itself and accidentally end the network improperly or prematurely.

3. Check the connections to other computers (on a LocalTalk/10Base2 network) or to the hub (on a 10BaseT network). You might try a different port on the hub if you suspect the current port might be faulty.

4. On a LocalTalk/10Base2 network, check for proper termination at this Mac or at the end of the network chain — wherever is appropriate. If the network isn't terminated, you may have trouble getting this Mac and/or others to connect.

You may have other hardware troubles, such as bad transceivers, cabling, or connectors, but this is tough to know without thoroughly troubleshooting the software on your Mac.

Check software

The first thing you need to check before troubleshooting the software connections is to make sure all the appropriate Mac networking software has been loaded at startup. A series of extensions and control panels are necessary for the Mac to successfully find and work with a network; you'll need all the software loaded before your Mac can get connected.

Assuming you're using Mac OS 7.6 or higher, the software you need loaded includes the following:

✦ AppleShare extension

✦ AppleTalk control panel (it's the Network control panel in earlier Mac OS versions)

✦ Ethernet (built-in) extension

✦ Open Transport libraries (Open Transport library, AppleTalk library, Internet library, OpenTptAppleTalkLib, OpenTptInternetLib, OpenTransportLib)

✦ Shared Library Manager (and Shared Library Manager PPC for Power Macs)

✦ File Sharing control panel, File Sharing extension, File Sharing library (for peer-to-peer networks)

✦ Printer Share (for sharing non-PostScript printers)

To begin troubleshooting, open the AppleTalk control panel (assuming you plan to use AppleTalk). Choose the appropriate networking interface—LocalTalk or Ethernet. (If you have two Ethernet listings, choose the Ethernet built-in option if you're using your Mac's original Ethernet connection or choose the Ethernet slot option if you're using an Ethernet expansion card.) If you receive an error at this point, follow these steps:

1. Try restarting and choose again.

2. If this doesn't work, open the Extension Manager and make sure you're loading the appropriate drivers for your network interface or card. The Ethernet (built-in) extension is required for Ethernet on most Macs. You should also ensure other networking extensions are present. Restart and choose again.

3. If you have no luck, open the Extension Manager and choose Mac OS All from the pull-down menu of extension sets. Restart and try to choose the network.

4. If you still can't select a network architecture, suspect a hardware problem and move on to the next section.

5. If you can select your networking hardware in the AppleTalk control panel, move on to the Chooser. Open the Chooser and turn on AppleTalk in the lower-right corner.

If you've gotten this far, you've probably solved the problem. Go ahead and log in to other computers or servers using the AppleShare icon in the Chooser.

Check hardware again

If you can't get the AppleTalk control panel to choose the hardware you'd like to use for networking, and you're completely sure the Mac is loading all the correct extensions, it's possible there's either a cabling problem or a hardware problem.

If you're receiving an actual error message about 5 to 10 seconds after trying to switch to Ethernet — "Could not switch to EtherTalk," "An error occurred when attempting to switch", or something similar — there's a good chance something is wrong with your Ethernet network. The seconds-long delay is a result of the Mac OS polling the Ethernet hardware to learn what sort of network is connected and what networking zones are available. When the Mac OS returns the error message, it means the Mac was unable to locate a network.

Here are some possible solutions:

✦ You need to activate AppleTalk in the Chooser.

✦ There's a problem with the cabling, ports, or transceivers on your Macs and/or hub connections.

✦ There may be a problem with the System file. See Chapter 33 for information on performing a System file reinstall.

✦ You may have an incompatible third-party hard disk driver.

✦ Your Ethernet card has a hardware setting that directs Ethernet data to the 10BaseT port, but you're using the 10Base2 port (or something similar). If your card has more than one interface, check its documentation.

If AppleTalk is active and your wiring seems in order, try zapping PRAM to free up the option and enable you to choose the Ethernet solution. Disconnect and then reconnect the transceiver or network cable from the computer.

If these approaches don't work, the delayed error message may be the result of a problem with the Ethernet hardware itself (either the expansion card or Ethernet circuitry in your Mac). Take the card or Mac to a service center.

If the error message is immediate, the problem is likely with the Mac OS extensions that govern that hardware. Try a clean install of the Mac OS and/or a clean installation of the drivers for your expansion card. If you're using built-in Ethernet, try starting up with only Mac extensions to see if there's a conflict with another extension or driver. (Chapter 32 covers extension troubleshooting.)

Note

Just so you know it's okay to give up, here's a true statement: Ethernet ports can just go bad. During the writing of this book, the built-in Ethernet port on my main Mac went dead for a reason that remains inexplicable. I was sitting at the machine when the port stopped working, and nothing else odd was going on. My solution: I installed a new (faster, more exciting) Ethernet card, and things are working great.

If the AppleTalk control panel allows you to select hardware without popping up an error message, but nothing else changes in the control panel, this may not be indicative of a problem. Instead, it's just telling you you're connected to a network that has no AppleTalk zones. Or, if the connection is a LocalTalk connection, you might not be connected to a network at all; LocalTalk connections don't have to be active for your Mac to be happy. If you think you're supposed to be seeing zones, it's possible that something is wrong with the cabling at your Mac or that another driver is interfering with your use of the printer port. Try turning off any serial-port control panels or applications that use the serial ports, and then restart if the problem persists. Otherwise, check your cabling carefully and make sure there's really a network for you to connect to.

If the problem is you can't select AppleTalk in the Chooser, this also suggests that the port is currently being controlled by another program or driver. Clear the port and try again. You can also restart and zap PRAM to clear the port, and then try again to choose your networking hardware in the AppleTalk control panel.

The network is down

When the network goes down (that is, when most or all of the network becomes unavailable to your users) the important question to ask is what networking architecture is being used? If you're using LocalTalk or 10Base2 Ethernet, a physical break in the chain of network connections can cause all or part of the network to become unavailable. If you're using 10BaseT hardware, you should start troubleshooting by taking a look at the Ethernet hub or switch you're using.

Note that in this section I'm talking about networks that have been working but suddenly stop working (or partially stop working) for some reason. If you've never gotten a particular Mac to work on the network, consult the previous section, "Can't connect a Mac."

LocalTalk and 10Base2

These daisy-chain-style networks aren't much fun to troubleshoot in the case of a downed network. To test for a break in the network, you'll likely need to walk from workstation to workstation, checking behind each to make sure the wiring for the network is still intact. A single bad cable, transceiver, or connection can keep an entire daisy-chained network from working correctly. You may spend a bit of time tracking down breaks. (In some cases you'll notice that a number of Macs downstream from a problem may be affected, while Macs upstream can still complete a network connection, or similar circumstances. If something like that is happening, look at the Macs toward the middle that may be causing the break.)

In general, the network should continue to function even if something is wrong with one of the Macs in that network. A configuration problem, an issue with AppleTalk, or even a Mac that's been shut down generally won't affect the network. What you're looking for are physical breaks or damage to the network.

Here's how to find them:

1. Check each networking transceiver to ensure that both the incoming and outgoing connectors are plugged in. Check the quality of the connections and make sure the connectors are secure and unbroken.

2. Note whether each transceiver is properly connected to its port on the back of the Mac. (For Ethernet that's the AAUI port, and for LocalTalk that's the printer port. Check that the transceiver is connected to the printer port, not the modem port or others).

3. Check for proper termination wherever it's necessary (usually at each end of the entire network, unless the network is terminated at a bridge or hub).

4. Check each length of networking cable for breaks, tears, crimps, or anything else that suggests damage.

Most of the time you'll find that the network suddenly goes down because a poorly placed cable gets kicked under the table or a computer is disconnected and/or moved without sufficient forethought. It's perfectly all right to move Macs and printers around on the network, but you'll need to make sure doing so doesn't create a permanent break in the cabling. It's a good idea to do networking rearranging after hours, because disconnecting daisy-chained cable causes interruptions for the entire network.

But there's another time you may find that the network won't come back up — after you've worked on it. If you've recently added machines and things are working well, check the following:

✦ Ensure proper connections and proper termination.

✦ It may sound crazy, but make sure every computer's cabling and transceivers are plugged in, and in the right order. You could accidentally have an extra length of cable or two that starts at one Mac's network connection but goes nowhere. (I've seen it happen. All that cable can get confusing.)

✦ Check your cable lengths and the number of nodes on the network, as discussed in Chapter 17. LocalTalk is limited to 32 devices and 1,800 feet of cabling; PhoneNet lowers that number to 24 devices. 10Base2 can only handle about 600 feet in total cable length.

✦ If you can, test your new transceivers to see if they're the problem. The best way to do this is to create a small network of two nodes, and then test each transceiver along with one you know works properly. That way, you can test all your transceivers quickly by swapping them into your mini-network.

10BaseT

In the case of a 10BaseT network, the entire network being down is an easy problem to troubleshoot — there's something wrong with your hub. In such a network, problems on one Mac don't create problems for the entire network, at least not from a hardware point of view. If a server crashes or a particularly popular Mac that's running file sharing shuts down, it can affect everyone on the network. But that's not a hardware problem.

Ethernet hubs aren't terribly friendly for troubleshooting. Depending on how complicated they are, they usually work or they don't work. You can try flipping t he hub's power switch and moving connections around to see if a particular port has gone bad, but there's not much else you can do but have the hub serviced. (Check your hub or switches manual for diagnostic capabilities that may be built into the hub.)

Note   At the time of writing, a few Ethernet problems had been identified with the Power Macintosh G3 series, including issues that were resolved with the Mac OS 8.1 release. If you are having trouble with 10BaseT Ethernet connections on a Power Macintosh G3 machine (including trouble with auto-sensing hubs, problems with built-in Ethernet causing crashes, and other issues), upgrade to the latest OS version by visiting Apple's support site (www.apple.com/support) for information on downloading an update.

Software Issues

Your Mac network is likely using one or more of three different networking protocols: AppleTalk, TCP/IP, or MacIPX, the Novell NetWare standard. You may also be connecting to a Windows NT network using either AppleTalk (which NT can support in a limited way) or DAVE, an add-on client from Thursby software.

Software configuration is the key to most networking problems; in fact, network management is the arcana of the computing industry that, in many cases, results in thousands of dollars being spent to train individuals who make very healthy salaries keeping corporate and organizational networks up and running. Although the Mac isn't as difficult to run as all that, it certainly offers its share of networking problems.

This section covers Open Transport and its support for AppleTalk and TCP/IP. If you have a Mac and/or a version of the Mac OS that doesn't support Open Transport, the advice in the AppleTalk and TCP/IP sections should still apply, for the most part. The difference is in the names of the control panel more than anything else. The AppleTalk control panel is handled by the Network control panel in older versions; File Sharing is Sharing Setup in previous Mac OSes; and TCP/IP is MacTCP in earlier implementations.

Evangelista tip: Novell and NT

Having trouble with your Mac's connection to a Novell or NT network? You probably already know the basics: To connect to a Novell NetWare network, you need the MacIPX software. If you've already got it (it should come with the NetWare distribution), you'll want to look into updating it (see Chapter 17 and `www.novell.com/` for more info). If you need to hook up to an NT network, NT does offer AppleTalk services; however, the experts currently recommend using Thursby Software's DAVE client software, which is also discussed in Chapter 17.

If you're using NT for AppleTalk services, you may encounter an interesting problem called the *dancing icon syndrome*. This can happen with AppleTalk servers on non-Mac platforms, such as Linux, Windows NT, and Novell NetWare. (The problem may be limited to Mac OS 8.1.) When the server volume is mounted on the Mac client, file icons in the server window move around, making regular Finder tasks tough. The official Windows NT software fixes should be available on the Microsoft Web site or via Microsoft's helpline phone support.

For Novell-bound Mac users, Evangelista Yuval Kossovsky has this advice:

"There is a Mac IPX client for NuBus machines and one for PCI-based Macs. 'CLT 511' is the Novell IPX client for PCI machines. There is also a special update for Mac OS 8.

"Here's a quick connection tip: When the IPX client cannot find the server or NDS tree and the frame type is correct, change the frame type to an incorrect one and then change it back. This usually resets the connection. Also, to make a Mac mount a Novell volume at bootup, make an alias of the volume and put it in the Startup Items folder."

Try `http://support.novell.com/products` on the Web for this update and future updates, including Mac client software.

Open Transport

On the newest macs, and any Mac using Mac OS 7.6 or above, Open Transport is the underlying networking technology. But who cares? If you'll be using a network or the Internet, the Open Transport libraries need to be in your System Folder. And, "Open Transport" is what Apple usually calls updates to the Mac's networking that are posted on the Apple Web site periodically for downloading. (The installers are also included with new Mac OS released.) Otherwise, the name Open Transport isn't really all that important.

What's important is the distinction between Open Transport and so-called classic networking. Open Transport introduced the new, more efficient control panels — AppleTalk, File Sharing, Modem, TCP/IP, PPP — to replace the classic networking approach, which was a hodge-podge of networking solutions. Open Tranport provides one unified layer of networking, on top of which different protocols — such as AppleTalk and TCP/IP — can be used to communicate with the outside world.

In the early updates to Open Transport, a lot of work was being done to bring it up to speed, get it compatible with nearly all Mac programs, and get it to work on most Macs. For the most part, that effort has been successful, and you'll not come across too many hassles with Open Transport in later releases. In fact, it's reliable enough that Mac OS versions beyond Mac OS 7.6 don't support classic networking anymore.

Here are a few of the lingering issues:

✦ Computers running the Apple IP Gateway and AppleTalk Internet Router shouldn't be upgraded to Open Transport. Stick with classic networking (which also means sticking with an OS prior to Mac OS 7.6).

✦ Use the most recent version of PPP dialer software and AOL that you can get your hands on. Check the Open Transport Read Me file for more information.

✦ Power Macintosh and Performa 5200/5300/6200/6300 models can have a hardware problem that keeps them from using Open Transport successfully. The Mac OS 8 or higher installation will test for this problem, as will the 5xxx/6xxx Tester program available from Apple's Support Web site.

In general, some aging Mac programs that implemented special networking features — or otherwise "hacked" into MacTCP or AppleTalk in a way not recommended by Apple — may not work correctly with Open Transport. If you're using an older version of Open Transport, it's certainly recommended that you upgrade to a newer version of OT, a newer Mac OS, or both. You may experience many other problems; check the Read Me file that came with your version of Open Transport for details.

AppleTalk

As mentioned in the section "Can't connect a Mac," one of the main issues in troubleshooting AppleTalk is making sure all the appropriate extensions are loaded. In Mac OS 7.6 and above, those extensions changed somewhat in name (and function, in some cases) from their previous incarnations, with control panels such as Network and extensions such as EtherTalk giving way to AppleTalk and Ethernet (built-in) — names and functions that follow a bit more logically.

These more recent controls for your network give you backward compatibility (you can still hook up a machine that's running an older OS version) and a few extra capabilities. Troubleshooting and getting your network to work properly requires that these extensions and control panels work in concert toward the end goal of enabling your Mac to communicate with other computers. Take a look at how this works and what you can do to test and troubleshoot when the system fails.

Note   Are you missing any important icons? If you can't find the AppleShare icon, AppleTalk control panel, or the File Sharing options, this is a sure sign you don't have all the appropriate extensions loaded. Head back to the "Can't connect a Mac" section and make sure you've got all the right software in your System Folder. This is one of the most common causes of networking problems, especially when you first start putting together the network.

How it should work

One of the keys to getting an AppleTalk-based network to work is — surprise! — choosing the hardware that AppleTalk is going to use. You do that by heading to the AppleTalk control panel:

1. When you first open the control panel, you may be warned that AppleTalk isn't active and that it should be initialized when you close the AppleTalk control panel. If that sounds like a good idea (and it probably is) click Yes. The AppleTalk control panel will then appear.

2. In the control panel, choose the hardware you'll be using for your AppleTalk network. If it's Ethernet hardware, choose the entry for the particular circuitry you'll be using. Regular Ethernet or Ethernet (built-in) suggests the port that's built into most non-Performa Macs. If you have an entry that says Ethernet slot *xx* (where *xx* is a two-letter address), this indicates an Ethernet expansion card. Select it if that's what's wired to the network.

3. At this point you should also choose the correct zone for this Mac if you can. Zones are set up using network-administration software and server software; however, even if you use file sharing, you need to choose a particular zone that will serve as the home for your Mac. (If you just have a couple Macs in your own office, you probably don't have any zones to choose from.) Now you can close the control panel.

4. In the Chooser, find the AppleTalk selector; it should already be turned on. To set up a network connection, click on the AppleShare icon. Choose the correct zone if you're given the option. Now you should be able to choose a server (or a Mac on the network that's running file sharing) and log in to it using a name and password.

That's the ideal scenario. You've already looked at what to do if you can't select the network topology you want to work with — that's what the entire first part of this chapter is about. And if you can't manage to select AppleTalk in the Chooser, that also is covered in the section "Can't connect a Mac." But what if you're having trouble with file sharing itself? Or what if you need to know more about your AppleTalk connection? Then, you need to dig a bit deeper.

Note
Interested in knowing more about your AppleTalk connection? For more advanced users and administrators, the AppleTalk control panel offers additional information and options (especially useful if you need to know some specific addressing issues regarding your network adapter). Choose Edit ⟿ User Mode from the menu, and then choose Advanced for a more complicated AppleTalk control panel. You can choose Administration to set a password and lock the AppleTalk settings—usually a good idea in a shared lab environment.

File sharing won't work

The basics of file sharing are discussed in Chapter 17, which, among other things, shows you how to get up and running on a peer-to-peer network of Macs. But if you're having trouble getting file sharing to start up, you might feel stuck in the mud. The symptom: You're clicking the Start button in the File Sharing control panel and it won't start up — you either get an error message that says "File sharing could not be enabled" or it just never stops trying to start up.

If you have all the proper extensions loaded and AppleTalk is active, receiving this message suggests a software problem — specifically, a problem with corruption. You'll need to dig into your Preferences folder to find the solution.

Note
This is probably a good time to mention that it never hurts to back up the Users and Groups preferences file or the File Sharing folder in the Preferences folder. If you are forced to delete any of these files, replacing them from a clean backup is much easier than rebuilding them from scratch.

Here are some things to try:

✦ *Delete the User and Groups preferences file in the Preferences folder located in the System Folder.* (You can also just drag it to the desktop as a preliminary measure.) Try to start up file sharing again.

✦ *Drag the File Sharing folder from the Preferences folder to the desktop.* Try file sharing again. If it works this time, you can throw away the folder.

✦ *Delete AppleShare PDS.* This invisible file is in the main directory of your hard drive, and it's likely corrupted if you're having trouble getting file sharing to start and you've already tried the other two files. Unfortunately, you'll need to make the file visible first, and then delete it. (See the sidebar "ResEdit: Making invisible files visible.") Once you've done that, you can try starting up file sharing again.

✦ *Check for extension conflicts.* You may be having a conflict between the File Sharing extension and other extensions in your system. Try restarting your Mac with the Mac OS All extensions option selected. If file sharing now works, you've got a conflict with a non-Mac OS extension. Check Chapter 32 for troubleshooting tips.

✦ *Run Disk First Aid.* A bad block or other trouble with the desktop database can hinder file sharing. You should also rebuild the Desktop file.

✦ *Zap PRAM.* You may want to delete all these files, then immediately restart and Zap PRAM. Check your AppleTalk settings in the AppleTalk control panel, then start up file sharing again. It should work this time.

You should also make sure you have some free RAM and hard-drive space — file sharing needs a bit of both (about 800K of RAM and 1MB of hard drive space) to start up properly.

Note

Apple's Tech Info Library also recommends that you reinstall the networking software and/or the Mac OS if you're experiencing problems that can't seem to be fixed or after having used a third-party file sharing program.

File sharing security

Although file sharing security isn't strictly troubleshooting, I would like to mention it quickly — after all, trouble may crop up because you're not being careful enough when securing your Macs.

ResEdit: Making invisible files visible

You need to be fairly comfortable with your Mac skills before you use ResEdit, which is a low-level Macintosh programming tool designed to mess files up beyond recognition. (At least, that's what the program does in the wrong hands.) In the right hands, you can quickly use it to find and de-cloak that pesky AppleShare PDS file.

Find ResEdit online, in Apple's FTP directories (www.apple.com/support/) Start ResEdit. Close the File window that opens and select File ⇨ Get File/Folder Info. Now, find the AppleShare PDS file on the main level of your Mac's startup hard drive. Highlight AppleShare PDS and click Get Info.

This brings up a dialog box that tells you a lot of interesting stuff about Mac files, but it lets you change some of that stuff, too. Notice toward the bottom of the window that this file has a check next to the word Invisible; click once to uncheck that option. Click the close box on the window. When asked if you want to save info before closing, choose Yes.

Now the file should be visible. Quit ResEdit, and then head over to your Mac's hard drive. Open it and find the AppleShare PDS file. Drag it to the Trash and begin testing file sharing again.

The bottom line to security is this: Be careful with your Sharing permissions, especially if your LAN also has an Internet connection. (Permissions are set in the Sharing control panel, and they determine what capabilities are granted to certain users or groups of users. For instance, you can decide whether or not a user has the authority to save files in a particular folder, or if that user is only allowed to read files in the folder.) It's best to make a habit of setting the permissions so that every person you want to have access to your Mac has to provide a password and have an account, and gets access only to specific parts of your drive. Even a well-meaning visitor can trash an important document or application. Don't give them the opportunity.

On the CD-ROM

If you're a system administrator, you can check the status of your Mac LAN's security using a shareware program, found on the included CD-ROM, called Network Security Guard from MR Mac (www.mrmac.com/). The program will check your connected Macs and generate reports on Macs that have file sharing enabled, those that allow guest access, those that have the user name as password (or other obvious passwords that you can tell it to search for), and similar reports. This is invaluable information if you're trying to manage a larger group of Macs and need to (kindly) suggest to users that they maintain security on the network.

So how do you set permissions? By using the Sharing command. Choose a hard drive on which to impose a permissions lockout, and then choose File ➪ Sharing from that Mac's menu bar. In the resulting dialog box, you can choose which users or groups you want to give permissions to and which permissions they get — read, write, both, or none. If you have more than one user who needs a special permission set, that's when you'll head to Users and Groups on this Mac and create a new group. Note that you can then either copy those permissions to all enclosed folders or you can go to each individual folder and set permissions.

It's important, as the system administrator or "Mac person" in your office, that you avoid allowing people to log in as guests and with simple passwords. Mac networks can be very secure, in theory, even on the Internet with a firewall — as long as users are vigilant about that security. If you have a smaller office where you can gather everyone together and chat about things, you might mention this, and train them to keep their Macs secure.

Obviously, the best security comes — especially in larger offices — from using only an AppleShare (or NetWare/Windows NT) server solution for connectivity instead of allowing the Macs to access file sharing. File sharing is really about empowering individual Macs to control their own security and networking; in a larger office, though, that isn't necessarily practical or wise. It's better to run a server computer and control how *everyone* logs in and accesses shared resources.

In fact, you can disable file sharing on your workgroup's Macs, if necessary, by unchecking the File Sharing control panel, File Sharing extension, and File Sharing shared library in the Mac's Extensions Manager or otherwise moving the File Sharing system files to their respective Extensions (Disabled) and Control Panels (Disabled) folders in the System Folder. This will keep any users from turning on file sharing and compromising the security of their network (or, at least, their Macs) to outsiders.

By the way, while you're taking inventory of the file sharing settings on your networked Macs, it's a good idea to take a look at the Web Sharing control panel as well. If your network is hooked up to the Internet, it's possible that your Mac users are broadcasting a special Web directory (called Web Pages) to anyone with a Web browser. This might not be a problem, unless they've set weird permissions for the folder or the folder holds your top secret plans for a better mousetrap. In any case, check for security holes and disable the control panel if it makes you uncomfortable.

Do you administer a network of file sharing Macs? It's a good idea to update a single machine's Users and Groups (in the preferences folder) whenever you add a new user, and then distribute that data file to each Mac on the network. (This keeps things nice and uniform.) You should also back up that master Users and Groups data file so you can restore any Mac's corrupt Users and Groups data without being forced to enter the data manually.

Sharing trouble

Once you get file sharing up and running, you could still run into the occasional snag. A couple of these are well known:

✦ *Crashing.* Corruption in a preferences file or an extensions conflict. Start up with Mac OS All extensions enabled and try to reproduce the file sharing crash. If you can't, troubleshoot for an extensions conflict. If you can get the Mac to crash, try deleting the preferences files as outlined in the previous section.

✦ *Can't unmount a volume.* Often with removable media, you'll get a message that says you can't eject the cartridge of a disk because it's being shared; file sharing has gotten confused and believes the media is in use. (This was supposedly fixed in Mac OS 7.5.1.) If the media really isn't in use (ask around among your networked friends or colleagues), you can disable file sharing, eject the disk, and re-enable file sharing. In Mac OS 7.5 and earlier, you may find that restarting the Mac is the only way to get the disk ejected.

✦ *Can't see the whole remote disk.* File sharing (through Mac OS version 8.1) is limited to sharing 4GB volumes. To see an entire volume of over 4GB across the network, you should partition the drive into chunks of 4GB or smaller.

✦ *Can't log onto a file sharing Mac.* Make sure file sharing is enabled on the Mac. If you can access the Mac but it won't accept your user ID, make sure that Mac has included you as part of its Users and Groups entries. (If you've had to troubleshoot by deleting preference files, you may need to reconstruct the Users and Groups profiles.) If you do exist in the Users and Groups data and everything else seems to work, that Users and Groups file may be corrupt. Drag it to the desktop, restart file sharing on that Mac, and create another user profile. If you can log in, you'll need to delete the Users and Groups data file and redefine them for that Mac.

TCP/IP

Problems with TCP/IP itself are pretty rare; you'll have more trouble with your PPP dialer if you're using one to connect to the Internet. For the most part, PPP problems are simply modem problems, so you should consult Chapter 26 for hints on getting connected to your ISP.

The TCP/IP control panel doesn't cause too much trouble, as long as all your Open Transport networking extensions are in place and you've got your TCP/IP addresses and settings entered correctly. You should get these numbers directly from your network administrator or ISP; make sure you enter them exactly as they're supposed to be entered. Easily the most common TCP/IP problem is a transposed IP address.

The other big problem with TCP/IP is its ability to load and unload on demand — this usually works, but not always. If your Mac signs itself on at times (or can't seem to sign on at all other times), this option may be to blame. To change it, you'll need to dig into the TCP/IP control panel:

1. With the TCP/IP control panel open, choose Edit ⇨ User Mode from the menu bar.
2. Choose Advanced and click OK.
3. Click the Option button that now appears in the TCP/IP control panel.
4. In the TCP/IP Options dialog box, change the way that TCP/IP will now load.

Depending on how your user settings are set, you may already see the Options button in the TCP/IP control panel; in that case, you just need to worry about steps 3 and 4.

Here are some problem symptoms and potential cures:

✦ *Internet connection not working.* This problem is often more specific (as with the other bullets in this section), so if you're having trouble with your TCP/IP connection, you should narrow it down a bit first. If the PPP connection was successful, the problem is probably with the TCP/IP control panel. Can you do *anything* on the Internet? Can you check your e-mail or get Usenet newgroups? If you can do that but can't surf the Web, your problem is probably with the DNS server entries. If you can surf the Web but can't get e-mail, you may have set up your e-mail server and/or news server settings incorrectly in the Internet Config or Internet Setup Assistant.

✦ *TCP/IP not loading.* If you're using an older Internet program, and it's the first Internet program you've run, it's possible that TCP/IP is not loading on demand. To get around this problem, choose the Options button in the TCP/IP control panel and uncheck the option Load only when needed. You should also check the Options window to make sure TCP/IP is set to Active.

✦ *DNS can't be found.* A Web browser will report it can't find the domain name server (and, thus, figure out how to find a Web site) for one of two reasons: either the Mac isn't connected to the Internet or the DNS addresses are wrong. (The DNS computers could also be down, so call your ISP if trouble persists.) If your PPP connection seems to be working, or if your hub is flashing its lights in response to a solid Internet connection, the problem is most likely with the IP addresses you've entered in the TCP/IP control panel for your DNS computers. Check them again and correct them.

✦ *Can't get e-mail and/or Usenet news.* You need to set the correct e-mail and news server addresses in Internet Config or the Internet Setup Assistant. Be aware that not all mail and news programs use the Internet Config settings, so you may have to individually set the addresses in your e-mail and/or news programs (see Figure 27-1).

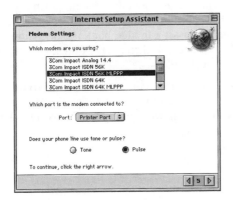

Figure 27-1: You can run the Internet Setup Assistant at any time to change the default mail and news servers for your Mac.

✦ *Internet connection dials itself.* You may find that your PPP dialer will attempt to log onto the Internet as the Mac starts up or during the time that the Mac is running, even if an Internet application is running. (If a Web browser or e-mail program *is* running, suspect it first; look for a self-refreshing Web page or a scheduled e-mail check.) In this case, go to the TCP/IP Options window and check the option Load only when needed. TCP/IP may be trying to constantly maintain an Internet connection. (This problem can also be attributed to older versions of MacPPP and FreePPP, two popular Internet dialers. For some reason, these earlier versions had a bug that caused them to dial out for no reason every few hours. If you suspect your PPP dialer, upgrade it.)

Loading TCP/IP only when needed is a good idea if you use a dial-up connection or you have very little RAM in your system, but it should generally be kept on for direct (Ethernet-based) connections to the Internet. TCP/IP may also need to be on all the time if you use a special bridge or other device to get Internet access for your local area network.

Summary

✦ Troubleshooting a network requires a close look at the hardware and cabling, followed by software troubleshooting, and then an even closer look at the hardware. Many networking problems are due to a bad wire or a bad connection, with AppleTalk and Chooser problems a close second. Only after exhausting these options should you even wonder if there might be something wrong with your networking ports.

✦ 10Base2 and LocalTalk networks often go down for very little reason: Because every computer connection is required to keep the network running happily, any problems with the wiring or transceivers on any of the machines can bring the network crashing down. In these cases, it pays to be organized. 10BaseT networks are easier; if they go down, blame it on the hub.

✦ Open Transport and AppleTalk have their own little incompatibilities, but for the most part the trouble is in configuration. AppleTalk especially can be confusing, and—if it gets used a lot—it can kick back the occasional error. Many AppleTalk problems can be attributed to corrupt files. Fortunately, most of these problems are also easy to fix.

✦ TCP/IP shouldn't give you much trouble except that you need to be meticulous when entering IP addresses and other values. Get those right and only one or two potential problems will pop up to give you Internet headaches.

✦   ✦   ✦

Gaming, Multimedia, and DOS Issues

I t's no fun to spend hard-earned money and a little elbow grease installing a state-of-the-art video card, only to be less than overwhelmed by the speed increase you witness. There can be a couple of reasons a video accelerator might fail to speed things up, and most of them are configuration issues that can be easily solved.

Speaking of configuration, getting game controllers — such as high-end joysticks and gamepads — to work correctly can be a study in arcana. If there's anywhere the Mac has let users down in the past, it's here, with the ADB port being used as a poor excuse for a gaming port. Fortunately, that's changing. You'll just need to make sure you have the latest drivers and software.

On the DOS emulation front, you've probably got two concerns: running Windows in its full splendor, and bleeding every last ounce of performance out of your emulation solution. Now, I'm sure not going to help you troubleshoot Windows; plenty of books *much* bigger than this one are devoted to that task. But you will explore, in this chapter, some possible solutions for an emulator that's giving you a little grief or a Windows solution that could use just a bit more power.

3D and Acceleration

You buy the card, get it home, follow all the instructions in Chapter 18, and you perform, in your own humble estimation, a fabulous job of it. Then you fire up your Mac and nothing spectacular seems to happen. There's two possible reasons for this:

✦ *Nothing spectacular is supposed to happen.* This is especially true if the card you've bought is an add-on 3D card. Voodoo cards and some QuickDraw 3D RAVE accelerators only kick in when they're being used with a program — often a game or multimedia title — designed to be accelerated. In general, you'll get regular performance with these cards with other programs.

✦ *The configuration is wrong.* For successful 3D acceleration, the card's software components and extensions should be loaded and running with the Mac OS. In addition, you need an application or title that's designed to be accelerated in the first place. If you're working with the latter, then the former may be causing your problems; you need to install and use the correct extensions for your 3D hardware.

Unless you encounter a vendor-specific defect, you're unlikely to have many problems beyond configuration. However, you need to have all the necessary components present for the card to work, and you need the card to be properly installed. Here are some steps for fixing problems with your 3-D card:

1. If you suspect you're having 3D problems, you can isolate those problems and get to the root of the issue by first determining which 3D technology you're trying to use.

2. Move on to the software specific to that 3D technology. Both QuickDraw 3D and 3Dfx Voodoo technologies require specific system extensions. Your card may also require special drivers.

3. If neither of those get the card to kick in, suspect a conflict between those extensions or a problem with the application you're trying to use.

4. Finally, if troubleshooting the extensions or application doesn't solve your problem, you can suspect that it's a hardware issue.

One way to solve 3D acceleration problems is to rerun the installation program that came with the card. This should install any drivers for the card that are missing and may be necessary to configure the card. The one thing to watch out for, though, is the installation's propensity to overwrite upgrades to your Mac OS; don't let it overwrite QuickDraw 3D, QuickTime, or similar technologies if you know that your current versions of those extensions are newer.

If your Mac OS extensions are newer than the 3-D card's versions, you might want to consult the accelerator card manufacturer's Web site to see if it has released an update to the installer. The company may also have specific recommendations regarding the product's interaction with your newer release of Mac technology or the Mac OS. Often a manufacturer will upgrade its installation when a new version of the QuickDraw 3D technology is made available by Apple, and you can download that upgrade (or read about the work-around) from the manufacturer's Web site.

QuickDraw 3D

Because QuickDraw 3D is written by Apple and supported from within the Mac OS, it's very well integrated for a number of tasks. For instance, you can accelerate QuickDraw 3D graphics within a window; with Voodoo 3D, you have to be viewing the acceleration full screen, one of the main reasons that Voodoo acceleration is pretty much limited to the arena of games.

But with that integration comes a certain amount of confusion. Sometimes it's tough to tell exactly which extensions you need to have active for 3-D acceleration to work. Remember, QuickDraw 3D is the required technology for creating the 3D objects and manipulating them in the Mac OS — QuickDraw 3D *RAVE* is the acceleration technology that makes the 3D graphics render more quickly. So, you need both technologies present to get QuickDraw 3D–accelerated graphics cards and applications to work together correctly.

Loading trouble

To begin, check to make sure all the required QuickDraw 3D extensions appear in the Extensions folder on your Mac (or that they're checked to load in the Extensions Manager). Those extensions are as follows:

✦ QuickDraw 3D

✦ QuickDraw 3D IR

✦ QuickDraw 3D RAVE

✦ QuickDraw 3D Viewer

If you get a message that says "QuickDraw 3D could not be found," that's a good indication you're missing one or more of the preceding extensions. If they are present (and the Mac has been restarted), it's possible that you're receiving the message because you're running low on application memory. Try closing other applications and restarting the Mac, and then run the QuickDraw-enabled application again (with no other applications loaded).

If you still have trouble, you may simply not have enough RAM to run QuickDraw 3D and the application. If you feel you have plenty of RAM, increase the problem application's allocated RAM slightly (select the application's icon and choose File ⇨ Get Info). If all else fails, try a clean install of the Mac OS in case the extensions (or some other aspect of the Mac OS) have become corrupted.

Note These days, QuickDraw 3D is generally installed along with the QuickTime distribution, so if you can't find an option to help you reinstall QuickDraw 3D, look to the QuickTime installer. Also, note that QuickDraw 3D is a PowerPC-only technology that can require quite a bit of RAM, so this won't work with older Macs.

Acceleration issues

Aside from having all the QuickDraw extensions loaded, including QuickDraw 3D RAVE, the most important part of using QuickDraw 3D RAVE acceleration is running a program — usually a game — that supports RAVE. You'll find that not all of them do, and games written specifically for the Voodoo chipset from 3Dfx aren't necessarily designed to be accelerated by a QuickDraw 3D accelerator card. (Some cards do both types of 3D acceleration, and some games do both, too.)

It's always a good idea to check the game publisher's Web site to see if it has updated the game to support RAVE drivers or created a patch for the game that includes the support. In the computer gaming world, games get released as soon as they possibly can — sometimes with other support files, patches, and upgrades being released weeks later through the mail or via a Web site. Check often if it seems acceleration isn't working well or if acceleration isn't yet present in the game.

If you're using a 3D card for higher-end multimedia or design 3D acceleration, the main concern is making sure you're loading the correct extensions for your video card (see Figure 28-1), so study the card's manual carefully. You'll also want to check your Extensions folder for any extension conflicts; Apple has its own graphic accelerator extensions that may interfere with the operation of your card, as may extensions left over from a previous video card. Also check the video card manufacturer's Web site for updates to the extensions you currently have installed.

In a number of cases, built-in 3D acceleration only works at 16-bit color depths (thousands of colors), not 8-bit (256 colors) or 24-bit (millions of colors). Check your documentation regarding your particular Mac model — this is certainly true of the Power Macintosh 5500/6500 series of Macs, the 20th Anniversary Mac, and many Power Computing models that featured ATI-based 3D acceleration.

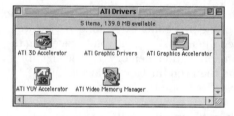

Figure 28-1: The ATI chipset in a Power Computing PowerCenter Pro comes with five files for the Extensions folder.

Note Don't forget that some game drawing functions require Game Sprockets as well as the appropriate acceleration extensions. See the Game Sprockets discussion later in this chapter.

Voodoo

Overall, Voodoo acceleration is simpler than QuickDraw 3D RAVE, but it does still require attention to the extensions loaded on your machine. You'll also want to make sure your card and monitor are configured correctly.

If the Voodoo accelerator card you're using is a 3-D card only, it needs to be connected to the existing 2D card in your Mac. To do that, you generally attach a cable to the 2D card's RGB (DB15) port, and connect the cable to the video-in port on the Voodoo card. From there, you hook a VGA (HD15) monitor cable into the Voodoo card, although you may need an adapter if you're using an Apple monitor. Check these cables for proper configuration if you're having trouble getting either the card or your monitor to work after installation.

Voodoo accelerators will generally only support multisync monitors (because they need to resync to support full-screen 3D), and they require PCI-based Power Macintosh computers. Voodoo cards can also add quite a bit to the RAM requirements of your favorite games, usually needing 32MB of RAM or more for successful game play.

QuickDraw 3D: When things slow down

Apple's Tech Info Library contains a tech note that was originally part of the Power Computing tech database, which Apple incorporated into its own support Web site when Power Computing sold its assets to Apple. The note discusses the built-in ATI RAGE II chipset on the Power Computing machine, although the chipset is actually a popular add-on in many Macs.

The note discusses problems that occur when video memory gets low, which manifest themselves with 3D objects that slowly begin to lose their texture and detail as QuickDraw allows these things to drop out in the interest of preserving VRAM. This effect is especially noticeable if you're increasing the window size while viewing a complex 3D object; it's less likely to be noticeable while playing games. Eventually, the card will run out of memory and the QuickDraw functions will revert back to software-only, resulting in slower performance. The answer: Get more VRAM or render less complex objects.

You'll also have to have the correct software installed. QuickDraw 3D and QuickDraw 3D RAVE are probably still required, as may be the DrawSprocket from Apple's Game Sprockets. (In fact, some Voodoo accelerators work as QuickDraw 3D RAVE accelerators, too, but sometimes only in full-screen modes.)

In addition to the above, your 3Dfx card will likely require a few additional drivers:

✦ 3Dfx RAVE driver extension

✦ 3Dfx shared library file

✦ Graphics library file

All of these will need to be placed in the Extensions folder. Check your documentation for the exact name and other required extensions.

Your Voodoo card will also require full-screen games specifically written to take advantage of Voodoo (or QuickDraw 3D RAVE, in some cases) acceleration. This means games that tout that they're Voodoo-, 3Dfx- or Glide-compatible, all of which refer to pretty much the same thing. (The Glide API is a programmer's interface for writing accelerated 3D routines.)

Troubleshooting

If you have trouble with a pass-through style add-on Voodoo accelerator, your problems are likely to revolve around the cables and adapters you need to get the card working. If you install the card and immediately have trouble, check the cables and adapters first. Some of these troubleshooting hints are more applicable to one type of accelerator over the other, but you may find any of them useful for a particular problem.

Here are some common issues:

✦ *Cable doesn't fit on a pass-through Voodoo system.* Make sure you've attached the RGB port (DB15) to the 2D video card. Some video cards feature both RGB and VGA (HD15) ports, but the cable is designed for one RGB and one VGA port. So, use RGB on the Mac's video and use VGA on the Voodoo card's video-in port.

✦ *Monitor is blank on a Voodoo system.* Check the pass-though cable between your 2D and Voodoo card. Also check the connection from the Voodoo card to your monitor. If you've installed an adapter for the monitor's connection to the Voodoo card, test that adapter as well. (If you can, plug it into another VGA port for testing with your monitor.) Test for trouble with the Voodoo card by reinstalling the monitor on the 2-D card, and then testing to see if the original video card is putting out a signal and that the monitor works.

✦ *Works fine until you load a game, and then goes blank using a Voodoo card.* Wait a few moments to make sure the game isn't just slow. Make sure the game supports either QuickDraw 3D RAVE or Voodoo acceleration. If not, try restarting with extensions off (hold down the Shift key during startup) and running the game again. You may have a conflict between video drivers, especially if you have both the Voodoo drivers and another series of 3D drivers loaded on the same system. (Techworks, maker of the Power3D card, identifies a conflict with some ATI 3D drivers.)

✦ *The screen goes blank using any accelerator.* If the light on your monitor is orange instead of green, the monitor may have gone to sleep. Try disabling monitor sleep in the Energy Saver control panel. (You may need to restart.)

✦ *Sound stutters during gameplay with any accelerator.* There's an identified problem with many 3D acceleration cards and the Catalyst motherboard used in Power Macintosh 7200 machine and many of the Mac clone systems. Look for driver updates from the card manufacturer.

✦ *Things don't look any different.* Check for game settings and/or special drivers for the game itself, which must support the 3D acceleration technology you're using. You may need to use a different version of the game program that's specifically enabled for your type of 3-D acceleration. You may also need a patch or update program for the game that's been released on the game publisher's Web site.

✦ *Things are working, but dark.* Some accelerators have trouble with managing monitor gamma, resulting in a dark screen. Look for brightness settings in the game's preference settings or turn the brightness up on your monitor.

If it feels like the problem doesn't fall in any of these categories, you can try zapping PRAM and reinstalling the software drivers for the card. You should also power your Mac all the way down, test that all video cables are securely installed, and start the machine back up to make sure it is properly sensing the video adapters and cables. You can also try installing the card in a different PCI slot; accelerator cards and some video cards can be sensitive to which slot they're installed in. And, while you're inside the Mac, make sure you press the motherboard reset button if one is present.

Sprockets and Controllers

If you're having trouble with a game controller, you probably either have an ADB conflict or overload, or your software isn't configured correctly. To test for an ADB-related problem, see Chapter 24.

There are three basic ways to configure game controllers on the Macintosh:

✦ **Mouse-substitute.** Using an application or control panel for the settings, the game controller is calibrated so that it works effectively when the mouse option is chosen in the game being played.

✦ **Game-based.** Individual games (especially games that are a few years old) can come with drivers designed for the more popular models of joystick or controller. These games will often support basic controls on all joysticks, along with support for specialized controllers, such as flight yokes and throttle systems.

✦ **Sprockets-based.** Each device you have gets an Input Sprocket driver that's stored in the Extensions folder, kind of like the drivers for fax modems and printers that eventually show up in the Chooser (except that sprocket drivers don't show up in the Chooser — they show up in a standard interface that can be written into Mac games). You need to have the sprocket for your particular controller in the Extensions folder if you're going to effectively use a game that works with Sprockets (see Figure 28-2).

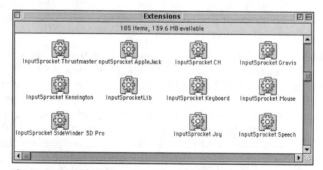

Figure 28-2: The Input Sprocket drivers. Some games or other installations will add a whole slew of them to your System folder.

So, configuration problems you run into will probably have to do with missing drivers or controller descriptions necessary for each type of game. If your game's support for controllers is mouse-based, there's really only so much you can do — usually you'll be able to configure certain settings in a control panel, or you can physically reconfigure the joystick using dials and settings while you're testing the game itself. You may also be able to program the game controller to do certain things (represent key presses, for example) when you click a particular button. For instance, the CH Products Gamepad control panel enables you to assign tasks to each programmable button (see Figure 28-3).

Figure 28-3: The Gamepad control panel gives you control over the function of each button.

You may find that certain games already have built-in configurations for the controller you're trying to use, in which case you may need to disable the control panel that governs that controller and/or configure the controller from within the game. Usually, the more popular the game and the controller, the more likely it is you can configure the controller from directly inside the game.

The best all-around solution is a controller that takes advantage of Game Sprockets. In this case, you simply need to make sure the Input Sprocket driver for your particular controller appears in the Extensions folder on your Mac. If you don't have an Input Sprocket driver, check your installation disks and the manufacturer's Web site. You may also find the driver on the installation media for the game in question. Game Sprockets is still gaining popularity, so, for a time at least, the entire distribution tends to come with every game that supports the Sprockets. Check the CD for a driver that works with your joystick.

If you can't find a driver — either a game-based driver or a Sprocket driver — check your controller's manual for substitutes. Sometimes a particular controller is designed to emulate a more popular product by the same company or a well-known controller from another company in the industry.

PC Compatibility

PC compatibility means three things: file exchange, expansion cards, and emulation software. You want your Mac to be capable of mounting PC disks and reading their contents, you may want to run Windows applications using an add-in card, and you may also be interested in getting DOS and Windows applications running using a software emulator on your high-end PowerPC-based Mac.

As far as floppy and file-format compatibility, most of the problems you encounter will be issues with configuration, although you'll run across the occasional preferences file that needs a stern talking to.

Input device conflicts: Drivers and control panels

The Advanced Gravis Frequently Asked Questions site (www.gravis.com) addresses a couple of interesting problems that can affect how well your game controller integrates into your system.

The first of these is a specific issue with the extension that Gravis uses for some of their Mac devices, called the Firebird GA extension. (You should examine your System folder to see if your game controller has a similar extension.) The extension works in the background, polling the ADB bus, preventing the Energy Saver control panel from putting the Mac to sleep and conserve energy. The solution is to disable the extension and load each game set manually.

Another problem that some game controllers can have is a conflict with mouse-management software like Kensington Mouseworks, which can try to control every device on the ADB bus. If you have trouble getting an input device to work correctly and you're using an advanced mouse or trackball, check the mouse software for controls for excluding certain ADB addresses or devices. (See Chapter 24 for more information on the Mouseworks control panel.)

The PC Compatibility Cards from Apple, Reply, Orange Micro, and Radius introduce a disturbing variable into the configuration and troubleshooting of a Macintosh — DOS and Windows. With these two somewhere near your system, you'll encounter a few problems that are way, way outside the scope of this text.

Instead, in this section we'll focus on only two compatibility issues: Getting an Intel-compatible chip to work with the Mac's components and getting Windows and the Mac OS to coexist peacefully enough that they can share peripherals and swap data. These are no small tasks, but they're handled surprisingly well by the PC Setup control panel that ships with many of these cards.

If you're not using one of the cards, but you are using a powerful Power Macintosh, you may be more interested in putting SoftWindows or VirtualPC to use in running Windows and DOS applications. If this is the case, a few unique issues should be addressed in the configuration and troubleshooting of these applications, as well.

Floppies and files

To mount a DOS-formatted disk or removable media cartridge, your Mac needs to be armed with the appropriate drivers for the device and the PC Exchange control panel, a Mac OS add-on that's responsible for most of the cross-platform disk handling tasks. So, if you're having trouble with a DOS-formatted disk — especially if you're getting a message that says "Disk is unreadable" or "Is not a Macintosh disk" — check to make sure the PC Exchange control panel is being properly loaded at startup. If it doesn't appear in the Control Panels menu under the Apple menu, check the Extensions Manager to make sure PC Exchange is enabled.

I get so used to being able to use DOS-formatted disks that I'm sometimes surprised it doesn't work when I restart with extensions off by holding down the Shift key as the Mac starts up. If you stick a PC disk in when the PC Exchange control panel hasn't been loaded, the Mac can't read the disk. The Finder then tries to entice you into formatting the disk, which will erase all the data on the disk. Don't do it. Restart so that the PC Exchange extension can load.

PC Exchange won't work with Macs that don't include an Apple SuperDrive (the Mac Plus and before, along with early releases of the Mac SE and the Mac II) and will only work with properly formatted 720K and 1.44MB DOS floppy disks. (In my experience, you'll have more luck with 1.44MB floppies.) Apple warns that you shouldn't try to verify or fix a DOS floppy with a Macintosh disk doctor program. Take the disk to a DOS or Windows machine and run a disk doctor program there, instead.

Trouble with long filenames and removable media

If you're having a problem seeing the Windows 95 long filenames associated with files on a DOS-formatted floppy, you need to make sure you've upgraded to PC Exchange 2.2 or higher (included with the Mac OS 8.1 upgrade). This is also true if you're having trouble with an Iomega Zip cartridge, which is better supported with the 2.2 version.

Depending on the version of PC Exchange you have, the control panel has the built-in ability to mount many different types of DOS-formatted media, including many removable drives and cartridge drives. You should begin by inserting the media and seeing if it appears on the desktop. Iomega Zip and Jaz drives, for instance, support the PC Exchange control panel natively, enabling DOS-formatted Zip and Jaz cartridges to appear on the desktop seamlessly.

You may need to mount other removable drives manually. To do this:

1. Open the PC Exchange control panel and click the Options button.

2. Wait for the Mac to locate any recognized SCSI devices that are PC formatted.

3. Choose the drive. It should then mount on the desktop. Close the control panel.

Your removable drive may not appear for two reasons. First, it may have its own update that will enable it to work more closely with the PC Exchange control panel — look for updated drivers on the manufacturer's Web site. Second, it might not work correctly because PC Exchange is comparing the drive against an internal list of drives it supports. If PC Exchange doesn't support the drive or media you're trying to mount, you'll need to upgrade PC Exchange or contact the manufacturer to see if a workaround is available.

Can't see more than 1GB

PC Exchange has a limitation, even in recent versions: It doesn't see DOS-formatted media that's over 1GB in size if it's in the regular FAT (File Allocation Table) format of pre-Windows 95 volumes. In Windows 95 OSR 2 (OEM Service Release #2) and in Windows 98, the underlying file system has been upgraded to FAT32, which, like HFS Plus for Macs, supports larger drives and smaller allocation blocks. Using PC Exchange 2.2 or higher, you can see these drives.

Otherwise, the solution is to repartition the PC media so that only 1GB is formatted to the regular FAT specification at once.

Freezes and crashes

If your Mac freezes or crashes when trying to work with a DOS-formatted floppy, suspect an extension conflict. It's possible the PC Exchange extension is in conflict with another extension on your system. You can try restarting with only the Mac OS extensions active, or troubleshoot the extension conflict as discussed in Chapter 32.

Symptoms of a conflict also include the Mac not being able to read a DOS floppy that you know is correctly formatted, the Mac crashing while mounting the disk, or the Mac crashing while reading the disk.

Loading PC files

If you're trying to load a PC document into a Macintosh program, PC Exchange will attempt to help you with that as well. It does so by using a table of filename extensions (the three letters in the DOS filename that are used to identify the type of document) that corresponds to a Macintosh program designed to open that file. Many Macintosh programs are able to directly open or import files created in their Windows counterparts, or even in competing Windows applications.

If you double-click a PC file and a window appears asking you which application should be used to load the file, pick the appropriate application from the list provided.

If you double-click a PC file, and it doesn't give you a window of choices — but it also doesn't load in the correct application — you should head to the PC Exchange control panel to change the association. Open the control panel and select that file name extension's entry (for instance, .DOC for Microsoft Word for Windows files). Now, click the Change button to change the association (using a standard Open dialog box) to another Mac application. Find the Mac application in the dialog box and click OK.

If the file attempts to load in the correct application but fails, this may be a sign that the application isn't equipped to deal with this particular type of document — at least, not directly. The file may need to be translated. For that, you'll want to launch the application, choose File ➪ Open, and attempt to open the DOS document from the Open dialog window.

Why must you use the File ⇨ Open command? Because the application now has more complete control over the process. Using the Open command from within the program causes the program to attempt to *import* a foreign file format. In fact, in some programs you can choose the type of file directly in the Open dialog box; if it's a WordPerfect for Windows document, for instance, you can pull down the File Type (or similar) menu and choose the WordPerfect for Windows entry. Now the application knows how to translate the DOS/Windows document.

If the document still won't open, and you have Mac OS 7.6 or higher on your Mac, the problem may be solved by installing MacLinkPlus, which is included on the Mac OS CD-ROM. (You can also buy this utility separately or upgrade it with more translators from DataViz, Inc., at www.dataviz.com.) With this utility, the Mac application will have additional translators at its disposal. With these translators properly installed (make sure MacLinkPlus has been installed from the Mac OS CD-ROM and that the control panel is active), the application's Open dialog should have many more translation choices (see Figure 28-4). Select the DOS file you're trying to open, select the appropriate translator, and then click the Open button.

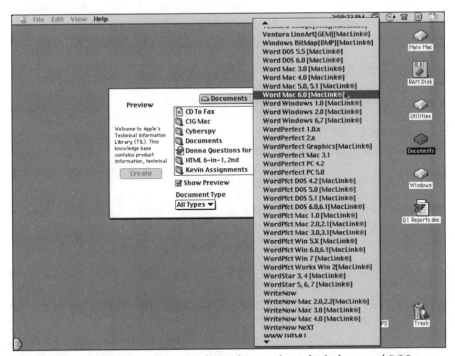

Figure 28-4: MacLinkPlus offers translators for a variety of Windows and DOS applications.

PC Cards

The DOS and PC Compatibility Cards (and the associated software) do a surprisingly good job of integrating themselves into a Mac and functioning side by side with the Mac's processor. In general, things should be as trouble-free as you can expect from Windows and the Mac OS, with the understanding that crashes on one system have the potential to affect the other system, and giving the PC Compatibility Card access to the Mac's peripherals can sometimes result in unexpected consequences.

You can expect a few limitations regarding the typical PC Compatibility Card:

✦ The Apple, Reply, and Radius (along with some of the earlier Orange Micro cards) are not designed to run any OS other than DOS or Windows 3.1, and they can have some fits when running Windows 95. (The OS itself will usually work fine; however, some important parts of it don't work correctly, hampering compatibility. Specifically, most of these cards lack 32-bit device drivers that enable Windows 95 to run in a full-compatibility mode. This limits some of the applications that the PC Card is able to run in Windows 95, especially multimedia titles and advanced games.

✦ PC Compatibility Cards are generally designed to use the Mac's serial ports for serial communication (to modems, for instance). Unfortunately, incompatibilities between typical PC serial ports and Mac serial ports tend to cause modem connections to run very slowly for the PC Card. Some cards offer their own serial ports (many of the cards from Orange Micro do, for example), and Apple has offered a PCI-based serial/parallel card for PC-Compatible Macs that allows you to use Intel-compatible peripherals.

✦ Printers and modems that rely heavily on the Mac OS to function often won't work when accessed from the PC environment. Specifically, GeoPort modems and LaserWriter Select 300 and Personal LaserWriter printers aren't supported, along with some other third-party models of both modems and printers. You'll have better luck with hardware-only modems and PostScript printers when trying to access them from DOS or Windows.

✦ Most PC Compatibility Cards are designed to share a video monitor with the Mac, switching back and forth in response to a hot-key sequence. This means the PC Setup software needs to properly set up and use the video card while in PC Compatibility mode. The PC Cards work best with very standard, multisync monitors, and, preferably, a second monitor that hooks directly into the VGA port on the PC Card.

✦ Working with removable media from the PC Compatibility environment can sometimes create trouble, especially with disks such as the Iomega Zip that tend to mount themselves on the Mac desktop.

The following troubleshooting issues are more or less applicable to the entire line of PC Compatibility Cards. Some of them also affect the older DOS Compatibility card. If the issue affects only OrangePC Cards, I'll mention that specifically.

Note

The first thing you should do is update the PC Setup software you're using with your Apple-brand PC Compatibility Card if you haven't for a while. The exception is the card in a Quadra 610 — the last available upgrade for that machine is PC Setup 1.0.2.

PC doesn't start up

If you've installed the card and its software, and you can't get the card to start up (either the options are grayed out in the PC Setup control panel or you get an error message), you need to begin your troubleshooting by isolating a potential software problem, and then move on to evaluating the hardware. To begin, follow these steps:

1. Check that the control panel is properly installed and turned on. You may need to restart after installing or moving the control panel.

2. Make sure you've chosen a valid DOS or Windows startup volume in the control panel. On most of the cards, this can't be a DOS-formatted hard drive in your Mac; it needs to be a disk container on a Mac-formatted drive. (You can use the DOS-formatted hard drive as the D drive.)

3. Check to make sure you don't have an extension conflict. Try restarting with only the basic Mac OS extensions and the extensions necessary for your PC Compatibility Card.

4. Try throwing away your PC Setup, Detente (Reply), or OrangePCi preferences, especially if you've recently upgraded the software. Restart and try again.

5. Restart and zap PRAM. Restore the settings in the PC Card's control panel and try again.

6. Reinstall the PC Card's software. Look for a newer version on the manufacturer's Web site.

7. Open the case and make sure the card is properly seated in its slot. If it's a PCI card, try changing the slot it's in. If you can put it in the bus master slot (the one closest to the Mac's processor), go ahead and try that.

8. Hit the reset button on your logic board to reset the PCI bus.

If none of these work, you might try the card in another Mac, or create a clean install of the Mac OS and try installing the card and the software all over again. You should also try the card with and without any additional RAM installed on the card. Be careful not to confuse a monitor problem with a PC Card problem; if the monitor switches to black but nothing happens, suspect the monitor and monitor connection.

PC starts up black

This is probably a problem with the monitor settings, connection, or the monitor itself. If the monitor is the same one you use for your Mac (or you otherwise know it to be in working order), you should troubleshoot the connection in the back — make sure all the cabling is as it should be — and troubleshoot the PC Setup (or

Detente or OrangePCi) control panel. Specifically, you want to make sure the control is set for the correct monitor resolution and refresh rate.

Apple lists a certain number of approved monitors for use with a PC Compatibility Card; consult that list (in your manual or in Apple's Tech Info library) to make sure your monitor is compatible. If your monitor has a VGA connector, you can also try hooking the monitor directly to the PC Card to make sure it isn't a problem with the cabling you're using to connect the Mac and PC to the same monitor.

Monitor trouble

The PC Card may not be properly sensing the monitor. You can fix this by setting the monitor to a different setting other than the automatic one in the PC Card's control panel. You should also consult your card's manual for instructions regarding specific monitors and video chipsets.

In many cases, you may get odd or high-end monitor options in Windows that your monitor doesn't support, so be wary when changing resolutions and color depths. You may find, for instance, that the card gives you the choice of 24-bit color or a very high resolution. Generally 800x600 or 1,024x768 and 16-bit colors are the highest you'll get from the PC Card. (Earlier cards offer lower resolution and color depths.)

If the screen appears with a large black border around it, you've chosen a resolution for the PC environment that's lower than the monitor is designed (or adapted) to support. Either change the setting on your monitor's VGA-to-RGB adapter or increase the resolution in Windows.

Newer PC-compatibility cards from Apple and Reply feature an ATI chipset that should be auto-sensed by Windows, which then chooses the appropriate driver. During installation, Windows 95 will ask you to choose the type of monitor you're using — you should do so, telling it as closely as possible the model you have.

If you have a fixed-frequency monitor, you may experience some trouble with video playback (running Video for Windows, and so on) in the Windows environment. Some video games and multimedia titles may be poorly synchronized between the audio and video. The only answer is to upgrade the monitor to a multisync model.

DOS won't boot

Make sure you have a valid DOS driver container selected in the DOS card's control panel as the C drive. If you suspect that there's something wrong with the drive container, you should be able to boot DOS by inserting a DOS system disk in the floppy drive and starting up the PC.

If DOS still won't boot, but it's switching to a blank screen, it's possible that the DOS card itself has crashed or hung and needs to be physically reset. Usually you can do this in the PC Card's control panel. If that still doesn't work (unlikely, but possible), you may want to shut the Mac all the way down so that the PC Card no longer gets power. Try starting up again, and then test the card.

You should also test for extension conflicts and look for an update for the PC Card software. If necessary, you can reinstall the PC Card software and/or create a new drive container and attempt to install DOS and Windows in the new container. You should also make sure the card is properly seated in its PCI slot. You might try the card in a different slot (preferably the bus master slot), especially if you've recently installed another PCI card.

Modem setup

One of the biggest headaches with a PC Compatibility Card is getting it to function correctly with a Mac modem when you need to connect the PC environment over phone lines. Because of inconsistencies between the Mac's RS-422 serial port and the RS-232 serial ports that Windows expects to deal with, the results will usually be less than pleasing.

To use your Mac's modem in the PC environment, it needs to be a hardware-based Hayes compatible modem — preferably one that's similar to a PC model by the same manufacturer and has simply been repurposed for Mac use, with nearly all its functions implemented within the modem itself. You'll have very little luck with software-based modems (for example, some Global Village Teleport and Apple internal GeoPort modems) that rely heavily on a control panel and system extension to work properly. And you'll have absolutely no luck with a GeoPort Telecom Adapter, which simply isn't supported by PC Compatibility Cards.

The basic problem you'll encounter when configuring your Mac modem in Windows is you can't get hardware to handshake and flow control to work from the PC environment to the Mac modem. So, as discussed in Chapter 16, you're severely limited in the throughput you can expect between the modem and the computer — at least, the throughput that the PC can manage without using hardware flow control. In my experience, the best-case scenario is a true connection of 9.6 Kbps and an overall (compressed, error corrected) connection of perhaps 19.2 Kbps, with 14.4 or 9.6 Kbps more likely.

To set up the modem, you should select the following in the DOS or Windows environment:

1. In the Mac environment, turn off any applications that might be using or polling the modem port. This includes programs such as a fax program or a PPP dialer.

2. In the PC Card's control panel, map the modem port to COM 1.

3. In Windows, go to the Control Panel folder and create a new modem profile. Specify a "standard 9600" modem.

4. Change the options as follows: Choose not to use the FIFO UART, choose Xon/Xoff flow control, and choose 19,200 bps as the modem's top speed.

Now you should be able to use the modem through Windows. Note that this setup is only necessary if you're using the Mac's serial port for modem communications; if your OrangePC Card has its own serial ports or your Apple/Reply PC Compatibility Card has been augmented by Apple's Serial/Parallel expansion card, you should be able to set up an Intel-compatible modem with no trouble using the PC serial port.

You may be able to get the modem to work and still have software that won't use the Mac modem appropriately or at all. (I've had trouble with America Online in the past, unless I connect over a TCP/IP connection to the service.) The basic problem is this: Not all RS-232 signals are available to the PC Card when it's remapped to a Mac serial port. Carrier Detect (CD), Data Set Ready (DSR), Request to Send (RTS), and Ring Indicator (RI) are all unavailable to the DOS or Windows program. If your application or serial device requires these signals, you won't be able to get it to work.

But if your DOS/Windows program allows for some advanced modem configuration, you may be able to implement a workaround. The first thing you can try is dig into the program's preferences and tell it that the modem is a Hayes-compatible 9,600 bps modem, which usually will persuade the program to talk to the modem without using these signals. If that's not the case, refer to Chapter 26 and your modem's manual to help you dig into the AT command set and disable the modem's need to detect a carrier and use hard flow control. If you can manage that, you can probably use the modem at speeds between 9,600 and 19,200 bps.

Crashes and errors on the Mac

A crash of the PC can sometimes bring down the Mac, although more often you should be able to hot-key back to the Mac environment and restart the PC from the PC Card's control panel.

Crashes on the Mac itself can occur sometimes, especially with out-of-date PC Setup software. If your Mac crashes on startup, it may be because it's trying to start the PC as the Mac starts up—which is one option in the PC Setup control panel. A crash at this point could keep you from getting to the Mac OS to troubleshoot the problem. The solution is to start up with extensions off, open the PC Setup control panel, and turn off the Auto-startup option. You can then restart the Mac with regular extensions loading. Once the Mac has started up, you can troubleshoot the problem with the PC Card from the Finder.

You can also encounter a problem if the PC Setup control panel is set to map a serial port to a COM port and also has Auto-startup selected. In that case, you may have a conflict with your Mac modem software that results in crashes, freezes, or other errors from within your Mac's modem-oriented applications. It's best to set the PC Setup control panel to not map any of the serial ports to COM ports until you're ready to the use the PC and have turned off other modem-based Mac programs and/or extensions.

Note

Apple recommends that you not rebuild the desktop while auto-start is active. In fact, it's probably a good idea (in my opinion) to leave auto-start off completely. It seems to cause more trouble than it addresses, including overall system slowdowns and occasional errors.

To avoid crashes on the Mac, your first step is to update to the latest version of PC Setup that your Mac can handle. Many bug fixes and other issues are addressed with the later releases of the PC Setup software.

The PC Setup preferences can become corrupted, resulting in error messages such as "PC Setup, Unimplemented Trap" and some random crashing or freezing. If you experience this, you can drag the PC Setup preferences file (in the Preferences folder in the System Folder) to the desktop and restart the Mac. Run PC Setup to see if the problem recurs. If it doesn't, you can throw away the preferences file.

Open Transport can cause compatibility issues with the PC Setup control panel. Check the Read Me file that came with your PC Setup installation to determine which version(s) of the Mac OS and Open Transport are required for proper operation of your PC Compatibility Card. Remember also that the PC Card is a complex component in your Mac and that new versions of the Mac OS will sometimes require the card to be specifically supported with a software update. That may take time to get from Apple, so check the Read Me file and installation instructions before you upgrade to a major new version of the Mac OS.

RAM modules installed on some cards under specific circumstances can cause crashes. Try booting the card without the RAM module installed to isolate the problem. (If this doesn't work either, your problem lies elsewhere.) If the card works while sharing memory with the Mac, upgrade to the latest version of PC Setup and try installing the RAM module again. If it still doesn't work, the problem may lie with the module itself.

Crashes on the PC side

Many PC Compatibility Cards only support Windows 95 or 98 in the most roundabout way, with *real mode* drivers required for some of the components to work correctly. (Real mode is a backward-compatible mode in Windows 95 that enables it to work with driver programs designed for older versions of DOS and Windows.) In day-to-day use, this may slow your work down slightly, but it shouldn't affect many Windows programs. However, it can keep you from working with anything that requires a *32-bit clean* Windows system (one that uses no real mode drivers).

More often than not, it's Windows' high-end graphics and gaming technologies that require 32-bit clean operation. That includes *DirectX support* as well as some other Windows multimedia technologies. You shouldn't attempt to install DirectX on an Apple or Reply card (newer Orange Micro cards have 32-bit drivers that support these Windows technologies). If certain games, multimedia programs, or even the Office Assistant in Microsoft Office for Windows cause crashes in your Windows environment, try to avoid using them, unless you're able to obtain 32-bit drivers for the PC Card.

Although Apple has expressed no interest in writing these drivers, there's speculation at the time of writing that Orange Micro may make their drivers (which are already available for their cards) available for owners of other card brands. (There's no guarantee that this will happen, however.) Check `www.orangemicro.com` for details.

Software emulators

If you've got a fast Power Macintosh and have opted for SoftWindows or VirtualPC, you'll probably find that you have slightly fewer problems than owners of PC Compatibility Cards; you shouldn't have too much trouble getting Windows software to work correctly, although the trade-off is a pretty serious speed hit compared to a physical DOS card.

Probably the biggest problem you'll encounter with these emulation programs is when you don't (or can't) allocate them enough RAM to run properly. They tend to be very hungry for RAM, which isn't too surprising; after all, they're emulating either the Windows environment (SoftWindows) or an entire Intel-compatible PC (RealPC, VirtualPC), both of which require at least as much RAM as a typical Mac. If you plan to use one of these programs extensively, I highly recommend you double the amount of RAM in your Mac so that you can dedicate a large chunk of RAM to the emulation program while still being able to get things done in the Mac environment.

Printers and modems

Software emulators suffer from a few of the same problems PC Cards encounter, including certain limitations with dealing with Mac modems and printing issues. Fortunately, both of the major emulation companies offer some significant workarounds — after all, the emulation program is ultimately a Mac application, not a Windows machine. If you have problems printing or using a modem, make sure the software program supports the modem (check its documentation and Read Me files). Next, make sure the program's special drivers are loaded in Windows to make those Mac peripherals work with the Windows environment.

In some cases, you'll find the most convenient way to fix an interface problem with an emulator (a mouse, display, modem, printer, or something similar that once worked and no longer does) is to restart the emulator with a new DOS drive container image. On the CD used to install your emulator, you'll likely find one of these images that can be copied to your hard drive and used immediately to boot the environment. You can then assign the older container to be the D or E drive, for instance, and copy over any important documents. Unfortunately, the way Windows installs programs will likely require you to reinstall them for the new drive container instead of simply dragging them over.

To avoid this, though, it's recommended you change the Windows settings for monitors, printers, modems, and other peripherals as rarely as possible. In many cases, the installed environment is already optimized for working with your Mac peripherals, and changing these settings can cause hours of headaches later. Work closely with the software's documentation to learn what's best left alone.

Note

GeoPort and software-based modems will often work with emulation programs, but you may need to disable flow control and change some other settings, according to the emulator's documentation.

Mice

It's important not to change the mouse driver in the Windows environment, because the emulator needs to use a special driver to enable the Mac mouse to work in both the Mac and Windows environments at the same time. When you move into DOS (and perhaps some other operating systems, if your emulator supports them) you may need to specifically load a DOS mouse driver to get things to work correctly. In Windows 95, for instance, you can type **mouse** and press the Return key at a DOS window prompt to enable a DOS-based mouse driver. You can also install this command in the Windows 95 autoexec.bat file to load the driver automatically.

If your emulator doesn't feature a mouse driver for DOS, look for an update from the software publisher.

If you have a programmable mouse, you can probably program one of the mouse buttons to mimic the right-click of a Windows mouse in the emulated environment. For SoftWindows, the programmable key should emulate the equals (=) sign; in VirtualPC, it should be programmed to emulate Shift-Tab.

CD-ROMs

Emulation environments can have some trouble with third-party CD-ROM drives, especially those that use the FWB CD-ROM kit software. In most cases, workarounds exist. Look for updates on the publisher's Web sites. If you're having trouble getting PC CD-ROMs to appear in the emulated environment, make sure the ISO9660 File Access option is checked in the CD-ROM Toolkit control panel and/or that the ISO9660 File Access extension appears in your Extensions folder and is loaded at startup.

You should then make sure the CD-ROM Toolkit control panel is set up to enable mounting of any ISO 9660 volumes of "dual-format" Apple HFS CD-ROMs. This allows a hybrid CD to work with the DOS environment.

In other cases, you may find that access to FWB-based CD-ROM drives is very slow. Turn off caching or acceleration in the CD-ROM Toolkit control panel to increase performance in the Windows environment.

Summary

✦ If you plan to use a lot of 3D applications or games, you'll want your accelerator in tip-top condition. Many recent Power Macs include 2D and 3D acceleration, but they require the correct QuickDraw 3D drivers to make things work well. Often this is managed by system extensions, which you'll want to load correctly for best performance.

✦ With 3Dfx Voodoo cards, things can get even a bit more complicated, because they're designed as add-ons for regular 2D cards. Make certain you have all the cabling, setup and software drivers correct. Next, as with QuickDraw 3D, make sure your program or game supports the 3D technology you're trying to use.

✦ Setting up game controllers is a mess on the Mac. If you're lucky, both your program and your controller support the Input Sprocket, which makes it a piece of cake to select your particular controller from within the game itself. In other cases, you may need to configure the controller manually, choose a game profile in the game controller's control panel or load a controller profile into the particular game that you're using. For dedicated gamers, this usually means surfing the Web sites of the controller manufacturer and game developer to get the right match.

✦ Almost any modern Mac can deal directly with Windows and DOS floppies and files, but you'll need to dig into the PC Exchange control panel to make sure nothing is lost in the translation. If you've got a Wintel file you simply must edit in a Mac program, there's probably a way to get that done easily.

✦ If you've got a PC Compatibility Card, you've got a really powerful way to deal with Windows documents and applications. However, things can break down a bit when you use an unsupported OS or you try to access Mac peripherals. A couple of workarounds make life a little easier, but the sad fact is everything doesn't always work correctly.

✦ For Windows and PC emulation software, the good news is some clever programming has made these into great applications that can fool almost any PC application into running on top of the Mac OS. The hit you take is with some minor compatibility issues — and emulation is a lot slower than a new PC Compatibility Card, at least, for now. Someday soon, high-speed G3 and G4 processors may help emulation programs take on the Pentium II chip and beyond.

✦   ✦   ✦

PowerBook Problems

◆ ◆ ◆ ◆

In This Chapter

Startup and power problems

Batteries and battery care

Other PowerBook issues

◆ ◆ ◆ ◆

Stranger things have happened than a PowerBook not lighting up when you hit the Power key. The all-in-one PowerBooks are convenient, state-of-the-art and, in some ways, amazing; almost the same technology that can require a minitower case for a desktop computer can fit in the small space that's taken up by a PowerBook. At the same time, though, all these components — so close together — can offer up a few special quirks, as can the software and hardware required to tie all of them up in such a nice, neat little package.

The PowerBooks have their own power management hardware and software that tend to differentiate them from desktop Macs. They also have their own interfaces types — docks, bays, and PC Card slots — that you don't find in desktop models. In the same way, they rely on LCD technologies and batteries for power, two things that aren't much a part of the desktop computing world at this point.

So, PowerBooks have their own unique sets of problems aside from those already touched on in earlier chapters. (For instance, you can troubleshoot SCSI, serial port and ADB problems on PowerBooks much the same way you do with desktop Macs.) This chapter takes a look at troubleshooting PowerBook-specific problems as well as offering workarounds and solutions for a few known problems with various PowerBook models.

Startup, Shutdown, and Power

As you may already know, Macs can be trouble to get started up; that's because of the whole Power key system that's designed to be functional, easy, and cool. With many Intel-compatible PC models (or with a VCR or blender, for that matter) you push a button or throw a switch — even if that switch is on the back of the machine, way down below the desk, behind the trash can, and around the corner from the cat's scratching post.

With PowerBooks, powering on can become even more complex. To turn the PowerBook on, you need to have it in the correct mode, you need to have some source of power (with a good charge in it) hooked up to the Mac, and you need to have the screen ready to register that something is going on and there's a reason for it to be awake. Because PowerBook displays don't have an LED indicator to tell you what's going on like most desktop monitors do, it can be tough to tell if a PowerBook is even turned on, much less if the Mac OS is started up and everything else is working properly.

If you're having trouble getting starting with a PowerBook, you'll need to isolate the problem. If the trouble is getting your PowerBook to turn on, check the items that follow to see if you can solve or isolate the problem:

✦ *Check the batteries.* On some Mac models, the batteries feature an external LED indicator. On others, you need to remove the battery to see the indicator. (Pre–3400 series PowerBooks don't have either.) If you suspect that the battery isn't full charged, plug in the power adapter. If you think the battery is charged, take it out and replace it to ensure it's properly connected. If you can test the PowerBook with a battery you know is good (or if it fires up when you use the power adapter), the battery may be dead; have a service center check it out.

✦ *Check the power adapter.* Make sure the power adapter is properly attached to the PowerBook and that it's plugged into a working power outlet or surge protector. The power adapter should get warm after a few minutes of being plugged in. Check the power brick and its connection to the outlet cable — these often come loose, even if they don't look loose from a distance. If you've charged the batteries recently, your PowerBook still may not start up if the power connector is only half-way plugged in or otherwise faulty. Also, make sure you're using the right power supply for your particular PowerBook — they are not all interchangeable.

✦ *Is the power outlet good?* Don't forget to try different locations in your building to make sure there isn't something wrong with the power socket your PowerBook is plugged into.

✦ *Is the SCSI cable plugged in?* If you have the SCSI Disk Mode cable plugged in, shut the Mac down and unplug the cable. If another SCSI cable is plugged in but the connection isn't properly terminated, you may have trouble starting the PowerBook, or it may have crashed.

✦ *Is it asleep?* Try tapping the spacebar or another key to see if the PowerBook is in Sleep mode and needs to be awakened.

✦ *Is the screen brightness set wrong?* It's possible that the PowerBook is turned on, but you can't see the screen because its brightness setting is turned too far down. Reset the brightness setting to a middle level, and then test to make sure it's working, it's not in Sleep mode, and so on.

You may also have luck if you remove the battery (or batteries) from the PowerBook for a few minutes, and then try to restart with only the power adapter. If that works, plug the battery back in and make sure it's completely and properly connected. Next, check your PowerBook utilities to make sure the battery is charging. (Depending on the Mac OS version and PowerBook you have, you should see a menu bar icon or a control strip indicator that tells you the battery is being recharged.)

It's also possible that the Mac has crashed while in Sleep mode. If you suspect this is the case (and nothing else so far has worked), you can hit Ctrl-⌘-Power to perform a hard reset of the PowerBook. If that doesn't work, check the back of the PowerBook for a Reset button and push that button to reset the PowerBook. (Resetting is covered in the next section.)

Shutdown, sleep, and reset

If you suspect that your Mac has crashed or hung and you can't get it to reset, you have some options. Aside from Ctrl-⌘-Power, you can do a couple of different things to reset PowerBooks, depending on the model. Earlier Mac models have both a Reset and an Interrupt button. The Reset button is marked with a small triangle, and it performs the same function as turning the PowerBook's power on and off—that is, it performs a *hard reset*, not just a typical restart. The Interrupt button is marked with a small circle, generally used by programmers to get access to the command-line debugger interface. (The key combination ⌘-Power works does this same thing on some PowerBook and Mac models.)

If you think your PowerBook has frozen or hung, don't forget to try the steps for dealing with a frozen Mac outlined in Chapter 30 *first.* These include waiting, testing external ADB connections, and forcing the current application to quit using the ⌘-Option-Esc key sequence. If these attempts fail, though, you should reset your PowerBook.

After you've reset it, you can troubleshoot the nature of the freeze as you would with any Macintosh. The only difference is PowerBooks are more prone to freezes while in Sleep mode.

Resetting

A hard reset, unlike the Mac OS's Restart command, will erase the contents of a RAM disk, if one is present. A hard reset on some models can also return values in PRAM to their defaults, requiring you to change settings in your control panels.

The steps to follow to restart particular Mac models are listed below:

✦ **PowerBook 100.** The PowerBook 100 has no Power button, so it usually enables you to start the Mac by pressing any key on the keyboard. It does have both Reset and Interrupt buttons, which are found on the left side of the PowerBook (when you're facing the screen). The Reset button is the closer of the two to the front of the machine.

✦ **PowerBook 100 series.** The Power button is found on the back of the unit inside the back panel. You'll need to open the back panel door to gain access to the Power button. In most cases, you should be able to perform a hard reset on these PowerBooks by holding down the Power button for a few seconds and waiting until the PowerBook shuts down completely. (The Reset and Interrupt buttons are recessed into the back of the case, requiring a paper clip to use them.)

✦ **PowerBook Duo series.** These machines have two power buttons — one on the keyboard and one on the back of the PowerBook (if you're facing the screen, reach your right hand around the back to find it). To perform a hard reset the PowerBook, hold down the Ctrl-⌘-Power keys. To hard reset, hold down the rear power button for five seconds or so.

✦ **PowerBook 500 series.** These PowerBooks feature a keyboard power button. To reset power on these models, use the familiar keystrokes Ctrl-⌘-Power for a soft reset. If that doesn't work, you can use Ctrl-Option-⌘-Power for a hard reset. If you have trouble starting up, you may have luck if you hold down the Power key for a few seconds. (These key combinations work for the Duo 280 and 280c, too, incidentally.)

✦ **PowerBook 5300/190 series**. These PowerBooks have two Power buttons — a keyboard Power key and a button that 's behind the rear access panel below the video connector. To reset these Macs, use the Ctrl-⌘-Power key sequence. To shut the PowerBook down, press the Power button. If you have trouble shutting the PowerBook down or starting it up, hold in the Power button for a few seconds. It can also be hard reset using the button on the back panel.

✦ **PowerBook 1400 series**. This PowerBook has one Power key (on the keyboard) and a Reset button, found behind the rear access panel between the serial port and the ADB port. Try resetting with Ctrl-⌘-Power, but if it doesn't work, you can press the Reset button to restart the PowerBook.

✦ **PowerBook 3400/G3 3500 series**. These PowerBooks have the typical keyboard Power key and can be reset using the Ctrl-⌘-Power key sequence. If that's not working, you can use the Reset button, located behind the rear access panel next to the 10BaseT Ethernet connector.

✦ **PowerBook G3 series.** These units have a keyboard Power key and you can perform a soft reset with the Ctrl-⌘-Power key sequence. For a hard reset, the G3 series has its own unique key combination: Shift-Function-Ctrl-Power. The Function key (Fn) is a new key with this series.

Sleep problems

PowerBooks will occasionally crash or freeze when they go into Sleep mode or when the screen dims. If this happens to you, use the following methods to isolate the problem:

✦ *Are you running a screen saver or background application?* Third-party screen savers and power management programs can affect the PowerBook while it's in Sleep mode. Other programs, such as background virus checkers, hard-drive integrity checkers and datebook alerts can also get confused by Sleep or screen-dimming modes. Check for an update or workaround from the software publisher.

✦ *Are you connected to an external monitor?* Restart, disconnect the monitor, put the PowerBook in Sleep mode, and see if the crash happens again. If the crash doesn't happen, a program you're running may be incompatible with dual-monitor support while the PowerBook is in Sleep mode. If you're connected to AC power, try disabling the Sleep mode.

✦ *Update your hard disk driver.* Use Drive Setup or your hard-drive utility program (Silverlining or FWB Disk Tool Kit) to update the driver for your hard disk.

✦ *Troubleshoot conflicts.* Find out if there's a known issue with the Sleep or dimming features and the applications you regularly use. Also, troubleshoot for an extensions conflict (see Chapter 32 for more on conflict troubleshooting).

If none of these seems to be the problem, you should try zapping PRAM and, if necessary, deal with the Power Manager. Beyond that, these Sleep crashes may happen when a System file is corrupt. See Chapters 30 and 33 for troubleshooting tips and quick replacement advice for a corrupt System file.

Reset the Power Manager

Resetting the Power Manager is a pretty big deal in the PowerBook world — it's one way you can get the PowerBook to work better when it's on battery power, when it won't seem to start any other way (especially with PowerBook 5300 and 190 models) and when the PowerBook is exhibiting odd behavior. The Power Manager is automatically reset when you zap PRAM on a PowerBook (which is done the same way as with desktop Macs — see Chapter 30), but you may come across times when it's best to reset it on its own, too.

Interestingly, Apple says that one of the most common reasons for a Power Manager corruption results from plugging the AC adapter into the PowerBook first, and then into the wall (the way you plug in most appliances and electronics). Apple recommends instead that you plug the adapter into the wall socket or surge protector first, and then into the PowerBook's AC connector. You should also avoid turning off the PowerBook without using the Shut Down command.

You can reset the Power Manager in response to a number of symptoms, including the following:

✦ Battery power fails after a short time even after fully recharging the batteries.

✦ The PowerBook appears to be dead, even with AC power connected.

✦ The battery displays bizarre consumption patterns, fails to recharge, or recharges only after an inordinate amount of time (usually days).

✦ When connected to AC power, the PowerBook starts itself up immediately after accepting the Shut Down command and powering completely off.

Note

Like zapping PRAM, resetting the Power Manager is both a fix for many different issues and a fix of last resort. Although it may solve your problem (especially if the problem seems to be power-related), you should exhaust all other troubleshooting options first. Also, don't forget that resetting PRAM or the Power Manager on a PowerBook will delete data on a RAM disk.

Unfortunately, the process is different for just about every PowerBook model, because it tends to focus on the Reset switch. The following is a quick rundown of how to reset the Power Manager for different PowerBook models.

PowerBook 100

1. Unplug the AC adapter and remove the battery.

2. On the rear of the unit you'll find the battery contact switch. Flip it to the down position.

3. Let the PowerBook sit without any power for about five minutes.

4. Simultaneously press the Reset and Interrupt buttons (on the left side of the unit), holding them in for 15 seconds.

5. Reinstall the battery, reconnect the AC adapter (if you're using one), flip the battery contact switch to the up position, and then start up the PowerBook to test it.

PowerBook 140, 145, 145 B, and 170

1. Unplug the AC adapter and remove the battery.

2. Let the PowerBook sit without any power for about five minutes.

3. Using two paper clips, simultaneously press the Reset and Interrupt buttons (on the left side of the unit), holding them in for 10 seconds.

4. Reinstall the battery, reconnect the AC adapter (if you're using one), and start up the PowerBook to test it.

PowerBook 160, 165, or 180

1. Unplug the AC adapter and remove the battery.

2. Let the PowerBook sit without any power for about five minutes.

3. Reinstall the battery, reconnect the AC adapter (if you're using one), and start up the PowerBook to test it.

If this doesn't reset the Power Manager (that is, if the PowerBook seems to continue experiencing the same troubles that you've previously identified as problems with the Power Manager), follow the instructions for the PowerBook 140 series.

PowerBook 150

1. Unplug the AC adapter and remove the battery.

2. Press the Reset button (on the back of the PowerBook) and hold it in for 10 seconds.

3. Plug the AC adapter back into the wall socket or surge protector. Reconnect it to the PowerBook.

4. Push the Reset button quickly. You'll hear a sound or pop from the speaker.

5. Push the main power button, on the back of the PowerBook. It should power up.

If the power comes on, you can insert the battery. If the PowerBook doesn't start after this, it may require service.

PowerBook 500 series

1. Unplug the AC adapter and remove the battery.

2. Let the PowerBook sit without any power for about five minutes.

3. Simultaneously press the Ctrl-Option-⌘-Power keys, holding them in for 10 seconds.

4. Reinstall the battery, reconnect the AC adapter (if you're using one), and start up the PowerBook to test it.

PowerBook Duo Series

Duos work a little differently. You should be able to reset the Power Manager by holding in the Duo's Power button (on the back of the machine) for about 45 seconds. If this doesn't solve the problem, remove the battery and AC adapter, and then let the Duo sit without power for about ten minutes.

Note   Apple notes in its Tech Info library that one way to reset the Power Manager in a Duo is to remove the internal backup battery. The procedure is not recommended by Apple and will void your warranty (if you happen to still have one). Take it to a service center.

PowerBook 190/5300, 1400, 2400, 3400/G3 (3500)

The only difference among these models is the location of the Reset button, which is discussed in the section "Shut down, sleep, and reset."

1. If the computer is on, shut it down.

2. Hold down the Reset button for 20 seconds. The PowerBook should restart.

3. If the computer does not restart, repeat step 2 a few times.

PowerBook G3 Series

1. If the computer is on, shut it down.

2. Simultaneously press the Shift-Function-Ctrl-Power keys on the keyboard.

3. Press the Power key on the keyboard. The PowerBook should turn on.

PowerBook 5300 or 190 That Won't Power On

If you've got a 190/5300 series PowerBook that appears to be completely dead, this might be a particular Power Manager issue. You need to do the following to reanimate the PowerBook:

1. Unplug the AC adapter and remove the battery.

2. Press the Reset button on the back of the PowerBook and hold it in for about 45 seconds.

3. Plug the AC Adapter into the wall outlet or a surge protector.

4. Reattach only the AC Adapter to the PowerBook. Don't install the battery.

5. Press the Reset button one more time, and the PowerBook should start up after a brief pause.

Crash when Finder loads

If you've just reset the Power Manager and your PowerBook crashes as the Finder loads, it may be because the Mac's Date and Time clock has been reset to its base date, which is usually 1904 (some Macs and PowerBooks reset to 1956 or 1980). The date gets reset as if the PRAM battery was removed when the Power Manager is reset (at least, sometimes it does). This can conflict with some extensions, especially the Claris Instant Organizer extension used with Claris Organizer. Others may also be affected.

The answer is to force a quit (⌘-Shift-Esc) to get the Finder to continue loading. If this doesn't work, restart the Mac with Extensions Off (hold down the Shift key as the Mac starts up), and then reset the clock using the Time and Date control panel once the Finder has loaded. Restart again to load extensions and avoid the crash.

Reset after zapping PRAM

Many newer Mac models can sometimes appear to go dead or into Sleep mode immediately after you've zapped PRAM. Apple lists the PowerBook 190, 5300, and 1400, in its Tech Info Library, although this problem seems to affect the 3400/G3 3500 series as well. Zapping PRAM in these machines also resets the Power Manager, so additional steps must be taken to get the PowerBook to come up after zapping PRAM.

Here are the augmented zap PRAM instructions for these PowerBook models:

1. Shut down the PowerBook (don't restart).

2. Power up the machine and hold down the ⌘-Option-P-R keys.

3. After one startup chime, the screen will go black and the green Sleep LED will light up.

4. Press the PowerBook's Reset button (see previous section for location). After what may be a brief wait, the PowerBook should come back on.

This might not be the last of it. If the PowerBook powers up but then shuts down again, hit the Reset button. Now, if the PowerBook doesn't come on, try turning it on from the Power key on the keyboard.

Batteries and Battery Life

The batteries in PowerBooks have changed quite a bit over the past few years, improving in both the amount of power they offer to the PowerBook and the length of time that the PowerBook can remain working on a single charge of the battery. The difference between the original PowerBook 100's 16MHz 68000 processor and the PowerPC 750 processors in the PowerBook G3 Series notebooks is astounding. It's no small wonder that battery technology has had to play a little catch-up.

And that's not to mention the huge color displays, the CD-ROM and DVD-ROM drives, and the large amounts of RAM and hard drive space that we ask today's PowerBooks to deal with. In fact, this is where the real battery drain is; the minute voltage required for a processor on its own is nothing compared to what power is needed by a removable media drive, color screen, or a hard disk.

So, battery problems can really arise from two sources: First, there can be something wrong with the battery itself or the way the battery is operating. These range from trouble with "intelligent" batteries (batteries that have their own diagnostic capabilities, like those in the PowerBook 500 series) to batteries with a more chemically based *memory-effect*—the battery gets so used to being recharged over and over again when it's only consumed half its power, that it begins to think it's run out of juice when it's only half-discharged.

Battery types and issues

Each PowerBook form factor pretty much requires a slightly different type of battery. Not only do the batteries come in different shapes, with specific types of latches and closures, but they can also vary in the actual technology (usually the chemical makeup) used to create the battery. Each of these batteries needs to be treated a bit differently, and each has its own troubleshooting issues.

All PowerBook batteries require proper disposal when dead. You can't just throw them away. Most of these batteries can be dangerous, explosive, or water-reactive in the wrong circumstances, requiring them to be treated as hazardous waste. Return the battery to an authorized Apple service center, which can then return the battery to Apple or its third-party manufacturer, if appropriate. (Call ahead to the service center to ensure they perform this service.)

Table 29-1 shows the different types of batteries, Apple model numbers, and the PowerBooks that they work with.

<table>
<tr><td colspan="4" align="center">Table 29-1
PowerBook Batteries</td></tr>
<tr><td>*PowerBook*</td><td>*Battery Type*</td><td>*Part Number*</td><td>*Notes*</td></tr>
<tr><td>100</td><td>Lead-acid</td><td>M3053</td><td>Works with no other PowerBooks</td></tr>
<tr><td>140, 145, 145b, 150, 170</td><td>2.5 amp Nickel-Cadmium (Ni-Cad)</td><td>M5417</td><td>Works with 160, 165, 165c, 180, 180c, but not recommended due to short battery life</td></tr>
<tr><td>160, 180</td><td>2.8 amp Ni-Cad</td><td>M5653</td><td>Works with 140, 140b, 150, 160, 165, 165c, 170, 180c</td></tr>
<tr><td>165c, 180c</td><td>2.9 amp Ni-Cad</td><td>M5654</td><td>Works with all 100 series except 100, most life of all Ni-Cads</td></tr>
<tr><td>500 series</td><td>Nickel Metal Hydride (NiMH)</td><td>M1908</td><td>Special "intelligent" battery</td></tr>
</table>

PowerBook	Battery Type	Part Number	Notes
5300/190 series	NiMH	M3254	Can be recognized by 3400 and G3 (3500), but can't be swapped with newer battery types
Duo 210/230	NiMH	M7782	Type I battery, works in all Duo models, but offers low battery life in others
Duo 250, 270c, 280	NiMH	M1499	Type II battery, twice the life of Type I. Required new battery charger. Works in any Duo; requires PowerBook Duo Enabler 1.0 (or System 7.5 or above)
Duo 280, 280c, 2300c	NiMH	M2780	Type III battery, more power, works in any Duo; requires PowerBook Duo Enable 2.0 or System 7.5; some Duo battery chargers also need to be updated to deal with these batteries
1400 series	30 watt-hour NiMH	M2538	
2400 series	29 watt-hour Lithium Ion (LiIon)	M5876	
3400 series	32 watt-hour LiIon	M5139	3400 supports 5300/190 battery, but at decreased battery life
G3 (3500)	47 watt-hour LiIon	M4895	G3 supports 3400 and 5300/190 batteries, but at decreased battery life
G3 Series (BTO)	LiIon	M6385	

Lead Acid

The PowerBook 100 uses a lead-acid battery, which can't be interchanged with any other PowerBook battery. The lead-acid batteries don't experience battery memory-effect issues, but they should also be maintained at some level of a charge for them to continue to be useful. After a certain amount of time between charges, the battery will lose its entire charge, and then it will begin a process called *sulfation*. This is when the lead electrodes in the battery begin to convert to lead sulfate, which ruins the battery. This can happen after as few as three months of idle time. The PowerBook 100 battery should never be fully discharged.

The PowerBook 100 battery isn't actively marketed by Apple, although a number of third-party manufacturers still offer them. You should also be able to get them from an Apple authorized dealer.

Nickel-cadmium (NiCad)

These batteries are used in all 100-series PowerBooks except the PowerBook 100 itself. The later versions of the NiCad batteries have the most battery life and can be used in all compatible models. Battery model number M5654 should be used with all color 100-series PowerBooks.

These batteries can experience memory-effect issues, causing the battery to hold a smaller and smaller charge after each recharge. To counteract this effect, you can fully discharge the battery by leaving the PowerBook on until it shuts itself down (or until it gets very close to quitting, complains strongly, and goes into Sleep mode), and then recharge the battery overnight.

This may still not help, in which case, you can try using a third-party recharging station that does a *deep discharge* (fully discharges the battery) before recharging it. Software utilities are also designed to discharge the battery, and Apple service centers can perform a deep discharge and reconditioning on many batteries. If your storing these batteries, NiCad batteries should hold a charge for about 2 months and should be able to take a recharge for 6 to 12 months, according to Apple.

Nickel Metal Hydride (NiMH)

These batteries are used in the Duo series, the 500 series, and the 5300/190 series of PowerBooks. The batteries are interchangable within each PowerBook series, but cannot be exchanged between series (for example, you can't use a Duo battery with a 500 series PowerBook).

The Duo series used three different battery models: the Type I, Type II, and Type III. Although any Duo running System 7.5 or higher (or the appropriate enabler) can run with any of the batteries, the Type III is recommended for all of them, as it offers the most battery life. The Duo's batteries can experience battery memory-effect, which can be fixed with a manual reconditioning or with software reconditioning.

To manually recondition the battery, fully discharge the battery by leaving the PowerBook on until it quits (or until it gets very close to quitting, complains strongly, and goes into Sleep mode), and then recharge the battery overnight.

If you'd prefer to use software, the Battery Tools 2.0 utility can be downloaded from Apple's Support Web site (www.apple.com/support/).

Duo battery charger updates

Certain Duo battery charger models from Apple are only designed to charge certain battery types, while others need to be updated to work with Type III batteries. If you're getting a red light when you pop your battery into a Duo charger from Apple, you either have the older charger or your newer charger needs an update.

If the Apple Duo battery charger's model number is M7778, it will only charge Type I batteries. A recharger with a model number of M1812 will charge all three types of Duo batteries, but may need to be updated to use a Type III battery. If your M1812 battery charger needs to be updated, Apple recommends the following steps:

1. Shut down the Duo and make sure a Type III battery has been installed. (If you're running System 7.5.1, the Type III Battery extension must be installed.)

2. Plug the Duo's power adapter into an AC outlet. Snap the recharger onto the side of the power adapter.

3. Plug the power adapter cable into the power adapter port on the back of the Duo computer. Turn on the Duo to download the update to the charger.

The PowerBook 500 series uses its own "intelligent" batteries, which are able to report quite a bit of information to the PowerBook, including battery monitors, temperature settings, and other indicators on the Control Strip. These batteries can experience memory-effect and should be reconditioned manually or using the Intelligent Battery Update available from Apple's Support Web site.

The 5300/190 series uses a NiMH battery that will fit into the 3400 series and G3 (3500) series, but will offer those PowerBook models much lower battery life. The 5300/190 series can't be used with any other batteries, though, because they lack the technology to use the more advanced LiIon battery. The 5300/190 battery can experience memory-effect and can be reconditioned manually or using software that came with your PowerBook.

LiIon

Lithium Ion (LiIon) batteries are used in the PowerBook 1400, 2400, 3400, G3 (3500) and G3 (BTO) series of PowerBooks. Although you may be able to physically cram a LiIon battery into a 5300/190 series PowerBook, don't do it — the 5300/190 series isn't designed to work with these batteries.

You can identify a LiIon battery by the four small LEDs on the battery (usually on the part of the battery that's actually installed in the PowerBook, although the G3 BTO series batteries put the LEDs on the outside). These four LEDs indicate percentages of full-charge left, from 25 to 100 percent.

LiIon batteries are subject to memory-effect and can be manually reconditioned. Fully discharge the battery by leaving the PowerBook on until it quits (or until it gets very close to quitting, complains strongly, and goes into Sleep mode), and then recharge the battery overnight.

Battery life

A number of different factors come together to affect your PowerBook's battery life, including the age of the batteries, memory-effect, your charging habits and the charger that you use. Although all of these are important (as are deep-discharging tactics on all batteries but the lead-acid variety in the PowerBook 100), you can more easily control other factors on a day-to-day basis that may, arguably, have an even more dramatic effect on your PowerBook's battery consumption habits.

Some items that can change the speed at which the battery's power is consumed include the following:

✦ The amount of RAM you have installed in the PowerBook.

✦ The brightness setting for the PowerBook's display, as well as whether or not backlighting is turned on.

✦ The amount of time spent accessing the hard disk, floppy, CD-ROM, or DVD-ROM drive.

✦ Settings in the Energy Saver and/or PowerBook Settings control panels, including the operating mode of the processor and the amount of idle time before power management kicks in.

✦ Peripherals, including internal modems, ADB devices, and PC cards.

Memory

Although you probably need the amount of RAM (or more) that you already have in your system (especially if you're a designer or professional who needs a lot of RAM), you may be able to get by without upgrading RAM, and in the meantime add a little to the PowerBook's battery life, by conserving the RAM used by the PowerBook; minimize the number of extra extensions and control panels you use by paring them down in the Extensions Manager.

RAM is power hungry, but not as much as a hard drive or CD-ROM drive. So, having a whole lot of RAM can be a good choice, too. For PowerBook owners, using a RAM disk is certainly an intelligent option, especially if you know you'll be using certain saved data a lot while on a plane trip or otherwise away from AC power. Place your data files on the RAM disk and save them to the hard drive as infrequently as possible (every 15 minutes or so).

Be aware that you could lose the data on a RAM disk if you shut down the PowerBook, zap PRAM, or reset the Power Manager. (You can do these things by allowing the Mac's power levels to get very low, removing a battery for a length of time or leaving the PowerBook in Sleep mode for a long time so that the batteries drain and the PowerBook shuts down.) Otherwise, RAM disk data should survive a regular restart.

Cross-Reference   Chapter 6 has more on RAM settings and RAM disk controls, both of which are just as applicable for PowerBooks.

Settings and controls

Turn down the physical brightness control for your PowerBook's display to conserve battery life. You should also turn the backlighting delay settings to minimum accepted levels, so that the delay is very short before backlighting kicks off. In bright light situations, you'll probably be able to compute without backlighting.

Don't use screen savers with PowerBooks. The picture can only burn into a PowerBook's LCD display after months of being displayed, unchanged on the screen. So, a screen saver isn't necessary for short-term screen protection. Plus, a screen saver accesses the hard drive, uses processor cycles, leaves the backlighting on, and keeps the dimming controls from kicking off to conserve power. Instead, set the screen to dim and blank after a few minutes. (These controls are in the PowerBook, PowerBook Settings, or Energy Saver control panel. See Figure 29-1.)

Mac Evangelista tip: RAM disk for startup

You can really get into this battery saving thing, as Evangelista Garry Halliday, from Sacramento, California, proves with his tip for getting the most out of battery life by using a RAM Disk as your PowerBook's startup disk. Actually, it sounds like a great idea. Just remember to save your actual documents and data to the hard drive occasionally, just in case of catastrophe. You'll also need a decent amount of RAM, at least 32MB, for this plan to work:

"Want to maximize your running time when operating off your battery? Create a RAM disk large enough to hold a slimmed down System Folder and an application such as SimpleText or TextEdit. I use a 20MB RAM disk, and have room to spare. Put these files on the RAM disk, and restart by holding down ⌘-Option-Shift-Delete. This will boot your PowerBook from the RAM disk without having to change the Startup disk with the control panel each time you restart. Select the RAM disk to save your work, and you can work easily twice as long because your hard disk hardly ever gets accessed."

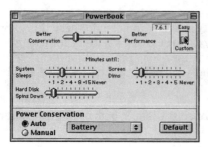

Figure 29-1: The PowerBook control panel for energy saving settings. Note the Custom button, which offers you additional settings.

Here are some other recommendations for controls you'll find in the PowerBook (or PowerBook Settings, or Energy Saver) control panel. You may need to click the Custom button in the control panel (if one exists) to see all these settings. Also, the names of each conservation function vary slightly between control panels, but they should make sense:

✦ Move the slider control toward Better Conservation to set automatic controls designed to save battery life. Otherwise, choose Manual conservation controls and change the following settings:

- Slide the System Sleeps control down to only a few minutes (two to four) using the PowerBook control panel.

- Slide the Screen Dims setting to one minute. (PowerBooks recover very quickly from a dim screen.)

- Slide the Hard Disk Spins Down settings to between one and four minutes.

- Enable the Allow Processor Cycling option, if available. This option slows the processor (causing it to draw less energy) when it's been idle for a few minutes.

You should also use the Special ⇨ Sleep command whenever you plan to stop using the PowerBook for five minutes or more. You should shut the PowerBook all the way down if you plan to stop using it for 30 minutes or more, unless you have a RAM disk whose contents need to be preserved.

You can get shareware utilities designed to automatically save and restore the contents of a RAM disk, including AppDisk (Maverick Software), RAM Disk Backup (John Rethorst), and ramBunctious (Elden Wood). Download the latest versions from www.download.com.

Random acts of conservation

There are a couple of other things you can do to conserve power when working with a PowerBook on batteries. They include the following:

✦ Open the Chooser and turn off AppleTalk (if your PowerBook is not connected to a network. (If it is connected to a network, you're likely in a place with an AC socket available, so use it.) According to Apple, this saves power and lets the PowerBook wake up faster.

✦ Turn off Virtual Memory, which uses the hard disk to allow your PowerBook to load more programs for multitasking, making it seem as if you have extra RAM. Accessing the hard drive drains power. Likewise, don't use Connectix RAMDoubler (or disable it for battery sessions).

✦ Use fewer feature-driven programs. Some programs are written specifically for PowerBooks or are so slight in features that they don't often access the hard drive. Use those. Or, if you can get away with it, write your memos in SimpleText, and then translate them to Word or ClarisWorks and spell-check them once you're connected to AC power.

✦ Avoid games and educational titles that require the CD-ROM drive or play a lot of QuickTime movies, sounds, or other files that need to be loaded from the hard drive.

✦ Don't use external peripherals, internal modems or PC Cards while connected to battery power. If you do use them, use them quickly, and then disable them. For PC cards, pop them out when done.

✦ Don't use external ADB devices unless they're low-power ADB devices that are designed for PowerBooks. Avoid external keyboards, joysticks, game controllers, and ADB-powered modems while on battery power.

Don't forget to recondition your battery when you can—either manually or using a special charging station that reconditions batteries. Apple recommends that you perform one or the other of these procedures every 90 days or so.

Also, travel with spare, charged batteries on long trips. Some PowerBook models still only last two hours on battery power under the best circumstances. Check your PowerBook manual to see if you can swap batteries while the PowerBook is in Sleep mode—nearly all PowerBooks support this feature. You usually only have a few seconds to make the swap happen, though, so do it quickly to maintain the information in RAM. (If your PowerBook supports two batteries, swap them one at a time.)

Battery not charging

There are a couple of different reasons a battery might not charge, including a problem with the battery, the batteries age-old death, need for reconditioning, or a Power Manager circuit problem. The first thing you should probably do is try to deep discharge the battery and recharge it, to see if it's working. If you have a battery reconditioning unit, you might use that, or take the battery in for service.

It's also possible that a short on the logic board could cause this problem, especially if you notice that the PowerBook will only run with the battery and AC adapter connected, and that it dies quickly on battery power alone, even if the battery seems fully charged. You should try resetting the Power Manager first, as described earlier in this chapter. If that doesn't work, though, it's possible that the Power Manager circuit inside the PowerBook has gone bad and needs to be replaced — a reasonably inexpensive fix most of the time.

Other PowerBook Issues

Specific PowerBooks can suffer from specific problems, some of which are beyond the scope of this chapter. Fortunately, PowerBook issues are easy to search for in Apple's online Tech Info Library. Just call up `http://til.info.apple.com` on the Web and enter your PowerBook model or the model series in the search engine ("PowerBook 140") or just do a more general search on PowerBook and the problem area ("PowerBook, display").

But some problems can generally be applied to a number of different PowerBook models (and one or two issues that are model-specific but interesting nonetheless). Take a look at the following issues if you're having PowerBook troubles.

Mac Expert tip: Parts is parts

PowerBooks have a lot of plastic on them, and some of that plastic (and a few other parts) like to snap, bend, fold, or break. Rich Voelker, owner of Voelker Research (`www.voelker.com`) in Colorado Springs, Colorado, has compiled quite a list of little annoyances, as well as what some of them will likely cost you when you stop by the Mac shop to have them fixed — if it's something that can be fixed.

Allow me to step back and present his list of typical problems, prices, and fixes:

(continued)

(continued)

✦ *PowerBook 100-180c.* The AC adapter's insulator ring likes to break, requiring a $70 replacement for the whole adapter. (If you continue to use a fractured AC adapter, you will be seeing your dealer later for the Power Manager circuit.) The Power Manager circuit can go bad, resulting in repairs costing about $75 for parts and labor. If the battery's voltage is less than 6.8vdc, you can try to recondition it. (Voelker would do that for about $50.) If that doesn't work, you'll pay $70 for the new battery. In many cases and under some circumstances replacement of the $2 AC adapter end plug may also work.

✦ *Trackball.* If the button is broken, you'll pay about $75 in labor to have it fixed. If the trackball isn't tracking properly it can be disassembled and cleaned for $50 or so of labor. If the trackball assembly can't be fixed, it'll cost around $110 plus labor for a new trackball assembly.

✦ *PowerBook 500 series.* The Power Manager circuit can go, costing about $75 for parts and labor. The display access cover seems to fall off a lot, especially if you poke at it to see what's under there. It can be replaced for the cost of parts (about $13) and labor ($25 on a good day), but be aware that this is rarely the problem if you're having trouble with the display housing. The display housing screw posts are often broken, causing the access cover to break off. If the whole display assembly needs replacing, the kit from Apple will include a new access cover. The display latch can also be snapped, requiring about $50 in labor and parts. (It's difficult to install on a PowerBook 500.) If the intelligent battery needs reconditioning (using the "Apple Confidential" method it'll cost a flat hour of labor.

✦ *PowerBook 5300.* Warranty issues covered may include a loose AC jack, split bezel, loose trackpad (not the button), PC Card–generated crashing, or broken display hinge. If it's not under the warranty extension, the loose power port repair should run about $75, with the cable reseating about a $50 shop charge.

✦ *PowerBook 1400cs.* The passive matrix display can sometimes exhibit a horizontal gray line, especially noticeable at lower brightness levels. This is, for the most part, normal. Don't try to get anyone to fix it; it can't be fixed and is within legal specifications for this type of display.

✦ *Plastic parts.* In general, plastic parts are harder to get than the other stuff—because someone has to reverse engineer (that is, figure out) the Apple naming scheme for the parts. To complicate things even more, the costs on the parts are relatively low, further discouraging a technician from searching out the part number. Most PowerBook plastics are less than $50 and typically run between $10 and $25. Display access covers are about $15 and I/O access doors are about $8 to $10. If you've cracked or lost something, ask your Apple dealer—he or she should be able to get the part for you from Apple.

PC Card issues

PC Cards are generally pretty easy to work with using the Mac OS and PowerBooks. Like most Mac things, they're visual, they give great sensory feedback, and it makes no sense that you're actually supposed to drag them to the Trash can. (Yikes!) Still, you can run into a little trouble:

✦ *Size matters.* Remember the types of PC Cards and the types you can use. The types, by the way, refer only to the height of the card. Type I cards are very thin (usually memory cards) and can be put in either PC Card slot — two can fit at one time. Type II cards are also thin, and two of them can fit at once. A Type III card (often a miniature hard disk or a paging card) will fill both slots, although it plugs into the lower slot. So, you can't use any other cards if you have a Type III card installed.

✦ *Eject problems.* If a PC Card fails to eject when you drag it to the Trash can or highlight it in the Finder and choose File ➪ Put Away, you can attempt to physically eject the card. Straighten a paper clip and stick it in the tiny hole next to the PC Card slot to force the card to pop out of its slot. If it still won't come out, you can pull it out with needlenose pliers or your fingernails. Once the card is out, try inserting the paper clip again and listen for the spring mechanism to release. Check the card to make sure it's designed for a PowerBook and fits the slot correctly. You'll sometimes find that the bottom slot on your PowerBook is easier to use for oddly shaped cards.

Note

PC Cards designed for data storage on the Newton OS platform are not compatible with PowerBooks, although most modems and a few Ethernet cards can work with both.

✦ *Modem not recognized.* If you insert a PC Card and nothing happens, this could be a sign you are using a PowerBook 500 series PowerBook with an add-on PC Card cage. In early releases of the PCMCIA Expansion Module, modem cards didn't show up on the desktop. You can check the Control Strip for the PCMCIA Quick Eject component, which lets you know that the PC Card is mounted. Otherwise, check your modem software to see if you have an option to change the software's modem port setting to "upper card slot" or "lower card slot." If one of those options appears, your modem has been recognized. (You may still need to choose the modem brand and other settings.)

✦ *"PC Card in use" error message.* PC Cards can sometimes get stuck during use, giving you an error message when you try to eject them, even though no other applications are running. If this happens to a modem card, open the modem software you're using and make sure the modem is not set to auto-answer or auto-dial. (If you must, you can use Chapter 26 as a guide for resetting the modem using terminal program.) If the card is a storage card, try turning off File Sharing, ejecting the card, and then turning it back on again. If neither works, try restarting with Extensions Off, and then try ejecting the card again in the Finder.

Ports and Internals

PowerBooks have varying numbers of ports and support for external devices; even the most modern PowerBooks have opted to include only a single serial port for communicating with serial devices. (If you have an Apple portable computer that includes USB ports — only a vague rumor at the time of writing — consult Chapter 10 for information on using USB.) This single serial port scenario can cause a few headaches. (Basic PowerBook serial configuration tips are back in Chapter 20.)

Printer/Modem port

In most cases, an internal modem will simply work with your modem software. The serial port on PowerBooks that only have one (a printer/modem combo port) is a LocalTalk-capable port, but it's usually mapped as a modem port. (At least, as far as the Mac OS is concerned. In the Chooser and in control panels, you'll usually see the name Printer/Modem port.) So, you should usually be able to use an internal modem and print at the same time, to either a serial printer or a LocalTalk printer.

The exception is when you have a modem program that doesn't support the Apple Communications Toolbox. In this case, you'll need to choose one of the following options for your internal modem (through the PowerBook, PowerBook Setup, PowerPort, or Express Modem control panel), depending on your model: Internal, Compatible, or "Use internal modem instead of serial port." This reroutes the serial port so that it uses the internal modem; the errant application believes it's using the modem port, but it's really using the internal modem.

Unfortunately, this creates a situation where you can't use the serial port for any other task while that setting remains the way it is — including printing through that port to a serial printer. You won't be able to use a serial device until you turn off that modem program and switch the port back to its default mode in the PowerBook, PowerBook Setup, PowerPort, or Express Modem control panel. (The port can be used for LocalTalk connections, so you can print via a LocalTalk printer, if you'd like. Set up the printer as directed in Chapter 15.)

Video port

You may encounter a few problems with the external video port. If you're not getting a picture on the screen, check to make sure the cable is correctly connected to the video-out port; if your PowerBook requires an adapter (most do), make sure it's secure as well. It's best to put your PowerBook in Sleep mode or shut it down before switching the video adapter cable; that way, it can sync correctly to the monitor. Most earlier PowerBook video adapters support an RGB port, which requires an additional RGB-to-VGA adapter. The most recent PowerBooks include a VGA port for video out.

If you're only getting 640x400 or 640x480 resolution on the external monitor, it could be because the monitor is set incorrectly. Check the Monitors or Monitors & Sound control panel to set the second monitor's resolution. You may also have video mirroring turned on (or your PowerBook may only have a video-mirroring capability), in which case the image has to be the exact same on both screens. If the PowerBook is the more limited display, the external monitor will default to the lower resolution. If the external monitor is more limited, then the PowerBook screen will be forced to use a lower resolution. (The PowerBook screen will appear with a border around it to make it take up less screen space.)

5300/190 repair extension

I'll mention one model-specific issue: The PowerBook 5300/190 is under an Apple repair extension program that extends Apple's willingness to repair certain components of the machines for seven years, under very specific circumstances. (If your PowerBook 5300's serial number ends in the letters *AA* you probably don't qualify.)

Here's how to tell if your PowerBook qualifies:

✦ On either model, the AC power connector becomes loose or inoperative. Affected serial numbers are xx605xxxxxx and below.

✦ On either model, using a device in the expansion bay in combination with a PC Card causes the Mac OS to freeze. (You can move the mouse, but clicking has no effect.) Affected serial numbers are xx605xxxxxx and below.

✦ On either model, the display bezel and housing cracks and/or separates at the hinge. Affected serial numbers are xx622xxxxxx and below.

✦ On either model, the bottom case plastics (including the palm rest, trackpad button, center clutch cover, and CPU stiffener) can crack or develop faults. Affected serial numbers are xx622xxxxxx and below.

✦ On the PowerBook 5300, it takes twice as long to boot from AC power as it does from a battery only. Affected serial numbers are xx605xxxxxx and below.

✦ On the 5300, devices drop off of a larger LocalTalk network. Affected serial numbers are xx622xxxxxx and below.

If one of these seems true, take your PowerBook to an authorized service center or call Apple's customer service department (1-800-SOS-APPL) for instructions.

Temperature

PowerBooks are small devices that can be somewhat susceptible to temperature shifts, both hot and cold. For this reason, never leave your PowerBook in a hot car, in direct sunlight, or in other extreme temperature situations. If this does happen, allow the PowerBook to cool gradually to room temperature before turning it on.

Don't expose the PowerBook to extreme cold, either. If you leave the PowerBook in the car or near an open window on a freezing or near-freezing night (or in similar conditions in a car or elsewhere during the day), allow the PowerBook to gradually warm to room temperature before turning it on. When a PowerBook gets very cold, its internals can seize, thereby causing a catastrophic hard drive failure, for instance, the moment you turn the PowerBook on.

Always use the PowerBook's feet when you're using the PowerBook on a smooth surface; the feet help to dissipate heat through the bottom of the machine, which keeps internal components from overheating and causing crashes, freezes, or internal damage.

When using a PowerBook with an external monitor, don't close the PowerBook unless you've also turned the screen off; check your PowerBook's documentation for details. With certain PowerBook models, you can start up the PowerBook using an external keyboard and an external monitor while the PowerBook itself is still closed. This will leave the PowerBook's screen turned off, and the PowerBook will treat the main monitor as if it's the only monitor.

Otherwise, don't close the screen while the PowerBook is active if your model doesn't support this feature. The screen can build up heat that can damage components. If you do use the PowerBook with external components, at least keep the screen open a few inches to allow heat to dissipate.

Cleaning

You can clean the outside surfaces of the PowerBook itself (when it's completely shut down) with a clean, slightly damp cloth (not wet, just a tad damp). Use a computer vacuum to clean the keys of the PowerBook and the edges around the keyboard and screen. Use a clean, lint-free, nonabrasive cloth and a mild glass cleaner (applied to the cloth, not the screen) to clean the PowerBook's screen.

To clean a PowerBook's trackball, follow these steps. (Note: *Do not* use *any* liquids on the trackball components or elsewhere inside the PowerBook):

Mac Evangelista tip: Shipping concerns

Working as a Macintosh technician, Lisa Devlin learned quite a bit about properly packaging and shipping a PowerBook—advice you can use whether you need to overnight your PowerBook for service or just need to pack it for a move or flight overseas. Here are her thoughts:

"Sturdy boxes (not too large) and packaging material are critical. So is insurance for the shipment. Antistatic wrap should be used whenever possible as a precaution. Soft form-fitting foam (the stuff that's sold in rolls) is good to pack PowerBooks in, peanuts are too unstable, and using newspaper as padding is just asking for trouble. Bubble wrap is okay if the PowerBook is first put in some antistatic wrap or otherwise protected from static.

"Never, ever ship a PowerBook Duo inside a Duo Dock. Both units can be damaged by rough handling or static. It's also best to remove PC Cards, cables, and so on when shipping to avoid damage from jostling or static. Oh, and make sure the PowerBook is off, not in Sleep mode. It's a good idea to back up data before shipment, just in case.

"It is also extremely important to inspect the box carefully upon receipt. If it appears damaged, even slightly, in any way, contact the shipping company before opening it. Make sure the shipping company has a representative there when the box is opened if the box is visibly damaged. (I once repaired a machine that was damaged during shipping, and because the shipping company was not present when the box was opened, they refused to pay for the damage, which was considerable.)"

1. Remove the trackball's retaining ring by turning it counterclockwise about 1/4 of a turn. (You should be able to use your fingertips or fingernails.)

2. Remove the ring and the trackball.

3. Locate the rollers inside the trackball housing and wipe them with a lint-free cloth, a cotton swap, or even your finger.

4. Clean the trackball with a dry towel.

5. Reinsert the trackball and its retaining ring.

With a trackpad, clean the surface only with a dry cloth or towel; don't allow water near the trackpad or at the edges, where it could slip through at the seams.

Spills

Spilling liquid on your Mac's keyboard is one thing, but spilling something on your PowerBook is quite another. After all, below that keyboard is the entire computer. If you do spill something on your keyboard, you probably shouldn't wait to get the PowerBook to a technician before you take some action. (If you do want to wait, though, at least turn the PowerBook over, shake out the liquid, and try to carry it upside down to the service center.)

At this point, there are no guarantees. Liquid will most often kill all or part of a PowerBook, depending on how much was spilled, how corrosive the liquid is, and how sticky things get.

Note

It's a good idea to know exactly where your PowerBook's tools (Torx and Phillips screwdrivers in the correct sizes) are at all times, as well as an antistatic, lint-free towel. Your PowerBook's carry case would probably be an ideal spot for these things. You should also familiarize yourself with these instructions and the instructions for opening your PowerBook (in Chapter 20) *before* disaster strikes, just so that you have an idea what to do the second liquid touches your PowerBook.

Here are some quick steps to follow if you spill something on a PowerBook:

1. Immediately unplug the PowerBook and remove the batteries. (You can fret over your lost data later, unless the data is worth more than the PowerBook, in which case you can quickly hit ⌘-S to save, and then pull the battery and plug.)

2. Put the machine on its front side to drain liquid while you look for your PowerBook tools (if you need tools). Hold it firmly and shake it to try and release liquid. If you need to leave it for a moment, you might try standing the PowerBook on the top edge of its screen and the bottom edge of its keyboard casing, forming an upside-down V with the screen and keyboard facing down.

3. If you feel competent to do so, open the PowerBook's case (see Chapter 20 for step-by-step instructions on each different form factor), at least to the point that you have the keyboard popped out. Shake the keyboard clear of liquid and blot it with an antistatic, lint-free towel (not a paper towel or a dirty towel). If you don't have such a towel, just shake. You can also blot surfaces in the PowerBook that have spills, but be very careful that you aren't just moving liquid around or leaving towel residue on components. There is still a charge in the logic board (thanks to the backup battery, among other things), so you should avoid moving liquid around on it.

Now it's decision time. If a local Apple authorized dealer is open and reasonably close, keep the PowerBook open and/or upside down and take it to that dealer. Explain to them the problem and see if they can look at it on an emergency basis.

If you can't get to a service center immediately, you might consider using a hair dryer on a *cool* setting to dry things off as much as possible. If you're lucky, you'll be able to concentrate your efforts on the keyboard; make sure you drain, sponge, and dry the keyboard completely. Don't get the hair dryer too close to components, and don't use a hot setting.

With these things accomplished, get to the service center as quickly as possible. Do not turn the PowerBook on again, no matter how well you think you've cleaned it up.

The keyboard will likely be lost regardless of what you spilled on it. If it's water, it might survive, but you need to get it out of the PowerBook and dried very quickly. Other parts of the PowerBook might survive water, tea, or something similar. A soft drink can be more troublesome, but a clever use of compressed air on a fully disassembled PowerBook by a service technician might still save it, or parts of it.

Your best defense, however, is avoidance. Do what you can to avoid spilling anything on your PowerBook. Be much more vigilant about this than you are about spilling on a desktop keyboard. One spill can ruin a whole PowerBook, so take that into consideration when you eat or drink around it.

Summary

✦ There are times when a PowerBook simply won't power on; this may even happen more often than with desktop Macs because of the elusive Power Manager that PowerBooks require. There are more ways to get power into a PowerBook than a desktop Mac, so there are more problems associated with power.

✦ If you need to reset your PowerBook, there's a slightly different procedure for each major PowerBook series. You can also do some specific things to troubleshoot startup problems and crashing that happen right as the PowerBook starts up.

✦ Working with batteries is a big part of using a PowerBook. Aside from getting the correct replacements, you should also troubleshoot your batteries to make sure they're really going bad before you decide to replace them. PowerBook batteries do need to be replaced every few years, but there are plenty of other problems that contribute to battery failure. You can also do quite a bit to conserve battery power to keep your PowerBook running longer when it's not plugged in.

✦ PowerBooks can experience some odd little problems or habits that you can try to break them of — issues such as problems with ports, video-out capabilities, and PC Cards. Plus, certain models have their own issues, including being part of an Apple Repair Extension program that might make sense of some trouble you're having.

✦ Finally, check out the emergency procedures for a PowerBook that has encountered its worst enemy — liquid. Read them before it happens so you know exactly what to do.

✦   ✦   ✦

Tweak and Recover the Mac OS

If your problem is in the Mac's operating system software, its solution will likely be found in these pages. Part IV introduces you to the basic techniques and specific problems associated with the Mac OS, including how to troubleshoot crashing programs, freezes in the Finder, and specific error messages. You'll also look at preventative measures you can take to avoid system software problems, including intelligent approaches to managing your System Folder and other parts of the Mac OS installation. Finally, if that installation needs a complete refresher, you'll find strategies for backing up your Mac and starting all over again with a clean installation of (or an upgrade to) your Mac OS software.

First Aid for Ailing Mac Systems

In Chapter 21 I introduce the varied world of Mac troubleshooting by looking at the factors determining whether problems on a Mac are software or hardware related. Chapters 22 through 29 detail some of the basic hardware problems that can strike your Mac—along with problems generated by software interactions with that hardware.

In this chapter (and through to the end of the book) I discuss some software-only types of problems. These issues generally aren't related to problems with a particular piece of hardware or a hardware technology such as SCSI. Instead, these problems happen almost exclusively in software, usually manifesting themselves when you're just trying to get some work done with the keyboard and mouse.

From this chapter, which identifies the basics of software troubleshooting and shows you how to get up and running quickly, you can move on to the others in Part IV. Those other chapters focus on cleaning and maintaining your Mac, resolving system conflicts, and, when absolutely necessary, reinstalling the Mac OS.

Software First Aid

Because software falls into two basic categories— applications and system software—the software first aid you'll perform focuses, in most cases, on the convergence of these two types of software. On one hand, your system software is responsible for all the input, output, and process management that goes on in your Mac. On the other, the application software is required for you, the human in this equation, to get something done.

In some cases, your troubles are caused by a specific problem with a specific application. In most other cases, though, your problem is in the interaction between an application (or applications) and the system software. An application may misbehave, the system software may misbehave, or something else may create problems that cause a blip in the communications between these two. That, ultimately, is what leads to instability, resulting in crashes and freezes on your Mac.

First aid techniques

As discussed briefly in Chapter 21, you'll encounter three different, basic types of problems that create trouble with your applications and system software:

✦ **Bugs.** Bugs are problem areas in applications or the system software that do things they shouldn't do. These often result in crashes or hangs, depending on the bug, although they can sometimes just result in strange behavior or a program not doing what it's supposed to do.

✦ **Conflicts.** Conflicts occur between specific programs and system software fragments. Generally, these problems are between system extensions and applications, although a very common subset of these errors focuses on two system extensions that don't get along. (These extension conflicts are common enough to be covered by their own chapter, Chapter 32.) In either case, they tend to cause crashes and hang-ups and can sometimes seem very mysterious.

✦ **Corruption.** Corruption occurs when an important file gets overwritten with either bad or nonsensical information. This can also causes crashes, hangs or other problems. Corruption can sometimes be avoided with proper maintenance, as detailed in Chapter 31. However, corruption's also a small fact of life when dealing with a computer; it will crop up, forcing you to do a little first aid to see if you can solve the problem quickly. (Corruption is usually the result of a bug in a program, although any crash has the potential to result in corrupt files that can then crash the system again at some later time.)

These are really the three different problems that can affect software. Each of them generally has a solution, although you're likely to prefer that none of these problems ever happen, as they can be a pain to troubleshoot and solve. Let's look at those solutions quickly before getting into the actual diagnosis. Like any good boy or girl scout, you should first learn the *technique* of first aid, and then how to apply it to your victim.

Bugs

If the problem looks to be a software bug, your best fix is to find an update on the software publisher's customer service Web site. Many times bugs are actually known issues that have been fixed, worked around, or otherwise dealt with by the company in question. Check Apple's Tech Info Library for clues and read the Read Me file that came with the program. You can also check Mac OS Web sites, chat groups, or mailing lists to see if others are encountering the same bug; if they are, there's a chance the problem will become known to the software publisher and fixed more quickly.

Other than a programming fix, the only real first aid solution is to create your own workarounds—don't download a Java applet if there's a bug in your Web browser that makes the Java applets crash, for instance. Or, remember a certain procedure for saving your documents when using a particular program or a particular order of steps when printing to a problematic printer.

After first aid, if you can reproduce the bug accurately and on demand (or fairly closely so), come up with whatever diagnosis you can and report the bug to the offending program's publisher. You'll likely find some mechanism for reporting bugs on their Web site or through their customer service center. At the very least, knowing that you can reproduce the bug will help you convince the customer service folks that the problem exists and needs to be looked into.

Note

It's usually important for your technical support representative to know quite a bit about your computer to help you troubleshoot or report bugs. A program like Apple System Profiler can be helpful. If you need to take a screenshot, you can usually use ⌘-Shift-3 to take a PICT file of the screen that is then saved in the root folder of your startup disk. The keystrokes ⌘-Shift-4 in Mac OS 8.0 and above gives you little cross-hairs that enable you to take a screen shot of any particular area of the screen. Just drag from one corner to the other with the mouse.

Conflicts

Often overlooked is the Read Me file, a fairly standard addition to a typical software installer or distribution disk. If you look at your program's disks or CD-ROM, you'll likely find a Read Me file that will help you determine some of the known conflicts that have been revealed during the program's testing. Workarounds are usually discussed, including common extensions and programs that should be disabled, upgraded, or avoided when working with the problem application.

If you can't seem to find a known issue statement but still suspect a conflict, your first aid solution is to disable all possible offenders; use the Extensions Manager to restart with only the Mac OS Base extensions enabled, for instance, or turn off other possible conflicts such as file sharing, background printing, Virtual Memory, and some of the other typical Mac OS offenders. If your program still acts up, you'll need to decide if it's worthwhile to continue to use it in the short term. (You can try to limp by until the company writes an update patch by saving your work constantly or running the program without others in the background and restarting the Mac often.)

After first aid, you should try to troubleshoot the exact nature of the conflict as discussed in Chapter 32. You should also look to update the software, if possible, or choose other extensions and/or programs that don't have a similar conflict. You can also report the conflict to the software publisher, if it's reproducible, to see if they can help you troubleshoot or create a workaround.

Corruption

Overwhelmingly, corruption means a preferences file (in the Preferences folder) has gone bad, but it can also refer to corruption in RAM, in PRAM, or in other files on the hard drive. If you suspect corruption is crashing your program, the first aid solution is to try throwing out its preferences file, and then restart and try the program again. If you suspect disk corruption, load and save important data to a different disk.

Over the long term, you should look for the source of corruption. It could be a problem application, a large crash that caused bad data to be written, or a more insidious problem — even a computer virus. To properly root out corruption, see specific crash and freeze descriptions later in this chapter and consult Chapter 31 for more on maintaining your system, properly uninstalling programs, and dealing with viruses.

Note   You'll see advice in this book and elsewhere that encourages you to sometimes trash your preferences files when testing for corruption. This is almost never a fatal mistake; preferences files as a rule are to be rewritten by standard Mac programs if the program can't find its preferences file. If you're wary, though, just drag the preferences file out onto the Mac's desktop or into another folder outside the System Folder. You can then test to see if the file was corrupt. If the problem behavior goes away once the file has been disabled, the file is corrupt, and it's safe to trash the file. If the problem persists you can move the file back to the Preference folder.

Software symptoms

With a little technique under your belt, it's time to observe the symptoms of software failures. The symptoms are generally pretty similar — crashes, freezes, hangs, and bizarre behavior. Sometimes you can get the Mac to start up or a program to start up. Sometimes you can't do something as simple as print from your application.

The symptoms you'll likely encounter when working with programs are as follows:

✦ **Errors.** You get an error message while working with the program that doesn't force the program to quit or shut down. Generally, you receive these messages in an alert dialog box (in Mac OS 8.0 and above these dialogs are outlined in red), which tells you that the last command you attempted could not be completed because something went wrong.

✦ **Crashes.** In this situation, you get an error message that is accompanied by the immediate shutdown of the program. Sometimes these error messages offer explanations, other times the program has unexpectedly quit.

✦ **Freezes.** The Mac locks up completely, not allowing you to type, move the mouse, or issue commands of any kind. This often isn't accompanied by an error message, and it leaves you no choice but to restart the Mac using the Cntrl-⌘-Power restart sequence or a physical power switch on the Mac.

✦ **Hangs.** This is like a freeze (symptomatically), but you can still use your mouse to click things — it's just that nothing on screen responds. The first thing to do is stop clicking things and wait. This behavior usually results from the program getting itself into a logic loop that causes it to stop responding to input from the mouse or keyboard. Overloading the input queue with clicks or keystrokes won't help. If, after a reasonable interval, the program doesn't pop back to life, you can use the ⌘-Shift-Esc key sequence to attempt to force quit the program.

✦ **Bizarre behavior.** This can be almost anything, but it certainly includes the screen becoming pixelated, program commands simply failing to work, or issues such as files not being saved correctly, documents disappearing, or windows behaving oddly.

Once you pin down the symptoms, you can quickly diagnose the basic problem — bug, conflict, or corruption. you're then ready to put your learned technique to use for your first aid fix.

To begin, take a look at some first aid steps you can take in diagnosing and testing based on the symptoms.

Error Messages

Hopefully, the extent of the problems you'll have with your Mac are focused on error messages. Error messages sometimes provide a decent idea of what happened and why, at least giving you a fighting chance to figure out what's wrong.

Error messages that don't crash the application will usually have a reasonable solution. Sometimes an error will point you to a hardware issue — perhaps the Chooser or your modem is configured incorrectly. Often an error message will let you know that there isn't enough memory for a particular request or function; in this case, you usually try to increase memory for that application or quit other applications that may be using that memory. Other errors have similar solutions.

Most of the error messages you see that don't result in a crashed application (crashes are covered in the next section) are pretty straightforward. You'll be asked to replace a disk, troubleshoot a port, or pick a printer. Just read your Mac's complaint and consult the related chapter(s) in this book.

However, some more generalized issues can crop up in the Finder and in applications that might be caused by a variety of issues. Here are a few of those very common errors and some solutions to try.

"Not enough memory" error message

This message will likely appear to most Mac users at one time or another. Although it may be a symptom of a bug or corruption, it's usually the result of a conflict; specifically, the program has tried to use more RAM than it's been assigned.

Here's a quick checklist of the things you can do to combat an out-of-memory issue:

✦ Check the state of RAM in the About This Computer dialog box.

✦ Raise the application RAM available to the troubled program.

✦ Restart the Mac.

✦ Check for a program update or bug fix from the application's publisher.

You can check the Mac's overall memory situation by switching to the Finder and choosing the About This Computer command from the Apple menu. In that window, check to see how much of the Application's RAM is being used and what the largest unused block of memory is. If the application's RAM is nearly used (indicated by a full bar, as shown in Figure 30-1) and there's still room in the largest unused block, it's likely that your application just needs more RAM assigned to it.

Figure 30-1: The About This Computer dialog box tells you how much RAM is being consumed by the Mac OS and applications.

You can change the RAM settings for a particular application this way:

1. Shut down the application.

2. Find the application's original icon. Highlight it and choose File ➪ Get Info from the Finder's menu.

3. In the Get Info box, enter higher values for Minimum Size and Preferred Size under the Memory Requirements section.

4. Close the Get Info box.

Now you can relaunch the program and see if the memory errors persist.

Note

If you got the memory error and found that there was very little memory left in the largest unused block, it's possible that you're using nearly all of the Mac's RAM for the Mac OS and your running applications. In that case, you may need to shut down the problem program, shut down some other applications that you're not currently using, and relaunch the program to use it.

But what do you do if you're getting "out-of-memory" errors all over the place (or you get the errors even when there seems to be plenty of memory available)? In this case, there's a good chance that memory has become fragmented. When memory fragmentation occurs, a form of corruption has set in; a number of programs have been opened and closed on this Mac, and those programs, once closed, haven't always done a stellar job of releasing all the RAM they were using. After a while, these fragments of leftover code become a problem, because the Mac is trying to take notice of them and track them to keep them from causing trouble. If memory gets fragmented enough, you'll get odd out-of-memory errors that can only be cured by restarting the Mac.

You could also have a bug in your application that causes it to use memory inefficiently, or *leak memory,* meaning it begins to take up all the available memory because it's not handling its assigned memory well. In either case, a recurring "Out of Memory" error message will result because the program isn't working correctly, not because of any problems on your end. If you suspect this is the case, surf the publisher's Web site and check for an update or bug fix for the program in question.

Explore your memory settings

If you have repeated problems with "Out of Memory" error messages, your Mac may be telling you something—add more memory. But if you need to squeeze that RAM a bit to make things work in the short term, you might be able to get a little extra RAM from your Mac to make that application run more cleanly.

The obvious place to start is to use as few extensions and control panels as you can. Try to pare down your Extensions Manager so that you're only using the most important extensions you need to run. You can also lower the requirements of some applications by managing your fonts a bit. If you have tons of different fonts in your Fonts folder, try moving all the nonessential ones to another folder (you could create a Fonts - Disabled folder in the System Folder or use one of the shareware solutions on the included CD for font management).

(continued)

(continued)

The real savings, though, may come about in the Memory control panel. You can gain some RAM back by lowering the amount used for disk cache or by doing away with a RAM disk, although both of these solutions can decrease performance. One way to boost the amount of RAM available to your Mac is to turn on or turn up the amount of Virtual Memory in the Memory control panel. Virtual memory enables your Mac to use a portion of the hard drive to swap data in and out of RAM, allowing you to work with more and larger applications at one time. Of course, this is a trade-off, too, because it'll slow down your Mac's performance quite a bit. When you can, buy more RAM to get the best of both worlds.

"Disk is full" error message

This one usually crops up when, you guessed it, your disk is full. In general, it happens when you're trying to copy or save a document to the drive in question, or when you're otherwise transferring data (it could happen as you check for new e-mail or surf the Web, for instance, because both save data to the hard drive while you're working). Be especially wary when you're creating digital audio, video, or working with high-end photographic images, all of which can require an enormous amount of disk space.

The solution, in most cases, is to clean some of your stuff off the disk and try to copy or save again.

If the disk isn't really full, though, you could have some disk damage or fragmentation problems with the drive — both of which are solved with a combination of Disk First Aid and a disk doctor program from a company like Norton or Micromat. (Chapter 23 has a lot more on using these programs.)

Remember, there can be some interesting culprits on your drive that are taking up the space. Check your e-mail program's folders, the "downloads" folder in the AOL or Web browser's folder, and your Web browser's folder in the Preferences folder. All of these can be storing untold hidden megabytes that can be eating up space on your drive.

This error can also result from running a very old program (likely one written before the release of System 7.0) that incorrectly calculates available disk space. In this case, your best bet is to try and use a newer program or look for an update for the current one.

"File not found" or "File system error" message

If you see either of these error messages, and after checking for the obvious (such as the file not actually being where it should be or a network volume that suddenly disappears) you still have problems, your Mac could be experiencing some sort of file corruption or problem with the desktop database files. Because Macs are pretty good at tracking files and disks, you'll usually get an error that says something like "Please insert the disk _____ " if you've managed to eject a floppy disk or removable media disk that's currently in use.

So, getting a "File not found" error message means something fishy is going on. If your Mac is part of a network, that's one thing to suspect; it's possible that an application was expecting to find an active network connection and an important file, but the network connection went down.

Much of the time, though, this error results from a disk or disk directory error. You should try a few things. The immediate concern is to save any work that you have open. Try to save or use the Save As command to save any open work you have. You might consider trying to save the document(s) to another floppy disk or removable disk if you're concerned that there's something wrong with your hard drive.

You should next follow the basic storage media troubleshooting plan:

✦ Rebuild the desktop using a tool such as Micromat's Techtool.

✦ Reboot using a boot disk or a system CD (if the problem is with your startup disk) and run Disk First Aid to diagnose the drive.

✦ Run a disk doctor program such as Micromat Techtool 2 or Norton Utilities.

Program Crashes

When a program crashes, you'll generally get an error message along with the famous Mac bomb icon. The program has tried to do something that the operating system feels is illegal. You'll also often get an error message or number that tells you, for instance, that you have a Type 11 error. In many, many cases, these errors are pretty much meaningless. It's tough to troubleshoot based on them, so I'll discuss them more generally.

The error codes are really meant for programmers. Looking at a long list of these codes tells you what each of them is supposed to mean, but they can mean some very complicated and confusing things. They're also not really supposed to show up in programs. When they do, they're usually the result of bugs.

On the CD-ROM

Are you really interested in the program codes? Check out the shareware resources Apple Error Codes and Easy Errors, both located on the CD-ROM included with this book.

What follows is a more general discussion of what's going on with your Mac when it crashes and what you can do about it. There are really three basic types of crashes, all of which usually offer the same result: a program disappears, sometimes leaving the system unstable and sometimes allowing you to continue computing. For the most part, the same software problems that cause other problems cause crashes: bugs, conflicts, and corruption. There are a few clues to show you which is which, but some of it is guesswork:

✦ *Error message or code.* This sort of crash manages to pop up an alert box (usually with a bomb in it) that tells you something untoward has happened, so the Mac OS is making the program go away. This is a controlled sort of crash that usually sees your system recovering safely to the Finder. If you get an error message, you can suspect any of the three types of problems, although bugs and conflicts are more likely.

✦ *Unexpectedly quit.* This sort of crash usually leaves you wondering for a moment — the application just disappears into oblivion, followed by a message in the Finder telling you the program unexpectedly quit. It's abrupt, but the Finder almost always recovers. All three problems can cause this, but if it's reproducible, suspect a bug in the program.

✦ *No message.* In this case, the program just quits, disappears, or otherwise becomes inaccessible. This sort of crash is a bit more rare and usually accompanied by increased instability, although you may be able to work in the Finder or other applications for a while. This suggests a larger system problem, possibly a conflict.

So what can you do about a crash? It's important to be able to isolate the crash by taking a few different factors into play, including what you've done recently and how persistent the error is. Your first aid goal is to get past the crash, save your work, and restart your Mac; after any crash, the Mac may be too unstable for more than a few minutes worth of work. Use the Special ➪ Restart command to get your Mac back in fighting shape as soon as you've saved your critical data in other non-crashed applications.

The bigger issue, though, is isolating the crash and figuring out why it happened. You will eventually encounter a crash, and it's not always indicative of a larger problem. Some crashes are just once-in-a-while sorts of problems. Here are some basic things to look into:

✦ *Has your Mac been on for quite a while or have you been running many different programs?* If so, you can suspect memory fragmentation or corruption. Eventually, every Mac needs to be restarted just to clear out RAM and begin anew. If you don't run many programs, your Mac may last months without a restart, but crashing programs after a long working stint are one sign of a Mac that's just, well, tired.

✦ *Have you added anything recently?* If you've recently installed something new, such as a new hardware driver, a new extension, or a new application, it may be the source of a conflict that's suddenly causing the crashing application to have more trouble than it has in the past. Read the program's Read Me file and go to the manufacturer's Web site to check for any known incompatibilities, and then troubleshoot conflicts as outlined in Chapter 32.

✦ *Have you upgraded the Mac OS recently?* This may cause problems or incompatibilities in programs that had been working well in the past. If there's been a recent Mac OS release, check for bug fixes and updates on the software program publisher's Web site or through their customer service representatives.

✦ *Did anything precipitate the crash?* Sometimes you can pinpoint the source of new, consistent crashes. For instance, say your Mac was hit with a power surge or crashes spectacularly during a long file operation, a network connection, or an Internet session. Any crash like this — especially a freeze or a hang — can cause corruption in the desktop files, Internet preferences, or elsewhere. This corruption can then cause crashing.

✦ *Is the crashing consistent?* If your Mac crashes every time you try to load a QuickTime movie over the Internet in your Web browser, you're well on your way to pinpointing a bug, conflict, or corruption problem that has a definite source. It may seem like an obvious example, but crashes can be so frustrating that you forget to make a mental or written note of what was happening when the crash occurred. A reproducible crash is much easier to fix.

Once you've done some work trying to isolate the crash, you're on your way to fixing the situation. The key is to decide what sort of problem is likely — bug, conflict, or corruption. You then can put your first aid techniques to work.

Aside from general application crashes, there are some specific types of crashes — with either particular characteristics or telltale error codes — that bear a little more discussion.

Type 11 errors and "FPU not found" error messages

Although less and less frequent as the Mac OS ages, these error messages were particularly prevalent during the transition to Power Macintosh computers and then again to PCI-based Power Macs. The real trick to them is they don't mean much of anything and were for a time used as catch-alls for other problems. Some of them related to the transition from older 68000-based programs to PowerPC-native programs, but only barely.

When you can't get rid of the error message

In an ideal world, the Mac would handle every application crash with aplomb, forcing the errant program to quit with dignity and allowing you to move back to the Finder and save anything that's open without too much hassle. But this is not yet a perfect world. (Rumor has it that it will be a perfect world after Mac OS X is released, but, as of this writing, that remains to be seen. It may be a better world, though, with protected memory and preemptive multitasking giving the Mac OS more control over misbehaving programs.)

Many of your programs, when they crash, will recover to the Finder. But sometimes you'll find that trying to dismiss an error message alert box causes more problems, such as an error alert box that keeps reappearing. In other cases, you'll find that trying to dismiss the error causes or is followed by a worse error.

In these situations there are three things that can happen and two things you can do to try and head them off:

A freeze. If the Mac freezes after an error message, you can try to troubleshoot the freeze as discussed later in this chapter. You'll likely need to restart your Mac and move on, though.

Force Quit. If an application hangs on its own after an error (or otherwise becomes erratic), you can try to force the program to quit. The keystrokes ⌘-Shift-Esc will bring up a Force Quit dialog box allowing you to manually "crash" the program and recover to the Finder.

Endless alerts. If you can't seem to do anything about the alerts showing up over and over again, you can try one desperate measure before throwing in the towel and restarting—drop into the programmer's box. With the ⌘-Power key sequence, you can bring up the programmer's box. Type **G F** and hit Return. This might recover the Mac to the Finder, which will be very unstable but may allow you to save your work in other applications.

Whatever you do, your goal should be to save your work and restart the Mac. Any crash can make your Mac too unstable to continue working. If you try to keep going on, you'll likely encounter another crash or freeze within minutes.

Type 11 errors are really just "miscellaneous" errors, an error message that occurred often when the Mac OS engineers were transitioning the Mac OS, but are less common now that the kinks have been worked out of the PowerPC code and any errors are mapped to other error messages. FPU error messages aren't really accurate, at least on PowerPC machines; they usually just mean the Mac has jumped to an invalid memory address and is trying to work with bad data. (On pre-PowerPC machines, they usually are actually errors with the floating point unit.)

If you're getting a lot of Type 11 or FPU-type errors on a PowerPC machine, the chances are good that a simple Mac OS update will solve the bulk of these problems. In Mac OS 7.6.1 and above, many of the crashes were eliminated or given error types that were more meaningfully worded. They also don't cause as many forced reboots, enabling the program to quit gracefully to the Finder instead.

Type 41 errors and Finder or Bus error messages

These types of errors often occur as the Finder is loading or soon after it's been loaded, but before you can get much work done. They basically point to a corrupted Finder, Finder preferences, or (occasionally) a corrupt System file on your startup disk. Sometimes a quick restart will cause the problem to go away for a time, but it's often back with a vengeance.

The Finder can become corrupted as a result of a system crash, a problem with an application, or an overall maintenance issue. Over the longer term, you should check your hard drive for errors and look into possible conflicts on your system. You'll occasionally find that trouble with your hard disk driver will cause Finder corruption.

The quick answer is a Mac OS reinstallation, or, if you have a draggable System Folder (a complete, current Mac OS installation on CD-ROM or another removable media), you can drag the corrupted System file to the Trash and copy a new System file in its place.

Expert tip: System reinstallation

If it looks like the Finder and/or System are corrupt, sometimes the best thing you can do is perform a shortcut reinstallation. A full clean install is probably the better choice, but this shortcut is a great first aid tool that many professional Mac managers use when they need to get their Macs up and running immediately. When you get a little down time, go back and see if you can figure out what caused the System corruption in the first place. At that time, you should especially consider using a disk doctor program and a clean reinstall.

But if you've got to get the Mac up quickly, try this advice from Glenn Schunemann, Macintosh consultant for academic information technology services at the University of Maryland, College Park:

"I've found a way to do a 'shortcut' clean system install, when an existing system is already on the disk and the system is the cause of the problem. What I do is trash the Finder and System file and then reinstall (not clean install) the system from CD. This way the installation has no choice but to replace the Finder and System file. This works most of the time, and it beats the heck out of copying over all the third-party control panels and extensions!"

(See Chapter 33 for more on Mac OS installations.)

Internet-related crashing

Did the crash occur in your Web browser? This could be a strong sign of corruption, especially if the crashes seem to be gaining frequency and are not necessarily reproducible. (Your first Web browser troubleshooting should probably focus on multimedia plug-ins, which can be too soon on the market.) One symptom of corrupt Internet preferences is crashing in multiple Internet programs — Web browser, e-mail, FTP, and so on.

The Internet Preferences file takes a beating and Web browsers tend to crash a lot, so the file seems to get its share of corruption. If you suspect this is the case, reach into the Preferences folder and drag the Internet Preferences file onto the desktop or to the Trash. Restart your Mac and run your Internet tools again.

Note

If the crashing seems focused on the browser, you can also consider trashing the browser's preferences and history file, and resetting the browser cache. Some users swear that trashing the Global History file in the Netscape directory can solve problems with both Netscape and Internet Explorer if both are on the system.

You may also be able to attribute Web browser crashes to multimedia plug-ins that are sometimes brought to market very quickly and not completely tested. (Or, they may crash when a poorly coded Web page is encountered.) In these cases, the error should be fairly reproducible; it occurs when your browser attempts to load a particular type of multimedia data, a Java applet, or something similar. If this is happening and you need to get browsing quickly, you should be able to change the browser's preferences so that it ignores the offending sort of data. Later, you should check for updated versions of the plug-in software.

Freezes and Hangs

Usually without so much as a little bit of happy help from the Mac OS (in the form of an error message, perhaps), a freeze simply locks up the screen so that nothing moves; it resembles what happens to your TV when you've hit the Pause button on your VCR. A true freeze will bring the mouse cursor to a screeching halt. No matter what you do, you can't move the mouse and no activity can take place on the screen.

A subset of these freezes is something that's called an *endless loop* or a hang, a program gets caught doing the same thing over and over again without giving much control back to the computer or allowing you to move on to other things. That's really just a crash, but it can have the symptoms of a freeze: The program just sits there. The difference is you can usually move your mouse pointer around on the screen, even if it doesn't move terribly smoothly.

A freeze can be caused by any of the three major software problems (a bug, a conflict, or corruption) but a bug is far and away the most likely cause (especially a bug that causes a conflict). You'll also find that the problem is often actually triggered by a process that's running in the background — such as the Printer Share software, HP background printing, AppleTalk, or other networking activity.

Freezes are also often related to memory. If you have a program that regularly causes freezing, one step to overcome this is to add more application RAM in its Get Info box.

As far as first aid goes, though, there isn't too much you can do about a freeze; you can try to recover from it, but it's unlikely. The real trick is to make sure you actually know the Mac has *completely* frozen. Otherwise, you may be losing data when you don't need to, if simply out of frustration.

When it seems your Mac has frozen, perform all the following steps to make sure it's really a system freeze and not a hang, crash, or other problem:

1. Check your mouse, keyboard, and other ADB connections. A really good way to emulate a freeze (and make you feel sheepish at the same time) is to kick your ADB cabling loose, resulting in a mouse pointer that won't move. If your mouse or keyboard is unplugged, try plugging them back in to see if you regain control. (Note: Apple recommends against adding ADB devices while the Mac is powered on, although purely anecdotal evidence suggests that you probably won't destroy anything if you occasionally have to replug an ADB device.)

2. Watch the screen carefully to make sure you're not seeing any activity. If you have a menu bar clock, a visual keystroke indicator, or any icons that generally flash but aren't, there's a chance that you really are experiencing a freeze or a hang.

3. Wait. This is especially true if you're working with high-end graphics, animation, movies, audio, the Internet, scanning. or anything that is talking over a network or to peripherals. In fact, anytime your Mac seems to have crashed is a good time to get up and stretch or look into getting yourself a refreshing beverage. Even the menu bar clock can stop updating while an application struggles to get past something. And these apparent freezes can last up to ten minutes or so. If you can help it, wait that long before trying to quit the program or restart the Mac.

4. If you're absolutely convinced the program isn't responding, you should try the keyboard. ⌘-. (period) and/or the Esc key may convince the program to stop what it's doing and move on. Try pressing ⌘-S to save your work. And try ⌘-Q to get the program to quit peacefully. If that doesn't work, try a forced quit. Press the ⌘-Shift-Esc keys at the same time and attempt to bring up a Force Quit alert box. If it appears, click the Force Quit button to attempt to quit the application abruptly and recover to the Finder.

5. Before giving up completely, hit ⌘-Power. If a dialog box appears with a small prompt, enter **G F** (including the space) and hit Return. This may recover you to the Finder, or it may freeze your Mac once and for all.

6. If those don't work, you may really be dealing with a freeze. It's time to restart the machine. Using the keyboard, hit Ctrl-⌘-Power to force the Mac to restart immediately. If this doesn't work, double-check that your keyboard is connected. (This is a great time to find out that the problem is ADB after all, because it won't notice the keystrokes and nothing will happen.) If all seems correctly configured, use the Mac's hardware reset key or button to cycle the Mac's power. (If your Mac has no reset button or key, turn it off and on again.

In rare cases a freeze might actually force you to unplug the Mac and plug it back in again.)

If the force quit or any of the other measures — beyond plugging in ADB or waiting — is successful, immediately save your work and try to restart your Mac. The system is likely very unstable.

Once you've recovered from the freeze, it's time for your detective work. You can troubleshoot a freeze much as you would a crash, but focus on RAM issues, conflicts (especially background and extension conflicts), and corruption in the application or process that was running during the freeze. For instance, delete unfinished print jobs in the PrintMonitor Documents folder (in the System Folder), delete Finder preferences, and delete Internet preferences or others that might have been related to the programs that were running during the freeze.

Freezes are often hardware/software conflicts, too. Troubleshoot your printing connections, network connections, SCSI connections, and other peripherals and peripheral drivers with help from Chapters 21 through 29 in this book. Identify the part of the system that seems active when the bug or conflict occurs (if the freeze is reproducible), and then look to those particular applications or subsystems as the likely cause.

Heat and internal problems cause freezes

Your Mac is designed to run under reasonably optimum conditions and with a minimum of modification to the Mac's case and innards. A tightly packed minitower case might have everything you need to get by, but it also might reduce the flow of air inside the case, leading to increased heat build-up. Similar problems can result from working with your Mac at high altitudes, above room temperature, or after a cold session in the basement or in the trunk of your car.

You should always work with your Mac within its ideal temperature range — usually between about 40 to 75 degrees Fahrenheit. A little hotter or cooler may not do much damage, depending on other factors. But if your Mac has been exposed to extreme cold or heat, just turning it on without allowing it to return to room temperature can damage it severely.

Overheating, especially, causes freezes and crashes. Running with a processor upgrade that doesn't have proper heat dissipation (a heat sink or fan), leaving the case off your Mac for extended periods, or running the Mac in a humid or hot room without decent ventilation could all lead up to seemingly random crashes and freezes. One sign that overheating could be causing a problem is a Mac that computes well soon after being turned on, but begins to have unexplained crashes or freezes after 30 minutes or so of work.

Freezes can also suggest something is wrong on your logic board or with another component in your Mac. If all else fails, consult Apple or your clone's manufacturer to see if there are any known issues related to freezes on your particular Mac model or logic board. Make note of the circumstances and any patterns to the freezes or crashing, to help them better troubleshoot the issue with you.

Bizarre Behavior

Certain problems are a bit tougher to classify, even though they're not necessarily impossible to track down and solve. Some of these are long-known issues, whereas others can be symptoms of larger problems.

Icons and aliases

The classic rebuild-your-desktop scenario is brought about when your Mac begins to inexplicably lose its unique icons or aliases begin to fail. Because of fragmentation or other issues within the desktop database files, the icons are no longer associated with the correct programs and documents, resulting in their use of more generic-looking icons. Similarly, aliases tend to lose their relationship with the original document or program as damage creeps into the desktop database.

Other symptoms of desktop database problems include slow access in the Finder, slow startups, and slow file operations in applications. Generic document icons can also be a sign, although some applications don't necessarily have special icons for their saved documents.

The answer? Rebuild the desktop. Hold down the ⌘-Option keys as the Mac starts up; usually you should hold down the keys all the way through the sequence until you see a dialog box that asks you if you want to rebuild the desktop file (see Figure 30-2).

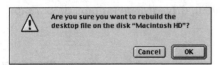

Figure 30-2: The Mac is responding to a ⌘-Option startup request.

Choose OK and then be prepared to wait — in most cases, the bigger your drive is, the longer this process will take.

In Mac OS 7.5 and newer, Apple recommends that you turn off most extensions in the Extensions Manager, and then restart to rebuild the desktop. The one exception to this is Macintosh Easy Open (or Mac OS Easy Open), which Apple recommends you leave loaded in the Extensions Manager.

If your drive is heavily fragmented or you're experiencing problems outside of rebuilding the desktop, it's a good idea to run Disk First Aid and/or a disk doctor program before relying completely on rebuilding the desktop. The desktop database files are likely to become corrupted again more quickly if the drive itself is in bad shape. You should also run a disk doctor program if you find that rebuilding the desktop doesn't fix your generic icon issues.

Another way to rebuild the desktop file — and arguably a better way — is to use TechTool or TechTool Pro. TechTool preserves the comment fields in Get Info boxes and completely deletes the desktop's files in a reasonably safe way, making for a more reliable rebuild process.

Slow startup, crashes, or freezes while word processing

Sometimes unexplained crashes and freezes can actually be attributed to corrupt fonts. Problems that can be attributed to this issue include unexplained crashing on startup, crashes after a clean install (if you've manually copied the contents of the previous Fonts folder to the new Fonts folder), crashes that occur as an application starts up, or crashes when choosing fonts in an application.

If you can manage to load and isolate the problem to particular fonts that crash your system when you switch them in an application, try to restore those fonts from installation disks or a backup. If you can't isolate the fonts, perform a clean install or replace your entire font directory from a backup. You can also troubleshoot fonts much the same way as you troubleshoot extensions, as discussed in Chapter 32.

Slow disk, disappearing files, bad menus, beeps

If your Mac is constantly crunching the hard drive, files are disappearing, corruption seems rampant, or the system seems almost painfully sluggish, you're probably dealing with a drive problem, drive fragmentation, or, perhaps, a computer virus.

Expert tip: The why of rebuilding

So what's going on with all the desktop rebuilding and funny looking icons? Reed Jackson, Apple Computer system engineer, gives the scoop:

"The Mac stores a files creator and type record in an invisible area of the Get Info window. When those values change, or are not present in the file, your file may appear in icon view as a generic, dog-eared document icon.

"To remedy this ailment, first rebuild the desktop. This process examines all of the file and creator settings and several other values and corrects any that are misadjusted.

"Also, you can launch the application that the file was created in, and then, using the File ⇨ Open command, choose the file that is affected and open it. Now, save the file with a new name, and verify that the new file has the correct custom document icon from that application."

The presence of a virus is also indicated by bizarre beeps, dialog boxes announcing nontechnical sorts of things (such as "Merry Christmas" or "Don't panic"), and problems with your menus, especially in programs such as the applications in Microsoft Office.

If Norton or TechTool can't solve your problems, and you've been through the hard drive troubleshooting tips discussed in Chapter 23, you might consider whether or not you have a computer virus. Most Mac viruses (and there are relatively few of them) prey on the desktop database and the file system, trying to create problems with your folders and files.

See Chapter 31 for definitions, tips, and troubleshooting advice regarding viruses.

Summary

✦ Before looking at the specific software problems you'll run up against, it's important to get a little technique down, as with any first aid procedure. The splints, tourniquets, and bandages of software first aid come into play when you're dealing with bugs, conflicts, and corruption.

✦ The different types of software issues you'll deal with include error messages, crashes, freezes, and just plain strange behavior. Although all of these can be caused by hardware issues, there are certain symptoms that suggest very clearly that you have a software problem that needs to be addressed.

✦ Error messages can be pretty straightforward, although error codes that show up in those messages aren't always useful. Most of the codes are really designed for programmers who are debugging their programs. Once the program is released to the general public, the codes can be less useful. Still, there are general things you can learn about the codes to help you troubleshoot.

✦ Crashes and freezes can be frustrating, but you can deal with a lot of them through some clever elimination. It's important to get to the source of the problem, and then determine what sort of problem is causing the crash and whether or not you can isolate and reproduce it. Of course, your first aid issue might just be that you need to get the computer running again — there's a right way to do that, as well.

✦ The rest of the software problems you'll encounter can be a little odd at first, but these quirks are facts of life on the Mac platform. If your Mac is acting a little strange, there are a couple of symptoms you can look for that will help you determine why.

✦   ✦   ✦

Clean and Maintain Your Mac OS

Many problems you encounter can be solved by regularly maintaining your system with hard-disk tools, virus protection, and a backup plan. If you keep up with these three things, you're likely to have fewer problems than if you simply use your Mac without regard for maintenance. The process certainly doesn't need to be exhausting, although you do need to be thorough. In fact, the best way to achieve harmonic system maintenance levels is to create a schedule and stick to it.

Obviously this chapter includes a little upgrading advice; you need to get a disk doctor program such as Norton Utilities or Micromat TechTool 2. Check to see which is most compatible with your system and the latest Mac OS upgrade. Each has its own specialty, with Norton focused on crash and file-corruption prevention, and TechTool focused on providing a total solution for your Mac's troubleshooting tasks.

As you'll see by the end of this chapter, you need a good virus checker. I make some recommendations later, but I want to mention up front that a virus checker is a good idea, especially if you use your Mac for business or education (and losing your data would be costly) and/or you spend a lot of time on the Internet.

Regular Maintenance and Care

You should follow a pretty straightforward checklist to maintain a happy, working Mac system. Aside from some of the tips elsewhere in the book (correct installations, avoiding conflicts, upgrading, and working with the latest programs and software drivers), the most important thing you can do to keep your Mac running flawlessly is to create a schedule of maintenance and stick to that plan. In many cases, you might even be able to get your software to do it for you (see Figure 31-1).

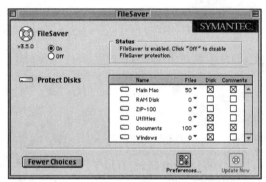

Figure 31-1: Norton Utilities includes tools that enable you to automate certain maintenance tasks.

Scheduled care

What are the things you should do? I'll discuss two types of maintenance: the daily stuff and the time-based issues. Daily, you should do the following when you're working with your Mac:

✦ *Turn the computer on and off no more than once a day.* If you want to turn it on in the morning and off in the evening, fine. Otherwise, you'll extend its life by leaving it turned on; just turn off the monitor (or set it to Sleep mode in the Energy Saver control panel) to conserve energy.

✦ *When shutting down or restarting the computer, use the Special menu commands.* On many Macs you can use the Power key to shut down, too, but the point is this: Don't just kill the power, turn off your surge protector, or throw the power switch. This keeps the Mac from shutting down in an orderly way, including writing some last-minute files and closing everything out before restarting or shutting down.

✦ *Restart occasionally.* If you use many different applications and documents in one computing session, it's a good idea to restart your machine occasionally to guard against memory fragmentation and subsequent crashes. If you restart when you come back from lunch, for instance, or before switching over to a marathon Web session, you might encounter fewer unexpected crashes and restarts.

✦ *Maintain files and check drive space.* It may seem silly, but it's actually a good idea to make a point of deleting files, throughout the day, instead of putting it off until you can sit down and delete in one session. The reasoning here is it helps to keep your drive from filling up, which can cause errors and crashes if temporary files and data documents suddenly can't be written to a full disk. It's also a bit easier to manage your Mac that way.

Just doing these things will help keep you up and running on a regular basis, but you can do more to ensure a relatively error-free computing existence. Each of the following tasks has a recommended frequency; you may not need to do them quite as often, but it's certainly a good idea. Indeed, you might find it's useful to set a calendar program or alarm clock to remind yourself to do these things — if your disk doctor program doesn't do it for you.

✦ *A few times a week:* Back up your hard drive(s) or your network according to a preplanned rotation. (See Chapter 7 for more on backup planning.)

✦ *Every week:* If you spend a lot of time downloading files, transferring documents, or working with files from the Internet or an online service, it's a good idea to run a virus-checking program once a week. You should also update the virus definitions by downloading them every month to every three months from your virus-protection software publisher's Web site.

✦ *Every month:* Rebuild the desktop file. This will keep it from getting out of control and causing trouble that eventually requires a disk-fixing session or worse.

✦ *Every three months:* Check the level of fragmentation on your hard drive and defragment if necessary. Defragmenting not only optimizes the drive for speed, it guards against potential problems. A heavily fragmented drive can lead to file corruption.

✦ *Every three months:* Do a little seasonal cleaning (or spring cleaning) to your drive, archiving and/or deleting files you don't need on the drive or don't need at all. This includes preferences files and other system-level stuff that may just be taking up space. (Spring cleaning is discussed later in this chapter.)

Note

There's actually a product called Spring Cleaning, from Aladdin Systems (www.aladdinsys.com/), which does this same sort of thing by helping you track down superfluous preference files, uninstall unwanted programs, and generally give your Mac the once-over to report on any files or configurations that could be cleaned up on your Mac.

✦ *Every three months:* Hold a special Web surfing session during which you check for updates to your favorite software by surfing the software publisher's Web sites. This includes your virus definition files if you have a virus-protection program.

✦ *Every six months:* Perform a major hard-drive maintenance session, including a complete check of the disk (boot from another drive or a floppy), an update to the Mac OS if it's available (and reportedly free of major bugs), and an update to your hard-disk driver, if necessary.

✦ *Every one to two years:* Perform a clean install of the Mac OS. If you have a new version of the OS or you're installing a new hard drive, that's a great time to clean install, especially because you may need to troubleshoot your extensions anyway after installing a new version of the Mac OS. (This isn't always true, but you should check the Read Me file and proceed with caution.) Even if you're not upgrading, it's a good idea to reinstall every few years just to clean things up a bit.

This checklist alone should keep your Mac out of trouble, most of the time. With a solid maintenance schedule, you'll find that the only problems that crop up will be hardware failures and problems that you expect, such as slight file corruption, minor fragmentation, and the occasional virus. In any case, you're prepared and ready to deal with these minor evils.

The other side of maintenance: Hardware

Most of the maintenance discussed in this chapter covers software. However, it's also a good idea to adopt a maintenance routine for your hardware, too.

The items to concentrate on most are those that move — the keyboard, mouse, and perhaps your printer. Your keyboard and mouse can probably use cleanings once a month or so; a trackball can usually use a little more cleaning (at least pull the ball and blow out any dust or dirt). See Chapter 24 for more on cleaning input devices. Obviously, you should clean your monitor whenever it needs it. Use the special solutions described in Chapter 25.

The inside of your computer might be able to do with an occasional dusting — every six months to a year depending on how clean the area is around your Mac. Although you shouldn't blow compressed air directly on the circuit boards inside your Mac, you can use a small vacuum cleaner designed for use around electronics. You should also try to clean out the power supply fan (don't open the power supply — just vacuum the back of it) and clean any dust away from ports on the back of the Mac.

In the same time frame, it's a good idea to dust or vacuum your scanner, printer's paper tray, and the power supplies for external hard drives, and even run a commercial disk cleaner through the floppy drive and make good use of a CD-ROM cleaner. And while you're at it, you might as well do what you can to arrange that jumble of power cables and connectors.

Spring cleaning

Over time the Mac OS and its subsidiary files simply begin to bloat. Old applications leave Read Me files, SimpleText versions, and preferences files littered all over the drive. Programs install fonts you don't really want or need. Temporary document files get left in your document directories. Even saved game documents start to take up unwanted space.

Eventually, these small files will cause fragmentation and the sheer volume of them will give you all sorts of headaches, including less room for your *new* stuff, important temporary files, Virtual Memory, and other things that together can cause a few crashes. You should take the time to run through your hard drive once a season to see if you can't find some stuff that's worth deleting.

Duplicate applications

To begin your spring cleaning ritual, use the Find File command in the Finder to gather together duplicate files and see how many you can do away with. Different programs tend to come with their own versions of some old standards, and you may find you have a certain number of the same files or applications inhabiting your drive (see Figure 31-2).

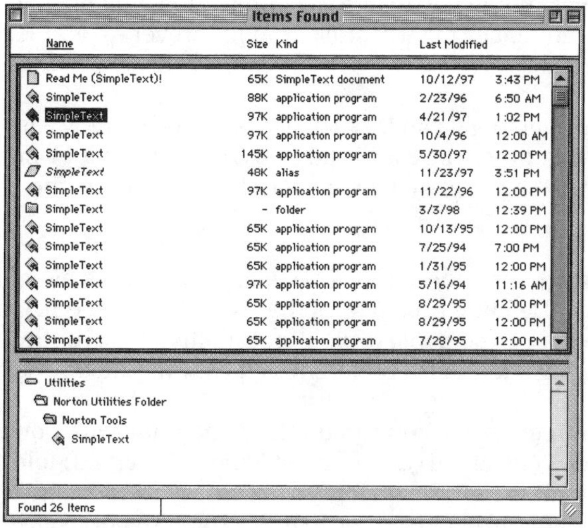

Name	Size	Kind	Last Modified	
Read Me (SimpleText)!	65K	SimpleText document	10/12/97	3:43 PM
SimpleText	88K	application program	2/23/96	6:50 AM
SimpleText	97K	application program	4/21/97	1:02 PM
SimpleText	97K	application program	10/4/96	12:00 AM
SimpleText	145K	application program	5/30/97	12:00 PM
SimpleText	48K	alias	11/23/97	3:51 PM
SimpleText	97K	application program	11/22/96	12:00 PM
SimpleText	-	folder	3/3/98	12:39 PM
SimpleText	65K	application program	10/13/95	12:00 PM
SimpleText	65K	application program	7/25/94	7:00 PM
SimpleText	65K	application program	1/31/95	12:00 PM
SimpleText	97K	application program	5/16/94	11:16 AM
SimpleText	65K	application program	8/29/95	12:00 PM
SimpleText	65K	application program	8/29/95	12:00 PM
SimpleText	65K	application program	7/28/95	12:00 PM

Utilities
  Norton Utilities Folder
    Norton Tools
      SimpleText

Found 26 Items

Figure 31-2: Using Find File you can see how many files or documents are wasting space on your hard drive.

Want to know some of the common culprits? Because many of these files are distributed and installed by a number of manufacturers (as part of bundling agreements and other arrangements), I'd put even money on the likelihood that you have the following duplicate files on your drive:

✦ SimpleText

✦ StuffIt Expander

✦ DropStuff with Expander Enhancer

✦ Internet Config

✦ TeachText

✦ MoviePlayer

✦ Hypercard Player

✦ QuickTime Plug-in for Web browsers

You may encounter others. The point is you can probably do just fine with only one copy of each of these programs. Using Find File and the Finder, check each file to see which is the most recent copy (you can use the File ➾ Get Info command to find out what the version number of each is) and delete the rest.

Preferences, fonts, and extensions

The next step is to comb through the System Folder and look for duplicates or leftovers that are ready to be trashed. One of the prime possibilities is the Preferences folder, where nearly every application you ever install and run on your Mac will place one or more files. When you delete the application, you may be surprised to know that the preferences file will stick around forever — or at least until you clean the folder manually.

Gathering preferences files for deletion is an inexact science — I generally run through and delete any files that I recognize and can absolutely say that I won't be using the associated application anymore. If I've deleted the application, the preferences file can go, too.

Of course, if there's a file in there that doesn't look familiar or you think might be necessary, by all means skip it. Deleting preferences files is really just a quick way to get back some file-storage space and avoid a slight possibility of corruption due to drive fragmentation — leaving a few extra preferences files won't do any harm.

Once you've moved on from preferences, you can do the same thing with your Fonts folder and the Extensions (Disabled) and Control Panels (Disabled) folder. If you see extensions in those folders that are no longer necessary (for example, they worked with an application that you've deleted or hardware you're not using anymore) you can toss them, too, and save some more storage space. Fonts are a special case; the fewer fonts you have in the Fonts folder, the faster your Mac will boot and applications that use the fonts will start up. It's always a good idea to clean out the Fonts folder of any fonts you never use. (You can also boot a little faster if you combine your existing fonts into fewer font suitcases, as described in Chapter 26.)

Want to see what the font looks like? In the Finder, you can double-click a font suitcase to see a visual representation of the font, as shown in Figure 31-3.

Figure 31-3: You can check out the font before trashing it.

Note

You should also consider organizing your fonts into suitcases, as described in Chapter 26, to keep things orderly and under control in the Font folder.

Evangelista tip: Don't trick your Mac out

Some of the best advice is the most simple. While you're going through this spring cleaning process, you might also take careful inventory of your System Folder and decide what, exactly, you need on your Mac to survive. A program such as InformINIT, on the CD-ROM included with this book, might help.

Or, you can go to an extreme. How about using *only* Mac OS extensions? It's possible you could get away with it, or something close. (That'll mean staying away from Global Village products, Microsoft software, 3Dfx, PC networking, and non-Apple printers and hard drives, among some other interesting programs.) Here's a tip direct from Evangelista Allan Schwartz (www.concentric.net/~Ams):

"Extension (init) conflicts can potentially waste a lot of your time. Should you ever use third-party inits? My philosophy is if it's unlikely that Apple Quality Assurance has tested an init as part of their release cycle QA, I don't want to use it—I don't want to have to test it.

"Sometimes, I fix severe system problems by dragging the System Folder into the trash and reinstalling from the 7.6 CD. It's helpful not to have too much investment in System Folder customization."

Sound good to you? If you're serious about it, you'll probably want to follow the Evangelista tips in Chapter 32 that recommend using Labels to track file changes in your System Folder. Then every few weeks, tool through your Extensions and Control Panels folders to make sure no errant application has installed something new. If it has, you'll have to pull it and try to do without the application at fault, or make an exception in this one case. (Remember, some games and multimedia titles will drop in extensions, too. Maybe you can leave them in until you're done with the game, and then toss 'em!)

Temporary files

Applications on your Mac will often take advantage of a hidden folder, called Temporary Items, that resides on your hard drive. It'll store in that folder temporary files that are on as the Mac is being used and the application is open. For the most part, there's really no point in mucking around in that directory.

However, sometimes those temporary files will escape and end up saved on your hard drive, either in the Trash (as rescued items) or in your documents directory as work files that got saved when the application experienced a crash or some other oddity.

In any case, after awhile these files can start to pile up a bit. They're usually ripe for deletion; you either needed to dig into the file or you didn't. If you didn't, and the file has gotten on in age, maybe it's okay to delete it.

There's no particular standard for naming temporary files; you can try "temp," "work," and similar words in a Find File search. You should also comb through your document folders (especially when you're getting ready to archive and delete them) and look for temporary files that can be deleted so your compressed archives or backups take up less storage space.

Attachments and downloads

Another place to look for potential spring cleaning victims is in any directory that stores e-mail attachments or downloads you've received over the Internet or through an online service. (Check your e-mail program's folder, your Web browser's folder, and online services' folders such as those for AOL and CompuServe.) You'll find you've often already read, installed, used, or otherwise dealt with an attachment, yet it lingers in a download or attachment folder on your hard drive for quite some time — if not forever. Some e-mail programs are set to automatically delete these downloads after a certain amount of time, but others might not have any plans for these files.

In Find File, use "attach" or "download" as a keyword and search for files and/or folders that have these files in them. Check the dates carefully and be sure you don't delete anything important.

You should also travel individually to your e-mail program's storage folders; they may be in the System Folder, in the application's folder, or even in the Preferences folder. In those folders you may find extra files — attachments, cache files, old mail — that are ready to be deleted. While you're busy doing these things, you might want to stop by the Preferences or Options menu in your e-mail and online programs to see if you can tell it to delete downloads after a certain amount of time.

Deleting applications

Part of your spring cleaning might involve getting rid of any applications you no longer need on the system. This might be an older version that you've upgraded or a program that you've decided didn't suit your needs.

Deleting an application involves more than simply taking the application folder and dragging it to the Trash. You'll want to think about a few other issues, too, including the following:

✦ Do you have any documents currently stored in the application's folder that you'd like to keep? Make sure you don't have anything else important in that folder or a subfolder, either.

✦ Do you have some means of translating the documents you are keeping? If you're deleting Microsoft Word, for instance, make sure your copy of ClarisWorks (AppleWorks) or Nisus Writer can translate all those Word documents you held onto.

✦ Is there a Read Me file or a manual that tells you what files the program installed on your system? Applications can install extra folders (such as the Microsoft Office folder on many Macs), put stuff in the System Folder (such as the Claris folder), or install extensions or control panels that work with the application. Try to round all of these up when you're planning to throw away the application.

✦ Did the program have a preferences file? If so, grab it from the Preferences folder.

One trick I recommend: If you're serious about deleting the application, create a folder and place it on your desktop or on the main level of your hard drive. Call it "Files to Delete" or whatever you like. Put all the files related to this application that you're extracting from your drive into this folder. Now compute for a few days.

If things start to go nuts (and you haven't changed anything else), you may need to replace one of the extensions, preferences, or other files you thought you were supposed to delete; it may turn out it wasn't part of this application's installation after all. Plus, this system gives you a week or so to use the application again if you find a document hiding somewhere that requires it.

Otherwise, drag the Files to Delete folder to the Trash and choose Special ➪ Empty Trash to delete it!

Defragmenting and optimizing

When you've used your hard drive for a number of weeks or months, it can begin to get fragmented. This fragmentation is a result of the way the Mac stores files on a hard drive. While it still can (that is, while there's still free and open space on the hard drive), the file will be written *contiguously* — the whole file will be written to one section of the drive. But if there isn't a large enough area on the drive, the file will have to be broken up into smaller pieces to be stored on the drive. The Mac will keep track of the pieces so it can find them again later.

This doesn't necessarily have to happen when the drive is almost full. It can happen on a drive that's only half full if the drive is fragmented enough. The fragmentation is the result of files being saved to the drive, and then moved or deleted from that drive. When the files are deleted, a new hole is created where that file used to be.

To further illustrate, imagine yourself in a public library. Because library patrons rarely take home entire shelves of books, they open up small holes on shelves all around the library when they check out books. Even if the library gets to where it's only half-full of books, the shelves are limited to the size of books (or number of contiguous books, such as an entire series of encyclopedias) that would fit into a particular opening.

Fragments of space are what make up the drive's fragmentation level. If the drive is unfragmented, an entire file can load immediately after it's found by the hard drive's read head. Fragmentation forces the hard drive read head to spin up and seek out many different parts of the drive to load one particular file. As a result, access slows down, sometimes considerably.

All of this seeking and spinning also makes for more opportunities for an error to occur, which can result in file corruption or parts of a file being lost because the Mac's desktop database (where this data is stored) becomes too bloated, slow, or fragmented itself.

Note   As with any sort of hard disk maintenance, it's a good idea to disable file sharing and print sharing on a particular Mac if you normally allow people to log into the computer. Network users are unlikely to do damage, but it's possible they could interfere with the disk fixing or defragmentation problem.

Defragment the drive

You should regularly defragment your hard drive every three months or so. During the process, a disk doctor application reads the fragmented parts of files, and then writes them back to the drive in a more contiguous manner. It cycles through the entire drive, finding ways to write the files and rewrite them so that the puzzle comes together and most, if not all, of the files are written contiguously.

Most defragmenting programs give you the opportunity to choose how meticulous you want the defragmentation process to be — that is, if you want it to be done quickly for minimal results or if it should be an intensive session that results in nearly 100 percent defragmentation. The latter is certainly recommended when you have the time, although partial defragmentation is OK for maintenance purposes (see Figure 31-4).

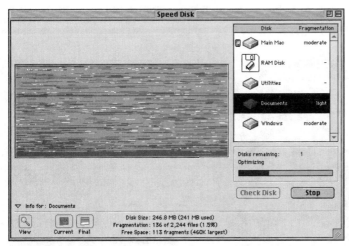

Figure 31-4: Defragmenting a drive to speed it up and keep files a little more secure

Most of these programs will enable you to ascertain the drive's level of fragmentation before going through the optimization process; if the drive is heavily fragmented, the program may also recommend that you run the file saver or disk-fixer portion of the program to make sure the fragmentation hasn't already created errors. After the drive is fixed, you can defragment the drive and swear to maintain it more closely.

Note

If you have a drive that's been formatted using the Mac OS Extended (HFS Plus) format, you need to use a defragmentation tool that's been designed for that type of drive. Older versions of Norton Utilities and other programs can damage these drives if used on the newer format. Make sure you have an updated version of Norton Utilities, TechTool Pro, or whatever other tool you use for defragmentation that specifically claims to be HFS Plus-compatible. Plus Optimizer, another tool from Alsoft (www.alsoft.com/), is specifically designed to work with HFS Plus disks.

Optimize the drive

If you have time this session, you can also choose to have your defragmentation program optimize the drive, which is simply an extension (a little more time consuming) of the standard defragmenting process. When you choose to optimize a hard drive, the program not only writes the files contiguously, it actually writes them in a special order, according to a special algorithm created by the programmers. This scheme for optimizing can even be geared toward a particular type of application to help you get the most performance out of your drive (see Figure 31-5).

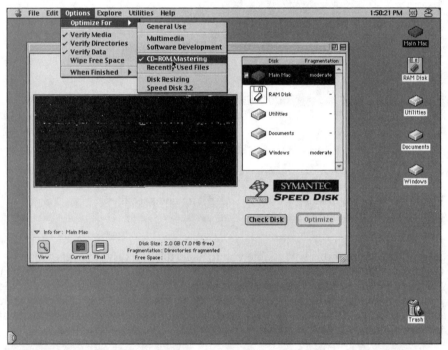

Figure 31-5: Norton Utilities enables you to optimize the drive for a number of different purposes and applications.

For instance, an optimization scheme might write all the documents in one section of the drive and all the applications in another, or it might do a quick optimization that simply creates a large contiguous space — perfect for multimedia files that need to be digitized from an audio or video source.

Note   If you have Norton Utilities or another disk doctor program that can perform optimizations, look carefully at the different optimization schemes it offers. Some of them can be very useful for a particular situation, such as optimizing the drive for CD-ROM mastering or for software development. You can also choose more general uses for every day optimization.

Evangelistas and Experts: Optimizing

Although defragmenting is generally considered a good idea, people certainly don't always agree on how to go about optimizing—or if one should do it at all. Rich Voelker of Voelker Research thinks an optimization is of dubious value. In fact, he advises avoiding just about any process that spends too much time rearranging important files on your hard drive. Instead, he says, the best way to optimize or defragment a drive (although it may be somewhat impractical) is to back up the entire drive, format it, and then copy all your files back from the backup media. That way the Mac can lay everything down in a defragmented state, without fear of data loss. And you don't even have to buy a special program.

Other tips have come in from Evangelistas around the world, with their own opinions on defragmentation and optimization. In all cases, don't forget that a backup is a good idea:

"I use Turbo Disk from the Turbo Toolkit (FWB) to optimize my hard disk. With a cleaned up System Folder, the Mac boots much quicker. For this optimization, it is necessary to run Turbo Disk from a secondary bootable drive or volume. The manual explains how to copy Turbo Toolkit to a secondary bootable device, and temporarily make the secondary device the startup volume in the Startup Disk control panel. There's an easier way, however. As you're booting, with the secondary device turned on, press Shift-Option-⌘-Delete. This temporarily boots the Mac from an alternate startup disk, without the need to reset the original boot disk. Once the Mac starts up from this alternate disk, press Shift. This turns all extensions off, which is important because an extension can interfere with the optimization process and freeze Turbo Disk. This results in a system halt and, most probably, the risk of some files getting corrupted." — George Pluimakers

"I'm a hard-drive *crasher* because of two things. First, I use the Internet constantly and second, I don't do enough disk repairs and defrags. Think of it this way. Every time you write and erase a file, you have a chance of messing up your hard drive. Internet usage is about as heavy of a write/erase scenario as the normal user can come up with. So, I use a multi-tiered approach to minimize my crashes. The idea is this: If I mess up the file directory of one hard disk partition, I don't lose the other partitions due to file directory problems.

"I've partitioned my hard drive into three partitions: One is my boot drive and application drive. The second contains all my documents and work (which makes backing up critical files a snap). The third has all my Internet software, downloads, and caches. I run Norton Utilities now, and regularly fix the tiny problems that crop up. Because my drive is partitioned, I only have to do this regularly on my third partition. This saves a lot of time. Finally, I use a RAM disk for my Web browsing cache. It's a bit faster than getting the info off of the hard drive, but more importantly, if I do have a problem, I don't get phantom cache files anymore that are half-written or half-deleted. I find that my regular Web pages are news-related and change regularly anyway, so I don't mind not having my cache on disk from startup to startup." — Jon Steltenpohl

Viruses

Historically, the Mac has only had to deal with a relatively small percentage of viruses compared to the number that have been created to infect Intel-compatible computers. In fact, there's a certain line of thinking out there that says Mac users are almost so statistically unlikely to encounter a virus that making a big deal out of them is unimportant.

I'm not quite in that camp. For one thing, the fast and furious pace at which the Internet is becoming a part of most Mac owners' computing experience makes for a solid opportunity to distribute viruses. And the Mac isn't exactly impervious; the lack of viruses is probably more the result of a lack of interest than it is in the security of the operating system or some other inherent Mac advantage. There are more viruses on the Intel-compatible PC platform because there are more computers to infect, thereby allowing these virus authors to cause more trouble.

However, more viruses are appearing on the Macintosh — specifically, viruses that are cross-platform. The Microsoft Visual Basic for Applications macro viruses (probably the type you're most likely to encounter in the near future) can hop right from a Windows-based PC onto a Macintosh running Microsoft Office. It's likely that other cross-platform viruses, perhaps written to exploit holes in Java (a technology that allows programs to run on many different operating systems) or other cross-platform solutions will be just as capable of infecting the Mac as any other computers.

So, the threat is real. My Mac has gotten only a few viruses that I'm aware of, and all of them (again, all the viruses I've caught) were either Microsoft macro viruses or viruses specific to a particular application (for instance, Hypercard-based viruses). Other than that, I've been lucky. Still, surfing the Internet, sharing floppies, swapping Zip disks, and sitting on a large computer network are all high-risk activities that leave you more susceptible to viruses.

What is a virus?

First and foremost, a virus is a program, and its main goal is to replicate itself as much as it possibly can. It wants to copy itself onto new hard drives, new removable media, and new computers over networks. Viruses are often designed to infect low-level operating system code so that they can self-replicate whenever certain commands are invoked on the computer or when a particular event, such as a new floppy disk being inserted or a new computer appearing on the network.

Viruses can be malicious, but they don't have to be. Many viruses are relatively harmless; they self-replicate and try to distribute themselves to more and more computers, but then at some prescribed date and time, they pop up season's greetings or peace messages on screen. Still other viruses are designed to be annoying by moving the cursor around the screen, popping up dialog boxes, or affecting the display. Of course, these can still cause problems as there's a good chance they'll crash an application or the entire system, potentially affecting data.

The worst viruses are those that attempt to destroy data and files on your Mac. These viruses may try to infect the hard disk driver software, the system software, or even the desktop database. They erase files, mess up your folders, and attack the disk's structure itself, introducing errors. In some cases, they can manage to erase or mangle your entire hard drive. It's very rare that this happens, especially on a Mac, but it can happen. (See Table 31-1 for a list of some Mac viruses.)

Table 31-1
Sample Macintosh Viruses

Virus	What It Does
Autostart 9805	Exploits a hole in QuickTime to copy itself to available disk volumes, and then creates invisible files on the hard drive. Causes extensive disk or network activity and can overwrite some files with bad data. (Technically a worm, not a virus — see the sidebar "Non-viruses: Other malicious code.")
Code 252	Infects applications and some system files. Displays a message that says "You have a virus. Ha Ha Ha. Now erasing all disks...[etc.]" before deleting itself. Does no other damage on purpose, although it can crash the machine and cause damage.
Init 17	Displays the message "From the depths of Cyberspace." It's been known to do some damage, especially to 68000-based Macs.
Init 29	Infects all types of files and spreads rapidly on the system. May display the following message when a disk is inserted in the floppy drive: "The disk needs minor repairs. Do you want to repair it?" Can cause many unintentional problems.
Init 1984	On Friday the 13th, the virus damages files by renaming them, changing file dates and sometimes deleting files. Infects system extensions only. (Init-M is a similar virus.)
nVIR B	Infects applications and the System file, but does no significant damage. Has a number of strains, including AIDS, CLAP, Hpat, Jude, nFlu. Will sometimes beep or say "Don't panic" if speech is enabled.
MDEF	Infects the System file, doing no intentional damage. Can cause crashes. Has a number of strains, including Garfield, Top Cat, C, D.
T4	May keep extensions from loading or make the hard drive unbootable (depending on the version number). Strains include A, B, and C.
Zuc	Causes the mouse pointer to move around on the screen whenever the mouse is held down and an infected application is running. Only infects applications.

Non-viruses: Other malicious code

Along with viruses, which are self-replicating programs that attach themselves to other programs, there are two other major types of problem programs—Trojan horses and worms. A Trojan horse is rogue code that (probably) does something malicious, but is disguised as a program that does something interesting. An example would be a program that says it will get you free Internet access but actually erases your hard drive when executed.

Worms are even more like viruses—they're self-replicated, but they don't attach themselves to programs. Like viruses, they're sometimes malevolent and sometimes they don't do much of anything. An example of a worm is the AutoStart 9805 worm, which has just been discovered at the time of writing.

The AutoStart 9805 worm only affects Power Macintosh systems. Using the AutoStart feature in QuickTime 2.0, 2.5 and 3.0, the worm launches itself when an infected disk or other media is mounted on the Mac's desktop. If that Mac isn't already infected, the worm copies itself to the Extensions folder as a program called Desktop Printer Spooler. Now whenever the Mac is restarted, this worm program is run.

After infecting all the drives it can, the worm looks for files ending with "data", "cod", and "csa". When a targeted file is found, it is damaged by the worm overwriting the data fork with random data. The current workaround is to disable AutoStart in the QuickTime control panel, although the major Mac virus detectors are capable of detecting and destroying the worm.

What's not a virus?

There are a number of hoaxes out there that seem to be forever circulating on the Internet. Some people compare them to "urban legends": stories such as the one about the little boy who wants postcards before he dies from leukemia or the frantic warnings about body parts being farmed by prostitutes. These chain-mail type ventures are very popular in e-mail.

Some of these e-mail hoaxes show up in the form of virus alerts that have been released by the U.S. government, Microsoft, a university, or some other organization that seems credible. Surprisingly, most of the alerts I've read have glaring misspelling and grammatical errors that seem to indicate that they're hoaxes, but that deters few people.

When one of these notices arrives in your In box, don't forward it, and don't believe it. Unless you've heard otherwise from a very reliable source, the following statements will always be true about viruses:

✦ Regular, text e-mail messages cannot be infected with a virus.

✦ A virus is almost always distributed by attaching itself to a program, which can be an attachment to an e-mail message. The infected program must be executed, however, before the virus can infect anything.

✦ Unless it's exploiting a security hole in your Web browser, a virus can't be executed simply by loading a particular Web page.

You really shouldn't worry at all about the possibility that a virus is being transmitted through an e-mail message. Instead, you should focus on being sure that files you download from Internet sites and unsolicited e-mail attachments don't have viruses. (You can also suspect a floppy disk given to you by a colleague or friend if viral symptoms show up in your Mac.) Get a good virus-protection program and scan files you think may be a problem before you launch them.

Note

You'll hear many pundits say that a text e-mail can never be infected with a virus. And, in the current state of technology, that's completely accurate. The problem I have with this blanket statement, though, is it's always possible that some form of scripting or macro language will be popularly instituted by e-mail programs, at which time a virus infection — such as by the Word macro virus — may be possible. Javascript, for instance, is a scripting language that consists of text commands embedded in Web pages. These commands turn Web pages into running programs. As long as the host applications themselves remain secure (Web browsers won't allow anything but the most innocuous data to be saved and executed on your Mac by a remote site), you won't have any problems. But if an e-mail application comes along that processes text-based scripting instructions *and* allows access to the user's hard drive (through a bug or by mistake, as with Word Basic), e-mail messages could, ultimately, contain viruses or Trojan horses.

Viral symptoms

Although virus authors tend to do their best to hide their viruses (at least until they want them to be found through a dialog box or file damage), there are some symptoms that you can associate with a virus, assuming you've eliminated other troubleshooting possibilities. Although you should always have a virus checker handy, especially to investigate odd behavior, remember that it's far more likely that your problem is related to an extension or hardware conflict, program bug, or file corruption.

That said, here are some symptoms that might suggest a viral infection:

✦ You experience seemingly automated behavior on your Mac that can't otherwise be explained (such as files moving on their own, the mouse pointer being affected, dialog boxes appearing).

✦ A launched program doesn't appear or appears after a significant and unusual delay.

✦ The system unexpectedly restarts after accepting a disk, running a program, or mounting a removable media disk.

◆ Extensive, unexplained disk activity occurs, especially when no programs are running and/or when the Mac has been started with extensions off.

◆ Files and folders become corrupted or disappear.

◆ File sizes, creation dates, names, or other file details change automatically.

In general, these situations describe the action of viruses at the Mac OS level. Program-level viruses do more specific things, usually messing with your ability to use that program. Hypercard viruses infect Hypercard programs, for instance, whereas Word Basic viruses affect your ability to use Microsoft Word correctly.

Detection and cleaning

If you're a high-risk, connected Mac user, you should consider getting yourself a virus-protection program. These programs generally run in the background, checking files as they appear on your hard drives or in a removable media device. You can also program them to check for viruses at specific times during the day and/or week. Popular antivirus programs include the following:

◆ Symantec (www.symantec.com), makers of Symantec Anti-Virus for Macintosh

◆ Network Associates (www.nai.com), makers of VirusScan for Macintosh

◆ Dr. Solomon's (www.drsolomon.com), makers of Virex for Macintosh (Dr. Solomon's has recently be bought by Network Associates, so this URL may change at some point.)

When a virus-protection program detects an infected file, it will generally try to isolate that file by letting you know it has a problem and, sometimes, giving you the option of moving the file (perhaps to a folder of infected files to help you keep track of them).You then have the option of simply deleting the files and restoring them from a backup (after testing the backup for viruses) or trying to clean the virus from the infected file.

Cleaning is something you should worry about only if you absolutely must have the file's contents — otherwise, I'd recommend deleting and then restoring the file, because most infected files are applications or system files that can be replaced. If the infected file is a document, you might be desperate to get it clean. Run the virus cleaner and see what happens.

Should you run the virus program all the time to check files? If it annoys you, I recommend you back off to scheduled virus sweeps that occur once or twice a week, as long as they work logically within your backup schedule. (May sure you rotate your backups so that viruses can be dealt with using backup copies of documents and applications.) If you don't mind the additional protection, keep the virus program running. It can't hurt.

The only thing that *can* hurt is not updating your virus definitions. The major virus-protection publishers come out with updates every few months (sometimes every month) that include more virus definitions, better weapons, and protection from new viruses. Stop by the virus program publisher's site and update frequently.

Word Basic viruses

The Word Basic macro viruses are a strain that infect Word documents by infiltrating the Normal template. Using Word's built-in customization and macro abilities, these viruses subtly change Word's behavior, causing both minor and major problems. What's worse, you're only likely to discover this after the virus has been in Word for a while, possibly even spreading the virus by distributing infected documents.

Note Actually, these macros are often called Visual Basic for Applications macros because they can affect a few different Microsoft applications, including Microsoft Excel. Although the Word macro viruses are much more pervasive, you may find that an occasional Excel document acts oddly. Check that document with a virus checker.

The regular Concept virus — the first one to really appear on the scene — forces your documents to be saved as templates, which are difficult to work with. The virus remains in the newly saved template file, infecting the next computer to which the file is transmitted.

The solution is to download the Macro Virus Protection Tool from Microsoft's Web site. (Try `microsoft.com/macword` and look for a link to the downloads.) Run the tool according to the instructions that come with it. This tool basically adds a capability to Word that prohibits macros from automatically running if they're in new documents. Now, whenever a file comes up with a macro attached to it, a dialog box will appear that allows you to save the file again, while Word strips the macro from it.

Note This capability is built into Word 98. By default, Word 98 will ask you if you want to run macros embedded in a Word document. If you don't know why the document would have macros (or if the document is otherwise foreign to you), choose not to load them.

Unfortunately, that solution doesn't work well for another strain, the CAP virus, because it manages to infiltrate the Normal template itself, intercepting any attempts to alter the templates attached to files — which means the Microsoft virus protection tool can't even be loaded.

To get around this one, you'll need to be a little creative:

1. Close Word.

2. Find the Templates folder and move the Normal template to the desktop.

3. Restart Word.

4. Use the File ➪ Open command to find the document you want to load.

5. When you find the file, hold down the Shift key and click Open.

6. Keep the Shift key down as the file loads (this disables macros).

7. Save the file with a new name.

8. Delete the file.

This works great when it works, but even newer strains seem to affect the Shift key macro disabling, making it impossible to load a cleaned version of the file. The only solution seems to be to drag out the Normal template, and then avoid loading the infected files into Word. The next time you open Word, a clean Normal template will be created, and you can go on about your business. Meanwhile, toss the infected documents.

If you don't toss those documents, don't ever open the infected documents again in Word 6.0. You'll also need to search your drive and find any documents that have turned into Microsoft Word Template files (*.dot) instead of regular Microsoft Word files (*.doc). Check the icon, which is slightly different for a template file.

If you absolutely must get the data out of the documents, you might try copying and pasting the document's contents into a *different* application, and then cleaning out the Normal template and going from there. Or, open the file through ClarisWorks and let it (or MacLinksPlus) translate from Word's template file format. Even if you can't open the file directly, you can try opening it as an RTF file. This may allow you access to the text inside the file so you can copy and paste it into another document. I stress, though, that you don't load the file at all back into Word. It'll infect the Normal template again, and you'll have to start over.

You may have some luck with the very latest virus checkers — Symantec, Network Associates, or one of the others that specifically treats Word Macro viruses. Unfortunately, they probably can't wipe the virus from a particular file; they can just help you determine that the file is infected. You should also have luck opening most of these infected files if you upgrade to Word 98 or higher.

This sort of virus is particularly insidious, because you'll likely end up tossing the infected documents, and you may have been working with infected documents for quite a while. Luckily, the problem is limited to the documents themselves — no directories, applications, device drivers, or anything else will have been infected. These macro viruses offer a great reason to keep a good backup of your documents.

Summary

✦ The best way to keep too many unexpected problems from cropping up is to have a schedule and a plan for maintaining your Mac. This means both a daily routine and a routine for doing various things at one week, one month, three months, and other intervals. A Mac is like a car in this respect; aside from some of them approaching car-like prices, they do need some regular maintenance to behave well over a number of years of service.

✦ Regular maintenance also means the occasional spring cleaning session and regularly defragmenting your hard drive. Cleaning up your Mac's system files generally results in more disk space, fewer fragmentation problems, and fewer file corruption problems. The same is true of defragmenting and optimizing your hard drive, except that you also enjoy the added benefit of a speedier computer after an optimization.

✦ Aside from regular maintenance, you should also work to protect your Mac from virus infections. They're not the most common problems you'll encounter, but they can cause serious trauma in your daily computing life. Having the right tools on hand to combat viruses is essential.

✦ The most likely virus infestation you'll experience will not be with a typical Mac OS virus; you're much more likely to get a Word Basic virus, but only if you use Microsoft Word 6.0. If you do, be aware that a number of viral strains exist that will force you to stop what you're doing and troubleshoot Word when they hit. Many of the professional-level virus checkers can track these viruses, so use them if you work with and share many Word documents.

✦　✦　✦

Resolve System Folder Conflicts

32

Y ou've truly graduated in the world of Mac troubleshooting when you finally undergo an important, time-consuming, and extremely annoying rite of passage — troubleshooting extension conflicts. Even though the role and usage of extensions has changed and grown dramatically over the past ten years of Mac OS upgrades, the basics have remained remarkably the same. Some extensions conflict with others, causing problems at startup and during other times you're computing.

Other times, extension conflicts with specific applications cause known or unknown issues that either the application publisher or the extension author may or may not plan to do anything about. In these cases it's important to identify the problem and move on with a solution or a workaround.

The extensions and control panels themselves can sometimes be set in ways that upset programs and other extensions, especially that troublemaking Memory control panel. In this chapter, you'll look specifically at the Memory control panel to see what settings tend to play well with others.

Identify Extension Conflicts

Although I've been talking about extensions all throughout this text, they probably deserve a reasonable straightforward definition at this point. Extensions are small bits of code that augment the Mac OS in some way, by either adding hooks for a full-fledged application to work with or by adding some capability to the Mac itself.

In This Chapter

How conflicts occur

Finding extension conflicts

Using extension conflict software

Resolving the conflict

Other System Folder conflicts

◆ ◆ ◆ ◆

What's an extension?

Actually, the definition of an extension is a bit more elusive than that, so being completely accurate depends on how technical you want to get. The easy answer is extensions are small bits of code that load as the Mac is starting up and patch the Mac OS in a way that extends the Mac's capabilities. This is mostly true, although that's really only one type of extension, called an *INIT*. Other extensions, such as RDEVs (Chooser devices) and shared libraries, don't necessarily patch the Mac OS, although they are part of the initialization process.

In fact, extensions don't even need to be stored in the Extensions folder. If a particular extension needs a user interface, it'll most likely be stored in the Control Panels folder, even if it has INIT qualities. This is an interesting point: all control panels are not extensions, but those that need to talk to the user are generally stored in the Control Panels folder.

The distinction isn't terribly important, however. What is important is that your Mac looks at both the Extensions and the Control Panels folders as it starts up in an attempt to read and activate all the items with INIT resources stored in those folders. It then tries to enable them all to do what they were created to do — extend the Mac OS.

Most extensions do this by patching parts of the code that initially loads from the *Mac OS ROMs* — the Read Only Memory chips situated on the logic board that help the Startup Manager get the basic Mac OS up and running. In fact, the Mac OS on your hard drive (in nearly all Mac models) is also designed to patch the code that's loaded from those ROMs so that the software routines (called *traps* in programming lingo) are updated to the latest fixes and capabilities.

Most extensions also try to patch these traps, adding some interesting new capability to the Mac OS in the process. I like to think of these as "But if..." patches. The extension might patch a particular trap that's designed to do a specific task, *but if* the application asks that trap to do something slightly different, then the extension code is there to help out. (Of course, that's not always the case — some extensions completely change the Mac OS behavior.)

The extensions then sit in RAM as part of the memory allocation known as the *system heap* (which is the portion of memory called Mac OS in the About This Computer dialog box). Whenever their services are required, they're asked to perform their duties using the RAM they've been allocated in the system heap. They can also request additional RAM if they need to perform some quick function, and then they release the additional RAM back to the Mac OS — ideally.

Extensions are loaded, in alphabetical order, as the Mac starts up (that's when you'll see the icons on the startup screen). After all the INITs in the Extensions folder load, the Control Panels folder comes next, followed by anything else that's in the main System Folder that needs to be loaded as an extension. If you need to, though, you can change the order in which these files load. Within their own folders, you can use special characters and name changes to alter the loading order. Or, you can place control panels in the Extensions folder, if necessary, to get them to load early (assuming they have INIT resources). If you want the control panel to maintain its place in the hierarchical Control Panels menu under the Apple menu, you can add an alias in the Control Panels folder found in the System Folder.

Note
How do you know when an extension is patching the Mac OS? As the Mac starts up, the system extension icons (and some of the Control Panel icons, if they have extension-like aspects to them) scoot across the bottom of the screen as each loads. You'll notice that some of them offer animated feedback or some other indication that everything has proceeded normally and looks fine. In other cases, you may be hit with an extension icon with a big X through it. This indicates that the extension hasn't loaded for some reason—perhaps due to a conflict, although it might also not load because there isn't enough RAM or the extension can't find the hardware or software it's supposed to be working with.

What's a conflict?

The system extension's attempt to extend the Mac OS doesn't always work. When this happens because another piece of software interferes (or if the extension fails subsequently because it interacts poorly with another piece of software), it's called a *conflict*.

In some cases, the extension may be conflicting with a part of the Mac OS, especially if the Mac OS has been updated and the extension attempts to do something that's no longer allowed. It's also possible the Mac OS offers a new ability or a built-in fix that now conflicts with the extension or renders it superfluous. These can be distressing conflicts, because it's usually a sign that the extension's publisher needs to update the extension to deal with the Mac OS. Apple will rarely accommodate an individual extension unless it breaks due to a bug Apple introduces into the Mac OS. (And then that software publisher might still be out of luck.)

In other cases, the extension might be in conflict with another extension that's already trying to patch the same trap. This can lead to the second extension being disabled or unable to load, an immediate crash, or an instability that will manifest itself later in that computing session. In fact, the process by which extensions patch the OS offers one interesting solution in these cases: Sometimes you can just change the order in which an extension loads and thereby solve the conflict. This is actually an important distinction, because it has ramifications for troubleshooting; not only may you need to find two or more extensions in conflict, but you may even need to determine if changing the *order* in which they load can fix the problem.

A third sort of conflict arises when a particular extension can't be used at the same time as a particular application is being run (or vice-versa, depending on your point of view). In these cases, you'll either have to hope the software publishers work out a solution that enables the two to coexist, or you'll end up pulling whichever one you need to use less (or looking for an alternative).

What's not a conflict?

You may find that your problem isn't an extension conflict, but that you can't get an extension to work correctly or to load when it's supposed to, even if it's in the Extensions Manager.

If you don't appear to be enjoying the functions that a particular extension is supposed to add to your Mac, you should look into the following before assuming you have a conflict:

✦ *Have you restarted?* You need to restart your Mac after making any changes in the Extensions Manager so that the proper configuration can be loaded by the Mac.

✦ *Did you disable extensions?* I've done this before: I start up with the Shift key to test one little item, and then I pretend to be all surprised when, 30 minutes later, I try to print to my network printer. Make sure a full extensions set is chosen in the Extensions Manager (preferably one of your own custom sets), and restart the Mac.

✦ *Is the extension really there?* It's possible for you or Extensions Manager to get a bit confused. Open the Extensions folder itself to make sure the extension is really there and that it's the only copy of the extension in that folder. If you find duplicates, drag them to the Extensions (Disabled) folder or the Trash. If you're concerned that Extensions Manager seems to be misreporting extensions, try throwing away the Extensions Manager preferences file.

✦ *Does the extension have a buddy?* In some cases, more than one extension is necessary to accomplish something, one extension needs to be loaded soon after another extension, and/or they're all designed to work together. Check the extension's documentation to see if it needs to be loaded with another.

✦ *Is the load order wrong?* Try changing the load order for the extension by altering its name slightly. (Extensions load in alphabetical order.) Add a space in front of the name to move it toward the top of the load order; use a bullet character (Option-8) to move it toward the bottom of the order. Experiment to see if either help.

✦ *Is the file in the wrong folder?* The Extensions Manager will report extensions and control panels that are in the Extensions, Control Panels, and System files and some other parts of the System Folder. Although most extensions and control panels try to correctly place themselves in the proper directory, something may have changed. Check to make sure you have each type of system software item in its respective folder and, more importantly, that you don't have an important extension accidentally stashed away in the Eudora folder, Claris folder, or one of the other unrelated folders that's been created inside the System Folder.

If you check all these things and the extension still doesn't load correctly or it shows up with an X through it, there are three possibilities: The first is a conflict with another extension that isn't dramatic enough to cause a crash or error. Go ahead and troubleshoot the extension. The second possibility is corruption in the extension; try replacing it from your installation media or from a backup. Third — the extension may not be intended for your Mac. Check your documentation, the extension's documentation or a shareware extensions helper such as InformINIT (see the "Conflict Resolution" section, later in this chapter) to see if you really need the extension at all.

Diagnosis: Conflict

Conflicts aren't always easy to diagnose, because they range from the very straightforward — a crash during extension loading or an X-ed out extension icon — to the very subtle. Some extension conflicts only occur when certain applications are active or when another conflict is present. In fact, some extension conflicts can occur based on when the troubled extensions are loaded; load A before B and you get a crash, but load B before A and you have a happy, stable Mac. (Well, at least as far as extensions go.)

Although these symptoms could also be attributed to other problems, in many cases the following are good indicators that you may have an extension conflict on your hands:

✦ A system crash occurs while the Mac is starting up, after the Mac OS splash screen has appeared and extensions icons have begun to flash across the screen.

✦ An X appears through one of the extension icons as the Mac is starting up.

✦ Problems occur shortly after installing a new application or utility program that included its own extensions.

✦ Problems occur shortly after installing a new version of the Mac OS or when using a newly installed application.

✦ An extension doesn't load (or an extension's functionality doesn't seem to have been added to the Mac OS) even if no errors, crashes, or messages appeared.

✦ The trouble disappears when the Mac is started up with extensions off or when you use only Mac OS system extensions sets in the Extensions Manager.

✦ Consistent crashes or errors happen when the extension might logically be put to use — for instance, when a network user tries to print (using the Printer Share extension) to your Mac's printer. This might also happen in multiple applications when they try to perform similar commands (such as Open, Save, or Print, if you have extensions that patch these commands).

✦ Trouble occurs when an application that's associated with a particular extension is launched (for instance, when a personal calendar program attempts to set off an appointment alarm that's handled by an extension).

✦ You seem to be having trouble that can't be explained in another way. It's especially true that extension conflicts between extensions and applications are a major cause of trouble on Macs.

Conflicts can sometimes have a certain feel to them. Because they work very much like software bugs (and can sometimes be attributed to bugs) conflicts are usually easily reproducible — the same crash or error happens over and over again. It's likely that the conflict will occur when you do the exact same thing in a problem application, such as when choosing a particular command or following a series of steps. When you think you've identified a possible pattern, do your best to verify and document what you're doing and consider what may be causing it.

Extension conflicts can often be identified by *what's* not working; that is, if a problem is occurring with printing or network access, it's likely to have something to do with the networking or printing extensions you have on your Mac. (This is especially true if you have add-ons that extend the Mac's native abilities for performing certain tasks or accessing peripherals.)

If you suspect an extension conflict, one way to tell if an extension conflict is the likely culprit is to start the Mac with extensions off. You can do this a number of ways:

✦ Hold down the Shift key while the Mac starts up until you see the "Extensions Off" message in the Welcome to Mac OS message box. If you don't see this message, make sure you're holding down the Shift key just after the Mac's startup tone and before anything else happens.

✦ In the Finder, open the Extensions Manager and turn off all extensions by choosing the All Off set. Restart the Mac.

✦ As the Mac starts up, hold down the spacebar. This will cause the Extensions Manager to appear as the first few extensions are loading. You can then choose the All Off option and click the Continue button to continue the startup process with extensions off. (Note: in some cases, this will not turn off all extensions, because one or two may load before the Extensions Manager appears. If you're still getting crashes, try restarting and holding down the Shift key.)

If you can start with extensions off, reproduce the circumstances that led to the error, and the error doesn't manifest itself, you're a step closer to diagnosing a conflict. (If the error does happen, it may be a bug in the particular application or in the Mac OS.)

Your next step is to do the same thing with only the Mac OS Base and the Mac OS All extension sets chosen in the Extensions Manager. From the Finder, choose the Extensions Manager control panel. In that control panel, choose the extension set Mac OS Base, as shown in Figure 32-1. Now, restart and check for the error. If the error reappears, you might be experiencing a conflict with an extension that's in the Mac OS Base set. Move on to the Conflict Resolution section of this chapter.

If the error is still gone, you should head to the Extensions Manager again and choose the Mac OS All extension set. Restart the Mac and, once the Finder appears, test again for the problem. If you encounter the error at this point, there's a chance the conflict is with one of the Apple extensions. If you still can't re-create the problem, there's a good chance that you've stumbled upon a conflict with a third-party extension.

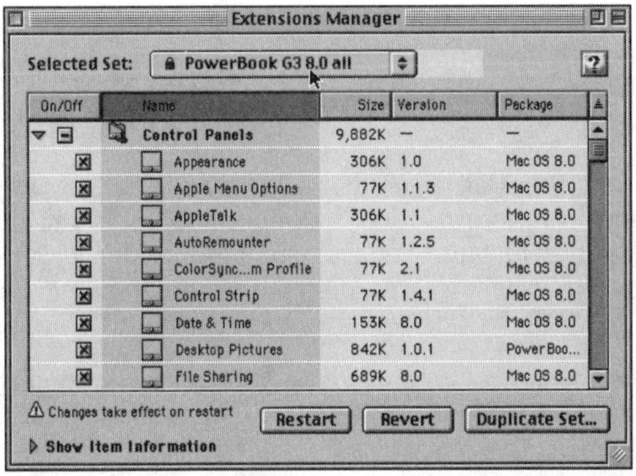

Figure 32-1: Use the Extensions Manager to load only the extensions that ship with the Mac OS, and then test for the error.

Another important way to determine whether or not you're dealing with an extension conflict is by doing a little reading. Specifically, read the Read Me file associated with anything that you've recently installed or the file that came with the application that is exhibiting trouble. It's generally accepted that a Read Me file that accompanies an application or utility (or Read Me First file, Release Notes, an About file, or the program's main documentation) will include information on known conflicts, especially as they relate to the Mac OS and/or extensions.

Also, don't forget the Apple-provided Read Me files, especially those that come with your Mac OS system software upgrades, as well as any subsequent upgrades to separate parts of the Mac OS installation (like updates to Open Transport or QuickTime). Those Read Me files should point out known issues and conflicts with both Apple-written software and many popular third-party products.

In Mac OS 7.6 and above installations, the Read Me files are even gathered together in one place on your hard drive — in the Mac OS Read Me Files folder, located in the root folder of your startup drive.

If the Read Me file isn't much help, or one isn't available for the application in question, you should try contacting the customer service department or Web site for the application (or utility or extension add-on) that is causing your trouble. Another good place to check for conflict information is at the Apple Support Web site (`www.apple.com/support`). Common extension conflicts with popular applications or utilities will often be discussed in the Mac media and on Mac-related Web sites, too.

Note   I've recommend both before, but Ted Landau's MacFixIt site (`www.macfixit.com/`) is a wonderful resource for learning about conflicts and other OS issues. And, of course, I'll track issues as they come up on the Mac-Upgrade site (`www.mac-upgrade.com/`).

Evangelista tip: Visualize the new guys

Here's a very cool (and popular among the Mac digerati) tip for managing the System Folder. One of the main problems you'll run into in conflict troubleshooting is you don't always know when an application decides to plunk its extensions down in the System Folder. Sometimes you notice while you're installing the program and sometimes . . . well, sometimes you have other things to do.

So the trick is, how can you keep track of the old extensions so you can tell immediately what new ones have been added? Use one of the most basic Finder features that no one has ever really found a good use for — labels! This one was submitted by a few folks, including Reed Jackson (Apple Computer), Wayne H. Deese, Martin Step (Kitchener, Ontario), and Skillman Hunter (Acrobytes Software):

If you've just done a clean install, received a new Mac, or have a System Folder setup that is working great right now, label your System Folder items. Open the System Folder and make sure the view is set to As List in the menu bar. Option-click all the right-facing arrows (this opens up all the subfolders), and then use the Find ➪ Select All command to select every file in the System Folder and its subfolders. Now, use the File ➪ Label command to set the label for every single System Folder item to the color of your choice. When a new extension, control panel, file, or font is added, you'll know about it, because the new item won't have a label.

This works great for individual folders — for example, Extensions, Control Panels, Fonts — within the System Folder, too, if you'd prefer to track them separately.

Conflict Resolution

If you've turned off all extensions and the problem has gone away (or if it went away with the Mac OS extensions on, but others off), you've probably diagnosed an extension conflict. Congratulations. Now the real fun begins.

There are several ways to resolve a conflict resolution. The easiest way is to identify the conflict as a known issue and follow the advice of the software publisher: Disable the extension, stop using the application, or apply whatever upgrades, fixes, or workarounds the publisher or some other troubleshooting expert recommends. But this won't always work, because you might not even be sure which extensions and/or applications are in conflict.

So, you're limited to the three more work-intensive approaches to conflict resolution, all of which somehow require you to constantly restart your computer and fiddle with your settings — sometimes for weeks straight without food or water and with very little sleep — until you find the extension that's creating the conflict. Go ahead and choose whichever type of troubleshooting makes you feel good. Quickly, the methods are as follows:

✦ *Identify the extension.* There's a good chance that this approach will end in frustration, but you can attempt to find the problem extension according to its function, and then disable it to see if it's the cause. This is useful only when you feel very sure that you know exactly what the conflict might be.

✦ *Conflict search.* Using either the Extensions Manager or the Finder to conduct your search, you logically pour through all the extensions, turning on one or more at a time to test for the error or crash.

✦ *Conflict software.* If you're like me, you might just opt for this solution. It's much more fun to let a piece of software manage your conflict resolution for you. The only problem: Some of these software programs have a steep learning curve that can be considerably complicated.

Identify the extension

If you have a good idea what the conflicting extension *does*, this might be the quickest way to conflict resolution. You don't necessarily need to know the extension's name. Instead, you need to have a notion of what the extension patches or what sort of routines it affects or adds in the Mac OS.

From this deduction, you can dig into the System Folder to figure out which extension is responsible for the behavior you think is part of the problem. For instance, you know it has something to do with your Open File dialog box, but you're simply not sure which extension could be causing that problem.

For this, you can begin by using the Extensions Manager. Here's the drill:

1. Open the Extensions Manager from the Control Panels folder (or menu item on the Apple menu).

2. If you have an option at the bottom of the window labeled Show Item Information, click the arrow next to that option.

3. Now select the extension or control panel about which you'd like to get information. That extension's information shows up in the small window at the bottom of the Extensions Manager.

As you scroll through the extensions, you'll find that some of them offer you some idea of what the extension is for, and others don't quite give you as much description as you'd like (see Figure 32-2). In either case, you might find out what you need to know about a particular extension.

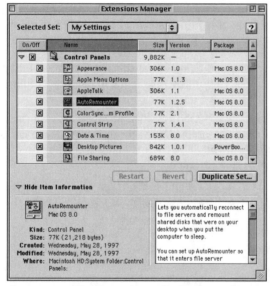

Figure 32-2: The Extensions Manager can give you extra information about extensions and control panels.

If your Mac is crashing while trying to load an extension, you'll find that it's tougher to troubleshoot, because the Mac doesn't get all the way to the Finder for you to access the Extensions Manager. In this case, you should start up your Mac and watch carefully to see which extensions get loaded (from their icons across the bottom of the startup screen) and which extensions appear right as the Mac crashes. Consider that the problem could really be one of the extensions very near the last one you see on the screen; not every extension's icon appears on the startup screen, and it's likely that the extension causing the crash isn't getting an opportunity to display its icon.

Now, start up with extensions off (hold down the Shift key while restarting) and wait until the Finder appears. Open the Extensions Manager and find the last extension that appeared on the startup screen. (You may need to open the actual Extensions folder to see the full-sized icons of each extension to help you determine which is the right one.) Once you find the extension, focus on testing the next few extensions that continue from the identified extension in alphabetically order. Test those extensions according to the discussion in "Conduct a conflict search" later in this chapter.

Once you've determined what the questionable extension does and you've decided to assume it's your culprit, open Extensions Manager and click to remove the check mark next to that extension's entry. Now restart the Mac and test for the error. If it doesn't show up after diligent testing, you might have correctly identified the conflict. Now you just need to ask around (or surf to the publisher's Web site) and figure out why the conflict occurs.

Note

Remember that the problem may be the result of your problem extension conflicting with another one of the extensions that's usually loaded prior to the problem extension. You might want to conduct a conflict search beginning with your Mac's first extension and going through all the others that lead up to your problem extension. While you're testing those extensions, you should also be loading the extension that you've identified as the problem. (That is, if I've identified extension F as a problem, I'll load extensions A and F and test, and then I'll load A, B, and F and test, and so on until I reproduce the error.) If you find that having another extension loaded makes the problem appear, you may have completely isolated the conflict.

Shareware: Get *more* info

If the Extensions Manager doesn't give you enough information, you'll want to turn your attention to a shareware solution. A number of them exist to help you figure out what the various extensions do and how they may create a conflict.

Probably the most popular of these programs is InformInit (http://cafe.ambrosi-asw.com/DEF/informINIT.html), a multipage document that lists an amazing number of extensions from Apple and third-party software and hardware companies. InformINIT includes a wealth of information, including discussions concerning which extensions are "officially" compatible with certain versions of the Mac OS. It also has fairly extensive troubleshooting information, including incompatibilities, issues that deal with RAM allocation, and suggestions for best use, sometimes from the authors of the extensions themselves.

Extension Overload (www.mir.com.my/~cmteng) is a similar product designed to tell you all about many of the extensions you might encounter in the Extensions folder. It's a little easier on the eyes than InformINIT, making it a bit easier to find a particular extension.

Some other shareware solutions for conflict catching (both recommended by InformINIT's Dan Frakes) include Macworld Installer Tracker (www5.zdnet.com/mac/download.html), which tracks application installations, creating a log of every file that's been added to your Mac and SysCompare, a program that takes a snapshot of your System Folder, and then compares it with the current state of the folder whenever you need to see what's been added.

Conduct a conflict search

If you're not sure what extension is causing the trouble, you can perform a conflict search, the time-honored tradition of testing out each extension until the problem extension loads and begins causing errors or crashes. Like any troubleshooting, the point is to isolate the extension so you can pinpoint what's causing the trouble and then do something about it.

The process by which you isolate an extension, though, can work a couple of different ways, include the one-at-a-time method, the few-at-a-time method, and the binary-tree search method. Each has its advantages (at least, in certain situations), although all three can be very time consuming. There's a lot of restarting in conflict searches.

Remember throughout these searches that you need to test for the conflict by doing whatever you've identified is the problem — working with an application, copying files, accessing the Internet, and so on. If you need a certain base of extensions to make that task work, you should test those first for conflicts. Then, load them every time as part of your base of extensions while you're testing the other extensions.

One-at-a-time method

With this method, the plan is to turn off all extensions (or turn off all non-Apple extensions) and add each extension one at a time (in alphabetical order, in the order of loading: extensions, control panels, System Folder files) in the Extensions Manager. You then restart and test to see if the problem occurs. If it doesn't, you add another extension.

Most of the time I would avoid this method like the plague, at least for starters, because it can be incredibly time consuming. But I supposed it might be useful for troubleshooting situations where you feel that a limited number of extensions may be causing the problem, or that the problem is caused by two or more extensions conflicting with one another.

Few-at-a-time method

In this one, the plan is to turn off all extensions (or turn off all non-Apple extensions), and then re-enable them a few extensions at a time — between three and five, let's say — in alphabetical order, in the order in which they're loading: extensions, control panels, and then System Folder files. Next, restart the Mac and test for a conflict. If the conflict doesn't happen, you can assume, for the moment, that the problem isn't in that particular group, so you add another set of extensions to the mix. Restart again, test again.

Once you're able to reproduce the error or crash, you'll need to go back and disable all the extensions you just added, and then re-enable them one at a time, restarting and testing each. This will allow you to pinpoint the exact extension that's causing trouble.

This type of troubleshooting is a little less annoying, and probably the best approach if you have a reasonable number of extensions. If you can find the problem in three or four restarts, at least you haven't yet lost the entire afternoon to this process. (You still need to test and make sure that the conflict isn't between an earlier extension and this problem extension.)

Binary-tree search

This one has a cool-sounding name that harkens back to the programming concept from which it derives its logic. Fortunately, the name is really the only thing that's complicated about this approach.

The basic point is to continue to divide all of your extensions in half until you isolate the extension that's giving you trouble. By the way, for this one, you might find it useful to bypass the Extensions Manager and head straight for the System Folder, even though Apple recommends you away from it these days. Open the Extensions folder and the Extensions (Disabled) folder. Use these two folders for splitting the extensions in halves.

Here's the process:

1. Start by splitting all extensions into two groups (alphabetically is best). Enable the first group in the Extensions Manager or by dragging those files into the Extensions folder — or, conversely, by dragging the second group *out* of the Extensions folder.

2. Restart and test for a conflict. If you don't find the conflict, enable the other group of extensions, restart and test those. Now the conflict should show up — if you still don't find the conflict, you'll need to try another method, because you have a conflict between two or more extensions.

3. Split the group that has the conflict into two groups, enable one of those groups, restart, and test for the conflict again. If you don't find the conflict, switch to the other group, restart, and test. This other group should have the conflict. If it does, split this group in two and repeat.

4. Continue the process until you're down to the single extension that's causing the problem.

If at any point you test both halves and find out that the problem is no longer occurring, this means that the conflict is between two extensions that have just been separated into different groups. At this point, take these two groups and put them back together again, and then use one of the first two methods to troubleshoot the entire group.

Confirmation

Even after you identify the extension that's causing the problem, you may not be done troubleshooting. The problem is you need to make sure the extension is causing the problem all by itself—and it's not in conflict with another extension. Although the binary-tree search addresses this problem, the others don't do quite as good of a job; if the conflict is between two extensions, you probably saw the results of the conflict after you enabled the *second* extension.

To test whether or not the extension causes a conflict on its own, isolate it. In the Extensions Manager, turn off all extensions except that one, and then restart and test it. (If you can't test for the error or crash without other extensions, enable those, too. Or, if you were already using the Mac OS base as your testing base, enable the Mac OS base and the problem extension.) If it creates the problem, you know the extension itself is causing the problem—or it's conflicting with your necessary base of extensions. In either case, you should probably try to upgrade it, switch it for a similar extension, or dump it, if you can.

If that extension doesn't cause the problem to appear, you're back to the races. Now you've got to integrate this extension into your base of extensions (even if it's the only one) and start to troubleshoot all the others again. (If you were enabling your extensions in alphabetical order, you may only need to test against extensions that came before the problem extension in order.) You've eliminated one, and you've got at least one more to find following the same procedures.

Of course, you should cut yourself some slack. Once you've found one extension that you know is part of the problem, head back to the sections "Diagnosis: Conflict" and "Identify the extension" to see if you can reason out the problem with this extension from an associated Read Me file or from the extension author's Web site. If you can't find any additional material on this extension, use InformINIT or a similar product to learn about it, see who wrote it, and research any potential conflicts.

Conflict management software

The Extensions Manager has been a welcome addition since its appearance in System 7.5 and overhaul in Mac OS 7.6 and above, but it doesn't do everything. Specifically, it doesn't do everything that Conflict Catcher, a commercial product from Casady and Greene (www.casadyg.com) does. Conflict Catcher is designed to root out problem extensions by literally taking over your Mac and performing the troubleshooting itself. You still need to be there, but Conflict Catcher can run you through the mundane parts. (Bring a good book.)

Before installing Conflict Catcher, read its Read Me file and associated startup documentation carefully; it's recommended that you turn off all extensions before installing the product, and there are some incompatibilities you need to know about, including some that occur with certain third-party keyboards (Conflict Catcher makes use of the keyboard as you're starting up your Mac, much like Extensions Manager.)

Once you have it installed, the software looks something like the Extensions Manager, but instead of checkmarking files to set them to load at startup, you highlight them. Conflict Catcher will occasionally let you know when it feels choosing a particular extension for loading is a bad idea. You can manage your extensions much as you would with the Extensions Manager, and Conflict Catcher includes a few additional features, such as the ability to drag and drop an extension to change its load order.

The real fun starts when you put Conflict Catcher to the test in tracking down an extension conflict. You tell the program you have a problem by clicking the Conflict Test button in the Conflict Catcher window. Next, Conflict Catcher asks you a number of questions about the conflict you're having. Give the test a name, choose the files you think may be causing the problem, and specify which extensions shouldn't be turned off (because they're required to keep your particular Mac running). Figure 32-3 shows Conflict Catcher's test mode.

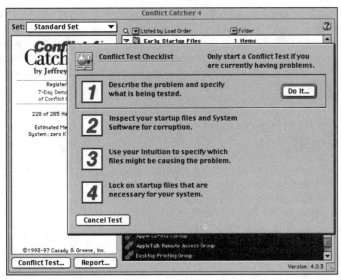

Figure 32-3: The step-by-step process tells Conflict Catcher how to proceed with the test.

With all that set, things go into motion. Conflict Catcher begins after you restart the computer. Only a few extensions load, and then you're asked to test for the problem. If the problem occurs, you tell Conflict Catcher. If it doesn't occur, you tell Conflict Catcher that, too, and you continue the process of restarting. In essence, Conflict Catcher is performing the conflict search I described earlier in this chapter.

Conflict Catcher generally does a thorough job of looking for the conflict and will often catch things you might not have. It helps to have some idea of what's going wrong, and you may have to play with things a bit to get Conflict Catcher on the right track; for instance, you'll need to figure out exactly which extensions need to be loaded as part of your testing base so that the error can be testing for properly. (If you think the error is with Printer Share, for instance, you're going to have to have all the AppleTalk and networking extensions and control panels active to test Printer Share.)

If you want startup management software to work well for you, there are two important things to remember when dealing with the software: First, install it before you have a problem. Second, get to know it well, setting it up to manage your different extension sets and allowing it to help you clean out your System Folder a bit. If you get used to working with the program before disaster strikes, you'll be more ready to deal with it when the problems do set in.

Note   Before using any startup manager other than the Mac's own Extensions Manager, check the software publisher's Web site, the Mac news sites, and anywhere else you can think of for news of conflicts between the management software and your version of the Mac OS, especially if a new version has recently been released. I would have talked about Now Startup Manager (www.qualcomm.com) as well as Conflict Catcher, but as of this writing it still hasn't been updated for the latest OS releases. Under those circumstances, it's important to avoid any startup manager, as they need to be updated to understand changes in the Mac OS.

Solving the conflict

Having identified the conflicting extension or extensions, you're ready to try to solve the problem. As a first-aid solution, you'll want to disable the extension or even isolate it from the System Folder completed to avoid accidentally re-enabling it and starting the process over again at some point in the future. But you've got some other options for dealing with the conflict, too:

✦ *Gather information.* Check the Read Me file, documentation, and Web sites for all the software that's in conflict (extensions, control panels, applications). See if any of them acknowledge the problem or can point you in the right direction. You might also check newsgroups or mailing lists to see if you can find an answer to the issue. (See Appendix B for various online resources.)

✦ *Check for an update.* Surf to the software publisher's Web site and see if the extension has been updated for some reason. This includes drivers, utilities, and other extensions designed to work with hardware from a particular company. Often those companies will update their drivers and utilities when it becomes clear that the latest Mac OS is not working correctly with their software. If they don't have an update, register a bug report or complaint and tell them as clearly as possible what the conflict is and how you are able to reproduce it. If the conflict is with an application, check for an application update as well.

✦ *Check for corruption; replace with backup.* You may want to run any software that's part of a conflict by your disk doctor program to see if it's corrupted or if other disk problems are affecting it. (Note that many shared libraries and some extensions will be reported by older disk doctors as broken when they're not. Make sure you have the latest version of your disk doctor software.) Even if you don't find corruption, you can try replacing the conflicting extension with another clean copy from your installation media or from a backup. You should also try all the standard remedies — rebuild the desktop, defragment the drive, and fix any errors on the drive with a disk doctor program. If you're working with a control panel or application that has a preferences file, try trashing that file, too.

✦ *Change the load order.* If you've identified a conflict between two different extensions, you should try changing one of the extension's names so that it loads in a different order than previously. If extension A was loading before extension B, change B's name so that it now loads before extension A. You can change the extension's name just as you would any file's: Click once on the name of the file and wait a few seconds until the name becomes highlighted. To load the extension toward the beginning of the process, add a space to the beginning of the name; to load toward the end, add a bullet point (Option-8) to the beginning of the name. This solution may work if your conflict is between the extension and an application — just move the extension close to the beginning or the end of the load order and see if that makes a difference.

✦ *Increase memory allocation.* If the extension is a few years old, it may be conflicting with new memory requirement in the Mac OS. Few extensions enable you to change their memory allocation easily, but you can check to see if the extension in question can have its allocation changed. To test for that, select the extension and choose File ➪ Get Info. If the Get Info dialog box includes a Memory Requirements section, you can change the memory allocation. (You may first need to disable the extension and restart.) Up the extension's memory requirements slightly — sometimes only 15- to 20KB will work — to see if that helps the conflict. You can also consider raising a conflicting application's memory requirements slightly.

✦ *Replace the software.* If you've identified the problem extension and can't come up with an update, you might want to fish around for a replacement that can do remarkably the same thing, especially if the extension is a shareware add-on (or, if a shareware equivalent is available). Check `www.download.com` and `www.macsoftware.com` for possible replacement candidates. If you can replace an application that's in conflict with this particular extension, and the extension is more important, try working with the new application and see if the problem can be avoided.

✦ *Manage the conflict.* If you use Extensions Manager or a similar extensions management utility, you might be able to create a new set of extensions designed to avoid the conflict; for instance, an extension that conflicts with Microsoft Word could be disabled in a set of extensions you call Use Word, and then re-enabled in another set you call General Use. When you need to switch back to General Use, you'll select that set in the management software and restart your Mac. It'll be a little painful and time consuming, but it'll work around the problem (see Figure 32-4).

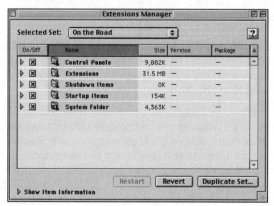

Figure 32-4: Use unique extension sets to work around conflicts between an extension and an application.

✦ *Live without the software.* If you can't come up with a more equitable solution, your best plan may be to drag the extension to the Trash and empty the Trash. This at least keeps the extension from accidentally being activated again and causing more trouble or data loss. And you may one day begin to forget that loveable little extension. Time heals.

Even if one of the preceding solutions works, consider that the extension may be a troublemaker in the future, too, especially since the same popular extensions tend to show up on the conflict radar screen over and over again. Why? Because they do something that Apple doesn't support in every OS, or they patch the OS in a very sophisticated way that's also a delicate process — in fact, most of the time it's against Apple's own guidelines. Although certainly worthy of your consideration, Connectix's RAM Doubler and Speed Doubler extensions are examples of extensions that are notorious for breaking with every new Mac OS update, because they patch the system at such a low level. Fortunately, most companies that make a living writing these patches are quick to update for every Mac OS version when necessary.

Other System Extension Issues

A couple of other factors in that System Folder — aside from extensions, preferences, and the system files themselves — can cause a little trouble. These, too, can create conflicts with extensions, control panels, applications, and utilities. Specifically I'm talking about some standard Apple control panels that enable you to set Mac OS parameters that may cause conflicts.

Control panels, software drivers for hardware peripherals, the networking control panels, shared libraries and the Chooser can all cause their own sets of problems. Fortunately, those are all covered in other sections of this book dedicated to the specific area of trouble. What follows are software-only issues that haven't been addressed elsewhere.

Memory control panel

The memory settings can affect the Mac OS's stability in a number of different ways. Depending on the Mac model and Mac OS version you're using, you may have a few different options in that control panel that can affect system stability (see Figure 32-5).

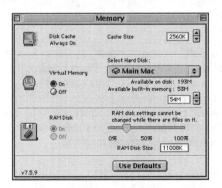

Figure 32-5: Settings in the Memory control panel can affect stability and performance.

If you're having trouble that has some of the symptoms of a software conflict but can't be attributed to a particular extension or group extensions, the problem may lie with the Memory control panel. Here are the settings you're likely to encounter and some possible problems:

✦ **Disk cache.** Most modern applications deal well with healthy disk caches settings, although older Macs and older versions of the Mac OS (especially pre-System 7.5) generally didn't use the cache settings for optimum speed. These days, the cache should be set to about 32K for every MB of RAM your

Mac has. Some applications (especially some programs in the graphics, 3D, and multimedia categories) will specify that you turn the cache settings down to its lowest level because the program itself has its own cache scheme. This may also be true of third-party caching programs and extensions like Connectix Speed Doubler, which acts as a substitute for built-in cache.

✦ **RAM disk.** A RAM disk enables you to treat a portion of RAM as a hard disk, saving data as you would any other media, only considerably faster. The RAM disk can survive a restart, but will be wiped clean if the Mac is shut down or the power is lost to the Mac. RAM disks don't cause many conflicts aside from increasing the size of the system heap memory allocation. The larger the RAM disk, the less space you have for running applications.

✦ **Virtual memory.** This one can cause conflicts, especially with some graphics, animation, and multimedia applications that require only the use of fast RAM for optimal performance. Because virtual memory uses hard drive space to augment RAM, it's useful for Mac OS systems that are a little crunched for space in memory. It usually causes few problems, but buying more physical memory is always a better solution than relying on virtual memory, especially for high-end creative tasks. On older Macs, virtual memory goes hand-in-hand with *32-bit addressing*, another Memory control panel option that enables an older Mac see more physical memory than it was originally designed to work with. It can cause occasional trouble with very old applications and control panels, but is mostly harmless. (There's one special case worth noting: You can't select an HFS Plus formatted hard drive for virtual memory usage on a pre-PowerPC Macintosh.)

Note

When setting the virtual memory size and disk, a good number to choose is a few megabytes over the actual, physical amount of RAM you have in your Mac. (If you have 32MB of RAM, choose 33MB of virtual memory or so.) This makes for a good speed compromise. Also, make sure you choose a drive that has enough free memory, plus quite a bit to spare. A conflict can arise if you put the squeeze on the drive by filling it completely with application and data files when virtual memory — or any other important part of the Mac OS system software — is trying to use it.

✦ **Modern memory manager.** An option on early Power Macs running a pre-Mac OS 7.6 version of the software, the modern memory manager doesn't cause too many conflicts, because it's now always on. In the early days of the PowerPC transition, though, some 68000-based programs ran better with the memory manager turned off.

Energy Saver

This panel can cause a little trouble — usually mysterious sleep times and a propensity to dim the monitor when you don't feel like having it dimmed. If you're suffering from something of the sort, here are a few strategies to follow regarding the control panel:

✦ *Know your settings.* If you've never taken a look at the Energy Saver control panel, familiarize yourself with it. It might explain behavior you weren't aware was being controlled — such as the monitor dimming or the hard drive spinning down so that it takes a moment to unfreeze the cursor as it starts up again.

✦ *If you make changes, make sure the panel is active.* If you change the sleep settings, and then immediately disable the control panel from the Extensions Manager, you might still experience the older settings. Make sure to restart at least once with the panel active and displaying the new settings.

✦ *Use the right Energy Saver.* There are two distinct versions of Energy Saver — one for NuBus-based Macs and one for PCI-based Macs. The older version often gets lost when you upgrade the Mac 8.0 or higher. If you can't find Energy Saver on your Mac (and your Mac is NuBus-based), try selectively reinstalling it from your Mac's original System CD.

✦ *Check twice.* Some versions of the Energy Saver control panel won't always save the Scheduled Shutdown settings correctly, causing your Mac to shut down at unexpected times (or not at all). If you set the shutdown time, switch back to the Sleep Settings before closing the control panel. That will save the settings. Check the panel again to make sure.

✦ *Preferences, not PRAM.* If you feel the Energy Saver control panel is acting wacky, and you suspect a settings corruption, there's no direct need to zap PRAM; try throwing away the Energy Saver preferences file first, because this is where all Energy Saver settings are stored. Some other issue in PRAM could be interfering, but it's unlikely. Deleting the Energy Saver settings will cause them to revert to defaults, so you'll want to open the control panel after deleting the preferences and restarting, and then set your Energy Saver choices as usual.

✦ *Avoid other sleep utilities.* Make sure you're not running other utilities — including screen savers, screen dimmers, and third-party sleep software — that might be interfering with Energy Saver.

✦ *Turn off Energy Saver when working with low-level utilities.* As a precaution, it's a good idea to turn off the Energy Saver control panel (leave it active, but disabled) when you plan to use Drive Setup, Norton Utilities, or any utility that digs deep into your system. This keeps the Mac from trying to sleep or spin down the drive while things are being worked on. In my experience, some Macs simply crash more often when trying to wake from a sleep, and this can be a real problem with low-level utilities.

Fonts

Although some font problems related to printing are covered in Chapter 26, it should be noted that two basic software-only problems can cause fonts to conflict with other utilities and applications, potentially creating errors or crashing the OS.

Test for these if you suspect a font may be causing the trouble or if your extensions conflict search comes up empty:

✦ *Too many fonts.* If your Font folder is overloaded, you may swamp applications as they start up or cause them to grind to a halt. You may also find that too many fonts will cause the application's memory allocation to be quickly filled, resulting in out of memory errors in the application itself. To avoid this, limit the number of fonts in the Fonts folder at a given time by managing them with font management software or dragging them out manually to a Fonts (disabled) or similar folder.

✦ *Corrupt fonts.* A corrupt font can crash either an application as it's loading, crash the application while it's in use or, sometimes, crash the Mac OS as it's starting up. If you suspect a particular font, try to isolate and test it by choosing it in an application and using it for typing and printing. If the program crashes, examine the font with a disk doctor program or replace it with a fresh copy from your installation media or a backup.

As you might guess, the most obvious way to check for font corruption and a subsequent conflict is to follow the same procedure as for extension conflicts — disable them all, and then start adding them back in a few at a time and testing.

If you have a reproducible error when starting ClarisWorks, for instance, start by quitting all programs but the Finder. Next, move all the fonts but Geneva and Chicago from the Fonts folder to another folder, and then restart ClarisWorks and test for conflicts. If those two fonts don't cause a conflict, quit to the Finder, move in five more fonts, and test again.

Eventually you may be able to find which font in particular is causing the problem. If you do, isolate it further by only loading it into the application. Test it with other applications as well. If you can, replace it with a fresh copy of the font and test that, too. If not, see if a disk doctor program can identify the problem with the file.

Summary

✦ Extensions are small bits of Mac OS system software that extend the operating system in some way, usually adding features that allow you to do more with your Mac or allow the Mac to communicate directly with a particular peripheral. These extensions are stored in the System Folder in the Extensions and Control Panels folders. (Some control panels are also extensions, because they load low-level code into the OS at startup time.)

✦ A conflict occurs when two extensions unsuccessfully try to patch the same part of the OS, extending functionality in either two different directions or in a way that overlaps and causes errors. These conflicts can be tough to isolate, because they either cause a random error message, crash early in the startup, or just create a slightly less stable system for regular computing. Extension conflicts should be considered when other types of hardware and software troubleshooting fail.

✦ To test for a conflict, you usually turn off most of your extensions, and then following a predetermined algorithm, turn on one or more extensions at a time, restart, and test again. This process can be time consuming, which is why many users opt for extensions management software that's above and beyond the capabilities of Extensions Manager. Some of this software can actually do most of the troubleshooting for you, with a little guidance.

✦ Once you have the conflict in your sights, you can do something about it. If the conflict isn't already known by the manufacturers, make it known and see if you can coax a response out of them. Also, take the time to research the conflict and see if there's a viable solution. As an alternative, you can replace the extensions or conflicting application with one known to cause fewer headaches.

✦ Finally, you'll find that extensions aren't the only things in the System Folder than can cause conflicts; aside from software drivers and control panels discussed elsewhere in the text, a few choice software-only issues can crop up and cause trouble.

✦   ✦   ✦

In Case of
Emergency:
Reinstall Mac OS

I hear from too many readers and other computer users that they plan — soon after finding a problem — to erase their hard drive and start over again. To me, this is disturbing. I want you to think of a reinstall as the last recourse, not the first. That's why it's back here in the back, next to the pages and pages of boring listings you'll find in the appendixes. It's even got an ominous chapter number — 33 — which suggests foreboding and wariness. I didn't even pick 33 on purpose. It was just the next number available.

If you've gotten to this point, you either have a problem with your Mac that is so irrevocably perplexing that you're ready to give up, or, in a more rational moment, you've decided that your Mac has been chugging along for a few years and might be happy with a complete overhaul. There's an adage for that one (if it ain't broke, don't fix it), but I can't help but agree that, under some circumstances, it's okay to reinstall for maintenance purposes.

In fact, one good reason to reinstall the Mac OS is because you've decided to reformat your hard drive in the Mac OS Extended format (called HFS Plus), which is discussed in Chapter 27. This advanced file system, introduced in Mac OS 8.1, gives you access to a number of new features, not the least of which is increased storage space. You should approach HFS Plus with caution, but once the decision is made, you'll probably need to reinstall the Mac OS. (Some utilities can implement HFS Plus without a reinstallation, as discussed in Chapter 27, but if these utilities fail you'll need both a backup plan and a reinstallation of the Mac OS.)

Finally, if you plan to install a new version of the Mac OS, I'm certainly not going to try to stop you. But you have an interesting decision to make in this regard, as well. Should you perform a clean install? Instead of upgrading the files in your current System Folder, a clean installation places the new version of the Mac OS in a new System Folder. That leaves all your old extensions, control panels, and fonts in the old System Folder, but it also means you can move them to the new one at your leisure. If you're lucky, this will do away with any nagging problems you have and might increase stability. If you're unlucky, a clean install can be a big pain in the backside.

Note   Displaying wanton disregard for people to whom Apple doesn't send free Power Macintosh computers for evaluation, I refer constantly to the use of the Mac OS Install CD-ROM in this chapter. If you don't have a CD-ROM drive and are planning to use Mac OS installation floppies, this chapter will still, basically, apply to you. Just keep a Disk Tools floppy on hand for starting up your Mac, if necessary, and realize that you may not have as many options as I discuss. If you don't have a CD-ROM drive and want to use Mac OS 8 or above, contact Apple. If your Mac is supported, they'll offer you floppy disks at an additional cost. (It's conceivable that Mac OS 8.5 and above won't offer a floppy option direct from Apple, because they'll be designed for PowerPC processors only, and all Apple PowerPC machines have CD-ROM drives. If your CD-ROM drive no longer works or you have some other need for floppy disks, it's possible that Apple will make floppy disk *images* available on the Mac OS CD, which you can then use to create floppy disks using Apple's Disk Copy program.)

Should You Reinstall?

Reinstalling the Mac OS isn't something you should take lightly. Although it may seem like an easy fix for a tough problem — just pop in the CD and start installing — the process is far more complicated than that.

For one thing, a reinstallation should never be seen as a first-aid solution to a hardware or software problem. In almost all cases it's important that you take the time to troubleshoot your problem and isolate its cause, even if there's not much you can do about it. At least you'll have a better idea of what may have caused the problem you're experiencing. (If you don't have time at that moment because you're trying to get something important done, take the first aid approach and work around the problem. When you do get a free moment, however, you should come back to the problem and try to find its root cause.) With any luck, you'll be able to fix the problem without resorting to a new copy of the Mac OS.

And a reinstallation won't necessarily guarantee success in solving the problem. Although a clean install of the Mac OS may solve some problems (for example, preference-file corruption or trouble with the Mac's basic fonts), it won't solve larger issues (such as fragmentation, disk errors, or a bad hard disk driver). Likewise, installing the Mac OS over itself to fix missing files or corruption generally won't work; the Mac OS installer won't overwrite newer files and can't do much of anything about third-party extensions that may be causing problems for your Mac. In addition, it won't overwrite or replace files already in the System Folder, no matter how corrupted those existing files might be.

The Mac OS isn't really as fragile as you might be led to believe, even with the possibility of bugs, conflicts, and corruption. After many years of use, I'd say that the Mac OS rarely needs to be reinstalled and only for the most drastic of reasons. If you think you might be able to avoid a reinstall, you probably can. Unless you have a problem that sincerely requires you to reformat your hard drive or replace it with a new one, you can probably troubleshoot your current Mac OS system and repair it so that it's stable again. Most of the time.

Don't reinstall

Before you consider reinstallation, then, take a look at some of the main issues that reinstallation doesn't address. In these cases, it's important to troubleshoot first and see if you can come to some conclusion as to why the error is occurring.

Reinstallation won't cure or solve the following:

✦ *Trouble with your file system or hard drive.* If you need to rebuild the desktop, run Disk First Aid, mount drives, install hard-disk drivers, defragment, disk fix, or recover deleted files, a reinstallation won't help (except insofar as newer Mac OS Installers do a cursory check of the drive to see if it has remarkable file-system damage. This is not a substitute for disk fixing).

✦ *Virus infection.* Viruses don't just attack the system files, they infect individual files on your Mac outside the System Folder files (in most cases). Some viruses can also infect the desktop database, low-level portions of your hard disk, or hidden files on the drive. In all of these cases, a reinstallation would simply give the virus more fresh files to infect.

✦ *SCSI trouble and most hardware issues.* The only thing a reinstallation could do to help with hardware trouble would be to include the installation of an Apple-written extension or control panel designed to interact with hardware. Otherwise, SCSI voodoo, network cabling, printing, scanners, and input devices all need to be examined directly when problems occur.

✦ *System Folder conflicts.* Reinstallation will rarely help you recover from a System Folder conflict, because these sort of conflicts don't often arise between two or more Apple-written extensions (which are the only extensions reinstalled when the Mac OS is installed). Instead, conflicts usually crop up between third-party extensions and the Mac OS or between extensions and applications, neither of which is addressed when you reinstall.

✦ *Bugs or file corruption.* If your Mac OS files have bugs, that's not going to change when you reinstall unless you're installing an upgrade to the Mac OS.

And bugs in other programs won't be affected by a reinstall. Unless you perform a clean installation, a reinstall won't alter the effects of file corruption, because the installation process won't overwrite corrupt files that are already in the System Folder or elsewhere on the hard drive.

So, if you have one of these sorts of problems, you have your work cut out for you. Jump back into the troubleshooting chapters (Chapters 21 through 32) and see what you can find out about your particular problems. Reinstallation has its place, but the first step is to thoroughly explore the troubleshooting and repair options at your disposal. If you get through them all and still can't figure out what's wrong, then it's time to contemplate a reinstall.

Do reinstall

In a few cases reinstallation (or a clean installation) of the Mac OS makes sense. Sometimes you can reinstall just a part of the Mac OS distribution and get good results, too. Most of the time, though, it won't really be a good idea to reinstall until you've exhausted most of your other options. Then, in cases where you've diagnosed a problem but can't fix it by moving files around, you may need to reinstall the OS or portions of it.

In other cases, you may decide the drastic steps required to reinstall are worth some goal beyond simple troubleshooting; it gives you a chance to start over, an opportunity to work with a fresh system, or it may help avoid problems caused by upgrading over and over again. Here are some possible reasons to go ahead and perform a reinstallation or clean installation of the Mac OS:

✦ *Beyond repair.* If your System Folder is shot — many files are missing, shared libraries have been misplaced, extensions and control panels are everywhere — you should probably consider a clean installation so you can start over again with your Mac. This is especially true if, regardless of what you do, you can't seem to get the startup disk to boot the Mac.

✦ *Clean start.* If the Mac is causing so many headaches that it's worth it for you to start over with a new System Folder — or if you've even considered erasing the entire drive or just chucking the system out the window — maybe a reinstall is warranted. If you are considering such drastic steps, consider how you're going to back up all your data, too.

✦ *Formatting and partitioning.* If you've decided to format and/or partition your hard drive, you'll likely need to reinstall the Mac OS after that's been accomplished. This can be a really good idea if you plan to upgrade to HFS Plus, too, because you get not only a better file system, but also a fresh start with a clean installation and a chance to control what gets installed on the Mac.

✦ *Need a file.* If you've deleted a file or a series of files that were written by Apple and necessary for the System Folder, you'll probably need to reinstall those from the Mac OS CD. In some cases you may be able to perform a custom installation and add the files you need. In other cases, the best plan may be to perform a clean installation, and then drag files from that new installation into the old System Folder.

✦ *System or Finder corrupt.* In these cases, you may have no choice but to reinstall the Mac OS if you can't get the machine booted because of corruption in the most important files on your Mac. In such cases, it's best to have a backup of these files, but not many people do.

These are valid reasons for wanting to reinstall the Mac OS. Of vital concern here, though, is that you must reinstall correctly to bring about the desired effect. There are different ways to go about that and, if your problems are severe, such reinstallations can be time consuming.

Reinstalling Mac OS

If you've decided that a reinstallation of the Mac OS is a good plan for your current needs, you're ready to move forward. You'll want to take care that a number of precautions are in place, because a reinstallation is a major undertaking that, while not likely to cause damage, could create trouble with your Mac as you get it up and running.

Pre-flight check

Although a reinstallation can take a few hours to completely accomplish, depending on how you perform it, it could take a few weeks for you to shake out all the issues associated with the change over. Fortunately, most Mac applications are resilient to this sort of change, as long as you take the appropriate precautions before forging ahead.

Do these things before reinstalling:

✦ *Backup.* You should have a nearly complete backup of your hard drive before proceeding with a clean installation or reinstallation. Although you won't always need the backup, it's a good idea to have a saved record of your current System Folder and all its components. Although they may be causing some trouble with bugs or corruption, at least you'll have the option of examining the old System Folder's structure to compare it to the new System Folder to troubleshoot problems.

✦ *Gather all drivers.* You'll need drivers and installers for all your peripherals and many of your software add-ons. If you perform a clean install, the best way to complete the task is to reinstall everything — the Mac OS, your printer drivers, scanner extensions, Claris and Microsoft applications, utilities, and anything else that might need to add something to the System Folder. It's possible to simply drag those files over to the new System Folder, but that might defeat the purpose, because you could be dragging corrupt or bug-riddled files.

✦ *Fix the disk.* Before performing a reinstallation, do everything you can to rebuild the desktop, fix the disk, and optimize it. Understandably, some problems necessitating a reinstallation will make it difficult to perform these tasks, but you'll be much more likely to enjoy long-term stability if you do manage to complete some basic disk maintenance.

✦ *Have startup alternatives.* Be prepared for the possibility that your hard drive won't be able to work as the startup disk at some point in the reinstallation process. Also, be wary of booting from your most recent Mac OS installation CD; you'll sometimes find that small incompatibilities in the "universal System Folder" used to make these CDs bootable will affect your ability to get the Mac started. As a backup, have on hand two items — a bootable disk ("Disk Tools" should work) and the original Mac OS CD that came with your system, if you had one. This is especially true for clone Mac models. If you have a non-Apple CD-ROM that didn't come with your Mac, you should attempt to make a boot floppy that includes in its System Folder the driver for your CD-ROM drive.

Apple recommends that, before performing any sort of installation, you open the Extensions Manager and choose the Mac OS All set of extensions. This keeps your third-party add-on extensions from interfering with the installation process, which is unlikely, but conceivable. Obviously, if your clone or upgraded Mac requires certain extensions to operate beyond the Mac OS All, you should enable those, too.

You should also pay careful attention to your Energy Saver settings, preferably turning off Energy Saver for the duration of the installation. (You should leave the control panel active in the Extensions Manager, but set the control panel to Never for sleeping and dimming the screen, and restart the Mac before installing.)

Although some recommend it, you probably don't need to boot from the installation CD-ROM to install or update the OS. Instead, just make sure you have the CDs and/or startup disks mentioned previously.

If you feel like being thorough, you should also restart and zap PRAM before committing to a long installation. It isn't necessary, but might help in rare circumstances.

With these things at the ready, it's time to forge ahead. Your next step will be to decide what type of installation you need to perform.

Although it's not official advice, don't forget to find any files you may need immediately — important files for work, your checkbook data, your tax papers in case of a surprise audit — and back them up to a removable cartridge or disk of some sort where you can get at them while you're undergoing this process. You may need to borrow another Mac or run down to the copy store to get something done while yours is in the throes of installation or to deal with any problems that crop up as a result.

Types of installation

Before you perform the installation, you should stop to consider exactly what you're trying to accomplish and what sort of installation will be best for that goal. You can take three different approaches.

A *complete installation* will install the Mac OS on a drive that hasn't had the Mac OS on it previously. If you choose to perform a complete installation on a drive that does already have a Mac installation present, the installer will either update the current OS or it will add files that are missing from the current version that's installed on the hard drive.

A *custom installation* will enable you to choose specific installers that will launch and install their wares on your drive. In fact, you can also selectively install files from each of the individual installers. For instance, you can decide to launch just the Text-to-Speech installer, or even install just some of the components (such as the Speech Manager extension) that are a part of Text-to-Speech. Custom installations are a good idea if you know that you've never added a particular technology to your Macintosh or if you know that certain drivers and extensions are giving you trouble, and you'd like to remove the originals from the System Folder and install fresh copies. This wouldn't help in the case of a virus, but might help with a problem such as file corruption.

A clean installation generally means you're installing a new System Folder and all its (Apple-based) contents onto a drive that already has a valid System Folder. You can do this for any number of reasons, but most of the time it's done for troubleshooting purposes. The Mac OS installer program (in Mac OS 7.6 or higher) offers an option that enables you to choose a clean install, making it a simple matter to add a second System Folder to your drive instead of overwriting the existing System Folder.

To do this, the installer disables the existing System Folder, renames it Previous System Folder, but leaves it on your Mac's hard drive. This allows you to access it once the new system is installed so that you can drag over extensions, fonts, and other elements that you want to hold onto.

After renaming the old System Folder, the Installer then creates a new System Folder and installs a fresh version of the Mac OS. This becomes your main, startup System Folder, excluding any of the custom, third-party software, extra extensions, software drivers, and fonts that were in your original System Folder, as well as starting over with new preferences files and settings in your control panels. This is usually a basic Mac OS installation, but it could be customized to include extensions and system files from more or fewer of the "extra" installers offered when you choose a full installation, as discussed in the next section. As far as all the third-party stuff goes, you'll need to install it on your own.

Regular installation

The Mac OS installer program went through a fairly significant change in Mac OS 7.6, and has since transformed even further. The installation program itself does a couple of significant things. First, it walks you through the installation process more carefully than had Mac OS installers in the past. Second, it has really become a basic launcher or starting point for a series of other installers that make up the entire Mac OS installer CD-ROM. (Compare this to Mac OS 7.1, which originally came on seven disks!)

If you plan to do a full installation and don't need the benefit of a clean install, you can simply load the Mac OS installer and begin the process. This is ideal if you're installing on a new drive, installing on a newly formatted and partitioned drive, or if you're installing over your old Mac OS because you or a disk-fix program has been forced to throw out corrupted system files. (If you know what those files are, you might want to custom install them — check the section, "Custom installation," later in this chapter.)

When you run the Mac OS installer, one of the first things it does is check the hard drive to make sure you have enough hard drive space for a standard installation. If you don't, you'll be asked to choose another disk or delete files from the current disk before moving on. If you plan to do a new installation or a clean installation, you'll need to adhere to this warning. If you're planning a custom installation or you're reinstalling the Mac OS over itself, you can skip the warning and click Continue (see Figure 33-1).

Next, you'll be introduced to and asked to agree with the licensing agreement — click the Continue and Agree or OK buttons if you agree with everything you read. If not, don't install the OS.

Figure 33-1: The Mac OS installer lets you know if it thinks you're running a bit low on disk space.

The installer then shows you the basic installation screen, where you can choose from among the *extra* installers you want to launch during this session. (These installers have been identified as extra, because they don't appeal to every sort of user. On the other hand, Open Transport and networking files are installed with all full Mac OS installations because they're considered standard.) You click to put an "X" in the check box next to each of the installers that you'd like to launch during this installation session.

At this point, you can also choose to customize the installation. In essence, this gives you access to options that enable you to turn off the installer for the Mac OS, the Mac OS InfoCenter, Internet Access, and Open Transport. (There may be newer installers in future versions that can also be controlled by selecting the Customize option.) Using this customizing control, you can select only the Mac OS for installation, for instance, or select a few installers that install extra features, without bothering to install the basics.

You can also choose the Options button at this point to determine whether or not you want the Mac OS installer to attempt to install a new Apple hard disk driver. If you have reason to believe that you shouldn't — or if you have a Mac clone or you're installing onto a non-Apple disk — click to remove the "X" next to this option.

Once you've chosen all the installers you want launched, click Start. The Installer will then take a few moments to check your hard drive for errors (this is basically the same procedure that Disk First Aid goes through). If all goes well, the first installation program in your series will pop up and begin installing things. The Mac will work through the rest of its installers until it's installed everything (or encounters an error). At the end, you click Continue to install more things or Restart to begin your Mac using the new system software.

Note   If you get an error message from the installer telling you that it can't update the version of the Mac OS that's on your hard drive, it's probably because the installed version is later than the version on the installation CD, for example, you're trying to install Mac OS 7.5.5 over Mac OS 8.0. If that's the case, and you really want to install the older version, you should probably perform a clean install, described later in this chapter.

Custom installation

To customize your installation, you can do one of two things. The first thing is to head to the main Mac OS installation program and run it as discussed in the previous section, choosing the Customize button in the main installation window. You can then choose whether or not you'll install the basic Mac OS along with the Internet connectivity features and PPP software for Open Transport. Click Start and the hard-drive checking and installation process begins.

Once the secondary installers open, however, you'll have another chance at customization. In each of these, you'll have the opportunity to choose from three different installation options:

✦ **Easy install.** Installs all of the Apple-recommended files, usually so that you have full capabilities.

✦ **Custom install.** Allows you to use the installer to add only certain related components. This is good if you'd like to reinstall drivers or extensions that you've accidentally deleted or that have become corrupted (see Figure 33-2).

✦ **Custom remove.** Helps you remove components controlled by this installer that have already been installed on your Mac. To uninstall a particular component, click to place an "X" next to that item.

Figure 33-2: Choosing Custom Install gives you access to all the components controlled by this installer.

Using the Custom Install option, you're given the opportunity to choose exactly which components controlled by that installer you'd like to add to your hard drive. Click the check box next to each item that you'd like installed. Note also that you can get information about what each item does by clicking the small information ("i") icon that floats way to the right next to each item.

Once you've chosen all the items you need, click the Install button. The installer will copy the appropriate components to your System Folder, and then move on to the next installer. If it's reached the last of the installers you asked to use, you'll be asked to Continue (to access any installers you didn't choose the first time around) or Restart the Mac.

Clean install

The idea with a clean install is to either update your Mac to a new version or reinstall the Mac OS on your hard drive, but without disturbing a copy of the System Folder that's already been installed on the drive. With a regular installation, you'll install Mac OS files right into the existing System Folder, which might result in the same problems you're trying to avoid if you've got corruption or conflicts in your current System Folder.

Bypass the test: Quicker custom installation

If you know the exact component (and its associated installer) that you need to add to your Mac to get everything working, you might prefer to bypass the hard drive check. It's nice that Apple has built this into the installer in Mac OS 7.6 and higher, because very few people are diligent enough to check their drive before installing. But if you're planning a simple, quick installation, waiting to test the entire drive can be frustrating. (This may also be necessary if you have a Mac that's been upgraded with a newer processor, a processor daughtercard, or a similar upgrade. Sometimes the installer will choke when it finds a processor it's not familiar with. If so, try to bypass the main installer and go directly to the specific installer you want to use.)

The answer is to dig around on your Mac OS Installation CD and find the specific installer you're looking for. This bypasses the main Mac OS installer program, enabling you to quickly add just the components in which you're interested.

In the CD's main root-level folder in the Finder, use the scrollbars to scroll down below the visible icons. You should see a folder that says Install Pieces, Installer Programs, or something similar. Open that folder and you'll be presented with icons for all the various installers available. These are the individual installers that the main Mac OS installer calls once it's done checking your drive. Launch one of these installers and you'll bypass the drive test, heading straight for the installation itself. (Note that the actual Mac OS installer is available in here, too, just in case you really feel like cheating.) This may not be true in Mac OS versions beyond Mac OS 8.1, although I hope it is.

Instead, a clean install disables the old System Folder and installs a brand new one. This gives you a chance to start over again with a completely new installation. Assuming your hard drive and other hardware items aren't giving you any trouble, you may be able to quickly avoid problems that are currently plaguing you. Maybe. (See the pros and cons of reinstalling the Mac OS earlier in this chapter for a full discussion.)

So why not just format the drive and do a full installation? Because you only need to format the drive if you're partitioning to create more virtual drives, formatting to get past an extreme fragmentation problem, or if you've reformatted in HFS Plus format. Otherwise, formatting the drive is overkill.

Keeping the old System Folder has three additional advantages. First, it allows you to see exactly how the old System Folder was arranged. This can be helpful when something doesn't work with the new System Folder installation and you wonder why. (For instance, you can easily answer questions such as the following: What extensions were necessary for using my CD-Recordable drive? Just head for your old System Folder and examine its contents to see what's missing.)

Second, having the old System Folder gives you something to go back to, if necessary. This is especially true if you're not having trouble with the old system, but you decide to perform a clean install as a precaution, in case an updated version of the Mac OS is buggy or doesn't work well with your Mac. If either of these is the case, you can disable the new System Folder, re-enable the old one, and restart the Mac.

Third, keeping the old System Folder will allow you to move components — such as third-party extensions and drivers — directly to the new System Folder, without requiring you to reinstall all that software. Again, this isn't the best idea if you were having a conflict or other trouble; in that case, reinstall everything from the original media just to make sure you're solving the problem. But if you're just updating to the new OS, you'll find it's easier to drag your third-party extensions to the new System Folder than it is to scare up all those old installation disks and CDs.

The easy way to effect a clean install is to allow the Mac OS installer to do it for you. In Mac OS 7.6 or above, simply check the Perform Clean Installation option that appears in the regular Mac OS Installer window (see Figure 33-3). Next, proceed as usual with the installation.

Figure 33-3: The easy way to perform a clean installation

If you don't have a Perform Clean Installation option in your installer, you're using an older Mac OS version. That's OK, though — just hold down ⌘-Shift-K while the installer window is open. This should pop up an option that enables you to choose how the installation will be performed — by updating an existing System Folder or installing a new System Folder (see Figure 33-4).

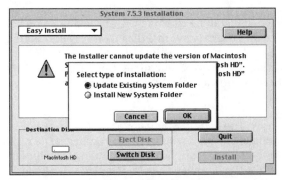

Figure 33-4: In earlier OS versions you can perform a clean install if you know the secret keystrokes.

If the keystrokes result in an error message telling you that you can't perform a clean install, it's possible that you've attempted to perform a clean install from a System CD that's only designed to upgrade an existing System Folder. These CDs are often distributed free; Apple designs them so that they can't create a new installation on their own. Instead, you'll need to create a clean install of the earlier OS, and then use this upgrade CD to update that new, clean version.

Unbless and clean install

If you'd like to perform without the aid of the Clean Install option in newer OS installers or the ⌘-Shift-K sequence in older installers, you can do so fairly simply. You just need to unbless the old System Folder before launching the installer. This can be a little dangerous; if you're forced to abort the installation or otherwise reboot your Mac, it won't be able to start from the hard drive. Be sure you have bootable CDs and Disk Tools disks ready.

To unbless the System Folder, open it up and move the System file to the Extensions (Disabled) folder. (You can choose another folder, such as the Fonts folder, or you can move the System file to another folder outside of the System Folder, if you like.) Now close the System Folder.

Rename the System Folder to something like Previous System Folder. Launch the installation program.

If it's unable to find a blessed System Folder, the installer should happily "Easy" or "Custom" install the Mac OS onto the drive in a new folder called System Folder. This will be a clean install of the OS.

Installation errors

You generally won't get errors when installing the Mac OS, especially if you've followed the precautions of checking the drive with a disk fix utility and optimizing it — an important step — before performing a huge installation session. If you haven't though, you may be flirting with errors. Of course, the errors could come about for other reasons, too. Here's a quick look at potential errors and their solutions.

✦ *Unable to quit all applications.* The installer may have trouble quitting applications that are running in the background when you begin the process. In most cases, the installer quits every application, including the Finder, to avoid potential conflicts while the installation is taking place. To get around this you should restart the Mac with only Mac OS extensions running and nothing active in the Startup Items folder (you can manage that through the Extensions Manager). Next, immediately run the installer after the restart has completed (don't run other applications first).

✦ *Disk errors.* If the installer stops, quits, or complains due to a disk write error (or a disk full error), you need to quit the installation and check the drive to make sure it has enough disk space for the installation. If that's not the problem, restart and run a disk fix utility. You should also consider booting from a CD-ROM, and then running the utility to get the full effect of the fixes. Defragment the drive as well, and then try the installation again. If you continue to get errors, you may need to back up your data and files, and then test the drive for physical errors (using Drive Setup or your drive management software) and reformat (see Chapter 27 for details on formatting).

✦ *Read errors.* If the installer has trouble reading something from its own media, there could be a problem with the available RAM for the installer (restart and run only the installer with only the Mac OS All Full extensions running.) Although it's unlikely the problem, you can also give the installer more RAM in its Get Info window. (You may need to copy the installer and its installation files to your hard drive to get this setting to take.) More likely, there's something physically wrong with your installation media. If you can isolate the particular installer that's causing the problem (such as the OpenDoc or QuickDraw 3D installer), try eliminating those in a custom installer, and then install again. If necessary, you can install those components from another Mac OS CD or by downloading their latest installers from Apple's file library.

✦ *Conflicts, crashes.* Again, if the installer program crashes, you should try restarting with only the Mac OS extensions enabled and without any other applications running. If crashes persist, you may have a corrupt Mac OS–related extension; troubleshoot the extension conflict and/or try restarting and installing with fewer or no extensions enabled, followed by a clean install to create a new System Folder.

Summary

✦ Reinstalling the Mac OS should be an option of last resort, not first. If you plan to reinstall the Mac OS because you're having trouble with your system software, you should first try all the troubleshooting advice in earlier chapters. Often, reinstalling the Mac OS won't solve corruption or conflict issues, especially if you install it over an existing version.

✦ You should reinstall the OS if you've formatted the drive, are upgrading to a newer version of the OS, or have exhausted all other troubleshooting possibilities. In this case, you have three different installation options: an easy install, a custom install, or a clean install.

✦ Easy and custom installs enable you to install the Mac OS on a drive that doesn't currently have a valid System Folder. If the System Folder does exist, its contents will be updated and overwritten by the installer.

✦ A clean install will enable you to create a new System Folder on a hard drive that already has a System Folder. For troubleshooting and as a precaution, this has many advantages. You can continue to consult the older System Folder, you can revert to it if necessary, and you can slowly move extensions and drivers from the earlier System Folder to the new one without being forced to reinstall all your utilities and drivers.

✦   ✦   ✦

Vendor Listings

T his appendix lists the Macintosh peripheral vendors discussed in this book, along with their contact information. A Web site is often the best way to get information, which is why Web sites are included throughout the text of the book when referring to a company. If you're interested in getting in touch with a particular company through more traditional means, though, here's the contact information you'll need.

Apple Computer, Inc.

Apple Computer, Inc. (www.apple.com)
1 Infinite Loop
Cupertino, CA 95014-2084
408-996-1010

Type of Support	Number to Call
Standard — support for the first 90 days you own an Apple product	800-500-7078
Application — support for software, such as QuickTime	512-873-4300
Apple Support Line — paid support calls after 90 days	888-APL-VALU
Professional — support for helpdesk professionals	888-APL-VALU
Automated — general information and frequently asked questions	800-SOS-APPL

Online Shopping

APS Technologies (www.apstech.com)
800-395-5871, 816-483-1600
6131 Deramus Street
Kansas City, MO 64120
sales@apstech.com

Club Mac (www.club-mac.com)
Customer Service 800-258-2622
Fax 949-768-9354
Monday — Friday 6 a.m. — 6 p.m. PST
7 Hammond Street
Irvine, CA 92618
custsvc@club-mac.com

Cyberian Outpost (www.cybout.com)
800-856-9800, 860-927-2050
Fax 860-927-8375
P.O. Box 636
Kent, CN 06757
sales@outpost

MacConnection (www.macconnection.com)
Customer Service Department: 800-800-0018
PC Connection
528 Route 13
Milford, NH 03055

Other World Computing (www.macsales.com)
800-275-4576
Monday — Friday 8:30 a.m. — 8 p.m.; Saturday 10 a.m. — 5 p.m.
224 West Judd Street
Woodstock, IL 60098
compsales@aol.com

Adapters, Ports, Input cards

Belkin Components (www.belkin.com)
800-2-BELKIN
Fax 310-898-1111
P.O. Box 5649
Compton, CA 90224-5649

Griffin Technology (www.nashville.net/~griffin/)
615-255-0990
Fax 615-255-8040
820 Fesslers Pkwy, Suite 315
Nashville, TN 37210
griffin@telalink.net

Infowave (www.infowave.com)
800-663-6222, 604-473-3600
Fax 604-473-3699
Infowave Wireless Messaging Inc.
Attention: Customer Service Group
4664 Lougheed Highway, Suite 188
Burnaby, British Columbia
Canada V5C 6B7

Interex, Inc. (www.interex.com)
800-513-9744
8447 E. 35th Street North
Wichita, Kansas 67226

Kernel Productions (www.kernel.com)
302-456-3026
Tech support fax 302-456-3124
Monday—Friday 7 a.m.—7 p.m. EST

Keyspan (www.keyspan.com)
510-222-0131
Fax 510-222-0323
3095 Richmond Parkway, #207
Richmond, CA USA 94806
info@keyspan.com

Momentum, Inc. (www.momentuminc.net)
425-893-8100
Fax 425-893-8200
sales@momentuminc.net
support@momentuminc.net

Proline Distribution (www.proline.com)
A division of Casa Blanca Works, Inc.
415-461-2227
Fax 415-461-2249
148 Bon Air Center
Greenbrae, CA 94904
info@proline.com

TechCessories (www.techcessories.com)
800-480-TECH (8324)
Fax 408-954-1984
2031 O-Toole Avenue
San Jose, CA 95131

USR Systems (www.3Com.com)
(US Robotics and 3Com have merged)
800-NET-3Com, 800-638-3266, 408-764-5000
Fax 408-764-5001
3Com Corporation
5400 Bayfront Plaza
Santa Clara, CA 95052-8145

Utilities, Drive Maintenance, and Backup Systems

Aladdin Systems, Inc. (www.aladdinsys.com)
408-761-6200
Fax 408-761-6206
165 Westridge Drive
Watsonville, CA 95076
service@aladdinsys.com

Alsoft Inc. (www.Alsoft.com/)
800-ALSOFT1, 800-257-6381, 281-353-4090
Fax 281-353-9868
Monday — Friday 8:30 a.m. — 5:30 p.m. CT
P.O. Box 927
Spring, TX 77383-0927
Tech.Support@Alsoft.com

Dantz (www.dantz.com)
925-253-3000
Fax 925-253-9099
4 Orinda Way, Building C
Orinda, CA 94563
customer_service@ntz.com

MicroMat Computer Systems, Inc. (www.micromat.com)
800-829-6227, 707-837-8012, 707-838-4231 (automated)
Fax 707-837-0209
Monday—Friday 9 a.m.—5 p.m. PST
8868 Lakewood Drive
Windsor, CA 95492
info@micromat.com

Symantec Corporation (www.symantec.com)
800-441-7234, 541-334-6054
Fax 541-984-8020
175 West Broadway
Eugene, OR 97401

Software Applications

Adobe Systems Incorporated (www.adobe.com)
800-833-6687, 408-536-6000
Fax 408-537-6000
345 Park Avenue
San Jose, California 95110-2704

FileMaker, Inc. (www.filemaker.com)
800-544-8554, 800-800-8954 (automated)
Monday—Friday 6 a.m.—6 p.m. PST
P.O. Box 58168
Santa Clara, CA 95052-8168

Microsoft Corporation(www.microsoft.com)
800-426-9400
1 Microsoft Way
Redmond, WA 98052
info@microsoft.com

Clone Vendors

APS Technologies (www.apstech.com)
816-483-1600
6131 Deramus Street
Kansas City, MO 64120

Mactell Corporation (www.mactell.com)
888-MACTELL, 512-323-6000
Fax 512-323-6394
7000 Cameron Road
Austin, Texas 78752-2828
info@mactell.com

Motorola, Inc. (www.mot.com)
847-576-5000
1303 East Algonquin Road
Schaumburg, IL 60196 USA

Radius, Inc. (www.radius.com)
650-404-6000, 800-5-RADIUS
460 East Middlefield Road
Mountain View, CA 94043
support@radius.com

UMAX Technologies, Inc. (www.umax.com)
800-562-0311, 510-651-4000
Fax 510-651-8834
BBS 510-651-2550
3561 Gateway Boulevard
Fremont, CA USA 94538

Processor Upgrades

Mactell Corporation(www.mactell.com)
888-MACTELL, 512-323-6000
Fax 512-323-6394
7000 Cameron Road
Austin, Texas 78752-2828
info@mactell.com

MicroMac Technology (www.micromac.com)
714-362-1000
Fax 714-362-5428
27121 Aliso Creek Road, Suite 125
Aliso Viejo, CA 92656-3364
sales@micromac.com

Newer Technology, Inc. (www.newertech.com)
800-678-DRAM (3726), 316-943-0222
Fax 316-943-4515
4848 W. Irving Street
Wichita, KS 67209 U.S.A.
info@newertech.com

PowerLogix (www.powerlogix.com)
512-795-2978
Fax 512-795-2981
8760A Research Boulevard, Suite 240
Austin, TX 78758
info@powerlogix.com

Sonnet Technologies (www.sonnettech.com)
800-786-6260, 714-261-2800
Fax 714-261-2461
18004 Sky Park Circle, MS 260
Irvine, CA 92614
sales@sonnettech.com

XLR8 (www.xlr8.com)
800-513-9744
8447 E. 35th Street N.
Wichita, KS 67226-1344

Logic Boards

MilagroMac (www.milagromac.com/upgrades.html)
714-723-1056
Fax 714-673-7238
P.O. Box 5240
Newport Beach, CA 92662
milagro@pacbell.net

NEXCOMP (www.nexcomp.com)
888-GET-A-MAC, 281-469-4061
Monday — Friday 9 a.m. — 6 p.m. CT
Nexus Communications
11115 Mills Road, Suite 112
Cypress, TX 77429
sales@nexcomp.com

We Love Macs (www.lovemacs.com)
408-725-8046
Fax 408-744-0307
8 a.m. — 8 p.m. PST
P.O. Box 700063
San Jose, CA 95170-0063
lovemacs@net-shopping.com

Storage Devices/SCSI

Adaptec, Inc. (www.adaptec.com)
408-945-8600
Fax 408-262-2533
691 South Milpitas Boulevard
Milpitas, CA 95035
salesbtc@corp.adaptec.com

Drivesavers (www.drivesavers.com)
800-440-1904, 415-382-2000
Fax 415-883-0780
400 Bel Marin Keys Boulevard
Novato, CA 94949
customerservice@drivesavers.com

Hitachi (www.hitachi.co.jp)
800-241-6558
Fax 770-279-5699
P.O. Box 4650
Norcross, GA 30091
webmaster@hitachi.co.jp

IBM North America (www.ibm.com)
800-IBM-4YOU, 770-863-1234
Fax 770-863-3030
1133 Westchester Avenue
White Plains, NY 10604

Initio Corporation (www.initio.com)
800-99-INITIO, 408-577-1919
Fax 408-577-0640
BBS 408-577-0431
Monday — Friday 8 a.m. — 5 p.m. PST
2188-B Del Franco Street
San Jose, CA 95131-1575
sales@initio.com

Panasonic (www.panasonic.com)
201-348-7000, 800-PANASYS (automated)
1 Panasonic Way
Secaucus, NJ 07094
pcpchelpdesk@panasonic.com

Toshiba America, Inc.
(212) 596-0600
1251 Sixth Avenue, Suite 4100
New York, NY 10020

CD, DVD, Removable Drives

Casa Blanca Works (www.proline.com/cbwindex.html)
415-461-2227
Fax 415-461-2249
148 Bon Air Center
Greenbrae, CA 94904
info@proline.com

Castlewood Systems, Inc. (www.castlewoodsystems.com)
510-224-9900
Fax 510-224-9901
5000 Hopyard Road, Suite 330
Pleasanton, CA 94588
castlewood@castlewoodsystems.com

e4 (www.e4.com)
408-441-6060
Fax 408-441-6070
1731 Technology Drive, Suite 800
San Jose, CA 95110
info@e4.com

FWB Software LLC (www.fwb.com)
650-482-4800
Fax 650-482-4858
2750 El Camino Real
Redwood City, CA 94061-3911
info@fwb.com

Imation (www.imation.com)
888-466-3456, 612-704-4000
Fax 800-537-4675
1 Imation Place
Oakdale, MN 55128-3414
info@imation.com

Iomega (www.iomega.com)
800-my-stuff, 801-778-1000
1821 West Iomega Way
Roy, UT 84067

NEC (www.nec.com)
800-338-9549, 800-366-0476 (automated)
Fax 630-775-7900
BBS 978-635-4706
1250 Arlington Heights Boulevard
Itasco, IL 60143

Philips (www.philips.com)
800-326-6586, 423-521-4316
Fax 423-521-4586
P.O. Box 14810
1 Philips Drive
Knoxville, TN 37914

Pinnacle Micro (www.pinnaclemicro.com)
800-553-7070, 714-789-3000
Fax 714-789-3150
140 Technology Drive, Suite 500
Irvine, CA 92618
fasteddie@codenet.net

Pioneer (www.pioneer.com)
800-421-1404
Fax 310-952-2247
P.O. Box 1763
Long Beach, CA 90801
product.pse@pioneerservice.com

Plextor (www.plextor.com)
800-886-3935, 408-980-1838
Fax 408-986-1010
BBS 408-986-1569/1474
4255 Burton Drive
Santa Clara, CA 95054
info@plextor.com

Ricoh (www.ricohcorp.com)
webmaster@ricohcorp.com

Sanyo (www.sanyo.com)
818-998-7322
Fax 818-701-4170
21350 Lassen Street
Chatsworth, CA 91311

Software Architects (www.softarch.com)
425-487-0122
Fax 425-487-0467
19102 North Creek Parkway, #101
Bothell, Washington 98011
sales@softarch.com

Syquest Technology, Inc. (www.syquest.com)
510-226-4000
Fax 510-226-4100
BBS 510-656-0473
47071 Bayside Parkway
Fremont, CA 94538
sales@syquest.com

Teac (www.teac.com)
213-726-0303
Fax 213-727-7656
7733 Telegraph Road
Montebello, CA 90640
webmaster@teac.com

Yamaha Corporation of America (www.yamaha.com)
714-522-9011
6600 Orangethorpe Avenue
Buena Park, CA 90620
infostation@yamaha.com

Input Devices

Adesso, Inc. (www.adessoinc.com)
310-216-7777
Fax 310-216-7898
100 Corporate Pointe, Suite 230
Culver City, CA 90230
info@adessoinc.com

APS Technologies (www.apstech.com)
800-395-5871, 816-483-1600
6131 Deramus Street
Kansas City, MO 64120
sales@apstech.com

CalComp Technology, Inc. (www.calcomp.com)
714-821-2000
Fax 714-821-2832
2411 West La Palma Avenue
Anaheim, CA 92801-2689

Cirque (www.glidepoint.com)
801-467-1100
Fax 801-467-0208
433 West Lawndale Drive
Salt Lake City, UT 84115-2916
info@cirque.com

Gefen Systems (www.gefen.com)
800-545-6900
Fax 818-884-3108
6261 Variel Avenue, Suite C
Woodland Hills, CA 91367
gsinfo@gefen.com

Kensington (www.kensington.com)
800-280-8318
Fax 650-572-9675
Attn: Customer Service or Sales
2855 Campus Drive
San Mateo, CA 94403
info@kensington.com

MacAlley (www.macally.com)
626-338-8787
Fax 626-338-3585
Mace Group, Inc.
5101 Commerce Drive
Baldwin Park, CA 91706
info@macally.com

Microspeed (www.microspeed.com)
510-259-1270
Fax 510-259-1291
2495 Industrial Parkway West
Hayward, CA 94545-5007
info@microspeed.com

Qtronix (www.qtronix.com)
408-467-1888
Fax 408-467-1880
1746 Junction Avenue, Suite E.
San Jose, CA 95112

Wacom Technology Corporation (www.wacom.com)
360-896-9833, 800-922-9348 (U.S. only)
Fax 360-896-9724
BBS 360-896-9714
1311 SE Cardinal Court
Vancouver, WA 98683
sales@wacom.com

Special Needs Input Devices

Alva Access Group (www.aagi.com)
510-923-6280
Fax 510-923-6270

tty 510-923-6286
5801 Christie Avenue, Suite 475
Emeryville, CA 94608
info@aagi.com

Dragon System's PowerSecretary (www.dragonsys.com)
617-965-5200
Fax 617-527-0372
320 Nevada Street
Newton, MA 02160 USA
info@dragonsys.com

Duxbury Systems, Inc. (www.duxburysystems.com)
978-486-9766
Fax 978-486-9712
435 King Street
P.O. Box 1504
Littleton, MA 01460 USA
info@duxsys.com

R.J. Cooper and Associates (www.rjcooper.com)
800-RJCooper, 714-661-6904
Fax 714-240-9785
24843 Del Prado #283
Dana Point, CA 92629
rj@rjcooper.com

Synapse Adaptive (www.synapseadaptive.com)
888-285-9988, 415-455-9700
Fax 415-455-9801
3095 Kerner Boulevard, Suite S
San Rafael, CA 94901
info@synapseadaptive.com

Touch Screens

ELO TouchSystems, Inc. (www.elotouch.com)
800-557-1458, 510-608-3200
Fax 510-608-3277
6500 Kaiser Drive
Fremont, CA 94555
eloinfo@elotouch.com

Information Display Systems (www.idisplay.com)
302-764-8602
ids@idisplay.com

KeyTec, Inc. (www.magictouch.com)
800-MAGIC-89, 972-234-8617
Fax 972-234-8542
sales@magictouch.com

MouseTouch Technologies, Inc. (www.mousetouch.com)
806-274-7296
Fax 806-274-7298
505 West 10th Street
Borger, TX 79007
sales@mousetouch.com

PixelTouch (www.pixeltouch.com)
909-923-6124
KDS Pixel Touch
1840 Carlos Street, Building 15 A
Ontario, CA 91761

Touch Screens Inc. (www.touchwindow.com)
800-753-2441, 770-921-8436
Fax 770-921-8494
5761 Four Winds Drive
Lilburn, GA 30247
info@touchwindow.com

Troll Touch (www.trolltouch.com)
805-257-1160
Fax 805-257-1161
25510 Stanford Avenue, Suite 106
Valencia, CA 91355-1131
trolltouch@earthlink.net

Scanners

Agfa Division (www.agfa.com)
201-440-2500
Fax 201-440-5733
100 Challenger Road
Ridgefield Park, NJ 07660

Caere (www.caere.com)
800-535-7226, 408-395-7000
BBS 408-395-1631
100 Cooper Court
Los Gatos, CA 95032
ocr_sales@caere.com

Epson (www.epson.com)
800-442-2007, 310-782-0770
20770 Madrona Avenue
Torrance, CA 90503

Hewlett-Packard (www.hp.com)
650-857-1501
Fax 650-857-5518
3000 Hanover Street
Palo Alto, CA 94304-1185

La Cie Ltd. (www.lacie.com)
503-844-4500
Fax 503-844-4508
22985 NW Evergreen Parkway
Hillsboro, OR 97124
sales@cie.com

Linocolor (www.linocolor.com)
888-LINOCOLOR
Fax 516-233-2166
8320 Old Corthaus Road, Suite 200
Vienna, VA 22182
info@linocolor.com

MicroTek (www.microtek.com)
310-297-5000, 310-297-5101 (automated)
Fax 310-297-5050
Monday — Friday 7 a.m. — 5 p.m. PST

Polaroid Corporation (www.polaroid.com)
800-432-5355, 781-386-2000
549 Technology Square
Cambridge, MA 02130

UMAX Technologies, Inc. (www.umax.com)
510-651-4000, 800-286-6186 (automated)
Fax 510-651-8834
BBS 510-651-2550
3561 Gateway Boulevard
Fremont, CA 94538

Visioneer (www.visioneer.com)
510-608-6300, 888-368-9633 (automated)
Fax 716-871-2138
34800 Campus Drive
Fremont, CA 94555

Digital Cameras

Eastman Kodak Co. (www.kodak.com)
800-235-6325
Monday—Friday 9 a.m.—8 p.m. EDT
343 State Street
Rochester, NY 14650-0229

Olympus (www.olympus.com)
516-844-5000
Fax 516-844-5930
Two Corporate Center Drive
Melville, NY 11747-3157

Nikon, Inc. (www.nikon.com)
800-52-NIKON, 516-547-4200
Fax 516-547-0299
1300 Walt Whitman Road
Melville, NY 11747-3064

Casio Computer Co., LTD. (www.casio.com)
800-962-2746
1-6-2 Honmachi
Shibuya-ku
Tokyo 151-8543, Japan
qvsupport@casio-usa.com

✦   ✦   ✦

Online Resources

The Internet has quickly become the information source of first resort when it comes to the Macintosh world. If you're looking for information on troubleshooting, upgrading, particular peripheral issues, or daily news bites to keep you informed on Mac goings-on, fire up your Web browser and check out these sites. (Actually, a few are FTP sites where you can download files directly; you can use a Web browser for these, too, or an FTP program such as Fetch for Macintosh.)

Apple Web Sites

These are all sites handled under the corporate banner of Apple Computer, and they feature news, information, support, and developer information. Apple's site is reasonably complete, and you'll often find what you want, although not always by simply surfing. When in doubt, use the Search textbox to see if you can find what you're looking for.

www.apple.com/

This is the index page for the entire Apple USA Web site, including links to the latest news items, product information, and support.

www.apple.com/hotnews/

This page gives you the latest on Apple technologies, products, and tradeshow appearances, as well as the occasional feature story on people who work at or with Apple. It's a good place to find product, technology, and service announcements, as well as good news about Apple.

www.apple.com/support/

This is the index page for Apple's support site, including links to the Technical Information Library, the Software Update Center and links to others support resources such as the troubleshooting guide and the Apple Specifications database.

http://til.info.apple.com/

You can get to this site from the Support pages, but it's certainly a good idea to have the URL memorized, especially if Mac upgrade or repair is your livelihood, hobby, or specialty. Thousands of technical articles discuss problems and issues that have been brought up by Apple engineers, technicians, and telephone support staffers. (See section later in this appendix.)

www.apple.com/developer/

These pages, intended for Mac OS programmers and developers, also offer good information on how Apple's technology works and what the latest additions are through news items and press releases.

http://product.info.apple.com/productinfo/datasheets/index.html

The AppleFacts Online Archive on Apple's main Web site is a great resource for learning about past Mac models, including an in-depth look at capabilities and specifications.

www.apple.com/store/

This is Apple's online store for configuration and purchasing Apple products.

International Apple Site Index Pages	
Area	*URL*
Asia Pacific	www.asia.apple.com/
Australia	www.apple.com.au/
Belgium	www.apple.be/
Brazil	www.apple.com.br/
Canada	www.apple.ca/
Chile	www.applechile.cl/
Czech Republic	www.apple.cz/
Denmark	www.apple.dk/
Europe	www.euro.apple.com/

Area	URL
Finland	www.apple.fi/
France	www.apple.fr/
Germany	www.apple.de/
Holland	www.apple.nl/
Hong Kong	http://appleclub.com.hk/
Hungary	www.apple.hu/
Iceland	www.apple.is/
Japan	www.apple.co.jp/
Latin America/ Caribbean	www.latinamerica.apple.com/
Mexico	www.apple.com.mx/
New Zealand	www.apple.co.nz/
Norway	www.apple.co.no/
Poland	www.apple.com.pl/
South Africa	www.apple.co.za/
Spain	www.apple.es/
Sweden	www.apple.se/
Switzerland	www.apple.ch/
Taiwan	www.apple.com.tw/
Turkey	www.bilkom.com.tr/
United Kingdom	www.uk.euro.apple.com/

Shopping

Various sites on the Web can help you shop for a new Mac, a used Mac, or an upgrade peripheral that you'd like to install in your existing Mac. These sites are by no means the only ways to shop online (nor am I necessarily endorsing any of them if they are commercial sites), but they might help get you started on your quest for cool new Mac stuff.

www.amcoex.com/

Here you'll find American Computer Exchange's regular listings of used buying and selling prices on the Web.

www.club-mac.com/

Club Mac really does feel like a club, of sorts, especially when you sign up for their weekly e-mail sales sheet. Plus, they often have great prices, discounts, and close-outs.

www.outpost.com/

Cyberian Outpost is a complete resource for software, books, accessories, Macs and peripherals. Another good place to shop, Cyberian Outpost is known for its "Coming Soon" lists which feature manufacturers' announcements for not-yet-released products.

www.macsales.com/

This site has been improving its look and feel for quite a while now, but you often can't beat Other World for great prices on Macs, PowerBooks, and other equipment. It's a no-frills kind of Web site, but that's part of what makes it fun.

www.mac-deals.com/

This Web site keeps track of all sort of deals on Macs, upgrades, and peripherals on other sites around the world. Includes searches, special reports (such as MacWorld Expo price lists and where to find the best deals on particular upgrades), and even some news and quality reports.

www.smalldog.com/

Small Dog Electronics is another favorite Mac, upgrade, and peripheral vendor.

www.enproindia.com/macguide/

The Mac OS Buyer's guide is a Web site devoted to comparisons of retail prices on Mac OS computer systems and peripherals.

http://mac.computertown.com/

Here are the Mac-specific pages of ComputerTown, a popular store and information resource for Mac users, especially in the San Francisco Bay Area. They're an authorized electronic reseller, though, which means they can sell Apple products directly over the Web.

Used Parts and Classified Sales Sites

Site Name	URL
Shreve Systems	www.shrevesystems.com/
NEXCOMP	www.nexcomp.com/
MilagroMac	www.milagromac.com/
We Love Macs!	www.lovemacs.com/
Insanely Great Classifieds	www.insanely-great.com/class.html
ClassMac	www.classmac.com/
Mac Trading Post	www.mymac2u.com/themactradingpost/
Classic Macs	www.unitus.ml.org/cmsales/
PowerDeals (PowerBook classifieds)	www.powerdeals.com/
Usenet—Macs for Sale	comp.forsale.computers.mac
Usenet—Mac Systems For Sale	comp.sys.mac.forsale
Usenet—Mac Systems Wanted	comp.sys.mac.wanted

Note

Interested in visiting the Usenet classifieds boards? You may need a special program to access Usenet. Cyberdog, Outlook Express, Netscape Communicator (in the Messenger module), and Microsoft Mail and News can all access Usenet newsgroups. Newswatcher from John Norstad is a great shareware choice for this task.

Mac News

Mac news Web sites are incredibly popular and successful, with many different players trying their hand at Web-based Mac journalism. Some of them pull it off better than others (including those participants who *actually are* professional journalists). But if you're interested in Mac news, you won't want for opportunities to read some.

www.macsurfer.com/

Features Mac-related headline news from the popular Mac-oriented Web sites and other news organizations around the Web.

www.maccentral.com/

One of the premiere Mac news sites, with features and stories that change daily, including popular columnists, consumer advocacy, and rumor-squashing reports.

www.macosrumors.com/

The much-heralded (and sometimes maligned) rumor source covering possibilities and probabilities in the world of Macs and Apple Computer.

www.macnn.com/

Mac-related headline news, updated many times a day. Hosts the MacNN Reviews and MacNN Reality, another rumor report.

www.webintosh.com/

Daily headlines, columns, and product reviews, includes a stock-watch report, news on other sites, and product previews.

www.macaddict.com/

Online arm of the popular Mac magazine offers regular news, commentaries, and special reports on its Web site.

www.macweek.com/

Once the Mac world's weekly professional tabloid journal, MacWeek is now only on the Web, although its news is keeping pace with the rest. Articles featuring professional insider stories and leader's opinions change at least weekly, and often more frequently.

www.macreport.com/

The new weekly magazine for Mac users and professionals includes some online news, but most of it comes in the form of a free weekly PDF or text document. It may, at some point, become a weekly print newspaper.

www.tidbits.com/

Adam Engst's venerable e-mail–based Mac newsletter has a large audience base of happy readers. The list is distributed weekly and includes news, commentary, and product reviews and roundups.

www.gcsf.com/

Home of MWJ, the weekly journal of Macintosh news and analysis. To get your weekly dose of MWJ's analysis requires a monthly subscription, although you'll find information about the newsletter and occasional free versions on the site.

www.ogrady.com/

O'Grady's PowerPage is a news, analysis, and reviews site dedicated to all things PowerBook. Features info on specific PowerBook models, rumors regarding upcoming models, and links to sites for more information about PowerBooks.

www.mactimes.com/soho/

SOHO Macintosh News and Tips features just what it says: news and tips for the small office/home office Mac users.

Mac Advocacy

These sites focus on analyzing the news, rallying the troops, or responding to more mainstream articles, columns, or criticisms of all things Mac. They may not be the most reliable sites when it comes to product information or updated or unbiased looks at Apple Computer, but they're sure to prove enjoyable and, occasionally, more right than not.

www.evangelist.macaddict.com/

The official Web site of the Evangelist, a mailing list started by Guy Kawasaki to spread good news among Mac users. The list also has a useful side; if you need to formulate an argument, find a particular product, or encourage a company to write a Mac version of their software, post your request to the Evangelist and you'll likely be inundated with replies, strategems, and encouragement.

www.mackido.com/

Opinions on many things Mac-related and some things not. Mackido's specialty is focusing on the major media's view of Apple and what they get wrong in their arguments.

www.macmarines.com/

The Mac Marines fight against injustice, misinformation, and general evilness in the computing world—at least, as they define it. The truth is, they don't seem to update too often, although they do have a great links page.

www.apple.com/whymac/

The Why Mac pages on Apple's site include feel-good information such as Apple's advertising and benchmarks, along with reports, facts, and opinions that may help you convince others to buy more Macs (or allow you to keep the Mac you have).

Upgrade and Troubleshoot

Here's the meat — some of the best sites to find information about your Mac model, new Mac upgrades, hardware problems, software issues, and the latest conflicts, bugs, and other errors.

www.mac-upgrade.com/

The companion site for this book, repository for updates, news, information and reviews of upgrades and hardware troubleshooting for Macs.

www.macfixit.com/

An excellent resource for regular updates, news, and information on maintaining your Mac and troubleshooting software and Mac OS problems. Ted Landau is author of the highly regarded *Sad Macs, Bombs, and Other Disasters*.

www.everymac.com/

This site lists and discusses specifications and other tidbits about nearly every Macintosh model ever made, especially including the many different clone vendors, both large and small, that have made and sold Macs internationally.

www.xlr8yourmac.com/

News, reviews, and performance evaluations of various upgrades for the latest Mac models, including upgrade processor cards, RAM, graphics cards, and other speed-ups.

http://junior.apk.net/~rjl/performa/

Problems and solutions focus specifically on Performa models and their owners, offering advice for updates, workarounds, and other issues specific to Apple's consumer models.

www.micromac.com/

Aside from selling a wide variety of upgrading products, Micromac also offers an excellent specifications search service on their Web site. Just choose your Mac model from a menu, and the search will give you all the specifications for the model including RAM types and possible upgrades.

www.mactimes.com/lowend/

Low-End Mac offers news, insights, and special reports on the different upgrades and updates you can add to aging Mac models to make them hum again.

http://msproul.rutgers.edu/macintosh/PCIcards.html

PCI Cards for Macintosh is a resource compiled by Mark Sproul. It lists manufacturers and model numbers of all the PCI cards for Mac Mark has found on the Net and elsewhere.

www.powermacintosh.com/

The Power Macintosh Resource Page offers news, tips, problem workarounds, and other information about PowerPC-based Macs.

Internet Services

These links lead variously to Mac-based Internet Service Providers, Web server specialists, and other sites that can help you get the most out of an Internet connection.

www.macconnect.com/

This national, Mac-only Internet Service Provider offers expert help on getting your Mac online as well as other services, such as Web serving.

www.alternativemedia.com/index.html

Alternative Media is a small Web-hosting and Mac-based design firm.

www.digitalforest.net

Digital Forest offers Mac OS server colocation (they'll look after your Web server computer for you) as well as FileMaker Pro database serving over the Web.

www.kepler-solutions.com

Kepler Internet solutions also offers colocation, Web serving, Web design, and other services, all with a Mac-centric flare.

www.56k.com/

Find ISPs that specialize in high-speed Internet service, including 56 Kbps modem service, ISDN, ADSL, and other technologies.

www.xdsl.com/

The Telechoice xDSL report offers information on high-speed DSL technologies, adoption, and other news from around the U.S.

Software

Want Mac shareware, freeware, drivers, or other downloads? Look no further. Included in this list are many, many ways to access the venerable InfoMac FTP collection on various mirror sites around the world. Either use Fetch, Anarchie, or a similar FTP program—or just enter the FTP URL in your browser to access hundreds of Mac-related files.

www.download.com/

This cross-platform shareware/freeware service will automatically sense that you are using a Macintosh (depending on your Web browser) and show you the Macintosh interface, enabling you to search or browse for downloadable software.

www.kagi.com/

This site is easily the most popular shareware payment system for Mac programmers and users. Here you'll find listings for many, many different Mac shareware authors, who allow you to use this interface to pay for and register their products.

www.macdownload.com/

Macworld Magazine has created this Web site to catalog and chronicle the Mac shareware world, including ratings and recommendations.

www.pht.com/info-mac/

This Web interface is a front-end and home page for the Info-Mac archive, the popular and probably largest collection of Mac-related shareware, freeware, and other types of downloadables. The Info-Mac FTP archive is *mirrored* to a number of different FTP sites.

Table B-3
InfoMac FTP Mirrors

Location	URL
US: Apple	`ftp://mirror.apple.com/mirrors/Info-Mac.Archive/`
US: AOL	`ftp://mirrors.aol.com/pub/info-mac/`
US: Washington University, St. Louis	`ftp://wuarchive.wustl.edu/systems/mac/info-mac/`
US: Arizona Macintosh Users Group	`ftp://ftp.amug.org/pub/mirrors/info-mac/`
US: University of Hawaii	`ftp://ftp.hawaii.edu/mirrors/info-mac/`
US: University of Delaware	`ftp://fiesta.tsc.udel.edu/pub/mirrors/info-mac/`
Australia: Australian National University	`ftp://sunsite.anu.edu.au/pub/mac/info-mac/`
Austria: Vienna University	`ftp://ftp.univie.ac.at/systems/mac/info-mac/`
Canada: AGT Limited	`ftp://ftp.agt.net/pub/info-mac/`
Colombia: University of Los Andes	`ftp://ftping.uniandes.edu.co/pub/Info-Mac`
Finland: Finnish Academic and Research	`ftp://ftp.funet.fi/pub/mac/info-mac/`
France: FranceNet	`ftp://ftp.francenet.fr/pub/miroirs/info-mac/`
Germany: University of Hannover	`ftp://ftp.rrzn.uni-hannover.de/pub/info-mac/`
Hong Kong: HK SuperNet	`ftp://ftp.hk.super.net/pub/mirror/info-mac/`
Israel: Israel Institute of Technology	`ftp://ftp.technion.ac.il/pub/unsupported/mac/info-mac/`
Italy: CNUCE Institute of CNR	`ftp://cnuce-arch.cnr.it/pub/info-mac/`
Japan: Osaka University	`ftp://ftp.center.osaka-u.ac.jp/info-mac/`
Korea: Pohang University of Science and Technology	`ftp://hwarang.postech.ac.kr/pub/mac/info-mac/`
Netherlands: EuroNet Internet	`ftp://ftp.euro.net/Mac/info-mac/`
New Zealand: Victoria University of Wellington	`ftp://ftp.vuw.ac.nz/info-mac/`

(continued)

Table B-3 *(continued)*

Location	URL
Norway: University of Oslo	`ftp://mac.uio.no/info-mac/`
Singapore: National University of Singapore	`ftp://ftp.nus.sg/pub/mac/`
South Africa: The Internet Solution	`ftp://ftp.is.co.za/info-mac/`
Spain: Universitat Rovira i Virgili	`ftp://ftp.urv.es/pub/mirror/info-mac/`
Sweden: Swedish University Network	`ftp://ftp.sunet.se/pub/mac/info-mac/`
Switzerland: Swiss Academic & Research Network	`ftp://sunsite.cnlab-switch.ch/mirror/info-mac/`
Taiwan: National Chiao Tung University	`ftp://nctuccca.edu.tw/Macintosh/info-mac/`
Turkey: Bilkent University Preparatory School	`ftp://ftp.bups.bilkent.edu.tr/pub/info-mac/`
UK: Imperial College Department of Computing	`ftp://src.doc.ic.ac.uk/packages/info-mac/`

Multimedia and Gaming

Digital video, MIDI, digital audio, 3D, and straight gaming news are all covered in this section.

www.mac-dvr.com/DV/

The monthly scoop on the world of creating digital video, including a catalog of links to other sites that cover digital video with varying degrees of Mac, cross-platform, or other focuses.

www.el-dorado.ca.us/~dmnews/

Digital Movie News is a site about creating digital movies and other content, purporting to offer reviews, tips, and other tidbits about content creation software and hardware.

www.computersandmusic.com/

It's a store for computer musical equipment, but it's also a great information source regarding digital audio and MIDI. Its strong leanings toward Mac solutions don't hurt, either.

www.sims.berkeley.edu/~jwang/cgi/av-faq/

Macintosh AV FAQ for tips on AV-style Macs.

www.3dfx.com/

3Dfx, Inc. maintains quite a bit of information about the Voodoo 3D acceleration technologies, including news, companies, games, developers, and other things that are affecting 3D gaming.

www.imgmagazine.com/

Web site for Inside Mac Games magazine, includes recent news, previews of the current issue, and links to recently posted game demos.

www.macledge.com/

The Mac Gamer's Ledge is a full-fledged e-zine dedicated to Mac gaming, including news, reviews, and an extensive download library of demos, shareware games, and freeware add-ons.

www.tikabik.com/

Yet another gamers' site that includes industry news, 3-D news, reviews, demos, and other special features.

Searching the TIL

I thought the Tech Info Library (TIL) deserved its own section. If you need troubleshooting information directly from Apple, this is the best way to get it without waiting on hold for their tech support people. (In fact, they might charge you for the call, too, making the Web interface for the TIL an even better deal.)

Unfortunately, this means you'll need to search the TIL, which can take a little getting used to. The interface for searching the TIL may change at some point, but until it does, these instructions may help you do a better job of searching for a particular article. Remember that it takes a little patience, cleverness and tenacity to get the right article to pop-up in the TIL. But if your Mac is experiencing a common enough problem, and you've done a good job isolating it, you may have luck finding an answer in here.

Here's how to search the TIL:

1. Bring up `http://til.info.apple.com/` in your Web browser.

2. You'll see the search interface. Enter keywords in the text box, separating each with a comma. (Words not separated by commas are treated as a single phrase. If you search for "PowerBook 1400" you'll get articles that include the two words "PowerBook" and "1400" right next to one another. If you search for "PowerBook, 1400" you'll get articles that include any of the following: both words, both words separated by other words, and articles that include one or the other of the words.)

3. Choose the parts of the TIL articles that you'd like to search from the menu above the keyword text box. (It's often a good idea to begin searching article titles, because you're more likely to get the information you need from an article that includes your keywords in the title. If that doesn't net you much information, you can broaden the search by returning to this page and choosing Search For:, which searches the text of all articles.)

4. You can limit your search to certain types of hardware or software in the pull-down menu.

5. Choose how you want the articles listed (by relevance is usually the best choice).

6. With all these options selected, click the Search button.

A results page generated by the search engine will include a list of articles that may or may not have the answer you're looking for. If you chose to have the articles listed by relevance, those that seem to have the best match for your keywords are listed near the top. If not, you can hit the Back button in your browser to enter different keywords or broaden your search.

I can offer a couple of other hints to help you find the article you need:

✦ If you can't find an article using very particular keywords, try to back away from those keywords and broaden the search. If keywords such as "PowerBook 1400, modem, connection" don't get you the article you want, try a search with just "PowerBook, modem" or even "PowerBook." You'll have more articles to wade through, but this way you might find what you're looking for.

✦ Try all known variations of Apple's names for technologies if your keywords don't find a particular article. Different people write the technical articles and they don't all use the same style conventions. For instance, you can come up with different articles by entering the keywords "HFS+," "HFS Plus," and "Mac OS Extended format", even though those keywords refer to the same Apple technology. Even knowing an Apple code name, such as "Rhapsody" or "Copeland", will sometimes return results.

✦ Try different spellings, words, or other keywords, even if they aren't Apple technologies. For example, "specifications" might get more or different results than "information," or "telephone" might get better or different results than "phone." "Mouse" and "mice" return completely different results, as do "notebook" and "laptop." In other words, experiment.

Most of all, you need to be persistent. If all else fails, drop back from the TIL and search the entire Apple Web site. (There should be a search box on the main Apple index page at www.apple.com/.) This may not result in answers to specific questions, but it will show you any Tech Notes articles (developer info), parts of the Apple Web site, or news items that involve the product or technology that's giving you trouble.

✦   ✦   ✦

What's on the CD-ROM

Included with this book is a CD-ROM that contains a number of demo, freeware, and shareware programs available for your use and testing. The CD-ROM is designed to be as friendly as possible and offers a complete listing of its contents. I've also included a listing here of some of the best tools available on the disc, as well as some instructions for accessing its contents.

How to Use the CD-ROM

The CD-ROM offers a few important files you can use to read about the CD-ROM contents and how to access its files.

Files and folders on the main level of the CD-ROM include the following:

- ✦ **Read Me.** The Read Me file is a text file (you should be able to view it using SimpleText, BBEdit Lite or any word processor) that contains the very latest information I was able to include at the time the CD-ROM was created, including information that may have changed relative to this appendix. You should read the Read Me file for information about any major changes that affect the CD-ROM.

- ✦ **Contents.** The contents file is a text file that includes a listing of the CD-ROM's contents and the folders and subfolders that contain the files. This file isn't as pretty as the HTML interface but will be useful if you'd like to manually locate and drag a particular archive to your hard drive.

✦ **StuffIt Expander.** Aladdin System's archive expansion utility is available on the CD-ROM. If you don't already have a StuffIt Expander version on your hard drive, you'll need to "unstuff" many of the other software distributions stored on the CD-ROM in a compressed format. If you need StuffIt Expander, simply drag the StuffIt Expander folder from the CD-ROM to your hard drive (or a folder within your hard drive). You can then either double-click a StuffIt archive (distinguished for its .SIT filename extension) or you can drag the archive onto the StuffIt icon.

Note

If you prefer, you may want to use the StuffIt installer, which is located in the Backup Utilities folder on the CD-ROM. Double-click the installer to launch it and install StuffIt Expander on your hard drive.

✦ **Netscape Navigator** or **Internet Explorer.** If you don't already have a Web browser installed on your Mac (or if you'd like to upgrade to one of the newer versions included on this CD-ROM), pick either Netscape Navigator or Internet Explorer from this CD-ROM. A Web browser will be necessary for viewing the HTML documents used as contents pages on the CD-ROM.

✦ **index.html.** This HTML document displays just like a Web page would in either Netscape Navigator or Internet Explorer. (If you use some other Web browser such as Cyberdog, Mosaic, or MacWeb, this page should work fine in those browsers, too.)

✦ **html.** This folder includes the other HTML files that make up the CD-ROM's interface.

✦ **archives.** This folder contains the subfolders and archives used to store the freeware, shareware, and demo files.

To view the CD-ROM's contents, use the File ⇨ Open File command in Internet Explorer or the File ⇨ Open Page command in Netscape Navigator. This should bring up an Open dialog box. In that dialog box, choose the CD-ROM, and select the file index.html. Click OK to load the file in the Web browser and begin viewing the CD-ROM's contents.

Alternatively, you should be able to open the CD-ROM window and double-click the index.html document to have it load in your Web browser.

When viewing the HTML interface to the CD-ROM, the blue, underlined text represents a hyperlink, which, when clicked, will take you to a new document. (Notice that you may also be able to click folder icons and other icons to move around.)

You'll encounter four different types of links on the CD-ROM:

✦ **Local pages.** These links take you to another HTML document that has been created on the CD-ROM. The new page will tell you more about the files stored on the CD-ROM.

✦ **Web links.** These hyperlinks will take you to a particular site on the World Wide Web. To access them, you'll need an active connection to the Internet either through your office network or through an Internet Service Provider. If you use a PPP connection, America Online, or a similar dial-up solution, you'll need to have the connection active before accessing one of these links. (The link should say clearly whether or not it's a Web link.)

✦ **Mail links.** Some of the links on the CD-ROM (usually those that have a name as the underlined text) are e-mail addresses. Click one of these and the associated e-mail address will pop up in your e-mail program or in the browser's e-mail window, if it has e-mail capability. (If this doesn't happen, you need to set the e-mail preferences in your browser program and/or the e-mail settings in the Internet Config file on your hard drive. If you have Mac OS 8.0 or above, you can use the Internet Assistant to set your e-mail preferences.)

✦ **Files.** The last of the links you'll encounter are links to the actual files that are stored on the CD-ROM. In most cases, when you click one of these links, you'll be asked where you want to save the file. Choose a folder on your hard drive, and click OK to save the file.

Note

If you click a file link and things don't work the way you planned (you get an error, for instance, instead of a Save dialog box), click and hold the mouse button while you're pointed at the file link. This should bring up a menu in Netscape Navigator and Internet Explorer that will provide you with the option Save This Link As (Navigator) or Download Link to Disk (IE).

If you'd prefer to forgo the HTML interface and just want to get at the file archives themselves, double-click the `archives` folder on the CD-ROM and double-click a subfolder to start your quest for the file in question.

Once you have the file on your hard drive, you may need to double-click the file or drag it to the StuffIt Expander icon to get it to decompress and install itself on your hard drive. If after decompression a new installer file of some sort appears, double-click that file to install the software.

Once the software is properly installed, you can delete the original archive without fear; it will remain on the CD-ROM if you need to access it again.

CD-ROM Contents

Each piece of software included on this CD-ROM has its own licensing agreement or a similar document that you should read to completely understand how it's being distributed and what you need to do (if anything) to continue to use the software in good faith.

Types of Software

In general, there are three different types of software you'll encounter on this CD:

+ **Freeware.** With this sort of software, the author is allowing you to use the program for as long as you need or want to use it without requiring payment. It's made available freely, either for everyone or under certain circumstances (like for non-profit use). In most cases this does not mean the software is "public domain" software—that is, the author still controls rights to the software and hasn't released the source code or any copyrights.

+ **Shareware.** Often called try-before-you-buy software, these programs are freely available and distributed, but require a payment for continued use after a certain amount of time has passed or a certain amount of use has been noted by the program. Shareware programs, written by small companies or individuals and designed as an intermediate step between expensive commercial software and freeware, are often reasonably priced. If you find you enjoy using a program, I encourage you to register the program by paying for it and thereby receiving a registration code that can be used to turn off any shareware notices or turn on any additional features in the program. The program's distribution should include instructions for registering, although you'll also sometimes find instructions by choosing the About This option from the Apple menu while the program is running in the foreground.

+ **Demos.** Demonstration software is usually a limited version of a commercial application that's available for you to try out for a few days. (Other demonstration versions can be used as often as you like, but only have limited features.) In either case, you can use the program for as long as it continues to work or given certain limitations. If you like the program, you'll need to purchase it and install the full version separately.

Programs on the CD-ROM

The following are the software programs included on the CD-ROM. They're arranged according to the categories used to catalog them.

Note

Other software programs are discussed on the CD-ROM, but if a particular program isn't listed here, the file archive isn't on the CD-ROM. Instead, the descriptions on the CD-ROM point you to the Web pages or download sites for some great programs that I wasn't able to include on the CD-ROM itself.

Internet Utilities

Netscape Navigator
Author: *Netscape, Inc.*
The most popular Web browser includes Java, Javascript, multimedia, and support for special Netscape commands.

Microsoft Internet Explorer
Author: *Microsoft Corporation*
Very popular browser now comes as the default browser for Mac OS installations. Supports Java, multimedia, and special IE-only features such as Internet channels.

Backup Utilities

Drag'n'Back and Drag'n'Back Lite
Author: *Enterprise Software*
Back up your Mac's hard drive without complex setup; just drag folders and files that need to be backed up and set the rotation schedule.

StuffIt Expander
Author: *Aladdin Systems*
This freeware utility enables you to expand compressed files and archives stored in the popular StuffIt compressed file format. Just drag a compressed file onto the StuffIt Expander icon to expand. (Works with other common Mac file formats. In conjunction with the shareware version of DropStuff with Expander Enhancer, StuffIt can expand many DOS and UNIX compression schemes, too.)

ZipIt
Author: *Tom Brown*
ZipIt is a Macintosh program that zips and unzips archives in a format fully compatible with PKZip for the IBM and zip implementations on other systems.

Super Save
Author: *Michael Kamprath, Claireware Software*
Super Save is a data protection utility. It performs two functions that help you preserve your work in case your system should accidentally shut down or crash. First, it saves all the keystrokes you make to a convenient save file. Secondly, it will periodically tell the current application to save the document you are working on.

Keeper
Author: *Michael Hamel, ADInstruments, LTD.*
Keeper is an easy-to-use backup and archive application for the Macintosh.

Synk
Author: *Randall Voth*
Synk is a backup/synchronization program that can resolve aliases and archive old files. It runs on all Macintosh computers except Mac Plus, Classic, and PowerBook 100.

Keystroke Recorder
Author: *Hal Gumbert*
Keystroke Recorder is an extension that records each keystroke into a file for later retrieval. It's a great last resort for recovering data after a system crash.

RAM Utilities

Memory Usage Monitor
Author: *Stephen Becker*
Most Mac crashes can be attributed to the way memory resources are handled. Memory Usage Monitor was designed to help you address this issue by providing a way to dynamically monitor memory demands on your computer, and increase the stability of your machine's configurations. You can use this program to track which activities lead to memory configuration issues.

AppDisk
Author: *Maverick Software*
AppDisk is a RAM disk program that enables you to use extra RAM as a super-fast hard disk. AppDisk RAM disks can be mounted and unmounted without restarting your Mac, so it's easy to change the size and use different RAM disks for different applications.

RAM Disk Backup
Author: *John Rethorst*
Automatically back up your RAM disk to a disk drive when you shut down your Mac, and restore the RAM disk when you start up your Mac.

Memory Mapper
Author: *Jintek, LLC*
Memory Mapper determines the boundaries of objects in memory by examining low-memory globals, querying the Process Manager, and checking the page state of each piece of memory (if Virtual Memory is on). Consequently, Memory Mapper requires System 7.

Startup and System Utilities

TechTool (freeware version)
Author: *MicroMat Computer Systems*
The freeware version of TechTool can be used to analyze your Mac and take a look at the hardware and software configuration. It's also useful for some specific housecleaning tasks such as rebuilding the desktop and zapping PRAM completely and effectively.

InformINIT
Author: *Dan Frakes*
InformINIT is a DocMaker application that provides information on a mind-boggling number of System Folder files — control panels, extensions, system folder contents, and more — from both Apple and third-party developers. Information includes file descriptions, who needs what, version numbers, RAM consumption, and helpful tips (even a few "secrets"). Where appropriate, files that are mainly used together are organized into groups. Live URLs to information sources on the Web are provided for files that require extensive discussion.

Conflict Catcher
Author: *Casady & Green*
Conflict Catcher offers detailed information on thousands of files as well as links to individual vendor information, including Web address, update address, e-mail address, phone, fax, and physical address. It also provides powerful tools to manage plug-ins and filters as well as fonts, control panels, startup files, and extensions.

Mac Identifier
Author: *Maurice Volashi, Flux Software*
Mac Identifier was designed for Mac OS 7.5 (or later) users who can't stand the thought of their Macintosh not knowing its own model designation or what it looks like. It is also useful for network administrators who manage networks consisting of any 7.5 (or greater)–based Macintoshes.

Extension Overload
Author: *Teng Chou Ming*
Extension Overload 2.5 reviews 590 extensions and 223 control panels commonly found in the Extensions folder and Control Panel folder on every Mac. For those who do not know much about extensions and control panels, this program gives you some insight so you can decide which ones are necessary for your computer and which are not.

Speed Tester
Author: *Brian Bergstrand*
Speed Tester is based on a program called CheckTicks. This program makes 10,000 calls to GetNextEvent(), and then quits. Speed Tester expands on this idea. It lets you perform multiple runs of the tests (up to five) to obtain a true average, instead of relying on one test run. It includes a GetNextEvent() test, an integer test, a floating-point test, and a graphics test. Also included is a small database of Macs to compare your times to.

TattleTech
Author: *John Mancino, Decision Maker's Software*
TattleTech is a Mac hardware and software profiler that reports over 850 distinct items of information about the Mac on which it is running.

AutoBoot
Author: *Karl Pottie*
AutoBoot is a control panel/system extension that will restart your Macintosh after a system error (bomb) or a freeze-up has occurred. AutoBoot ensures maximal availability of unattended Macs.

Keep It Up
Author: *Karl Pottie*
KIU watches certain applications and monitors if they are still running. If an application no longer runs because it unexpectedly quit or because the user quit it, KIU will attempt to relaunch this application (and open certain documents) or restart the computer. This will ensure your application is always running and available.

Symbionts
Author: *Nivek Research*
Symbionts is an extension that monitors the startup process. It displays the name and number of bytes of memory each system extension allocates from the system heap. The name and number appear beneath the extension's icon, and since the name is usually truncated, Symbionts also displays it in the menu bar. Symbionts even shows the icons for those extensions that don't normally reveal themselves.

Respond!
Author: *Shawn Lee*
Respond! is a control panel that brings a limited form of preemptive multitasking to the Macintosh right now. And it runs on any Mac, 68k or PowerPC, with System 7.0 or later. No more waiting for Mac OS X. Even in Mac OS 8, if you hold down a menu in the Finder, processes will not continue in the background. With Respond!, you can be holding down a menu (particularly useful with Sticky Menus in Mac OS 8), or clicking in a zoom or close box (or the WindowShade collapse box in Mac OS 8), or dragging a window or the thumb of a scroll bar, and processes will continue in the background.

Snitch

Author: *Nifty Neato Software*

Snitch is a Finder enhancement that extends the Get Info command, allowing you to view and edit a variety of different information about a file, alias, folder, or disk. Snitch itself is also extendible, enabling other software developers to create new uses for it.

Font and Text Utilities

Fontasee Deluxe

Author: *WM Enterprises*

A program that prints banners, headlines, and information about all the fonts in the fonts folder.

Fonts Manager

Author: *Edwin Hopkins, Æ°dvantage*

Fonts Manager is similar to the Mac OS Extensions Manager, but it manages fonts instead of control panels and extensions. It allows the enabling and disabling of font suitcases and printer fonts in sets. It supports the viewing and printing of font samples, exporting of sets, importing of saved sets, balloon help, and a tutorial topics system.

BBEdit Lite

Author: *Bare Bones Software*

The premiere Mac-based text editing program in a freeware version that has fewer capabilities but is still very useful for text manipulation. Reads files larger than SimpleText, changes between DOS, Mac, and UNIX text formats, and offers very strong search-and-replace capabilities.

CopyPaste

Author: *Script Software*

This software features 100 extra clipboards, clipboard processing, saving clips through restarts, application switching, clipboard archives, and Internet tools.

iSearch

Author: *Script Software*

iSearch lets you perform Boolean and literal text searches through files, folders, disks, and CDs. It has an accelerated search engine that can work equally fast in the background while you carry on your work. It uses drag and drop to define search locations and remembers the most frequent locations used, listing them in a Search in: drop-down menu.

UltraFind
Author: *UltraDesign*
UltraFind is a fast and flexible text search and file management program for the Macintosh. Its text search feature shows words in context (in their original sentence), searches in both live or preindexed modes, and even includes a built-in thesaurus; this allows you to find documents related to a particular topic on your hard disks, in text indexes, on the World Wide Web, and in newsgroups.

UltraFind Text Indexer
Author: *UltraDesign*
Text Indexer 2.0 is a modern indexing engine for Mac and PowerPC that pre-indexes your documents, making text searches not just fast, but instant.

SmartKeys
Author: *Maurice Volashi, Flux Software*
Helps you type in four ways. First, it automatically corrects typing that violates conventional typesetting rules, such as typing more than one consecutive space. Second, it automatically corrects fast typing errors, which result in words that are misspelled, such as "teh" for "the" and "THe" for "The". Third, it can require modifiers to engage the Caps Lock and the Help key, making them more difficult to press inadvertently. Finally, in the event of a system crash, it can keep a log of what was typed.

Multimedia Utilities

Sound Machine
Author: *Rod Kennedy*
Sound Machine plays many of the commonly found sound files on the Internet. It can be used as a stand-alone player or as a helper application with your Web browser.

Convert Machine
Author: *Rod Kennedy*
Convert Machine is a powerful sound file conversion program. Most audio files dropped onto the application can be converted to AIFF, AU, WAVE, SDII, or MooV format in either mono or stereo, with any of a number of compressions and arbitrary sampling rates. It is ideal for converting audio files to formats commonly used on the web.

iView
Author: *Script Software*
Powerful and easy-to-use tool for processing images, movies, QuickTimeVR, animation, clip art, and sound; works with Canvas, QuarkXPress, Illustrator, and Freehand files; and also provides font cataloging and archiving.

SoundApp
Author: *Norman Franke*
SoundApp can play and convert sound files in a large number of formats. It supports MPEG, QuickTime, WAVE, AIFF, Psion, MOD/S3M, and many others. It can use playlists to group favorite files for playback and is AppleScriptable.

SCSI and Disk Utilities

Mt. Everything
Author: *Horst Pralow*
Mt. Everything is a control panel to help you manage your SCSI-bus and the devices connected to it.

CacheSaver
Author: *St. Clair Software*
CacheSaver periodically saves (or flushes) the disk cache, thus minimizing data loss should your Macintosh crash while you are working. You can set CacheSaver to flush the cache whenever your Mac is idle for more than a specific amount of time, or it can do it automatically at regular intervals. CacheSaver also provides a hotkey so you can flush the disk cache manually.

Disk Charmer
Author: *Fabrizio Oddone*
With Disk Charmer, you can erase any kind of disk, even using foreign formats such as MS-DOS. Set the minimum allocation block size with the Mac OS Extended format to free up trapped disk space. Create oversize disks by reducing catalog space (you gain 8K on 800K disks, 18K on 1.4M disks, 1.5M on Zip disks), initialize floppy disks in the background, copy floppy disks, verify floppy disk media, create DiskCopy disk images from floppies, and recreate floppies from DiskCopy or DiskDup+ disk images.

Drive Monitor
Author: *Jude Giampaolo*
Drive Monitor displays a window that lists the vitals for all of the currently mounted drives. Drive Monitor 3.x is PowerPC only. Users of 68k-based machines may be interested in one of the 2.x versions. Drive Monitor 3.x also requires MacOS 8.0 or newer.

DiskSurveyor
Author: *Tom Luhrs, Twilight Software*
DiskSurveyor shows you, graphically, what or who's hogging space on your hard drive. And you can create DiskSummary files that list all the files found on CD-ROMs or any other volume. No longer will you have to waste valuable time navigating through folder after folder, trying to figure out which files need to be archived or trashed to free up precious disk space.

Alias Assistant
Author: *Maurice Volashi, Flux Software*
Enables your Macintosh to automatically delete all the alias files associated with an original file when the original file is emptied from the Trash.

PowerBook Utilities

BatteryAmnesia
Author: *Jeremy Kezer*
BatteryAmnesia is a utility for any PowerBook that uses a nickel-cadmium (NiCad) battery or nickel-hydride (NiMH) battery. Over time, these batteries are susceptible to a memory effect, which can reduce their battery capacity. The memory effect can be cured by fully discharging the battery before recharging it.

LCD Screen Tester
Author: *The Syzygy Cult*
This is a small, useful application for people with active matrix PowerBooks who would like to test their screen for stuck pixels. It floods your screen with red, green, blue, white, and black to make the culprit stuck pixel (or subpixel) show its ugly head. This is so you can show your Apple Dealer that there is a problem with your screen and that it needs to be replaced. This will only be useful for people with active matrix screens.

Networking and Security

IPNetRouter
Author: *Sustainable Softworks*
IPNetRouter provides IP multihoming and routing under Macintosh Open Transport. With IPNetRouter, you can use multiple IP interfaces at the same time (such as Ethernet and OT/PPP) and specify additional routes for communicating with more than one IP gateway. The built-in IP Masquerading feature allows an entire network to simultaneously share a single Internet connection and end-user account.

Sentry
Author: *Quade Publishing*
Sentry cdev 4.0.2 monitors your computer's usage.

The Block
Author: *Marc Mennigmann*
The block is a clever access protection utility for your Mac.

Chooser User
Author: *Maurice Volashi, Flux Software*
Lets you control who can change the owner name of a Mac. It also allows the owner name to be changed at startup, either manually or automatically.

FCB Inspector
Author: *Maurice Volashi, Flux Software*
Allows users to peek at a Macintosh's list of open files. It also provides information about these files on demand and can close any that aren't crucial to system operation.

Miscellaneous Utilities

Dvorak keyboard layout
Author: *Joseph J. Strout*
Gives you a Dvorak-like keyboard layout for use with the Mac OS. This one is specifically designed for people who want to rearrange the keycaps on an existing Mac keyboard.

Finder Killer
Author: *Thomas J. Bovo*
FinderKiller will kill the Finder (well, actually it just quits the Finder). It has no dialog boxes, no user interface, and does not attempt to relaunch the Finder.

Finder Reset
Author: *Thomas J. Bovo*
FinderReset will quit the Finder but then issue a relaunch command to the Finder so it restarts immediately.

Apple Spec Database
Author: *Apple*
Apple Spec Database contains the technical specifications for many Apple computer models, and therefore provides a convenient reference for determining your model's features to help you make critical upgrading decisions. Updates to the database can be found at `www.apple.com/support/`.

✦   ✦   ✦

Index

NUMBERS AND SYMBOLS

K

Kensington
  cleaning products for mice and
    trackballs, 636
  other input devices by, 258
  Turbo Mouse by, 253–254
key frames rate, QuickTime, 329
Keyboard control panel, changing
    keyboard layout with, 259–260
keyboards
  as input devices, 42, 44–45
  changing layout for, 259–260
  cleaning up after a spill, 637–638
  compatibility between PCs and Macs,
    44–45
  considerations for upgrading, 5, 6
  Dvorak layout, 259–260
  ergonomic, 257–263
  for users with special needs, 267
  increasing productivity by upgrading,
    18, 72
  original for Mac Classic, 258
  removing key caps from, 637, 638
  sources for, 257–258
  troubleshooting, 633, 637–638
  typical for Macs, 45
  with built-in trackpads, scanners, or
    joystick-like pointers, 260–261
KeyTec, MagicTouch series touch
    screens, add-ons, and monitors, 267
kilobytes (K), 31
kiosk presentations, using touch screens
    for, 266–267
Kodak, Web site address, 283
Korg, audio I/O cards by, 361

L

LaCie Ltd., Web site address, 283
LANs. *See* local area networks (LANs)

laser printers, 53, 374–377
  advantages over other printers, 375
  cost per page, 371–372
  RAM use in, 375–376
  speed of versus inkjet printers, 5
  tips for shipping, 378
  toner for, 376–377
  typical RAM quantities for, 376
LaserWriter 8 printer driver, using with
    non-Apple-branded printers,
    682–683
LaserWriter, printer problems, 682–683
lead acid batteries, PowerBook 100,
    753–754
Level 1 cache memory, 32
Level 2 cache memory, 32
Level 3 cache memory, 32
LiIon (lithium ion) batteries, PowerBook,
    755–756
lines per inch (lpi), effect on halftone
    images, 370
LineShare, serial port sharing software,
    461
Linocolor, Web site address, 283
local area networks (LANs)
  communicating with other computers
    over, 56
  increasing speed of by upgrading, 66
LocalTalk network
  architecture, 433–435
  basic installation of transceiver and
    cabling, 451
  bridges, 452–454
  cabling and solutions manufacturers,
    451
  cabling for small local area networks,
    56, 432, 433–434, 452
  connecting to Ethernet networks,
    452–455
  hardware and cabling needed for
    installing, 450
  hubs for, 452

(continued)

(continued)

R

Radius Corp.

    PC-compatibility hardware by, 493

    upgrading PC-compatibility cards, 500–501

    Web site address for, 334

Radius/Reply

    add-on cards for serial and parallel ports, 494

    PC-compatibility cards, 497–498

    upgrading PC-compatibility cards, 500–501

RAID (Redundant Array of Inexpensive Drives)

    adding, 204–205

    setting up, 205–206

RAM (Random Access Memory), 29–30

    adding, 168–177

    checking allocation of, 167

    effect of adding additional on laser printer speed, 375–376

    effect of in digital video playback, 321

    increasing system speed by adding, 14, 16, 67–70

    installing, 174–176

    interleaving, 174

    measuring, 31

    PC emulator software requirements for, 738

    software requirements from version to version, 65

    system bottlenecks caused by lack of, 64, 65

    troubleshooting startup problems, 588–589

    upgrade table, 169–173

    working with, 167–168

RAM disk

    creating, 166

    shareware utilities for automatically saving and restoring contents of, 758

RAM modules, 30–31

RAM settings, checking, 165–167

RamDoubler (Connectix) utility, increasing system speed with, 14

Ramp Networks, Internet routers by, 466

random access memory. *See* RAM (Random Access Memory)

RAVE, QuickDraw 3D acceleration virtual engine, 472–473

    acceleration issues, 722

    choosing a RAVE video card, 477–478

RCA video plugs, 329

Ready to Send command, from modem to computer, 400

RealAudio codecs, 347

RealPC (Insignia Corporation), PC emulation software, 57

reblessing the System Folder, 606–608

recordable CD-ROM discs, creating, 224–225

Reduced Instruction Set Computing (RISC) architecture, 28

Redundant Array of Inexpensive Drives (RAID)

    adding, 204–205

    setting up, 205–206

refresh rate, for monitors, 295–296

    changing to solve display movement problems, 649

reinstalling Mac OS

    clean install, 847–850

    custom installation, 846–847

    deciding on type of installation, 843–844

    installation errors, 850–851

    pre-flight check, 841–843

    regular installation, 844–846

    tips for a quicker custom installation, 847

    unblessing the System Folder and doing a clean install, 850

(continued)

(continued)

(continued)

(continued)

IDG BOOKS WORLDWIDE, INC.
END-USER LICENSE AGREEMENT

4. **Restrictions On Use of Individual Programs.** You must follow the individual requirements and restrictions detailed for each individual program in Appendix C in this Book. These limitations are also contained in the individual license agreements recorded on the Software Media. These limitations may include a requirement that after using the program for a specified period of time, the user must pay a registration fee or discontinue use. By opening the Software packet(s), you will be agreeing to abide by the licenses and restrictions for these individual programs that are detailed in Appendix C and on the Software Media. None of the material on this Software Media or listed in this Book may ever be redistributed, in original or modified form, for commercial purposes.

5. **Limited Warranty.**

> **a)** IDGB warrants that the Software and Software Media are free from defects in materials and workmanship under normal use for a period of sixty (60) days from the date of purchase of this Book. If IDGB receives notification within the warranty period of defects in materials or workmanship, IDGB will replace the defective Software Media.

> **(b) IDGB AND THE AUTHOR OF THE BOOK DISCLAIM ALL OTHER WARRANTIES, EXPRESS OR IMPLIED, INCLUDING WITHOUT LIMITATION IMPLIED WARRANTIES OF MERCHANTABILITY AND FITNESS FOR A PARTICULAR PURPOSE, WITH RESPECT TO THE SOFTWARE, THE PROGRAMS, THE SOURCE CODE CONTAINED THEREIN, AND/OR THE TECHNIQUES DESCRIBED IN THIS BOOK. IDGB DOES NOT WARRANT THAT THE FUNCTIONS CONTAINED IN THE SOFTWARE WILL MEET YOUR REQUIREMENTS OR THAT THE OPERATION OF THE SOFTWARE WILL BE ERROR FREE.**

> **(c)** This limited warranty gives you specific legal rights, and you may have other rights that vary from jurisdiction to jurisdiction.

6. **Remedies.**

> **(a)** IDGB's entire liability and your exclusive remedy for defects in materials and workmanship shall be limited to replacement of the Software Media, which may be returned to IDGB with a copy of your receipt at the following address: Software Media Fulfillment Department, Attn.: *Macworld Mac Upgrade and Repair Bible*, IDG Books Worldwide, Inc., 7260 Shadeland Station, Ste. 100, Indianapolis, IN 46256, or call 1-800-762-2974. Please allow three to four weeks for delivery. This Limited Warranty is void if failure of the Software Media has resulted from accident, abuse, or misapplication. Any replacement Software Media
> will be warranted for the remainder of the original warranty period or thirty (30) days, whichever is longer.

(b) In no event shall IDGB or the author be liable for any damages whatsoever (including without limitation damages for loss of business profits, business interruption, loss of business information, or any other pecuniary loss) arising from the use of or inability to use the Book or the Software, even if IDGB has been advised of the possibility of such damages.

(c) Because some jurisdictions do not allow the exclusion or limitation of liability for consequential or incidental damages, the above limitation or exclusion may not apply to you.

7. <u>**U.S. Government Restricted Rights.**</u> Use, duplication, or disclosure of the Software by the U.S. Government is subject to restrictions stated in paragraph (c)(1)(ii) of the Rights in Technical Data and Computer Software clause of DFARS 252.227-7013, and in subparagraphs (a) through (d) of the Commercial Computer—Restricted Rights clause at FAR 52.227-19, and in similar clauses in the NASA FAR supplement, when applicable.

8. <u>**General.**</u> This Agreement constitutes the entire understanding of the parties and revokes and supersedes all prior agreements, oral or written, between them and may not be modified or amended except in a writing signed by both parties hereto that specifically refers to this Agreement. This Agreement shall take precedence over any other documents that may be in conflict herewith. If any one or more provisions contained in this Agreement are held by any court or tribunal to be invalid, illegal, or otherwise unenforceable, each and every other provision shall remain in full force and effect.

my2cents.idgbooks.com

CD-ROM Installation Instructions

To view the CD-ROM's contents, use the File ⇨ Open File command in Internet Explorer or the File ⇨ Open Page command in Netscape Navigator. This should result in an Open dialog box. In that dialog box, choose the CD-ROM, and select the file *index html*. Click OK to load the file in the Web browser and begin viewing the CD-ROM's contents.

Alternatively, open the CD-ROM window and double-click the *index.html* document to have it load in your Web browser.

When viewing the HTML interface to the CD-ROM, the blue, underlined text represents a hyperlink, which, when clicked, will take you to a new document. (Notice that you may also be able to click folder icons and other icons to move around.)

There are actually four different types of links you'll encounter on the CD-ROM:

+ **Local pages.** These links just take you to another HTML document that has been created on the CD-ROM. That new page will tell you more about the files that are stored on the CD-ROM.

+ **Web links.** These hyperlinks will take you somewhere on the World Wide Web. To access them, you'll need an active connection to the Internet, either through your office network or through an Internet Service Provider. If you use a PPP connection, America Online, or a similar dial-up solution, you'll need to have the connection active before accessing one of these links. (The link should say clearly whether or not it's a Web link.)

+ **Mail links.** Some of the links on the CD-ROM (usually those that have a name as the underlined text) are e-mail addresses. Click one of these and the associated e-mail address will pop up in your e-mail program or in the browser's e-mail window, if it has e-mail capability. (If this doesn't happen, you need to set the e-mail preferences in your browser program and/or the e-mail settings in Internet Config file on your hard drive. If you have Mac OS 8.0 or above, you can use the Internet Assistant to set your e-mail preferences.)

+ **Files.** The last of the links you'll encounter are links to the actual files stored on the CD-ROM. In most cases, you'll click one of these links, and then you'll be asked where you want to save the file. Choose a folder on your hard drive, and click OK to save the file.

Note

If you click a file link and things don't work the way you planned (you get an error, for instance, instead of a Save dialog box), click and hold the mouse button while you're pointed at the file link. This should bring up a menu in Netscape Navigator and Internet Explorer that will present you with the option Save This Link As (Navigator) or Download Link to Disk (IE). This opens a Save dialog box, which enables you to save the file somewhere on your hard drive.

If you'd prefer to forgo the HTML interface and just want to get at the file archives themselves, double-click the *archives* folder on the CD-ROM and then double-click a subfolder to start your quest for the file in question.

Once you have the file on your hard drive, you may need to double-click the file or drag it to the StuffIt Expander icon to get it to decompress and install itself on your hard drive. If after decompression a new installer file of some sort results, double-click that file to install the software.

Once the software is properly installed, you can delete the original archive without fear; it will remain on the CD-ROM if you need to access it again.

For more information about what is on the CD-ROM, see Appendix C.